# 'Courage Was Not Enough'

# 'Courage Was Not Enough'

No.218 (Bomber) Squadron

Weston-Super-Mare's Own, 1936-1942

by

Steve Smith

www.bombercommandbooks.com

Also by Steve Smith and published by Mention the War Limited:


*A Stirling Effort: Short Stirling Operations at RAF Downham Market 1942-44*

*In Time: 218 (Gold Coast) Squadron 1944-45*

*A Short War: The History of 623 Squadron RAF*


First published 2020 by Mention the War Ltd., 25 Cromwell Street, Merthyr Tydfil, CF47 8RY.

Copyright 2020 © Steve Smith

Cover design: Topics - The Creative Partnership www.topicsdesign.co.uk

A CIP catalogue reference for this book is available from the British Library.

ISBN 9781911255628

'I say to the House as I said to ministers who have joined this government, I have nothing to offer but blood, toil, tears, and sweat. We have before us an ordeal of the most grievous kind. We have before us many, many months of struggle and suffering. You ask, what is our policy? I can say: It is to wage war, by sea, land and air, with all our might and with all the strength that God can give us; to wage war against a monstrous tyranny, never surpassed in the dark, lamentable catalogue of human crime.'

Prime Minister Winston Churchill

# Contents

# Acknowledgements

This book would not have been possible without the tremendous help of so many people. Their time, guidance and above all knowledge was generously shared.

I want to firstly thank the families of the veterans. So many have freely given their time and provided me with a wealth of information. They are too numerous to mention, but you know who you are, and I will forever be grateful to you.

I would like to thank and acknowledge two good friends, Simon Hepworth, and Chris Ward. Each have helped greatly with this book and my previous efforts. Another friend who I want to thank is the respected author and historian, Ken Marshall. The book has benefited greatly by Ken's tireless help, advice and guidance.

Lastly, I would also like to thank the following for their assistance and support, Dr Theo Boiten, Errol Martyn, Bob Collis, Hans Nauta, Jonathan Falconer, Bob Body, Kelvin Youngs, Joss Leqlercq, Dave Richardson, Arnaud Gillet, Andy Long, Gildas Saozanet, Luc Vervoort, Martin Gleeson, David Fell, Malcom Barrass, Marc Doucet, Peter Wheeler, Pavel Vancata, Bertrand Hugot, Di Ablewhite and Dee Boneham MBE, Andy Bullock, Soren Flensted.

An excessively big thank you to the Marham Aviation Heritage Centre and particularly the excellent help from Mark Every.

Lastly, I would also like to thank the help of two excellent web sites / forums who have provided on numerous occasions the answers to many difficult questions, RAF Commands and 12 O' Clock High.

# Dedication

This book is humbly dedication to the memory of the young men and women, aircrew, ground crew and the WAAF who served on No.218 (Bomber) Squadron between 1936-1945.

---

*Also, in memory of my late father, 'Mick' who passed away in 2019.*

*Lastly a big thank you to my wife Jill, for her love and support.*

# Foreword

As the researcher at the Marham Aviation Heritage Centre in Norfolk, I have, as part of my daily routine, the need to read through a great deal of reference material. For me, the sign of a good book is the desire to continue reading beyond the item I was specifically researching, getting involved in an unfolding story and immersing myself deeper within the subject. Although a distraction no doubt, it is a somewhat pleasant one and also a fringe benefit of the researcher's role when you come across such a book. Steve's previous titles established his reputation for detailed and engaging aviation history. This current book is informative, meticulously researched and expertly written book,and is testament to the passion he has for 218 (Gold Coast) Squadron and the importance in keeping its history alive. Through hard work and years of research he has been able to document some of the stories and name some of the participants and characters behind the basic data commonly found in the archives or Operational Record Books.

Covering a period where the Squadron was equipped with five different aircraft types and moved base location as many times, from overseas to the fields of Norfolk, the tales told are enough to keep both the casual reader and aviation history enthusiast engrossed and satisfied in equal amounts.

As a part of RAF Marham's history, and to a wider extent this corner of the North Norfolk countryside, 218 (Gold Coast) Squadron's relationship to my own work and that of my colleagues is extremely close, having this book is an excellent addition to our Heritage Centre toolbox, one that will no doubt be read and reread many times over.


Mark Every

Former Chief Technician Armourer with Nos. 2, 12 and 31 Squadrons.
Served Gulf War One, Yugoslavia, Bosnia, Iraq, Afghanistan and Libya.

# Preface

This is the story of an ordinary squadron, no different than any other within the ranks of the RAF between 1936-1942. However, what sets this squadron apart is its varied and at times costly transition between roles and groups within Bomber Command.

Re-formed in the mid 1930s, the Golden Age of the pre-war RAF No.218 (Bomber) Squadron spent the first three years' operating with No.1 Group, RAF Bomber Command equipped with the sleek but absolute Hawker Hind. The squadron then progressed onto the new Fairey Battle in 1938. In 1939 and now a part of the AASF the squadron found itself in France, almost twenty years since it departed after the defeat of the Kaiser's Germany in the Great War. During the German 'Blitzkrieg' of May 1940 the squadron found itself facing overwhelming odds. Operating the lightly armed Battle in the face of fast, modern and heavily armed Bf109s and Bf110s the squadron crews faced almost certain death. The dedication and bravery of these young men has never been fully recognised due mainly to the absents of the Squadron Operational Records Book for May 1940. Decimated within weeks of the German offensive the squadron was withdrawn from the front line. What was left of the squadron was sent back to England to reform. Their aircraft were gone, as was many friends and comrades but the fighting spirit of the squadron was unbroken. With the squadron's arrival back in England re-equipment with the Bristol Blenheim quickly followed. Once fully converted operations would commence under the control of No.2 Group RAF Bomber Command. Daylight operations against the Invasion barges were initially undertaken. These were quickly followed by solitary attacks against key targets with the aid of cloud. These near suicidal raids would require crews to fly into the occupied territories and Germany in daylight alone and armed with only two .303 machine guns for defence.

The skill and tenacity of the crew was pitted against not only the weather but a capable and deadly enemy. With the Battle of Britain won, the squadron once again found itself on the move. In total contrast to what it had been its primary role since its formation, daylight bomber operations it found itself chosen to convert to the night bomber role. With the change of role came yet another move. The flat fens of East Anglia would be the squadron's new home. Chosen to operate the Vickers Wellington with No.3 Group RAF Bomber Command, No.218 Squadrons new nocturnal role would witness its participation in the early night-time offensive.

Conversion to the massive four engine Short Stirling beckoned as the tempo of operations and losses increased. Night after night the squadron would operate against distant targets, losses grew as the German defenders fought desperately to blunt the destructive power of Bomber Command.

This is the story of one squadron, a close-knit band of men and women who pitted their skill and courage against a formidable foe. The squadron, like No.3 Group gets extraordinarily little publicity and recognition for its contribution to the success of the bomber offensive.

I have tried to ensure historical accuracy, however, I apologise in advance for any errors that will inevitably creep in. Much of the squadron's early history especially between 1936-1939 can be found over just three pages of the Squadron Operational Records Book. Likewise, the squadron's brief and bloody operations of May 1940 are missing from the Operational Records Book. I have used when possible other primary source material to fill in the gaps. The accuracy of which can vary. In putting this book together, I have been overwhelmed by the bravery and sacrifice of those who served within the squadrons ranks. Sadly, this courage, and that of the groups it served have been all too often overshadowed by the more glamorous squadrons and groups so preferred by authors and historians. There is a massive void in photographs depicting the squadron, especially the Hawker Hind and Bristol Blenheim period. I apologise now for the lack of photographic coverage in these chapters.

Finally, this is the history of a squadron and the brave young men and women who served on it. A generation we owe so much, but now tend to ignore and ridicule in these present times. This was a generation of heroes who would fight and die for King and Country. I have not attempted to include Bomber Commands many trials and tribulations and strategies, simply because it is outside the scope of this history.

*Steve Smith*

*2020*

# Chapter 1: 1936 - From the Shadows

On Monday, March 16th, 1936 No.218 (Bomber) Squadron was officially reformed at RAF Upper Heyford, Oxford. The squadron which had last flown actively in June 1919 had like so many others been unceremoniously disbanded by the still relatively new Royal Air Force during the ruthless cutbacks of post-war Britain.

The nucleus of the new squadron was formed by hiving off one of the three existing flights of No.57 (Bomber) Squadron which was also based at Upper Heyford. Records conflict as to what flight formed the fledgeling squadron, 57 Squadron state 'C' Flight while 218 Squadron record 'A' Flight. Regardless of the flight, the squadron would initially be commanded by Flight Lieutenant Basil Carey, formally of 57 Squadron. Thirty-one-year-old Carey had previously seen active service in India with No.28 Squadron flying the Airco DH.9A light bomber from Risalpur over the inhospitable North-West Frontier. Joining F/Lt Carey would be thirty-two-year-old Pilot Officer Alexander Olney, one flight sergeant, two sergeants, five corporals and nine aircraftsmen. Unlike 57 Squadron which was equipped with the Hawker Hart, 218 would be equipped with six sleek Hawker Hinds powered by the new Rolls Royce Kestrel V engine.

*Two Vickers Weybridge built Hawker Harts of No.57 Squadron. Note the very distinctive squadron numbers of the fuselage.*

The Hind was an improved Hawker Hart bomber defined by Specification G.7/34, and was purchased by the RAF as an interim aircraft, while more modern monoplane bombers such as the Fairey Battle, which the squadron would ultimately convert to were still in development. Structural elements were a mixture of steel and duralumin with the wings being fabric-covered, the main differences compared to the earlier Hart was a new power plant.

Both squadrons were under the direct control of the A.O.C.-in-C Central Area, part of the Air Defence of Great Britain a forerunner to Bomber Command. The Central Areas HQ was at Abingdon commanded by Air Commodore H.B Nicholl CBE. Day to day activity of both squadrons was organised and directed by Squadron Leader Francis Reeve a commander with considerable experience.

On Friday, March 27th both squadrons flew north to No.2 Armament Training Camp at North Coates in Lincolnshire, it would be the start of many visits by both squadrons. The airfield at North Coates was established in 1926 to accompany the formation of an Armament Practice Camp (APC). Initial tented accommodation and the four wooden huts inherited from the army were used as messes, HQ and armoury. These very basic facilities were gradually replaced in the 1930s by firstly portable timber and canvas Bessonneau hangars and then permanent hangars, admin buildings and also hosted an air observers' school. From 1927 onwards, two bomber squadrons would be deployed to the airfield for 4 weeks at a time for range practice on nearby Theddlethorpe Range and Donna Nook Range.

In January 1932 RAF North Coates Fitties became No 2 Armament Training Camp (ATC). By now many RAuxAF and Fleet Air Arm units were among the many visitors as the prospect of war in Europe loomed. The Air Observers' School set up in January 1936 began to train personnel selected for part-time observer duties in the disciplines of bomb aiming and air gunnery.

*Seen here in 1937, RAF North Coates (Fitties). By the time the squadron arrived for its first practice camp the station had grown considerably since the Great War.*

The reforming of No.218 Squadron was no coincidence. The comfortable sense of security which had characterised the twenties were rapidly disappearing. In the Far East Japan had invaded Manchuria, then China. Closer to home in July 1932 the Nazi party achieved their biggest election success, becoming the largest political force in the Reichstag thus giving them almost unparalleled influential over consecutive German governments. In only six months, on January 30th, 1933, Adolf Hitler was sworn in as Chancellor. Throughout 1935 the political alliance of the Axis powers was slowly but clearly evident, the Japanese Government gave their American counterparts notice of intention to terminate the Washington Naval Treaty. In March, Germany repudiated the Treaty of Versailles, at the same time declaring openly the intention to re-arm. The Luftwaffe was officially formed, and the existence of the new service made public by Hermann Goering, the flamboyant WW1 veteran who now headed the new Luftwaffe. Six months later the Italian Army under direct orders of Mussolini launched a brutal assault on Abyssinia. The rumblings of future conflicts were at least to the crews of 218 Squadron something they read about, but not influence, all they could do was concentrate on the job in hand, building a squadron and preparing.

The squadrons arrival at North Coates coincided with some partially adverse weather, for the lower ranks this meant eating and sleeping under canvas, never an enjoyable experience. The airfields proximity to the Humber Estuary and the North Sea was also challenging with quickly changeable weather conditions. During the winter months, such was the conditions that from October the station was effectively closed and would re-open on March 1st the following year. Over the next four weeks, both flights of No.57 and the single flight of 218 Squadron dropped 724 practice bombs and fired over 29,777 rounds of ammunition. To spice up the training and improve efficiency, and at the same time promote inter squadron competitiveness a competition was devised which would be held each year, the prestigious Armament Officers Trophy, affectionally known as 'The Cock'. The 1936 competition would be one of the toughest to date, standards were high bringing out the very best in the 'light' and 'medium' bomber squadrons. All the light bomber squadrons wanted to win for their squadron, however, there could be just one winner. With a bombing accuracy of just 67.3 yards in the long-range bombing tests, the Hawker Hart equipped No.57 Squadron was crowned winners. It was a magnificent result for the squadron, unfortunately, 218 Squadron's performance is unknown. On April 25th both Squadrons returned to RAF Upper Hayford and the relatively modern and comfortable surroundings of a front-line bomber station.

May 1st, 1936 was busy for many reasons. It would record the arrival on the squadron of three sergeant pilots from No.57 Squadron, regrettably only the identity of one, Sergeant George Dodsworth is known. Frustratingly, neither squadron felt it important to record their names or movement. Across the airfield, No.57 Squadron finally bade farewell to the Hawker Hart and was re-equipping with the Hawker Hind. Friday, May 1st, 1936 was also noticeable for the creation of four new independent groups with the reorganisation of the Home Commands. This restructuring resulted in the Central Area being split and renamed No. 1 (Bomber) Group and No. 2 (Bomber) Group, the Western Area being renamed No. 3 (Bomber) Group and No. 1 Air Defence Group being renamed No. 6 (Auxiliary) Group. Number 1 (Bomber) Group would as from the 1st of May would comprise of the following station and units.

**RAF Abington** :
Station Flight
No.15 and 40 (Bomber) Squadrons
No.98 and 104 (Bomber) Squadrons (one flight only)

**RAF Bircham Newton** :
No.18 (Bomber) Squadron
No.21 - 34 - 49 (Bomber) Squadrons (one flight each)

**RAF Upper Heyford** :
No.57 (Bomber) Squadron
No.218 (Bomber) Squadron (one flight)

The spring and early summer months of 1936 were spent refining the exceedingly high level of skills required by a 'Peace-Time' Royal Air Force. In May it is understood that the squadron along with 57 Squadron travelled south to RAF Northolt, a station located north of London. Over the coming months, both squadrons would be affiliated to the Air Fighting Development Establishment (AFDE). The main objective of this affiliation was to determine due to the ever-changing characteristics of bomber development and performance the most effective and suitable formations to be flown, not only for accuracy but mutual protection. The increase in speed particular for the light bombers and weaponry had the effect that new tactics needed to be developed, not only for the bomber-boys but the fighter pilots also. The notion of attacks from astern, a tactic used over the battlefields of France and Belgium during the Great War was then the accepted method of attack, almost twenty years on, this same method of attack was still generally believed to be the only effective way of dealing with the bombers. For the bombers, especially the Hawker Hind equipped squadrons a technique of collective mutual defence was needed, concentrated defensive fire from a compact formation was believed to be the only effective answer. Both 57 and 218 Squadrons would work closely with the Gloster Gauntlet Mk.II equipped No.111 (Fighter) Squadron commanded by Squadron Leader George Howard DFC. After numerous experiments with the fighters at Northolt and Upper Heyford, the conclusion was reached that the formation giving the most advantage in flexibility, manoeuvring and defensive power was a unit of five aircraft.

*No.218 (Bomber) Squadron Hawker Hind*

This formation was provisionally referred to as the 'Up and Down' formation, trials also concluded that if the squadron was operating in flights of two and possibly three, they should format in the following "Vic' formation until a fighter attack developed. If fighters were encountered the squadron should take up a line astern formation with the following formation stepped down from the leading flight, all the while the flights remained in the 'Up and Down' formation. The role of the Hawker Hind in any future war was clear from its concept, medium to low-level daylight bombing. To train the pilots in this method of attack both squadrons began practising low-level bombing. A series of cross-country flights were organised to represent operational conditions, bombing heights varied from 200 feet to 1000 feet. On May 21st both squadrons put on a demonstration in front of the members of the Imperial Defence College at Porton Bombing Range, Wiltshire. Two flights from 57 and the single 218 flight put on an impressive display of bombing, 72 bombs were dropped in salvos, all of which landed in a target area of just 50 feet square. The squadrons of RAF Upper Heyford welcomed thousands of spectators on May 24th when the annual Empire Air Day took place. The Empire Air Day started in 1934 giving the British public a rare opportunity to visit a Royal Air Force station and view up close the day-to-day activities. According to a speech in the House of Commons by Anthony Muirhead MC and Bar the Conservative MP he is on record as saying *'The idea of Empire Air Day is that the public should be enabled to see the Royal Air Force at its everyday work. As many stations as possible... are opened to the public on payment of a small charge for admission'*. At each station, a programme of flying was arranged despite the unfavourable weather conditions. During the afternoon Upper Heyford was visited by Air Commodore Alexander Cunningham CBE OBE, senior air staff officer Air Defence of Great Britain and the groups commanding officer, Air Commodore Owen Boyd MC AFC

*Sergeant Charles Pay. Photographs of the squadron's NCO pilots are extremely rare pre-war.*

OBE. Upper Heyford was visited by General Nakhichevan, the Iranian Chief of Staff and six Iranian officers on June 26th, they were accompanied by Squadron Leader Henry Walker MC DFC.

The squadron Operational Records Book makes one of its very rare entries in July, recording the arrival of two new pilots from No.7 Flying Training School (FTS) based at RAF Peterborough. These recently qualified pilots were Acting Pilot Officer Frank Beales and Kenneth Sharpe. Tragedy struck on the 16th when Gloster Gauntlet Mk.II K5264 of No.111 (Fighter) Squadron crashed returning to Northolt after completing an exercise with the squadrons of RAF Upper Heyford. The pilot, Pilot Officer Geoffrey Cornwall crashed near Knotty Green, Beaconsfield when he blacked out in a loop and crashed killing him instantly. Both squadrons were involved in a three-day joint exercise starting on July 27th. Also participating would be the Royal Observer Corps of No.1 and 18 Observer Group, the 1st Anti-Aircraft Division and the fighters of No.11 Group. Given the squadrons previous training at low level, it came as something of a surprise that they were tasked with carrying out mock daylight raids on London from the dizzy height of 25,000 feet. This was pushing the Hinds and the crews in their open cockpit to their limits. The wearing of oxygen masks was a novelty to most, so was the altitude. Additional clothing was quickly issued to the crews who were instructed to remain at this height for the duration of the attacks. On the 28th, ten crews drawn from both squadrons visited a number of Observer posts on the Norfolk and Suffolk coast. In August, the squadron again found itself on attachment, initially to Old Sarum Airfield situated northeast of Salisbury, Wiltshire. For over a month the squadron trained in the reconnaissance / Army Co-Operation role. This new role also meant that the squadron would operate further along the south coast with visits to both RAF Tangmere and Ford.

On August 24th the squadron welcomed three new pilots, Acting Pilot Officers Geoffrey Beavis, Howard 'Sniffer' Sharpe and twenty-one-year-old Sergeant John Jarvis, all three arrived via No.11 Flying Training School (FTS) Wittering.  Within a week the squadron was bolstered with the arrival of two more pilots, from RAF College Cranwell, Pilot Officer Edward Culverwell from No.2 FTS Digby and Acting Pilot Officer Alan Rogers. It would be the start of a long association with the squadron for Alan Rogers. With the influx of pilots, the squadron now began to find its own identity, since its formation, it had been to some extent overshadowed by its parent squadron while effectively acting as its third flight. Almost all day-to-day activities were organised by Squadron Leader Francis Reeve. Where 57 Squadron went, 218 would undoubtedly follow.  On September 4th, the squadrons of Upper Heyford bade farewell to their vastly experienced station commander, Air Commodore George Reid, DSO MC, he was replaced by another Great War veteran, Canadian fighter ace, Wing Commander Joseph Fall DSC, AFC who was posted in from the Home Aircraft Depot, Henlow.

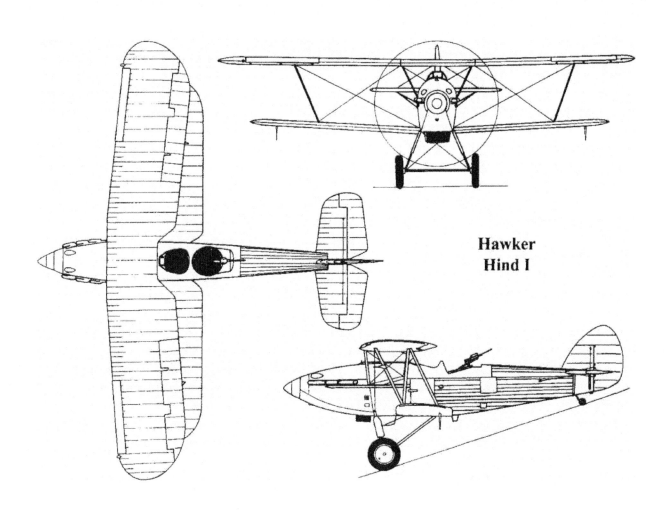

**Hawker
Hind I**

The squadrons reliance on 57 squadron began to change on September 7th when Flying Officer Terence Morton was posted in from No.7 (Bomber) Squadron based at RAF Finningley as 218 Squadron Adjutant, he was quickly followed by Sergeant William Pay from No.1 (Fighter) Squadron, RAF Tangmere. Before qualifying as a Pilot, William Charles Pay was a Wireless Operator with No.500 Squadron based at RAF Manston. On the 29 September 1935, he was successful in his application for pilot training and was posted to No.3 FTS qualifying as a Pilot on the June 5th, 1936.

On Tuesday, September 22nd the prestigious Armament Officers Bombing Trophy was officially present to No.57 Squadron by none other than the officer commanding No.1 Group, Air Commodore Owen Boyd OBE MC AFC at a special ceremony. The crews of 218 Squadron could only look on. The squadron lost P/O Beales on September 20th, if but temporarily, when he was attached to the School of Air Navigation based at RAF Manston for a short navigation course. In his absence the squadron welcomed Australian Pilot Officer Harry Daish from No.3 FTS, Grantham. A native of Sydney, Australia he had gained his wings with No.1 FTS Point Cook, Victoria, Australia. He along with a specially selected group of six Australian pilots were chosen to join the RAF (UK) on a five-year Short Service Commission. Like Pilot Officer Rogers, he would make a name for himself on the squadron. The irrepressible Squadron Leader Reeves was attached to the Air Ministry on September 29th, the command of 57 Squadron and its 218 Squadron flight was passed onto Flight Lieutenant Kenneth Lea-Cox. October began with the departure of Flight Lieutenant Basil Cary to RAF Station, Calshot. In December 1937, 32-year-old Cary would along with four other pilots captain five Saro London flying boats to Australia with No.204 (General Recognisance) Squadron, a distance of some 25,000 sea miles. The squadron returned to No.2 Armament Training camp, North Coates Fitties on October 4th, unlike its first visit in March the squadron had now found its own identity and had with the influx of new pilots a squadron-camaraderie that would be vital in the months and years to come. Within days of the squadron's arrival tragedy struck. Aloft just before 8 am Sergeant George 'Ginger' Dodsworth and his observer/gunner, Sergeant Walter Devoil were participating in dive-bombing practice at Theddlethorpe Ranges. Whilst banking at 800 feet the upper wing badly distorted resulting in the Hind crashing into the sea a short distance from the shore at 08.10 hours. An eye-witness on his way to work reported that the aircraft was on fire before crashing. Boats were quickly sent to the scene in the hope there were survivors. With the rear section of Hind K5516 still visible above the waves the rescuers were quickly on the scene. Sadly, both crew were found dead, the crumpled wreckage would be eventually recovered and brought back to North Coates for examination. It was a tragic accident, the squadron had not suffered any fatalities since the Great War, it was a rather sombre mess that night. Given the exact cause of the loss of K5516 was still unknown restrictions were immediately imposed on the squadron, crews were warned to keep well within permissible guidelines when pulling out of dives and aerobatics were strictly forbidden.

**Tuesday October 6th 1936**
*Hawker Hind*
*Mk.I K5516*
*Contract No : 404654/35*
*Taken On Charge : 06/05/1936*
*Struck Off Charge : 23/10/1936*
*Structural Fatigue*

*Pilot : Sergeant  George Chapman Dodsworth **Killed.***
*Observer : Acting Sergeant Walter James Devoil **Killed.***

*The broken remains of the Rolls Royce Kestrel engine of Hawker Hind K5516. Seen here on the floor of the SHQ hangar at North Coates.*

While at North Coates Fitties the squadron lost another pilot, if under more agreeable circumstances. On October 15th, Pilot Officer Alexander Olney was posted to No.60 Squadron based at Kohat, India. He would spend the next six years serving in the Middle and the Far East. The squadrons detachment to North Coates continued, however, the weather like the mood on the squadron since the death of two friends was disheartening. Strong winds blowing in from the North Sea made training particularly difficult, with the squadron still unaware of the cause of the accident on the 6th the flying limitations were still in place, this added to the increasingly inclement weather was having an effect. With the departure of F/Lt Cary, the squadron welcomed Flight Lieutenant Arnold Louis Christian from RAF Uxbridge on October 20th, this would be Arnold's first command, if only in a temporary capacity. Although born in London in 1906 Arnold was a bit of a mixed bag, he was the son of Vincent Cristini and Gertrude Barley, however his grandfather, Francesco Cristini, a professor of languages was from Naples while his grandmother, Eulalie Bon was from Paris. On settling in England, the family anglicised their surname from Cristini to Christian. Commissioned as a pilot officer in October 1930 he served initially with No.54 (Fighter) Squadron flying the Bristol Bulldog before a spell with No.207 (Bomber) Squadron at RAF Bircham Newton and then Sudan in 1936. His arrival coincided with the squadrons premature return to RAF Upper Heyford due to a combination of weather and structural concerns to the Hinds airframe. Saturday, October 24th was the day that 218 Squadron officially became independent

*The squadron's first commanding officer pictured here prior to joining the RAF. Flight Lieutenant Arnold Louis Christian.*

of 57 Squadron, from that date all training, administration and operational decisions were solely the responsibility of the squadron commander. It was a momentous day, 57 Squadron had nurtured and guided the squadron over the previous months, now it was time for 218 Squadron to demonstrate that it could perform at the highest peacetime levels. Flight Lieutenant Christian's occupancy as squadron commanding officer came to an all to brief conclusion on November 2nd with the arrival of Squadron Leader Francis Shales from No.40 (Bomber) Squadron where he served as a flight commander. Thirty-nine-year-old Shales was a veteran of the Great War, he had served with the Duke of Cornwall's Light Infantry in 1915 before transfer to the Royal Flying Corps. Having held the fort until the arrival of S/Ldr Shales, Arnold Christian was soon posted. A series of spells instructing with No.5 Elementary Flying Training School (EFTS) and No.13 Operational Training Unit (OTU) resulted in promotion to squadron leader and the award of a Mentioned In Dispatches. In November 1940 he was posted to the Bristol Blenheim equipped No.105 Squadron as 'B' Flight Commander. On Christmas Eve 1940 he was promoted to wing commander and given command of the squadron on the departure of Wing Commander Cyril Coggle. Sadly, this popular and courageous wing commander was killed on May 8th, 1941 while leading an attack on a large German convoy at the entrance of Hafrsfjord, Norway.

It was inevitable that with the squadrons recent independence it would fall under the scrutinising gaze of those in high command. On November 27th, none other than Air Chief Marshall Sir John Steel, AOC in C, Bomber Command visit the squadron. It was the squadrons first official visit and Squadron Leader Shales was not going to leave anything to chance, everything was cleaned, polished and painted and then cleaned again. On November 30th, the squadron temporally lost the services of Pilot Officer Edward 'Eddie' Culverwell who was posted on detachment to No.1 FTS at RAF Leuchars for training on Torpedo Spotter Reconnaissance aircraft, it was the first of a number of moves for this young pilot officer.

A squadron Hind was severely damaged on December 12th in rather bizarre circumstances when some recently erected scaffolding collapsed, causing considerable damage. The squadron was not slow in attributing the blame squarely on the local contractors, T.H Kingerlee and Son Ltd, the aircraft never returned to the squadron.

### Sunday December 12th 1936
*Hawker Hind*
*Mk.I K5517*
*Contract No : 404654/35*
*Taken On Charge : 06/05/1936*

Following closely on the visit of Air Chief Marshal Steel the squadron welcomed No.1 Group's A.O.C, Air Commodore Owen Boyd OBE, MC, AFC. Finally, and to the relief of the whole squadron, and the rest of RAF Upper Heyford the final official visit took place on December 7th with the arrival of Air Chief Marshal Sir Robert Brooke-Popham. The same day, Pilot Officer Culverwell fresh from his detachment from RAF Leuchars was again on the move, this time to RAF Calshot, Hampshire for more nautical training. The squadron welcomed the return of P/O Beales on completion of his Navigation Course at Manston on the 19th, it was the last posting in or out of the squadron before the Christmas Festivities. Thus 1936 came to an end, for the squadron it had been a steep learning curve since its formation in March. Having effectively served as a third flight to the established 57 Squadron, it had been rather over shadowed, now with a new commanding officer and growing confidence the squadron could with some justification hold its head high and look forward to the coming year.

# Chapter 2: 1937 - Tension in Europe

*A young-looking Eric Arthur Hunt. Photographed when he received his pilot's licence in 1935.*

January 1937 began with a flurry of postings with the long-awaited and welcomed addition of a second flight. On the 4th, Acting Pilot Officers Charles Crew, Stewart Coultes-Woods and Eric Hunt arrived from No.8 FTS. Number 18 (Bomber) Squadron provided Pilot Officers William Warren, William Newton Howes, Anthony Beck and lastly Russell Oxley. The same day as the arrival of seven new pilots the squadron finally lost it roving P/O Culverwell who for the last time found himself on the move, this time to RAF Gosport. Sadly, he would be killed on June 13th, 1941 while serving with Coastal Command. At the time of his death, he was leading a small detachment of Bristol Beauforts of 22 Squadron on a special night-time shipping strike from Wick, Scotland. His aircraft, W6521 crashed off the Norwegian coast while searching for the German Cruiser Lutzow. He was a squadron leader the time of his death. The squadron participated in the first of two large Fighter Command tactical exercise starting on January 7th, both flights were involved in evaluating the defensive capabilities of the command, the light bombers of No.1 Group played the enemy intruders. Pilot Officer 'Sniffer' Smythe departed on the 13th posted to No.1 Group HQ for duty as Personnel Assistant (PA) to the recently appointed A.O.C, No.1 Group, Air Commodore Sydney Smith O.B.E. Born into a wealthy family, 'Sniffer' was part of the Lyons confectionary business empire. At the outbreak of war, he would serve with some distinction as a flight commander with No.214 Squadron where he completed a hectic first tour. After a period of rest, he returned to the squadron in July 1942 this time as commanding officer. He ended the war with a DSO, DFC and AFC retiring from the RAF in 1958. On the 21st the squadron participated in the second of the large Fighter Command exercises to test the country's defences in the face of enemy attack from the air. The squadron lost one of its more recent arrivals on 26th when Pilot Officer Stewart Coutts-Wood was posted No.21 (B) Squadron based at RAF Lympne. He was still on the squadron when war was declared and operated throughout the 'Phoney-War' up until the German capture of Dunkirk. What was left of the squadron was moved north to Lossiemouth in July 1940 after suffering heavy casualties. Posted to No.13 OTU for as an instructor, 25-year-old Stewart Farquharson - Coutts Wood DFC was tragically killed when the Blenheim he was flying collided with another 13 OTU aircraft during a formation exercise on October 8th 1940.

With the rapid re-armament of the military in Germany from 1936 onwards the British Government finally began to realise the possible threat this posed. With a resurgence in all aspects of aviation in Germany those with the purse strings in White Hall were quick to ensure that the Royal Air Force was given higher priority in terms of rearmament than the other senior services, this decision was to ensure that there would be parity with Germany. In Britain, a growing number of new modern designs were slowly entering service or about to. For the squadron at least these new designs were something that they could only read about, as a recently formed squadron, they were aware that they were way down the pecking order for conversion. Training was essential for any squadron and 218 was no different, this training ranged from individual pilots being posted for specific courses or the whole squadron being detached. For the young pilots it was an exciting era to be flying in the RAF, they were truly the 'Golden Years'.

Major Bremmer of the Finnish Airforce was attached to RAF Upper Heyford from February 9th, his brief visit was to become acquainted with the operational organisation of a light bomber squadron, his stay was concluded on the 13th. Prior to his arrival Pilot Officer Kenneth Sharpe was posted on detachment to the Air Armament School, he was followed by Pilot Officer Russell Oxley who attended a Parachute Course at RAF Manston, Kent. Another accident occurred on February 17th when one of the squadrons few non officer pilots damaged Hind K5390. Twenty-Year-Old Sergeant John Jarvis was taxing to the hangar when he encountered some soft ground, taken unawares the Hind tipped up onto its nose, smashing the propellor, both crew members were shaken but uninjured.

## Wednesday 17th February 1937
*Hawker Hind*
*Mk.I K5390*
*Contract No : 404654/35*
*Taken On Charge : 23/03/1936*
*Repaired On Site :*
*Pilot : Sergeant John Jarvis 590478*
*Observer/Gunner : Unknown*


The squadron recorded damage to yet another aircraft in similar circumstances on February 20th. Pilot Officer William Newton Howes was at the controls of K6629 when he was obliged to make a forced landing at RAF Odiham after becoming lost on a cross country training flight. While taxing too fast towards the hangar the Hind encountered a match of boggy ground the consequence of which was the Hind came to a rapid halt, the nose dug in and the aircraft, and its occupants found themselves in a precarious position.

## Saturday February 20th 1937
*Hawker Hind*
*Mk.I K6629*
*Contract No : 424397/35*
*Taken On Charge : 16/11/1936*
*Repaired On Site :*
*Pilot : Pilot Officer William Newton-Howes 37297*
*Observer/Gunner: Unknown*


The squadron lost two pilots on March 15th, Pilot Officer Terence Moreton to No.90 (B) Squadron, and Pilot Officer William Warren to No.226 (B) Squadron. Terence Berkeley Morton would survive the war and was awarded the DSO in June 1945 having survived three operational tours, sadly he died in 1946. On the 23rd Pilot Officer Beck was attached to Air Navigation School for a short navigation course, the same day Pilot Officer Alan Rogers assumed the post of squadron Adjutant. Even the squadron commanding Officer, S/Ldr Shales was not excluded from attending training courses, on March 30th he travelled south to RAF Biggin Hill, Kent to attend a course at the school of Anti-Aircraft Defence. This was a joint Army - RAF establishment located near

Bromley. The course was quickly followed by a further course at the School of Artillery at Shoeburyness, situated on the Essex coast a few miles east of Southend-On- Sea. The gunnery school was the training ground and experimental site where new guns were evaluated and tested.

The squadrons annual trip to armament camp commenced on April 24th, unlike the previous year the squadron flew north to RAF West Freugh, Scotland and No 4 Armament Practice Camp. It was along with 107 Squadron the first to visit since opening. If the crews thought that North Coates Fitties was bleak, they were in for a surprise. The Air Ministry had purchased 2700 acres of land for £19,400 in August 1936, realising that they needed more land they absorbed land at East Freugh. It opened in January 1937, four months later the squadron found on its arrival that conditions and facilities were at best rudimentary. Other than Australian Pilot Officer Harry Daish departure to London on May 7th, in connection of the coronation of King George VI and the arrival of RAF Upper Heyford's station commander, Wing Commander Joseph Fall DSC, AFC on the 20th the detachment was noticeable by its lack of excitement. The squadron returned to RAF Upper Heyford on May 24th and were shocked to discover their popular commanding officer, S/Ldr Shales time at the helm would be brought to an early conclusion.

*Seen here while serving in the Far East. Australian Harry Daish wearing a rather stylish moustache. He was one of the squadron's more charismatic individuals.*

The growing popularity of the Empire Air Day was graphically illustrated by the attendance of over five thousand paying visitors to RAF Upper Heyford on May 1st. The squadron gave a faultless display of dive bombing in glorious weather. Apart from the 5000 plus crowd also attending was the prominent British Conservative politician Viscount Swinton and Sir Edward Ellington. Chief of Air Staff, Sir Edward was the architect of a plan known as 'Scheme F'. This schemes objective was to increase the size of the Royal Air Force to 187 front line squadrons. The concept was that for every two fighter squadrons, there would be a need for five bomber squadrons, this reflected the dominance of the bomber strategy at the time. This proposal introduced in 1936 was planned to be achieved within three years to counter the threat from Hitler's Germany. He was also responsible for the break-up of the command known as "Air Defence of Great Britain", this break up effectively created RAF Fighter Command, RAF Bomber Command, RAF Coastal Command and RAF Training Command.

The new squadron commander, twenty-eight-year-old James Cunningham arrived on June 1st, and was immediately promoted to squadron leader, however he would not replace S/Ldr Shales just yet. James Charles Cunningham had already experience of command having previously served with the Hawker Hind equipped No.49 Squadron. June 1937 found No.1 Group in a healthy position; the following squadrons fell under its command.

RAF Abingdon      : Nos XV, 40 and 62 Squadrons, plus Station Flight.
RAF Upper Heyford : Nos 18, 57, 218, 113 and 233 Squadrons
RAF Harwell       : Nos 105, 266 and 107 squadrons
RAF Bicester      : Nos 101 and 90 Squadrons
RAF Lympne        : Nos 21 and 34 Squadrons
RAF Usworth       : Nos 103 and 33 Squadrons
RAF Cranwell      : Nos 62 and 108 Squadrons

All the above squadrons were equipped with the Hawker Hind except Nos.105 and 266 Squadrons which were operating the Hawker Audax. Number 101 Squadron flew the ungainly twin engined Boulton Paul Overstrands while No.90 Squadron were in the process of converting to the new and exciting Bristol Blenheim. The squadron lost another pilot on the 3rd when Pilot Officer Russell Oxley was posted to No.15 Squadron. He would eventually serve with distinction with No.50 Squadron gaining the DFC in 1941 and then a DSO while commanding the squadron in 1942. He survived the war retiring in 1960. On June 14th, Squadron Leader Cunningham official assumed command of the squadron, S/Ldr Shales was posted to No.1 School of Technical Training (Apprentices) Halton, he retired due to ill heath in 1940. With the departure of some of the squadrons more experienced pilots the squadron was bolstered with the arrival of four recently qualified pilots. Acting Pilot Officers Thomas Brock, John Mahoney and David Devoto, plus the slightly more experienced Pilot Officer John Innes-Crump who had joined the RAF in 1934.

The squadron recorded another flying accident on the June 22nd when Sergeant Edward Fleet inadvertently landed 200 yards short of the designated landing ground at RAF Abbotsinch on return from a formation training flight. The Hind hit the boundary ditch which was not visible to the young pilot owing to the length of the grass resulting in damage to the undercarriage and propellor.

**Tuesday June 22nd 1937**
*Hawker Hind*
*Mk.I K5392*
*Contract No : 404654/35*
*Taken On Charge : 24/03/1936*
*Repaired On Site :*
*Pilot : Sergeant Edward Fleet 365741*
*Observer/Gunner : Unknown*

On July 7th, a rather tanned Flying Officer Richard Seys DFC arrived fresh from his posting from Palestine where he had served with 14 Squadron flying the cumbersome Fairey Gordon two-seat light bomber and utility aircraft. He would immediately take up the post of flight commander. The summer of 1937 found RAF Upper Heyford's squadrons on the move, the first squadron to vacate was No.233 (B) Squadron in early July, followed in August by No.113 (B) Squadron who moved to RAF Grantham and 3 Group control.

While carrying out an Observer Corps calibration exercise over Lincolnshire on July 15th Sergeant William Pay encountered heavy rain and almost zero visibility. With conditions quickly deteriorating he was obliged to force-land at Kirby Bellars, two miles SW of Melton Mowbray hitting a tree in the process. Although both crew members were only slightly injured, they were admitted to hospital for observation.

**Thursday July 15th 1937**
*Hawker Hind*
*Mk.I K6630*
*Contract No : 404654/35*
*Taken On Charge : 16/11/1936*
*Struck Off Charge : 13/09/1937*
*Total Flying Hours : 115hrs 35mins*
*Pilot : Sergeant William Pay 512972*
*Observer/Gunner : Corporal John Davis*

Yet another accident occurred on the night of July 28th when Pilot Officer David Devoto flattened out too soon while making his approach to Upper Heyford on what was his first night landing. Misjudging his height, he landed on one wheel buckling it and damaging the wing in the process. The damage was such that the Hind was Struck off Charge.

**Wednesday July 28th 1937**
*Hawker Hind*
*Mk.I K3391*
*Contract No : 404654/35*
*Taken On Charge : 24/03/1936*
*Struck Off Charge : 06/09/1937*
*Total Flying Hours : 302hrs 45mins*
*Pilot : Pilot Officer David Devoto 39228*
*Observer/Gunner : Unknown.*

In September Pilot Officer John Culloch Middlemore Hughes was posted from RAF Cranwell. John was born at Bromsgrove, Worcestershire on 13th February 1917. He attended Haileybury College from 1930 to 1934 and entered the RAF College Cranwell in September 1935 as a Flight Cadet joining C Squadron. A keen sportsman Hughes represented the college in Squash, Soccer, Cricket and Tennis. Over the following months and years, he would become instrumental in the success of the squadron. The growing tension in Europe was increased when Mussolini visited Germany on a five-day state visit in September 1937. During a radio broadcast both Hitler and Mussolini spoke at a rally in Berlin that was heard by millions around the world in a radio broadcast. Hitler went first and spoke of the *"common ideals and interests inspiring Italy and Germany."* Mussolini, delivering his speech in German, made the first public acknowledgement that Italy had troops in Spain when he said, *"Where words are insufficient to carry on the fight we turn to weapons. We have done this in Spain, where thousands of Italian Fascist volunteers have lost their lives.*

Both Britain and France balked at Spain's demand to condemn Germany and Italy as aggressors and allow arms exports to the Spanish government, fearing it would worsen the general situation in Europe. Both Britain and France needed time, time to re-arm, time to reorganise and time to prepare for what many believed to be the inevitable war.

Pilot Officer Geoffrey Beavis was posted to the Air Armament School on September 6th, it is the last time he is mentioned in the squadron ORB. Sadly, he would be killed on January 17th, 1939 while at the controls of a Miles Mentor (L4414) from RAF Eastchurch Station Flight. Flying with Air Vice-Marshal H.M. Cave-Browne-Cave, C.B, D.S.O., D.F.C. the aircraft crashed at Butley, 20 miles

*John Hughes perhaps more than most optimised the courage and professionalism of the pilots arriving on the squadron at this time. He would play a pivotal role in the squadron's history.*

north of Ipswich killing Beavis outright. Air Vice-Marshal Cave-Browne survived with severe head injuries, he was at the time Air Officer Commanding No. 25 (Armament) Group.

The recent spate of accidents continued on September 16th with the total loss of Hind K6628. Canadian, Pilot Officer John Mahoney was on a Tactical Exercise and on route from Scotland to RAF Thonaby when he became lost due to the inexperience of the observer and the incorrect setting of the aircrafts compass. Having vainly circled several times in an attempt to find a suitable landing area Mahoney finally found what he believed to be the idea spot. Not satisfied with his first approach he came around for another, however on this occasion he overshot. The Hind, which was reported to have been carrying seven small bombs crashed into a low stone wall on the Boldron Road between Barnard Castle and Bowes, County Durham. The pilot was severely cut to the face, Corporal Davies suffered a broken ankle. Both were bruised and suffering from shock. Fortunately, a L.N.E.R delivery lorry was quickly on the scene and took airman to the local village of Bowes from where they were quickly taken by ambulance to Catterick Hospital. The mangled Hind was recovered and transported to RAF Catterick, were it was deemed beyond repair and stuck of charge.

**Thursday September 16th 1937**

*Hawker Hind*
*Mk.I K6628*
*Contract No : 424397/35*
*Taken On Charge : 20/11/1936*
*Struck Off Charge : 08/01/1938*
*Total Flying Hours : 229hrs 10mins*
*Pilot : Pilot Officer John Jennings Edward Mahoney 40182*
*Observer/Gunner : Corporal Davies.*

*Another rare photograph, which captures the wrecked Hawker Hind flown by Pilot Officer Mahoney.*

The squadron welcomed another batch of pilots the first week of October, these were acting Pilot Officers James Calvert and Robert Balls, both fresh from training. On the 4th Flying Officer Hughes took over the duties of squadron adjutant from F/O Rogers. The role of squadron Adjutant came with responsibility, he would assist the commanding officer with administration, organise flying training, aircraft serviceability, postings and of course leave. As such, the adjutant was usually a man with significant influence within the squadron.

November 1937 would be remembered for the number of flying accidents suffered by the squadron. With the worsening weather the crews found themselves at the mercy of the wintery conditions. Exposed to the elements in their open cockpits and with basic navigation instruments the crews found themselves often flying in low cloud, rain, sleet and snow. These conditions were challenging even for experienced pilots, for the junior pilots, it must have been truly daunting. It was not long before the recently posted P/O Calvert blotted his record book. Having lost himself while on a cross country flight, Calvert sought the sanctuary of RAF Usworth. In quickly fading light the recently qualified pilot came into land too fast resulting in the buckling to the undercarriage and rear wheel. Having gained his wings with No.5 FTS on July 29th, 1937, and with only 3 hours flying time on the Hind the subsequent investigation placed the error squarely on the young pilot shoulders stating it was an '*Error of Judgement*'.

**Friday November 5th 1937**
*Hawker Hind*
*Mk.I K6633*
*Contract No : 424397/35*
*Taken On Charge : 30/11/1936*
*Repaired on Site :*
*Pilot : Pilot Officer James Calvert 39491*
*Observer/Gunner : Unknown.*

The run of accidents continued, four days later Pilot Officer Charles Crews was returning from a cross country flight in Hind K5457 when he undershot his approach to RAF Usworth and hit the boundary fence due to strong cross winds. Thankfully both crew members were uninjured however the Hind required minor repair. Unlike James Calvert, Charles Crews was an experienced pilot having gained his wing in August 1936 and had acquired over 200 flying hours on the Hawker Hind.

**Tuesday November 9th 1937**
*Hawker Hind*
*Mk.I K5457*
*Contract No : 404654/35*
*Taken On Charge : Not recorded*
*Repaired on Site :*
*Pilot : Pilot Officer Charles Arthur Reginald Crews 37795*
*Observer/Gunner : Unknown.*

The A.O.C No.1 Group arrived at RAF Upper Heyford on the 9th for the station's annual inspection. Joining the AOC was former squadron pilot P/O 'Sniffer' Smythe. All three squadrons, No.18, 57 and 218 were presented to the Air Officer Commanding. The final accident of the month sadly resulted in the death of both crew members. On the afternoon of November 26th Pilot Officer Eric Arthur Hunt and his observer, Aircraftsman 1st Class Joseph Thomas was scheduled to carry out a cross country flight with part of the route over the Irish Sea. The Hind was seen emerging from clouds at around 300 feet just off the Cambrian coast, probably in an attempt to establish their position. Witnesses reported hearing the Kestrel Mk.V engine misfiring and smoke and sparks were observed trailing behind the aircraft. Pilot Officer Hunt turned inshore, the aircraft rapidly lost what little height it had and was seen to make a steep turn to starboard, immediately the Hinds lower wing touched the surface of the freezing waters of the Irish Sea with catastrophic results.

Instantly the Hind was seen to cartwheel into the sea off the coastal town of Workington situated at the mouth of the River Derwent on the west coast of Cumbria. Witness John Courter reported, *" I heard the two-airman cry for help when the aircraft hit the water. They went down, and then one appeared on the tail, then another joined him. I shouted for them to hang on as a rowing boat was on its way"*. Sadly neither heard that rescue was on the horizon, John Courter, *" It would appear that one of them was on the back of another as they swam for shore, there was a bit of a struggle and they went down together. One came up and appeared to be making an effort to swim, he cried for help, then just floated."*

Another witness, a Mr Harry McCullough of Lawson Street, Workington was standing on Workington Pier and was attracted to the terrific noise and knew immediately something was wrong. *'The 'plane never got more than a yard above the water for the last quarter of a mile. It sank quickly, but I saw two men clinging close together on the under- carriage. They let go and appeared to be trying to swim'.*

The body of Arthur Hunt was quickly located, it would appear from the witnesses that he had vainly tried to save his crew mate in the freezing sea. It took nine hours before the body of the 20-year-old observer from Merionethshire, North Wales was found. His body was discovered at low tide amongst the rocks a mere 200 yards from the scene of the accident by a Mr Monkhouse. The wreckage of the Hind, which was less than 50 yards offshore was towed into Workington Dockrills by a Irish and Scottish Herring Drifter. Arthur Hunt was born on October 8th, 1916 the only son of Mr and Mrs A.V Hunt of Lower Bedington, Wirral. He was educated at Birkenhead School leaving to work at Messrs Lever Bros of Port Sunlight in the laboratory department as a junior chemist, the department his father was a manager. He left to join the RAF in 1936 having previous gained his pilot's licence in 1935, he joined the squadron on January 4th, 1937 on completion of his flying training at No.8 Flying Training School, Filton. He was at the time of his death an experienced pilot, having notched up 290 flying hours, 142 of which was on the Hind. A local newspaper reported that the aircraft was en-route from RAF Turnhouse to RAF Hooton Park.

### Friday November 26th 1937
*Hawker Hind*
*Mk.I K6632*
*Contract No : 424397/35*
*Taken On Charge : 03/12/1936*
*Struck Off Charge: 05/04/1938*
*Total Fling Hours : 301hrs 30mins*
*Pilot : Pilot Officer Eric Arthur Hunt. 37808* **Killed**
*Observer/Gunner : Aircraftsman Joseph Thomas 527003.* **Killed**

The day after the tragedy three new pilots arrived on the squadron, Pilot Officers Richard How, Michael Fox and the aristocratic sounding Norman Harvey de Capelles Brouad found themselves at RAF Upper Heyford. One can only imagine the atmosphere on the squadron, it had been almost a year since the squadron lost a crew in a fatal accident.

The final month of 1937 found the squadron at Upper Heyford joining No.18 and 57 Squadrons over the festivities. Rumours that the squadron had been chosen to convert to the fast and modern Fairey Battle had been circulating for a few weeks, the whole squadron was excited at the prospect of converting. The recent run of accidents had not quite finished with the squadron. On December 8th, the recently posted P/O Brouad was on a training flight when he undershot his approach and struck a hedge with his undercarriage damaging the aircraft in the process.

**Wednesday December 8th 1937**
*Hawker Hind*
*Mk.I K5457*
*Contract No : 404654/35*
*Taken On Charge :  On strength of 57 Squadron*
*Pilot : Pilot Officer Norman Harvey de Capelles Brouad*
*Observer/Gunner : Unknown.*

There is no report of any injuries to the crew, the Hind which is recorded as being on the strength of 57 Squadron sustained only minor damage and was repaired on site.  At the time of the crash Norman Brossard had the grand total of 4 hours experience flying the Hawker Hind. Interestingly, on February 18th, 1938 the London Gazette reported that Pilot Officer Norman Brouad had relinquished his short service commission on account of ill-heath. Whether this was a direct result of the crash is unknown.

It had been a tough year for the squadron, it first full year on the Hawker Hind had brought a few challenges which the squadron had faced and overcome. The recent spate of accidents and the death of two crew members had tainted what was otherwise an excellent year's work. The squadron was finding its own unique identity and everyone from the lowest erk to the squadron commander was working hard to put 218 Squadron on the map. The rumours that the squadron was to be re-equipped with the Fairey Battle were persisting and were the talk of the mess. The crews were excited at the prospect of flying the new light bomber just entering service within No.1 Group and 218 Squadron would be the first of RAF Upper Heyfords three resident squadrons to convert, it was a tremendous boost to morale.

*The squadrons last recorded Hind incident. A rather bent looking Hind K3767.*

# Chapter 3: 1938 - Munich Agreement

*Five of the squadron's aircraft high above the clouds. Hawker Hind K6755, K5392 K5389, K6631 and K6633.*

The year started with the arrival on January 4th of the squadrons new commanding officer, Squadron Leader Lewin Bowring Duggan. Thirty-Nine-Year-old Duggan was a Great War veteran having initially served with the 1st Battalion, Hertfordshire Regiment as a 2nd Lt on the Western Front. His flying experience prior to his arrival was distantly nautical. He was seconded for service in the RAF on July 30th, 1918, where he was granted a temporary commission as 2nd Lt (A. and S). The February 1919 RAF Air Force Lists records his appointment to a commission in that service as a land and seaplane pilot dated July 30th, 1918. In January 1927 Duggan was posted to No.23 Group Headquarters based at St Vincent's, Grantham. Further posting followed, still with the rank of Flight Lieutenant he had his first taste of command when he took charge of 421 (Fleet Spotter) Flight based at Gosport from July 9th, 1928 until the Flight was disbanded on April 26th 1929.

His next command was of 447 (Fleet Spotter) Flight aboard HMS Furious from April 26th 1929 until February 19th 1931. He was replaced by Flt Lt J B Heath, RN. It is understood that Lewin also served aboard the Aircraft Carrier HMS Glorious. Next was a posting to the RAF Training Base at RAF Leuchers in April 1931.His last home service was as adjutant at RAF Abingdon before he was posted to Hinaidi in Iraq in November 1935 where he was employed on photographic staff duties in which he specialised in 1923. The departing Squadron Leader Cunningham was posted to the Staff College at Andover. Sadly, he would be killed within weeks of war being declared. On September 29th, 1939 the now Wing Commander Cunningham lead the Hampden equipped 144 Squadron on a daylight operation to Heligoland to attack German shipping. Intercepted by

Bf109s of 1./ZG26 the squadron lost five of the twelve crews dispatched including Wing Commander Cunningham who was shot down by Uffz Pirsch. RAF Upper Heyford welcomed the arrival of the Long-Range Development Unit (LRDU) and its large and heavy Vickers Wellesley aircraft on January 1st 1938, the station was fast becoming overcrowded and rumours once again began circulating of a possible move. The eagerly awaited re-equipping of the Fairey Battle commenced on January 17th with the arrival of the squadrons first aircraft, Stockport built Battle Mk.I, K7647. The squadrons association with the Hind was not quite over, or accidents with them. On January 18th, Pilot Officer Frank Beales was involved in a collision at RAF Usworth. Beales had become bogged down in mud in Hind K3767 and was awaiting towing when without warning a Hind of 103 Squadron smashed into the side of the aircraft. The pilot of the 103 Squadron aircraft, P/O Lowne had taken off without permission and without checking for obstructions! Damage was quickly repaired, this was the squadron's last incident with the Hawker Hind.

**Wednesday January 18th 1938**

*Hawker Hind*
*Mk.I K3767*
*Contract No : 424397/35*
*Taken On Charge : On strength of 57 Squadron*
*Pilot : Pilot Officer Frank Beales*
*Observer/Gunner : Unknown.*

The Fairey Battle was a single-engine light bomber designed and manufactured by the Fairey Aviation Company. It was developed during the mid-1930s as a monoplane successor to the Hawker Hart and Hind biplanes. The Battle was powered by the same Rolls-Royce Merlin piston engine that powered the Hawker Hurricane and Supermarine Spitfire. The Battle however was much heavier, with its three-man crew and bomb load. Though a great improvement over the Hart and Hind the Battle was relatively slow and limited in range. Unfortunately like its predecessors it was lightly armed, a single forward firing .303 machine gun was mounted in the starboard wing fired by the pilot, this was supplemented by manually aimed .303 Vickers K machine gun in the rear.

The Battle had a relatively clean design, having adopted a slim oval-shaped fuselage which was manufactured in two sections. The forward section, in front of the cockpit, relied mainly upon a steel tubular structure to support the weight of the nose-mounted engine the rear section was of a metal monocoque structure comprised hoop frames and Z-section stringers which was built on jigs. The structure of the aircraft involved several innovations and firsts for Fairey, it had the distinction of being the company's first low-wing monoplane it also was the first light-alloy stressed-skin construction aircraft to be produced by the firm.

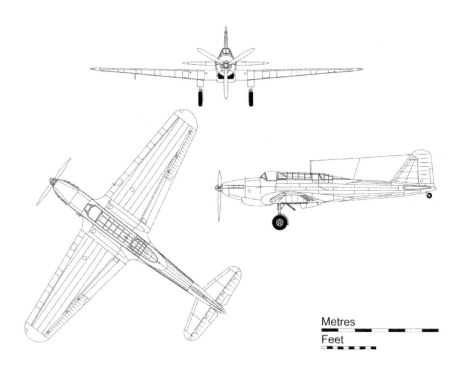

Fairey Battle Mk.I

The wing of the Battle used a two-part construction, the centre section being integral with the fuselage. The internal structure of the wings relied upon steel spars which varied in dimension towards the wing tips, the ailerons, elevators and rudder all were metal-framed with fabric coverings, while the split trailing edge flaps were entirely composed of metal.

The Battle was designed with a single enclosed cockpit to accommodate a crew of three, these typically being a pilot, observer/navigator and radio operator/air gunner. The pilot and gunner were seated in a tandem arrangement in the cockpit. The observer's position, who served as the bomb aimer, was situated directly beneath the pilot's seat sighting was performed in the prone position through a sliding panel in the floor of the fuselage using the Mk. VII Course Setting Bomb Sight. Complete with a continuous glazed canopy, which was much appreciated by the crews after the open cockpits of the Hind.

The Battle had a standard bomb load of four 250lb bombs which were carried in cells neatly concealed in the internal space in both wings. These could be augmented with a further two 250lb bombed or anti-personnel clusters fitted to external bomb racks. As with all aircraft of the time forward visibility while on the ground was extremely poor, however once airborne the pilot had excellent views, the cockpit was modern when compared to the Hind with many additional dials and was roomy and comfortable and thankfully fitted with a heating system.

By the time that the Battle was entering service in late 1937 the increase in performance and capabilities of fighter aircraft had outstripped the modest performance gains that the light bomber had achieved over its biplane predecessors. The early variants of the Battle lacked an armoured cockpit and self-sealing fuel tanks. The Battle was considered well-armoured by the standards of the 1930s. No RAF bombers were fitted with self-sealing tanks at the beginning of the war, although they were hastily fitted once the necessity was made apparent, however that was in the future. For now, the squadron was just content to be converting. During January, a steady flow of Battles began to arrive, on the 20th K7651 and K7652 were delivered followed on the 21st by K7653. On the 24th K7654 was taken on charge followed by K7655 and K7656 on the 26th. The last four Battles quickly followed, K7657 arrived on the 27th and on the last day of the month K7658, K7659 and K7660 were accepted.

February began with the role of squadron Adjutant once again changing hands, Pilot Officer Hughes relinquishing the post and the former Adjutant, P/O Alan Rogers taking over for a second term. By February 11th the squadron recieved the last of its Battles via Messrs Fairey Aviation Co, making the squadron total of sixteen Battle Mk.Is ( 12. I.E and 4 I.R ) these were;

| Serial | Delivered | Maker | Contract |
|--------|-----------|-------|----------|
| K7647 | 17/01/1938 | Fairey Stockport, Hayes | 424738/35 |
| K7651 | 20/01/1938 | Fairey Stockport, Hayes | 424738/35 |
| K7652 | 20/01/1938 | Fairey Stockport, Hayes | 424738/35 |
| K7653 | 21/01/1938 | Fairey Stockport, Hayes | 424738/35 |
| K7654 | 24/01/1938 | Fairey Stockport, Hayes | 424738/35 |
| K7655 | 26/01/1938 | Fairey Stockport, Hayes | 424738/35 |
| K7656 | 26/01/1938 | Fairey Stockport, Hayes | 424738/35 |
| K7657 | 27/01/1938 | Fairey Stockport, Hayes | 424738/35 |
| K7658 | 31/01/1938 | Fairey Stockport, Hayes | 424738/35 |
| K7659 | 31/01/1938 | Fairey Stockport, Hayes | 424738/35 |
| K7660 | 31/01/1938 | Fairey Stockport, Hayes | 424738/35 |
| K7661 | 02/02/1938 | Fairey Stockport, Hayes | 424738/35 |

| K7663 | 10/02/1938 | Fairey Stockport, Hayes | 424738/35 |
|---|---|---|---|
| K7664 | 10/02/1938 | Fairey Stockport, Hayes | 424738/35 |
| K7665 | 10/02/1938 | Fairey Stockport, Hayes | 424738/35 |
| K7666 | 10/02/1938 | Fairey Stockport, Hayes | 424738/35 |

There followed an intensive period of training, the pilots especially had their work cut out getting to grips with the complexity of a modern aircraft and the increase in cockpit instrumentation, at the same time mastering the Rolls Royce Mk.I engine. For the ground crews it was also a period of adjustment and learning. The majority had been trained on fabric covered aircraft, although the Hind was a mixture of steel and aluminium it was still a big learning curve. For the engine fitters the change from the 700hp Rolls Royce Kestrel V to the 950hp Rolls Royce Mk.I engine fitted to the Battles would have been equally challenging.

Change was not just confined to squadron level, at Group HQ the incumbent Air Commodore Sydney Smith O.B.E was posted to Headquarters, Bomber Command of the February 28th, he was replaced by Air Vice Marshal Patrick Henry Playfair CB, CVO, MC. It was not long before new group commander made his presence felt when he visited RAF Upper Heyford on March 21st. This visit may possibly have been to inspect the aircraft of the Long-Range Development Unit and the squadrons recently acquired Battles. On March 16th Squadron Leader Duggan visited RAF Boscombe Down by air, flying Battle K7651, he was accompanied on the flight by P/O Richmond who would act as navigator. Within 40 minutes the crew had touched down, a meeting with the station commander followed and a quick check on the facilities was undertaken. One can only speculate that the visit was in preparation for the squadrons move. On March 28th, the squadron participated in a Group Navigation exercise, all available Battles and crews were involved which would see the squadron visit Flimston Down, Bircham Newton and Abington.

Inevitably the first mishap was not long in coming. On March 29th, P/O David Devoto was ordered to carry out a two-part training exercise. The first part was attack at low level a pre-selected target at Royston, Hertfordshire. On completion of the attack, the crew were then to practice low level oblique photography visiting towns including Bassingbourn and Hitching. It was at this stage P/O Devoto experienced engine trouble and was obliged to land with his undercarriage retracted. A newspaper article in the Essex Newsman date April 2nd, 1938, states that the Battle had engine failure while at 1000 feet and was forced to make a wheels up landing in a corn field between Little Dunmow and Bishop Stortford Road. RAF mechanics from nearby RAF Debden were quickly on the scene as were the local constabulary. The reporter quotes an eye-witness to the events, 'The pilot was about twenty, he stepped out of the plane after the crash as if nothing had happened and was as cool as a cucumber! Thankfully, no one was injured, and the damage was reported to consist of a smashed propellor and damaged under surface, this quickly repaired on the squadron.

## Tuesday March 29th 1938

*Fairey Battle*
*Mk.I K7652*
*Contract No : 424738/35*
*Taken On Charge : 27/01/1938*
*Pilot : Pilot Officer David Devoto*
*Observer/Bomb aimer: Unknown.*
*Gunner / Wireless Operator : Unknown*

Another Group Navigation Exercise was flown on March 31st, unlike the previous flight which was flown at 4000 feet, this would undertaken at 12,000 feet. The route was unchanged, however cloud made this a more challenging exercise. The squadron was informed that it would be leaving the familiar surroundings of Oxfordshire in early April, it was no surprise given the rather cramped conditions at Upper Heyford. The squadrons new home would be RAF Boscombe Down in Wiltshire. The main squadron party arrived on April 22nd, 1938, that same day the station transferred from No.4 Group control to No.1 Group control. The two resident squadrons, 51 and 58 Squadron and their Armstrong Whitworth Whitley and Avro Anson's travelled north to Yorkshire where they and the group would eventually make its home. The station had been in the capable hands of 58 Squadrons, Wing Commander John Potter, this changed on April 29th with the arrival from RAF Turnhouse of Wing Commander Gerard Oddie DFC, AFC.

*One of the earliest photographs of a squadron Fairey Battle taken at RAF Boscombe Down soon after the squadron's arrival.*

*Above: Fairey Battle Mk.I K7660 'L' seen here at its dispersal at RAF Boscombe Down.*

The airfield first opened in October 1917 and was operated as a Royal Flying Corps Training Depot Station. The airfield was initially known as Royal Flying Corps Station Red House Farm and trained aircrews for operational roles in France during the Great War.  Between opening and early 1919 the station accommodated No. 6 Training Depot, No. 11 Training Depot and No. 14 Training Depot. At the end of the war in November 1918, the airfield became an aircraft storage unit until 1920 when it closed and was returned to agricultural use.

*Below: The Air Ministry Form 78 Movement Card which records the movement of K7660 from joining No.218 Squadron on January 21st, 1938 until it was eventually Struck Off Charge June 30th 1940.*

In 1930 the site reopened as Royal Air Force Boscombe Down as a bomber station in the Air Defence of Great Britain command. The first unit to operate from the new airfield was No. 9 Squadron which started operating the Vickers Virginia heavy bomber on February 26th, 1930. 218 Squadron welcomed a newly qualified pilot in the first week of May, Pilot Officer Walter Harry Shaw. Walter had just finished his pilot training at No.6 FTS RAF Netheravon. He carried out his first flight on May 9th when he accompanied A Flight commander, P/O Harry Daish on a low-level bombing exercise in Battle K7760. It was the beginning of a long and action-packed association with the squadron. The following day the squadron carried out a tactical exercise with squadrons of No.11 (Fighter) Group. The squadron was intercepted by four Hawker Furys who attempted to carry an attack, the Battles with a slight edge on speed had the advantage.

The squadron notched up another flying accident on May 18th. After completing an hours training of circuits and landings Pilot Officer Michael Fox line up on Boscombe Downs grass runway for the final time on completion of an otherwise successful sixty minutes flying. However, on this occasion the undercarriage refused to lower and despite every effort by the pilot it remained firmly retracted. With no alternative P/O Fox brought

*Taken in October 1932 on obtaining his pilot's License. A youthful looking Walter Harry Shaw. His flying logbook has been pivotal in recording the squadrons war in France.*

Battle K7661 into land on its belly, the landing was harder than anticipated and in the process Battle K7661 suffered severe damage. None of the crew were injured during the landing but damage was such that the aircraft was Struck Off Charge.

## Wednesday May 18th 1938
*Fairey Battle*
*Mk.I K7661*
*Contract No : 424738/35*
*Taken On Charge : 02/02/1938*
*Struck Off Charge : Not recorded*
*Total Flying Hours 80hrs*
*Pilot : Pilot Officer Michael Frederick Henry Fox*
*Observer/Bomb aimer: Unknown.*
*Gunner / Wireless Operator : Unknown*

On the morning of May 23rd, the squadron flew to RAF Harwell to join forces with 105 and 226 Squadrons on a mass formation exercise to advertise the forth coming Empire Air Day. With 105 Squadrons commanding officer, Squadron Leader Geoffrey Tuttle DFC in the vanguard, 218 made up the rear squadron with S/Ldr Duggan leading. The formation consisting of 24 Battles flew in a mass line astern formation visiting Cheltenham, Gloucester, Avonmouth, Hereford, Worcester, Kidderminster, Leamington, Banbury and finally back to Boscombe Down. June 1st found the squadron once again travelling north to the annual month long detachment to RAF West Freugh and No.4 Armament Training Camp. The visit in June was much more to the squadrons liking, hopefully the hated wind and rain that seemed to dominate the visits during the winter months would be replaced by more favourable weather conditions. It was while the squadron was on detachment that another accident occurred. Pilot Officer Charles Crews had just completed a high-level bombing sortie and was in the process of landing when he made a heavier than normal touch-down buckling the tail wheel in the process. Damage was minor and repaired on site.

**Thursday June 16th 1938**
*Fairey Battle*
*Mk.I K7657*
*Contract No : 424738/35*
*Taken On Charge : 27/01/1938*
*Repaired On Site*
*Pilot : Pilot Officer Charles Crews*
*Observer/Bomb aimer: Unknown.*
*Gunner / Wireless Operator : Unknown*

The only notable event in July 1938 was a minor accident while taxying by P/O John Mahoney of the 9th when he was slightly too heavy when applying the brakes. On the 16th the squadron along with 88 Squadron carried out a flying display on the official opening of Luton Airport which was followed by a large-scale Observer Corps Exercise on the 18th.

**Saturday July 9th 1938**
*Fairey Battle*
*Mk.I K7665*
*Contract No : 424738/35*
*Taken On Charge : 10/02/1938*
*Repaired On Site*
*Pilot : Pilot Officer John Mahoney*
*Observer/Bomb aimer: Unknown.*
*Gunner / Wireless Operator : Unknown*

August began with both resident Boscombe Down squadrons taking part in a three-day Air Defence of Great Britain Exercise starting on the 5th. All three commands, Bomber, Fighter and Coastal Commands were involved from 09:00 hours on Friday 5th until 16:00 hours Sunday August 7th. The squadrons of No.1 Group formed part of the attacking force (Eastlands) and simulated raids were carried out by mass formations and by individual squadrons attacking key industrial targets from the direction of the North Sea.

Sadly 88 Squadron recorded the loss of a Battle when it suffered engine failure north of London on the last day resulting in the death of the observer when his parachute failed to deploy at a sufficient height. A new Fairey Battle squadron was formed at Boscombe Down on August 8th, No.150 Squadron. Its temporary squadron commander was 218 Squadron's 'B' Flight Commander, Flying Officer John Innes Crump who transferred the same day. The role of flight commander was taken over by the respected F/O Alan Rogers.

The squadron recorded yet another landing accident on the 22nd when P/O David Devoto overshot his landing in heavy rain and ran into the boundary fence owing to bad visibility through the windscreen.

**Monday August 22nd 1938**
*Fairey Battle*
*Mk.I K7664*
*Contract No : 424738/35*
*Taken On Charge : 10/02/1938*
*Repaired On Site*
*Pilot : Pilot Officer David Devoto*
*Observer/Bomb aimer: Unknown.*
*Gunner / Wireless Operator : Unknown*

The run of bad luck for Pilot Officer Devoto's luck continued the following day, having hit the boundary fence on landing on the 22nd he was involved in yet another incident the following night. Returning from a night time training exercise he failed to keep a visual check on his position using the Glim light flares, this resulted in him undershooting his approach and hitting the boundary fence. Thankfully, the damage was minor, but the real damage was to the pilot and his crew's confidence and nerves.

**Tuesday August 23rd 1938**

*Fairey Battle*
*Mk.I K7653*
*Contract No : 424738/35*
*Taken On Charge : 20/01/1938*
*Repaired On Site*
*Pilot : Pilot Officer David Devoto*
*Observer/Bomb aimer: Unknown.*
*Gunner / Wireless Operator : Unknown*

The run of accidents continued, on the 27th the recently posted Pilot Officer William Wright failed to lower the undercarriage of Battle K7657 while landing, it was a basic and costly mistake. This was the second incident involving K7657, it had only just return to flying condition after the damaged sustained on June 16th. William Wright had gained his wings in March 1938 and was at the time a reservist on 1 year's active list.

**Saturday August 27th 1938**
*Fairey Battle*
*Mk.I K7657*
*Contract No : 424738/35*
*Taken On Charge : 27/01/1938*
*Repaired On Site*
*Pilot : Pilot Officer William Wright*
*Observer/Bomb aimer: Unknown.*
*Gunner / Wireless Operator : Unknown*

The months following the German seizure of Austria saw a new wave of tension sweep over Europe. It soon became evident that Hitler, was casting covetous eyes toward the Sudetenland in Czechoslovakia. Meanwhile, the ruthless persecution of minorities was drastically put into effect in Austria by the Nazis.

Throughout the early summer of 1938 the tension between Germany and Czechoslovakia mounted. Germany launched a "War of nerves" against the latter, and it became evident that Hitler was bent on securing his territorial designs on the Sudetenland, even at the risk of a general war. By the middle of September, the crisis was nearing a climax, and all over Europe armies were put on a war footing. The British Government tried to halt the threatened catastrophe when Prime Minister Chamberlain went to Germany for several conferences with Hitler, but this effort appeared fruitless

*Ron Gill (1ˢᵗ left) seen here at RAF Boscombe Down. Wireless operator /gunner Ron took a number of wonderful photographs but sadly the identity of the young men with him were not recorded.*

42

as the latter remained inexorable in his demands upon Czechoslovakia. The period would forever be remembered as the *'Munich Crisis'*. On August 29th the squadron partially mobilised, all personnel were inoculated, and the squadron's Battles had the peace-time 218 painted out and a new code, **SV** applied. Group HQ put into operation a number of precautionary plans which had been agreed for such an eventuality. The following is taken via RAF Station Boscombe Down's Records Book.

*The European situation has become extremely critical through the failure of the German-Czechoslovakian negotiations concerning the Sudeten Germans. Royal Airforce Station Boscombe Down, under the command of Wing Commander G.S Oddie DFC AFC, finally completed its mobilisation scheme and plans for the formation of No.75 (B) Wing comprising of No.88 (B) Squadron and No.218 (B) Squadron RAF Boscombe Down.*

*On mobilisation being ordered No.75 Wing will proceed overseas and be in readiness for immediate active service as a part of the advanced Air Striking Force. During the month or September 1938, No.s 88 and 218 (B) Squadrons were being given annual leave. On Saturday, September 17th, 1938 orders were given by HQ No.1 (B) Group to recall from leave the squadron commanders, and the station intelligence officers and proceed to No.1 Group HQ for a conference on September 20th, 1938. The Station Mobilization Scheme was reviewed and revised. All aircraft were made serviceable by available personnel. On Monday, September 26th 1938, all Officers and airman were recalled from leave. Certain Naval reservists employed in a civilian capacity reported to their mobilisation pools. Orders were received to collect certain vehicles from the Maintenance Units. Approximately 40 vehicles were collected and held in readiness for departure oversea of No.75 (B) Wing. All Identification numbers on aircraft were obliterated. The wives and children of all married officers and Airman were told to hold themselves in readiness for evacuation of the married quarters. All civilians were fitted and issued with respirators. Crisis period ended with the signing of the Munich Agreement.*

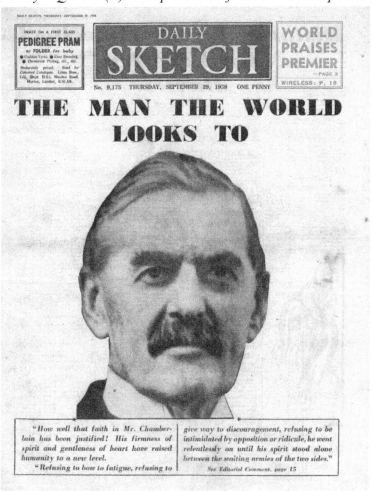

*His tireless actions would ultimately fail, but Prime Minister Chamberlain's pursuit of peace gave the RAF a few precious months to prepare for the inevitable.*

October began with yet another change in squadron Adjutant, on the 1st Flying Officer Charles Crews took over the role that he would occupy until the start of hostilities. On October 9th, Wing Commander Oddie AFC DFC relinquished command of RAF Station Boscombe Down on appointment to H.M.S Nelson for duty as Fleet Aviation Officer. Temporary command of the station was passed to Squadron Leader Duggan.

During the first few weeks of October the squadron began exchanging its Mk.I engine Battles for the improved Merlin Mk.II.    The original power plant had looked good on the drawing board, however it did not achieve the performance that was needed under operational conditions.  With the Mk.II engines gradually becoming available the squadrons slowly began to convert, in October it was 218 Squadron's turn. The newer 1030hp Merlin G Mk.II engine was an improvement, and other than a few minor alterations to the engine controls the pilots had very little to master.  The squadron's Battles were flown north to RAF Grantham, Lincolnshire the home of No.185 Squadron. The recently formed 185 Squadron had transferred to No.5 Group and were to lose their MK.II powered Battles in exchange for 218 Squadron's Mk.I powered aircraft.

### No.218 (B) Squadron Fairey Battle Mk.I with Merlin MK.II Engine

| Serial | Delivered | Maker | Contract |
|--------|-----------|-------|----------|
| K9251 | 10/10/1938 via 185 Sqdn | Faireys, Stockport | 522745/37 |
| K9323 | 10/10/1938 via 185 Sqdn | Faireys, Stockport | 522745/37 |
| K9324 | 10/10/1938 via 185 Sqdn | Faireys, Stockport | 522745/37 |
| K9325 | 10/10/1938 via 185 Sqdn | Faireys, Stockport | 522745/37 |
| K9326 | 10/10/1938 via 185 Sqdn | Faireys, Stockport | 522745/37 |
| K9327 | 10/10/1938 via 185 Sqdn | Faireys, Stockport | 522745/37 |
| K9328 | 10/10/1938 via 185 Sqdn | Faireys, Stockport | 522745/37 |
| K9329 | 10/10/1938 via 185 Sqdn | Faireys, Stockport | 522745/37 |
| K9252 | 11/10/1938 via 185 Sqdn | Faireys, Stockport | 522745/37 |
| K9253 | 11/10/1938 via 185 Sqdn | Faireys, Stockport | 522745/37 |
| K9254 | 11/10/1938 via 185 Sqdn | Faireys, Stockport | 522745/37 |

| K9255 | 11/10/1938 via 185 Sqdn | Faireys, Stockport | 522745/37 |
|---|---|---|---|
| K9256 | 11/10/1938 via 185 Sqdn | Faireys, Stockport | 522745/37 |
| K9260 | 11/10/1938 via 185 Sqdn | Faireys, Stockport | 522745/37 |
| K9273 | 11/10/1938 via 185 Sqdn | Faireys, Stockport | 522745/37 |
| K9353 | 20/10/1938 | Faireys, Stockport | 522745/37 |
| K9354 | 24/10/1938 | Faireys, Stockport | 522745/37 |
| K9355 | 24/10/1938 | Faireys, Stockport | 522745/37 |
| K9356 | 26/10/1938 | Faireys, Stockport | 522745/37 |
| K9357 | 24/10/1938 | Faireys, Stockport | 522745/37 |
| K9384 | 17/11/1938 | Faireys, Stockport | 522745/36 |

Boscombe Down was visited by The Inspector General, Sir Edward Ellington GCB, CMG, CBE, on November 1st, 1938, he spent the day inspecting the station and the squadron. The squadron pilots busied themselves carrying out a few test flights with the new Battles while the ground crews especially were keen to give their new charges a thorough check over. The new squadron code letters were applied, and the aircraft's serial which had been painted in large white numbers on the underside of the wings were painted over. Pilot Officer Shaw displayed some cool nerves and considerable flying skill on the 5th when 15 minutes into a forced landing exercise the control column of Battle K9356 suddenly jammed. With only forward and partially laterally movement, and the control column refusing to be pulled back, the young pilot was in serious trouble. Showing considerable calm P/O Shaw brought K9356 in for landing using only the Battles large dive flaps in the fully up position, when 10 feet above the ground he cut the engine bringing the aircraft in for a bumpy but safe landing. On inspection it was found that the clock winder had wrapped around the control column, it had been a lucky escape for the young Walter Shaw. Shaw was not the average pilot on the squadron, he had an eventful career prior to his arrival on the squadron;

*My mother used to buy flying books for me; I remember two of them called 'The Aeroplane and Flight'. I was interested in the First World War flying aces, especially Baron von Richthofen, the Red Baron. That is when I first wanted to be a pilot. Fortunately, in my late 20s my mother arranged for me to learn to fly at Skegness Flying Club and I qualified there for A and B Pilot's Licences, I always wore a red silk scarf on all my Operational Flights. Following an advertisement in the paper where they were asking for people to enrol with RAF reserve, I applied and was accepted. Then I went to Brough airfield near Hull and did two weeks flying on B2 trainers, the first light training aircraft with side-by-side seating. I had the rank of Sergeant, but I never wore the uniform because it was just the reserve.*

*After that I went out to Malaya to be part of a group that was going to start an airline in Malaya. We had a light aircraft we used to for joyriding passengers and cross-country flights in. Unfortunately, the idea dropped and I came home. Then I applied for a short service commission in the RAF and was accepted. First as I could already fly, we went to a civilian training school at Desford. After a month I was posted back to the RAF for two weeks training at Uxbridge. There we did wear uniform as acting pilot officers and were involved with the discipline of the Airforce. Drill, marching etc. and studying King's Regulations. We were also measured for mess kit and went through gas training with and without gas masks, and then I was posted. I went to no. 6 training school at Netheravon and we did tactics, bombing, firing etc. At the end of the course my instructor thought I would make a fighter pilot but there was a long waiting list as the Squadrons were not fully established, so I elected to go on to Fairey Battle bombers. At the*

*New Zealander Ian Richmond. He would over the coming years prove himself to be a courageous and skilled bomber pilot.*

*end of the course, we got our wings, and I was posted to 218 Squadron at Boscombe Down. There I met the CO, Wing Cdr Duggan who briefed me on the ethics of being an officer. Also, a new post had started, and he made me the Squadron intelligence officer. Then I met the Flight Commander Harry Daish. He was a good type, an Australian, and got me used to flying Fairey Battle bombers and I gradually got used to my duties as Intelligence Officer.*

The squadron was by the beginning on November 1938 equipped with 16 I.E aircraft plus 5 I.R as per Bomber Command orders BC/843. The final batch of five aircraft were collected by the squadron direct from the Fairey factory at Stockport. A few squadron pilots were flown to the Austin works at Longbridge on the 14th to collect and return a number of Battles for 150 Squadron, why the pilots of 150 Squadron were unable to collect their new aircraft is unknown. Throughout November the squadron busied itself with training, to give an example of the varied day to day activities the following flights were recorded in the flying logbook of 'A' Flights Pilot Officer Richmond.

| Date | Aircraft | Flight Details | Duration |
|------|----------|----------------|----------|
| 03/11/1938 | Battle K9254 | To Abington. | 25mins |
| 03/11/1938 | Battle K9254 | Back to Boscombe Down. | 25mins |
| 04/11/1938 | Battle K9254 | Forced Landing Practice. | 1hr 10mins |
| 07/11/1938 | Battle K9254 | Test of Regional control. | 55mins |
| 07/11/1938 | Battle K9254 | Formation Practice. | 55mins |
| 08/11/1938 | Battle K9254 | Reconnaissance Flight (Winchester railway) | 50mins |
| 10/11/1938 | Battle K9251 | Night Flying Training. | 15mins |
| 14/11/1938 | Battle K9255 | Cross Country Flight. | 1hr 50mins |
| 22/11/1938 | Battle K9252 | Tactical Exercise. | 4hrs30mins |
| 24/11/1938 | BattleK9328 | Formation Cross Country. | 3hrs |
| 24/11/1938 | Battle K9328 | Local Circuit and Landings. | 30mins |
| 25/11/1938 | Battle K9255 | Photography Training. | 1hr 05mins |
| 28/11/1938 | Battle K9255 | Forced Landing Practice / Local formation flying. | 1hr 50mins |
| 29/11/1938 | Battle K9255 | Formation Flight to Grimsby Regional D/F Test. | 2hrs 35mins |

The visits by high ranking officers continued with the arrival on the 14th of Bomber Command's Commander-In-Chief, Air Chief Marshal Sir Edgar Ludlow Hewitt KCB, CMG DSO MC, who carried out a formal inspected of the station and the squadron. The squadron welcomed Squadron Leader George Warrington on November 18th. Born in Calcutta, India in 1908 he joined the RAF in 1929. Granted a Short Service Commission in June 1929 he had served firstly with No.501 (Bomber) Squadron then had a spell on float planes at Leuchars, Gosport and finally Calshort before spending four years with the Home Aircraft Deport (Engineering) Group.

After the excellent effort by P/O Shaw in landing his Battle on the 5th the young officer blotted his record book when he undershot his landing on return from a night flying test at Boscombe Down on the 22nd. The investigation into the crash pulled no punches blaming the accident on *'mishandling'*

**Tuesday November 22nd 1938**

*Fairey Battle*
*Mk.I K9254*
*Contract No :522745/37*
*Taken On Charge : 11/10/1938*
*Repaired on Site*
*Pilot : Pilot Officer Walter Shaw*
*Observer/Bomb aimer: Unknown.*
*Gunner / Wireless Operator : Unknown*

Sweeping changes introduced by the Air Ministry to the command structure of the squadrons of Bomber Command were implemented on December 1st. The squadron would now be commanded by an officer with wing commander rank, while the flights would be managed by either a squadron leader or flight lieutenant. The engineering officer would also have to be a flight lieutenant of flying officer rank.

The squadron was presented with the squadron crest by Air Vice Marshal Patrick Playfair, KBE, CB, CVO, MC during the A.O.C Annual inspection on December 6th. His Majesty the King had graciously consented to the adoption of the Hourglass as the squadrons crest with the motto **IN TIME.** The hourglass representing

the fact the squadron was originally formed in April 1918, near the end of the First World War, the sand having almost run through. The squadrons motto again symbolises the squadrons late participation in the Great War.

On December 29th RAF Boscombe Down welcomed its new commanding officer in the form of Group Captain Wann. Archibald Herbert Wann was born in 1895 had had for much of his military career been involved with Airships and the Royal Navy. He was one of only five people to survive the R38 explosion over the Humber in 1921. He later acted as Registrar during the Court of Inquiry into the loss of the R101 in 1930.

A marked increase in bombing practice, air to air and air to ground firing swept the squadron during December, little or no emphasis had been placed on these two vital activities when not on detachment to the Armament Camps, now a new determination seemed to grip the squadron. This trend would continue over the winter. The following is a record of flights in the Flying Logbook of P/O Shaw of 'B' Flight for December.

| Date | Aircraft | Flight Details | Duration |
|---|---|---|---|
| 06/12/1938 | Battle K9252 | Regional Control Test. | 35mins |
| 07/12/1938 | Battle K9252 | Blind Flying Practice. | 1hr 20mins |
| 08/11/1938 | Battle K9255 | Night Flying Test. | 20mins |
| 08/12/1938 | Battle K9255 | Night-time Circuit and Landings. | 1hr 40mins |
| 12/12/1938 | Battle K9255 | Low Level Bombing Practice. | 20mins |
| 12/12/1938 | Battle K9255 | Low Level Bombing Practice. | 25mins |
| 12/12/1938 | Battle K9255 | Low Level Bombing Practice. | 45min |
| 13/12/1938 | Battle K9255 | Low Level Bombing Practice. | 30min |
| 15/12/1938 | Battle K9251 | Air Test. | 25mins |
| 16/12/1938 | Battle K9255 | Air Firing at Markers in sea. | 1hr 15hrs |
| 16/12/1938 | Battle K9256 | Air Firing at markers in sea. | 1hr 30mins |
| 29/12/1938 | Battle K9384 | Forced Landing Practice. | 25mins |

Christmas 1938 was spent in traditional RAF fashion, little did the squadron realise as they were tucking into the Roast Turkey, that this would be the last Christmas they and the country would enjoy at peace in six years. For the squadron, the year had been an exciting one, the conversion to the Fairey Battle had taken place and despite a number of accidents the transition went remarkably smoothly. The unfortunate deaths by drowning of two colleagues blighted what would have been an outstanding safety record for the year. In comparison to its sister squadron, 88, it had an exceptional record.

# Chapter 4: 1939 – Dark Clouds Over Europe

On January 8th, 1939 the newly promoted Wing Commander Duggan lead ten crews north to No.5 Armament Training School at RAF Penrhos, Caernarvonshire. It would be the squadron's first visit to this rain and wind-swept aerodrome. For the best part of three weeks the squadron carried out an intensive programme of gunnery practice interspersed with both low and high-level bombing.

While the squadron busied itself over the Welsh coast the British Prime Minister Neville Chamberlain and the foreign minister Lord Halifax were meeting with their French counterparts Édouard Daladier and Georges Bonnet in Paris. It was a show of solidarity to both the Germans and Italians. Italy, ever boastful had made territorial demands on the French in relation to some of their colonial interests. On January 12th, Neville Chamberlain and Lord Halifax travelled on to Rome and met with the swaggering Benito Mussolini. Chamberlain naively hoped to persuade Mussolini to advise Hitler not to continue his aggressive demands and war like rhetoric. Mussolini willingly agreed promising that both Italy and Germany wanted peace. On January 23rd, Prime Minister

*A fresh faced and recently qualified Pilot Officer Michael Robin.*

Neville Chamberlain launched a recruitment drive with the goal of mobilizing 30 million Britons for the voluntary civil defence army, it was a sign of things to come. On February 6th, the three Battle squadrons of RAF Boscombe Down, Nos 88, 150 and 218 carried out a mass wing formation flight, the target being Leicester. Once airborne the formation led by 218 Squadron headed for Leicester taking in Swindon and Worcester at 10,000 feet on the way. It was on the outward flight that trouble started for P/O Michael Robin at the controls of Battle K9252. Flying as No.4 in the forward formation the following squadron crews were amazed to see the passenger aboard K9252 take to his parachute. The squadron initially believed that the crew were in trouble, but details later emerged that the passenger, fellow pilot P/O Arthur Imrie *'mistook the movement of the pilot's hand when opening hood for alternative evacuation signal'.* The young Rhodesian landed safely, however from that day on he was known as *'Bail-out Imrie!*

The following day the squadron was scheduled for a cross country exercise with a stopover at RAF Henlow in Bedfordshire for refuelling. The outward flight went without incident however on landing at Henlow one of the squadrons sergeant pilots, John Horner made a heavy landing which resulted in the port undercarriage leg partially retracting. The Battle came to a shuddering stop inflicting damaged to the port wing, the crew were shaken but otherwise uninjured. Sergeant Horner was an experienced pilot having logged some 576 flying hours, 140 of which were on the Battle.

### Tuesday February 7th 1939
*Fairey Battle*
*Mk.I K9323*
*Contract No :522745/37*
*Taken on Charge: 10/10/1938*
*Repaired on site.*
*Pilot: Sergeant John Horner*
*Observer/Bomb aimer: Unknown.*
*Gunner / Wireless Operator: Unknown*

The recent series of wing size formation flights continued throughout February and as the month progressed these would evolve into mass formations of 8, 9 and even 10 squadrons flying the length and breadth of the country. On the 9th, Boscombe Down provided three squadrons for an attack on Falmouth. The responsibility of leading the formation was given to 218 Squadron and Wing Commander Duggan. The exercise was cancelled due to complete cloud cover of the 'target'. With the British public concerned about the news emanating from Germany and Italy it was felt that a show of military force would help strengthen the publics resolve and relieve some of their apprehension. Another exercise was flown on February 13th when the squadron flew north to Skegness on the Lincolnshire coast. The return flight would take in the fashionable Bournemouth on the south coast and Bristol. Aloft of over 3 hours the squadron eventually started to land back at Boscombe Down late afternoon. All was well until Sergeant Charles Owen misjudged his approach and undershot the landing. Holding off too high, the Battle stalled from 10 feet resulting in a bone shaking bounce on contact with the grass runway, the Battle and its crew were catapulted up again until eventually gravity came to the aid of the inexperienced pilot. Thankfully on this occasion the usually temperamental undercarriage held up to the abuse, but wisely the aircraft was sent for a complete overhaul.

### Monday February 13th 1939
*Fairey Battle*
*Mk.I K9260*
*Contract No :522745/37*
*Taken on Charge: 11/10/1938*
*Repaired on site.*
*Pilot: Sergeant Charles Owen*
*Observer/Bomb aimer: Unknown.*
*Gunner / Wireless Operator: Unknown*

On the 16th Boscombe Down provided three squadrons on what was one of the largest mass Group Exercises to date. Each of the group's bases would form into one wing, as usual 88 and 218 were teamed together and formed No.1 Wing, while 150 Squadron joined the Harwell squadrons to help form No.3 Wing. In all 5 Wings participated and the honour of leading the whole armada was again given to 218 Squadron. A total of one hundred and ten Fairey Battles of No.1 Group would visit Bristol, Halton, Debden and then head south to Tilbury Docks which was the 'target' for the exercise. Tilbury was situated on the north shore of the River Thames, 25 miles downstream of London Bridge. Having delivered the attack, the formation turned for home skirting north London. The squadron began landing just before dusk, it had been an exhilarating day for all concerned, for the public watching below the sight and sound of the Battles would have been a spectacular.

This show of force was again repeated on the 24th when over 120 Battles again visited Bristol, Halton and Debden as well as Tunbridge Wells. These flights went a long way to steady an increasingly worried population. For the squadron, the last week of February was spent carrying out increasingly frequent bombing and gunnery exercises. Number 150 Squadron departed for a month-long detachment to No.1 A.T.S at Catfoss on February 27th. March 1st, 1939 would see the squadron affiliated to the seaside town of Weston-super-Mare, Somerset. Under the guidance of the Municipal Liaison Scheme

*Aircraftman Kenneth Gregory in his civilian clothes ready to go on leave while based at RAF Boscombe Down. He would be killed on May 11th, 1940.*

squadrons would be affiliated to towns and cities to promote regional alliances. This would provide the squadron with a territorial 'home' and gave the town or city a vested interest in the activities and welfare of 'their' adopted squadron. Why Weston-super-Mare was chosen is unclear, but a genuine friendship between the town and squadron was forged. Other than the usual training sorties being carried out March was uneventful and incident free. On March 12th, Boscombe Down welcomed Nos 18, 57 and 63 Squadrons on attachment for bombing trails at Larkhill bombing range situated on Salisbury Plan. The following day Wing Commander Allen Hesketh DFC assumed command of 150 Squadron with the departure of Wing Commander William MacDonald DFC. On March 16th Wing Commander Kenneth Elliott DSO was appointed commanding officer of 88 Squadron. Pilot Officer Richmond was aloft on an Air-Test on the morning of the 16th after a 40-hour inspection of Battle K9329. After 15 minutes aloft the young Kiwi brought the Battle in for landing, he selected the undercarriage lever to down only to find it would not lower. Despite Richmond's best efforts and violent manoeuvres, the undercarriage refused to budge. In the end the arduous task of lowering by hand using the hand crank was undertaken, 28 tiring turns later the undercarriage finally locked.   fighter affiliation exercises were flown during the month, one such exercise was on the 20th when the squadron mixed it with 'A' Flight of 43 Squadron and their Hawker Hurricanes. With the ever-deteriorating situation in Europe RAF Boscombe Down was ordered to prepare to mobilise on April 3rd, an additional sixteen vehicles were collected and parked ready for use. Crews were ordered back from leave and all the squadron aircraft were prepared. Only days before the German battleship *Tirpitz*

51

was launched in Wilhelmshaven. Adolf Hitler attended the ceremony and made a speech that included a response to Neville Chamberlain's pledge of supporting Poland, saying *"If they [Britain and France] expect the Germany of today to sit patiently by until the very last day while they create satellite States and set them against Germany, then they are mistaking the Germany of today for the Germany of before the war."* The ominous signs of war spread their evil shadow over the whole of Europe.

March had been an accident free month, however April was not so lucky. On April 11th, Pilot Officer Robert Balls was returning from a night navigational exercise when he overshot his approach, realising this Balls opened up the Merlin engine and raised the undercarriage and flaps to go around for a second attempt. This proved his undoing, the Battle hit the ground and slide to a halt ripping off the propellor in the process. Although culpable the inexperience pilot was cleared of any blame. The following morning it was discovered that a film of oil had restricted his forward vision, this was made all the worse from the glare of landing lights positioned around the airfield. The Battle required extensive repair and was sent to 1472M at Locking as a non-flying Instructional Airframe. Stockbridge built Battle K9260 had been involved in a similar accident on February 13th.

### Tuesday April 11th 1939
*Fairey Battle*
*Mk.I K9260*
*Contract No :522745/37*
*Taken On Charge: 11/10/1938*
*Beyond Repair*
*Pilot: Pilot Officer Robert Balls*
*Observer/Bomb aimer: Unknown.*
*Gunner / Wireless Operator: LAC Ron Gill*

*Pilot Officer Ball sitting on the cockpit and Pilot Officer Robin inspected the badly bent Battle K9260 after it overshot its landing on the night of April 11th 1939.*

Regardless of the worsening political situation sweeping across Europe the annual Empire Air Day took place on May 20th as planned. It was an ideal opportunity to show both the Germans and Italians the strength of the RAF and the modern aircraft now equipping its squadrons.

*Another view of Battle K9260. Standing on the wing in Ron Gill. Ron joined the squadron in 1938 on completion of his training at RAF Cranwell.*

The squadron began rehearsals on May 10th when sixty Battles of No.1 Group carried out a mass formation flight, 218 contributing 12 Battles. A follow up rehearsal was flown on the 18th fine turning the display. The worlds media would be watching and none more closely than those from Germany and Italy, everything had to be perfect. The weather on the morning of May 20th was ideal, twelve Battles led by Wing Commander Duggan lifted off from Boscombe Downs grass runway and once airborne formed up into an immaculate diamond formation. Once satisfied, W/Cdr Duggan then headed first to Netheravon airfield, then Stockbridge, Winchester and Guilford. The fighter base at RAF Kenley was visited next before heading to Hanworth airfield, Reading and finally RAF Odiham. Having been aloft for nearly 3 hours the squadron performed two low level bombing routines in front of a near capacity crowd of 14,000 people back at Boscombe Down. In the afternoon Air Chief Marshall Edgar Ludlow Hewitt KCB, CMG, DSO, MC, officer command RAF Bomber Command, accompanied by No.1 Group commanding officer, Air Vice Marshal Patrick Playfair, arrived by air at Boscombe Down to inspect the squadrons.

Several selected pilots were despatched to RAF Mildenhall in early May for a training course on the still relatively new Lorenz blind landing device. Developed by C Lorenz AG in Berlin the system was first used in 1932 at the Berlin-Tempelhof Central Airport primarily for its civil airlines. The device allowed an aircraft to approach an airport at night or in bad weather. The pilot when approaching the runway would tune his radio to the broadcast frequency and listen for the signal. If he heard a series of dots, he knew he was off the runway centreline to the left (the *dot-sector*) and had to turn to the right to line up with the runway. If he was to the right, he would hear a series of dashes instead (the *dash-sector*) and turned left. The key to the operation of the system was an area in the middle where the two signals overlapped. The dots of the one signal "filled in" the dashes of the other, resulting in a steady tone known as the *equi-signal*. By adjusting his path until he heard the equi-signal, the pilot could align his aircraft with the runway for landing. Two of the pilots selected were F/O Richmond and P/O Max Freeman they arrived at Mildenhall on May 15th and immediately began training. Richmond's first flight was in Anson L9155 his tutor was one of the RAF's pioneers in signals / radar development, Squadron Leader Robert Blucke AFC. A veteran of the Great War he was the first ever pilot to be detected by radar while serving with the Experimental Section of the Royal Aircraft Establishment. His skill in radar would see him command the Wireless Investigation Development Unit before joining the Directorate of the Flying Training at the Air Ministry. He became the station commander of Holme-On-Spalding Moor in 1942 and then station commander of RAF Ludford Magna. In 1945 he took command of No.1 Group.

For the next four days Richmond along with P/O Freeman would be aloft flying three sometimes four practice sorties a day, on 18th Richmond was at the controls of Percival Gull, P1752, a graceful four-seater touring aircraft built by Percival Aircraft Limited which had been fitted with a blacken out canopy hood. Flying Officer Richmond had missed the excitement of the Empire Flying Day while attached to

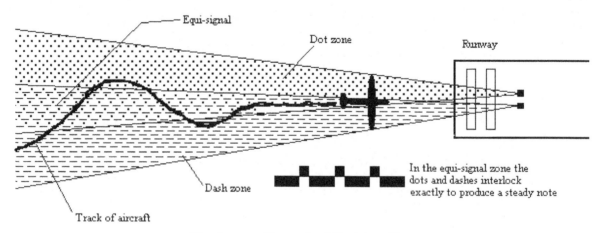

**The Lorenz Beam for Blind Landing**

Mildenhall, however upon his return he was given to two important flights to perform. On May 30th he was given the responsibility of flying Battle K9326 from Bournemouth to Southampton, his passenger was Mr Dwyer of New Zealand Public Service, a member of the Imperial Defence College. Mr Dwyer was at the time coming to the end of his year long appointment, he was the first New Zealand civilian to hold the post. On the return trip to Bournemouth during late afternoon Richmond was accompanied by Lieutenant Colonel Charles Balfour Davey MC of the Gordon Highlanders.

June began with the squadron on paper at least expanding to three flights. This additional flight would bring the squadrons total aircraft and crews to 24 I.E and 8 I.R. On the 6th the squadron participated in yet another Group Tactical exercise carried out at the unfamiliar height of 20,000 feet. A section of 'A' Flight lead by F/O Shaw was given a low-level bombing exercise on the 9th. The target was the grass airfield at Lands' End, the most south-westerly airfield in mainland Britain. A joint Army and Air Force exercise began on the 12th. Dozens of MT vehicles arrived at Boscombe Down on their way to Milford on Sea where they would be camped. It was agreed that the convoy would be attacked allowing both the 'Brown types' and the squadron to undertake some realistic practice. Both A and B Flights took it in turns to attack the convoy near Abingdon over the next few days. The attacks carried out between 1000 - 3000 feet were undertaken with real vigour by the squadron who were keen to show the Army how vulnerable to attack from the air they were. Number 88 Squadron lost a Battle and sadly recorded the death of one of the crew on the 20th. Battle K9249 was returning to Boscombe Down on completion of a night flying exercise when suddenly the Merlin caught fire. Realising immediately that the aircraft was doomed the order was given by P/O Donald Foster to abandon the aircraft. Sadly, Sergeant Harrison Ing appeared to leave it too late as his body was found close to the smouldering wreckage. Pilot Officer Donald Foster would ultimately join 218 Squadron and serve with some distinction. On June 27th, Air Ministry orders were received instructing the squadron that reequipping for the third flight should be started immediately. Another exercise with the Army was carried out on the 28th, on this occasion with the Lincolnshire Regiment, frustratingly low cloud prevented most crews from carrying out any attacks.

July would see the arrival of the first of 11 factory fresh Battles collected direct from the Austin Works at Longbridge, Birmingham, these aircraft would be used to form the third flight. Selected crews were given the task of shuttling pilots to the Austin factory. These flights started on July 3rd, when P/O John Crane headed to Birmingham, aboard his aircraft were F/O Richmond and Sergeant Horner. Richmond flew home Battle L5202 while John Horner piloted Battle L5201. Both these aircraft were equipped with a Rolls Royce Mk.IV Merlin engine which gave slightly more power.

### No.218 (B) Squadron Fairey Battle Mk.I - Delivered July 1939

| Serial | Delivered | Maker | Contract |
|---|---|---|---|
| L5194 | 03/07/1939 | Austin, Longbridge | 540408/36 |
| L5195 | 03/07/1939 | Austin, Longbridge | 540408/36 |
| L5197 | 03/07/1939 | Austin, Longbridge | 540408/36 |
| L5199 | 03/07/1939 | Austin, Longbridge | 540408/36 |

| L5202 | 03/07/1939 | Austin, Longbridge | 540408/36 |
|-------|------------|--------------------|-----------|
| L5193 | 05/07/1939 | Austin, Longbridge | 540408/36 |
| L5196 | 05/07/1939 | Austin, Longbridge | 540408/36 |
| L5201 | 10/07/1939 | Austin, Longbridge | 540408/36 |
| L5198 | 12/07/1939 | Austin, Longbridge | 540408/36 |
| L5203 | 12/07/1939 | Austin, Longbridge | 540408/36 |
| L5200 | 14/07/1939 | Austin, Longbridge | 540408/36 |

Three aircraft of 'A' Flight were involved in another co-operation exercise with the Army on July 3rd. The sections target was the 3rd Division Royal Engineers which were attacked throughout the day from as low as 1000 feet. These exercises, although useful, gave the participating crews misplaced confidence in the effectiveness of low-level attacks and more worryingly the ability of the Battle to survive such an attack. Between July 7th and 9th, a large-scale Regional Air Exercise took place, all Bomber Command squadrons along with the fighter squadrons of No.11 Fighter Group participated. No.75 Wings 88 and 218 Squadron acted as both friendly and enemy bombers. On the morning of the 9th, six aircraft took off from Boscombe Down and headed towards the south coast and out over the choppy English Channel. The formation at 9,000 feet flew to a point 3 miles off the French coastal town of Le Tréport and circled. Acting as the enemy force the formation then headed back towards the English coast, the first destination was Winchester, followed by Salisbury before finally making a low-level attack on Crewkerne a sleepy town in Somerset, situated 9 miles south-west of Yeovil. After refuelling, the exercise was again repeated in the afternoon, but this time the squadron acted as a 'friendly' force. On the 11th the squadron joined 103 Squadron from RAF Benson on an exercise that would see it fly over France for the first time since February 1919. The squadron lead by Wing Commander Duggan flying at a little over 3000 feet majestically made their way over the familiar French towns and cities of Le Treport, Orleans, Le Mans and finally Barfleur. For the French civilians below, the presence of 18 Fairey Battles of the RAF would have been a welcoming sight given situation with Nazi Germany. This show of force was again repeated on the 25th when the squadron once again visited Le Treport, Le Mans, however on this occasion the French Capital, Paris was also visited.

The last month of peace in Europe, was from the squadron perspective a busy one. A four-day exercise commenced on August 3rd, both the squadron and station took part in what would become one of the last major Home Defence Exercise undertaken. Boscombe Down defences posts were manned and the ground defences were put on alert, everyone was put on a war footing. The squadron first sortie was on the 5th, however low cloud and heavy rain cancelled the squadrons involvement. The following day a section managed to get away, however the weather intervened again, P/O Shaw was obliged to abandon the flight when his Battle, K9253 developed a serious oil leak requiring him to land at the earliest opportunity.

Tragedy struck on August 11th when acting Flight Lieutenant William Kinane at the controls of Battle K9328 hit the top of an electrical pylon at Carlton resulting in the death of all three crew. Taking off from Boscombe Down mid-morning, F/Lt Kinane was leading a section of three Battles as a part of the attacking force for the morning exercise. Flying at low level as briefed, the section comprised of F/Lt Kinane, P/O Max Freeman and Sergeant Wilfred Herring.

Heading towards Carlton the section had just flown over the brow of the hill when suddenly and without warning, a line of 87 feet high electrical pylons and their hanging electrical cables loomed in front of them. Flying slightly lower than his companions F/Lt Kinane did not see the danger

*Three of the squadron's wireless operator / gunners seen here at RAF Boscombe Down a few weeks before the squadron moved to France. Aircraftman Davies, Ellis and Chamberlain.*

until it was too late. The wing of the Battle hit the steel girders breaking off two and pulling down two cables. There was a blinding flash as the Battle now with a wing ablaze headed towards its destruction. Pilot Officer Max Freeman reported;

*I was flying in the formation slightly behind the other aircraft and slightly higher. We were carrying out a exercise in connection with the Home Defence Exercise. At mid-day we came over Carlton and saw the high-tension wires and pylons second before I saw the other aircraft hit them. There was a blue flash and the aircraft immediately burst into flames and crashed. I circled and later landed at Cranfield aerodrome and reported the incident.*

There was truly little the young Australian pilot could have done in the circumstances, such was the damaged to the wing, pieces of which were found in the grounds of Carlton Playing fields, the Battle and it doomed crew hit a large Ash tree splitting it in half. The Battle then somersaulted and immediately burst into flames crashing onto the cricket pavilion killing the pilot and the 28-year-old observer, Sergeant Peter Allan instantly. Miraculously the wireless operator / gunner, AC Ivor Roberts was found alive still strapped into his seat, the rear section was still relatively intact. The crews pre-packed picnic basket was found only yards from the tail section, seemingly undamaged by the fire. One of the first on the scene was Mr Bevington, and his son, who showing commendable courage pulled the airman, complete with seat straps, parachute and wireless leads from the blazing wreckage. Farm labourer Thomas Betts came to their assistance, more help arrived in the form of students from the college, however, the explosion of one of the fuel tanks prevented any further efforts. The severely burnt Roberts was quickly transferred to Cranfield Station Sick Quarters. Although semi-conscious, he seemed initially to be in a stable condition, however, despite the best effort Dr W Thomas, a flight lieutenant serving at RAF Cranfield the young Welshman succumbed to his injuries at 4.30 pm Sunday 13th. Mr Bevington described the events on this Friday morning;

*A pre-war photograph of William Kinane. His premature death was a tragic blow to the squadron. A natural pilot, he would have achieved great things on the squadron and in the RAF.*

*I had just looked at my watch and it was 11.55 am when I heard the aeroplanes approaching. They were low and one hit the pylon causing a light and a flash. It was coming straight for us and my boy shouted to my housekeeper who was in doors to run out of the front door. By this time, it had hit the tree and I saw flames rushing upwards. As I was behind the house, I thought it had hit it. As I ran forward a piece of flying wood almost hit me. I went near to the wreckage and when I was about three feet away, I saw something that looked like a bundle move. My son was with me and when we turned it over, we found it was a man. I shouted for my assistant, Mr Thomas Betts and he came to help lift the man out. I kept trying to put out the man burning clothes by fanning them with my hat. When we had him clear I cut off his headphones, his parachute straps which held him in his seat. Mr Betts put out the fire on his clothing by wrapping him up in sacks. We then wrapped him in blankets to prevent him getting cold. We tried to get the second man out, but the heat was too much. When I found the injured man, I could see the legs of another nearer the wings, but I could not get to him although I beat all the flames out with my cap. As soon as the injured man was able to speak, he asked "How is the pilot? there are two men in there"*

Mr Bevington, his 21-year-old son and Mr Betts all sustained burns to their hands in their efforts to save the crew. They had shown considerable bravery at no small risk to themselves. The bodies of the two dead airmen were initially taken to the cricket pavilion before collection and transporting back to Cranfield. Twenty-one-year-old William 'Bill' Kinane was given a full-dress military funeral on the afternoon of Wednesday 16th August at Cranfield (SS Peter and Paul) Churchyard. In attendance was Group Captain William Dunn DSC, station commander RAF Cranfield and 218 Squadrons commanding officer, Wing Commander Duggan. The coffin draped in a Union Jack was carried by 218 Squadron pilots, Flight Lieutenant Rogers, Flying Officer Hughes and Crew, and Pilot Officers Freeman and Robin.

William Kinane was the youngest of five siblings and the only boy. He attended the Christian Brother College, Perth where his athletic talents soon become evident. He set a then new record for the high jump and was a skilled lifesaver and footballer. William, or Billy as he was often called had started an engineering course at university when he decided to become a pilot, attending Point Cook. On graduation he was selected to join the RAF and set sail for England. Having gained his wings in December 1936 he joined 'B' Flight 142 Squadron in May 1937. In June 1937 he was posted to the newly formed 82 Squadron where he commanded 'B' Flight until his posting to 218 Squadron in February 1938 where it is believed he would eventually command the newly formed 'C' Flight. At the time of his death he had flown a total of 163 hours on the Battle. Aircraftman Ivor Roberts of the Rhondda Valley was taken back to Wales and buried at St Athan. The 21-year-old was the son of Albert Roberts, prior to the war he had lived and worked in Gelli, a small village in the Rhondda. Two crews flew to St Athan for the funeral on the 16th, in attendance was Pilot Officers Thynne, Shaw and Sergeant Malpass.

*A recent photograph of the badly worn grave of William Kinane.*

There is a tragic postscript to the death of Peter Allan, the day he died he was to travel to Biggin Hill, Kent to collect his wife and 8-month-old child and bring them back to RAF Boscombe Down to live in the married quarters. Since his arrival on 218 Squadron in June his family had remained in Kent. Born in Edinburgh, Peter had previously spent 3 years at RAF Biggin Hill. It was while stationed at the famous fighter base that he met and married Lily Parker. Like his pilot, Peter Allan was buried on Wednesday 16th at St Giles Churchyard, Farnborough, Kent. The squadron was represented by 'A' Flight commander, Flight Lieutenant Daish, also attending was 88 Squadron's commanding officer, Wing Commander K Elliott DSO and Peter Allan's former station commander, Wing Commander R Grice. The coffin draped in a Union flag was carried by fellow sergeant observers and pilots from the squadron, these were, Sergeant Dormer, Baxter, Burdett, Mullis and Ruffell-Hazel. Sadly, on a visit to the church in 2000, the author discovered that the original headstone had been removed. The 87-foot high pylon which Battle K9328 struck still stands today next to the former Carlton (St Margaret's) School. These pylons were erected in the late 30s and were one of the first sections of the UK's national electricity grid. In 1939, their appearance would have posed a relatively new and unexpected hazard for low flying crews. The subsequent investigation into the crash attributed the cause to the young Australian flying below the minimum authorised height and showing 'excessive zeal while flying'.

**Friday August 11th 1939**
*Fairey Battle*
*Mk.I K9328*
*Contract No :522745/37*
*Taken On Charge : 10/10/1938*
*Struck Off Charge.*
*Pilot : Acting Flight Lieutenant William Kinane 39466* **Killed**
*Observer/Bomb aimer: Sergeant Peter Aitken Allan 511195* **Killed**
*Gunner / Wireless Operator : Aircraftman 1st Class Ivor Roberts 536007* **Killed**

One can only imagine the atmosphere on the squadron, three young lives tragically lost in what should have been a routine exercise. These were the first fatalities suffered by the squadron since November 1937. It was a sobering and painful lesson for everyone. Four days later, the recently qualified Pilot Officer Geoffrey Rhind with only 3 hours experience on the Battle failed to lower his undercarriage when landing after a circuit and landing exercise.

**Tuesday August 15th 1939**
*Fairey Battle*
*Mk.I K9253*
*Contract No : 522745/37*
*Taken On Charge : 11/10/1938*
*Repaired On Site.*
*Pilot : Acting Pilot Officer Geoffrey Arthur Cyril Rhind*
*Observer/Bomb aimer: Unknown*
*Gunner / Wireless Operator : Unknown.*

Perhaps due to this elementary pilot error or simple coincidence, P/O Rhind found himself posted to 35 Squadron based at RAF Benson prior to the squadrons move to France. He was tragically killed in a flying accident on October 29th, 1939. On the 19th, 12 Battles, led by Wing Commander Duggan headed to Weston Super Mare. After spending 30 minutes flying in perfect formation over the seaside town, the squadron landed at 3pm at the Municipal Airport. The Battles were parked together along the fenced off crowd line eagerly watched by what appeared to be hundreds of spectators. Here they were formally welcomed by the Deputy Mayor, Alderman J.G Western. After the official civic welcome by the Deputy Mayor in the Airports main building the twelve pilots were provided with afternoon tea ably performed by the airport manager, Flight Lieutenant W.E Knowlden. With the official part of the visit over, the crews returned to the aircraft and mingled with the crowds who were eager to inspect the Battles up close and ask the assembled crews questions. At one point, the engine cowling of Battle K9329 was removed for closer inspection and the Deputy Mayor took great delight in being photographed. On August 20th, the British and French governments were shocked to discover that Nazi Germany and the Soviet Union had agreed a trade pact between the two countries. Such was the alarm in the Britain that Members of Parliament were summoned back to London for a special session to discuss the implications. Further revelations followed on the 23rd when both the Soviets and the Germans agreed not to attack each other and to remain neutral if attacked by a third power, known as the *Treaty of Non-aggression.*

On August 24th, 1939, Parliament passed the Emergency Powers (Defence) Act, giving the government broad powers in order to conduct war effectively, it was the beginning of the end for peace in Europe. The same day the Royal Auxiliary Air Force and Royal Air Force Volunteer Reserve were merged into the RAF and brought to active service. Orders were received at of No.1 Group HQ to mobilise prior to proceeding to France as an Advanced Air Striking Force (AASF). The plans for such a move had already been drawn

*Seen here with the Mayor of Weston-super-Mare. Sadly, only the identity five of the officers shown here are known. 1st left Pilot Officer Crane, 5th left Flying Officer Hughes, centre Squadron Leader Warrington. 5th from right, Pilot Officer Robin, 2nd on right Pilot Officer Richmond.*

*The squadron's Fairey Battles lined-up at the airfield at Weston-super-Mare during their last peace-time engagement.*

up and finalised weeks prior. For the squadron, its association with No.1 Group was over, it was now a squadron of the Allied Air Striking Force. At 23:00 hour of the 24th, 218 Squadron received orders to mobilise. The squadron strength stood at 16 Fairey Battles equipped with the Merlin Mk.II, plus a reserve of four aircraft and four additional pilots. The squadron along with 88 Squadron would form No.75 Wing, which consisted of 41 officers, 5 warrant officers 62 senior non-commissioned officers and 674 other ranks. The command structure on this day was.

### No.75 Wing August 24th 1939

Group Captain Archibald Herbert Wann : Commanding Officer
Squadron Leader Eric John Daubery Routh : Operations
Flight Lieutenant Franklin Herbert Worlledge : Intelligence
Flight Lieutenant William Lawson Whitlock : Adjutant
Wing Commander Kenneth Riversdale Elliot DSO :Officer Commanding No.88 Squadron
Squadron Leader Thomas Charles Dickens : No.88 Squadron
Wing Commander Lewin Bowring Duggan : Officer Commanding No.218 Squadron
Squadron Leader George Ninian Warrington : No.218 Squadron

The morning of the 25th was predominately spent ensuring that the aircraft were ready for war, everything was packed and sorted into ever larger piles of stores and equipment ready for transportation. The Reservists began to arrive one-by-one from their civilian peace-time jobs. For the pilots, never had they been so focused on the performance of 'their' aircraft while on air-tests, everything had to be bang-on!

The ground crews especially work feverishly to ensure everything was perfect with their charges. The remainder of August would see the squadron effectively pack and crate tons of equipment ranging from engines to pots and pans. It was around this time the squadron's pre-war **SV** codes were removed, and the squadron's new **HA** codes applied.

Over the 29th and 30th, every available pilot from 'A' - 'B' and 'C' Flights was airborne on either an Air-Test or local flying practice, the only absentees were 'C' Flights P/O Robert Givens and the soon to be posted P/O Rhine. At the end of the days flying on August 30th, the squadron establishment was 21 Battles, of which 18 were serviceable, while 3 were undergoing routine maintenance checks.  On the 30th, the 4th Battalion of the Wiltshire Regiment TA arrived at Boscombe Down to man the ground defences and airfield security.  The German invasion of Poland began at 4:44am on the morning of September 1st, 1939, the British Prime Minister Neville Chamberlain appeared before the House of Commons shortly after 6:00pm that evening.  Shattered by the news from Poland, the Prime Minister must have known that war was inevitable, in a passionate speech he told the packed house *"It now only remains for us to set our teeth and to enter upon this struggle, which we ourselves earnestly endeavoured to avoid, with determination to see it through to the end"*, Chamberlain declared. *"We shall enter it with a clear conscience, with the support of the Dominions and the British Empire, and the moral approval of the greater part of the world"*.

At 9pm that night the British Ambassador to Germany Sir Neville Henderson handed an ultimatum to Joachim von Ribbentrop. It declared that unless the British government received "satisfactory assurances" that Germany was prepared to withdraw from Polish territory, *"His Majesty's Government will without hesitation fulfil their obligation to Poland."* One hour later, the French ambassador delivered an identical note. The country and world held its breath.

# Chapter 5: 1939 – War With Germany

At around 09:15 hours on the morning of September 2nd, Group Captain Wann, S/Ldr Ronald Thorpe, (75 Wing Medical Officer) F/O William Macken, (Armament) P/O Eric Macro, (Equipment) and 46 other ranks departed RAF Boscombe Down in six civil transport aircraft for Auberive-sur-Suippe airfield
At 13:45 hours No.75 Wing's forward sea party comprising of 95 airmen departed for Auberive under the overall command of the recently promoted S/Ldr Worlledge. Flight Lieutenant John Hughes was responsible for the 43 airmen of 218 Squadron. The squadrons of Boscombe Down were made ready for an afternoon departure, the first squadron away was 88 Squadron lead by Wing Commander Elliot DSO who departed at 14:00 hours with sixteen Battles. Seventy minutes later, Wing Commander Duggan took off followed by fifteen squadron Battles, plus a solitary aircraft of 88 Squadron. Slowly gaining altitude the Battles formed up into two flights. Once at formed, the formation headed to the coast of south-east England, over the Hop fields of Kent and out over the English Channel.

## Formation No.1

| Serial | Pilot | Observer | Wireless Op/Gunner |
|---|---|---|---|
| K9324 (No.1) | Wing Commander Duggan | Sergeant Ruffell Hazel | Aircraftman Gill |
| K9353 (No.2) | Flight Sergeant Fleet | Sergeant Baxter | Aircraftman Richardson |
| K9355 (No.3) | Pilot Officer Thynne | Sergeant Pike | Aircraftman Colnourn |
| K9323 (No.6) | Flight Lieutenant Daish | Sergeant Malpass | Aircraftman Jones |
| K9327 (No.4) | Pilot Officer Shaw | Sergeant Morgan | Aircraftman Fisher |
| K9326 (No.5) | Sergeant Horner | Sergeant Young | Aircraftman Davies (035) |
| K9329 (No.9) | Pilot Officer Richmond | Sergeant Jennings | Aircraftman Ellis |
| K9325 (No.8) | Flight Sergeant Herring | Sergeant Butt | Aircraftman Davies (992) |

## Formation No.2

| Serial | Pilot | Observer | Wireless Op/Gunner |
|---|---|---|---|
| K9251 (No.1) | Squadron Leader Warrington | Sergeant Burkett | Aircraftman Gregory |
| K9252 ( No.2) | Flying Officer Hulbert | Sergeant Deverill | Aircraftman Wiltshire |
| K9254 (No.3) | Pilot Officer Warring | Sergeant Harris | Aircraftman Jones (388) |

| K9256 (No.6) | Flying Officer Rogers | Sergeant Andrews | Aircraftman Connerlley |
|---|---|---|---|
| K9255 ( No.4) | Pilot Officer Reeves | Sergeant Stubbs | Aircraftman Drummond |
| K9356 ( No.5) | Sergeant Owen | Sergeant Farmes | Aircraftman Forrester |
| K9357 (No.9) | Pilot Officer Crane | Flight Sergeant Wavell | Aircraftman Evans |
| K9273 ( No.8) | Pilot Officer Robin | Sergeant Lowndes | Aircraftman Cranley |

Strangely, the recent batch of Battles (L Series) delivered in July were not taken to France, most would be returned to No.22 M.U during September in the squadron's absence. The squadron for some unknown reason would re-equipped with the Battles they had first been given back in October 1938!

All thirty-two Battles and civilian aircraft safely reached Auberive, on landing they were immediately dispersed. Auberive-sur-Suippe airfield was a large flat field bounded on the south by low pine trees. To the north was the village that bore the airfield's name. Situated a few miles south east of Rheims it would be the home for the squadron for the next 8 months. Pilot Officer Walter Shaw; *'The Squadron took off in strength at about 2 pm to an airfield we now know to be Auberive, near Rheims. We landed and at each dispersal point were already 4 x 250 lb. bombs but we were told that as, yet war had not been declared'. The accommodation was very limited and austere. I was lucky and was based in a bare room in the Town Hall and used our camp kit which we used to laugh at as Scout's kit. The NCOs were billeted in haylofts and one was near a pigsty! It was a very rude awakening to active service.*
*The following morning, we went to the airfield and there was a French Army unit who prepared breakfast for us all. We had a ladle of stewed apple and a chunk of very dark French chocolate, which was not very substantial or nice!'*

Back in England, a visibly tired looking Neville Chamberlain informed the House of Commons that no reply had yet been received from Germany regarding the previous night's ultimatum. The whole of Europe was hoping for a miracle, it never came.

The following morning, Sunday September 3rd at 9:00am Britain gave Germany a deadline of 11:00am to announce that it was prepared to withdraw its troops from Poland or else a state of war would exist between Britain and Germany. The deadline passed with no response. At 11:15am Neville Chamberlain announced on BBC Radio that Britain and Germany were at war. *"You can imagine what a bitter blow it is to me that all my long struggle to win peace has failed"*, Chamberlain said, sounding dispirited. *"Yet I cannot believe that there is anything more or anything different that I could have done and that would have been more successful ... We and France are today, in fulfilment of our obligations, going to the aid of Poland, who is so bravely resisting this wicked and unprovoked attack upon her people. We have a clear conscience. We have done all that any country could do to establish peace, but a situation in which no word given by Germany's ruler could be trusted and no people or country could feel themselves safe had become intolerable. And now that we have resolved to finish it, I know that you will all play your part with calmness and courage".*

On the afternoon of the 4th, the squadron commenced flying, if but only air-tests. Disappointingly, 4 Battles were found to have minor engine problems while one aircraft, K9323 was declared unserviceable. This aircraft was the usual mount of 'A' Flights C/O F/Lt Daish. The Forward Sea Party arrived during the late afternoon of the 4th, the Wing was almost complete and on paper at least, ready for action. Over the next week both, 88 and 218 Squadrons flew numerous air-tests and local recognition flights. Just before teatime on the 10th, F/Lt Whitlock the Wing adjutant and F/O Henry Copeland, Wing Signals Officer arrived by air from Boscombe Down. At 15:30 hours the squadron provided a section led by Wing Commander Duggan on a local reconnaissance flight to Rheims, Nancy, Bitche and finally the town of Sierck-les-Bains, situated just a few miles from the German border, all three crews returned safely just after 5pm. On the

morning of the 11th orders were received from Group HQ at Rheims, that one squadron was to depart Auberive and re-locate to Mourmellon airfield. Who decided what squadron was to vacate is unclear, but at 19:00 hours the advance party of 88 Squadron set off for their new home. The following day, the main party and sixteen Battles departed, it was a sad day for both squadrons as they had served side-by-side since April 1938. On the 12th and 13th, P/O Shaw was tasked with ferrying Battle K9324 to Rheims where it was given a compass swing. Mechanics typically use one of two methods to swing the compass on an aircraft. They either perform it on a compass rose at an airfield or used a calibrated master compass to align the aircraft during the swing, neither were available at

*A sight that would become all too frequent over the months to come. Despite AASF HQ's rather naive attempt to discredit the fighter and its pilots the Bf109 proved to be a deadly opponent.*

Auberive. On the 14th, the first official visit took place, Sir Ludlow-Hewitt, Commander in Chief, Bomber Command and Air Vice Marshal Patrick Playfair, Air Officer Commanding AASF, arrived at Auberive.

On the 17th, three Battles led by 'A' Flights F/Lt Daish flying K9329 departed Auberive at 14:45 hours and quickly proceed to Thionville. On reaching the town and establishing their position the crews were briefed to carry out a reconnaissance along the Franco-German frontier. The route was to take the section firstly to Lauterbourg a small town nestled on the border, then to fly parallel along the frontier visiting both Metz and Verdun on the way before returning. However, a navigational error on the part of Sergeant David Malpass, observer in the lead Battle resulted in the section crossing the border into Germany and flying over Karlsruhe! Situated on the right bank of the Rhine, the city lies between the Mannheim/Ludwigshafen and was a major arms producer. Luck was most definitely on their side, the three Battles did not encounter any opposition, quickly realising the error, F/Lt Daish, P/O Harold Waring (K9256) and F/Sgt John Mitchell (K9355) quickly turned for the relative safety of the Frontier, they landed shortly after 15:00 hours. It was not entirely the way the squadron wanted to enter German airspace, but it had crossed into Nazis Germany for the first time. Just after 10am the following morning seven Morane SS fighters from the Coupe de Chasse arrived at Auberive to discuss a joint operation to be flown on Tuesday 19th. Unfortunately, low cloud and drizzle meant that the operation was cancelled, however there was some good news, the squadrons Main Party under the able command of Flight Lieutenant John Hughes arrived, tired but otherwise in good order just before tea-time.

The setback due to the weather was quickly forgotten when the following day Wing Commander Duggan led two sections away just after 1pm on a high-level reconnaissance flight ten miles into German airspace. The crews involved in the squadrons first planned foray over Germany were;

| Serial | Pilot | Observer | Wireless Op/Gunner |
|--------|-------|----------|--------------------|
| K9254 | Wing Commander Duggan | Sergeant Ruffell Hazel | Aircraftman Gill |
| K9353 | Flight Sergeant Fleet | Sergeant Baxter | Aircraftman Colhourn |
| K9327 | F/O Hughes | Flight Sergeant Wavell | Aircraftman Evans |
| K9325 | Flight Sergeant Herring | Sergeant Butt | Aircraftman Davies (992) |
| K9251 | Squadron Leader Warrington | Sergeant Burdett | Aircraftman Gregory |
| K9256 | Flight Lieutenant Rogers | Sergeant Andres | Corporal Connerley |

After gaining altitude the six Battles circled Auberive waiting for the promised escort of seven French Morane fighters. Frustratingly the French fighters did not materialise, defiantly, W/Cdr Duggan then took the dangerous decision to continue with the planned operation. The six aircraft took up the standard No.1 Group Defensive Formation and headed into Germany at 23,000 feet, almost the operational ceiling of the Battle. This altitude was possible as the Battles were not carrying bombs. The formation did a sweeping loop taking in Hoheinod, Waldfischbach and other unassuming Germany towns that would have been oblivious to the 18 RAF airman slowly passing above then. The German defences offered no opposition from either flak or fighters. Once the photographs had been taken the squadron swung for home, however unlike the outward trip the weather conditions had quickly deteriorated. The return flight was carried out over an almost solid cloud base making navigation almost impossible. Unable to locate Auberive the squadron forced landed at the Aero Club at Gray, 20 miles ENE of Dijon due to shortage of petrol. While descending into the cloud, F/O Hughes collided with the tail of the sub leader, S/Ldr Warrington, both aircraft were damaged but thankfully not seriously and were able to make a successful landing. Wing Commander Duggan was the first to land at 16:40 hours, within 15 minutes the remaining crews were safely on the ground, given the time, the crews were forced to spend the night at Gray.

**Wednesday September 20th 1939**
*Fairey Battle*
*Mk.I K9327*
*Contract No : 522745/36*
*Taken on Charge: 10/10/1938*
*Repaired on Site.*
*Pilot: Flying Officer John Hughes*
*Observer/Bomb aimer: Flight Sergeant Wavell*
*Gunner / Wireless Operator: Aircraftman Evans*

**Wednesday September 20th 1939**

*Fairey Battle*
*Mk.I K9251*
*Contract No : 522745/36*
*Taken On Charge : 10/10/1938*
*Repaired on Site.*
*Pilot : Squadron Leader Warrington*
*Observer/Bomb aimer:  Sergeant Burdett*
*Gunner / Wireless Operator: Aircraftman Gregor*

On the afternoon of the 21st, 'A' Flight's  P/O Richmond departed for Gray at the controls of K9324, loaded aboard were the spares required to make good the damaged to both Battles. The four airworthy Battles again led by W/Cdr Duggan landed back at Auberive just after lunch. The repairs to the two damaged aircraft were completed by late afternoon, the section led by P/O Richmond returned just after dusk. Unbeknown to the crews at Auberive, 88 Squadron had been in action on the morning of the 20th and lost two of their number to Bf109 fighters.  Just after 10am the three Battles lead by F/O Lawrence Baker set course for Sarreguemines on the Franco-German border. It was here that the flight was attacked by Bf109s of 5./JG3. In the ensuring encounter one aircraft was shot down in flames, while another force landed. Flying Officer Baker managed to return claiming the destruction of a Bf109 fighter, the first aerial 'kill' of the war by the RAF. The following day, P/O Shaw led a section on a reconnaissance of the frontier, unlike the previous operation this would be carried out at 1,500 feet. On the morning of the 22$^{nd}$, P/O Shaw led a section on a reconnaissance of the frontier. Once again the operation would be carried out at just 1,500 feet. Departing at 11:45 hours the Battles headed for Sarreguemines on the Franco-German border. Here they swung to port and headed towards the French town of Lauterbourg.  This unassuming town was the easternmost commune in France and uncomfortably positioned between the French Maginot and German Siegfried-lines. Once again, no opposition was encountered, and the only sighting was of a small transport convoy.  In the afternoon, S/Ldr Warrington led a section on a similar reconnaissance operation but in the opposite direction. Both the French and AASF HQ were keen to utilise the Battle squadrons, the French especially were keen for the whole Franco-German Border to be regularly photographed. Initially, unwilling to fly into German airspace these sorties were carried out on the French side of the border, the photographs being taken obliquely.  This changed on September 19th when the Battles penetrated 10 miles into Germany, this would be further increased to 20 miles. This push into Germany was however not without its dangers, Air Vice Marshal Patrick Playfair was keenly aware of the defensive limitations of his Battle squadrons, and the further the squadrons penetrated the more his concerns grew. It was Playfair who pushed for greater coordination between the French fighter squadrons and his light bombers.

Number 75 Wing's motor transport convoy arrived at Auberive on the 23rd consisting of an impressive 105 vehicles, including prime movers. The urgently needed vehicles were quickly divided between 88 and 218 Squadrons, much to the delight of all concerned. The squadron was detailed and briefed for another high-level reconnaissance operation over Germany on the afternoon of the 23rd. Discussions with the local French fighter wing had agreed that the six Battles would be escorted to Neustadt, Germany. Situated between the Haardt mountains and the eastern edge of the Palatinate Forest, it would be the squadrons deepest penetration into Germany to date. Disappointingly, the weather curtailed the operation shortly

*A section of squadron Battles tucked in close for mutual protection. Shown are K9353 HA-J, K9324 HA-B and K9325 HA-D*

before take-off. There were however nagging doubts about the reliability of the French regardless of their confidant promises of escort cover for the operation.

The airfield defences were tested on the 27th when three Battles carried out a mock low-level attack. All non-essential personnel quickly found sanctuary in the recently dug slit trenches dotted around the aerodrome. A rifle company of 50 men took up position and engaged the low flying Battles, or at least tried too. Given the drubbing inflicted to 88 Squadron on the 21st, it was agreed that the standard and accepted evasive tactics against fighter attacks needed to be improved or at least practised. Mid-morning, F/Lt Harry Daish, Sgt John Horner and P/O Ian Richmond were airborne. Just after 11pm the French fighters appeared as previously arranged. After some hand waving and friendly gestures both parties engaged in a series of staged dogfights. The fighters, Curtiss Hawks H75 of Groupe GC 1/4 based at Wez-Thuisy gave the section a real test. After carrying out various exhausting manoeuvres, it was established that a steep turn while still maintaining a tight formation was the best method of presenting the most challenging target and at the same time increasing the effectiveness of the rear gunner's fire. Over at Mourmelon-Le-Grand, 88 squadron had come up with their own method of dealing with the fighters. They opted for a system where a section of three aircraft would break away in an inverted 'Prince of Wales Feathers' manoeuvre and format at a lower altitude.

That same afternoon a high-level reconnaissance operation was scheduled for 15:45 hours, six Battles led by F/Lt Daish were to enter Germany to a depth of 20 miles unescorted. The six Battles slowly climbed to the briefed altitude of 23,000 feet and formed up into a boxed formation. Once established they headed towards the French border town of Biche. Using the towns large cathedral to pinpoint their position they set off in near perfect weather conditions. The formation soon passed over the Siegfried Line and into Germany, their objective was the town of Kaiserslautern nestled at the north end of the Palatinate Forest. Soon after crossing the border the crew of P/O Max Freeman were obliged to turn for home when the oxygen system aboard Battle K9355 failed. The formation flew untroubled apart from the freezing cold at 23,000 feet any activity from German artillery was to be recorded, especially along the front line and conveyed back to HQ immediately upon return. With the photographs taken, F/Lt Daish turned the formation for home, once again the whole trip had been undertaken without encountering any opposition.

The squadron HQ moved from its temporary location on the airfield to the village of Auberive on the 29th, with winter fast approaching, the rather basic conditions needed to be improved and quickly. During the afternoon, F/Lt Alan Roger's led a section of three Battles over the various French flak batteries dotted along No.75 Wing's frontier. Newly applied RAF roundels had the squadron slightly on edge, French aircraft recognition was on par with the British Army so a demonstration under controlled conditions was deemed to be the wisest, and safest option. The last operation of the month was undertaken by F/Lt Harry Daish who was aloft taking mosaic photographs of the airfield, Auberive village and St Hilaire. These photographs would be used by the Operations Officer in his preparation and planning for the defence against aerial attack should it come.

*The village of Auberive-sur-Suippe seen here pre-war. The whole area was devastated during the Great War.*

By the end of September, the squadron was beginning to settle into its new surroundings. The French countryside around the airfield was varied and wonderfully green and lush despite the horrors of the Great War. The airfield lacked many basic comforts that had been taken for granted back at Boscombe Down, but it was now home. Both air and ground crews had worked tirelessly to ensure that the squadron was at the very peak of efficiency, both in the air and on the ground. Unlike 88 Squadron there had been no encounters with the much-vaunted Bf109, however further along the front worrying news had filtered through that a flight of Battles had been lost. This was at odds with the dispatches from AASF HQ at Rheims who had a woeful disregard of the German opposition. It appeared that Rheims had a rather disparaging view of the performance of the German fighters and their pilots, a report from late September recorded.

IT HAS BEEN RELIABLY REPORTED THAT THE SLIGHTEST SIDE SLIP OR FLAT TURN WILL TROW OFF THE GERMAN FIGHTER PILOTS AIM. ENEMY FIGHTERS ATTACK IN LINE AHEAD OR LINE ASTERN FROM SLIGHTLY ABOVE OR BELOW. THEY THEN TURN

These naive reports emanating from Rheims would be quickly seen for what there were, delusional. The squadron had flown over Nazis Germany on three occasions, and to date suffered no losses. A total of 102 sorties had been flown, and apart from the collision while descending in cloud on the 20th there had been no incidents or accidents, but more importantly there had been no casualties. Squadron establishment at the end of the month was reported as, 18 serviceable Battles, with 3 under repair. Aircrew numbers stood at fifteen officer pilots, six NCO pilots with 20 observers and a further 20 air gunners.

*Wing Commander Duggan greets the Mayor of Auberive-sur-Suippes.*

The first week of October was a mixture of training and yet more recognition flights over the anti-aircraft defences along the front-line and French airfields. A trickle of recently posted pilots fresh from England were put through their paces by F/Lt Alan Rogers and P/O Arthur Imrie, there was lot for them to learn. Flight Lieutenant Rogers led six Battles on a fighter co-operation exercise on the 10th with six Curtis H75 fighters from Groupe GC 1/4 based at Wez-Thuisy. The six Battles firstly flew in box formation and were attacked from both above and below, next F/Lt Rogers had the formation divide into two sections flying line astern. After an hour, the exhausted crews returned to Auberive. It was a sobering de-briefing, all agreed that when flying in the standard box formation a steep turn was the best method of defence, nonetheless, they all agreed that they still made an easy target for the fighters. They concluded that their only hope was that a tight boxed formation might on first sight be considered formidable, and less likely to attack! It was wishful thinking. The following morning, F/Lt Daish and six Battles found themselves mixing it again with the French fighters, the same tactics as the previous day were flown and sadly the same conclusion was reached.

Further along the front, No.74 Wings 103 and 150 Squadron had since their arrival in France experienced a number of costly encounters with German fighters, 150 Squadron especially had taking a mauling. On September 30th, a formation of six Battles were ordered to carry out a photo reconnaissance north west of Saarbrucken, it was while over Germany they were attacked at 23,000 feet by Bf109s. One Battle had turned back early, but the remainder were subjected to a prolonged and savage attack. The fighters of 2./JG53 shot down four of the Battles and severely damaged the fifth which crashed in France, despite the reassurances from HQ that the Germans appeared not to press home their attacks, it was a massacre. These losses coupled with 88 Squadron effectively halted further Battle operations over Germany. Presumably, the senior staff at AASF HQ at Rheims had quickly come to realise that the pre-war doctrine of the bombers fighting their way to the target was now truly shattered.

On October 16th P/O Richmond led six Battles for yet more fighter practice. Over the previous two days the major topic of conversation was tactics and survival.

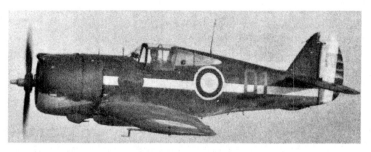

*A French Curtiss H-75 fighter. Probably the best fighter in the Armee de I'Air at the time of the German invasion. It could with an experienced pilot just hold its own against the Bf109E.*

Once again with the help of French Curtiss H.75 fighters the squadron put into practice a new method of defence. The Battles would fly in tight box formation, however now a running commentary would be broadcast by the gunner of the flight leader. This commentary would ensure that the flight stayed compact when taking evasive action, and secondly co-ordinate the defensive firepower from the rear gunners. Another tactic was tried, once the Battles had been engaged the formation would split into to two sub flights and make a very steep turn just as the fighters came within firing range. The tired crews, especially the Battle pilots arranged for a post practice conference with the French counterparts. The discussion seemed to confirm the crew's opinion, mutual co-ordination and tight turns made the attackers job harder, and at the same time exposed them to return fire, that was the theory at least. On the 17th, two crews, Sgt Charles Owen and P/O Michael Robin were aloft just after 3pm to demonstrate to the anti-aircraft gunners recently arrived from England the silhouette of the Fairey Battle. Shortly after, Pilot Officer Ian Richmond led a flight to calibrate the D/F station which had been installed on the north west corner of the aerodrome the day before. For ninety minutes the flight would fly at various altitudes and headings giving the ground station the opportunity to fine tune and calibrate the still relatively new and important apparatus, which over the winter months become invaluable.

On the 19th, the Secretary State for Air, Sir Kingsley Wood, accompanied by his staff, and representatives of the press and cinema visited AASF HQ and inspected the landing ground at St Hiliare. Sixteen crews were sent by road to St Hiliare for the visit, it was a good opportunity to meet old friends from 88 Squadron and discuss tactics. Sir Kingsley Wood spent the morning inspecting the Operations Room, Billets, Airmens' kitchen and canteen, photographic sections, MT Section. Finally, he was introduced to the pilots of 88 and 218 Squadrons. In the afternoon and on completion of his inspection, the Secretary of State for Air had a well-earned lunch in the Officers' Mess.

For the first time since the squadrons arrival high level bombing practice was carried out on the afternoon of the 21st. Nine crews were involved, attacking targets on the aerodrome from between 5,000 - 8,000 feet, bizarrely none of the Battles were loaded with bombs, so the accuracy or otherwise could not be judge. Observation on the ground however concluded that the dives were far too shallow to be effective. That evening a fire broke out in the large straw barn near the M.T section. The squadron Orderly Officer, P/O Robins telephoned HQ just after 1.30am stating that there was a fire. The St Hiliare Fire Picquet and the manual fire apparatus were loaded onto a light van and rushed to Auberive. While waiting the Fire trucks arrival, all available personnel at the airfield turned out to help contain the fire, eventually after a 20-minute delay the Fire Picuet finally arrived and quickly managed to bring the fire under control saving the adjoining farmhouse and buildings from destruction. Worryingly, it was later discovered that a lorry parked in the M.T section had been sabotaged, although there was no evidence that the fire was started deliberately, extra guards were posted. It was *Au revoir* on the 22nd to the French Air Party that had been stationed at Auberive since the squadron's arrival, P/O Shaw remembers fondly the hospitality of the French;

*A French unit prepared breakfast for us all initially. We were introduced to stewed apple and a chunk of very dark French chocolate for breakfast, it was not very substantial or nice. Eventually the officers were billeted in very good quarters in Auberive and the NCOs settled in their haylofts and got established and the dining hall had a very good kitchen for other ranks. So began the 'phoney war'. We liaised with a local French flying squadron flying Curtiss single engine fighters and we got to know them very well. They invited us out to a dinner at Ves Thuisy. Although we could not speak French, we all got on very well and sang the Marseillaise.*

At 01:30 hours on the morning of the 23rd AASF HQ sent a signal to No.75 Wing instructing the squadrons to standby on half hours' notice for a 'close support' operation that day. The squadron ground crews worked throughout the night and early morning to make ready nine fully bombed and armed Battles. There was an atmosphere of apprehension throughout the squadron, was this going to be the squadrons first bombing raid of the war. The whole squadron waited for instructions, however it was all in vain, at 10:00 hours the squadron was instructed to return to 2 hour readiness.

The installation of a new downward firing gun fitted to a squadron Battle had F/Lt Daish airborne on the morning of the 25th. Aloft in Battle K9323 just after 10:35 hours the crew tested the installation of a Vickers K gun fitted on a moveable mounting fixed to the bombing aperture. It was soon after 88 Squadrons costly encounter with the Bf109s that the Battle squadrons began carrying out some improvised modifications to their Battles to address the vulnerability to attack from behind and below. One of the first squadrons was 105 based at Villeneuve-les-Vertus. They installed a Vickers Gas Operated gun on a bracket attached to the bomb sight spigot aboard Battle K9486 on October 8th. This was inspected by Air Chief Marshal Sir R Brocke-Popham and Air Marshal Sir Charles Burnett on the 15th and operational trials started within four days. Number 74 Wing's 150 Squadron had also been busy, Sgt H Beddellon had installed a Vickers K Gun firing through the bombing aperture. This could be fired both forward and to the rear, although it had

*The view from the bomb aimers position in the Battle was at best restricted. The installation of a rearward and downward facing machine gun was not only cumbersome it was almost impossible to operate with any degree of accuracy.*

to be turned upside down when firing to the rear and required two sights!

It had been given approval from the very top after inspection at Reims by Air Chief Marshal Sir Edgar Ludlow-Hewitt, Air Officer Commander-in-Chief of Bomber Command, and Air Vice Marshall Phillip Playfair AOC-in-C of the AASF on the 24th. The modified Battle was flown to Fairey Aviation in Stockport for demonstration, within the month squadron were receiving the slightly adapted mounting direct from England. There is some uncertainty surrounding the origin of the new gun installation on the squadron. The idea may have been copied from 150 Squadron, but more likely 105 Squadron. The armourers of 218 produced an ad-hoc installation 'in-the-field' prior to any official blessing. Unlike 150 and 105 Squadrons, 'A' Flight commander, F/Lt Daish found the gun *'impracticable'*. Dive practice was carried out on the 25th and 26th, on the 27th Squadron Leader Warrington led a sub flight to attack various targets dotted around the airfield, manning the machine guns posts were all available pilots. It was hoped that seeing an attack from ground level would benefit the pilots when attacking ground targets. The pilots on the ground agreed that the diving Battles made difficult targets but needed to increase their speed on levelling out. No further flying was carried out until the 30th when S/Ldr Warrington led a flight on a fighter affiliation exercise with the Curtiss H75's from Wez-Thuisy. October had generally been a month of training, 105 flights were flown without incident or loss.

Yet more dive-bombing practice was undertaken on November 2nd, eight pilots carried out low level bombing and shallow dive-bombing attacks on the aerodrome from 1,000 feet using practice bombs. Following on the from the exercise on October 27th, a new tactic of zig-zagging away from the target on releasing the bombs was tried, all agreed it was a very effective method of eluding any ground fire in the target area, in theory anyway.

'A' Flight commander, F/Lt Daish was aloft just before lunch on the 3rd, joining him was 2nd Lieutenant Waddington of the Royal Artillery. The flight was carried out to check the AA gun emplacements situated 1 mile east of the aerodrome. The British Army unlike their French counterparts had a lot to learn about effective camouflage and concealment, this flight was to check just how well they had or had not concealed the guns. Two fortunate crews were chosen to sample the delights of Paris on the 3rd, it would be the start of a much sort after 48-hour leave. To compensate those left behind, the NAAFI opened a canteen and bar for the airman. Unfortunately, the cost of a pint of British beer was beyond most of the lowly paid airman and NCOs meagre wages. Not to be outdone, the bar manager stocked up with local French beer, which although not as good the beer back in Blighty, was much cheaper. It was around this time that news began to circulate about German parachute spies being dropped behind the Maginot Line. The French, already nervous, were particularly anxious to apprehend any spies and quickly quell the rumours that were sweeping along the front. At Auberive an increase in sentries and greater vigilance was the order of the day, especially after the mysterious fire and damaged vehicle the month before.

Continuing the effort to ensure that the French anti-aircraft gunners were fully familiar with the look and sound of the Battle, P/O Max Freeman flew Battle K9355 to Wez-Thuisy airfield on the morning of November 6th. It had been arranged for the local anti-aircraft gunners to have an opportunity to inspect the aircraft on the ground, however the French did not turn up as planned. Undeterred, P/O Freeman returned during the afternoon, but once again the unreliable French did not materialise. Pilot Officer Hugh Forth was obliged to land Battle K9273 HA-R with one wheel unlocked on return from a formation practice flight on the 7th. After circling the aerodrome for an hour, the experienced Forth brought the Battle into land, holding off until the last moment the aircraft made a textbook landing on the wet grass. Immediately the port undercarriage retracted inflicting minor damage to the wing and damaging the propellor, none of the crew were injured.

**Tuesday  November 7th 1939**
*Fairey Battle*
*Mk.I  K9273 HA-R*
*Contract No :522745/37*
*Taken On Charge : 11/10/1938*
*Repaired On Site.*
*Pilot : Pilot Officer Hugh Forth*
*Observer/Bomb aimer:  Sergeant Peter Stubbs*
*Gunner / Wireless Operator : Aircraftman Forrester*

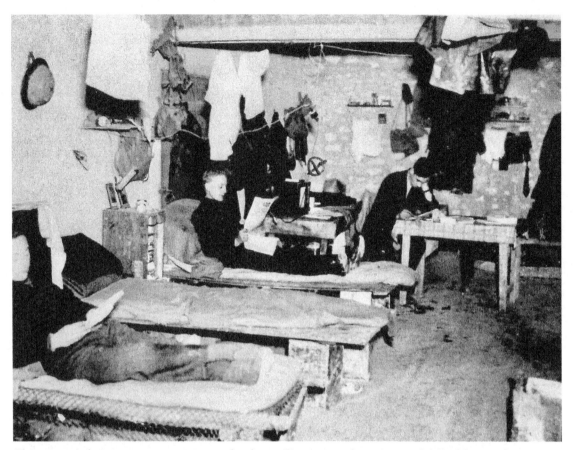

*The airmen's living quarters were somewhat basic. Freezing in the winter and full of flies in the summer the conditions could not have been any more different from those left behind at RAF Boscombe Down.*

At 24:00 hours on the night of the 9th, AASF HQ at Reims warned No.75 Wing HQ of an expected dawn attack by German bombers on both Auberive and Mourmelon airfields and precautionary measures were to be implemented. Wing Commander Duggan had the squadron's Battles dispersed even more than usual, all gun posts were manned, and non-essential personnel were ordered off the airfield. As dawn broke, the squadron was ready for the attack. By late morning there was still no sign of the German bombers, normality slowly crept over Auberive. On the positive side, all the squadron personnel had performed well given the circumstances, it had been a good practice for things to come.

There was an air of excitement sweeping around the messes on November 10th, the squadron was scheduled to carried out a low-level bombing programme at the bombing range at Morounvilliers, situated only 12 miles north-east from Rheims. For the first time since arriving in France the squadron was to drop live bombs. Each of the 13 Battles were loaded with two 250lb H.E G.P bombs fitted with a 11 seconds delay at Auberive then flown to Mourmelon airfield where they would be dispatched individually to the bombing range via a control officer. Given it was the first time that most of the pilots had dropped live bombs the squadron ORB recorded *'results were considered very good as a certain amount of error was due to the bombs bouncing'.* There was good reason to celebrate on return from Morounvilliers, New Zealander Ian Richmond was promoted to Flying Officer. The now F/O Richmond had served on the squadron since February 1938. Born in Nelson, New Zealand on September 23rd, 1915, he had learnt to fly with the Marlborough Aero Club in 1936, being awarded his 'A' Licence in July 1936. Making his own way to Britain he successfully applied for a short service commission and started training at 3 Elementary and

*A 250lb HE bomb being loaded to the wing bays of a Battle. It was back breaking work for the armourers, muscle power was the order of the day. The winter of 1939/40 proved to be exceptionally cold making their work even more difficult.*

Reserve Flying Training School in May 1937. Commissioned in July 1937 he was posted to 7 Flying Training School from where he joined the squadron.

| Pilot | Over | Short |
|---|---|---|
| Pilot Officer Shaw | 10 yards | 5 yards |
| Flight Sergeant Fleet | 5 yards | 10 yards |
| Flying Officer Richmond | 10 yards | 10 yards |
| Wing Commander Duggan | 30 yards | 5 yards |
| Flight Lieutenant Daish | 8 yards | 50 yards |
| Pilot Officer Freeman | 45 yards | 10 yards |
| Sergeant Owen | 10 yards | 60 yards |
| Pilot Officer Imrie | 35 yards | 20 yards |
| Squadron Leader Warrington | 100 yards | 10 yards |

| | | |
|---|---|---|
| Flying Officer Crews | 20 yards | 60 yards |
| Pilot Officer Crane | 70 yards | 180 yards |
| Flying Officer Hulbert | 100 yards | 15 yards |
| Flight Sergeant Mitchell | 250 yards | 5 yards |
| Flight Lieutenant Roger | 300 yards | 300 yards |

*Above: the dive bombing results of the live bombing practice over Morounvilliers.*

Armistice Day 1939 was cold and wet. There was no squadron parade, however, the two-minute silence was solemnly observed, all personnel were issued with poppies which were worn throughout the day. During late morning three crews, Pilot Officers Imrie and Robin and F/Sgt Herring practised low-level formation attacks on the aerodrome. The Royal Engineers started erecting a new hut for the N.A.A.F.I during the afternoon, and all ranks were overjoyed at the prospect of its completion, to add to the creature comforts, a piano arrived for the canteen. More training over the airfield was arranged for the 13th, this time the crews would be practising high-level diving bombing technics. The first aloft at 1407 hours was Pilot Officer Robert Thynne and crew in Battle K9356. At 14:20 hours P/O Thynne was seen from the ground to commence his first dive.

Observers on the ground watched as the Battle appeared to start its dive in a half roll. This manoeuvre was quickly followed by what to the witnesses below looked like a near-vertical dive from 6,000 feet. With the engine at half throttle, the Battle attained a vertical dive at 1,500 feet at which height P/O Thynne seemed to be trying to pull the aircraft out of its dive, by this time it was estimated the Battle was flying at almost 400mph. It was then, and to the total shock of those on the ground, the port wing suddenly sheared off. The main portion of the aircraft and the three helpless crew struck the ground and almost completely buried itself before it burst into flames. Wreckage was scattered over 150 yards from the point of impact. The exercise was immediately cancelled, and the crews ordered to land back at Auberive immediately. All flying was suspended as initially the cause of the accident was believed to be a structural failure. What was left of the Battle was collected for inspection by No.2 Salvage Section. With no Accident Inspector in France at the time the squadron was effectively grounded until the 20th while investigations were underway. The initial report submitted on November 13th put the blame squarely on the pilot, it recorded;

*The aircraft being put over the vertical at the commencement of the dive and attaining great speed and thus putting great strain on the wings. In this connection inexperience and, I think excessive ardour on the part of the pilot should be taken into account, for it was Pilot Officer Thynnes first practice on dive bombing, and he was apt to be over zealous to the extent of unnecessary risk sometime.*

Pilot Officer Robert *'Bobby'* Thynne had gained his wings in October 1938 having trained at No.3 F.T.S at Hatfield, he had at the time of his death 118 hours flying on the Battle so was far from inexperienced. A report dated November 19th submitted by Squadron Leader Geoffrey Tuttle DFC to the Under Secretary of Air, Accident Investigation Branch based at the Air Ministry, London reported ;

*I consider that the accident was due to the fact that the pilot allowed the aircraft to get beyond his control and that he then endeavoured to pull out of the dive too violently possibly by the use of the tail trimming gear as it is unlikely that he would have been able to pull the control column back very rapidly at the speed the aircraft was flying. I do not think that any useful purpose would be served in having any further investigation by the Accident Branch.*

Just after 04:00 hrs on the 13th a German aircraft was reported flying high over Auberive travelling west. This information was immediately telephoned to Group HQ, too high for the local anti-aircraft battery to engage it passed safely overhead. At 05:10 hours possibly the same enemy aircraft approached Auberive this time from the east flying much lower. On this occasion the local Anti-Aircraft Battery eagerly engaged but despite their best intentions the aircraft escaped. A major training exercise began to take shape on the 14th, AASF HQ at Rheims issued Training Exercise No.1 to the various wings including No.75. The exercises' main purpose was to ensure that communications from squadron level up to Wing HQ and ultimately AASF HQ worked satisfactorily under operational conditions if a German attack should develop. A conference was held at No.75 Wing HQ on the morning of the 15th. Group Captain Wann outlined the exercise to his staff including Wing Commander Duggan and 88 Squadron's Wing Commander Elliot DSO. The Battles squadrons of the AASF would be required to attack and stem the advance of an imaginary Germany invasion through Belgium and Holland. The squadrons would attack and destroy advancing enemy columns at low level and undertake tactical bombing sorties as and when ordered from Rheims (Code named *Panther* ). At 15:00 hours on the afternoon of November 5th the squadron buried the crew of K9356. The coffins were loaded onto the back of a squadron lorry and in miserable weather conditions the funeral procession slowly made its way to the Franco-British Cemetery at Epernay. The funeral cortege consisted of Group Captain Wann, Wing Commander Duggan, who oversaw the ceremony, officers and NCO from the squadron, Wing Commander Elliot DSO of 88 Squadron, and representatives from both No.75 Wing HQ, and a detachment from the French Air Force and French Calvary. There was one final twist in the tragic deaths of three young airman. The highly respected and experienced, Chief Inspector of Accidents at the Air Ministry W/Cdr (Ret) Vernon Brown in a memorandum dated November 28th expressed his doubts about the initial finding submitted by S/Ldr Tuttle DFC, Vernon Brown wrote;

*This is the first case of structural failure in the air to the Battle. It seems that the aircraft was seen to do a half roll at about 6000ft and it is apparent that the blame has been put on the pilot for doing this. I cannot however believe that a pilot would deliberately half roll his aircraft with his crew on board. I think it is much more likely that the half roll, if indeed that is what happened was an involuntary manoeuvre the result of something having gone wrong. To say there is 'no evidence of structural failure' seems a remarkable statement. As to whether an investigation now would serve any useful purpose, I can only venture an opinion, but I think it worthwhile, I will send someone to look at this. I think it would be more satisfactory then having the pieces of the wing sent to R.A.E and moreover, it might be possible to obtain further evidence on the spot.*

**Monday November 13th 1939**
*Fairey Battle*
*Mk.I K9356*
*Contract No :522745/37*
*Taken On Charge: 26/10/1938*
*SoC*
*Pilot : Pilot Officer Robert Thynne 40650 RAF, age 20* **Killed**
*Observer/Bomb aimer: Sergeant Richard Cecil Luscombe Pike, 580454 RAF* **Killed**
*Gunner / Wireless Operator: Aircraftman 1st Class Vivian William Liddle Richardson 550941 RAF, age 19* **Killed**

On the afternoon of the 16th, F/Lt James Sanders arrived from Wing HQ to assist in preparing the operations room for the practice exercise on the 17th. His role was twofold, firstly he would liaise between the squadron and group HQ at St Hilaire, and secondary, would be accessing the squadrons performance. The following is the sequence of events, bizarrely throughout the whole exercise, not one Battle left the ground.

*November 15th, 1939 was cold, wet, and depressing, replicating the mood of those attending the funeral of former friends. Here the funeral procession of Pilot Officer Robert 'Bobby' Thynne and crew. The three young airmen were given a full military burial at the Franco-British Cemetery at Epernay.*

**Exercise A.H.1**

| Time | Sequence of Events |
|---|---|
| *12.01hrs* | *Raid order received from wing* |
| *12.04hrs* | *Target plotted by the Intelligence Officer* |
| *12.08hrs* | *Raid routed by the squadron commander* |
| *12.10hrs* | *Distance calculated by Intelligence Officer* |
| *12.14hrs* | *Crews instructed by the squadron commander* |
| *12.14 1/2 hrs* | *Crews instructed by the Intelligence Officer* |
| *12.20 1/2 hrs* | *Maps marked out by crews instructed by raid leader* |
| *12.34hrs* | *Crews left crew room for aircraft.* |

| | |
|---|---|
| 12.41 1/2 hrs | Crews arrive at aircraft. |
| 12.45 1/2 hrs | Aircraft started (Delay owing to removal of bombs for reconnaissance) |
| 12.51hrs | Aircraft taxied out. |
| 12.53hrs | Aircraft took off. |
| 13.19 1/2 hrs | Reconnaissance commenced. |
| 13.43hrs | Reconnaissance completed |
| 14.30hrs | Aircraft landed. |
| 14.40hrs | Crews returned to crew room. |
| 14.55hrs | Form D despatched to wing |
| 14.57hrs | Films dispatched. |
| 15.15hrs | Form Y ready for dispatch to wing. |

The imaginary operation was led by F/Lt Rogers. During the fictitious reconnaissance flight the crews were ordered to keep a detailed log and report any troop movement, or anything of importance as though it was an actual raid. The 'operation' was to be flown at mere 150 feet. The section observed a large M.T column travelling west near the small town of Le Roche, Luxembourg. The river bridges at Bomal and Barvaux which spanned the rivers Ourthe and Aisne were seen to be used by troops and motorised vehicles, while at Hody, an improvised landing ground was observed occupied by single engine fighters! The operation was an outstanding success in theory. In reality, all that happen was the Battles taxied out to take off and then taxied back to the dispersal area. It was all rather surreal.

The second 'operation' was a tactical bombing exercise, once again farcical timings were to be rigidly adhered too. This raid, unlike the previous operation did however have a number of realistic scenarios which given the events of May 1940 proved remarkably accurate.

**Exercise A.H.2**

| Time | Sequence of Events |
|---|---|
| 12.49hrs | Raid order received from wing |
| 13.00hrs | Target plotted by the Intelligence Officer. Raid routed by the squadron commander. Distance calculated by Intelligence Officer |
| 13.08hrs | Crews instructed by the squadron commander. Crews instructed by the Intelligence Officer |
| 13.19hrs | Maps marked out by crews instructed by raid leader |
| 13.22hrs | Crews left crew room for aircraft. |
| 13.26hrs | First crews arrive at aircraft. |
| 13.34hrs | Last crews arrive at aircraft. |

| | |
|---|---|
| *13.47hrs* | *Taxy out (two aircraft difficult to start)* |
| *1350hrs* | *Aircraft take off.* |
| *14.24hrs* | *Bombs dropped.* |
| *15.14hrs* | *Aircraft landed at satellite aerodrome (Main aerodrome had been attacked and damaged )* |
| *15.34hrs* | *Crews returned to crew room.* |
| *16.11hrs* | *Form D despatched to wing by Dispatch Rider ( Telephone communications destroyed)* |
| *16.18hrs* | *Form Y ready for dispatch to wing.* |

The success, or otherwise of this operational exercise is unknown. What was gained from these fictitious raids is unknown, but what is clear is that at this stage of the war, the planners at AASF HQ at Reims, the staff at No.75 HQ at St Hilaire and the senior officers at squadron level had woefully little idea of modern warfare when compared to the Germans. The rigid pre-war mentality of fixed front lines, limited ground gains by the enemy in a similar fashion to the Great War was still very much evident. The following day, the Operations Room which had been a hive of activity was cleared, while F/Lt Sanders returned to No.75 HQ. There was some light relief on the 18th when a football match between the squadron and local Army personnel was played, to the squadron won 6 - 0.

Squadron Leader Warrington led nine crews to the live bombing range at Moronvilliers early on the morning of the 24th. The Ranges were situated about 12 miles east of Rheims, and were controlled by, and used almost extensively by the units of the French Air Force. Each of the Battles was loaded with 2 x 250lb GP HE bombs, unlike the previous visit the accuracy of the low-level bombing exercise was not recorded other than results were described as 'average'. With the weather quickly deteriorating training flights were becoming less frequent, on the 26th freezing winds of 35mph plus with gusts of 65mph swept the open expanse of Auberive, with no cover say a few trees the ground crews especially suffered in the exposed conditions. This did not stop the eagerly anticipated football match between the squadron's gunners v maintenance crews, the gunners on this occasion were victorious. Entertainment was once again on the menu, on the 28th a party of officers and airman visited Rheims Opera House to see a concert by Miss Josephine Baker, the black American-born French entertainer. Known for her erotic dancing and appearing practically nude onstage she was a sensation in the 1930s. The following day a number of officers again visited Rheims Opera House, this time by invitation of the A.O.C. Showing was the film, *'A Lion Has Wings'* a documentary style, propaganda war film directed by Adrian Brunel and staring Ralph Richardson. The film was followed by entertainment provided by Sir Seymour Hicks, the British actor and music hall performer and his Company. Former squadron equipment officer Ben Johnson remembers Reims for other reasons, *" Rheims had three separate brothels, one for the officers another for NCOs and the third 'other-ranks'. I remember when S/Ldr Gilman took a party of us on a visit. Inside the Brothel was spotless, a well-stocked bar, music and lovely company, few of which could speak English!"*

The squadron welcomed two new crews on November 29th, New Zealander, Pilot Officers William Anstey and Canadian Howard Wardle. William Anstey was born March 22nd, 1919 in New Zealand and had originally joined the RNZAF in 1938. He was granted a short service commission in the RAF as P/O on August 16th, 1939. Howard Wardle was born in Dauphin, Manitoba, Canada on August 14th, 1915. Pre-war Howard, or 'Hank' as he was called, worked as a bookkeeper. With war looming he and two friends sailed for England to join the RAF, only Hank was successful. In March 1939, he was granted a short service commission, and after completing his training and gaining his wings, he was posted in November 1939 to No.98 (Bomber) Squadron based at RAF Hucknall operating the Fairey Battle. Hank's stay was short lived, on November 29th, he along with his observer, Sergeant Edward Davidson and air gunner, Aircraftman 1st Class Albert Bailey were posted to 218 Squadron joining 'B' Flight. The last morning of the month was spent carrying out yet more shallow dive-bombing attacks on the aerodrome. In the afternoon, a sub section led by F/O Crews carried out even more practice attacks, but this time they practised the important get away manoeuvres. Visiting Auberive late afternoon was the Inspector General, AVM Sir Charles Burnett KCB, CBE, DSO who was accompanied by Air Vice-Marshal Playfair, the squadron commanding officer and six selected officers from the squadron were interviewed in the mess.

So ended November, other than the tragic death of three colleagues the month was remarkable for its monotony. Endless training flights were now part and parcel of life on the squadron. There were some welcome developments with the improvement in accommodation and facilities both on the airfield and in the village. Despite the worsening weather and the enforced grounding, a total of 117 sorties were flown. Away from the squadron, the Royal Engineers had been busy digging slit trenches in Auberive and clearing a new satellite strip and dispersal field a mile SW Aubérive. There was little settling in time for the two recent arrivals, just after breakfast on December 1st, Pilot Officers Anstey and Wardle were aloft with F/Lt Alan Rogers. For an hour in worsening weather Wardle and Anstey were put through their paces at the same time familiarising themselves with all the local landmarks, including flak positions and the nearest RAF and French airfields. In the afternoon P/O Crane and Forth were over Moronvilliers bombing range, on this occasion the bombs, 250lb High explosives failed to explode, it was later established that the detonators were faulty. The following day P/O Anstey and Wardle were up again, this time under the critical eye of Flying Officer Hughes. For an hour, the pair practised formation flying, this was far removed from what was taught in flying training school, here, over France, tight, compact formations meant survival. A rugby match against a combined French Army team was played on the 3rd. The French, who had a pool of over 5000 men to pick from, had amongst their ranks two pre-war internationals. In front of a crowd of over 4000 the squadrons first XV put in a spirited effort losing 9 - 0.

The Chancellor of the Exchequer, Sir John Simon visited No.75 Wing HQ on the 5th, on completion of his visit he took off from Auberive in his D.H Flamingo, escort was provided by a section of Battles led by 'A' Flight's commander F/Lt Daish to with 10 miles of Reims from where he continued direct to England. On the 7th, F/O Crews led a flight of six aircraft to practise close formation flying in preparation for an operation of the utmost secrecy. On the morning of the 8th, six Battles led by F/O Crews departed Auberive and headed towards Rheims. The weather was foul, rain and sleet greeted the crews as they formed up. Over the unofficial capital of the Champagne region the flight was to provide an air escort for King George VI who arrived at Rheims by train just after 09.00 hours. On reaching the city the King left by car traveling first to Ludes and then Tours-Sur-Marne. For 2 1/2 hours the flight circled the royal car at 1,500 feet in freezing weather conditions. Each of the aircraft experienced severe icing, the crews especially the wireless operator / gunner suffered numbing cold perched in the semi open gun position. Just after 10am the flight was relieved by another wing, the Battles started landing back at Auberive just before 11:00 hours. What possible protection a flight of Battles could have provided against a swarm of Bf109s or Bf110s is uncertain. Wing Commander Duggan, three officers and six men proceeded by car to Villeneuve-les-Vertus. Here they would join Group Captain Wann, S/Ldr Routh and other representatives from No.75 Wing in being inspected by His Majesty the King.

The squadron was given permission from Wing HQ to carry out air to ground firing practice on the 9th. A new firing range had been set up 300 yards north west of the aerodrome, a number of large circular white targets had been positioned on the ground for the gunners to practice with the rear Vickers gun. Twelve crews participated, unfortunately the results could not be accessed as the targets were not patched between attacks. There was some cause for celebration on the 10th, former F/Sgt John Mitchell was promoted to pilot officer. A large convoy of fast cars and motorcycles arrived at Auberive on the morning of the 13th, they heralded the arrival of The Chief of Air Staff, Air Chief Marshal Sir Cyril Newall and Lord Londonderry. Those crews not carrying out gun firing practice were lined up in full kit and inspected by

*Three squadron Battles looking rather battered and worn high over the French countryside.*

the Chief of Air Staff. The parade, conducted by W/Cdr Duggan was undertaken in freezing conditions, joining the squadron was No.75 Wing's commander, Group Captain Wann. These visits were not enjoyed by the members of the squadron, it was more for the visiting dignitaries' egos than any practical reason.

*The rear gunner of a Battle. This photograph clearly illustrates the exposed position of the gunner. The gunner had to endure both the freezing conditions and knowledge that they were extremely vulnerable to enemy machine gun and cannon fire.*

On the 14th another pointless training operation was organised similarly to the one undertaken on October 17th. "AASF Operational Training Instruction No.2" was to test the effectiveness of communications within the group. Once again F/Lt Sanders arrived from No.75 Wing, he would act as Intelligence Officer, on this occasion he was ably assisted by P/O Shaw. Every facet of planning was to be tested from receiving orders from Wing HQ, the briefings of crews right through to interrogation of returning crews. Throughout the day fictitious operations took place, reports on enemy activity, success or otherwise were passed onto the intelligence staff, which in turn was then passed on to Group HQ. By late afternoon, the exercise was brought to an early conclusion enabling the Operations Staff and flying personnel to attend a concert given by Mr Leslie Henson at Epernay. One could only hope the Germans were as obliging!

For the next five days, the squadron flew countless practice operations ranging from shallow bombing attacks, air to ground firing, rear gun firing and the usual formation flying exercises. Flying Officer Christopher Mackinnon, Wing Armament Officer, gave a lecture on Anti-Gas procedure to both air and ground crews on the 15th. The horrors of gas warfare were still very much a possibility, almost all those who attended the lecture would have known about the effects of gas in the Great War, it was something that everyone hoped would never be repeated. Number 75 Wing HQ had two distinguished visitors mid-month. On the 17th, former Prime Minister, The Right Honourable Neville Chamberlain paid a visit, he was followed the next day by the Australian Prime Minister, the Right Honourable Mr J.V Fairbairn. On the 19th leave started in earnest for the fortunate, under the command of F/O Richmond, a party of two complete crews, Richmond's and Sergeant Charles Owen's, plus 17 non-flying personnel set off back to England. A Tactical exercise was carried out by two sections on the late morning of December 20th. The purpose was to train the crews in attacking large army road convoys. A Convoy of General Sir John Dill's 1st Corps B.E.F obligingly drove up and down the Arras-Fresnes-Douai Road. The first section, led by P/O Shaw, were briefed to attack the convoy from low level while the second section led by F/Lt Rogers would attack the convoy in a shallow dive. The exercise, although useful, was more of a morale boost to the participating crews. With no opposition, the crews could with all justification enjoy the exercise and attack with care-free abandon.

With the now constant freezing conditions it was wisely agreed to check and test the guns should they be needed in the extreme weather. Battle, K9327, flown by F/O Crews was the first to be tested, both the fixed Browning and rear K gun had a light covering of oil applied. In an almost clear blue sky, the aircraft began its climb, at 6,000 feet the temperature was already zero. Every 2000 feet both guns were test-fired, at 14,000 feet the weapons were tested every 1000 feet until the Battle reached its maximum ceiling, 21,000 feet, at this height, the temperature was numbing -32. Much to the relief, both guns operated at their normal rate of fire. The test was again carried out in the afternoon, this time F/O Hughes was aloft in Battle K9252. On this occasion, both guns were heavily oiled. Hughes reached 22,000 feet with a temperature of -36 degrees. Both guns fired satisfactorily, no stoppages were reported on either gun. The squadron was required for yet another navigation and tactical exercise on the 23rd, on this occasion it was more navigational than tactical. Three sections would be involved. Two were allocated the Nantes and Abberville areas to reconnoitre at low level, while the third would patrol the Arras area at a high level and attack a specific target. Flying Officer Crews led No.1 Section, they had the furthest target to reach, they were aloft for some 3 1/2 hours. Flying Officer Freeman led section 2, his objective was a crossroad 3 miles west of Saint-Saëns. They were airborne for nearly 2 hours covering a distance of some 323 miles. The high-level section under the capable leadership of F/Lt Rogers were allocated Arras to attack from a height of 10,000 feet, all three flights were successfully carried out, and all nine Battles landed safely back at Auberive. An enemy reconnaissance aircraft flew over Auberive at 11:00hrs, the local A.A Battery engaged the aircraft estimated to be flying at 22,000 feet. The flak bursts were seen to explode slightly behind the aircraft which was later intercepted by Hawker Hurricanes. During the afternoon of the 23rd, the squadron held a Christmas party in the NAAFI hut for the children of the local village. Much hard work and late nights had been put in to ensure the children had a wonderful time. A well-stocked Christmas tree and a hearty meal went a long way to overcome the children's initial shyness. With the arrival of Santa Claus, the faces of the children beamed with excitement, each was presented with a toy much to their delight. The party ended with a rendition of God Save the King and a rather ropey "La Marseillaise" in French. Christmas Eve 1939 would see the squadron on stand-by from 07:00 hours. The planned navigation exercise was cancelled owing to a blanket of thick cloud and low-level fog that shrouded the region. For the squadron, it could not have been better, no flying. With the prospect of the fog dispersing remote, W/Cdr Duggan made what was left of the day a half day holiday. A Grand Concert Party by 'local talent' was held in the NAAFI at 20:00 hours. One of the biggest cheers was for a sketch depicting the operations staff at work, this given the recent exercises caused a barrage of friendly insults, much to the amusement of all. To add to the Christmas spirit, the canteen was granted an extension to 02.00 hours. Christmas Day 1939, the first on active service. As per tradition the NCOs arrived en-mass to the Officers mess. Here W/Cdr Duggan read out a Special Order of the Day from Air Vice Marshal Playfair;

*A Hawker Hurricane Mk.I of No.1 Squadron. The Hurricane squadrons bore the brunt of the bitter fighting over France in the early days, it was a testing time for all involved. Usually outnumbered and given scant warning of an attack, the pilot's, many of whom notched up a number of kill's would apply their hard won skills over Britain between June and October 1940.*

*The first snow fell on Auberive on December 27th, 1939, it heralded the start of a freezing few months for the squadron and particularly the ground crews who endured some harsh conditions. Here two remove the canvas cockpit coverall from snow-covered Battle K9324 HA-B. The Battle was one of the few to survive the French campaign, it eventually ended up in Australia and was finally Struck off Charge in March 1944.*

*I send to all ranks under my command Christmas Greetings and my best wishes for the New Year . In sending you these greetings, I wish to take advantage of the opportunity to express to you my deep appreciation of your excellent work and conduct since you came overseas. Your bearing and conduct in France and your cheerful acceptance of the conditions have laid a sure foundation for the ultimate success of our campaign. I am confident that the high standard that you have set will be maintained no matter what dangers, difficulties and discomfort you may be called upon to face, and I know that I can rely upon all ranks to uphold the high traditions of the service.*
*Good wishes and good luck to you all.*

At 12:30 hours, W/Cdr Duggan, officers and NCOs trudged to the NAAFI hut to serve the airman their Christmas Dinner. Due to the limited seating, three sittings were necessary. During each of the servings Christmas Cards from Their Majesties the King and Queen were distributed to each airman. At the end of each serving the Airman showed their appreciation and gave three cheers to W/Cdr Duggan and his band of tired, but merry helpers. The squadron cooks had excelled themselves and provided the usual traditional Turkey dinner with all the trimmings. Dessert was a steaming Christmas pudding liberally laced with French cognac!

In the evening Christmas was celebrated in the usual traditional manner in both the officers and sergeant messes. Pilot Officers Wardle, Robins and Anstey had pulled the short straw and served as orderly officers throughout the day, they had the unenviable task of keeping everyone under control, a not too easy task in the circumstances. Given the forecast weather conditions for Boxing Day, the squadron could with some confidence enjoy the squadrons first war-time Christmas in the best traditions of the RAF, getting drunk.

The following morning as predicted the whole region was blanketed in a thick layer of fog forestalling any flying, there was some excitement however on the ground. The airfields ambulance somehow managed to overturn while on its way to St.Hilaire. The driver, and the squadron medical officer, Squadron Leader Reginald Thorpe were slightly injured, the ambulance was extensively damaged in the crash, the cause of the accident was attributed to a slippery road!

Thankfully for S/Ldr Thorpe his injuries did not prevent him going on leave that afternoon, he along with three complete crews, those of Pilot Officers Crane, Forth and Sergeant Horner, plus 16 other ranks began the long journey home. Squadron Leader Thorpes replacement was the vastly experienced S/Ldr James Sandow who had received his permanent commission in the RAF back in 1933. The first heavy snow fell on December 27th, Auberive was covered in 3-4 inches, the flat Grand Est landscape looked picturesque, but for those having to work in the bitter conditions it was the start of a harsh

*Reported to be the officers mess. Here two airmen enjoy a pint. Behind them a Union flag and French Tricolour adorn the walls. Also visible are some hand painted RAF roundels.*

winter. A number of the more fortunate squadron airman travelled to Epernay to attend a concert by the hugely popular and darling of the BEF and AASF, Miss Gracie Fields on the afternoon of the 27th. Those left behind at Auberive were entertained in the NAAFI by Kirk Wilbur and 'Glamour' Girl, Miss Vickie Browne. It was probably not the best venue they had played, but the night was a roaring success. With fog still preventing any flying, S/Ldr Warrington and F/Lt Daish took a small party of airman to Rheims to see a variety show from the Casino De Paris on the 28th, this basically brought the month, and the year to a conclusion. The squadron welcomed 28-year-old Flight Lieutenant James Robert Gillman on the 28th, he had until the previous day served with 'A' Flight of No.12 Squadron based at Berry-su-Bac. On arriving on 218, Gillman was immediately promoted to acting squadron leader. An experienced Battle pilot, he had served with 12 Squadron since June 1938, on the squadrons arrival in France in September 1939, he and his crew were one of the first to fly on operations.

The squadron had been in France four months and apart from a few reconnaissance flights over the Franco-German Border in September there had been little action and no encounters with the Luftwaffe, unlike 88 Squadron. A total of 462 flights had been recorded, the vast majority of which were training flights, it was almost like pre-war England.

*Two ground crew preparing a Battle covered in overnight snow. The aircraft's 250lb bomb load is seen here underneath the starboard wing. The storing of the bombs next to the aircraft was primarily to speed up the bombing up process. It was also due to the lack of transport available.*

# Chapter 6: 1940 – Ice, Snow, and Heaps of Boredom!

January 1st, 1940 was freezing cold, snow flurries throughout the day resulted in the squadron ceasing work at noon. The following day, the squadron commander W/Cdr Duggan along with P/O Shaw and Rhodesian P/O Imrie departed on leave, command of the squadron was passed to S/Ldr Gillman.

A late morning navigation exercise was planned for a flight led by F/Lt Daish on the morning of the 2nd, freezing conditions overnight meant that the engine fitters experienced considerable difficulties coaxing the frozen Rolls Royce Merlin's into life.

After a delay of nearly two hours a sub flight managed to take off, a further delay of almost two hours resulted in a further two Battles getting away, the third Battle simply would not start. Once aloft the problems did not end, both exercises found navigation difficult due to the whole region being covered in a blanket of snow. A fighter co-operation flight was undertaken on the afternoon of the 3rd, Flying Officer Hughes, F/O Richmond and Sgt Dockrill were away just after 14:00 hours, they were to rendezvous with four Morane MS.406 fighters of GC III/6 based at Wez Thuisy. The fighters were encountered at 5,000 feet between Auberive and Reims just after 14:30 hours. The fighters split into pairs and over the next 90 minutes the nimble French Moranes put the Battle crews to the sword. Carrying out the standard defensive manoeuvre of turning into the attack in a steep turn initially worked, but the French pilots quickly changed tactics and got the better of their RAF counterparts.

Keeping a compact section for mutual defence the Battles predictably commenced a step turn when fighters approached from astern. The French now aware of the tactic waited until the Battles started to turn. Once committed a section of Moranes would quickly attack from the beam and below giving the Battles little if any chance. The observers tried valiantly to engage the fighters attacking from below with the 'K' gun mounted in the bomb aimers position, but opportunities were rare. It was a rather tired and concerned section that landed back at Auberive. It was the first occasion the squadron had exercised with GC III/6 since their arrive at Wez Thuisy on November 15th.

There was some reason to celebrate in the mess that night. Squadron Leader Warrington was posted to HQ RAF Component Field Force for engineering duties. Typically, there was a mess party to see the deputy squadron commander on his way. On returning to England after the fall of France, he would have a spell with No.11 OTU before taking command of the Vickers Wellington equipped No.215 Squadron operating in the Middle East. There followed a posting to India where he was promoted to Group Captain. While in India he commanded No.223 and No.221 Group. He was tragically killed in September 1945 when the boat he and his wife were sailing in struck a sea mine off the coast of Scotland killing them both.

The squadron did not fly a single sortie between January 5th and 9th. Squadron Leader Saunders from Wing HQ gave a lecture on the 5th. The subject, French night recognition. With practically no activity by the Battle squadrons of the AASF by day, it was agreed that the squadrons should be utilised at night. Night flying training was to begin as soon as the weather started to clear. On the 8th, Flying Officer Crews, P/O Robin and F/Sgt Herring and 14 other ranks departed Auberive just after lunch on some well-earned leave. A follow-up lecture by S/Ldr Saunders was again given on the evening of the 8th, just before commencement of a dusk landing exercise, the weather however intervened cancelling the planned flights.

With the weather improving slightly a major Air Exercise involving all the AASF Battle squadrons was scheduled for the 10th. Freezing condition overnight meant that the flight mechanics were up especially early preparing the frozen Battles, eleven crews were breakfasted and briefed by 06:00 hours. At 07:35

hours orders were received from Wing HQ, two sections were to attack a sizeable 'enemy' mechanised infantry column that was moving southeast from Dampierre and Neuchatel having landed at Dieppe. Despite the best efforts of the ground crews there was a reluctance on the part of the Merlin's to start-up in the freezing conditions. The first section away, led by F/O Richmond was finally aloft at 09:37hrs, the second section, led by F/O Hughes departed at 09:42hrs. Despite a few difficulties navigating to the target both sections located the 'target' and successfully attacked in a series of shallow dives. In the afternoon, a section led by P/O Mitchell departed Auberive at 13:30 hours to attack a 'fleeting target' south of Dieppe. While on route Battle K9327 flown by Sergeant Charles Owen suffered total engine failure requiring him to make a force landing at Monchy, 6 miles north-west of Compiegne, none of the crew was injured.

**Wednesday January 10th 1940**
*Fairey Battle*
*Mk.I K9327*
*Contract No :522745/36*
*Taken On Charge: 10/10/1938*
*Repaired on Site*
*Pilot: Sergeant Charles Owen*
*Observer/Bomb aimer: Sergeant Frank Dewar*
*Gunner / Wireless Operator: Aircraftman Robert Wiltshire*

Following close on the heels of P/O Mitchells flight was a sub flight once again led by F/O Hughes. Hughes had kicked off the day's activities, upon his return from the morning sortie his flight had been refuelled, briefed and 'bombed-up'. This sub flight, consisting of P/O Anstey and P/O Crane were ordered to attack a column of 30 light tanks and 30 transport vehicles situated south of Dieppe. A fourth and final section was briefed and depart just after 14:35 hours when the 'Wash-out' signal from Wing HQ was received, much to the crews' relief as it was doubtful if the section would have returned before dusk. It had been a hectic day for all the squadron, and unlike the other exercises, it gave the participating crews a taste of the intensity of operations that would follow. Throughout the day, which was sunny and clear but freezing, the crews took some comfort in seeing numerous other Battle squadrons proceeding to and from the target areas.

The following morning a section led by F/O Richmond took off to carry out a formation flight for the benefit of an Air Ministry photographer who flew in the Battle flown by F/Lt Daish. Just before lunch, the C-in-C Bomber Command Air Chief Marshal Sir Ludlow Hewitt arrived at Auberive where he was met by No.75 Wings Group Captain Wann and Squadron Leader Gillman. His visit was to say 'Goodbye' to the squadron, his time at the helm of Bomber Command was almost up. A new role with Close Support Command beckoned. Before departing Auberive, he spent considerable time talking to the crews and S/Ldr Gillman. The goodbyes were not quite over for the day, at 15:00 hours Air Commodore John Quinnell (S.A.S.O AASF) arrived unexpectedly to wish the squadron good luck as he was returning to England to command No 31 (Balloon Barrage) Group. Sergeant Owen and crew returned to Auberive just after 16:00 hours after their enforced stay at Monchy. Not that they were complaining, having spent the day and night in the company of a French Transport battalion. The French hospitality held no bounds, ensuring that the three British aviators were applied with as much wine and cheese they could manage. Thankfully, Sergeant Owen had recovered sufficiently to return to Auberive.

Despite the attention of No.2 Salvage Section, the Battles Merlin engine cut on several occasions on the return journey. Showing a good piece of flying skill, Owens made an excellent landing with a 'dead' prop without damage to Battle and its weary crew.

*One of a series of well-known photographs depicting a section of squadron Battles.*

The squadron was informed they were to be on standby from 09:00 hours the following morning, another full-scale exercise was to be undertaken, but this would be more *'realistic'*. Due to the reluctance of some of the Merlin engines to start up due to the severe frost the previous day, the flight mechanics were out at dispersal long before they were needed. There was a touch of aristocracy in the Operations Room on the 12th. HQ sent P/O Lord Waleran to act as Intelligence Officer for the days exercise. Lord William George Hood Walrond was born March 1905 in Mayfair, London and educated at Eton and Trinity Collage Oxford. Between 1927 and 1930 he held the post of Assistant Private Security to the Governor General of New Zealand. A pre-war member of the House of Lords, he drove in the 1939 Le Mans 24-hour rally finishing a creditable 4th. By 08:00 hours the Operations Room was fully manned and ready for the day's activities, out on the airfield nine Battles were fuelled and ready, the twenty-seven aircrew sat patiently waiting for the order to take off. Unhappily for the crews they were informed that they would not be needed much before noon, eventually just after 13:00 hours the squadron received orders to dispatch 3 sections. The first away after a hurried briefing was the section led by F/O Richmond, he was given a target at M.4141 (road junction 2 miles SW of Esclavelles close to Foret d' Eawy, north of Rouen) within five minutes the second section departed led by P/O Crane. This section was to attack M.3539 (Saint Saens). The final section took off at 13:45 hours, at the forefront was P/O Hughes, he was tasked with attacking M.3940 (an area near Maucombe, south of Dieppe).

Conditions were good, too good. As the sections turned into the selected targets south west of Blangy-sur-Bresle they immediate started flying into the wintery low sun. Added to the hazy conditions it made pinpointing selected targets even more difficult at 1,500 feet. The motorised convoys and columns that each of the sections were expecting did not materialise. Flying Officer Richmond and his section found the tail end of a mixed column which they attacked from low level near the village of Bois-Hatrel. An accurate assessment of numbers and types of vehicles was almost impossible as most were well hidden under trees

*A boyish looking Peter Stubbs.*

or shrouded in haze. Pilot Officer Crane's section unable to find their briefed target turned for home, shortly after 14:00 hours Cranes Battle suffered engine failure which resulted in a crash landing at Pommiers, 3 miles west of Soissons. Having come to rest after smashing through a hedge, P/O Crane leapt from his shattered Battle and indicated to the remainder of his flight circling above that he, and his crew were all uninjured. Fairey Battle K9357 was almost totally wrecked in the crash.

**Friday January 12th 1940**
*Fairey Battle*
*Mk.I K9357*
*Contract No :522745/36*
*Taken On Charge : 23/10/1938*
*Collected by No.21 AD Nantes, abandoned.*
*Pilot: Pilot Officer John Crane*
*Observer/Bomb aimer: Sergeant William Harris*
*Gunner / Wireless Operator: Aircraftman James Drummond*

This was not the only crash landing during the day, Pilot Officer Forth was flying as No.3 in F/O Hughes section when he too suffered engine failure. At around the same time as P/O Crews was crash-landing, Forth was making a forced landing near Noyon, 15 miles north east of Compiegne. In the ensuring crash the tail assembly unit of Battle K9254 was severely damaged.

**Friday January 12th 1940**
*Fairey Battle*
*Mk.I K9254*
*Contract No :522745/36*
*Taken On Charge : 11/10/1938*
*Collected by No.21 AD Nantes, abandoned.*
*Pilot : Pilot Officer Hugh Forth*
*Observer/Bomb aimer: Sergeant Peter Stubbs*
*Gunner / Wireless Operator: Aircraftmen Forrester*

Sergeant Peter Stubbs recalls the crash; *"Our engine was never right from take-off, and then while in formation it just gave-out and stopped. We came down in a frozen ploughed field. The undercarriage was ripped off and the fuselage broke in two. It was later established that the fuel pipe was blocked with mud because the ground crews just dragged the nozzle of the fuel line from the bowser through the muddy ground from one aircraft to another".*

The day's activities were not as intense as anticipated, the exercise flown on the 11th was in the opinion of the participating crews much more demanding, and as far more 'realistic', the crews were if anything disappointed. The mood soon changed on their arrival back at Auberive. During late afternoon, S/Ldr Gillman assembled his crews into the operations room and informed them that the following day they might be doing the real thing. Perhaps now, they were going to see action. All available Battles were to be fuelled and bombed up with 4 x 250lb instant impact fused bombs. Ground crews worked tirelessly until 22:45 hours preparing the Battles for the following day, after a tremendous effort on their part working in freezing conditions, eight Battles were fully serviceable with a further two requiring just an hour's work in the morning. Order B.19 (Code Word *'Meddling'*) had been received from Wing HQ late afternoon. The squadron would in the event of a possible German invasion be co-operating with the Army, its role would be to cause maximum disruption to the German line of communication and to attack and harass mechanical columns, troop concentrations and all types of military transport.

The following morning, the 13th, the whole squadron was at readiness by 0800 hours, frantic work by the hard-pressed ground crews had managed to complete the work on the two remaining Battles bringing the squadrons availability to ten aircraft. A further Battle, K9327 would be available by lunchtime. It was not the squadrons full strength, but it was the best they could manage. Three Battles were under repair, two with complete engine overhauls, a third was awaiting spares, added to the loss of two Battles the previous day almost a third of the squadron was unavailable. As the morning progressed, it again became apparent that the expected German threat was not going to materialise, there was a huge sense of relief mixed with disappointment throughout the squadron. That evening a signal from Wing HQ was received cancelling all leave. On the morning of the 15th, hours before daybreak and in bitter conditions, the ground crews were ordered to the aerodrome and instructed to ready all eleven available aircraft in preparation for operations. The assembled aircrew were in the crew room by 05:20 hours, where W/Cdr Duggan recently returned from his leave, unravelled to his crews the current International situation and that they may be required to operate for real at an hour's notice. As per the previous day, the squadron waited for the call for action, which thankfully was never received.

During the late afternoon, F/O Hughes was detailed to inspect the satellite aerodrome, at Moscow Ferme, 2 miles WNW of Prosnes and decide on its suitability for landing and taking off with light and full bomb loads. In F/O Hughes' opinion it was not suitable. The day concluded with the arrival on the squadron of Air Commodore Henry Thorold DSC, DFC, Air Officer-in-Charge Salvage Organisation in France and AASF Engineer Staff Officer, Group Captain Seymour Benson.

This recent spell of activity was a result of '*The Mechelen Incident*' of January 10th, 1940, also known as the *Mechelen Affair*. A German aircraft, a Bf108, had crash-landed in neutral Belgium near Vucht within the Province of Limburg. Apart from the pilot, the aircraft was carrying Major Helmuth Reinberger, who was carrying the plans for *Fall Gelb* (Case Yellow), the German plans for the attack on the Low Countries. His capture and the subsequent discovery of the document prompted an immediate crisis in the Low Countries, once aware, the French and British authorities immediately put into action their defence strategies. On the 16th, Flight Lieutenant Alan Rodgers handed over his duties of squadron Adjutant to P/O Alexander Proudfoot and immediately took command of 'B' Flight from F/O Hulbert.

The squadron received orders at 11:15 hour on the morning of the 16th to remove the bombs from the Battles and return to formal duties. It was just as well, weather conditions continued to plummet with heavy snow throughout the region. The only activity throughout the day was a large column of French armour passing through Auberive-sur-Suippes. Overnight 3-5 inches of snow-covered Northern France. The freezing conditions made it almost impossible to travel from the billets to the dispersals, transport movement was restricted to an absolute minimum. However, as usual, it was left to the poor bloody ground crews to keep the

*The heavy canvas cover kept the snow off the engines but did not prevent them from freezing. Some ground crews would improvise and build small stoves and have them smouldering overnight. It was hazardous and required an airman close by at all times.*

aircraft from freezing up and fully serviceable if needed. The only protection for the Battles against the elements were heavy duty canvas covers, these were draped over the cockpit canopy, and framed tents were set up over the Merlin to keep the worst of the weather from freezing up the engines. French Representatives of 'Le Matin' a popular French newspaper along with an official Air Ministry photographer arrived on the 16th and took a number of photographs of the squadron personnel and aircraft. Despite the appalling weather, six aircraft, two sections of three were ordered to carry out a local formation practice flight on the morning of the 17th. After some coaxing only three Battles led by F/O Hulbert managed to get airborne. They visited Moronvilliers Range in the hope the ground targets would be visible from the air. As expected, the whole range was a blanket of snow and the flight cancelled. The same day, Sergeant Charles Owen collected Fairey Battle Mk. I P2203 from No.2 Servicing Flight at Rheims. This aircraft had only arrived in France on the 14th, and it would replace Battle K9357. With the weather conditions restricting practically all flying, it was no surprise that arrangements had been made for the squadrons of the AASF to use the Armament Training Station at Perpignan in the warmer south of France. Perpignan was in the centre of the Roussillon plain, 10 miles west of the Mediterranean coast and only 15 miles from the Border with Fascist Spain. On the 17th, Wing Commander Duggan assembled his section leaders and discussed the impending move south.

The first of many dusk landing practice flights started on the 19th. Pilot Officer Shaw was chosen to test the recently installed French L shaped flare path and the squadron's recently improvised night landing procedure. Prior to the test, P/O Shaw carried out a successful 15-minute air test in Battle K9324 late afternoon. Satisfied, he was aloft again at 16:15 hours in near total darkness. He completed two successful landings under the guidance of S/Ldr Gillman and F/Lt Daish.

No flights were flown on the 20th, 21st and 22nd, freezing conditions, snow and ice provided the crews with some welcome respite. This, unfortunately, did not extend to the flight mechanics who were ordered

*Two airmen stand guard besides Battle HA-A. This photograph gives an excellent view of the canvas engine cover. The winter of 1939/40 was hard on both men and aircraft.*

to ground run and test the engines of each of the squadrons Battles every morning. There was some relief from the cold, bus and M.T transporters took a party of officers and 160 airmen to St Hilaire for a concert by Mr Jack Buchanan, the Scottish theatre and film actor, plus singer and dancer Miss Joan Black and Company. They were joined by Syd Milward and his 'Nitwits' who provided the music. The band played unusual and popular versions of classic songs, usually in a humorous way. Much to the crowd's delight, glamour girl and singer Miss Primrose brought the evening to a conclusion. The concert which was almost exclusively attended by 218 Squadron was a tremendous success. At the end of the concert, both Mr Jack Buchanon and W/Cdr Duggan addressed the crowd resulting in a rousing cheer. The following morning a compass swing programme was planned at Mourmelon. This was the only location that was equipped. A circular concrete platform marked out in degree divisions accurately aligned with local magnetic north had been installed. The Battle was placed on the pad in a series of angular positions and the reading of the aircraft's magnetic compass is compared with the true heading on the pad. An overnight frost and temperatures below -10 resulted in difficulties starting not only the Battles Merlin's but the transport vehicles used to take the crews to the airfield. An hour later than planned, 'A' Flights P/O Richmond departed for Mourmelon at the controls of K9329. Within the hour P/O William Anstey departed in 'B' Flights P2183. Finally, at 14:00 hours P/O Shaw departed in another 'A' flight aircraft, Battle K9324.

On completion of the compass swing, F/O Richmond departed at 14:50 hours for the ten minute flight back to Auberive. On reaching base everything seemed to be in order until he selected the flap levers down. Richmond was surprised to discover they would not lower. As a result, the Battle floated over the aerodrome. This would not usually be a problem given the vastness of the grassed airfield however on this

93

occasion the Kiwis luck had run out. Having touched down, Richmond realised almost immediately that there was a real danger of a collision with a dispersed Battle. Richmond opened up the Merlin engine in an attempt to avoid the rapidly closing Battle, K9327 which was still undergoing maintenance since its arrival back from Monchy, but it was just too late. The starboard wing of Richmond's aircraft struck the engine of the parked Battle which was torn off resulting in a slightly uncomfortable crash landing. Flying Officer Richmond sustained a sprained ankle, while his crew were bruised and shocked but otherwise uninjured. The luckiest pair on the squadron were the two engine fitters working on the parked Battle, covered by a heavy-duty canvas tent they were oblivious to the danger until the wing tore through the canvas striking the Battle. Aircraftman Anderson was the only casualty on the ground, he was hit a glancing blow to the head and suffered concussion and immediately taken to hospital.

### Tuesday January 23rd 1940

*Fairey Battle*
*Mk.I  K9329*
*Contract No :522745/36*
*Taken On Charge : 10/10/1938*
*Collected by No.21 AD Nantes, abandoned.*
*Pilot : Flying Officer Ian Richmond*
*Observer/Bomb aimer: Sergeant Cederic Jennings*
*Gunner / Wireless Operator : Aircraftman Arthur Ellis*

*Flying Officer Ian Richmond.*

Both aircraft were collected by No.21 A.D based at Nantes where they would be eventually abandoned. A period of clear weather was the opportunity needed to continue with night take-off and practice flights. On the evening of the 24th, with an almost cloudless night sky and full moon F/O Hulbert, P/O Robin and Sergeant Charles Dockrill spent an hour perfecting these most hazardous routines. Thankfully, there were no incidents considering the icy conditions. The following night, which the squadron diarist described as *'marvellous'* would see the squadron continued with its night flying programme. Four crews were aloft just after 16:20 hours, on this occasion the recently installed flood lights were used, however such was the glow of the moon on the snow they were not really needed. Pilot Officer Robins collected Fairey Battle P2249 from No.2 Servicing Flight based at Rheims on the 26th, the Battle had only been in France 48 hours. Rapidly deteriorating weather meant there was no flying for the remainder of the month, which was just as well as the squadron was busy preparing for its move to the warmer climate of the practice Camp at Perpignan. On the 30th, three 3-ton transport lorries departed on the long journey south. The following day in filthy weather Air Marshal Arthur 'Ugly' Barratt AoC-in-Chief British Air Force in France, and W/Cdr James Fairweather DFC, SASO AASF HQ arrived by air at Auberive. Those aircrew and ground crew available were parade in the rain, thankfully the

94

parade was cut short and moved to the warmer and dryer Guard hut. Here Air Marshal Barratt spent considerable time talking with the air crews and reminded them of the *'Glorious and hectic times to come'*.

February 1<sup>st</sup> started with Auberive blanketed with fog forestalling any flying, as an alternative the Battles were ground tested in preparation for the flight to No.1 Armament Training Station. Pilot Officer 'Hank' Wardle drew the short straw and was given the responsibility of commanding the main rail party that departed just after 11 am. In the afternoon, W/Cdr Duggan had the essential equipment, bombsights, cameras and life jackets loaded into the Battles in preparation for an early departure the following morning. As a precaution, extra guards were placed around the dispersal areas. The morning of the 2nd found Auberive once again covered in fog, W/Cdr Duggan had his crews load up their personnel kits onto two lorries in the vain hope it would clear. By 08:30 hours it was apparent that the planned move was in serious doubt. By 10.30 hours the trip was officially cancelled. To keep the crews occupied, W/Cdr Duggan and S/Ldr Gillman briefed all the crews on the training schedule for the next few weeks, and what was expected from each of them.

Finally, on the morning of the 3rd clear freezing blue skies replaced the fog, everything was set for departure. Unfortunately, heavy rain over Perpignan had rendered the airfield unserviceable, frustrated, and eager to get away, W/Cdr Duggan decided that the squadron would undertake the journey in stages. The first stage would see the Battles land at a Slabanive, a civil airfield near Perpignan. After a hurried lunch and crew briefing, the squadron was again thwarted when reports were received that this airfield too was unserviceable. There was nothing they could do but wait, much to everyone's frustration. More frustration followed on the 4th, W/Cdr Duggan and his section managed to eventually take off at 13:35 hours but were immediately lost in low clouds making any attempt of forming up in possible, wisely the section returned to Auberive. Reports from Perpignan on the 5th and 6th prevented any further attempts to depart. The squadron had effectively not flown since January 25th, and everyone was becoming irritated. There was some cause for celebrating, P/O Harold Gerard Kelso Waring was promoted to Flying Officer. Keeping with tradition a mess party was organised. On the 6th, F/O Shaw, the Squadron Duty Officer rang Wing HQ and reported an enemy aircraft was seen flying over Auberive at 21:45 hours, strangely F/O Shaw reported that it appeared to come up from the ground?

A full six days late, the squadron was finally ready to depart, the weather was improving, just. All the crews were briefed on the morning of the 7th. Due to the conditions at Perpignan the squadron would not fly direct to the Armament Station as planned. They would fly to Lézignan-Corbières an airfield, 45 miles north, Perpignan was still unserviceable. Due to an unfavourable weather forecast on the original planned route it was decided to fly down the Rhone Valley, the route flown would be Base - Epernay - Dijon - Avignon - Lézignan-Corbières. Finally, and to the delight of everyone, W/Cdr Duggan and his section departed noon February 7th. There was some panic when the leader of the second flight, S/Ldr Gillman had difficulty starting his engine, thankfully this was quickly rectified, and 30 minutes behind the leader, he and his section finally got away. At 12:45 hours F/Lt Rogers, leader of the final section left. As forecast the squadron encountered low cloud and showers on route, it did little to dampen the enthusiasms of the crews. It was a small price to pay, they were finally airborne and on their way. By 16:20 hours each of the three flights had successfully landed at Lézignan-Corbières. The aircraft were quickly dispersed, engine and cockpits covered and picketed. As arranged the crews were met by M/T vehicles and taken to their billets, the officers would stay in the Grand Hotel while the airman bedded down at Hotel Darade in Narbonne.

News from Perpignan was encouraging, a strip of ground 500 yards by 50 yards had been prepared for their arrival, the rest of the airfield was a sea of water and mud. On the 8th, W/Cdr Duggan was airborne for the final short flight to the Armament Station, the rest of the section quickly followed. The run of bad luck continued, Sergeant Owen was forced to return to Lézignan-Corbières immediately after take-off due to mechanical problems. Bizarrely, and for reasons unknown W/Cdr Duggan and the remainder of his flight returned to Lézignan-Corbières due to a reported shortage of fuel? The remaining two flights eventually made the short trip to Perpignan. From above the airfield appeared more like a lake than an operational airfield. Red flags marked the 500-yard-long landing ground, it was short, but it was all that was available. Tons of sand had been put down over the previous few days in preparation for the squadron's arrival. All the Battles landed safely and were immediately inspected by the ever-willing ground crews. The officers quickly proceeded to their billet at the Grande and Perdix Hotels. The Grande would be used as the officer mess, while the NCOs were allocated rather less luxurious quarters on the airfield.

On the morning of 9th, and in the absence of W/Cdr Duggan the crews were briefed by F/O Mathews the No.1 ATS Armament Officer on the bombing and air firing ranges. In the afternoon, seven crews carried out individual low level 'stick' bombing attacks, the practice was marred by numerous minor problems. It was not the start of the squadron was hoping for. The exercise was again repeated during the late afternoon with only marginal improvement. Heavy rainfall overnight made take-off and landing even more difficult the following day. Regardless, W/Cdr Duggan and the remainder of his flight finally arrived at Perpignan on the afternoon of the 10th. Despite the conditions, a target-towing programme was arranged, but due to the mud, sand and water the drogue was torn to pieces on take-off and landing cancelling the flight. In its place, high-level dive-bombing practice was undertaken. Only ten bombs had been dropped before this too was brought to a premature end due to low cloud over the range, to add to an otherwise frustrating day, two Battles became bogged down while taxing in the sea of mud. A planned night flying programme was arranged for the evening of the 10th, but had to be cancelled due to the unserviceability of the airfield. On the morning of the 11th the lorries were loaded with equipment ready for the long journey back, this effectively ended any further night flying attempts! The whole detachment was quickly descending into a series of unforeseen howlers due mostly to the weather.

During the late morning of the 11th the squadron attempted another target-towing programme, this time both aircraft managed to get aloft. Despite one of the tow-aircraft returning early, the squadrons thirteen air observers managed to fire over 100 rounds each with the downward firing K gun, while the air gunners each fired 100 rounds with the rear machine gun. Over 20,000 rounds had been fired by the end of the day. Flight Sergeant George Greenfield, the squadrons senior armaments instructor had the unenviable task of trying to sort out how successful, or otherwise the practice had been. Somehow, despite the frequent jamming of the downward-firing Vickers he concluded that only 2.6 hits per 100 rounds fired actually hit the target. Most of the observers had little or no experience of using the underneath rearward firing gun which was proving difficult to aim and frequently jammed. It was not an encouraging performance, and the crews dislike of the gun quickly increased.

The squadron had planned to return to Auberive on the 12th taking off from the much-preferred Lézignan-Corbières airfield. Wing Commander Duggan had instructed his ground crews the previous day to prepare the squadron Battles for departure. However, the weather once again intervened. Forecast weather reports from No.75 Wing HQ announced severe conditions over the Rhone Valley and around Nantes with patches of dense fog and icing. Wisely, the commanding officer postponed the flight, much to the delight of the aircrews. The ORB reported *'The flying crews seemed exceptionally cheerful about it'*. Not so lucky was the recently promoted F/O Waring who was given the job of commanding the M/T convoy back to Auberive, he left at 09:00 hours. Thirty minutes later, P/O Wardle in charge of the rail party departed. With the weather for once sunny and bright, some officers and airman went on an excursion by bus to visit a nearby wine distillery. After sampling the various wines, the now invigorated group visited the beautiful seaside town of Narbonne. It was just the tonic the squadron needed after the frustrations of the previous two weeks.

The following day reports began to filter through that the weather to Nantes had improved, W/Cdr Duggan quickly ordered the squadron to prepare to leave with immediate effect. At 11:20 hours the first section of three Battles led by the indomitable W/Cdr Duggan departed on the first leg of the journey home. Thirty minutes later, F/Lt Rogers taxied his section out for take-off, while taxying Rogers discovered his elevator trimming tabs had jammed forcing him to abort his departure. Flying Officer Hughes quickly took over the role of flight leader. The second section departed at 12:25 hours, by this time 50-60mph winds with gusts up to 70mph were sweeping across the airfield making taxing in the muddy conditions extremely difficult. Once airborne the crews experienced strong headwinds with severe turbulence making the trip home rather uncomfortable. After nearly three hours airborne the first section landed at the snow-covered Nantes. At 15:30 hour the second section landed in quickly fading light. All the aircraft were covered and picketed down for the night. The officers left for the Central Hotel at Nantes while the NCOs and airman made do with the facilities on the station. At Auberive, P/O 'Hank' Wardle and the rail party had arrived tired, but in good order, like the British counterparts, the French Railway service was highly efficient even in wartime. The return leg to Auberive was planned for the morning of the 14th, the weather at Nantes was freezing but clear, ideal flying weather. Just before take-off, a message was received informing W/Cdr Duggan that there were near blizzard conditions at base and that the flight was to be cancelled until further orders. Happily, the officers returned to the warmth and comforts of the Central Hotel, while the other ranks made do with Nantes less glamourous facilities. The following afternoon both sections finally landed back at a snow covered Auberive, the Battles were dispersed and covered. Such was the freezing conditions that the aircraft could not be picketed due to the frozen ground, large iron grating were used in their place. Finally, the squadron was home, the 'Perpignan Saga' was thankfully over for all but one. While at Perpignan, Joe Stevens a mechanic developed a high temperature within days of his arrival by train. Joe recalls, *"I don't remember much, but was told by my good friend Jimmie James that I was walking around the billets talking and mumbling nonsense one night, sweat pouring out of me. I was taken to a French Hospital in town, next morning I awoke to find a big black French Orderly standing over me, it gave me quite a fright! The whole region was full of North African Troops. I don't remember too much, I seem to remember being told I had symptoms of meningitis. I ended up having a lumber puncture procedure carried out on me. All the time I was on my own, hardly anyone could speak English. By the time my temperature had come down and the drugs had started to work, the squadron had returned to Auberive, I was on my own. Finally, the doctors gave me the OK to leave, I was given a train ticket and headed first to Epernay which was about 20 miles from my base. On arrival, and in true traditions of the RAF I was immediately sent to No.75 Wing Base Hospital at Dieppe. This was run by the Army, and as can be expected I came into some stick from my fellow ward patients, all of which were Army bods. Eventually after what seems months, I returned to Auberive via Paris lugging all my kit, it was good to be back amongst my mates".*

There were very few positives from the whole sorry detachment, obviously the weather did not help and was instrumental in causing frustrating delays and cancellations. There was nothing the squadron could do about the weather, however in a report to No.75 Wing HQ W/Cdr Duggan pulled no punches about the facilities and inadequacies of the underneath K gun. In a section titled <u>Suggestion for Improvements</u> Duggan made it clear that the following needed urgent attention.

1. *There was no hangar lighting, all repairs / work had to cease late afternoon.*
2. *There were no night flying facilities.*
3. *No flood lights or beacons.*
4. *There was no canteen.*
5. *There were no stores, all equipment and replacement parts had to be provided by the squadron.*
6. *Additional transport needed.*
7. *Accommodation was 20 miles from the airfield.*

While most of the squadron was making their way south to the Armament Camp those left behind at Auberive welcomed on February 7th Flying Officer Terrence Newton and his Observer, Sergeant Robert Clapperton. There was no flying on the 16th due to heavy snowfall, it was an ideal opportunity to draw breath and try and forget the frustrations of the previous two weeks. While 218 Squadron was settling back into familiar surroundings, No.75 Wing was joined by No.103 Squadron on the 16th. Based at Bétheniville it was commanded by Wing Commander Henry Gemmel and had seen some action since its arrival in France.

*Wing Commander Duggan. Aged 41 and a veteran of the Great War his pride in the squadron held no bounds. He would do all he could for the men under his command.*

On the 18th, P/O Shaw and F/Sgt Fleet were driven to Rheims to collect two replacement Battles from No.2 Servicing Flight. Pilot Officer Shaw returned in Austin built Fairey Battle Mk.I L5237 a former 15 Squadron aircraft while F/Sgt Fleet returned in a former 40 Squadron machine, L5245. These two aircraft were replacements for K9329 and K9327. On the 20th F/O Hughes and P/O Wardle departed on some well-earned leave. The following day the squadron lost three of its longest serving and most capable pilots, F/Lt Daish, F/O's Crews and Richmond were posted on attachment to the Photographic Development Unit based at Heston, England. Flying Officer Crews would return to the squadron in March. Flight Lieutenant Harry Daish and P/O Richmond would both join 212 Squadron, a photographic reconnaissance unit. Richmond would eventually return to 218 Squadron in June. Australian Daish, would carve out a distinguished career in the Far East before returning to England in 1945. On the 24th, Sergeants Horner and Owen, who had been left behind at Plivot with an unserviceable Battle arrived back at Auberive by air.

A recent thaw coupled with heavy rain meant that Auberive was practically unserviceable, mud and large areas of water made take off and landings almost impossible. Finally, on the 27th, two crews managed to get airborne from Auberive late morning. Given the conditions at Auberive they were sent to Mourmelon aerodrome to carry out night flying practise. Sadly, conditions here were just as bad and the planned night flying was cancelled due to the weather. There was some good news in an otherwise gloomy few days, Pilot Officer Shaw was promoted to flying officer, and P/O Imrie returned from a short navigation course. On the last day of the month the weather improved sufficiently to allow three Battles to carry out a low-level bombing exercise over the Moronvilliers range. The results were disappointing, each Battle was loaded with 4 x 250lb 11 second delay bombs. One stick failed to explode, the pilot failing to fuse the bombs. The bombs on the remaining two Battles failed to drop owing to pilot error. Thus, ended February 1940, a month that the squadron wanted nothing more than to forget.

March 1st started with a full flying programme, three sections were detailed for low level bombing over Moronvilliers range. One section was tasked with local flying and practice low level attacks on transport vehicles along the Reims Road. While two aircraft were detailed and briefed for night cross country flights. Sergeant Horner and F/O Hulbert were away early evening, north of Dijon the Battle flown by F/O

*With the weather improving the snow and ice began to thaw inevitable leaving much of the airfield a sea of mud and water. Seen here, Flying Officer Hughes and Flying Officer Crews are in conversation. Behind them is Battle Mk.I K9323. It would be transferred to No.150 Squadron at the beginning of May.*

Hulbert crashed into Chambremont Woods, a densely wooded area near Cote de la Couche near Avot, Cote d'Or at approximately 21.30 hours. Flying Officer Eric Hulbert survived the crash with only a broken ankle, sadly his crew mates, Sergeant Frank Dewar the observer and the gunner Aircraftman Robert Wiltshire were killed. The squadron diarist recorded in the Operational Records Book that the aircraft crashed due to *'misinterpretation of the QDM and QDR and extremely bad weather in the area.'*

**Friday March 1st 1940**

*Fairey Battle*
*Mk.I K9252*
*Contract No :522745/36*
*Taken On Charge: 11/10/1938*
*Written Off. Abandoned No.3 Salvage Section, Rosieres.*
*Pilot: Flying Officer Eric Hulbert, injured.*
*Observer/Bomb aimer: Sergeant Frank Dewar 522984 RAF* **Killed.**
*Gunner / Wireless Operator: Aircraftman Robert Francis James Wiltshire 550694 RAF* **Killed.**

Twenty-Four-year-old Frank Dewar and 21-Year-old Aircraftman Robert Wiltshire were taken to Epernay Cemetery and buried with full military honours. Pre-war members of the squadron, they had been involved in one crash in January with Sgt Owen. Robert Wiltshire had joined the RAF at 16 in 1936, the son of Lt

*An unidentified member of the squadron 'Hanging out the Washing'. In the background the Church of Auberive-sur-Suippes.*

Commander Wiltshire RN he had written home to his parents in Exmouth, Devon a few days before his death that he was to be home on leave on March 19th, sadly this would never happen.

With the weather improving daily the squadron started training in earnest, navigational flights, low-level bombing practice at both Moronvilliers and St Hilaire ranges were flown on the 5th and the 7th. Squadron Leader Gillman and P/O D B Johnson and their crews, plus 16 other ranks departed for ten days leave on the 5th. It was well-timed, things would start becoming increasingly busy.

A large-scale exercise was flown on the 9th, code-named Exercise TX.8. Five sections were detailed to attack a convoy concentration in the Arras- Amiens area. Approaching the area at medium altitude, the convoy was sighted without difficulty. Once identified each of the sections took it in turns to attack the convoy from low-level. The exercise was continued on the 10th, for once everything seemed to go to plan. There were no early returns, no incidents and encouragingly no accidents. Yet another night flying programme was organised and brought to the attention of the crews, it had been a rather hit and miss affair over the previous winter months. Still at the mercy of the weather, every effort would be made to get the squadron operational at night. On the 14th, the use of self-towed drogues were experimented with over the Moronvilliers Ranges, however, a rapid change in weather put paid to the exercise. During the afternoon, a gale swept into the region, with wind speeds estimated between 70-80 mph all personnel were rushed to the airfield to secure the Battles and anything else that could be blown away. This prompt action saved almost everything except six shelter tents that ended up in trees 1/2 mile from the aerodrome. The following day was bright and sunny, giving the squadron the chance to complete the drogue exercise over Moronvilliers. During the evening, four-night cross countries were planned, three were successful. On the afternoon of the 16th, two sections practised fighter affiliation with three Hawker Hurricanes of No.1 Squadron. Flying Officer Robert Lorimer and P/O Peter Matthews and P/O Richard Lewis had flown their Hurricanes to Mourmelon on the 10th with the sole purpose of practice flights were the Battles of No.75 Wing's, 88, 103 and 218 Squadrons. The continual problems with night flying were addressed in a fashion on the 20th.

A specially prepared squadron Battle was aloft on the afternoon of the 20th. A heavy-duty blacken clothed hood was fixed over the cockpit to emulate night flying conditions. Flight Lieutenant Rogers would trial this homemade idea. After a few initial problems, it was found to be a satisfactory way of training. However, a vigilant lookout by the observer was essential. On the 21st news reached the squadron from Wing HQ that two crews would be required to carry out a reconnaissance / 'Nickel' raid over Mainz and Coblenz on the 22nd. There was an air of excitement throughout the squadron, the last time the squadron had flown over Germany was back in 1939! The main objective of the flight would be to carry out reconnaissance of the Rhine with 'Nickel' dropping as secondary importance. The two crews chosen were 'B' Flight commander, F/Lt Alan Rogers and Sgt Charles Dockrill. Throughout the afternoon the Battles were checked and then re-checked, the ground crews leaving nothing to chance. Sixteen bundles of 'Nickels' were loaded into each aircraft. Everything was ready for the squadrons first night flight over Germany in 1940. Both crews were briefed, and everything was ready, apart from the weather that once again forestalled the squadrons plans. It was only a 24-hour reprieve, the following night F/Lt Rogers took off at 22:10 hours at the controls of Fairey Battle P2249 HA-U, he was followed five minutes later by Sgt Dockrill in an unrecorded Battle.

**No.218 Squadron Sergeant Mess, March 1940**

<u>Six Row</u>
Willoughby
<u>Fifth Row</u>
Bulling, Woodmason
<u>Fourth Row</u>
Malpass, Andrews, Clapperton, Morgan, Dormer
<u>Third Row</u>
Owen, Horner, Stubbs, Barrnett, Dockrill, Collopy, Flisher, Farmes, Lounds, Burdett
<u>Second Row</u>
Baxter, Marsh, Edmunds, Wavell, Wynne, Jackson, Davison, Cock, Prosin, Pratt, Young
<u>Front Row</u>
Atkins, Darrington, Dolman, Wartaker, P/O Crane – W/Cdr Duggan, Etteride, Robbins, Greenfield, Ormswood

*A group of NCOs getting ready for a flight. Identified are, 2nd left Sgt Pratt, 3rd left, Sgt Woodmason and in the white overalls Sgt Clapperton.*

Flight Lieutenant Rogers headed towards the German town of Boppard, situated on the upper Middle Rhine, often known as the Rhine Gorge. Flying at 10,000 feet the crew encountered considerable flak and searchlight activity, something that they had never experienced. Before reaching Boppard, F/Lt Rogers turned to starboard and followed the Rhine south towards the more significant and much more industrialised town of Wiesbaden. Low cloud prevented any valuable reconnaissance, and any river traffic being observed. The sprawling city of Mainz was quickly located on the opposite bank of the Rhine from Wiesbaden. The 16 bundles of 'Nickels' were unceremoniously dropped by Corporal James Conneeley, the crew's rear gunner. Rogers reported on his return that the blackout over Germany was excellent, but extremely poor over France with Metz especially bad. Sergeant Dockrill also headed to Boppard, on arrival he turned to port and followed the Rhine north towards Linz, situated on the right bank of the river Rhine near Remagen, approximately 19 miles southeast of Bonn. Intense flak and searchlight activity were again encountered along the route. Unlike Rogers, Dockrill decided to lose altitude and brought his Battle down below the cloud. Flying between 4,500 - 5,000 feet many barges were observed just north of Boppard, the crew finally reached Linz without difficulty. Showing remarkable calm for their first operation the crew turned towards Mainz, aware of their presence flak again tried to engage the solitary Battle. Dockrill reported on his return that the flak was working in groups of four batteries. At one point a searchlight got rather close and showing some initiative Dockrill switched on the Battles navigation lights and at the same time flashed his recognition lights, this had the desired effect as the searchlights immediately disengaged. On reaching Mainz, Aircraftman Davies (136) dropped the 16 packages of 'Nickels' over the blacked-out city. Both crews landed safely at 01:20 and 01:25 hours. There was a real buzz around the squadron, finally, after so many obstacles 218 Squadron had flown its first operation of 1940.

The following night Flying Officer Shaw and P/O Imrie were detailed and briefed to carry out another reconnaissance flight. Flying Officer Shaw would fly over the Rivers Main and Rhine and 'Nickel' over Wiesbaden while P/O Imrie would 'Nickel' Frankfurt. The first away at 20:05 hours was the young Rhodesian, Arthur Imrie in Battle P2201. This crew experienced considerable opposition in the form of both flak and searchlights as they neared Frankfurt. Flying between 10,000 - 11,000 feet numerous searchlights beams were observed desperately criss-crossing the night sky searching for the lone Battle. In amongst the searchlights, flak and light tracer was being pumped aimlessly into the blackness. Further afield, the defences of both Darmstadt and Worms were reported to be active. Pilot Officer Imrie using the well-tested tactic of throttling back his engine and making a series of S turns managed to evade both the flak and searchlights. Pilot Officer Walter Shaw left Auberive at 20:45 hours in the recently arrived Battle, P2192.

He experienced little trouble over Germany, however they did encounter stronger than expected winds on the return flight which caused the aircraft to arrive over the French border well south of the intended track.

Effective use of the H/F and D/F Station at Villeneuve was made by the crew's wireless operator Leading Aircraftman Leonard Flisher who managed to bring the aircraft safely home, if a little late. Shaw wrote in his Flying Logbook " *Height 10,000 feet, Recco of Frankfurt and the Rhine. 4,000 feet searchlights and flak when we dropped nickels*".

Both operations obtained some useful information regarding the locations of German flak and searchlight units, but little else. The 25th, being Easter Monday was a holiday, most of the squadron personnel had the day off, apart from essential personnel. Another reconnaissance operation was planned for the 26th, two crews were chosen, Flying Officer Newton and Canadian P/O 'Hank' Wardle. They would fly along the Rhine south of Mainz to Worms and 'Nickel' the now familiar Wiesbaden. Unfortunately, the flight was cancelled due to adverse weather conditions over the Germany. On the 29th, both pilots and their crews were again briefed, disappointingly all-night flying was once cancelled owing to unfavourable weather conditions over the region during late afternoon.

*Above; Twenty-two-year-old Pilot Officer Frederick Sidney Bazalgette RAF*

March had been a challenging month, but rewarding, at long last the squadron found itself operating over Germany. It was only four operations but considering the fiasco of February it was a triumph for everyone on the squadron after all the hard work over the winter months. March would also be remembered for the desperate situation regarding the shortage of pilots on the squadron. A total of 10 pilots were either sick, on detachment, or away on leave. Flight Lieutenant Daish and F/O Richmond were still with the PDU at Heston. Flying Officer Freeman and Sgt Jupp were sick in England, Flying Officer Waring was in hospital while F/O Hulbert was convalescing with a broken ankle. Lastly, F/Sgt Edward Fleet had reverted to his basic pre-war trade. To add to the problems, Sergeant Owens, Horner and P/O Mitchell were on ten days leave as from the 12th and 19th. To offset this serious depletion in trained pilots, six replacements arrived during the latter part of the month. The first to arrive were Pilot Officers Rothes Meek, Henry Murray and Canadian Donald Smith. These were joined by Sergeant's Douglas Preston, Eric Marchand and finally, Pilot Officer Frederick Bazalgette.

April started with F/Lt Rogers and the recently posted crews flying to No.1 Armament Training Station at Perpignan for one week's intensive night flying training. Weather again intervened with the remaining crews training over Auberive and the Grand Est region of northern France. The lack of flying may have been the reason that Wing Commander Duggan left on the 6th for a spot of leave, with S/Ldr Gillman on sick leave command of the squadron passed to Flight Lieutenant Crews. Night flying was now priority, F/O Hughes practised take-off and landings with the Battle carrying a full bomb load. Fortunately, the robust undercarriage stood up to the tremendous strain applied to it when pushing its way through deep ruts and inches of mud. On the 7th five selected crews completed a 3-hour night cross country exercise.

Unlike the squadrons previous visit to Perpignan, this visit went to plan. On the 9th, seven crews started on the trip home, leaving behind the warmth and sun which had made the detachment even more pleasant. An overnight stay at Nantes due to weather conditions on route delayed the squadrons arrival until the 11th. One Battle, flown by P/O Bazalgette was left at Nantes requiring a new engine.

Back at Auberive, three Battles carried out a practice bombing attack on No. 5 Air Stores Park based at Verzenay Marne, (10 miles SE of Reims) at 1045 hours. For twenty minutes the Battles swooped down on the stores park, testing under 'real' conditions their pre-planned procedures for just such an event.

The squadron was visited by Marshal of the Royal Air Force, Lord Trenchard on the morning of the 11th. A formal inspection of the Operations Room and aerodrome was carried out. Acting Flight Lieutenant Crews was given the job of escorting the 'Father of the RAF' around the airfield and answering the numerous questions the ageing but still very sharp Air Marshal fired at him. With an eye for detail, Lord Trenchard spoke at length to both the air and ground crews and watched as a number of Battles were bombed up.

It was during the visit at around 11:30 hours a signal from Wing HQ was received instructing the squadron to bring half the squadron to 2 hours' notice, and the remainder at 4 hours' notice. For the next 48-hours the squadron stood-by and waited, the only activity being the return of S/Ldr Gillman from sick leave and on the 12th, and the appearance of P/O Bazalgette with his now repaired Battle on the 13th.

A bombing exercise over the Moronvilliers bombing range on the 17th was flown by two sub flights, on return to Auberive F/O Crane was unable to lower one of his wheels forcing him to land on just one wheel. Damage was minimal, the minor damage to the wing tip was repaired on site.

*Marshal of the Royal Air Force, Lord Trenchard talking to Flight Lieutenant Crews. On the extreme right is Flying Officer Hughes. Behind them is Fairey Battle P2249 HA-U. This aircraft was shot down on May 11th, 1940.*

## Wednesday April 17th 1940

*Fairey Battle*
*Mk.I (Serial unknown)*
*Contract No :*
*Taken On Charge :*
*Repaired on squadron*
*Pilot: Flying Officer John Crane, uninjured*
*Observer/Bomb aimer: Sergeant Ernest Farmes, uninjured*
*Gunner / Wireless Operator: Leading Aircraftman Herbert Baguley, uninjured*

The following day 4 sections of two aircraft each armed with 4 x 250lb bombs carried out a series of low-level navigational flights before returning to Auberive via Moronvilliers Bombing Range. Bad weather meant only the first two sections completed the exercise, while the 3rd and 4th sections returned to base. North of Soissons, the Battle of F/O Roths Meek was forced to make an emergency crash landing with a burst glycol tank. Showing commendable skill, F/O Meek brought the Battle in for a wheels-up landing at Saint-Christophe-à-Berry. What was more remarkable is that the landing was made with the four 250lb bombs still on board. The crew escaped shocked but otherwise uninjured.

## Thursday April 18th 1940

*Fairey Battle*
*Mk.I L5245*
*Contract No : 540408/36*
*Taken On Charge: 18/02/1940*
*No.1 Salvage Section*
*Pilot : Flying Officer Rothes Meek uninjured*
*Observer/Bomb aimer: Not Recorded*
*Gunner / Wireless Operator: Not Recorded.*

On the morning of April 20th orders were received from No.75 Wing HQ instructing the squadron to make ready four aircraft for a reconnaissance and Nickel dropping raid over the Rhine from Worms to south of Mainz. Flying Officer Newton and Pilot Officer Wardle would finally get the chance to operate after the two previously scrubbed briefings, they would be joined by 'A' Flight commander A/F/Lt Crews and Sergeant Horner. The first crew away was F/O Newton in Battle L5235 at 20:35 hours, they slowly climbed to 3,000 feet and headed towards the Franco-German border. Over Germany they turned towards their first objective, Worms. Located on the west bank of the river Rhine between the cities of Ludwigshafen and Mainz, it was famous for its wine, however it was also an important manufacturer of leather, machinery and chemicals. On reaching Worms at 10,000 feet the crew started their search for river traffic heading up the Rhine. Surprisingly, no flak was encountered. Unmolested they reached their second objective, Darmstadt at 21:55 hours. Once over the city the crew started dropping bundles of Nickels leaflets over the blacked-out city below. For seventeen minutes searchlights groped the night sky searching for the Battle. With this part of the operation complete the crew headed further up the Rhine towards Mainz. Dropping down to 6000 feet visibility was almost perfect, autobahns and railway lines were easily identified, but no shipping was seen. On reaching Mainz F/O Newton finally turned for home, on route he noted a blast furnace at Saarbautern and what appeared to be an airfield at Gernsheim, the crew landed at 23:30 hours.

*218 Squadron's Officer mess. Unfortunately, the identity of all those shown is unknown. It is however believed that the officer standing at the back beside the tricolour is P/O 'Hank' Wardle. The officer sitting down 2nd left is New Zealander Flying Officer Richmond talking with a spectacled intelligence officer. With him is Flying Officer Rogers and behind him Pilot Officer Crews.*

The next crew aloft was that of P/O 'Hank' Wardle at 20:55 hours at the controls of Battle P2201. The crew crossed the frontier without experiencing any trouble, however for some unexplained reason they found themselves over 80 miles south of their southernmost target of Worms. This could have been caused by a navigational error or faulty compass, sadly we will never know. In the clear conditions the numerous searchlights were easily visible over the Rhine, probably searching for F/O Newton. North of Kreilsheim and unbeknown to the crew they were being stalked by a Mannheim-Sandhofen based Bf109D flown Feldwebel Wilhelm Schmale of the 12(N)/JG2. At approximately 22:45 hours, and in all probability taken completely unawares the Battle was hit by machine gun fire which immediately set on fire the Battles engine. With the Merlin ablaze and illuminated by searchlights the young Canadian had no option then order the crew to bail out. Pilot Officer Wardle managed to take to his parachute, not so fortunate were his observer, Sergeant Edward Davidson and air gunner, Aircraftman 1st Class Albert Bailey. They were found in the burnt-out wreckage of the Battle at Wallhausen a municipality in the district of Schwäbisch Hall in Baden-Württemberg, Germany the following day. Quickly captured by a German soldier on a bicycle, Wardle was taken by car to the Luftwaffe Barracks at Kreilsheim where he stayed until the 21st. Howard

*German troops inspecting the wreckage of P/O 'Hank' Wardle's Fairey Battle on the morning of April 21st, 1940.*

Wardle in a report submitted upon his return to England stated that his aircraft crashed due to engine trouble, which subsequently burst into flames, he was obviously still unaware of the presence of the night fighter. In fact, this was the first recorded night fighter kill of WW2 on German soil. His two crew mates were buried with Full Military Honours on April 23rd, 1940 in the 'Plot of Honour' in the Kreilsheim's New Cemetery. A large number of Luftwaffe personnel stood honour guard, while a military band played. The service was conducted by the Chaplin of the airbase at Kreilsheim. It was all very dignified and lavish with echo's of WW1 about it, this would soon change.

After a short spell in Dulag Luft hospital, Wardle was sent to Oflag IXA (Spangenberg). In August he made his first escape attempt, one of the first from a camp by a RAF PoW, captured he was badly beaten resulting in partial deafness in one ear and a badly damaged leg, which left him with a permanent limp. He stayed at Oflag IXA until November 1940 when he was one of the first RAF officers transferred to Oflag IVC (Colditz). Involved in a number of unsuccessful escape attempts, he eventually teamed up with Major Ronald Littledale of The King's Royal Rifle Corps, Lieutenant Commander William Lawson Stephens RNVR and Captain Pat Reid, of The Royal Army Service Corps. After submitting their plan to the British Escape Committee these four determine individuals planned their escape for the night of October 14th, 1942. Everything hinged on absolute perfect timing, and a big dollop of luck.

**Saturday April 20th 1940**
*Fairey Battle*
*Mk.I  P2201*
*Contract No: 768880/38*
*Taken on Charge: 12/03/1940*
**Failed o Return**
*Pilot: Pilot Officer Howard Douglas Wardle 41761 RAF PoW*
*Observer/Bomb aimer: Sergeant Edward Davison, 563790 RAF* **Killed**
*Gunner / Wireless Operator: Aircraftman 1st Class Albert Bailey 552069 RAF* **Killed**


The four scaled roof tops, picked locks, dodge sentries and barking dogs before scaling the final barbed wire wall and making their escape from the supposedly escape proof Colditz. On reaching the outside, the group paired off, Wardle teaming up with Pat Reid. After what can only be described as a 'Boy' Own' journey through the heart of Nazis Germany, the pair arrived in Switzerland on October 18th, 1942. Pat Reid in his bestselling book the 'Colditz Story' stated that if it was not for Wardle, who on a number of occasions just picked him up and carried him when he was exhausted, he would never had escaped. Amazingly, the other pair also made it to the safety of Switzerland. Wardle completed his homerun by travelling with the aid of the French Resistance through France to the Spanish Border. On entering Spain disguised as a 6-foot-tall hairdresser called 'Raoul' he was imprisoned again. After a spell in Gibraltar, he arrived in England February 6th, 1944. He was recommended for the Military Cross on March 10th 1944, which he was duly awarded as per London Gazette dated 16 May 1944, for his *'continuous initiative, daring and resource over a period of two years, this officer has displayed the highest qualities of courage and determination'.* In 1944 he married June Porter and began ferrying bombers to the Middle and Far East. Towards the end of the war, Hank still ferrying bombers switched to flying bombers from Canada across the Atlantic to the United Kingdom. With the war ended, Hank remain in the air force, he was involved in a mid-air collision, which resulted in a crash in 1948, soon after he resigned his commission. Hank died 1995 in Ottawa, Canada.

The next crew to depart Auberive was that of 'A' Flight commander, F/Lt Crews. He was aloft in Battle P2192 at 2146 hours. Having crossed the Franco-German border the crew reached their first objective,

Mainz. Once over the city they successfully dropped their 'Nickels' from 7000 feet. Each of the Battles carried between 12-16 bundles of 'Nickels' which on this occasion were propaganda leaflets. These bundles measure 8 1/2 x 5 inch and were held together by a rubber band and dropped from the bomb aimers position. Their delivery was in theory to be calculated by the observer, the height and wind conditions at the time of dropping would determine the rate of full and spread, however few if any Observes did this calculation. Once again, searchlights were the main concern, working in sets of four they continually swept the night sky for the Battle. Flight Lieutenant Crews reported ' *Blue S/L much stronger than white, often dazzling'*. Dropping down to dangerously low altitude of 2,500 feet the crew searched the Rhine. From this height visibility was almost unlimited along the river and both banks. Blast Furnaces, railway lines and even a train were reported. With the operation complete they landed safely just after 0025 hours. The final aircraft to depart at 2220 hours was flown by Sergeant Horner. Unfortunately for the crew they were forced to return after just twenty minutes when the wireless set aboard Battle L5237 was found to be faulty, although there was a spare Battle available, it was considered by the squadron commander that the crew would not have sufficient time to carry out the operation in the time allocated to the squadron.

No operations were flown on the 21st, the news of the loss of P/O Wardle on his first operation would have quickly circulated around the squadron. Everyone, from the lowest Erk to the squadron commander was hoping that the crew had forced landed in France, however this was quickly discounted that evening when Hamburg Radio reported that a machine had been brought down at Kreilsheim and the pilot, P/O Wardle was a Prisoner of War, there was no news about his crew.

A Committee of Adjustment was assembled in the village at 11.00am of the 22nd to deal with the personal effects of P/O 'Hank' Wardle. Three of his fellow pilots, F/O Hughes and P/O's Smith and Murray observed as the young Canadians belongings were gathered, recorded and packed by the adjutant for their journey home to his family back in Canada. Sadly, this would become an all too familiar occurrence over the weeks and months ahead. During the early afternoon three Hawker Hurricanes arrived to inspect the airfield and facilities in preparation of a squadron move in the event of an emergency. Orders had been received via No.75 Wing HQ that new dispersal points were to be laid, seven to have telephones and a new exchange set up in preparation of the arrival of No.62 (Fighter) Wing Servicing Unit. Yet more orders from No.75 Wing HQ arrived just before lunch, six crews would be required to carry out another Reconnaissance and Nickel dropping raid that night. An early evening air test resulted in the withdrawal of one Battle due to engine problems. The first crew aloft was Canadian Pilot Officer Donald Smith at the controls of Battle P2249 at 21:13 hours. Seven minutes later Rhodesian Pilot Officer Imrie was on his way in Battle P2203. Pilot Officer Smith crossed the frontier at 10,000 feet dropping his 'Nickels' over Bad Kreuznach, a medieval spa town on the west side of the Rhine. Once delivered the crew turned towards Mainz losing altitude all the time until they reached the Rhine at 4000 feet. Hazy conditions prevented any observation, the crew returned to base just before mid-night, it had been a quiet trip. Pilot Officer Imrie on the other hand, on his second raid over Germany was continuously engage by searchlights throughout his sortie. On dispatching his leaflets over Bad Kreuznach, P/O Imrie followed the Rhine at 8000 feet to a well blacked out Mannheim. Once over Mannheim the cities searchlight defences quickly sprang into action, dozens of beams frantically scanned the sky for the Battle. In an attempt to confuse the Germans, P/O Imrie ordered his observer Sergeant Ernest Farmes to drop a parachute flare, it was a prudent order. Almost as soon as the flare ignited it had the immediate effect of extinguishing all the searchlights. With no searchlights to bother them, and the blacked-out city below, the crew caught a glimpse of an airfield, the concrete runways and hangars being clearly identified. The crew then headed north towards Worms, both stationary and moving barges were observed on both banks of the Rhine, the crew eventually landed at 00:01 hours. The third Battle airborne was flown by Sergeant John Horner at 22:13 hours, they reached the Rhine over

*A briefing prior to take off. On the right is Pilot Officer Charles Crews with telephone in hand. Next to him is Flying Officer Alan Rogers. The airman with the moustache is believed to be LAC Taylor and to his left holding the dog, Sergeant Farmes.*

Oppenheim at 2000 feet. Turning north they headed toward Mainz where they dropped their 'Nickels' at 23:26 hours. Once delivered the crew began their search along the Rhine. Three miles west of Worms and flying at only 3000 feet the Battle was located by a group of searchlights. Immediately they were engaged by flak, six bursts and light tracer exploded directly in front of the aircraft, Horner desperately tried to shake off the searchlight, *'I tried every evasive tactic I could at this stage, without effect'* he reported on his return. Still caught in the beams, flak exploded behind the Battle, thankfully the German gunners aim was marginally out, finally, and to the crew's immense relief they were finally clear. Undeterred they continued with their flight, flying at 2000 feet the crew easily identified roads and bridges but no barges or vessels on the Rhine. Finally, after 2 hours 44 minutes aloft Sergeant Horner landed Battle L5235 safely back at Auberive. The fourth crew aloft was skippered by Flying Officer Hughes at 22:33 hours.

On reaching an already alert Mainz the crew encountered isolated groups of searchlights. One group almost caught the crew in the beam's apex, by throwing the Battle about, at the same time turning on and off the Battles navigation lights F/O Hughes managed somehow to shake them off. With the 'Nickels' dropped the crew flew along the Rhine at 5000 feet. A few barges were reported as was a row of military type barracks, the crew landed safely back at base at 01.24 hours. Finally, at 23.10 hours the crew of Flying Officer John Crane departed. This crew had a relatively trouble-free operation, only one searchlight was reported, which was doused within 30 seconds! There was no opposition over Mainz as the last of the squadrons pamphlets slowly descended on to the city below. Losing altitude, the crew flew along the Rhine at the perilously low altitude of 2000 feet, condition were hazy making flying even more challenging. A large Wharf south of

Worms was observed, long white shadows from the interior lighting of a few open fronted sheds were easily visible in the inky blackness. With conditions quickly deteriorating the crew turned for home, landing Battle P2189 at 01:50 hours.  It had been an excellent effort by the crews and the squadron, and more importantly, all had returned.   There was no day flying on the 23rd, but two-night cross country flights were successfully undertaken. On the 24th, Wing HQ once again ordered the squadron to prepare six crews that night for a 'Nickel' raid. This was cancelled early evening due to weather.

Practice bombing and air firing were under taken at the St.Hilaire Ranges during late morning of the 25th, 28 sorties were completed just before lunch. A night flying programme was to be flown, but a change in the weather forced its cancellation.  Torrential rain hampered flying on the 26th, 27th and 28th, only a few isolated local night tests were flown. On the 28th, all available transport carried squadron personnel to the Parc Pommory to watch the cup final rugby match between No.71 Wing and No.75 Wing. Four of the players were drawn from 218 Squadron, unfortunately, F/Lt Alan Rogers broke his collar bone during a hard-fought match, victory alas went to No.71 Wing who won 6 - 0. This unfortunate injury in all probability saved Alan Rogers life. It was during the day that No.75 Wing HQ received further information via the International Red Cross confirming that P/O Wardle was a PoW, however there was still no news about his crew. The last few days of April were spent carrying out photographic Mosiac's of Rouvres airfield, the home of No.73 Squadron.   The injured F/Lt Rogers, P/O Imrie and 26 other ranks proceeded on 7 days leave, it would be the last by the squadron.

*Two guards stand beside a squadron Battle. The airfield at Auberive afforded little in the way of cover from the weather and German reconnaissance aircraft. Branches and cut down trees from a nearby pine forest were utilised where possible.*

# Chapter 7: 1940 – Bloody May

*Everything possibly needed is seen in this photograph of Battle K9254. Four x 250lb bombs, fuel and ammunition boxes all close at hand.*

Wednesday, May 1st, 1940 found 'B' flight carrying out practice bombing at the local ranges with No.88 Squadron. While 'B' Flight were away, a section carried out local flying exercise. The following day both flights were detailed for a cross country exercise in marginal weather. Pilot Officer Shaw led a section on a local flying trip on the morning of the 3rd. The weather was ideal, the French countryside was bathed in a thin layer of mist, above the sky was clear of clouds. The only sign of life was a few whispery contrails from high flying aircraft.

On May 1st, 1940, the squadron had the following Fairey Battles on strength.

| A/C | Serial | Delivered | Maker | Contract | Fate |
|---|---|---|---|---|---|
| 1 | **K9251 HA-K** | 10/10/1938 via 185 Sqdn | Faireys, Stockport | 522745/37 | *Abandon France June 1940* |
| 2 | **K9273 HA-R** | 11/10/1938 via 185 Sqdn | Faireys, Stockport | 522745/37 | *Abandon France May 1939* |
| 3 | **K9253 HA-J** | 11/10/1938 via 185 Sqdn | Faireys, Stockport | 522745/37 | Shot Down Ground Fire 12/5/1940 |

| 4 | K9323 | 10/10/1938 via 185 Sqdn | Faireys, Stockport | 522745/37 | To No.150 Sqdn 31/5/1940 |
|---|---|---|---|---|---|
| 5 | K9325 HA-D | 10/10/1938 via 185 Sqdn | Faireys, Stockport | 522745/37 | Shot Down Ground Fire 11/5/1940 |
| 6 | L5192 HA-P | 12/03/1940 via AASF | Austin, Longbridge | 540408/36 | *Abandon France May 1940* |
| 7 | L5232 | 05/03/1940 via AASF | Austin, Longbridge | 540408/37 | Believed shot down by Bf109s 14/5/1940 |
| 8 | L5235 HA-W | Unknown | Austin, Longbridge | 540408/38 | Believed shot down by Bf109s 14/5/1941 |
| 9 | L5237 | 18/02/1940 | Austin, Longbridge | 540408/39 | *To No.150 Sqdn 21/5/1940* |
| 10 | P2183 | 30/11/1939 via No.1 salvage | Fairey Stockport | 768880/38 | Shot Down Ground Fire 12/5/1940 |
| 11 | P2189 | 05/03/1940 via AASF | Fairey Stockport | 768880/38 | *Abandon France May 1939* |
| 12 | P2192 HA-E | 12/03/1940 via AASF | Fairey Stockport | 768880/38 | *Abandon France May 1940* |
| 13 | P2203 | 17/01/1940 | Fairey Stockport | 768880/38 | Shot Down Ground Fire 11/5/1940 |
| 14 | P2249 HA-U | 26/01/1940 via AASF | Fairey Stockport | 768880/38 | Shot Down Ground Fire 11/5/1940 |
| 15 | P2324 | 22/04/1940 via No.6 RSU | Fairey Stockport | 768880/38 | Believed shot down by Bf109s 14/5/1941 |
| 16 | P2326 | 19/04/1940 via AASF | Fairey Stockport | 768880/38 | Shot Down Ground Fire 11/5/1940 |
| 17 | P2315 | | Fairey Stockport | 768880/38 | To No.103 Squadron 23/05/1940 |

*LAC Taylor Wop/Ag passes a parachute to Sergeant observer Farmes. Note wing bullet badge on arm, the forerunner to the Wop/Ag half wing brevet.*

Early morning of the 5th, P/O Shaw was aloft on a weather-test in Battle P2324, interestingly his log book records that he was obliged to land at Wez-Thuisy airfield prior to his return to base, an interesting sentence is written against the flight details, *'Aircraft shot-up'*. Sadly, by what is not recorded. However, it is believed that he was the victim of 'friendly' fire emanating from an anti-aircraft battery.

In the afternoon, No.75 Wing Football Team played at a fete at Mourmelon where they were awarded a Bronze plaque. Formation flying using the R/T apparatus was flown on the morning of the 7th. During the afternoon, three Battles once again visited No.5 Air Stores Park and beat up the facility, probably testing any improvements since the squadrons last visit in April.

Austin built Fairey Battle L5422 was delivered on May 8th, its stay would be only a matter of days. On the morning of May 9th, a section was dispatched to the bombing ranges at Moronvilliers. Each of the Battles was armed with 4 x 250lb bombs, unknown to those involved it would be the last training exercise the squadron would undertake in France. At 02:30 hours on the morning of May 10th, the long anticipated German advance become a reality, Operation *'Fall Gelb'* had started. German divisions began rapidly advancing into Holland, Luxembourg and neutral Belgium, the alarm bells began to ring at No.75 Wing HQ at 04:00 hours, all three squadrons were brought to Readiness No.1, all aircraft would be on 4 hours readiness. At 04:50 hours, Betheniville airfield, the home of No.103 Squadron was bombed by Do17's of II/KG2, no aircraft or personnel were damaged or injured. At 0500 hours the squadrons received a new signal, changing the squadron Readiness to No.2, 50% of the squadron would be required on immediate standby, while the remaining aircraft would be on 4 hours. It was the turn of No.88 Squadron at Mourmelon at around 0535 hours to receive the attention of the Dorniers of III/KG3. Two Battles at readiness were damaged, one badly, thankfully only two personnel were hurt. The local flak battery put up a spirited defence but failed to deter the German bombers. It was obvious to everyone, even the French that this was the main German advance, at 07:45 hours No.75 Wing signalled its three squadrons the code word *'Meddling'* AASF Instruction No.7 for a German Invasion. Over at Auberive all the activity had not gone unnoticed, P/O Shaw recalls:

*The grave of 22-year-old Herbert Baguley.*

*On 10 May, the squadrons regular intelligence officer had gone on leave, I was the deputy. The morning of 10 May we got the code word, 'meddling', which meant Germans were going to invade. I got up exceedingly early and walked to the airfield. It was lovely countryside, fields and trees and seemed very peaceful as I reached the airfield. Four Heinkels flew over it at about 100 ft. They did not bomb, but I remember thinking to myself 'cheeky buggers. In the afternoon we heard that the Germans had started their attack and Panzer Divisions were advancing and we went out to attack them. The bombing tactics were low level bombing and strafing. The bombers experienced severe low flak and machine gun fire and if they went high, there were the ME 109s.*

At 12:20 hours two half sections from 218 and 103 Squadron were aloft following an order from Wing HQ.

```
Despatch two half sections each squadron to attack enemy mechanised column between AZ42
and Dippach. Town must be avoided. Position and troops as notified but special care to
be taken if target not found as indicated. Above sections may attack between AS55 and
AZ 39. Position of most advanced troops is at a point 31/2 miles south of Dippach and
another lot at Mont St.Martin, 10 miles SW of Dippach.
```

The identity of only three crews is known, that of F/Lt Hughes and F/O Crane and Sgt Owen in Battle P2315. The remainder from 218 Squadron are sadly not. The Operational Records Book for May 1940 is 'Missing' in all probability lost during the hectic withdrawal. Flying Officer John Crane was aloft in Battle L5232 and briefed to attack the Dippach - Luxemburgh Road. His crew comprised of Sergeant Wilfred Morgan, observer and rear gunner / wireless operator, Leading Aircraftman Herbert Baguley. The first pair departed at 14:30 hours, followed ten minutes later by the remaining pair. It is understood that both sections found and attacked targets.

The first section successfully attacked a stationary column of 20-30 vehicles on the Dippach - Luxemburgh Road. The second section attacked a column of about 20 vehicles one mile east of Dippach from low level scoring some hits with their bombs while at the same time experiencing accurate ground fire. Each of the Battles four gunners blazed away at the abundance of targets, for once even the much-hated rearward firing under-gun become useful. Flying Officer Crane was leading the first half section, when his Battle was hit by small arms fire. The rear .303 magazine exploded mortally wounding LAC Baguley and rendering the gun useless. Both section leaders considered that a low-level approach with a sharp turn to starboard followed by a low level get-away preferable. At 14:52 hours the first half section landed, followed a few minutes later by the second half section. All four Battles had been damaged, two badly. Sadly, soon after landing it was discovered that LAC Baguley was dead. It is thought that his .303 magazine had been hit by enemy ground gun fire and exploded, sending hot fragments of steel into his chest, puncturing his lung, the 22-year-old bled to death. He was buried on the 12th at Epernay French National Cemetery. Sergeant Owen was ordered to attack a convoy located on the Luxembourg Frontier Road. This he found and attacked from low-level experiencing considerable opposition from both light flak and small arms fire. Apart from several holes in his Battle, Sgt Owens and his crew, Sgt Andrews and LAC Cranley returned safely and reported at interrogation that each of their four 250lb bombs were seen to explode amongst the convoy.

Pilot Officer Shaw records the day's activities; '*We were lucky that day, we only had one casualty. It was a rear gunner who was hit by a ricochet bullet and unfortunately died. At that time, the Fairey Battle was underpowered, poorly armed*'

One of the squadron gunners, Corporal James Drummond exploits on this operation would be used as part of his citation for the DFM in a few short weeks. In comparison to the other squadrons of No.75 Wing, this

*A section of squadron Battles landing at Auberive. The Battles 54-foot wingspan is seen to good effect.*

the first day of the German advance 218 Squadron had been extremely fortunate. Tragically, No.103 Squadron reported the loss of three of the four Battles it dispatched, each of them the victim of the murderous ground fire. Over at Mourmelon, 88 Squadron reported four Battles damaged during the morning bombing. During the early evening they were again attacked, four JU88 dive bombers destroyed three Battles and set on fire one hangar, plus the ammunition and parachute store. The following day news from the front was anything but reassuring, the Germans had already passed the Meuse and Albert Canal near Maastricht, further south they were surging through the Ardennes, such was the speed of the advance the exact positions of the advancing German columns was unclear. At 08:30 hours instructions from Group HQ were received at Auberive, two half sections would be required to attack a bridge 2 miles north of St.Vith. The first section departed at 09:28 hours, this was led Sergeant Charles Dockrill in Battle P2203, his No.2 was Pilot Officer Henry Murray at the controls of Battle P2249. Twelve minute later the second section led by 'A' Flight commander, Flight Lieutenant Charles Crews took-off, he was followed by P/O Anthony Hudson in Battle K9325, one of the oldest aircraft on the squadron. Over Luxembourg the Battles encountered intense and continuous ground fire, every German column appeared to be equipped with both light and heavy calibre machine guns, many of which had been mounted on tripods along the roadside or on specially mounted vehicles. Such was the intensity of the defences all four crews were either shot down or obliged to force land. One of the first to succumb was the leader of the first section, Sergeant Dockrill. Flying as observer in P/O Murray's Battle was Sergeant Peter Stubbs, he recalls the tragic end of a brave crew;

*Our target was an area near St.Vith were the German tanks were massing to support the German spearhead into France. We were flying as a pair, about 200 yards apart at very low level equipped with 4 x 250lb bombs. Important modifications had been made to our aircraft, in that the bulky bomb aimers equipment was found to be useless as we hedge-hopped across the ground, so it was removed making way for the rear firing Vickers K Gun which would at least give us some protection against the intense ground fire. About 0930 hours we were airborne and heading towards the front, flying as low as possible to avoid the enemy fighters. However long before we reached the front-line positions marked on our maps we ran into a hail of machine gun and cannon fire, so rapid had been the German advance. Astonishingly, the further we flew behind the enemy line were found the roads packed with horse drawn transport, hauling supplies to the advancing German spearhead. The new K gun proved superb against these targets, as we swooped along the road, I fired off pans of ammunition. I could clearly see the chaos as the drivers fell from their carts and the horses crashed into ditches as they run amok in their death throes. It was then that Adams the W/op reported that Sergeant Dockrill was in trouble. The last he saw of it was the face of AC1 Kenneth Gregory, the crew's gunner as the flaming aircraft exploded at about 30 feet and hit the trees below.*

There were no survivors from the crew of Battle P2203 which crashed at Basbellain, a village in the commune of Troisvierges, in northern Luxembourg. The severely burned bodies were initially buried in a field grave close to the crash site. On May 27th, the bodies were exhumed and re-interred in the Municipal Cemetery of Niederbesslingen.

**Saturday May 11th 1940**
*Fairey Battle*
*Mk.I P2203*
*Contract No: 768880/38*
*Taken on Charge: 17/01/1940*
**Failed to Return**
*Pilot: Sergeant Charles James Ernest Dockrilll 563473 RAF* **Killed**
*Observer/Bomb aimer: Sergeant Percival Frank Dormer 563966 RAF* **Killed**

*Gunner / Wireless Operator: AC.1 Class Kenneth George Gregory 551303 **Killed***

Within seconds of the loss of Sergeant Dockrill the Battle of P/O Murray was also in trouble, Sgt Peter Stubbs describes the events that overtook his crew:

*Sergeant Charles Dockrill*

*It was obvious that we could not last much longer. The rattle of the bullets hitting the aircraft was continuous now, and cannon shells were tearing lumps out of the wings. As I lay on the floor firing at the enemy below, I could feel a couple of shells bend the armour plate beneath me. Soon flames leapt out of the engine and smoke and flames surrounded my pilot, P/O Murray. All I could see through the hatch was a forest of trees awfully close. Then there was a grinding crunch as we hit the ground hard. We had just cleared the trees and landed in a field beside a farmhouse at full speed. My 'Monkey' chain snapped with the impact and I shot forward hitting the instrument panel with my face as earth and stones poured through the open hatch. I crawled to the rear of the aircraft to climb out via the rear gunner's position and found my hand would not work. It had been hit by a cannon shell, but in the chaos, I had not noticed it. I was wondering how to climb out when the fuel tanks ruptured, pouring blazing petrol into the cabin. The heat was unbearable and a few second later I was outside the aircraft. My chest parachute had come undone, and the white silk was covered in my blood. The Germans continued to fire at us as we crouched behind our blazing Battle. About 100 yards away was what looked like a potato field with deep furrows. Knowing it would not be long before the bombs exploded in the heat of the fire, we decided our best chance of survival was to make a dash for it. Murray, my pilot was burnt, but Adams was uninjured. I was rather slower than the others and a bullet hit me in the elbow just as we made it to the first of the furrows. The German continued firing at us, we noticed around sixteen German soldiers walking towards our blazing Battle, they were cheering at their success, big grins and back slapping as they walked closer. Suddenly the bombs exploded, and lumps of aircraft, earth and debris screamed down on the field. I peered over the farrow, there was just a big hole where the Battle once was, and there was no Germans to be seen.*

The crew had come down near the village of Basbellain, they were quickly captured, and their wounds treated, they would remain Prisoners of War until liberated in 1945.

### Saturday May 11th 1940
*Fairey Battle*
*Mk.I  P2249 HA-U*
*Contract No : 768880/38*
*Taken On Charge :26/01/1940*
**Failed to Return**
*Pilot : Pilot Officer Henry Macale Murray 41051 RAF **PoW***
*Observer/Bomb aimer: Sergeant Peter Stubbs 5804568 RAF **PoW***
*Gunner / Wireless Operator: AC.2nd Class Ivan George Adams 628368 **PoW***

*The shattered and burnt-out wreckage of Pilot Officer Henry Murrays Fairey Battle P2249 HA-U.*

The second half section flying a few minutes behind would have been unaware of the fate of their friends, they too encountered the murderous ground fire as they raced at low level over the densely wooded Ardennes. The closer to their objective they flew the intensity of flak and machine gun fire increased, each of the Battles were continuously hit. Nearing the target F/O Crews instructed his No.2 over the R/T to turn

119

into the attack, almost immediately his Battle was mortally hit in the engine. Flames quickly began pouring out of the engine and glycol tank, while burning petrol covered the cockpit floor under the pilot's seat. Fighting with the controls it was obvious that the Battle was doomed. With his vision impaired by dense chocking smoke inside the cockpit and roaring flames from its engine quickly melting the engine cowling like a blow-torch F/O Crews wrestled with the controls as long as he could in the vain hope of finding a patch of clear ground to force land his Battle. Flying at a mere 100 feet, parachuting out was not an option, it would be suicide. With every second the heat and flames increased to a point that the young pilot could stand it no more, he ordered his crew to jump while at the same time he valiantly tried to coax as much height he could from his disintegrating Battle in an attempt to give him, and his two crew the best chance of survival. With his crew gone, Charles Crews pulled back on the control column, stood on his seat and jumped. Almost immediately after pulling the ripcord he was hitting the uppermost branches of the pine trees, fortunately his parachute was caught in the branches bringing his decent to a bone crushing stop. Winded and covered in cuts from the pines Charles swung from his harness, shocked, but very much alive. Within just a few yards, his air-gunner Sergeant Thomas Evans was also hanging in the branches, injured but alive. Sadly, the crew's observer was not as lucky, within 30 feet of the survivors the body of 20-year-old Sergeant Cederic Jennings lay, his parachute had only partially deployed and by a cruel twist of fate he had fallen between the densely grouped trees, he was killed instantly as he hit the ground. His body was buried close to the crash site 1mile south of Amelscheid, Belgium.

**Saturday May 11th 1940**
*Fairey Battle*
*Mk.1 P2326*
*Contract No: 768880/38*
*Taken On Charge :19/04/1940*
**Failed to Return**
*Pilot: Flight Lieutenant Charles Arthur Reginald Crews 37795 RAF* **PoW**
*Observer/Bomb aimer: Sergeant Cederic Maurice Jennings 580427 RAF* **Killed**
*Gunner / Wireless Operator LAC Thomas Stephen Evans 536059* **PoW**

After releasing themselves from their harness and clambering down the trees both Crews and Evans tried unsuccessfully to make their escape, the whole area was now in German hands making any escape impossible. Despite his capture Charles Crews was determined to get back to his wife, and home in Golders Green. Three failed escape attempts were finally rewarded in 1944 when feigning illness, he was shipped home from Sweden on the Arundel Castle, he arrived back in Britain September 15th, 1944, almost 4 years to the day he left Boscombe Down. Carmarthen born Leading Aircraftman Evan, who had just turned 21 a few short weeks prior spent the remainder of the war in various PoW Camps, he finished up at Stalag IIIA Luckenwalde where he was made to work in a coal mine. It is not known if the final Battle flown by F/O Anthony "Tony' Hudson managed to attack his target before he too made a forced landing in open fields near St Vith. All three crew members survived the murderous flak and the subsequent crash landing.

Quickly captured they were taken into captivity. Hudson was initially taken to the Oflag IX-A Spangenberg Castle. In a letter written to his mother in June 1940 Tony Hudson writes : *Just to let you know that I am still flourishing and have been transferred to another camp, this time I am living in a Castle perched high on top of a hill surrounded by the most lovely countryside, a place well known for its historical interest in Germany'.*

## Saturday May 11th 1940

*Fairey Battle*
*Mk.I  K9325  HA-D*
*Contract No: 522745/36*
*Taken on Charge :10/10/1938*
**Failed to Return**
*Pilot: Flying Officer Anthony John Hudson, 39125 RAF **PoW***
*Observer/Bomb aimer: Sergeant Neil Henry Thompson, 1310697 RAF **PoW***
*Gunner / Wireless Operator AC 1st Class Arthur Ellis, 550453 RAF **PoW***


Sergeant Peter Stubbs, who was aboard Battle P2249 recalls the events after the explosion of his Battle; *'I must have passed out shortly after the explosion due to a loss of blood. When I came to, the others had gone and there was a German soldier pointing his rifle at me and yelling at me to get up. Someone helped me off with my parachute and harness and I was marched into a farmyard. My little finger had been almost shot off and was held on by a mere thread of skin. I carried it along gently, like a valued possession. I was told to stand against a high wall with the others, piles of rifles were piled in front of us. Angry Germans, upset at the loss of their comrades shouted and gesticulated at us.*

*With the brick wall behind and the rifles in front, a thought went through my mind. Was this to be a firing squad in revenge. Just then a Luftwaffe officer ran into the farmhouse, shout and arguing with his army counterparts. He obviously won the argument, for he led us away to waiting cars. Murray, our New Zealand pilot was severely burnt bringing the Battle down, he was quickly driven away, we never saw him again. My injuries were now getting rather painful, the Luftwaffe Officer organised some bandages and a shot of morphine. I do not remember anything after that until I woke up that evening in the town of Prum. Here I was given a bowl of hot soup and locked in the Police cell for the night. Next morning, we were loaded into a car and driven for hours across Germany until late in the afternoon we arrived in the Spa town of Bad Neuenahr, near Coblenz. The car pulled up outside a Hospital and two nuns led me gently inside. There was a Convent next door, and all the nurses were Nuns. I stayed in the hospital for three weeks and found that in patching up my arm and hand, the Doctor had successfully stuck my little finger back on. Gently carrying it across Germany for a day and half had been worth it!'*

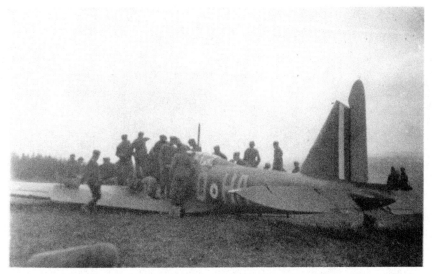

*The relatively intact Fairey Battle K9325 HA-D flown by Flying Officer Anthony John Hudson seen here being inspected by German troops and a few inquisitive civilians.*

*Once the fighting had moved on there was plenty of time to collect the hundreds of wrecks that littered the Belgium, Luxemburg, and French countryside. Here HA-D has had both wings removed and the aircrafts fuselage loaded onto a transporter.*

One can only speculate on what the atmosphere was like back at Auberive when it was realised that the four crews that had departed with such optimism were now missing. Both Charles Crews and Charles Dockrill and their crews were old hands, having served on the squadron at Boscombe Down. New Zealander Murray had been with the squadron since March, while Hudson was a relative newcomer to the squadron. It was a bitter pill to swallow, the loss of close friends was never easy, but there was no time to dwell. The rapid German advance would not allow them that luxury. Number 218 was not the only 75 Wing squadron to suffer, tragedy had also affected 88 Squadron at Mourmelon-le-Grand. Like, 218 Squadron, two half sections had been ordered to attack troop concentrations near Bouillon, ominously none returned. During late afternoon, a message from AASF HQ instructed the squadrons of No.75 Wing to 'Stand-off' immediately. All three squadrons were put on 3 hours readiness from 04:00 hours the following morning. Obviously expecting an increase in attacks directed against the airfields, AASF HQ also ordered that up to 50% of squadron strength could, at the OC 75 Wing discretion be dispersed to the satellite airfields up until 09:00 hours the following morning. It was a prudent move, at around 07:00 hours Mourmelon-le-Grand was bombed, half hour later it was the turn of Auberive. Three bombs were reported to have landed on the airfield, while a further four landed on the perimeter, none exploded. It was not until 16:00 hours that orders were received to dispatch a section to attack a strong mechanised column heading south from Paliseul towards Bouillon, a small town on the River Semois, and only two miles from the French border. After what would have been a rather hurried briefing three crews were selected for the operation. At round 16:30* hours they departed Auberive led by Sergeant John Horner at the controls of K9353. His number 2 was New Zealander P/O William Anstey in Battle L5192, the sections No.3, P/O Frederick Bazalgette was flying Battle P2183.   * ( P/O Anstey records take off time as 16:55 hrs in his log book )

123

*AC1 Arthur Ellis Wop/Ag would spend the rest of the war a guest of the Germans having survived the murderous flak over St Vith on May 11th, 1940.*

Unescorted the trio set off for Bouillon at 1000 feet, nearing Bouillon accurate anti-aircraft and small arms fire was encountered. Most of the anti-aircraft fire appeared to be coming up from a wood slightly west of the intended target. It was here the crews found fourteen to twenty armoured cars, light tanks and lorries all partially hidden. It was an excellent target and one the section leader immediately decided to attack. New Zealander, Pilot Officer William Anstey recalls the events that followed;

*'May 12th, 1940, I took off on my very first operational trip. The target was a motor convoy moving through Bouillon, north-east of Sedan. The payload was 4 x 250lb bombs. I flew as No.2 in the formation of three. The first indication that we were over enemy territory was the sound and sight of exploding shells. This was followed almost immediately by seeing the roundel of our leader's wing, which I was formatting on as closely as possible, suddenly disappear into a large gaping hole. A few seconds later smoke and flames began pouring from the leader's engine. He passed underneath me in what appeared to be a controlled shallow dive. His gunner gave me the 'thumbs-up' sign. A few minutes later the convoy was sighted and No.3 aircraft dropped his bombs and was last seen continuing on his course behind enemy lines. We dropped our bombs from 100 feet but were unable to observe the results as the machine gun and pom-pom fire was becoming too intense and accurate. On the route back were passed over the burning wreck of our leaders Battle. By now we were on our own and receiving the whole undivided attention of the enemy. We were flying at ground level and as we flew down a valley, we could see the tracer bullets coming down from either side. I will remember to my dying day seeing the black and white cows peacefully grazing in the valley as we were zig-zagging our way out of what seemed to us to be a valley from hell. Right then, I would have given anything to be one of those cows. After finally getting out of the valley in more or less one piece we found the front line and returned to our base without further incident. Our ground crew greeted us with the traditional open arms. After ascertaining we had dropped our bombs and fired our guns and the aircraft had flown alright, they transferred their attention to the aircraft. They proudly informed us that we had collected over seventy bullet holes from our fifteen-minute joy ride over enemy territory'.*

Sadly, despite what appeared to be a controlled decent there were no survivors from Flight Sergeant John Horner's aircraft, all three crew members perished. The Battle crashed on the slopes of a small rise 1000 yards south Sensenruth, 2 miles north of Bouillon at approximately 17:00 hours.

**Sunday May 12th 1940**
*Fairey Battle*
*Mk.I  K9353*  **HA-J**
*Contract No: 522745/36*
*Taken on Charge: 20/10/1938*
**Failed to Return**
*Pilot : Flight Sergeant John Bland Horner, 580159 RAF* **Killed.**
*Observer/Bomb aimer: Sergeant Leonard Charles Flisher, 564186 RAF* **Killed.**
*Gunner / Wireless Operator LAC Leslie Douglas Davies 537015 RAF* **Killed.**

The remains of the crew were initially buried close to the crash site. Later they were reburied in the local cemetery at Curfoz. All three were pre-war members of the squadron.

The Battle flown by Pilot Officer Frederick Bazalgette was also badly hit by the intense ground fire. Somehow despite his grievous wounds, the 22-year-old Bazalgette managed to crash land his Battle at Ferme de L' 'Esperance'. Hitting the uppermost branches of a row of pine trees the Battle came to rest on its nose. Although the area was still in French hands, the aircraft had come down on the wrong side of the River Meuse. The crew's rear gunner / wireless operator was LAC Harold Jones, he recalls the day's activities of that Sunday;

*'At around 16:20 hours we took off from Auberive to attack a convoy near Bouillon. As we approached the target, we encountered strong concentrated anti-aircraft fire. The leading aircraft, flown by Horner was hit, caught fire and dived into the ground exploding on impact. Our own aircraft was hit repeatedly but we were able continue and attack the target. On leaving the target is was clear that our pilot was gravely wounded. We could see the blood pouring along the inside of the fuselage, but it was just impossible to reach him. We were flying low and loosing height, we eventually crashed on outskirts of a deserted village called Donchery. The observer and I lifted the wounded pilot out of the aircraft and carried him to the shelter of nearby bushes and dressed his wounds. The observer, Harris and I set on fire the remains of our Battle. We then searched a nearby farm where we found a hand cart and a tablecloth which we used to transport our pilot. Having made our pilot as comfortable as possible on the cart and with the cloth wrapped around him, we began walking away from the village. Pushing the cart, I remember we crossed a railway line over a small bridge and soon after reached a road which ran parallel to the railway and also a river which was a little further on. I am not sure, but I think the road led to Nouvion. After a while, our pilot became very distressed and became rather delirious. In one of his more lucid moments, he asked us to stop and rest for the night. At various times we called out to the French soldiers asking for help, they did not reply.*

These were not the only losses suffered. Number 103 Squadron which had also sent a section to attack the convoy at Bouillon reported the loss of two crews, both the result of the murderous flak. It would have been a sombre Auberive when the realisation that the squadron had lost two more crews. The loss of six crews within 24 hours would have been something that no one on the squadron could have ever anticipated. There was however one small consolation, the return of P/O Anstey. He could at least give a first-hand account of the raid and the fate of the raid leader, and importantly, what the rest of the squadron could expect to encounter when called upon to operate. The squadron was not required on the 13th, although they were at readiness. Strangely Auberive was not visited by the Luftwaffe bombers throughout the day, unlike Betheniville, home of 103 Squadron which was bombed early morning and again during the afternoon. The village of Mourmelon-le-Grand was badly hit, and a number of French casualties reported, the airfield, and the Battles of 105 however escaped the Heinkel's attention.

*The twisted wreckage of Battle K9353 HA-J flown by Flight Sergeant John Bland Horner. It was along the road seen in the top photograph that elements of the 2nd Panzer Division used to push towards the Meuse.*

*Sergeant Leslie Davies from Cardiff was the eldest of six children. He had always wanted to join the RAF. Aged 18 he fulfilled that ambition when he joined up in 1936.*

*The grave of Pilot Officer Frederick Bazalgette.*

**Sunday May 12th 1940**
*Fairey Battle*
*Mk.I P2183*
*Contract No :768880/38*
*Taken On Charge :30/11/1939*
**Failed To Return**
*Pilot: Pilot Officer Frederick Sidney Bazalgette 70790, RAF.* **Killed**
*Observer/Bomb aimer: Sergeant William Harris 560630, RAF. Returned to squadron.*
*Gunner / Wireless Operator LAC Harold Jones, 526398, RAF. Returned to squadron.*

Leading Aircraftman Jones and Sergeant Harris and their gravely injured pilot were still attempting to reach the safety of the British, or French lines. After spending the night resting, they once again attempted to reach safety, LAC Jones continues.

*The next day we moved a short way along the river but had to once again stop as the pilot was becoming increasingly weak. Towards the evening I walked on along the riverbank and found that the railway curved across the river, but the bridge had been blown. I was unable to get a response from the soldiers on the other side and I crawled across the wreckage of the bridge and was then captured by our French Allies!*

*After 2-3 hours arguing with the French officer in charge of the battery of guns, he finally consented to provide a small boat, and an escort of soldiers for my return to my comrades. By this time it was very dark, but I was able to locate the place where I had left my friends. Unfortunately, my pilot was dead, still lying on the cart. There was no sign of Harris so I and my escort returned across the river, where despite the noise of the French guns and German bombing I fell into a very deep sleep.*

Sadly 22-year-old Frederick Bazalgette had succumbed to his wounds on the night of May 12th. Frederick is believed to have been initially buried in a make-shift grave between the River Meuse and the railway depot of Nouvion-sur-Meuse. In 1941 his grave was found and identified, on his hand he still wore a ring with his initials, also found in the grave was a bottle with his name engraved. The body was subsequently buried in the local cemetery at Nouvion-sur-Meuse. For his actions, Jones was recommended for a non-Immediate award of the Military Medal by the Air Marshal, Air Officer Commanding-in-Chief British Air Forces in France, but in the event, this was downgraded to a Mention in Despatches. (*London Gazette* 1 January 1941).

The first replacement Battles began to trickle in on the 12th and 13th, these were Austin-built L5422 which arrived on the 12th, the following day Stockport built Battle P2360 arrived. Their stay was brief.

The Germans bombers returned to Auberive airfield during the morning of May 14th. At around 10.10 hours a formation of bombers caused some inconvenience when a bomb cut the main telephone line between the squadron and No.75 Wing HQ at Saint Hilaire-le-Grand. The German offensive was still gaining ground despite the heroic actions of the Belgian and French Armies. Things had taken a more serious turn of events on the evening of the 13th when the Germans crossed the upper River Meuse. This thrust effectively threatened the area of Rheims, and the airfields of the AASF. During the night, a series of courageous attacks by the French Airforce had destroyed the important Dinant Bridges, they had also attacked with some success a large German column on the Cenay-Dinant Road. With the Dinant Bridges destroyed, attention was switched to three recently erected pontoon bridges at Sedan.

The following message was sent to the No.75 Wing HQ for the attack on the pontoon bridges;

> *Cancel my ops No.662, 13.5.1940. Confirming telephone conversation at 0100hrs and 0110hrs with Group Captain A.H.Wann. Requirement is now to attack the three pontoon bridges which the enemy are reported to have built 153 degrees AR4 30 miles and 140 degrees AR4 37. Strength of attack four half sections. Aim of attack, to destroy bridges. Tactics left to discretion of formation leader but attacks should be made early as light permits. One flight of fighters to be detailed by OC No.67 Wing to operate in support of bombers. Method of co-operation to be concerted between 75 and 67 Wings. Enemy fighter opposition strong in neighbourhood of target.*

The following targets and times were issued to the squadrons of No.75 Wing, who would make up the 3rd and final attacking force. No.76 Wing would attack first, followed by No.71 Wing, a total of 71 Battles would be involved in attacking various bridges and advancing German columns.

| Detail | Squadron | Target | Time Over Target | Force |
|--------|----------|--------|------------------|-------|
| No.1 | No.218 Squadron | Column on road between Bouillon and Givonne | 15:35 hours | 7 Battles |
| No.2 | No.218 Squadron | River bridge Douzy | 15:35hrs - 15:45hrs | 4 Battles |
| No.3 | No.103 Squadron | River bridge Mouzon | 15:35hrs - 15:45hrs | 4 Battles |
| No.4 | No.103 Squadron | River bridge 2 miles West Sedan | 15:35hrs - 15:45hrs | 4 Battles |
| No.5 | No.88 Squadron | River bridge 1 mile north of Villers | 15:35hrs - 15:45hrs | 4 Battles |
| No.6 | No.88 Squadron | Column on road between Bouillon and Givonne | 15:45 hours | 6 Battles |

Auberive was attacked by a number of Do17's of II/KG3 at around 08.30hrs causing little if any damage. A follow-up raid was carried out a few hours later by He111's of I/KG55, once again little damage was reported. The French High Command had called for a significant show of force to try and stem the German advance around Sedan. Arrangements were accordingly made for the whole strength of the Allied bombers in France to be hurled against the Sedan bridgehead in a series of waves. Just after mid-day the few French aircraft available went into action. Attacking bridges and columns of troops, they suffered losses so severe that their remaining operations for the day were cancelled. Now it was the turn of the AASF who would attack between 15:00 hours and 16:00 hours. The Germans were fully aware of the importance of the bridges and quickly strengthened the area, ominously this would include Bf109 fighter cover. The 218 ORB is missing for May, the exact time the squadron departed Auberive is unknown and the individual targets selected for the crews is also sadly missing.

The identity of the crews selected to attack the bridges south of Sedan from low level and the German columns around Bouillon are not known. However, there is some evidence to suggest that the following pilots and Battles participated.

| Detail | Serial | Code | Pilot | Known Target |
|--------|--------|------|-------|--------------|
| No.1 | L5422 | HA-R | Flying Officer Crane | Meuse Bridges |
| No.2 | L5235 | HA-W | Pilot Officer Imrie | Meuse Bridges |

| | | | | |
|---|---|---|---|---|
| No.3 | P2360 | ? | Pilot Officer Buttery | Meuse Bridges |
| No.4 | L5232 | ? | Pilot Officer Harris | Meuse Bridges |
| No.5 | P2189 | | F/O Hughes | Column on road between Bouillon and Givonne |
| No.6 | K9251 | HA-K | ? | Column on road between Bouillon and Givonne |
| No.7 | L5192 | HA-P | ? | Column on road between Bouillon and Givonne |
| No.8 | P2192 | HA-E | ? | Column on road between Bouillon and Givonne |
| No.9 | P2324 | ? | Flying Officer Foster | Column on road between Bouillon and Givonne |
| No.10 | ? | ? | Sergeant Marchand | Column on road between Bouillon and Givonne |
| No.11 | K9251 | | Sergeant Owen | Column on road between Bouillon and Givonne |

What is known is that they flew into a cauldron of both light and medium flak as well as small arms fire. Tragically also a number of Bf109s of JG53. Despite the defences over both targets the crews pressed home their attacks meeting withering fire, it was inevitable that despite their courage it was just a question of time before the first Battle was lost. The sequence of losses is not known, but five crews were brought down by a combination of flak and fighters.

**Tuesday May 14th 1940**
*Fairey Battle*
*Mk.I L5232*
*Contract No: 540408/36*
*Taken on Charge :05/03/1940*
***Failed to Return***
*Pilot: Pilot Officer William Arthur Reynolds Harris, 41582 RAF. Returned to squadron.*
*Observer/Bomb aimer: Sergeant Norman Basil Herriot 580956 RAF,* ***Killed***
*Gunner / Wireless Operator:  Aircraftman 1st Class William Robinson, 633727 RAF* ***Killed***

The circumstances surrounding the loss of Battle L5232 are unclear. Reported to have attacked the Bridge at Wadelincourt it is believed to have been shot down by a Bf109 flown by Oblt Ignaz Prestele of 1./JG53. The Battle crashed and burst into flames 500 yards north-east of the cemetery of Sauville situated north of Le Chasne taking with it two of its crew. The survivor, twenty-five-year-old P/O William Harris in a letter to his mother in Southern Rhodesia wrote; '*intense machine gun fire, petrol tanks blew up, I ordered the crew to bail-out but got no reply'.* Only the body of AC1 Robinson was initially determined, the body of Sgt Herriot being severely burnt. It was not until 1947 the body of Norman Herriot was officially identified, both were buried in the cemetery at Sauville. Although severely burnt, P/O Harris managed to eventually return to the squadron. Born in Japan in 1914, he would be awarded a DFC in 1945 for his time with No.356 Squadron flying Liberators in the Far East.

*Aircraftman 1st Class William Robinson. He is buried alongside his crew mate in the Sauville Cemetery.*

Sergeant Owen never reached his allocated target. On route he encountered seven JU87 Stukas. In the ensuring clash, LAC Cranley in the rear gun position claimed the destruction of one JU87. It was not all one sided, Battle K9251 sustained yet more damage, this time more extensive. Three large cannon holes in the rudder, courtesy of an encounter with a Bf109 and another half a dozen bullet holes in the fuselage effectively meant K9251 was grounded immediately on return.

### Tuesday May 14th 1940

*Fairey Battle*
*Mk.I L5422 HA-R*
*Contract No: 540408/36*
*Taken on Charge :12/05/1940*
**Failed to Return**
*Pilot: Flying Officer John Frederick Ryder Crane 39858 RAF* **Killed**
*Observer/Bomb aimer: Not used*
*Gunner / Wireless Operator; Aircraftman 1st Class Thomas William Holloway RAF PoW*

The crew opting to fly without an observer due to the low-level nature of the attack are believed to have been shot down by Oberlt Wildred Balfanz of Stab I/JG53 soon after attacking the bridge at Wadelincourt crashing between Bulson and Noyers-Pont Maugis at around 15:40 hours. There was only one survivor, 23-year-old Thomas Holloway of Worksop who would spend the rest of the war a PoW.

*The wreckage of Fairey Battle L5422 HA-R flown by Flying Officer John Frederick Ryder Crane.*

132

**Tuesday May 14th 1940**

*Fairey Battle*
*Mk.I  P2360*
*Contract No :768880/38*
*Taken on Charge :13/05/1940*
**Failed To Return**
*Pilot: Pilot Officer Robert Thomas Lothian Buttery, 70894 RAF **Killed***
*Observer/Bomb aimer: Not used*
*Gunner / Wireless Operator; Aircraftman 2nd Class William Coates Waterston 630224 RAF **Killed***

This crew also opted to leave the bomb aimer behind, thus in all probability saving his life. Briefed to attack the Wadelincourt bridge over the Meuse they also fell victim to the deadly Bf109s of JG53. Oberleutnant Hans Ohly of I./JG53 claimed a Battle south west of Sedan on this date, which may have been that flown by P/O Buttery. The location of the crash site is unknown and the bodies of the two crew, 23-year-old P/O Buttery and 19-year-old AC 2nd Class Waterston were sadly never found.

**Tuesday May 14th 1940**

*Fairey Battle*
*Mk.I  L5235 HA-W*
*Contract No: 540408/36*
*Taken on Charge: Unknown*
**Failed To Return**
*Pilot: Flying Officer Arthur MacDonald Imrie, 40711 RAF **PoW***
*Observer/Bomb aimer: Not used*
*Gunner / Wireless Operator; Leading Aircraftman Alfred James Taylor, 540413 RAF **Killed***

Rhodesian born Arthur Imrie made a successful forced landing in a small valley at Thelonne south of Sedan after encountering the Bf109s of JG53. Sadly, his gunner LAC Alfred Taylor was either killed outright or succumbed to his injuries very soon after the bullet riddled Battle belly landed. Twenty-One-year-old Fred Taylor was educated at Clifton School, Worcestershire where he won a bursary to the Victoria Technical School. He became a Leading Aircraftman on his 21st birthday having travelled to France with the squadron in September 1939. Arthur Imrie had joined the squadron in June 1937 a month after the publication of his Short Service Commission in May. Tall, fair haired and good looking, Arthur was one of the squadrons

*Aircraftman 2nd Class William Coates Waterston. The bodies of both William and his pilot were never found. They are commemorated at Runnymede Memorial.*

*The unmistakable Flying Officer Arthur MacDonald Imrie and his crew, LAC Alfred Taylor, Wireless operator / gunner, and Sergeant Farmes Observer. Behind them is Battle K9273 HA-R. This was one of the oldest aircraft on strength having arrived in October 1938. It was one of the aircraft left behind during the retreat.*

more noticeable pilots, both Arthur and Alfred obviously had confidence in each other's ability as they had flown regularly as a crew since September 1939.

**Tuesday May 14th 1940**
*Fairey Battle*
*Mk.I  P2324*
*Contract No: 768880/38*
*Taken on Charge :22/04/1940*
**Failed To Return**
*Pilot: Flying Officer Donald Alexander John Foster 39655 RAF **PoW***
*Observer/Bomb aimer: Not used*
*Gunner / Wireless Operator; Aircraftman Timothy John Bryan 531862 RAF **PoW***

The above crew were detailed to attack the advancing German columns between Bouillon and Givonne. They too are believed to have succumbed to the Bf109s of JG53 crashing in the area of Haraucourt, however there is compelling evidence to suggest that the Battle was brought down by ground fire. Both crew members were taken prisoner, a German Radio broadcast on May 20th confirmed both had been captured.

Twenty-six-year-old Canadian, Flying Officer Foster was burnt to the hands and face necessitating a stay in hospital. The wireless operator, gunner Aircraftman Timothy Bryan was one of the few airmen on the squadron who hailed from neutral Southern Ireland, born October 1917 in Cork. Timothy Bryan would escape from his prison of war camp in 1942 and is understood to have been hidden by a French family he had befriended while at Auberive. Sadly, he was re-captured and spent the remainder of the war a prisoner. The young Irishman would be incarcerated in a number of unusual PoW Camps starting with Stalag XXID (Posen), followed by stays in Stalag VIIIB Lamsdorf and Stalag VIIID. This camp was created in 1941 as the base camp for a number of work-camps (*Arbeitskommando*) for prisoners of war working in the mines and industries of Upper Silesia. This was again followed by spells in Stalag XXIA (Schildberg), Stalag 383 (Hohenfels) and finally Stalag IIIA at Luckenwalde, Brandenburg, 32 miles south of Berlin.

During the frantic action on the afternoon of May 14th the squadron lost five crews to a combination of both flak and fighters. Six airmen were killed, with a further five made PoW. One injured pilot managed to return to the squadron. What of the remaining crews? The No.75 Wing ORB states that only one Battle returned to Auberive. This is where the confusion regarding the actions on this day originates. It is the authors belief that the six remaining Battles, all of which were damaged to varying degrees either returned to Auberive or more likely were obliged to force land close-by in still Allied territory. The squadron suffered no further casualties from this operation, which would suggest that the remaining Battles reached the safety of the Allied territory.

What of the survivors who returned, four individuals are known, each of them was recommended for awards. The first was Sergeant pilot, Charles Dancaster Owen (590620). He was a pre-war member of the squadron and one of the original 16 pilots that departed RAF Boscombe Down in September 1939. The citation reads;

*"On the 14th May 1940, whilst carrying out a raid on Bouillon, he was attacked by a very heavy formation of enemy fighters. Although his aircraft was badly damaged Sergeant Owen pressed home his attack and by his skilful manoeuvring materially assisted his air gunner in shooting down one of the enemy fighters and having completed his mission brought his aircraft safely back to its base"*

Surprisingly, the recommendation was never agreed, this brave young pilot would not wear the DFM ribbon so courageously earned. He would eventually be awarded the DFC in 1945 while serving with No.163 Mosquito Squadron, part of 8 Group PFF Light Night Striking Force. Two DFMs were however granted, the first was awarded to Welshman Leading Aircraftsman Edward Joseph Evans, his citation reads;

*"On the 14th May 1940, this airman was wireless operator air gunner of the aircraft which on a bombing raid, was attacked by a force of Me 109s. Although heavily outnumbered Aircraftman Evans remained cool and withhold his fire until his gun could be used effectively. He shot down one enemy fighter and damaged others, causing them to break off the engagement. His courage and coolness in the face of heavy enemy opposition were largely responsible for the success of the raid and the safe return of the aircraft"*

*Two views of Flying Officer Arthur Imrie's Battle L5235 HA-W. The valley in which the young pilot forced landed at Thelonne south of Sedan is clearly evident.*

Fellow gunner, Corporal James Drummond was awarded an immediate DFM on his return from this operation, he had already mixed it with the Germans on May 11th, now 3 days later he was in the thick of the action again.

> On May 10th, 1940 this Air Gunner took off in a low-level bombing raid on an enemy column near Dippach and in the face of intense anti-aircraft fire, he added greatly to the success of the raid befall use of his gun on enemy troops. On May 14th, when taking part in another raid, his aircraft was attacked by a heavy formation of Me109s. With confidence and great courage, Corporal Drummond engaged the enemy fighters and as a result of his accurate fire, shot down one and inflicted damage on others. His coolness and accurate fire in the face of repeated attacks were to a very good extent responsible for the safe return of his aircraft.

Acting Flight Lieutenant John Hughes would be awarded the DFC for his actions on both the 11th and 14th, he had been on the squadron since September 1937.

> "During a period in May 1940 this officer led many successful raids. On one day an attack on an enemy column at Dippach. Four days later he successfully pressed home his bombing attack on a enemy position, although attacked by a strong force of Messerschmitt 109s, but by skilful manoeuvring his aircraft he enabled his gunner to shot down one enemy aircraft. Flight Lieutenant Hughes has shown magnificent leadership as a flight commander and, by his coolness and initiative, has maintained the excellent spirit and moral of all his flight personnel."

It is hard to imagine what the atmosphere was like for the survivors on the squadron on the evening of May 14th, with five crews missing or lost. The squadron had taken a severe mauling, those crews lucky enough to have survived had either returned with a damaged aircraft or more likely force landed in Allied territory. In four frantic days the squadron had lost 11 crews, how long could the squadron and its crews go on.

Given the rapid success of the advancing German Army, and the inability of the BEF and French Army to halt them the squadron, or what was left of it would in all probability be required the following day. As usual the hard working and conscientious ground crews worked throughout evening and into the early hours repairing the least damaged remaining Battles. The surviving pilots and gunners probably still shocked at the carnage they had witnessed would have wearily gone to their billets knowing that they would probably be called upon to face the murderous flak and fighters the following day. It was the blackest day for the squadron thus far. On the morning of Wednesday 15th, the surviving crews assembled in the briefing room awaiting fresh orders, the morning turned to afternoon and still no instructions were received from No.75 Wing HQ. Air Marshall Barratt obviously shocked by the losses the previous day issued orders to the effect that his depleted Battle squadrons would not be used on further daylight operations unless it was crucial, it was a wise order. There would have been a collective sigh of relief from the Battle crews who having witnessed the slaughter of friends and colleagues over the previous few days, would now at least have a chance of survival. Dornier Do17s of II/KG3 made a return visit to Auberive around 07:30am on the morning of the 15th. A dispersed Battle was listed in the No.75 Wing HQ Records Book as hit and set on fire, the subsequent fire ignited the four 250lb bombs destroying the Battle. Thankfully, there was no casualties. The author has not been able to identify this Battle.

*Welshman, Leading Aircraftsman Edward Joseph Evans.*

Although the lull in operations was welcome there was another problem, such was the German advance that the airfields of the AASF were now threatened. Plans had already been made for such a situation, however very few would have believed that they would ever be issued. AASF Administrative Instruction No.28 arrived on the afternoon of May 15th, instructing the squadron of its immediate withdrawal from Auberive. Wing Commander Duggan assembled his surviving senior officers and quickly briefed them of the situation, time was most definitely not on their side, immediate action needed to be taken. All available MT transport would be utilised to move all essential equipment, spares, office documentation and personnel luggage. Additional MT Transport would if required be supplied by Wing HQ. Out at the dispersals, all air worthy Battles were to be made ready to leave, these too were quickly loaded with various equipment, some personnel, others essential. To add to the general confusion the airfield was again attacked at around 13:50 hours, possibly by Do17s of II/KG3 who had paid a visit in the morning. The squadron's new home would be La Ferme de Moscou at Rheges. It was a vast airfield, well camouflage with a large dense wood on its western edge, it also boasted an excellent landing surface. A decision would have to be made on what Fairey Battles were airworthy, and what would remain. The identities of those Battles destined to remain at Auberive are unknown, however four are, HA-P L5192, damaged on the May 12th attack, HA-E P2192, HA-R K9273 (this was previously coded HA-T) and finally P2189. A small rear party stayed behind salvaging what they could and destroying anything which may have been beneficial to the advancing Germans. Flying Officer Walter Shaw makes an interesting point concerning replacement crews and interestingly aircraft at this time;

*'Our airfield was very severely bombed every day by about 20 bombers escorted by Luftwaffe fighters. By then we were losing crews and replacements came to fill the gaps. We lost some aircraft on the ground as well, but we were able to get replacements. Eventually we had to move from Auberive to our satellite airfield.*

What was left of the squadron arrived at Moscou Ferme in dribs and drabs. Movement on the French roads was painfully slow, hundreds of civilian cars and horse drawn carts carrying thousands of evacuees slowly shuffled from the advancing Germans.

Adding to the congestion were hundreds of French and Belgium lorries and thousands of dishevelled and demoralised soldiers. Joining 218 at Ferme Moscou would be 103 Squadron, they had fared slightly better than 218 having lost just five crews since May 10th. The squadrons stay at La Ferme de Moscou was brief, within 24 hours the squadron departed to Lucien Farm at Rhèges.

Surrounded on three sides by dense woodland the airfield was basically a stubbled field. There were no buildings, and the billets were 4 miles away at Bray-Sur-Seine. To add to the problems there was no water and no electricity and limited telephone communication. On the 17th a number of pilots were dispatched to Amiens to collect 9 replacement Battles, one of those chosen was F/O Walter Shaw. He flew to Amiens in Battle K9323 with LAC Harry Fisher in the back. For some unknown reason, the pilots returned empty handed. On the flight back to Lucien Ferme, LAC Fisher spotted a formation of 8 Do17s flying 4 miles astern and proceeding at right angles to them. Despite F/O Shaws attempt to engage the Dornier's slipped away.

*Battle P2189 HA-E was one of the aircraft left behind at Auberive.*

*The victors and the vanquished. HA-E tipped onto her nose gives temporary cover to a German motor cyclist while his colleagues look on.*

*Fairey Battle HA-P L5192 seen here at Auberive. This aircraft was damaged on the May 12th attack.*

AASF HQ recorded the aircraft state as of mid-day on the May 17th; it was depressing reading;

## No.75 WING

| Squadron | Availability 12:00 Hours |
|---|---|
| No.150 Squadron | 7 Fairey Battles |
| No.88 Squadron | 9 Fairey Battles |
| No.103 Squadron | 6 Fairey Battles |
| No.218 Squadron | 3 Fairey Battles |

A number of pilots returned to Amiens on the 18th in the hope that the urgently needed replacement aircraft could be collected. One of the pilots was Kiwi P/O William Anstey who ferried back Battle P2313. There are no records found to confirm if all 8 Battles were collected. The frantic need for replacement aircraft is obvious given the table above, the squadrons had the crews, it was the aircraft that was needed. The following gives the AASF aircraft state as at 9 am on Saturday May 18th, 1940.

| Squadron | Availability | Available Crews |
|---|---|---|
| No.12 Squadron | 4 Fairey Battles | 9 crews |
| No.88 Squadron | 7 Fairey Battles | 12 crews |
| No.103 Squadron | 4 Fairey Battles | 11 crews |
| No.105 Squadron | 2 Fairey Battles | 10 crews |
| No.142 Squadron | 6 Fairey Battles | 14 crews |
| No.150 Squadron | 7 Fairey Battles | 15 crews |
| No.218 Squadron | 2 Fairey Battles | 8 crews |
| No.226 Squadron | 1 Fairy Battle | 12 crews |
| **TOTALS** | **33** | **91 crews** |

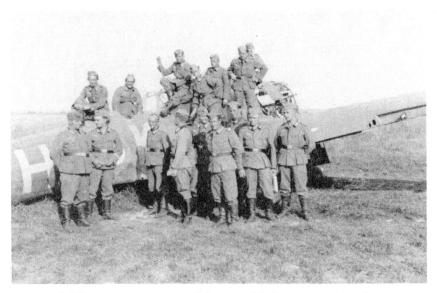
*Jubilant German troops celebrate beside Battle K9251 HA-K.*

The rapid advance on the ground on the morning of the 18th had the Allied commanders nervous, the Germans were moving in strength through the Gembloux gap and Sedan sweeping aside all opposition. As usual the French were requesting the intervention of the bombers of both the AASF and No.2 Group. Air Marshal Barratt who had previously halted all daylight operations by his Battle squadrons was now faced with a dilemma, should his depleted squadrons be deployed. In the end it was decided to use the Blenheims of No.2 Group.

However, the problems continued on the 19th when the French informed their British counterparts of two large, mechanised columns with infantry moving towards the Neufchatel-Montcornet road. It was clear to the British that the German intention was to cut the Allied forces in two and make a frantic push towards the coast. Air Marshal Barratt again turned to No.2 Group for help, however on this occasion it was refused. Given this and contradicting his previous orders Barratt had no choice but use his depleted Battle squadrons on a daylight operation. The order went out to his squadrons for a maximum effort at around 09:20 hours. The exact number of Battles deployed by 218 Squadron has never been established due to the lack of records, however three crews are known to have participated. New Zealander Pilot Officer William Anstey and his gunner AC Thomas were airborne at 10:00 hours in Battle P2313. They carried out a shallow dive-bombing attack on a convoy passing through Hauteville. This convoy was reported to include a number of mechanised vehicles and tanks. Diving from 7000 feet, P/O Anstey aimed his 4 x 250lbs bombs amongst the slowly moving packed convoy. Due to a barrage of anti-aircraft fire both he and AC Thomas were unable to observe the results. Also aloft was Flying Officer Walter Shaw in Battle K9323 flying with him was LAC Harry Fisher. They carried out a dive-bombing attack on a road near Conde village dropping 4 x 250lb bombs. The crew experience heavy ground fire from numerous vehicles hidden in trees. Smoke and fires were reported from both targets as the Battles turned for home. Also airborne was Sgt Owen in Battle P2315. Once again flying with LAC Patrick Cranley they carried out a high-level dive-bombing attack on enemy troops at Conde Village dropping 4 x 250lb. Light flak was plentiful and mixed with an abundance of small arms fire which emanated from all directions. Unlike many of the Battle crews their luck held. Apart from a few holes in the fuselage they returned uninjured. On leaving the target they had the satisfaction of seeing that they had started a large fire. Contrary to previous publications these three sorties dispel the often-quoted notion that 218 effectively did not operate after its drubbing on May 14th. The contribution may have been small but the effect on morale was massive given the confusion and disarray of the previous week. With the Battle squadrons back in the fight and quickly settling into their new airfields it was no surprise that the focus was now switched to nocturnal operations. Wing HQ issued Operational Order No.12 on the morning of the 20th instructing the squadrons to prepare for night operations. Work had already been carried out by 103 Squadron on the airfield, it is reasonable to assume that 218 Squadron would have helped. Number 103 Squadron were more experienced in nocturnal operations, their ORB clearly records the problems they encountered setting up the airfield for night operations. The height of the crops used to camouflage the airfields surface obscured the Glim Light flare path, so an electrically controlled flare path was set up using a generator taken from the chance light. This was designed with shielded lamps fitted onto small wire stands slightly taller than the crops. The flare path was capable of being dimmed and if needed switch off immediately by a master switch. It was an excellent piece of 'in-the-

*Battle K9251 HA-K. This shows that the Merlin engine was removed. It is not known if this was undertaken by the squadron prior to the squadrons retreat or by the victorious Germans.*

field' improvisation. That night a reported 30 aircraft of No.75 Wing carried out a sustained attack against targets at AR1 (Givet) AR2 (Dinant) AX1 (Eumay) between 02:00 hours and 03:30 hours. Their aim was simple, to cause maximum disruption and destruction to the Germans passing through these key points. Recent research can now confirm that 218 Squadron participated, flying its only night operation in May. Previous books have simply over-looked 218 Squadrons involvement primarily due to the lack of any documentation. The numbers of crews and their identity are sadly unknown, but the logbook of F/O Walter Shaw and Sgt Charles Owen again recorded their involvement. The squadron was tasked with attacking

*One of the squadron's aircraft left behind was the squadrons Miles Magister L5942 HA-G. It is not known if the aircraft was abandoned or had crashed. The photo was taken post May 24th, 1940. Note German soldiers.*

target AR2 (Dinant). Dinant was well known to the AASF Battle crews, situated in Belgium's Walloon Region, it was located on the banks of the Meuse River.

Flying Officer Shaw took off at 02:35 hours in Battle L5579 with him was Sgt Wynne and LAC Fisher. Conditions were not ideal, mist and haze made navigation to Dinant difficult. Eventually the crew reached the target area where they selected a heavily defended village slightly north of their primary objective. Three 250lb bombs were seen to exploded in the village which put up a considerable amount of ground fire, the fourth bomb exploded on a flak position. Flying Officer Walter Shaw was not quite finished, he attacked a few searchlights with his single forward firing machine gun, extinguishing two just for good measure. The crew reported upon their return what looked like ammunition exploding in the village. Sergeant Owen was airborne with Sgt Andrews and LAC Cranley aboard Battle P2215. They carried out a high-level dive-bombing attack on anti-aircraft and searchlights batteries in the Sedan area. For once the crew returned unscathed, the four bombs were successfully dropped and after a flight of 1 hour 50 minutes, the vast majority over enemy held territory Sgt Owen landed back at Lucien Farm, it was his fourth and last operation in France.

On Tuesday, 21st May the squadron received shattering news, they were to proceed to No.2 Base Area, Nantes leaving all their aircraft and equipment for disposal within the wing. It is understood that initially the squadron believed they were being pulled back for re-equipping. This would make sense, with only 8 fully trained crews and 5, possibly 6 airworthy Battles, the squadron was basically operating as a single flight. The following aircraft are known to have been transferred, the lack of records sadly means once again that the actual number of Battles and their identity will never be known.

| Serial | To | Fate |
|--------|-----|------|
| K9323 | No.150 Squadron | Returned to UK, passed on to 9 M.U 27/09/1940 |
| L5237 | No.150 Squadron | Returned to UK, damaged when overshot landing 11/09/1940 |
| L5579 | No.150 Squadron | Returned to UK, passed onto No.27 MU |
| L5514 | No.103 Squadron | Shot down attacking Chateau Roumont 26/05/1940 |
| P2315 | No.103 Squadron | Damaged attacking Ju87s, forced landed south of Paris 08/06/1940 |
| P2313 | No.88 Squadron | Blew up on take-off Les Grandes Chappelles 29/05/1940 |

Interestingly No.103 Squadron ORB records that they initially took over 218 Squadrons Battles, plus all the equipment and stores. Over the following few days everything was dispatched to Base area, this was supervised by 218 Squadrons equipment officer, F/O Taylor. On May 21st, No.103 Squadrons ORB records that it now had an impressive 31 Battles on strength. Just three days prior it was reported that it only had 4 serviceable Battles.

It would have been a somewhat demoralised squadron that began its journey to No.2 Base Area at Nantes, home of No.2 Aircraft Depot on the afternoon of the 21st. The brief euphoria of being back in the fight with successful operations flown on the 19th and 20th would have quickly faded as personnel kit only was loaded onto the transport by the now redundant air and ground crews. The squadron was instructed to move to the pre-war airfield at Chateau Bougon, 5 miles south-west of the Nantes, the home of No.98 Squadron. The author believes that in fact the squadron ended up at Saint-Aignan-Grandlieu approximately 8 miles SSW from Nantes and only 2 miles from Chateau Bougon airfield. Given the ever-changing situation on the ground and overcrowding at Chateau Bougon, plus the threat of bombing it would have made sense to try and disperse the ever-growing number of displaced RAF personnel away from what would have been a lucrative target. Importantly and affording some welcome cover was a large forest 1/2 mile from Saint-Aignan-Grandlieu. I have not been able to find any documents that record the activities of the squadron from May 21st, it is likely that once they arrived in the Nantes area, they quickly organised themselves into a functional, if but non-operational squadron. Thankfully, the weather was warm and dry making life somewhat more comfortable. Flying Officer Walter Shaw recalls this period;

*As a Squadron, we and the new replacements went from our satellite airfield to Nantes. We stayed in a tented camp — fortunately, it was summertime - with a view to eventually going back to Britain and exchanging our Fairey Battles for, we believed, American bombers. In the camp, about twice a week we had transport into Nantes. There was hardly any blackout, all the cafes were open, we found a lovely restaurant where we had hors d'oevres, langouste, salads, strawberries and cream and wonderful French wine. And this was while all hell was breaking loose, and the Germans were heading for Paris.*

To accommodate the squadron the N.A.A.F.I started to erect their tents on the afternoon of June 6th, one measured 60ft x 40ft, the other 40ft x 20ft with a kitchen. It was a step in the right direction. One piece of good news arrived on the 1st, Sergeant Neil Henry Thompson was reported a PoW by his parents. He had been shot down flying with F/O Hudson on May 11th. The gradual departure of squadron personnel began on June 2nd when 14 armourers were ordered to prepare for posting, it was the start of what would become an inescapable reduction in squadron personnel. News via the Red Cross arrived on the 3rd stating that Sergeant Peter Stubbs was alive and well, if but injured in a reserve hospital near Neuss. Early the following morning W/Cdr Duggan received a verbal message stating that the squadron was to stand-by to move back to the UK. Disappointedly, that same night another five armourers were posted to No.8 Servicing Flight. The very back bone of the squadron was unceremoniously removed from the squadron on the 4th. Given the situation, those in authority had decided that the squadrons personnel would be used to augment other units, 11 armourers were posted to No.21 A.D, plus 3 to No.16 Servicing Flight, surplus NCOs and airman were also posted No.21 A.D. In addition, 14 wireless operators/air gunners were posted to No.98 Squadron. These were to replace 98 Squadrons commissioned air gunners returning to the UK. It was not a welcome move, especially by the old hands many of whom had been with the squadron since Upper Heyford. The only good news was that once 98 Squadron had received replacements, they would return immediately to 218 Squadron. The squadron was not the only one to suffer, No.105 also started being stripped of its men. Both Wing Commander Duggan and Squadron Leader Keys of 105 Squadron attending a meeting at the Base Personnel Staff Office at 10am on the 5th where they were informed of the fate of both squadrons. To both Duggan and Keys dismay they were told that around 60 technical staff from both squadrons would have to remain behind to meet the current demands. Reluctantly they agreed, but still unhappy both requested a meeting with Group Captain Charles Carr, officer commanding No.2 Base Area. At around 20:00 hours both men put their case to the Group Captain, their question was simple, what could he do to prevent two fully operational squadrons from virtual disintegration. Sympathetic to their plight he promised to telephone BAFF HQ the following morning. A man of his word, he did, however the reply from BAFF HQ was blunt and to the point, *'Well aware of the consequences to the squadrons, but men were required and would need to be provided'.* To ensure there was no confusion and the order was carried out an Authorising Signal from B.R.S.O arrived stating *'Withdraw personnel from 218 - 105 Squadron as required'.* It was also on the 5th that Wing Commander Duggan received news that the boat to transport the squadron back to the UK had been ordered, yet another bombshell arrived from No.2 Base ordering that all cooks, butchers and remaining wireless operators were to remain behind. On the 6th the squadron diarist summed up the despair and frustration felt by all;

> *The probable posting of all the senior NCOs and other ground personnel is a virtual disintegration of the squadron. It is difficult to understand the reason for this as the squadron left the forward area fully operational believing it was too rapidly equip and return to the area of operations. Now, with only the pilots and observers and a very few ground personnel remaining it will take a considerable time before the squadron can operate again, and a further long period will elapse before the same co-operation between the ranks and between the sections can be completely re-established. It is generally felt that all the training and effort made by the squadron since it re-forming in 1936 has been wasted and particularly the period of waiting and training from September 1939 to May 1940 while with the AASF.*

Wing Commander Duggan had done all he could, the desperate situation in France had called for drastic measures. On the morning of May 7th, the squadron, or what was left of it consisted of 16 officers, 39 NCOs and 80 airmen, including two batmen who were in hospital. Just after 1 pm, a tired and emotional Wing Commander Duggan addressed the squadron. He thanked them for their hard work and explained that despite his tireless effort in trying to prevent the splitting up of the squadron, there was no choice. It was considered by the C-in-C to be more important that new units be formed at once, and as such, this action must be accepted cheerfully. With the lorries waiting the backbone of the squadron piled onto the trucks and set off, separating officers from NCOs and men, more importantly separating friends who had worked together for a period of 3 to 4 years. One such partnership was that of Flying Officer Walter Shaw and his gunner:

*I lost Leading Aircraftman Harry Fisher who was posted away, we said our farewells with a heavy heart. I later heard that unfortunately he was on board the Lancastria which was loaded with troops when the Luftwaffe came over and bombed it. It was sunk with a loss of 5000 lives, including Harry, but there was a news blackout on it because so soon after Dunkirk, it was felt it would upset the people*

There was some good new the following day, news was received that AC1 Arthur Ellis and AC2 Ivan Adams who were missing on May 11th were reported as prisoners of war. At the time, any good news was welcome. On the morning of June 10th, the squadron finally received orders to prepare to move that night, by noon all the tents had been taken down, and equipment returned to No.21 A.D stores. What was left of the personal gathered their personal luggage and kit and waited for the arrival of the transport. Frustratingly at 16:30 hours news from No.21 A.D was received stating that the move was postponed until 07:00 hour the following morning. There was nothing the squadron could do but try and find a place to settle down for the night, to add to the general gloom there was a possibility of rain, the first in a week. In anticipation of the early start the squadron was packed and already to leave by 06:00 hours when yet another message was received, departure was to be postponed to 15:00 hours. There was cause for celebration that afternoon when news reached the squadron that its first awards of the war had been won. A/F/Lt Hughes had been awarded the DFC, while Corporal Drummond and AC2 Evans had both been recommended for the DFM. More good news followed, Flying Officer Arthur Imrie, the tall blonde-haired Rhodesian was alive and a prisoner of war. The squadron moved off in lorries around 1.30pm on the afternoon of the 11th heading towards the railhead at Bougenais. What remained of the squadrons transport was handed over to No.21

Aircraft Depot. It was not until 17:30 hours the train departed via Nantes. It was at Nantes that Group Captain Carr, Squadron Leader Isaac Hodgson, No.2 Base Area HQ and Group Captain James McRae, officer commanding No.21 Aircraft Depot decided to say farewell to the squadrons returning to England. It was also at Nantes that the remnants of No.105 Squadron joined the train. Together both squadrons, tired and frustrated set off, slowly travelling throughout the night passing the beautiful French countryside not yet savaged by war or occupied. The train passed through Allencon and Argenton until finally arriving at Mezidon, Normandy at 09:40 hours the following morning. At Mezidon the train stopped for a few hours giving the occupants a chance to stretch their legs and be issued with rations. On the move again the train past the beautiful city of Caen then finally Cherbourg arriving at 13:40 hours. It was immediately obvious that there was utter confusion at Cherbourg, the whole port and surrounding area was packed with what appeared to be the whole BEF. Having entered the port area, the squadron was ordered by the Army Railway Transport Officer (R.T.O) to organise themselves at the quay side. At the same time the squadrons baggage was dispatched to another quay by the RAF Movement Control Officer! Once the mistake had been brought to the attention of both the RAF and Army the squadron personnel were on the march again, this time to re-join their baggage. It was becoming clear that no one had a clue what was happening, to add to the confusion, Cherbourg's Naval Harbour Officials were uncertain which quay the vessel taking the squadron home would birth. In the end both squadrons were told to fall-out and find somewhere to rest in an already overcrowded Dock Yard. Flying Officer Shaw recalls; *On the morning we arrived, we marched on to the quayside opposite a troopship full of army troops waiting to move off. They started giving us some abuse using rather unflattering language complaining bitterly about the Airforce not backing them. Our lads replied just as robustly telling them that they should be staying to fight. One or two actually pointed rifles at us, but fortunately their ship left.*

At around 19:00 hours the Harbour Master ordered the squadron to move to the end of the other quay and await the arrival of the Belgian Diesel vessel, Prins Albert. The squadron and its luggage moved to the quay and waited as ordered. To their dismay, the Prins Albert slid into the berth the squadron had only just vacated. After a few unflattering words aimed at the Navy the squadron trudged back to their original starting point and in fading light clambered board. Tired but thankful to finally be onboard, the squadron settled down for the unescorted night crossing, it was vastly different from their arrival in France just 10 months before.

# FRANCE 1940

## *Battles Left Behind*

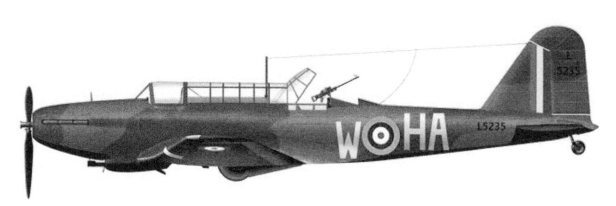

One of the most photographed squadron Battles was HA-W L5235 which was shot down on May 14th, 1940. In these photographs German troops take a few minutes to pose. These two photographs give a particularly good view of the landscape of the Ardennes. The aircraft crash landed at Thelonne.

*Above: Battle L5235. Note the dents along the leading edge on the starboard wing courtesy of field posts.*

*Below: A German solder sits in the cockpit, which only hours prior sat Pilot Officer A.M Imrie.*

*The following photographs show Battle K9325 HA-D flown by Flying Officer A.J Hudson. The Battle, and its three-man crew failed to return from the attack on St Vith on May 11ᵗʰ, 1940. Presumed damaged by flak the Battle forced landed in the fields close to the target area. The top photograph shows civilians taking an interest.*

*These two photographs again of Battle K9325 HA-D have curious local Belgian children looking inside the aircraft. The presence of youngsters would suggest that the area of the crash site was relatively safe and the fighting had moved quickly on.*

*A series of photograph depicting the shattered Battle P2189 HA-E. Above: Once again a magnet for German troop. Note the two bicycles. Below: A German motorcyclist views the wreckage while just below the port wing horse-drawn wagons are seen moving towards the front.*

*What appears to be German officers inspecting the wreckage. Note the staff car in the top photograph. Below. The rear fuselage of HA-E points towards the sky, the highest point in what appears to be a featureless landscape. The photos are believed to have been taken at Auberive-sur-Suippe.*

*The shattered wreckage of Battle L5422 HA-R. The aircraft was flown by Flying Officer J.F.R Crane who was sadly killed, the victim of an encounter with Bf109's of JG53. Above, a German soldier looks over the crash site. Note the French Army helmet on a makeshift grave. Below: the still smoulder wreckage of L5422 HA-R shot down May 14th, 1940.*

*Left: The wreckage of Battle L5422 HA-R in the trees. This photo gives a better view of the makeshift grave. Right. The Rolls Royce Merlin II from L5422. Below L5422 is seen here in amongst the trees next to the Noyers Pont Maugis Cemetery, Ardennes.*

*Austin built Battle Mk.I L5192 HA-P seen here abandoned at Auberive-sur-Suippe. Above: German troops obviously hard at work are photographed holding the tail fins of two 250lb bombs, the standard ordnance used on the Battle. Below : With the engine cowling and the propellor already removed it looks like HA-P was hurriedly deserted.*

*Two squadron abandoned Fairey Battles defiantly sit in long grass at what is believed to be Auberive. These battered and obviously long forgotten wrecks are HA-R and HA-P*

158

German troops clamber over Battle K9251 HA-K seen here abandon at Auberive-sur-Suippe. There is a possibility that the above photograph was taken at Moscou Farm after May 14th. Note the two German Henschel 33D1 trucks parked behind. There is significant damage to the horizontal stabilisers and trimming tabs, perhaps due enemy flak or fighters. Below, with the Merlin Mk.II engine removed.

*Stockport built Fairey Battle K9273 HA-R. Once again it is understood that this Battle was abandoned at Auberive on the squadrons move to Moscou Ferme in May. Once again German soldiers stop to survey the wreckage. Note the damage to the fuselage, a possible sign of bomb damage.*

*Above: Battle K9273 on what appears to be a wet day in May. Below : The Merlin II engine appears to have been removed in this picture which post dates the previous photos. K9273 had a long service with 218 joining the squadron in October 1938.*

# Chapter 8: June 1940 – 'Out of the Frying Pan'

*The vessel that brough both 218 and 105 Squadron home to England, Prins Albert.*

The squadron wearily began disembarking from Prins Albert at Southampton Docks around noon on June 13th. Towering over the exhausted evacuees was the imposing Netley Military Hospital, opened at the request of Queen Victoria for the troops returning from the Crimea. It was when completed the world's longest building. There was no fanfare or celebration for the survivors of the AASF Battle squadrons. The few survivors were just thankful they had escaped the desperate battles that were being fought over France.

A special train was scheduled to depart Southampton Docks at 13:00 hours, it had been laid on to take the squadron personnel direct to their new base at RAF Mildenhall, a pre-war regular airfield in the heart of Suffolk. However, the chaos that seemed to beset the squadron in France was present even back in England. What little the squadron had in way of luggage was off loaded and piled onto the quayside, it was not much. Both air and ground crews waited patiently for the order to move-out. The whole port seemed to be a mass of weary 'brown-types' being shouted at by angry looking sergeants barking orders. The customary *'Where was the bloody air force'* insults were still being aimed at anything in a blue uniform.

News soon reached Wing Commander Duggan that the departure had been put back an hour, this was followed by another order informing him that there would be yet further delays. Finally, at 17:30 hours the now fed-up and hungry members of both 218 and 105 Squadron finally departed, some unfriendly banter with the Army was exchanged as the train finally set off for Shippea Hill railway station on the Cambridge - Norwich line. Just before midnight the train pulled into the sleepy little station, situated a few miles north of RAF Mildenhall and RAF Lakenheath. The first to alight were the members of 218 Squadron with little in the way of personnel belongings and equipment leaving 105 to continue their journey to Thetford Station and RAF Honnington. In typical RAF fashion transport had been laid on in advance, once loaded the small convoy headed to Mildenhall. Despite the late hour food had been prepared in the dining hall, once fed the NCOs were allocated billets in the various huts and barrack blocks dotted around the station while the officers were given the more comfortable married quarters. It was the first time since the squadron left RAF Boscombe Down that squadron had slept in comfortable beds with hot running water and decent lavatories!

The following morning Wing Commander Duggan commandeered two offices in one of the massive pre-war hangars, they would be used as the squadron HQ. His first order was to send all non-essential personnel on three days special leave over a staggered period. For the first time since the German Blitzkrieg and what was to become known as 'Bloody May' the squadron could pause for breath, it needed too. Most of the squadron had been posted, losses had been grievous and to add insult to injury they had no equipment and no aircraft.

Now safely back in Britain the squadron battered but not beaten listened in dismay as Marshal of France Philippe Pétain delivered a radio address to the French people announcing his intention to ask for an armistice with Germany. On 21st June 1940, Hitler visited Compiègne, the site of the 1918 Armistice. In an act of arrogance and superiority the negotiations took place in the very railway carriage in which the 1918 Armistice was signed. Hitler purposely sat in the same chair in which Marshal Ferdinand Foch had sat when he faced the defeated German representatives. After listening to the reading of the preamble, Hitler left the carriage in a calculated gesture of disdain for the French delegates, and negotiations were turned over to Wilhelm Keitel, the Chief of Staff of OKW. The armistice was signed the next day at 18:36hrs (French time), by General Keitel for Germany and Huntziger for France.

The news that ACI Thomas William Holloway was safe and a PoW arrived on the 24th, sadly there was still no news about his pilot F/O John Crane. The surviving members of the squadron discovered their future on the afternoon of June 24th. The squadron received a signal from HQ Bomber Command stating that it was to be equipped immediately with the twin engine Bristol Blenheim Mk.IV medium bomber and be placed under the command of No.2 Group. The crews although trained on the single engine Fairey Battle were delighted with the prospect of converting to the Blenheim, it was a vast improvement over the hopelessly outclassed Battle. The following day at 00:35 hours the armistice and cease-fire went into effect, France had caved in.

Wasting no time, Wing Commander Duggan ordered Flight Lieutenant John Hughes DFC to work out a flying programme in anticipation of the arrival of the first Blenheim. The mood on the squadron was noticeably more buoyant, however it was short lived. On the 26th a signal was received informing the squadron that Wing Commander Duggan was to be replaced by Wing Commander Andrew Combe AFC of No.71 Wing with effect from June 28th, it was a bitter blow.

On June 26th, the first eight pilots were attached to No.17 Operational Training Unit based at RAF Upwood for Blenheim conversion, with the remaining pilots scheduled to convert on their return from leave on July 8th. The first four Blenheim's were scheduled to arrive on the 27th, Duggan immediately signalled Group HQ that their arrival was premature, the squadron had practically no ground staff, and maintenance equipment consisted of a few spanners and wrenches and there was no one with experience of the Bristol Mercury XV radial piston engines. In the signal he requested that delivery should be delayed until such a time the squadron could operate and maintain their charges. News was received the following day that Wing Commander Duggan's new posting would be No.3 School of Technical Training Blackpool.

The School, often referred to as Squires gate, was situated just beyond Stanley Park, located North East of the seaside town, it was not what Wing Commander Duggan had expected, but orders were orders. Since the signal of June 26th efforts had been made to contact Wing Commander Andrew Combe, when finally, they did manage to locate him he made it clear he was unaware of his posting to the squadron and until he

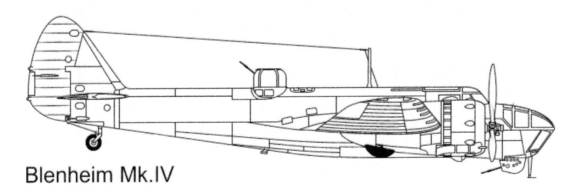

Blenheim Mk.IV

received his orders he was staying put! To add to the confusion the squadron had been signalled that it was to leave Mildenhall for RAF Oakington within days. Group Captain Roger Fields of No.71 Wing had been appointed station commander at RAF Oakington, however his whereabouts was unknown and until such a time he was found Wing Commander Duggan would assume command of RAF Oakington. Group Captain Fields had commanded No.71 Wing AASF in France and had been in the thick of the action with his two Battle squadrons, No.105 and No.150 and his two Blenheim units, No.114 and No.139 Squadron.

On the 29th, Wing Commander Duggan was flown in Miles Magister N3802 to Bomber Command HQ by Flying Officer Shaw to discuss the squadrons move and various issues about re-equipment. The same signal also confirmed that both 105 and 218 Squadron would operate from Oakington. There was one downside to the move, accommodation would be in tents until suitable buildings were completed. On the last day of the month Wing Commander Duggan made a visit to RAF Oakington, what he found was an airfield still under construction with many buildings unfinished and practically no creature comforts.

On Monday July 1st, 1940 the squadron is believed to have had the following pilots on strength.

| Wing Commander | Lewin Duggan Commanding Officer |
|---|---|
| Squadron Leader | James Gillman |
| Flight Lieutenant | John Hughes DFC 'A' Flight Commander |
| Flying Officer | Ian Richmond 'B' Flight Commander |
| Flying Officer | Walter Shaw |
| Flying Officer | Terrence Newton |
| Pilot Officer | William Anstey |
| Pilot Officer | Donald Smith |
| Pilot Officer | John Mitchell |
| Pilot Officer | Alexander Turnbull |
| Pilot Officer | William Wheelwright |
| Pilot Officer | George Agar |

| | |
|---|---|
| Pilot Officer | William Crosse |
| Pilot Officer | Rothes Meek |
| Pilot Officer | Johnson |
| Sergeant | Eric Marchand |
| Sergeant | Charles Owen |

Amongst the fifteen pilots only a handful had survived the slaughter of May 1940. It would be these men who would over the coming weeks guide the squadron back to operational readiness. With Oakington still incomplete and no squadron officially in residence a few squadron personnel arrived in readiness for its arrival. On July 4th, Pilot Officer Johnson the squadron equipment officer made an appearance, he was followed on the 5th by Flight Lieutenant Sanders the squadron Intelligence Officer and Flight Lieutenant Brill from No.71 Wing who would fill the post of Station Adjutant. More to the crews liking was the arrival of three new Mk.IV Blenheim's on July 5th, they were quickly joined Blenheim R3597 and R3674.

**No.218 Squadrons first batch of Bristol Blenheim Mk.IV June-July 1940.**

| Serial | Delivered | Maker | Contract |
|---|---|---|---|
| R3597 | 28.06.1940 via No.10 M.U | Rootes Securities Ltd | B.1485/39 |
| R3673 | 28.06.1940 via No.139 Sqdn | Rootes Securities Ltd | B.1485/40 |
| L9264 | 05.07.1940 via No.4 M.U | Rootes Securities Ltd | 551920/36 |
| P6959 | 05.07.1940 via No.80 M.U | Bristol, Filton | 774679/38 |
| P6960 | 05.07.1940 via No.80 M.U | Bristol, Filton | 774679/38 |

Two of the Blenheims were quickly dispersed while the third was unceremoniously pushed into a hangar after suffering a burst tail wheel on landing. The following day training started in earnest. Those pilots not part of the first batch selected for conversion carried out link trainer practice while the aircrews were given

165

*Poor quality photograph of Andrew Combe AFC with the Long-Range Development Unit.*

lectures on armament and signals. Over at Oakington, the tie line (B1489) to No.2 Group HQ and Willingham Exchange (Willingham 13) had been install and was working satisfactorily. Over the next few days pilots began to return from RAF Upwood on completion of their conversion, the first to return was Pilot Officer Alexander Turnbull on completion of his conversion course at No.17 O.T.U. Everything seemed to be moving in the right direction, however there was one pressing issue, spare parts and more importantly tools and equipment to service the Blenheims were almost non-existent. Mildenhall's resident squadron, No.149 did all they could to help but equipment specifically for the Blenheim was now a priority. With Wing Commander Duggan at Oakington, Squadron Leader James Gillman ordered New Zealander Flying Officer Ian Richmond to visit by air RAF Wyton and West Raynham in an attempt to obtain desperately needed spares. On the morning of the 8th the remaining pilots departed for RAF Upwood for conversion. That afternoon Wing Commander Andrew Combe made an appearance and introduced himself to the depleted crews. Andrew Nicholson Combe was born on July 7th, 1911 in Kensington, London into a wealthy banking family. He entered Cranwell in June 1930 and almost immediately started making a name for himself. He was awarded the Air Council Prize Cadet for two years and the prestigious Sword of Honour. In 1933 he was posted to No.201 (Flying Boat) Squadron based in Basra, there followed various postings in the Middle East until 1936 when he returned to England and completed an Armament Course at RAF Eastchurch on the Isle of Sheppey. In 1938 he was one of three pilots chosen to captain one of the three Vickers Wellesley of the Long Range Development Unit (L.R.D.F) under the command of Squadron Leader Richard Kellett to fly non-stop from Ismailia, Egypt to Darwin, Australian (7,162 miles) setting a then world distance record, for this he was awarded the AFC.

A planned day of flying training commenced at 10:00 hours on the morning of the 8th however it was short lived, the inexperienced pilots who were still getting to grips with the Blenheim managed to buckle the tail oleo leg on two Blenheims bringing training to a standstill. Just after midday 'A' Flights Flying Officer Richmond lifted off in the remaining airworthy Blenheim and headed to RAF Wattisham in the hope they could obtain two replacement oleo legs, his luck was in, the stores had three, all of which were speedily returned to Mildenhall. The recent issues of spare parts were discussed the following day when Squadron Leader Gillman drove to Oakington for a conference with Wing Commander Duggan. Without the spares and equipment, the squadron was effectively grounded. The promised delivery had still not materialised, and it was now becoming increasingly difficult to keep the three Blenheims airworthy even with the skill and dedication of the few ground staff. Heavy rain and almost zero visibility put pay to any flying over the next few days. The rain at least gave the mechanics time to carry out some urgently needed repairs. It was not until the late afternoon of the 11th that a number of cross-country flights were undertaken, the route being Mildenhall - Waddington - Sywell - Mildenhall. At 15:30 hours Wing Commander Combe AFC arrived by air once again, on the agenda was the lack of spares, things needed to be done and quickly. It was hoped that Combe could exert some pressure on speeding up delivery. The last of the pilots to

*Above left: Sergeant David Malpass. Seen here in France March 1940. He survived the French Campaign only to die over England in an avoidable flying accident. Above right: Sergeant Malpass' grave.*

undertake conversion departed for No.17 O.T.U on the morning Friday12th, they were Flight Lieutenant Hughes DFC, Flying Officer Shaw and Pilot Officers William Wheelwright, George Agar and the recently posted in Sergeant Donald Hoos. It was around this time the squadron were given some much-needed encouragement. It came from none other than Air Marshal Hugh Trenchard himself. Walter Shaw,

*We went to RAF Mildenhall and were called together one morning to be interviewed by Air Marshal Hugh Trenchard, who in fact had formed the RAF in 1918. He gathered us all and said that now we would start to be reunited and continue the war with zest against the Germans, which we did.*

A joint short cross country and map reading exercise was planned for the 13th, one of the crews briefed was Flying Officer Terrence Newton at the controls of Blenheim R3597. With the recent spate of serviceability problems, he was keen to add to his 71/2 hours flying time on Blenheim. Aboard were two observers, Sergeant David Malpass and Sergeant Joseph Routhledge. With favourable weather conditions both observers were eager to get some much-needed navigation experience and an opportunity to operate the rearward firing nose turret and the rear turret. The crew departed at 1055 hours on the now well used Mildenhall - Sywell route, at approximately 11:45 am F/O Newtons Blenheim was seen by a number of civilians flying extremely low over a farm on the Harrold-Sharnbrook Road, ten miles off the planned route. In making a pass over the farm the starboard wing tip was seen to clip the top of a 40-foot-high Ash tree damaging the aileron. The Blenheim started to bank to starboard which quickly steepened. Loosing height, the Blenheim struck the ground just north of Harrold disintegrating on impact, all the occupants were killed instantly in the ensuring blaze. The subsequent investigation by the Engineering Officer at Cranwell quickly determine that in a moment of high spirits the twenty-five-year-old had misjudged his height resulting in the deaths of all three. The finding of the Court of Enquiry reads:

> *'The accident was caused by the culpable negligence on the part of the pilot, involving disregards of orders. He flew unnecessarily low over a farm and in doing so struck a tree. The impact of which damaged his starboard wing and/ or aileron causing partial or complete loss of lateral control and the aircraft crashed into the ground.'*

The farm Terence Newton was buzzing was owned by Dennis Patrick Warren-Somerville, Terrence's uncle. Although born in Maresfield, Sussex, Terrence's had spent most of his adult life in Australia, where his parents lived in Melbourne, Australia. He was buried in Carlton Churchyard on July 18th, 1940, attending the funeral were his uncle and aunt. American Sergeant David Malpass was buried in Pembroke Dock Cemetery leaving a widow, while Sergeant Joseph Routledge was taken to his hometown of Penrith to be buried by his wife and family. Both Newton and Malpass had been with the squadron in France.

### Saturday July 13th 1940
*Bristol Blenheim*
*Mk.IV R3597*
*Contract No: B.1485/39*
*Taken on Charge :28/06/1940*
*Pilot Error*
*Pilot: Flying Officer Terrence Newton 39943 RAF* **Killed**
*Observer: Sergeant David Malpass 564042 RAF* **Killed**
*Observer: Sergeant Joseph Routledge 513919 RAF* **Killed**

On the afternoon and probably the result of the accident Wing Commander Combe finally took command of 218 Squadron on arrival from RAF West Raynham. There was no time to dwell over the loss, the following day the main party under the able charge of Pilot Officer John Mitchell set off by road for their new home, RAF Oakington. The squadron welcomed its first gunnery leader on the 15th, Pilot Officer Joseph Skinner who joined 'A' Flight. Much had been done in readiness for the squadron's arrival, no doubt due to the influence of Wing Commander Duggan who was still acting station commander. On the 16th the bomb store was completed and ready for use, it would become increasingly busy over the next few months. On the 19th Flight Lieutenant Hughes DFC flew to Wyton in the squadron Miles Magister to make arrangements for use of their Link Trainer. The squadron was now equipped with sixteen Mk.IV Blenheims most of which had been delivered direct from the factories. On the 20th, the first two Blenheims, P6960 and P6959 skippered by F/O Walter Shaw and P/O William Crosse were flown to RAF Wyton to have outer self-sealing tanks installed, these were collected on the 22nd by F/O Shaw and F/Lt Hughes DFC who had flown in two more aircraft for fitting.

Recent operations had tragically shown the necessity of self-sealing tanks. A flexible outer covering known as the 'Semape' were fitted to the 94-gallon tanks, they had proved successful without reducing the operational range of the Blenheim, also fitted at this time was armour plating for the oil tanks. Over the next few days, the training schedule was stepped up, with the increase in Luftwaffe activity over the south of England the threat of Invasion hung heavily over the country. In an effect to increase training two Avro Ansons, N5014 and N5010 arrived from Upper Heyford for the purpose of navigational training. It was not all flying, Squadron Leader Tom Pollitt started a series of lectures on the running and operational use of the Bristol Mercury Mk.XV engine. Not to be outdone the navigators were equally busy with a series of lectures by Squadron Leader Alfred Bax in the art of 'Blenheim daylight navigation'. Sergeant Charles Owen wrote-off Blenheim P6959 on a training flight on the 23rd. Leaving Oakington for a cross country flight the crew soon encountered a solid wall of low cloud which prevented the observer from establishing their exact location. After groping around for a break in the cloud they eventually chance upon the incomplete RAF Cheddington, Buckinghamshire. Sergeant Owen decided to land immediately however in his haste he misjudged his approach height, he undershot crashing through a large hedge resulting in the undercarriage collapsing. The crew clambered out dazed but otherwise uninjured.

**Tuesday July 23rd 1940**
*Bristol Blenheim*
*Mk.IV P6959*
*Contract No: 774679/38*
*Taken On Charge: 05/07/1940*
*Pilot Error*
*Pilot: Sergeant Charles Owen.*
*Observer: Unknown*
*Air Gunner: Unknown*


Some light relief was forthcoming on the 25th when F/O Shaw was chosen to fly Anson N5014 to RAF Wyton to collect two film production photographers and a Ministry of Defence photographer who had been given the job of taking stills for the forth coming release of *'March of Time'* a film about the Royal Air Force. Circling seven thousand feet above Wyton Shaw waited for the planned arrival of six Blenheims, unfortunately due to cloud they did not materialise. The photographers not wishing to waste a photo opportunity photographed a few massive clouds that menacingly drifted over Wyton, plus, much to their delight a number of inflight photos were taken of both Shaw and Sergeant Wayne at the controls of the Anson. For the next few days thunderstorms and heavy rain prevented the crews from becoming airborne, however the time was not wasted, classroom lectures and Link Training were put into immediate effect. The gunners were dispatched to a clay pigeon trap to master deflection shooting. A shot gun was purchased and fitted into a Bristol training turret to give the gunners further help. On Monday, July 29th two of the survivors from the carnage over France were awarded the Distinguished Flying Medal in a ceremony held at RAF Wyton.

Air gunners, Sergeants James Anthony Drummond, and Sergeant Edward Joseph Evans received their medals from Air Marshal Sir Charles Portal A.O.C -in-C Bomber Command. Both had been in the thick of the action during the desperate attempt to stop the German advance. Attending the ceremony were Wing Commander Duggan, officer commanding RAF Station Oakington and Wing Commander Combe, 218 Squadron Commanding Officer. Also present were Sgt Drummond's pilot and observer. Flight Lieutenant Hughes DFC and Sergeant Collopy. Sergeant pilot Eric Marchand and observer, Sgt Evans. On the same day, the squadron welcomed Flight Lieutenant George Newton from No.101 Squadron who would fill the vacant post of 'B' Flight commander. The last days of July were spent training, crews were now deemed sufficiently competent in navigation to be sent further afield. Two new routes were now being regularly flown, the first was Base-Northampton-Lincoln-Brough-York-Northampton-base while the other would see the crews heading west to Great Orme, a limestone headland on the north coast of Wales. The last day of the month was spent over Wainfleet Range, the squadron dropped a total of 108 bombs, results were reported as 'average'. By the end of July the squadron had received the following Blenheim Mk.IVs plus a short nosed Blenheim Mk.I for training.

*Sergeant Drummond receiving his DFM from Air Marshal Sir Charles Portal A.O.C -in-C Bomber Command. On the right is Sergeant Edward Joseph Evans.*

## Bristol Blenheim Mk.IV  Delivery July 1940

| Serial | Delivered | Maker | Contract |
|--------|-----------|-------|----------|
| T1863 | 15.07.1940 via No.27 M.U | Rootes Securities Ltd | B.1485/39 |
| T1864 | 15.07.1940 via No.27 M.U | Rootes Securities Ltd | 551920/36 |
| T1865 | 15.07.1940 via No.28 M.U | Rootes Securities Ltd | 774679/38 |
| T1888 | 15.07.1940 Via No.8 M.U | Rootes Securities Ltd | 774679/38 |
| N3563 | 16.07.1940 via No.38 M.U | A.V Roe and Co Ltd | 599371/36 |
| N3561 | 16.07.1940 via No.38 M.U | A.V Roe and Co Ltd | 599371/37 |
| N3585 | 16.07.1940 via No.38 M.U | A.V Roe and Co Ltd | 599371/38 |
| T1996 | 16.07.1940 Via No.27 M.U | Rootes Securities Ltd | 1485/39 |
| N3562 | 17.07.1940 Via No.38 M.U | A.V Roe and Co Ltd | 599371/39 |

| | | | |
|---|---|---|---|
| **L9306** | 24.07.1940 Via. 107 Sqdn | Rootes Securities Ltd | 551920/36 |
| **T1987** | 24.07.1940 Via 107 Sqdn | Rootes Securities Ltd | 1485/39 |
| **T1988** | 24.07.1940 Via 107 Sqdn | Rootes Securities Ltd | 1485/39 |
| **L9381** | 25.07.1940 Via No.4 M.U | Rootes Securities Ltd | 551920/36 |
| | | | |
| *L1137* <br><br>*(Blenheim Mk.I)* | 31.07.1940  Via No.27 M.U | Bristol, Filton | 5271114/36 |

July had been rollercoaster month, initially beset with frustration at the lack of spares and equipment, it was interspersed with moments of disappointment, amusement, and tragedy.  The departure of the respected and admired Wing Commander Duggan was a bitter blow, the nonappearance of not only the station commander, but also the squadron commander raised a few smiles in an otherwise dreary month.  The increased tempo in training, fresh new crews, and a steady supply of Blenheims meant that the squadron was almost ready to return to operations. It would be needed, in July alone No.2 Group had lost nearly forty crews on operations.

# Chapter 9: August to October 1940 – No. 2 Group

The first week on August was spent almost exclusively training, a high-level bombing programme over Wainfleet bombing range was flown the 3rd and 5th by both A and B Flights, 138 bombs were dropped in total, once again results were classed as average. On the 4th, F/O Shaw was given the job of ferrying F/Lt Hughes to Wattisham to collect a veteran Blenheim of No.107 Squadron, N6183. The aircraft would join 'B' Flight. A new pilot arrived from No.101 Squadron during the first week of August. Sergeant William Adam had served pre-war on No.18 Squadron and brought with him some welcomed experience of flying the Blenheim. There was cause for celebrations on the 6th, Flight Lieutenant John Hughes was presented with the Distinguished Flying Cross by His Majesty the King at Buckingham Palace. The announcement of the award had been published in the London Gazette back in June. The squadron welcomed P/O John Ross Stainton on the 6th, he would occupy the vacant Adjutant role. John Ross Stainton was born at Whitstable on May 27th, 1914, the son of a solicitor, and educated at Malvern College. He joined Imperial Airways as a trainee in 1933, serving his first postings at Alexandria, Khartoum and Brindisi. With the outbreak of the War John was in Rome, where he stayed until Italy entered the conflict in 1940. He made his way home by ship and joined the RAF. The squadron flew to West Raynham on the 7th for air firing practice over the Wash, a trip that would continue for the next week. The squadron's surplus gunners followed in the squadron's Anson. The Blenheim's Bristol gun turret was a rather basic design and proved

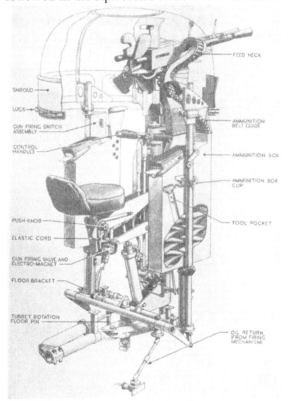

*The Blenheim's rear turret. The gunners now at least had a turret that afforded them some degree of protection from the weather. Power operated and equipped with a single .303 machine gun it proved just as ineffective as the Battle in fending off German fighters.*

reasonably easy to master, however the rearward firing .303 fitted into the nose for rearward defence was proving much more difficult. The observer had to lay on the floor of the nose and using rearward facing mirrors somehow aim at a fighter approaching from below and the rear. The whole concept looked good on the drawing board however in reality it proved extremely difficult to use. On conclusion of the day activities a total of 580 rounds had been fired, 274 hits were registered, once again the results were classified as 'average'.

On the afternoon of Thursday 8th August, the squadron was visited by the A.O.C of No.2 Group, Air Vice Marshal James Milne Robb, DSO, DFC AFC and Wing Commander Spencer. With the squadron almost ready to take its place on the front-line HQ 2 Group obviously believed a morale building visit was required.

That same afternoon at 1500 hours the squadron welcomed Squadron Leader Charles House from No.17 Operational Training Unit, he would assume command of 'A' Flight from the soon to be departing F/Lt Hughes DFC. Another Air firing exercise was flown on the 10th, it was a disaster, over 8400 rounds were expended the majority of which were from the rearward firing nose turret, only 42 hits were registered, a worrying 2% accuracy rate. With the squadron now almost totally trained on the Blenheim, the trusty old Avro Anson which had proved invaluable for training and ferrying crews were returned to their original units at RAF Upper Heyford departing on the 12th.

## Avro Anson Mk.I Training Aircraft

| Serial | Delivered | Maker | Contract |
|--------|-----------|-------|----------|
| N5010 | 25/07/1940 | Avro, Chadderton | 766119/38 |
| N5014 | 25/07/1940 | Avro, Chadderton | 766119/38 |

On late afternoon of the 14th instructions were received from 2 Group HQ that the squadron was to carry out training 'Sweeps' over the North Sea the following day. 'A' Flight was given the task, weather permitting. There was an air of excitement throughout the squadron when at 0930 hours the following morning Squadron Leader Charles House departed RAF Oakington in Blenheim P6960, five minutes later Flying Officer Walter Shaw was airborne in L9381, the last crew scheduled to depart at 0940 hours was Canadian Pilot Officer Donald Smith, but this was cancelled just before take-off as the Blenheim developed engine trouble. For the next two hours both crews kept a keen eye on any movement above, and below. The whole trip was an anti-climax, nothing was observed, but the effect on morale was infectious. Over the next few days the intensity of training was stepped up, both 'A' and 'B' Flights were airborne constantly, cross country flights, bombing exercises, long range navigation sorties over the Irish Sea and another North Sea sweep was flown, pressure was on all the squadron personnel to become operational. On the 18th 'B' Flight were airborne on a formation exercises when tragedy once again struck. Pilot Officer Alexander Turnbull recalls the events that cost the squadron two crews.

*Flight Lieutenant Newton, my acting flight commander, ordered me to lead the formation of four aircraft. The first three aircraft were to fly in vic and he himself was to fly at a distance directly behind me, as if leading a second section in box formation. He was to observe the formation and give orders to any member in it, as he thought necessary by RT. He asked me to fly at a reasonable height and to carry out turns increasing in steepness up to a rate three. Pilot Officers Wheelwright and Agar were to interchange in positions, No.2 and No.3. Before taking off, I made contact with all other members by RT and remained in contact with them up to the time of the collision. From the start, I climbed slowly up to 4,000-5,000 feet, by which time the other members had joined the formation and remained at this height throughout the flight. I carried out various turns, first rate 1, then a rate 1 1/2 and finally a rate 2 1/2. Pilot Officer Wheelwright, who at first was flying in No.2 position and latterly in position No.3 sometimes lost the formation in the turns. Flight Lieutenant Newton throughout the whole flight remained at a distance of about 250 yards from me. Ongoing into a left-hand turn at a rate 1 increasing to rate 2 1/2 I lost sight of P/O Wheelwright but concluded that he was underneath my port wing. I had almost completed the turn when a shout from my air gunner caused me to look backwards through my port 'blister'. I saw one aircraft diving to the ground followed by a trail of smoked another spinning slowly downwards, apparently inverted. My first thoughts were they had been shot down, so breaking off formation, I searched the sky for other aircraft for about 10-15 seconds. On looking downwards again, I was just in time to see the second aircraft hit the ground, still upside down. My height at the time of the accident was a little over 4000 feet.*

*The graves of two airmen who lost their lives on Sunday 18th August, 1940. Left: Aircraftman 1st Class Robert Harrison buried in the churchyard at Longstanton, Hampshire. It is understood that he was only flying on the fateful sortie having worked on one of Blenheim T1929 engines only hours before take-off. Right: Sergeant Robert Clapperton of Edinburgh, Scotland.*

Both aircraft crashed near Canterlupe, Farm, Grantchester, at approximately 11:45 hours, there were no survivors from either Blenheim. Flight Lieutenant George Newton was at the controls of Blenheim Mk.IV T1929, his four man crew comprised of Sergeant David Dennis, Observer and air gunner William Smith, also airborne with the crew was 23-year-old flight mechanic, Leading Aircraftman Robert Harrison. Their bodies were pulled from the smouldering wreckage. The other crew involved were skippered by Pilot Officer William Wheelwright who was flying Blenheim L9264, with him was 22-year-old Sergeant Observer Robert Clapperton and air gunner Sergeant John Bilton.

Unlike T1929, their aircraft did not catch fire, it simply disintegrated when it hit the ground. Canadian born Wheelwright had been granted short service commission as an Acting Pilot Officers on probation March 4th, 1939.

### Sunday August 18th 1940
*Bristol Blenheim*
*Mk.IV T1929*
*Contract No :1485/39*
*Taken on Charge: 03/08/1940*
*Collision*
*Pilot: Flight Lieutenant George Edward Newton, 37824 RAF,* **Killed.**
*Observer: Sergeant David Wesley Dennis, 755456 RAFVR,* **Killed.**
*Wireless Operator/Gunner: Sergeant William Leslie Smith, 900116 RAFVR,* **Killed.**
*Flight Mechanic: Aircraftman 1st Class Robert Hawley Harrison 911733 RAFVR* **Killed.**

**Sunday August 18th 1940**

*Bristol Blenheim*
*Mk.IV  L9264*
*Contract No : 551920/36*
*Taken On Charge: 05/07/1940*
*Collision*
*Pilot: Pilot Officer William Brian Wheelwright, 41763 RAF,* **Killed**
*Observer: Sergeant Robert White Clapperton, 530058 RAF* **Killed.**
*Wireless Operator/Gunner: Sergeant John Norman Bilton, 936831 RAFVR,* **Killed.**

The rest of the days flying programme was immediately cancelled as Oakington only fire tender was sent to the scene of the crash. The news of the accident stunned not only the squadron but the whole station. To lose two crews in such tragic circumstances was particularly hard especially after all the weeks of training. One can only speculate on the mood in the various messes that night.

Perhaps in an effort to maintain moral, the following day the squadron finally become 'Operational'. No.2 Group signal Ops 913 was received informing the squadron that one section would be required for operations and two battle sections would be on one hour standby from dawn in case of invasion. There was an air of excitement throughout the whole squadron. 218 Squadron was finally back in the front line, it had been a tremendous effort by the everyone involved.

The following morning there was an air of excitement throughout the squadron, it was an important day in the history of the squadron. The first aircraft aloft was 'B' Flight's Blenheim T.1996 HA-S at 0530hrs, at the controls was a 218 doyen, New Zealander Flight Lieutenant Ian Richmond. His target was Vlissingen aerodrome situated at the southern end of Walcheren island, south west Holland. At the time it was the home of the Dornier Do18 equipped Kü.Fl.Gr. 406 and the more dangerous, Bf109 equipped 6./JG 54. Five minutes later, 'A' Flight commander, Squadron Leader Charles House was aloft in T.1990 HA-J, his target was the airfield De Kooy located 38 miles North of Amsterdam. Both were armed with 4 x 250lb bombs, two with 11 second delay, the remainder 2 hours. Flight Lieutenant Richmond managed to locate and bomb his target from 14,000 feet without trouble. Squadron Leader House was obliged to return due to insufficient cloud cover, he brought his bomb load back to Oakington. In the afternoon it was the turn of 'A' Flight's Sergeant Gerald Clayton aboard T1864 HA-B. The all NCO crew departed at 14:20hrs, he was tasked with attacking the airfield at Haamstede, located on the tip of the Island of Schouwen, at the time it was the home of 4./JG54. Once again cloud prevented the completion of the operation.

The planned operations for the 20th were cancelled, thus it was back to flying training. 'A' Flight were over Wainfleet bombing range while 'B' Flight were given a navigational exercise. A formal Court of Inquiry into the accident on the 18th began under the Presidency of Wing Commander Denis Hensley Barrett of No.40 Squadron. A member of the court was Flight Lieutenant John Hughes DFC and Oakington's Engineering Officer, Flying Officer Harold Mathews also attended. The squadron was again in action on the morning of the 21st, when three 'B' Flight crews were detailed for another daylight sortie against German airfields. There was some excitement just before take-off, when a 'Red' air raid warning was received. Fortunately no enemy aircraft were seen, but in view of the ever present danger Wing Commander Duggan, Oakingtons still incumbent base commander immediately ordered that all ground transport vehicles that

*This is believed to be a photograph of the then Flight Lieutenant Charles House wedding to Dorothy Walker on Saturday 23rd October 1937 at the Salehurst Parish Church. Charles lived off the station preferring stay in the Lion Hotel situated in the High St at Ramsey, Huntingdonshire*

had up until recently been parked neatly outside the hangars be dispersed to a distance no less than 100 yards from the hangars and petrol dump.

The attacks on German airfields had begun in June before the main Battle of Britain had started. With the German occupation of their newly won airfields, it was no surprise, especially to the squadrons of 2 Group that something had to be done to make their stay as uncomfortable as possible. It would be the responsibility of the Blenheim Boys to cause as much interference and mayhem as possible. With the Luftwaffe throwing everything they had at destroying the airfields of No.11 and 12 Group Operational Instruction No.38 dated July 3rd, reached the squadrons, it read.

*'The enemy are using landing grounds in France, Belgium and Holland. The intention is to destroy as many aircraft on the ground as possible thus forcing the enemy to withdraw. Aircraft are to be escorted by fighters, or sections or individual aircraft using cloud cover when definite information is received from fighter reconnaissance'*

Number 218 Squadron would not be alone, they were joined by six other squadrons, the crews were fully aware that the task ahead of them was fraught with danger.

The first of the three Blenheim's away from Oakington departed at 10:55hrs skippered by Sergeant Charles Owen. His target was the airfield at Ypenburg, located 4 miles south east of Den Haag. Within five minutes fellow NCO, Flight Sergeant Hoos was airborne in Blenheim P.6959. Donald Hoos was given the German airfield at Brugge, situated 12 miles east of the town that bore its name. Like the previous day's operation, the weather would be the deciding factor in any success. Sergeant Owen wisely decided to abandon his attack, the expected cloud cover was simply insufficient to continue. Sergeant Hoos was forced to attack a target of opportunity near Stene south of Ostend due to lack of cloud over his primary target. He dropped his 4 x 250lb + 12 x 40lb bomb load from 6000ft meeting spasmodic flak. It was the turn of Pilot Officer Alexander Turnbull at 1125 hours, he was aloft in Bristol Blenheim L9306. He and his crew were more fortunate, scattered cloud at various heights meant that he could with some safety reach his attended target, the home of I./JG51, De Kooy airfield. He attacked from the lofty height of 12,000 feet, unsurprisingly the results were unobserved.

The bodies of four of the crew killed on the 18th were buried at Long Stanton (All Saints) Churchyard while their comrades were over the continent. Pilot Officer William Wheelwright, Sergeants Robert Clapperton, David Dennis and Aircraftman 1st Class Robert Harrison were laid to rest. The Bearer Party and Escort Party were provided by the station and squadron while the Attending Party consisted of 3 officers from the squadron and one officer and 16 other ranks from the 6th Royal Sussex Regiment. Flight Lieutenant Newton was buried on the 22nd at Barrowby (All Saints) Churchyard, Lincolnshire, Londoner Sergeant Smith was taken home to Streatham Park Cemetery and buried on August 25th, he was just 19 years old.

The squadron lost two of its longest serving pilots on 21st, in but temporarily. Pilot Officer John Mitchell and Pilot Officer William Anstey were both attached to RAF Upwood for dual training on the Blenheim. Twenty-five-year-old John had up until recently held the post of Squadron Adjutant. William had just returned from a month-long spell in Littleport Hospital, he was still not fully recovered even on his return. However, the slender built New Zealander was keen to get operational and readily agreed to go. After obtaining his private pilot licence he was accepted for military training at the RNZAF base at Wigram where he graduated in June 1939. Arriving in Britain in August 1939 he was posted to the Avro Anson equipped No.52 Squadron based at RAF Uxbridge. In November he was briefly posted to the Fairey Battle equipped No.98 squadron based at Hucknell before his arrival on No.218 Squadron on November 29th, 1939.

It was the turn of 'A' Flight to operate on the 23rd when again three aircraft were given individual targets. On the Battle Order was 'A' Flight Commander, Squadron Leader Charles House who with his crew, Observer Sergeant Percy 'Pete' Lefrevre and gunner Sergeant John Howard lifted off from Oakington's grass runway at 11:35 hours, their target was Bruges airfield. The crew's gunner takes up the story;

*'We were returning to England after completing our mission, due to circumstances beyond our control we were off course and flying in cloud by wireless bearing. The cloud cover broke and we were left in clear air our position then being south of Dunkirk. We were immediately subject to a heavy barrage of light flak, short afterwards we were engaged by three Me109 fighters. We held our own for a time but eventually we were hit in the port engine. I think it was light flak. The aircraft burst into flames. Communication in the aircraft was impossible but it seemed that S/Ldr House intended us to resort to our parachutes. I had great difficulty in leaving the machine but succeeded at a height of 800 feet. After leaving I saw no parachutes open and have every reason to believe that S/Ldr House and the Observer, Sgt Lefevre were in the machine when it crashed in flames. I was not allowed near the crash but from a distance it appeared to be scattered over a wide area, it would seem impossible for anyone to have survived it. The position of the crash was approximately 3 miles south of Calais'.*

Amazingly there was a witness to the events that unfolded. Mr Sainsart, the president of the Aero-Club of Calais reported that ' *A British aircraft was shot down on Friday 23rd at about 15:00 hrs at St Tricat, 6 miles south west of Calais. The aircraft was attacked over the forest of Guines by Messerschmitts and caught fire. One flyer remained with the aircraft and was burned, one jumped by parachute and made prisoner while the other likely jumped but fell into a tree in the commune of Hames-Bouches and was badly wounded. He was taken to the German Hospital at Gunes were he died the following day. The dead airman was buried at the scene of the crash by the Germans'*

Sergeant Howard was the first to leave Blenheim T.1990 and was quickly captured. He was taken by the Germans to the house of Mr Calais of Tricat, here he was initially questioned. Obviously in a state of shock he spoke nervously about his wife and child. He was lucky, other than a slight wound above his right eye, he was shaken but alive. The critically injured Squadron Leader House was taken from Hames-Boucres to Guines where he died in the German Field Hospital. His body was moved to the cemetery Chapel where he was placed in a coffin and subsequently buried. Hopelessly lost the crew had unknowingly almost reached the safety of the English coast but had for reasons unknown turn back towards France. The aircraft had been plotted and fixed by M/F and D/F on four separate occasions, twice over France, once over the English Channel and finally at 14:41 hours near Dungeness.

### Friday August 23rd 1940
*Bristol Blenheim*
*Mk.IV  T1990*
*Contract No : 1485/39*
*Taken On Charge : 03/08/1940*
*Enemy Action*
*Pilot : Squadron Leader Charles Constantine House, 32197 RAF **Killed***
*Observer : Sergeant Percy Thomas Lefevre, 516225 RAF **Killed.***
*Wireless Operator/Gunner: Sergeant John Howard, PoW*

Flight Lieutenant Walter Shaw followed close on the heels of his flight commander; he was tasked to attack the aerodrome at Ypenburg. The crew managed to reach their intended target but, on this occasion, the cloud proved their undoing, a solid blanket of cloud obscured the target. Hoping for a break in the cloud he circled the target at 4000 feet for twenty minutes before Shaw finally abandon the operation. Surprisingly, he met no opposition from either flak or fighter. It was the turn of 'A' Flights Deputy Flight Commander, Flight Lieutenant John Hughes DFC to depart at 14:45 hours. The crew which included the recently decorated Sergeant James Drummond DFM were given Antwerp airfield to attack. The crossing of the North Sea went without incident however as the crew groped their way inland, they started to encounter a wall of solid cloud. Undeterred they flew on, more in hope than judgement. Unfortunately, on reaching the target area the cloud was down to 1000 feet making any attack on the airfield suicidal. From an operational perspective, the day's activities were a total failure, two failed attacks and the loss of a flight commander. Once again, an air of despondency embraced the crews, it was becoming all too familiar!

The squadron was not required on the 25th, this did not mean it was idle, both flights were active. 'A' Flight were given instrument flying, perhaps due to the circumstances surrounding the loss of Squadron Leader House the previous day. While 'B' Flight were out on a cross country exercise. The planned trip to the Wainfleet Bombing Range had to be cancelled, due to the number of live unexploded bombs on it!! The squadron gunnery leader P/O Skinner attended a group Gunnery Officers Conference held at RAF Wyton on the morning of the 25th. He had the opportunity to request gunnery officers should be sent on a wireless operator's course, he believed it made operational sense that if trained the gunnery officer could fill in either roles. The squadron welcomed Sergeant Ronald Read and crew on the 25th, they were allocated to 'A' Flight. Six aircraft were required on 1-hour readiness (Stand-by-one) from 0450 hour to 0830 hours, these hours played havoc on the everyone's nerves. The crews often spent the time out at their dispersal reading books or newspapers, some of the more energetic types would play cricket or kick a ball about, anything to take their mind off the waiting. That night Bomber Command bombed Berlin for the first time in the war. Damage was slight and nobody was killed, but it came as a loss of face for Hermann Göring, who had boasted that Berlin would never be bombed. In retaliation, an enraged Hitler immediately switched the attacks directed against RAF Fighter Command airfields and authorised the bombing of London. This decision would have far reaching consequences not only of the Battle of Britain but the air war. The following day the squadron was required to provided three crews from both flights for operations. B Flights Sergeant Charles Owen was first away in Blenheim P6959 at 0950 hours, he was tasked to bomb Schellingwoude a former Dutch Naval Air Station located east of Amsterdam. Built on

*The grave of Squadron Leader Charles House at Guines Communal Cemetery, France.*

the artificial island of Zeeburg it housed a number of German maritime flying units equipped with both the Heinkel 115 and Dornier 18. Next away was New Zealander Flight Lieutenant Ian Richmond who was given the airfield at Schipol to attack, he and his crew departed Oakington at 1010 hours. Schiphol was at the time the home of the Heinkel He111 equipped Kampfgruppe 126. Immediately behind was 'B' Flight's Sergeant Geoffrey Morley and crew in Blenheim L9308, this crew undertaking their first operation was given the airfield at De Kooy. Both Richmond and Owens were unable to complete their operation due to insufficient cloud, Morley was more successful. He dropped his mixed bomb load from 6,000ft, in doing so he was greeted by a spirited wall of light flak from the airfield defences. During the afternoon, the important tie line connecting Oakington Operations Room to No.2 Group HQ was finally installed and fully operational. The arrival of Bristol Blenheim Mk.IV L8848 from No.XV Squadron on the afternoon of the 26th brought the squadrons total strength to twenty aircraft, eight per flight plus four in reserve. It was the turn of "B" Flight to welcome a new crew on the 26th. The recently promoted P/O Ross Mansfield arrived along with his observer, P/O Hugh Magee.

With no operations planned the for the next day the squadron looked forward to the arrival of an E.N.S.A concert party the following evening. Entertainment was increased when Oakingtons very own band made their debut performance, the evening by all accounts was a total success and did much to improve morale. The weather intervened on the 28th, the planned operations were again cancelled.

Airfields were again the priority on the 29th, the squadron detailed and briefed six crew, three from each flight. The first crews away were 'A' Flight's Pilot Officer William Crosse and Sergeant William Adam. This was P/O Crosse's first operation, he was tasked with attacking St Omer while Adams was given Merville airfield located 20 miles west of Lille, a place that was still fresh in the memory of the survivors of the AASF. Both sorties were unsuccessful due to insufficient cloud. 'B' Flights Pilot Officer George Agar and Sergeant Donald Hoos were next away, they were given Vlissingen and Brugge aerodromes to attack. Insufficient cloud once again prevented completion; both were back at Oakington within 80 minutes. The final two sorties were scrubbed.

A fighter affiliation exercise was panned for late afternoon, twelve squadron Blenheims were to participate, but in the end only six 'A' Flight crews departed for RAF Duxford. The plan was for the Czechoslovak-manned No.310 Squadron to try and attack various boxed formations. The exercise did not start well, Blenheim T1863 was declared unserviceable on arrival. As it turned out the whole exercise was a failure, the station commander at Duxford Group Captain Alfred Basil Wood-Hall was unwilling to spare his desperately needed fighters.

Since the squadrons arrival at Oakington the facilities had been rather basic. Contractors were still busy on the airfield and there was still much to be done to bring the whole station up to operational readiness. A step in the right direction was the squadrons move to the recently built offices on the southern side of the hangers at the end of August. With the squadron at full strength the few small offices originally allocated to them had become overcrowded. These new offices meant that the Stores, Maintenance and Armament sections could occupy the offices on the northern side without hindrance while the day to day running of the squadron could be conducted from the more spacious new offices.

That night the first official entertainment was given by the Officers Mess in the form of a Sherry Party. In attendance were officers from the Cambridge University Officers' Training Corps (UOTC), Colonel and Mrs Murray, Colonel Wannup, Lieutenants Cory Dixon, Cutts and Hodgson. There was also an element of divine intervention in the shape of Reverends Godchild and Leaney. With pre-war pomp the evening went according to plan, the station band were given centre stage and if the reports are accurate performed splendidly! A new Engineering Officer was to have arrived on the 30th, P/O Richard Dick-Larkam was to take over the responsibility of maintaining the squadrons aircraft, however for some strange reason he did not arrive. The last two days of August were spent carrying out yet more cross country and low flying exercises, it was an anti-climax. Only seventeen operations had been flown, of which only four were

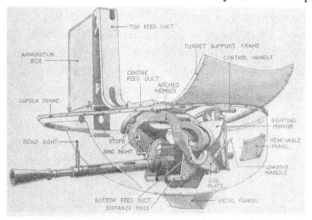 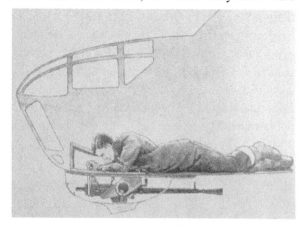

*The Blenheim Mk.IV was equipped with the rearward-firing turret equipped with a single Browning .303 machine gun. Like the Battle this was difficult to use and even more difficult to aim under operational conditions.*

successful. One crew had failed to return, and two had been lost while training, it was not a particularly good start to the squadrons operational debut in No.2 Group. Losses suffered by the group in August amounted to an alarming 37 Blenheim crews, daylight operations were taking their toll, but the group was doing their best to disrupt and cause confusion on the countless enemy airfields. The situation was just as grim for Fighter Command who were almost at their limit. A total of 126 Spitfire and Hurricane pilots had been killed, plus the crews of thirteen Blenheim fighters and seven Defiants.

September 1940 started with the squadron briefed to attack airfields in France, Belgium and Holland. Pilot Officer William Crosse was the first away in Blenheim L9381 at 1025 hours, he had the aerodrome at Bergen-Alkmaar as his objective. He was followed by 'B' Flight's Pilot Officer George Agar who had the unenviable task of bombing St Omer. New Zealand Flight Lieutenant Ian Richmond had the Belgian aerodrome at Hingene, situated 10 miles south-west of Antwerp. An hour later at 1230 hours Blenheim N3562 lifted off Oakingtons grass runway, at the controls was Canadian Pilot Officer Donald Smith undertaking his first operation, this crew had been given Evere aerodrome to attack.

Pilot Officers Crosse and Agar both managed to reach the enemy coast before they were forced to turn for home, the Met Officers forecast of cloud proved frustratingly inaccurate. The ever-resourceful Richmond also found limited cloud cover, but he and his crew decided to press on. Their persistence paid off, Hingene was located and their four 250lb bombs were successfully dropped. Pilot Officer Smith was unable to locate his primary target and turned for the secondary target of De Kooy. Running into the target at 4000 feet the crew meet a wall of light flak which thankfully proved inaccurate. More concerning was the appearance of a Bf109 which got to within 700 yards before Smith managed to reach the relative safety of the cloud. On the early evening, the station was visited by No.2 Group A.O.C, Air Vice Marshal James Milne Robb, DSO, DFC AFC. He talked at length with Wing Commander Duggan and Combe about the continuing if but slow improvement on the station and how the squadron was performing. The visit may have coincided with the completion of the main barrack blocks, a few squadron personnel, namely the ground crews were still sleeping under canvas.

On the 2nd the new station commander, Group Captain Roger Field arrived replacing Wing Commander Duggan. Lewin Bowring Duggan was born in January 1899, he had seen action in the trenches in the Great War with the 1st Battalion, Hertfordshire Regiment as a 2nd Lt before seconded for service in the RAF on July 30th, 1918. The inter-wars Flight found Duggan attached to both 421 and 447 Flights and serving aboard the aircraft carriers HMS Furious and Glorious. In November 1935 he was posted to Hinaidi in Iraq where he was employed on photographic staff duties in which he specialised. Promoted squadron leader 1st February 1936 he assumed command of No.218 (Bomber) Squadron on January 4th, 1938.

A spell of cloud free weather resulted in the squadron suspending operations and carrying out yet more training flights on the 3rd, this continued on the 4th and 5th. Operations throughout the group were being thwarted by insufficient cloud over the continent. To date the squadron had not undertaken any night raids unlike most Blenheim squadrons within the group, this would soon be rectified. With the ever-present threat of invasion, it was no surprise that group HQ instructed the squadron to begin night flying training. A training programme was immediately put into action, however there was one vital flaw, the majority of the Blenheims were not equipped with IFF.

Away from the station, Flight Lieutenant John Hughes, 'A' Flight's Deputy Flight Commander was sent to RAF Watton on the morning of the 4th to attend a Court Martial. A pilot of No.82 Squadron, Sergeant Arthur Barron was charged with *failing to carry out his duty* when he aborted an operation against Aalborg Aerodrome on August 13th due to lack of fuel. The pilot was subsequently cleared of the charge of cowardice at his Court Martial and returned to duty. Sadly, he was shot down and killed on July 20th, 1941

No.2 Group commander, Air Vice Marshal James Milne Robb, DSO, DFC AFC

while serving with No.139 Squadron, by which time he had been awarded a DFM. The real tragedy was that of the twelve Blenheims led by Wing Commander Edward Collis De Virac Lart DSO on the attack against Aalborg, eleven were shot down by a combination of flak and fighters. Twenty-year-old Arthur Barron and his crew were the only survivors. Why he was brought to trial is a blot on the group.

The squadron commander, Wing Commander Combe was aloft in Blenheim T1888 to test an IFF installation during the afternoon, also airborne was the recently promoted Squadron Leader James Gillman who was practising high altitude flying on oxygen, a novel experience for the crews accustomed to low-level operations. With no daylight operations scheduled for the 5th the squadrons attention turned to night flying practice. Sergeant Geoffrey Morley was aloft during the late afternoon carrying out further IFF tests, the results were encouraging. Wing Commander Combe carried out a practice dusk landing using the recently installed Glim Light Flares at 1930 hours, the runway beacons and floodlights were also used for the first time. Satisfied, Flight Lieutenant John Hughes and Flying Officer Walter Shaw were chosen to carry out the first take-off and landing at night from Oakington. In charge of night-flying was the recently arrived Sergeant Eric Marchand. The clear cloudless weather continued on the 6th, much to the dismay of not only the squadron, but Fighter Command who since the beginning of the month had been in a Herculean struggle with the Luftwaffe, there appeared to be no let-up in the battle. The squadron was on Standby from 0500 hours on the 7th, two section from both flights stood ready for action on what would turn out to be the turning point in the Battle for Britain. A message from No.2 Group HQ at noon stated, "INVASION ALERT No.2". Wing Commander Combe immediately recalled all personnel on leave and instructed his maintenance and repair sections to accelerate the servicing and repair on the five Blenheims currently unavailable for operations. Lack of concentration on the part of Sergeant Geoffrey Morley brought the wrath of not only the squadron commander but station commanding when he taxied Blenheim N3562 over a pile of gravel left by the contractors on the morning of the 7th. The rear fuselage, ailerons and rudder were peppered, and the undercarriage damaged. Wing Commander Duggan reported, *'Carelessness, the NCO pilot inclined to be rather full of himself'*

At 4:56pm on the late afternoon of September 7th 1940, the air raid sirens wailed as the Luftwaffe launched a massive raid on London. Over 350 bombers flew across the Channel from airfields in France and dropped 300 tons of bombs on the Dock yards and streets of London, it was the beginning of a new phase in the Battle of Britain. That night another message from group HQ arrived stating INVASION ALERT No.1, invasion maybe expected within 12 hours. Wing Commander Combe ordered all available aircraft to be bombed up and ready for immediate action the following morning. The squadron and the whole country waited for the German onslaught.

The previously planned day's activities were thrown out the window, and photographic reconnaissance flights against airfields and shipping made priority. The first two crews away just after 0930 hours were 'B' Flight's recently promoted Squadron Leader Kenneth Ault in Blenheim T1888 and Sergeant Eric Marchand aboard T.1863, both would be making their operational debut. The expected cloud cover once again promised by the Met officer failed to materialise. Squadron Leader Ault reached the Frisian Islands before aborting the operation, his target was the airfield at Leeuwarden. Further south, Sergeant Marchand was approaching the Dutch coastline at 5,000 feet, from this height he could see in the distance the flat polders were bathed in brilliant sunshine, the crew wisely turned for home.

*A Blenheim Mk.IV being bombed up with 4 x 250lb GPs. This photograph clearly shows the excellent forward visibility the observer had in comparison with the Fairey Battle. Under the nose can be seen the rearward facing .303 turret.*

Given the balls-up by the Met officer all further operations were postponed until the afternoon and the promise of cloud. 'B' Flights Flight Lieutenant Ian Richmond was away just after noon, he was given the area along the Dutch coast between the Island of Ameland and Ijmuiden to search. His task was to look for and photograph any signs of barge concentrations or coastal movement. Results were disappointing, a few photographs were taken, but exposure problems resulted in most showing just empty sea. Within five minutes Pilot Officer Alexander Turnbull was climbing away from Oakington, he and his crew were to carry out a photographic reconnaissance of the Dutch coast between Hamstede and Ijmuiden. The promised cloud now proved a hindrance, a solid mass of cloud forced Turnbull to complete the operation at the perilously low altitude of 1,800 feet. Thankfully, they encountered no flak or fighters, but photography proved impossible. An hour later Pilot Officer William Anstey was crossing the English Channel heading to Dunkirk. The entire route was flown in and amongst cloud at 15,000 feet. Hoping that they would be able to complete their operation, the crew were disappointed to find that within a mile of the French Coast the cloud suddenly stopped and then started again two miles inland. Fully aware of the importance of the operation the crew continued, and safety reached the of bank of cloud. Dropping down to 10,000 feet the crew skirted Dunkirk and it formidable flak defences and headed up the coast towards Ostend. Here they found a large concentration of barges in the Dock area and surrounding canals. Both light and heavy flak was encountered, thankfully the Germans gunners aim were slightly off. Ugly black bursts of flak exploded just 300 yards behind the Blenheim as they made their photo run from 10,000 feet. The crew were alarmed to see a Bf109 pass directly below them, thankfully they entered a dense bank of cloud before being detected. Undeterred the crew continued up the coast to Flushing and then Hamstede where 8/10th cloud prevented any further observation. On turning for home P/O Anstey dropped down to 3,000 feet, in doing so thick ice formed on the cockpit windscreen and the turret mechanism froze up, it was only when halfway across the North Sea forward visibility returned. The photographs of the barge concentration at Oostende resulted in the group attacking in force the following night. Flying Officer Walter Shaw was next away, like P/O Anstey he was given the area between Dunkirk and Flushing to search.

Arriving over Dunkirk at 7,000 feet it was soon apparent that any attempt to photograph was going to be spoilt by the mass of black-grey clouds and rain squalls which hid Dunkirk from any inquisitive eyes. This did not however deter the flak batteries who put up an accurate barrage of light and heavy flak which bracketed the Blenheim. Flying north along the coast the crew eventually arrived over Flushing where they encountered more favourable weather conditions. Flak once again erupted all around the Blenheim. In an attempt to shake it off F/O Shaw dropped the nose of the Blenheim and quickly headed out over the coast towards the relative safety of the sea. Levelling out at 500 feet the flak continued to burst a few hundred yards astern until finally and to the crew's relief it suddenly stopped. Within minutes the rear gunner Sergeant Ron Gill, a pre-war regular and veteran of AASF shouted out a warning that a Bf109 was closing in from astern. Dropping the Blenheim to wave top height the Bf109 opened fire from 600 yards, thankfully his aim was off as the bullets passed harmlessly below the Blenheim. Shaw took put the Blenheim into a tight turn giving Sergeant Gill an opportunity to engage the fighter with several good bursts. The fighter sheared off and was lost, Flying Officer Shaw reported in his flying Logbook, *"Me109 last seen streaking for the coast with black smoke pouring out of the engine"*. It had been a lucky escape.

The last operation of the day was carried out by two crews drawn from 'B' Flight. Just before six the pair departed Oakington and raced across the flat fens of East Anglia and out over the North Sea. Sergeant Gerald Clayton was at the controls of Blenheim L8848 HA-J. He and his crew were to carry out a

*Gerald Clayton photographed just prior to joining the RAF. Unusually Gerald is commemorated on a family headstone at St Mary and All Sant Churchyard, Hampshire. Note the incorrect date of his death.*

reconnaissance of the coast between Knocke and the Hague, while Sergeant Ronald Read and crew engaged on their first operation were given the coast between the Hague and Texel. Within two hours Sgt Read was back at his dispersal, insufficient cloud prevented him completing his task. Sadly, the crew of Sergeant Clayton failed to return and were reported as 'missing' back at Oakington. The circumstances surrounding the loss of the crew are unclear, no claims were made by any German fighter units although II./JG54 were active in the area. Rotterdam's flak defences engaged a Blenheim between 18:10 and 18:23 hours. It is not beyond the realms of possibility that L8848 was damaged by flak and Sergeant Clayton tried to make it back to Oakington. The squadron was the only one active during this time, the Coastal Command boys were further south over France. Blenheim, L8848 was believed to have crashed into the North Sea off the North West coast of Holland. Only the body of the gunner, Sergeant Gordon Taylor was recovered. The twenty-year-old's body washed ashore near Petten near marker Y.9368 on September 21st, he was buried the following day in the Petten Municipal Cemetery, Holland.

### Sunday September 8th 1940

*Bristol Blenheim*
*Mk.IV L8848 HA-J*
*Contract No: 551920/36*
*Taken On Charge: 26/08/1940*
**Failed To Return**
*Pilot : Sergeant Gerald Lawrence Clayton, 741533 RAFVR* **Killed**
*Observer: Sergeant Frederick Coish, 581203 RAF* **Killed**
*Wireless Operator/Gunner: Sergeant Gordon Taylor, 965631 RAFVR* **Killed.**


Gerald Lawrence Clayton was born on December 7th, 1916 in Oxfordshire the son of Charles Clayton, a wartime captain in the Royal Field Artillery who later became a respected architect, and his wife Olive (née Westbrook). Gerald attended the prestigious Brighton College (Chichester House) between 1930–1934. In 1937 he joined the Royal Air Force Volunteer Reserve, fulfilling a boyhood dream to serve with the RAF. Soon after the news of his son's death, Charles Clayton wrote to his son's headmaster. Obviously grieving he was frank about the conflict between his strict Christian philosophy and his thoughts of revenge, his father wrote, '*The loss strikes me to greater effort to see this madness through and get one's own back somehow. It took a lot of my faith in 'the other cheek' philosophy I'm afraid'.*

The squadron C/O Wing Commander Combe was aloft in the early evening, his destination was RAF Shawbury, Shropshire. As a part of No.2 Groups 'Withdrawal Plan', this former WW1 airfield situated a few miles north of the medieval town of Shrewsbury would be used in the event of a German invasion. Conditions were just as primitive as Oakington, but there was one bonus, there were no civilian contractors coming and going and no building works in progress. With Invasion Alert No.1 in place the squadron spent the morning of September 9th at readiness. There was an uneasy lull in the south of England, both the RAF and Luftwaffe were still licking their wounds from the previous days encounter. At 1630 hours practice blind take-offs were started in the squadrons dual control Blenheim Mk.I L1137 with F/Lt Richmond instructing. His first pupil was the squadron commander, Wing Commander Combe. He was followed by P/O Turnbull and Sgt Hoos again with Richmond in the righthand seat. At dusk both Turnbull and Hoos put their recently learnt skills into practice with take-off and landing practice in the Blenheim Mk.IV under the watchful of F/Lt Ian Richmond. There was growing urgency to get the squadron fully trained for night operations.

*Twenty-three-year-old observer, Sergeant Frederick Coish.*

Two aircraft of 'A' Flight were given photo reconnaissance tasks on the early afternoon of the 10th. Pilot Officer William Crosse was to search the enemy coast between Dunkirk to Flushing while Sergeant William Adam was given the area between Flushing and the Hague. Insufficient cloud over Dunkirk and Flushing forced P/O Crosse to abort his operation and they were back at their dispersal within two hours. A weather front over the North Sea and Holland meant the crew of Sgt Adam had to rely solely on DR navigation to reach their first target, Flushing. With no ground details visible and having reached what they believed to be the start of their search area Sgt Adam gingerly slipped into the clouds below. It was not until he was at the perilously low attitude of 1,200 feet that the ground finally become visible. To the crews alarm they found themselves inland of the heavily defended port of Zeebrugge, 40 miles south of their intended target. Setting course north the crew somehow managed to completely bypass their intended targets and now found themselves at the mercy of the flak defences of Rotterdam. Light flak immediately engaged the low flying Blenheim. Sergeant Adam desperately took what evasive action he could in an attempt to escape, just as the crew thought they were clear the starboard Bristol Mercury engine was hit, thankfully apart from a loud rattling noise the engine showed no sign of losing power. Adams pushed the throttles forward and climbed as quickly as possible to the safety of the clouds 4000 feet above, all the while the flak erupted around his Blenheim. They landed back at Oakington at 16:25 hours. The crew knew they had been extremely fortunate, luck was most definitely on their side groping around lost over Holland and Belgium in daylight was not a healthy occupation. That night a concert party consisting of local amateur entertainers from Cambridge gave a concert to all ranks in the N.A.A.F.I, it was a splendid evening, and all enjoyed few hours of normality

The crews of 'A' Flight were over Wainfleet bombing range during the morning of the 11th getting in some high level bombing practice. With the recent threat of invasion all training, apart from night flying had been put on hold. Interestingly the recent photo reconnaissance operations had all been flown without bombs. Squadron Leader Leslie Gibson, the squadron's Operations officer flew W/Cdr Duggan to RAF Thorney Island to take up his temporary post during the afternoon. One of 'B' Flight's Blenheim's, A.V Roe and Co Ltd built N3563 was flown to No.13 O.T.U at Bicester to be replaced by Blenheim L9327. Recent flights had established that N3563 was a comparatively slow machine compared to the others on the squadron, this was probably why it had not been used on operations since its arrival from No.38 M.U on July 16th. It was the crews of 'B' Flight who once again were aloft just after dusk for yet more night flying training. Pilot Officers Agar and Anstey along with F/Sgt Charles Owen spent two hours mastering take off and landings.

One of the lucky survivors was Sergeant William Woodmason.

*The squadron's reported a number of encounters with the famed Heinkel 113 fighter. Interestingly despite the crew's insistence of seeing the fighter only prototypes were built. The He113 never entered service with the Luftwaffe. The role of the Henkel 113 as a front-line fighter was a myth created by an extraordinarily successful Nazi propaganda and deception campaign.*

The training was planned to continue the following day however the weather intervened. A replacement aircraft, R3666 was delivered from No.5 MU during the afternoon, this machine would replace Sgt Claytons Blenheim, and like L8848 it would be lettered "J".

The morning of Friday 13th was wet and overcast, just the conditions required for operations. It would be the busiest day for the squadron since France. 'A' Flights Pilot Officer John Mitchell and Pilot Officer Donald Smith were away just after 06:30 hours. The crew of P/O Smith would be undertaking their first operation with the squadron, their objective was to report on any barge concentrations along the coast between Calais and Ostend. Pilot Officer Mitchell was to fly between the Hague and Haamstede and report any similar concentrations. Five minutes later 'B' Flights F/Lt Richmond DFC was aloft at the controls of Blenheim T1996 HA-S, within the thirty minutes he was back at dispersal with a faulty intercom. The problem was quickly identified, and Richmond eventually took off again at 09:10 hours. The veteran Richmond was given the area between Ostend and Flushing to search. All three crews encountered cloud at all heights on route, over France P/O Smith met a wall of solid cloud which started at 500 feet and continued up to 7,000 feet. It was obvious that for them the operation was over. The same conditions met P/O Mitchell and crew, however they decided to push on along the enemy coast in the hope of finding better conditions. Flying at 1,000 feet they began to encounter heavy rain which restricted viability even more, the crew wisely decided to turn for home. Somehow in the murk the observer Sergeant William Woodmason became lost, unable to fix their position and visibility almost nil the crew had to rely on luck to get home. Their luck was in, somehow the crew had flown parallel to the south coast of England until eventually contact with RAF Thorney Island was made, they had been aloft for nearly four hours. Flight Lieutenant Richmond had a close encounter with three Bf109s (reported as He113s) near Ostend, thankfully a bank of thick cloud gave the crew refuge, the fighters were not seen again. Deciding to remain in the relative safety of the clouds Richmond flew up the coast towards Knocke where to the crew's horror the protective cloud abruptly stopped. The ever-plucky Richmond turned his attention to the numerous inland waterways between Knocke and Zeebrugge. Flying at 800 feet they encountered intense light flak.

Thankfully the German gunners aim was off, obviously taken by surprise by the speed of the low flying Blenheim. With no new activity observed they too turned for home, landing at 1235hrs.

Just after midday Pilot Officer Ross Mansfield climbed away from Oakington at the controls of Blenheim L9306, it would be the crews first operation. Within the hour he was followed by fellow 'B' Flight crew skippered by Sergeant Donald Hoos at the helm of Blenheim N3573. Pilot Officer Mansfield operation was a wash-out, severe icing was encountered on route to Calais forcing the crew to abort the operation. Flying slightly north of Mansfield, Sgt Hoos found slightly better weather conditions. Overflying his intended starting point of Haamstede the crew emerged from the clouds inland above Dordrecht. Flying at 2,000 feet a visual reconnaissance of the waterways near IJsselmonde, east of Rotterdam was undertaken. It was here that a concentration of barges was found moored in pairs in the centre of the river, these were attacked with 2 x 250lb and 16 x 40lb bombs, results were unobserved. The last operation of the day was flown by Sergeant Charles Owen and crew of 'B' Flight who took off at 1435 hours. The crew were given the coastal strip between Ostend to Hamstede, including the waterways of Antwerp. With plenty of broken cloud the crew began their search. Near Zeebrugge the crew observed a convoy steaming out of the Scheldt Estuary towards the Mole of Zeebrugge, the convoy was made up of 6 or 7 oil tankers of approximately 2000 tons. Without hesitation the crew attacked the slow-moving convoy from 7000 feet, all the bombs were seen by the rear gunner to straddle the second vessel in the convoy. There followed an explosion with flames and dense smoke pouring out of what was reported to have been an oil tanker, but photographs developed back at Oakington indicated that in fact it was a destroyer. The triumphant crew landed back at base at 17:15 hours. That evening all the squadron was gathered and addressed by the groups Senior Air Staff Officer, Group Captain Hugh Pugh Lloyd MC, DFC. The assembled crews knew they were in the presence of an experienced and well-informed officer, he was no *'Chairborne-Warrior'*. A veteran of the Great War and with years of experience under his belt, Group Captain Lloyd proceeded to inform all present what he perceived to be the crucial factors that would over the coming weeks and months make all the difference.

1. *Discipline. Things like unpunctuality or slackness in various ways were indiscipline represented the first symptom of a deteriorating moral. It was important therefore, that slackness should not be allowed to gain hold anywhere at any time.*
2. *It was important that each member of aircrew should know as much as possible, without going deeply into details, of the duties and job of the other two members. This was undoubtably the most effective way to close co-operation and thorough teamwork inside the aircraft. All should do their best to learn as much as they could in their spare time, they would be well repaid in results.*

It was when discussing the invasion that G/C Lloyd prediction seemed uncannily accurate.

3. *If Hitler did not invade England before the end of the month, he would probably not attempt the task this year. Therefore, the invasion could be expected at any time within the next 14 days.*

Group Captain Lloyd's carefully crafted words had an immediate effect on an already jubilant squadron, it was just the tonic the squadron needed. From an operational perspective the day was the best thus far. The reported destruction of a 'destroyer' and attacks on a concentration of barges brought a great deal of satisfaction to the whole squadron, it appeared, at least on paper, to be hitting back.

The squadron was not required on the 14th, once again in an effort to start night operations three pilots were up at dusk in the squadron dual control Blenheim. Training continued on the 15th, 'B' Flight were over Wainfleet bombing ranges practicing high level and shallow dive-bombing practice. 'A' Flight were practicing the complexities of flying boxed formations consisting of six Blenheims for mutual protecting from attacking fighters. The squadron lost one of its longest serving and most respected pilots on this day, Flight Lieutenant John McCulloch Middlemore Hughes DFC. With his big smile and even bigger neatly groomed moustache, the willowy Hughes would be greatly missed. His contribution to the squadron was immeasurable. John was born at Bromsgrove, Worcestershire on 13th February 1917, the son of Lt, later doctor Percy Theodore Hughes and Emily Christabel Hughes. He attended Haileybury College from 1930 to 1934 then entered RAF College, Cranwell in September 1935. After gaining his wings and a Permanent Commission as a pilot officer on September 10th, 1937 he joined the squadron at RAF Boscombe Down. In August 1940 John answered the call by Fighter Command for pilots to replace those lost in action. In the south of England, the bravery and sheer tenacity of Fighter Command changed not just the course of the Battle for Britain but, the war. The action on September 15th was an overwhelming and decisive defeat for the Luftwaffe. The following day the squadron was ordered to carry out a combined reconnaissance / bombing operation along the enemy coast. It would turn out to be the squadrons most productive day since conversion to the Blenheim. Nine crews would be involved in operations ranging from Calais to Rotterdam. The first crew away was that of Pilot Officer William Crosse at 11:00 hours. They were given the coast between Calais and Ostend to search, over Ostend they spotted a convoy which was attacked from 4000 feet. Both the convoy and shore batteries put up an accurate barrage of light and medium flak which punctured the starboard wing. Such was the intensity of the flak Crosse was forced to take violent evasive action, to such an extent he found himself almost upside down at 1000 feet, thankfully his excellent piloting skills saved the day.

Sergeant Ron Read was next away in Blenheim N3625, he and his crew dropped their mixed 250lb and 40lb bomb load on the mole at Zeebrugge all the while engage by light flak emanating from the port. Squadron Leader Kenneth Ault soon followed, after taking a series of photographs of Zeebrugge the crew were lucky to escape the attention of three prowling Bf109s (once again reported as He113s) no doubt sent to search for Read's Blenheim. Using the available cloud, he continued to Ostende where he carried out a shallow diving attack from 4000 feet on the Docks. On leaving the target he once again encountered prowling Bf109s which he managed to lose in the cloud.

No more flights were ordered until after lunch when Kiwi Pilot Officer William Anstey of 'B' Flight flew direct to Oostende. Over the port he was met by a ferocious barrage of both light and heavy flak inter-mixed with heavy calibre tracer from the already alert flak defences. Picking out the quayside and a group of buildings close to the Docks mouth William put Blenheim N3573 into a shallow dive dropping his 2 x 250lb + 16 x 40lb bombs from 4000 feet. Buffeted by flak the young New Zealander dropped down to 1000 feet taking evasive action all the while. They landed back at Oakington at 1700 hours. Sergeant Geoffrey Morley and crew had to battle severe weather conditions on route to Calais, with the cloud down to 200 feet in places the young crew valiantly pressed on, sadly the conditions worsened as they neared the French coast. Unable to reach their objective they stumbled upon a convoy of 20 ships sailing in two lines towing a number of barges steaming north towards the safety of Dunkirk. Ignoring the wall of flak Sgt Morely attacked the convoy diagonally from 500 feet to the crew's shock only one 250 pounder dropped, the rest having hung up. Showing great courage, the crew made another attack, this was never a good idea as the element of surprise had gone. This time the flak gunners found the target. The Blenheim shuddered as flak punctured the starboard wing just behind the main fuel tank, thankfully there was no fire. Fortunately, on this occasion all the bombs apart from one container dropped, a number of 40lb bombs were seen exploding close to the barges. Miraculously the crew had somehow survived, after 58 minutes aloft the crew turned for home. The Docks at Dunkirk received the attention of Pilot Officer Ross Mansfield. Bristling with anti-aircraft guns the crew encountered an intense wall flak, wasting no time the bombs were dropped in the general Dock area. Once the bombs had gone Mansfield rapidly climbed into the relative safety of the clouds. They landed at Great Massingham on return.

Pilot Officer John Mitchell and crew attacked a concentration of barges in the Flushing - Veerse Canal but results were unobserved. Sergeant William Adam also found a small convoy of 3 ships and 12 barges in the mouth of the Scheldt, these were attacked from 3,500 feet but once again results were unobserved. The final operation of the day was undertaken by 'A' Flight's Pilot Officer Donald Smith in Blenheim T1863, they were given the Zeebrugge area to search. Over the North Sea the crew encountered a mass of cloud down to 600 feet, to add to their problems heavy rain made navigation difficult. With forward visibility down to a few hundred yards the crew found themselves south of target close to the heavily defended coastal port of Oostende. Somehow in the murk they chance upon a small convoy steaming towards the safety of the port. The young Canadian made two bombing runs over the convoy, on each occasion the bomb load failed to drop. Frustrated and angry and aware that a third attempt was pushing their luck the crew turned for Oakington landing at 17:30 hours.

It had been a marvellous effort by the whole squadron, nine sorties and more importantly, all had returned despite the best intentions of the German flak gunners and the weather. The crews had pressed home their attacks with a determination reminiscent of the low-level attacks on German columns in Belgium and Luxembourg in May. The squadron had dropped a total of sixteen 250 pounders and 108 forty-pounders, it was a marvellous effort by the whole squadron. These attacks on both the ports and convoys were, despite the obvious dangers inflicting some damage to the German merchant fleets. The transport ships Telde, Ceuta, Rolandseck, Palermo and Hans Leonhardt and at least 2 other freighters were damaged from RAF attacks during this period, all required Dock repair. Some good news arrived via Air Ministry on the 16th, Sergeant Howard, gunner to S/Ldr House was reported alive and well.

There was some light relief on the 17th, a barrage balloon was seen passing over the aerodrome just after breakfast, 'A' Flight's Squadron Leader Kenneth Ault took it upon himself to try and shoot it down. By the time he had collected the squadron gunnery leader and carried out the pre take off checks the balloon had almost disappeared. Despite both S/Ldr Aults and his gunner, P/O Skinner's best efforts the balloon remained aloft. They landed ignominiously back at Oakington to be greeted by much mockery over their apparent lack of shooting skills, their only response was the gun sights were unserviceable! The squadron's only other officer gunner, 31-year-old P/O Reginald Vaughan was posted to 144 Squadron at RAF Hemswell on the 17th, sadly he was to lose his life over Holland in May 1941.

*A typical barge concentration. Here a number of barges are seen in Boulogne Harbour. The 'heavies' of Bomber Command would attack these targets night after night during the summer of 1940.*

The squadron was once again visited by the A.O.C. Air Vice Marshal James Milne Robb, DSO, DFC AFC on the 18th. He arrived just after 11am flying his Percival Vega Gull. It was on this day, the commanding officer, W/Cdr Combe participated in shallow bombing practice over Wainfleet Sands, it was one of the few occasions he did. There was some cause for celebration in the mess that night, the respected F/O Shaw was promoted to acting Flight Lieutenant and would fill the vacancy left by the recently departed F/Lt Hughes DFC. Twenty-six-year-old Walter Shaw had joined the squadron in May 1938 on completion of his pilot training at No.6 F.T.S Netheravon, Wiltshire, he had served on 'A' Flight continuously since.

The following day it was fun and frolics with the Bren Carriers of the 6th Royal Sussex Regiment during a demonstration of how the aerodrome would be defended in the event of invasion. The squadron's aircraft would fulfil the role of German troop-carrying aircraft while the station's Miles Magister represented a long ranger fighter. In place of bombs, the Blenheims dropped bags of fish manure on the unfortunate 'Brown-Jobs'. In the ensuring chaos, which was more akin to a Charlie Chaplin film, a wealth of experience was supposedly gleaned.

It was not long after the exercise had concluded that the unfamiliar sound of a Jumo engine reverberated over Oakington. To the disbelief of everyone a Junker JU88 was seen attempting a landing with a feathered port engine, no sooner had the aircraft come to rest, the already highly motivated Bren Gun carrier crews raced to the scene. To add to the excitement two RAF fighters roared over the JU88 at less than 60 feet. The German crew consisting of one officer and three NCOs wisely gave no resistance and were quickly taken prisoner. The aircraft, JU88A-1 of 4.(F)/121 had been on a photo-reconnaissance flight.

*The only known photograph of a No.218 Squadron Bristol Blenheim. This was the personal mount of Flight Lieutenant Richmond. Rootes-built Bristol Blenheim Mk.IV T1996 HA-S arrived on the squadron August 3rd, 1940 from No.27 MU. It completed five operations, all with F/Lt Richmond.*

It was back to operations on the 20th, three crews were given reconnaissance sorties, 'B' Flight Sergeant Charles Owen flew the squadron's 50th Blenheim sortie, it should have been a cause for celebration however weather conditions once again prevented completion.

The growing pressure of becoming operational by night continued, five crews practiced dusk take off and landings, once confident, the practice continued in total darkness. A full day's fighter affiliation was flown on the morning of September 21st, six crews lead by W/Cdr Combe would practice evasive action against fighter attack. The attackers were six Hawker Hurricanes of No.1 Squadron, and six Supermarine Spitfires of No.266 (Rhodesia) Squadron, both of which were based at RAF Wittering. During the first half of the exercise the squadron flew in boxed formation and attempted to fend off the attackers with a concentration of fire power from the rear turrets. The second half was mainly taken up with the formation making steep turns towards the attacking fighters, giving the rear gunners an opportunity to engage. Like any practice the merits of such manoeuvres were impossible to determine, the fighter boys were confident that they would have shot down the Blenheims without too much difficulty given their recent experience. It was a rather tired and disillusioned bunch of aircrew who had to listen to the fighter pilots *lining shooting* over lunch at Wittering. After lunch, the squadron departed and headed back to RAF Oakington with the Hurricanes of No.1 Squadron flying as fighter escort. The Spitfires were given the task of attacking and breaking up the formation. Nearing base, the Blenheim crews had every right to think that they had got away with further strenuous aerobatics as familiar landmarks slowly passed below. With the Hurricanes flying protective cover the Blenheim formation broke up to come into land. With the first of the Blenheim's on final approach the Spitfires attacked. The escort and Blenheim crews were taken by complete surprise. Pandemonium ensured, the Spitfires attacked the slow flying Blenheims with ease, it was a classic 'bounce'.

On the late afternoon of the 22nd five crews were briefed to carry out individual sorties. A new name, and target appeared on the operations board, Gravelines. Located 15 miles south west of Dunkirk the once fortified town was situated at the mouth to the important canal which linked St Omer to the sea.

The recently promoted F/Lt Shaw was the first away, he encountered low cloud over the enemy coast between his intended search area of Boulogne and Calais. The sortie was saved when a merchant vessel and six barges was sighted off Wissant. Manoeuvring the Blenheim into attack accurate light flak from the shore and the merchant ship hosed the sky around Shaw's Blenheim as he made his run in from 3,000 feet. The rear gunner, Sergeant Ron Gill reported that the bombs had undershot, frustrated Shaw banked the Blenheim and made another attack, this time with his forward firing gun. The only casualty appeared to be a seaman on one of the barges who was seen to look anxiously over his shoulder as the bullets ricocheted off the deck, he was last seen jumping into the sea. Pilot Officer Mitchell's operation was a wash-out due to insufficient cloud, luckier was the crew of Pilot Officer Agar. They found sufficient cloud cover over most of their intended targets. After an unsuccessful attempt to find the airfield at Haamstede they bombed a small harbour on the north coast of the island of Beveland, once again the results were unobserved. B Flight's Sergeant Geoffrey Morley spent two hours flying between Rotterdam and Flushing before dropping his bomb load on the Docks of Flushing from 5,000 feet. A large convoy consisting of 52 ships was detected by the crew of Sergeant Read 3 miles off Zeebrugge, it was the largest convoy found to date. With plenty of cloud cover the plucky crew spent some time carefully counting the numbers of ships, their approximate tonnage and type. Once satisfied the crew made their attack singling out the last two ships, despite their best intentions the bombs fell short. Almost immediately the rear gunner reported two Bf109s approaching from the starboard quarter. Sergeant Read immediately pointed the Blenheim in the direction of a bank of cloud as the fighters closed to within 500 yards. Using every possible inch of cloud Read eventually found himself entering clear sky, to his horror the Bf109s had somehow manage to stay with the Blenheim. Wasting no time, the now desperate Read headed towards another bank of cloud where he managed to stay until within 10 miles off the coast of Great Yarmouth. To the crew's astonishment the rear gunner once again reported the presence of the two fighters. Incredibly they had stayed with the Blenheim across the North Sea, again Read quickly headed towards a convenient bank of cloud, this time the fighters were finally lost, they landed at 17:55 hours. It is highly unlikely that a Bf109 had the range to cross the North Sea and get back. What the crew reported is unknown. The squadron lost 'B' Flight's experienced Sergeant

Charles Owen in favourable circumstances on the 22nd when posted to Central Flying School at Upavon for an instructor's course.

While Wing Commander Combe and Group Captain Field were attending a group meeting at the Old Court House, Godmanchester the squadron carried out a number of rather monotonous fuel consumption tests during the morning of the 23rd. There was some excitement during the early evening when the unmistakable sound of a Rolls Royce Merlin caught everyone's attention. A solitary Spitfire landed on the grass runway with a reported defected undercarriage at 15:55 hours. Once safely dispersed the unmistakable figure of F/Lt Hughes DFC clambered out of the cockpit. With his large whiskery moustache and infectious smile, the news that this highly respected former flight commander was back on the squadron quickly filtered around the squadron. Everyone was delighted to see him again. With a certain amount of envy, the Blenheim pilots inspected the sleek fighter, none more so than 'B' Flight's F/Lt Richmond. Ian Richmond had gained some experience of flying the Spitfire while attached to the Photographic Development Unit at RAF Heston between February - March 1940. Once the 'defective' undercarriage was fixed the young Kiwi wasted no time in taking the fighter up for a flight. It was with some sadness that F/Lt Hughes departed just after tea-time. The squadron lost P/O Skinner on the 23rd, he was posted to No.38 squadron at RAF Marham.

A new tactic was trailed on the 25th, the recent spate of early returns due to insufficient cloud cover was proving frustrating and an unnecessary burden on the squadron. To prevent this, the squadron would dispatch a solitary crew to reconnoitre the enemy coast and send a message back to base reporting the conditions. This message would determine if the planned days operations would be carried out. The pilot chosen for this 'weather reconnaissance' sortie was 'A' Flights Pilot Officer Donald Smith who lifted off

*Nose art of Flight Lieutenant Richmond's Bristol Blenheim T1996. The word 'Verdammnis' or Damnation is seen below the Devil sitting on a bomb.*

from Oakington just after 06:30 hours in Blenheim T1863. The Canadian pilot was given strict instructions not to proceed further than the North Hinder Lightship, a well-known nautical landmark situated on the approach to Flushing. Deciding to ignore his orders, P/O Smith proceeded further inland than instructed, it was a risky decision given the defences. Satisfied with the cloud conditions Smith ordered his wireless operator / gunner Sergeant Rankine to send a message back to Oakington notifying them of suitable weather conditions. Unfortunately, the wireless transmitter was faulty as the message was not received, he landed back at base at 08:20 hours.

Given the favourable weather the squadron was allotted reconnaissance duties over the Channel ports. Seven crews would be given targets ranging from Antwerp to Boulogne, only two were successful. The irrepressible P/O Smith who carried out the early morning weather reconnaissance sortie found three small ships and a large merchantman of around 12,000 tons off the coast of Flushing. The Canadian wasted no time in carrying out a shallow diving attack. For once the German flak gunners were inaccurate, light flak was encountered but 50 yards behind the Blenheim as the 4 x 250 plus 4 x 40lb bombs were dropped. Frustratingly the bombs were seen to explode just short of the convoy, the Operational Records Book records, *'Pilot Officer Smith returned to base gloomily'*

Flight Lieutenant Richmond stumbled upon a large tanker escorted by four E-Boats in line-astern 50 miles off Calais. Owing to the distance from the enemy coast the New Zealander was hesitant to attack fearing that that they could be friendly. After circling several times and unable to positively identify the ships the crew decided to press on to their intended targets. Their decision paid off, a large cargo vessel was found beached just west of

*Supermarine Spitfire Mk.I X4593 UO-A of No.266 (Rhodesian) Squadron seen here during the Battle of Britain. The pilots of No.266 made sure the exercise was one the squadron would remember.*

Gravelines. Richmond made a low pass over the vessel, it appeared unmanned and undamaged. On his second pass his observer, Sergeant Albert Sweetland dropped the mixed 250lb and 40lb bomb load. Columns of sand erupted as the bombs straddled but missed the sitting target. Probably the result of the previous days poor results, Wing Commander Combe ordered a programme of bombing moving targets in the Wells area, both flights were involved. Unfortunately, the sea was too rough and the planned programmed was cancelled. With improved weather W/Cdr Combe ordered 'A' Flight back to the Wainfleet bombing ranges while 'B' Flight was sent on a fighter affiliation exercise with the squadrons of RAF Wittering. The formation of six Blenheim's lead by F/Lt Richmond flew on a predetermined route in box formation at 7,000 feet, the weather conditions were ideal. Over Market Harborough they were intercepted by twelve Spitfires of No.266 (Rhodesia) Squadron who made repeated attacks. Initially the squadron was able to evade the attacks by turning into their antagonists, however the Spitfires started to make head-on attacks which effectively prevented the squadron from reaching its intended target of Boston. The planned exercise after lunch had to be altered with the departure of No.266 Squadron to RAF Duxford, however this did not prevent the squadron from being 'bounced' by the Hurricanes of No.1 Squadron as they neared Oakington on the return flight. Wing Commander Duggan returned from his detachment at Thorney Island on the 27th, he had time to pick up some personnel items and say goodbye to the few pre-war survivors before he departed early the following morning to RAF Swanton Morely to take up his post as Station Commander. His long connection with the squadron which had begun in January 1938 was finally over.

The squadron was once again allocated reconnaissance operations on the 28th. The tactic of sending out a solitary crew to check on cloud cover was again tried and proved successful. Pilot Officer Alexander Turnbull and crew departed just after 0730 hours in Blenheim N3573. On nearing the enemy coast, the green fields of France were bathed in sunshine, there was not a cloud in sight. The unfavourable conditions were messaged back to Oakington where the planned morning operations were postponed. Reports from Group HQ seemed to indicate the conditions had improved by late afternoon when six crews were detailed to carry out reconnaissance flights over the enemy ports. The first away was Sergeant Morley in Blenheim L9327 at 1450 hours, he was back at his dispersal within 90 minutes due to lack of cloud. Pilot Officer John Mitchell was more successful, broken cloud was encountered giving the crew an opportunity to take photographs of both Zeebrugge and Bruges. On route to Oostende, the cloud suddenly vanished, expecting a volley of flak or fighters at any time the crew continued on in clear skies to their target unmolested. It was only when they had dropped their bombs that the flak opened up. Thankfully, the German gunners aim was off, but only just, dozens of flak bursts exploded slightly behind the Blenheim. 'A' Flights Sergeants William Adam and Donald Hoos both were forced to return early due to insufficient cloud. Flight Lieutenant Walter Shaw and crew found both cloud and an alert enemy. Having crossed the coast over Gravelines at 7000 feet they were meet by a wall of light accurate flak. It was only by Shaw flinging the Blenheim into a series of stomach-churning manoeuvres that saved the crew, eventually a perspiring Shaw managed to make his escape. With Dunkirk on the horizon, they made ready for their bomb run. The observer had singled out the oil tanks and the busy marshalling yards situated in the south of the town for their attention. Light flak once again burst around the Blenheim, however, unlike Gravelines is was not as accurate or intense. Positioned in the nose of the Blenheim, Sergeant Albert Wynne unloaded his 4 x 250lb and four 40lb bombs from 7,500 feet on the marshalling yards close to Dock No.5, results were unobserved as the Blenheim almost immediately entered a layer of cloud. Dropping down to 3,000 feet they headed out to sea, when ten miles off the coast the crew turned back flying parallel to the enemy coast until they re-crossed the coast near Nieuport, Belgium. Here the crew were subjected to murderous heavy calibre machine gun fire. Shaw once again took evasive action all the time taking photographs of the port below, finally satisfied they headed for home, it had been an eventful operation. The final operation was flown by Pilot Officer Turnbull, his second of the day, he was tasked with investigating enemy activity between Knocke and Haamstede. Flak was encountered almost immediately as the crew crossed the coast near Zeebrugge, with the enemy defences alerted the crew flew on towards Flushing where they were seen by a Bf109. Wasting no time Turnball made a steep diving turn into nearby clouds, it had been a close call as the fighter had closed to within 300 yards. Flying out to sea, the crew again turned inland to continue the sortie, by this time the whole area was alerted. The Blenheim was engaged by both light and heavy flak almost continuously, such was the intensity it was impossible to take photographs or bomb. The crew wisely turned for home landing at 17:40 hours.

It had been yet another frustrating day for the squadron, insufficient cloud had again thwarted the crew's efforts. It was not for the lack of trying. The day's activities had shown that the crews were prepared to risk everything to obtain the photographs so desperately needed, the squadron's resolve, and courage was not in question, it was the tactics being employed. The squadron was not required for operations on the 29th, during the afternoon for some curious reason known only to himself, Wing Commander Combe had 'A' Flight carrying evasive action against flak while flying in boxed formation. At the same time, 'B' Flight were also aloft carrying out formation flying at low level. One can only speculate on why given the squadron's recent tactics of operating individual aircraft the commanding officer had the squadron carrying out this type of training. The last day of the month was confined to just four training flights, it summed up an uninspiring month. The squadron had flown 51 operations, totalling 115 operationally hours, compared to 434 training hours, it was not a particularly impressive record. The 'Bouquets' a traveling concert party arrived on the station on the last evening of the month. Such was the size of the troupe the concert had to be held in the NAAFI Tent. The list of acts included the popular pre-war tenor Webster Booth, Mario de Pietro, one of the leading mandolinists in the country. Murray Ashford and Edgar Sawyer. A very entertaining evening ably assisted once again by the station band brought September 1940 to a conclusion.

The crews had no illusion as to the task in front of them, September had been a crucial month in the survival of the country, they had every reason to expect that October would be no different. The now standard pre-operation weather reconnaissance was flown by Sergeant Read on the morning of the 1st. As expected and contrary to the Met Officers briefing the weather over the continent was unsuitable for operations. Never one to let up on training, Wing Commander Combe had twelve crews aloft just before lunch carrying out formation practice. This was followed by a special practice reconnaissance flight in connection with a mechanised Brigade. The only incident in an otherwise routine day was the damage to Blenheim L9327 on return from the exercise. 'B' Flight's Sergeant Geoffrey Morley successfully landed on Oakington's grass runway and was taxying to its dispersal area when he instructed his observer, Sergeant Cave to open grills and raise flaps, inexplicably Cave reached for the undercarriage level and retracted the undercarriage. The Blenheim unceremoniously sank to shuddering halt, the shaken but uninjured crew clambered out to survey the damage. The port airscrew was bent backwards and the port mainplane was badly bent. Thankfully, the damage was not extensive, but the Blenheim which had only flown on three raids would not fly operationally with the squadron again. The investigation squarely attributed the blame on the shoulders of the crew recording it was a *'Clear case of carelessness'*. It was the second occasion the crew had been involved in a taxying accident.

## Tuesday October 1st 1940

*Bristol Blenheim*
*Mk.IV L9327*
*Contract No : 551920/36*
*Taken On Charge: 09/09/1940*
*Damaged, pilot error*
*Pilot : Sergeant Geoffrey Morley*
*Observer: Sergeant Cave*
*Wireless Operator/Gunner: Unknown*


The following morning twelve squadron Blenheim's were bombed up and on standby from 06:00 hours and remained on 30 minutes readiness until orders to stand down were received at 11:00 hours. Once again, the squadron was not required for operations and predictably W/Cdr Combe had the squadron airborne with yet more training. The C/O obviously felt that formation flying needed improving and that more practice was required. In varying weather, both flights stooged around in formation, something they had to date never been required to use operationally. Thursday, October 3rd began like any other day since the squadrons return from France, however this was to change dramatically at mid-day. Orders were received from No.2 Group HQ that four squadron Blenheim's would be required to attack targets in the heart of the German Ruhr. There was a real buzz of excitement around the squadron and Oakington. The squadron was finally being given a chance to bomb Germany. The first crew away was 'B' Flights Sergeant Donald Hoos and crew who departed at 1435 hours in Blenheim P6959 their target was an oil refinery at Sterkrade Holten. Using the cloud cover to their advantage the crew penetrated Germany crossing the Rhine at the perilously low altitude of 2,500 feet. The cloud which had aided their progress was now becoming increasingly dense and the further into the Ruhr the plucky crew flew the worse the visibility become. It was soon obvious that the primary target could not be found. Having come so far, the crew were determined to find a target. Between Wesel and Haltern the crew found and attacked the Coopler Ironworks which was nestled in amongst some woods. Regrettably, the bomb load narrowly missed the factory and hit a nearby house. Sergeant Hoos quickly climbed to the safety of the clouds and headed for home, landing in failing light at 18:15 hours. It had been a determined effort by this all NCO crew in difficult conditions. Following close on the heels of Sgt Hoos was Pilot Officer Mansfield and crew, they abandoned the operation after two hours. Sergeant Morley departed at 14:45 hours in Blenheim N6183, his objective was the oil works near

Reisholz. He too found Germany almost devoid of cloud, opting to find an alternative target the crew turned and headed towards the Maas River where a number of barges had been observed. At Heusden a concentration of around 50 barges made a worthwhile target. Encountering no opposition, Sgt Morley carried out a dummy run to try and pick out the most productive target.

Swinging around for the attack Sgt Cave, the crews Observer dropped the 4 x 250lb bombs scoring direct hits on the quayside, the 40lb bombs exploded close to a warehouse. Unharmed the crew returned to Oakington landing at 1755 hours.  The final sortie of the day was undertaken by New Zealander P/O Anstey and crew. They were briefed to attack a synthetic oil plant near Homburg. Again, inadequate cloud cover prevented the crew from attacking the primary target, flying northwards they attacked Rotterdam Docks from 5,000 feet encountering heavy flak which thankfully exploded just yards behind the Blenheim.

October 4th proved to be a busy but frustrating day, nine crews were detailed and briefed for attacks on targets in the Ruhr. None of the primary objectives was bombed, but some useful damaged was achieved. Pilot Officer Mansfield bombed Haamstede aerodrome from 900 feet inflicting damaged to the bomb dump. Pilot Officer Turnbull was briefed to attack an oil refinery north of Cologne. Insufficient cloud meant he returned to base. 'A' Flight commander, Squadron Leader Kenneth Ault was given Bremen Docks to attack in Blenheim T1888.  Lack of cloud cover prevented him from reaching this most dangerous of targets. Determined not to return with the bombload the crew sought out a target of opportunity. This they found in the shape of the seaplane base at  Schellingwoude. Prior to bombing, S/Ldr Ault decided to take a number of photographs. Making his first run over the target a series of photographs were taken. Satisfied, he turned around to make his bomb run.   This time the defences were ready, a barrage of light flak exploded all around the Blenheim. Shuddering under the impact, Ault quickly realised that any attempt to bomb was now suicidal. Light flak peppered the Blenheim's tail and rudder, Ault immediately started to jink the Blenheim from side to side in a desperate attempt to shake off the gunners. Finally, after what seemed a lifetime, the crew reached the safety of the sea, it had been a close call. Extensive damage was inflicted to the starboard engine, port aileron and the tailplane. Fortunately, none of the crew were injured. Most pilots would have turned for home, not S/Ldr Ault. On leaving the seaplane base, he headed to Ijmuiden, where he attacked a sizeable black merchant vessel, unfortunately the results were unobserved. It was the turn of Wing Commander Combe next in Blenheim T1865. He was given Salzbergen to attack. A lack of cloud prevented the squadron commander from penetrating further than the Zuider Zee. Shortly after crossing the Dutch coast, a convoy was briefly spotted near Ijmuiden. Deciding to attack the convoy, W/Cdr Combe turned to make his attack. Unfortunately, in doing so, the convoy was lost in the low cloud and dense sea mist. Surprisingly, W/Cdr Combe decided to bomb the convoy on its estimated position. Given the almost zero visibility and the briefest of sightings, it was a questionable decision. Not surprisingly the results were unobserved! Upon his return, W/Cdr Combe expressed his disappointment in not bombing Germany. It was a rather poor show from the squadron commanding officer given the lengths other crews had taken in trying to locate worthwhile targets. Given W/Cdr Combes previous efforts to improve both bombing accuracy and instil an aggressive fighting spirit within the squadron it was a rather poor show. Sergeant Marchand was given a synthetic oil plant at Homburg to bomb while Sergeant Read was given Leunen to attack. Both crews encountered diminishing cloud and decided to search out an alternative target, by a strange quirk

*Believed to show the squadron's sergeants at briefing while at RAF Oakington. Sadly, once again the photograph via the association records does not have any additional information other than a pencilled '218 1940' scribbled on the back.*

both selected the aerodrome at Haamstede. Sergeant Marchand flying Blenheim T1864 dropped his 4 x 250 pounders and 40 pounders from the perilously low altitude of 300 feet.

The crew of Sgt Read having identified the aerodrome was forced to give up when low cloud prevented an attack. Flight Sergeant Adam and crew attacked Rotterdam Dock as an alternative to his primary target of Emmerick. One of the most remarkable flights was that of Squadron Leader Gillman and crew who were detailed to attack the oil plant at Grevenbroich. Having crossed the Dutch coast at 13,000 feet S/Ldr Gillman entered the Ruhr south of Duisburg. Dropping to 8,000 feet to best use the available cloud cover, he turned south towards Dusseldorf. It was when nearing the city, he quickly noticed that the cloud that had thus far shielded him and had completely vanished. Courageously pressing on, the crew circled Dusseldorf picking out a factory to bomb. In near perfect visibility, the crew dropped their bomb load from 8,000 feet. The bomb bursts were unobserved. Realising that they may have used up all their luck they turned for home, landing Blenheim T1988 at the fighter base at R.A.F. West Malling, Kent. Remarkably given the near-perfect conditions over Germany, the crew did not encounter flak or fighter opposition. The final crew aloft was that of Pilot Officer Smith who departed at 12:34 hours in Blenheim T1863. They had the unenviable task of attacking Gelsenkirchen, deep inside the Ruhr. Having reached Adeldorn, it was soon apparent that the primary would not be reached due to lack of the promised cloud cover. Turning onto a reciprocal course P/O Smith reduced altitude and entered the cloud, eventually emerging half a mile off the Dutch Coast. Determined to reach his target P/O Smith flew north climbing to 10,000 feet before once again turning inland northeast of Haamstede in the hope of finding better conditions. The plucky crew got as far as the German city of Wesel before once again the lack of cloud forced the crew to abandon the target. In the end, they carried out a shallow diving attack from 1,200 feet on the Docks of Rotterdam. The bombs were seen to explode close to a lock. They eventually landed 5 hours after departing R.A.F. Oakington. It had been an excellent effort by most of the squadron in seeking out suitable targets to attack. The crews were not lacking in courage, just cloud cover. Flight Lieutenant Shaw attended a District Court Martial at R.A.F. Wyton on the morning of the October 4th. A crew from Horsham St Faith reported seeing an S.O.S. flashed from the sea while returning from a morning operation on the 6th, three aircraft of 'A' Flight was ordered to carry out a sweep over the North Sea covering an area 20 miles off Great Yarmouth. Pilot Officers Smith and William Crosse were joined by Sgt Adam who were aloft for over 3 hours scanning the sea. Unfortunately, nothing was sighted. There was some reason to rejoice, especially for the N.C.O.s. The new barrack blocks No.46 and 47 were finally finished, after living under canvas since their arrival the airman could now move in. Furniture was in short supply and there were no clothes lockers, but no one was complaining.

The squadron lost Sergeant Eric Marchand on the 6th when he was posted to No.12 Flying Training School based at R.A.F. Grantham. His observer, Sgt Harold Mason, was posted on detachment to No.10 RAAF Squadron, while the crews gunner Sgt John Moss was posted to No.206 Squadron based at R.A.F. Bircham Newton. Sadly, both would be killed on operations. It was back to Germany on the 7th, four 'A' Flight crews were allocated Ruhr targets, while five crews drawn from 'B' Flight were given reconnaissance duties. Some success was achieved by 'B' Flight, P/O George Agar carried out a shallow dive-bombing attack on 40-50 barges near the Maas estuary, some direct hits were observed. Sergeant Morley attacked a concentration of 40-50 sailing vessel off Sommelsdijk, Holland. Bombs were dropped from 3000 feet but

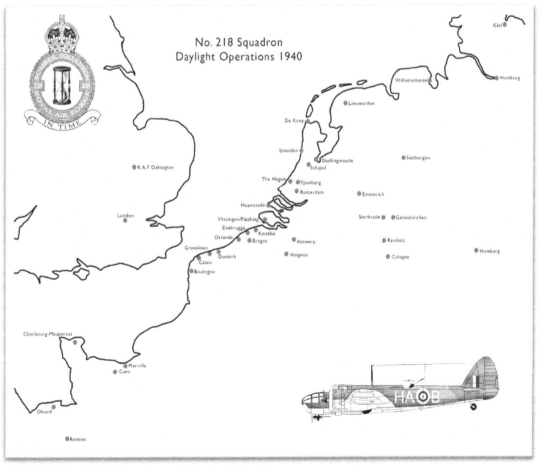

No. 218 Squadron
Daylight Operations 1940

disappointingly missed their target, in frustration the crew machine-gunned the ships. The planned sorties over Germany were cancelled due to insufficient cloud. Pilot Officer Peter Lambert arrived from No.17 O.T.U based at R.A.F. Upwood on the 7th. His arrival brought the squadron's total number of pilots to 17. It was the turn of 'A' flight on the 9th to achieve some success, three crews were given targets in Germany and for once the lack of cloud was not the problem. The first away at 1011hrs was P/O Mitchell in Blenheim N3585 with Emmerich his primary target. He was immediately followed by P/O Crosse and crew who were to attack Gelsenkirchen. The final crew aloft was the recently promoted F/Lt Shaw who was ordered to bomb Homburg. Pilot Officer Mitchell and crew encountered solid cloud that descended to 300 feet over the North Sea. Unable to make an accurate landfall and check their position the crew drifted north of track and ended up near a factory and railway goods yards and sidings near Warendorf, 14 miles E of Munster. Pilot Officer Mitchell took advantage of the low cloud and made a low-level attack from 500 feet, the bombs were seen to straddle the target. Pilot Officer Crosse encountered the same conditions, descending to 100 feet they passed uncomfortably close to the airfield at Wieringermeer, where many Bf109s were seen at their dispersals. Quickly putting as much distance between them and the Bf109s P/O Crosse dropped to just 20 feet above the ground, this was perilously low and any mistake would be catastrophic. As the crew neared the Dutch coast, the cloud lifted to 600 feet, believing that the conditions may have improved further north the crew headed towards Bergen-Alkmaar. Disappointingly, the cloud was almost at sea level. It was plainly obvious that neither the primary nor the secondary targets could be reached so reluctantly P/O Crosse turned for home. It was the crew of F/Lt Shaw in Blenheim P6960 that had the most frustrating encounter of the day. Unable to reach their primary target, they encountered a Heinkel He111 flying along the Dutch coast near the town of Oustvoorne. Not wanting to miss an opportunity to mix it with the bomber F/Lt Shaw gave chase. Catching up with the He111 Shaw opened up with his forward gun, to his dismay it refused to fire, drawing alongside and slightly ahead Sgt Ron Gill in the turret opened up at a range of 250 yards. His fire was accurate as tracer was seen to enter amidships, it was only now that the German crew opened fire. In an apparent effort to lose their antagonists the He111 pilot gently turned to port, there appeared to be no urgency from the German crew. Cutting across the bomber F/Lt Shaw managed to catch up and offered his gunner another opportunity to engage. Ron Gill opened fire, once again strikes were observed until again these to fell silent, the machine gun had jammed after 120 rounds. There was nothing to do but manoeuvre the Blenheim so that the rear firing blister gun could be brought to bear. Having positioned the Blenheim slightly in front of the Heinkel, F/Lt Shaw ordered Sgt Wynne the crews observer to engage, to everyone's annoyance after just 20 rounds this gun too fell silent, yet another jam. It was a bitterly disappointed crew that turned for home, what was said to the armourers is unknown upon their return. Damaged to Blenheim P6960 was a single bullet hole in the rudder. Wing Commander Combe, his flight commander S/Ldr Ault and P/O Smith were aloft just after 7 pm carrying out a series of night landings and local circuits on the 9th. The continual push towards night operations was still very much a priority. The following day the squadron welcomed the return of F/Lt Hughes D.F.C. who was piloting the R.A.F.'s latest and relatively new night fighter, the Bristol Beaufighter Mk.IF. The pilots on the squadron were particularly interested in this brutish and heavily armed aircraft which made its stablemate the Blenheim look somewhat obsolete. If the arrival of the Beaufighter was not enough excitement at 16:00 hours a very new aircraft landed on Oakington's grass runway. All the squadron came out to look over the massive four-engine Short Stirling. The sheer size of the No.7 Squadron Stirling staggered the assembled airman, it was the largest aircraft in Bomber Command's growing arsenal. The squadrons long-awaited debut flying night operations was scheduled for the night of the 11th. Six 'B' Flight crews led F/Lt Richmond were given invasion ports to attack that night. Each of the Battles was loaded with four 250lbs. Sadly, for all concerned, the operation was cancelled on account of fog. It was not until the 16th that the squadron was once again on the battle order. Flight Lieutenant Shaw was the first aloft just after 9 am flying the now customary weather reconnaissance flight, his message back to base was not encouraging, little cloud and weather unsuitable for operations over Germany. On his return flight, F/Lt Shaw briefly saw an aircraft flying in the opposite direction towards the Netherlands at a mere 100 feet above the sea. Sea mist and hazy conditions prevented immediate recognition. The mystery aircraft challenged the Blenheim by signalling by lamp the letter 'T'. Although 'T' was not the letter of the day, Shaw was still not sure of its identity. After losing altitude the Blenheim drew alongside the aircraft at 600 yards, it was only then that the black cross and bulbous nose of a Ju88 was instantly recognisable. Shaw immediately orders Sgt Gill to open fire on the Junkers. Ron Gill engaged with two well-aimed bursts, Shaw then turned into the Ju88 for a stern attack. The German pilot realising the danger opened the throttles of the powerful Jumo engines leaving the poor old Blenheim well behind. More in hope F/Lt Shaw opened fire with his single forward-firing gun, but by now the Ju88 was almost 800 yards in front, frustratingly the .303 rounds were seen falling short. They landed back at Oakington at 11:15 hours, happy that at least the guns did not jam on this occasion!

It was not until 1130 hours the first of the squadron's Blenheim departed. New Zealander P/O Anstey was the first away in Blenheim N3573, their target was Gravelines. He found a convoy of 13 ships off Gravelines which were attacked from 19,500 feet. Sergeant Donald followed in N3562, the crew encountered trouble even before they reached the English coast. Flying at 1,500 feet over Hastings the local anti-aircraft batteries opened fire, thankfully their aim, like their aircraft recognition was poor. The only damage caused was a few holes in the rudder and tail plane. Unable to attack the primary target of Boulogne due to insufficient cloud the crew returned to base. The docks at Calais were the intended target for P/O Turnbull, despite flying to within sight of the French coast at 17,500 feet he too was unable to find sufficient cover to complete his task. Squadron Leader Ault lifted off a few minutes before 1 pm in Blenheim T1888, by the time S/Ldr Ault had reached mid Channel he was flying at 16,000 feet, the coast of France could be clearly seen, more worryingly was the complete lack of cloud over his attended target, Dunkirk. Realising that any attempt to bomb was suicidal the crew turned for home, as they did so two German aircraft were seen flying 2000 feet directly above them. Squadron Leader Ault identified one as a Heinkel 113 while the other was either a Me110 (Jaguar) version or a Dornier 17. Carefully Ault lost height as quickly as he could without drawing attention to himself, thankfully both German aircraft kept on their course without noticing the lower flying Blenheim, it had been a close shave for the crew who landed shortly after 1400 hours. Why these attacks were attempted is questionable given the earlier unfavourable weather report submitted by F/Lt Shaw.

Some welcome news arrived on the 17th, a letter was received from Mrs Howard wife of Sgt Howard, air gunner lost with S/Ldr House in August. In her letter she wrote that *'My husband was in a prison camp and that his aircraft had been shot down in flames and he had saved himself by parachute, he landed with a wound over his eye and was taken prisoner almost immediately'*. The squadron received another letter, this time sent by Mr Bryan, father of L.A.C. Bryan. He was initially posted as missing and later 'Killed in Action' on May 14th. Mr Bryan informed the squadron that contrary to the earlier reports, his son was very much alive and had managed to parachute to safety and was now a prisoner of war. The Sergeants Mess and Quarters were finished and opened on the 18th along with the airman's dining area and kitchen. Things were finally improving. Nine squadron crews were allocated targets in Germany on the morning of October 19th. However, this was changed to attacks on enemy airfields within 60 miles of the coast due to lack of cloud cover. Four crews departed at 08:20 hours, frustratingly all returned without completing their allotted tasks on account of the weather conditions. It was on this day that F/Lt Shaw would start his 'special operations', below is the O.R.B. entry for this most unusual type of operation.

*F/Lt Shaw has been selected for special operational duties and is from today given, with his crew, a free hand to attack any self-evident military objective or military objective previously attacked, in Germany or the German occupied territory provided cloud cover is adequate at all times, whether or not the station is on duty. He is given full latitude as to when to go out on a mission, and the target to be attacked, or the weather conditions chosen are left to his judgement. This relieves F/Lt Shaw from other operational duties.*

The first of what would be known as "Roving Commission" flights was undertaken on the 21st, he departed RAF Oakington at 14:30 hours, the following is the entry in the Operational Records Book.

*F/Lt Shaws first operational flight this afternoon. He took off in rather poor visibility, choosing Dunkirk or Gravelines, or shipping in the neighbourhood as his target. Sgt Wynne and Sgt Gill were his crew. They broke cloud 4 miles west of Dunkirk. Cloud in that area was rather thin, with base at 10000ft-20000ft and visibility was poor. Near Dunkirk the crew saw two fairly large ships and circled them with the intention of making an attack. In the mist however they lost sight of them. A few moments later they came quite suddenly upon a convoy consisting of 14 ships led by a larger one escorted by 4 E Boats. F/Lt Shaw circled to approach the convoy from the rear and Sgt Wynne prepared the camera, until F/Lt Shaw told him to prepare to bomb quickly as possible and leave the camera alone. On the run up, the aircraft was challenged by a 3-star white flare, its reply was a stick of bombs which feel down the centre, along and slightly across the convoy. It is recorded that Sgt Wynne, the bomb aimer wore an expression of amazement as he saw where his bombs fell and exclaimed "GOOD HEAVENS, I'VE HIT IT" Of this there was no doubt, one ship was almost capsized, and its masts lay on the water and its hull seemed to be awash. Three other ships near it were heeling over when the Blenheim circled, and machine gunned them. The convoy dispersed rapidly while the E Boats dashed backwards and forwards apparently looking for survivor. During the attack, the crew met with considerable M.G and Pom-Pom fire. The aircraft was only at 2000 feet and the fire was accurate. Pom-Pom fire seemed to come particularly close. There was also a certain amount of heavy A.A fire from the shore but it was inaccurate. F/Lt Shaw returned to base at 16:55 hours. About an hour and a half later a telephone message was received from HQ 2 Group that a signal from the convoy to its base had been intercepted indicating that there were two dead and two wounded.*

It had been a splendid effort by the crew and justified the faith the commanding officer had in this experienced pilot and crew. The convoy attacked is understood to be that of 32 MS-Flotilla, which were transporting army soldiers.

A blanket of mist prevented operations for the next two days. It was not until the 24th that the squadron would operate, even then the weather would prevent the squadron from carrying out its original orders of attacking targets in the Ruhr. Unsuitable weather meant a change. The squadron would now attack the Channel ports and enemy shipping. As it turned out the squadron had some success, F/Lt Richmond was the first away at 0900 hours in Blenheim T1996, and his target was Zeebrugge. On reaching the enemy coast there was no sign of the forecast cloud, what he found,

*It was barges likes these the squadron actively sort out. Flat bottomed and used primarily for inland waterways they would have been rather uncomfortable crossing the choppy English Channel.*

however, was a small convoy of five ships. Wasting no time F/Lt Richmond immediately began his attack with both bombs and machine gunfire. His bombs exploded 50 yards from the rear boat, close but not close enough. However, the fire from the rear and blister guns was accurate as strikes were seen ricocheting off the decks. Having delivered his attack, F/Lt Richmond turned for base. Flying only a few hundred feet above the sea the Blenheim was without warning violently catapulted upwards, an explosion immediately below the aircraft brought a moment of panic to the crew. Thankfully, the experienced Richmond regained control within seconds. It is believed that a 250lb bomb had failed to release during the attack and dropped off on its own accord exploding on impact with the sea, as scary as it was, it could have been much worse, the bomb could have dropped on landing. Sergeant Morley flying Blenheim N6183 was given Flushing to attack, once again lack of cloud meant that the crew were obliged to seek out a target of opportunity, by chance they stumbled upon the convoy attacked by F/Lt Richmond. The already alert gunners greeted Morley with a barrage of accurate light flak and machine gunfire. Such was the intensity of his reception, Sgt Morley decided that his efforts would be better used on a less dangerous target. Flying south the crew found the airfield of Mardyck, situated west of Dunkirk. After flying over the aerodrome to take photographs, the crew made a dicey second run dropping their 4 x 250lb on the home of II./JG 51. Quickly turning for home, the crew were shocked to discover a Bf109 on their starboard bow only 500 feet lower. Both the Blenheim and the fighter entered a thin layer of cloud. Morley decided to gain altitude in the hope of thicker cloud above, to his horror on reaching 4,500 feet the cloud suddenly vanished and sitting just a few hundred yards to starboard was another Bf109 which immediately turned into attack. Putting the nose down the Blenheim raced towards the safety of the cloud below. Deciding it would be probably safer at low level the crew dropped down to with a few feet of the sea and headed for home.

Pilot Officer Crosse and crew set off for Gravelines at 09:11 hours. Crossing the coast to fix their position, once established they turned out to sea. On crossing the coast, the crew encountered accurate flak from a solitary barge and shore positions. Obviously slighted, Crosse turned and made a diving attack on the barge dropping one 250lb bomb and two 40lb bombs. Results were not observed but flak damage had been inflicted to the leading edge and tail plane. Deciding to find another target, Crosse flew south along the coast, approaching a small harbour the crew noticed a small vessel just outside the harbour entrance, instantly P/O Crosse decide to attack. Heavy flak from the nearby shore burst all around the Blenheim as it raced in at 1,500 feet to deliver the Coup de grâce. If the heavy flak was not troublesome enough light flak and heavy calibre machine gunfire emanating from the harbour crisscrossed the sky, thankfully the damage was restricted to just a few holes in the port wing, none of the crew observed the results of the bombing. Having used up all their luck, they turned for home landing at Oakington at 11:45 hours.

The ever-resourceful P/O Smith and crew were given Calais to attack, but the blanket of cloud that had accompanied the crew since leaving Oakington began to fade away as they neared the target. Selecting a marshalling yard and factory situated at Le Pont De Leu, on the outskirts of Calais the crew sped into the target at just 2000 feet. Intense and accurate flak greeted the crew damaging both wings, one shell ripping a large hole in the port wing just in front of the flaps. Undeterred Sgt Baxter, the crew's bomb aimer, dropped the entire bomb load in one salvo into the middle of the marshalling yard, the results were unobserved. Blenheim T1863 landed back at base just after 11 am, they had been aloft only 1 hour 55 minutes. The squadron lost 'B' Flight's P/O Alexander Stewart Turnbull on the 24th, posted to No.6 Operational Training Unit at RAF Sutton Bridge. Sadly, he would be killed in North Africa flying the Bristol Beaufighter with 153 Squadron, a night fighter unit. While on a convoy patrol the engine aboard Beaufighter IVF V8548 failed resulting in the aircraft ditching north of Cap Sigli, Algeria, at the time of his death he was a squadron leader.

With F/Lt Shaw attending a conference at RAF Wyton, P/O Mitchell would carry out a "Roving Commission" on the 25th. Unfortunately, the weather got the better of the crew who return without bombing. It was around this time that a rumour began to circulate that the squadron was going to convert to the Vickers Wellington and commence night bombing operations. Since its reformation back in 1936 218's primary role was day bombing. The handful of pre-war pilots and crews, including the ever increasing number of aircrew arriving from the O.T.U's had all been trained to operate in daylight. For the time at least, their role was still daylight bombing. Most dismissed the rumour, why change now was the feeling amongst the crews. Other than the solitary 'Roving" operation on the 25th, the squadron spent the next two days either practice bombing or at readiness.

The squadron was given a targets in northern Germany on the 27th. Squadron Leader Ault was given the unenviable task of attacking Hamburg. Soon after crossing the Dutch coast the promised cloud vanished, Hamburg was spared the 4 x 250 pounders. The crew flew south skirting the flat Dutch coastline. Eventually, they spotted a small merchant ship steaming towards Ijmuiden. The bombs were dropped but seen to fall 60 yards short. Sergeant Adam was given the important docks at Kiel. He returned without bombing. The crew of 'A' Flight's Pilot Officer Smith were briefed to attack Wilhelmshaven, not finding the expected cloud cover promised by the Met officer, the crew flew northwards along the Dutch coast in the hope that it may improve. After 20 minutes flying it was apparent that Wilhelmshaven could not be reached, turning back to look for a worthwhile target the crew located two Dornier 18 flying boats flying 500 feet below them. The two Do18s were flying in formation, P/O Smith decided to bomb the pair from above. Slowly catching up with the pair from astern and using what little cloud cover was available, Smith ordered his observer to bomb. It was at this moment the Dornier crews spotted the Blenheim, both aircraft swerved as the bombs exploded in the sea. Sergeant Baxter was adamant that if they had not been spotted, the explosions would have brought down the lumbering flying boats. Pilot Officer Smith quickly engaged the first flying boat opening fire with his front gun, drawing alongside Sgt Rankin opened fire from the rear

*The unmistakable Do18 Flying Boat. It would have probably been the most unconventional 'Kill' of the war if the bombs dropped by Sgt Baxter had found their mark.*

turret. As the crew turned away, black smoke was seen streaming from the Dornier's engine. Making another attack, the rear gun suddenly stopped due to a blockage. Sergeant Rankin informed his pilot that the second Dornier was approaching from astern, with the rear turret out of action, P/O Smith pushed the throttles forward and headed towards the nearest cloud and home.

New Zealander P/O Anstey and crew were also tasked with attacking Wilhelmshaven, finding the same conditions they were about to turn for home when Sgt Thomas the rear gunner noticed a significant splash in the sea below. It was then that an aircraft was spotted by Anstey about 20 miles distant, unsure of its identity Anstey changed course and headed towards the Dutch Coast but encountered severe icing soon after crossing, realising that any attempt to reach Wilhelmshaven was impossible he turned for home. Thirty miles off the English coast, the crew noticed an unexploded sea mine floating on the surface. These rogue mines were a serious hazard to allied shipping sailing along the east coast. Sergeant Tom Thomas the rear gunner opened fire with his single .303, after 270 rounds, a lot of swearing and much frustration it was decided to bomb the mine with a single 250lb bomb. This too failed to detonate the mine. By now the crew were getting low on fuel and after plotting the mine's position turned for base. Ten miles off the Norfolk coast four Royal Navy mine sweepers was spotted, using the Aldis Lamp Sgt John Jackson signalled the location of the mine, the signal was acknowledged as the crew set course for Oakington. Another crew aloft was F/Lt Shaw, given a free hand where to attack. He chose the North of Holland area as a likely hunting ground. Once again aloft in his favourite Blenheim, P6960 the crew crossed the North Sea at 3000 feet. Finding insufficient cloud, F/Lt Shaw headed towards Terschelling, 12 miles north of the island they encountered a convoy of what appeared to be 13 minesweepers steaming in two lines. Decided to attack, the crew raced into a barrage of flak, Sgt Wynne's aim was good but slightly too good as the 4 x 250 pounders exploded directly between the two columns of minesweepers. Making one more pass both the rear and blisters guns opened fire registering hits on two vessels. F/Lt Shaw takes up the encounters;

*Continuing our roving commissions, we encountered 14 enemy small ships three and a half miles off Dunkirk, two parallel columns of seven with a larger ship at their head, escorted by four E-boats. We started our bombing run and released all bombs straddling the two lines of boats being slightly diagonal to their course. On turning, we found that one of the ships was sinking and three more had been damaged and the rest of the vessels had scattered. When debriefing back at base, we were informed that German W/T signals had been intercepted confirming that the E-boats had picked up survivors and some bodies. A satisfactory result.*

A major sweep of the North Sea was carried out on the 28th, six crews drawn from 'B' Flight were away just after 10 am, forty minutes later, four crews of 'A' Flight were aloft, for nearly three hours the aircraft swept the sea looking for survivors of a ditched Dornier 18, nothing was found. Eager to make up for his disappointing 'Roving' operation the previous day F/Lt Shaw was the only crew aloft on the 29th. They were over a 10/10th cloud covered Holland desperately trying to find some landmark in the solid cloud. Unable to do so, F/Lt Walter Shaw turned on a receptacle course and headed back out over the sea in the hope the cloud would be better further south. Flying parallel to the coast the visibility began to improve slightly, people were seen out walking or cycling along the seafront. Some realising they were RAF waved vigorously as the Blenheim roared past at less than 1,200 feet.

The Blenheim approached the Hague at a mere 500 feet. Such was the surprise of this lone bomber that not one shot was fired. Within seconds they were the nearing the docks and port of Rotterdam, here six ships and a large crane lay directly in front of them. Selecting this as his target, Shaw gently pushed the nose down of his Blenheim and commenced a shallow dive. At 300 feet the four 250lb bombs were dropped in a salvo with a 11 second delay. By accident, the four 40 pounders were also dropped, these exploded on impact catapulting the Blenheim 100 feet upwards from the blast, at the same time showering the fuselage with fragments, one large piece penetrating close to the wireless set. Before the German defenders could engage the Blenheim, it was gone, it had been an excellent piece of airmanship by Shaw and his crew. It was on the 28th that new Officers' Mess was officially opened, much to the delight of the officers! It was opened just in time as members of No.7 Squadron began to arrive from RAF Leeming, with them they brought their massive Stirling bombers.

German naval and industrial targets were planned for the 30th. However, the weather once again forced a last-minute change. As an alternative, the squadron was given a number of new targets in Brittany and Normandy. Five new targets were chalked up on the Ops board, the airfields at Rennes, Caen, Dinard and finally Cherbourg - Maupertus. Sergeant Donald Hoos and crew were detailed to attack the aerodrome at Rennes, the home of the Heinkel He111 equipped KG27. Deciding that this distant target could not be reached given the lack of cloud, the crew attacked the docks at Cherbourg. Bombing from 6,000 feet the bomb load was dropped on four cargo ships moored close to a large warehouse. A mass of flak opened up, thankfully exploding a mere 50 yards astern of the Blenheim as it dived into the cloud bank for safety. Pilot Officer Mitchell spent most of his operation admiring the scenic views along the French coastline in the sunshine. He wasted no time in turning for home confident in the fact that Caen airfield would never be reached safely. Pilot Office Agar attacked five E Boats sailing off Cherbourg, his bombs landing within 30 yards of one showering it in water. Squadron Leader Ault was unable to reach his primary target, the airfield at Cherbourg - Maupertus due to insufficient cloud, instead he attacked three large cargo ships of about 5,000 tons off Pointe de Barfleur, reporting that one may have been damaged. Not one of the targets had been reached due to insufficient cloud, it was now becoming a regular occurrence and was slowly sapping at morale.

The squadron welcomed a recently qualified pilot in the form of Sergeant Bernard Madgwick from No.13 O.T.U on the 30th, he would be the last posting to arrive on the squadron at RAF Oakington. The last operation of the month was flown by the uncontainable F/Lt Shaw and crew who deciding to search the Hague -De Kooy area, they set off once again in Blenheim P6960. Arriving over the Hague the crew were met with a solid mass of cloud, slipping down to 1000 feet the crew picked out Ypenberg aerodrome in the murk. In an attempt make a pass over the hangars the aerodrome was lost in the cloud, deciding not to hang about F/Lt Shaw made for Soesterberg aerodrome instead. There was no mistake this time, the airfield was bombed from 600 feet, the 4 x 250lb and 4 x 40lbs were delivered accurately. In the rear turret, Sgt Ron Gill opened fire on a parade of German airman who rapidly scattered in all directions in a frantic attempt to miss the .303s ricocheting off the tarmac.

October can best be described as frustrating, despite the continuing determination of the crews the weather continued to thwart their efforts. Some useful damaged had been achieved, however the squadron was becoming increasingly frustrated. At the mercy of the weather the crews had to weigh up the dangers of continuing with an operation when the required cloud cover was absent. The pre-war press-on attitude was still very much prevalent as witnessed by the squadron's activities in May. On the plus side, 58 operations had been undertaken, all without loss. Towards the end of the month what started as a trickle became a wave of airman arriving from RAF Leeming, having been the soul occupants since their arrival, they were now in the minority.

# Chapter 10: November 1940 to July 1941 – Heavy Brigade

There were no operations flown until November 3rd when once again, F/Lt Walter Shaw carried out a 'Roving Commission' sortie over Holland. As it turned out this would be the last operation flown by the squadron on the Bristol Blenheim. The weather, that had dogged the squadron over the past few months once again resulted in the planned sortie over Germany being changed. In the end F/Lt Shaw attacked a large factory near the dock side at Flushing. Despite the 80-mph gale and heavy rain, Sgt Wynne placed the entire bomb load squarely on the target. Once again F/Lt Shaw recalls;

*On 3 November, we carried out another roving flight in very bad weather conditions. A strong wind was gusting up to 80 mph. We located the dock area at Flushing and dropped the bomb load on the installations. This was my last operational flight in a Blenheim. Shortly after this, pilots were gathered together in a crew room for a talk by a recruiting officer from Fighter Command and asked who would like to fly fighters and we all stood up. He then said 'night fighters' and we all sat down again!*

The previously voiced whispers about converting to the Wellington were finally confirmed at 1630 hours on November 3rd when a message from No.2 HQ confirmed that the squadron would re-equip immediately with the Vickers Wellington. Two dual control MkIa and 8 MkIc would be delivered as quickly as they became available. The trusty old Blenheims would be withdrawn at a rate of 2 per Wellington. The following Blenheims are known to have been still serving with the squadron at the time.

| Serial | Delivered | Maker | Contract | Flight | Ops Flown |
|--------|-----------|-------|----------|--------|-----------|
| R3666 | 12.09.1940 | Rootes Securities Ltd | B.1485/40 | A | 5 |
| P6960 | 05.07.1940 | Bristol, Filton | 774679/38 | A | 11 |
| T1863 | 15.07.1940 | Rootes Securities Ltd | B.1485/39 | A | 6 |
| T1864 | 15.07.1940 | Rootes Securities Ltd | 551920/36 | A | 7 |
| T1865 | 15.07.1940 | Rootes Securities Ltd | 774679/38 | A | 4 |
| T1888 | 15.07.1940 | Rootes Securities Ltd | 774679/38 | A | 12 |
| N3585 | 16.07.1940 | A.V Roe and Co Ltd | 599371/38 | A | 5 |
| N3625 | 08.08.1940 | A.V Roe and Co Ltd | 599371/39 | A | 3 |
| L9381 | 25.07.1940 | Rootes Securities Ltd | 551920/36 | A | 7 |
| P6959 | 05.07.1940 | Bristol, Filton | 774679/38 | B | 13 |
| T1987 | 24.07.1940 | Rootes Securities Ltd | 1485/39 | B | 4 |

| | | | | | |
|---|---|---|---|---|---|
| T1988 | 24.07.1940 | Rootes Securities Ltd | 1485/39 | B | 1 |
| T1996 | 16.07.1940 | Rootes Securities Ltd | 1485/39 | B | 5 |
| N3563 | 16.07.1940 | A.V Roe and Co Ltd | 599371/36 | B | 1 |
| N3561 | 16.07.1940 | A.V Roe and Co Ltd | 599371/37 | B | 3 |
| N3562 | 17.07.1940 | A.V Roe and Co Ltd | 599371/39 | B | 7 |
| N3573 | 20.08.1940 | A.V Roe and Co Ltd | 599371/39 | B | 13 |
| N6183 | 04.08.1940 | Bristol, Filton | 774679/38 | B | 5 |
| L9306 | 24.07.1940 | Rootes Securities Ltd | 551920/36 | B | 6 |
| L9298 | 08.08.1940 | Rootes Securities Ltd | 1485/39 | B | 7 |
| L9327 | 09.09.1940 | Rootes Securities Ltd | 551920/36 | B | 3 |
| T1987 | 24.07.1940 | Rootes Securities Ltd | 1485/39 | B | 4 |
| T1988 | 24.07.1940 | Rootes Securities Ltd | 1485/39 | B | 1 |
| T1996 | 16.07.1940 | Rootes Securities Ltd | 1485/39 | B | 5 |
| R3673 | 28.06.1940 | Rootes Securities Ltd | B.1485/40 | N/A | 0 |
| L1137(Blenheim Mk.I) | 31.07.1940 | Bristol, Filton | 5271114/36 | Training Aircraft | |

*The above details have been taken from various logbooks and the squadron's Operational Records Book, however the author cannot be certain of the accuracy.*

On the 3rd of November, Air Vice Marshal Robb DSO DFC AFC 2 Group commanding officer visited Oakington and spoke with the crews of 218 Squadron. He was sorry to lose them, especially having worked tirelessly to meet the challenges and demands of 2 Group H.Q since their return from France. It was not the only squadron AVM Robb would lose, No.15, 40 and 57 Squadrons would also transfer to No.3 Group within the month. The following day a signal was received notifying the squadron that from the 5th the squadron would be transferred to No.3 Group. There was some disappointment from the crews who were informed that the planned operation for the 5th was cancelled, they had hoped to celebrate Guy Fawkes Night in the appropriate manner over Hun land. Most, but not all the crews were sorry to lose the Blenheim, the squadron Operational Record Books recorded that *"Keen disappointment is felt at the prospect of losing the Blenheim which most of the pilots had grown to like "* The squadron lost one of its longest-serving sergeant observers, on the 5th. Sergeant Ernest Farmes, a pre-war veteran, was posted to No.101 Squadron, sadly he would be killed within a month on a reinforcement flight to the Middle East. With the Wellington equipped with two power-operated turrets, the squadron welcomed Flight Lieutenant Ian Magrath from Central Gunnery School (CGS) Warmwell. He arrived the same day as Sgt Farmes departed, he would be giving some hands-on training on the mechanical aspects of the Fraser Nash turrets. The prospect of re-equipping with the somewhat cumbersome Vickers Wellington was not to everyone's liking. Some pilots were not too keen on converting from daylight operations to nocturnal operations, especially some of the old hands. The Squadron Operational Records Book records the anxiety *" Views on this type are at present held in reserve, and any absence of optimism must be attributed to the single-minded affection for the Blenheim"*.

On arriving back in England in June 1940 and their new alliance with No.2 Group, few of the survivors could have believed that the squadron, or more accurately what was left of it could have turned its fortunes around so quickly and so effectively. Arriving at Oakington with no aircraft, no equipment and the vast majority of the air gunners and observers missing or posted there was a feeling of utter despondency. Under the capable leadership of W/Cdr Duggan and his senior captains, the squadron very quickly set about achieving the extremely high standards that all had come to expect. This they did, an influx of new crews and a steady delivery of aircraft meant the squadron quickly found itself back in the front line. The Bristol Blenheim played a big part in the recovery of the squadron's spirit and gave those that a fought so bravely over France a chance to hit back and a reasonable chance of survival. The crews showed time and time again that courage was not a problem on the squadron, nor were there complaints about the performance of the Blenheim. It was the type of operations the squadron found frustrating, the dangers of individual aircraft flying sorties over Germany and the occupied territories in daylight was an accepted occupational hazard. Time and time again the crews would experience the pre-operation tension, climb aboard the fully loaded Blenheim and cross the North Sea or English Channel only for the clouds that had been promised by the Met officer were not there. It was a hard decision having flown so far just to turn around, some did, others, the more press on types did not. If the squadron had begun night operations on the Blenheim in a similar fashion to the other 2 Group Squadrons, its future might have been very different. As it was its brief time with 2 Group was over, if anything the time was critical in building up the squadron's morale and confidence, something that it had been severely shaken in France. One immediate benefit of joining No.3 Group was that the squadron was no longer operational, 50% of the flying crews departed on 12 days leave that same day. On the morning of the 6th, those aircrews remaining would have been disappointed to see the arrival of a rather battered and weary duel control Wellington Mk.Ia, serial L4293. The aircraft was allotted to "B" Flight where it did not make a particularly good impression. Thankfully, the squadron took delivery of Wellington R1009 during the afternoon. This was a brand new Vickers built Mk.Ic fresh from No.23 Maintenance Unit. Equipped with two Bristol Pegasus XVIII engines, it was a vast improvement on the Mk.Ia that had so shocked the assembled crews earlier in the morning. The cumbersome 'Dustbin' turret had was removed and the aperture covered, two detachable .303 were fitted amidships. The front and rear turrets were equipped with twin browning .303s, the defensive capability over the Blenheim was increased two-fold. It also meant an increase in crew members, Pilot (Captain) second pilot, navigator, two wireless operators /air gunners and a rear gunner.

For the pilots, the conversion was going to be challenging given the size of the Wellington over the Blenheim. The wingspan was almost double that of the Blenheim, and it was twice as heavy. The first pilot to fly the Wellington was F/Lt Richmond on the 7th, he took off in R1009 and flew a number of circuits before carrying out a landing practice. Two more Wellington Mk.Ics arrived during the afternoon, R1008 and R1025, both from No.23 M.U. One of the Wellingtons was flown by a Czech pilot who was transported back to RAF East Wretham by P/O Smith in one of the Blenheims. At the time, the Czechs were also busy

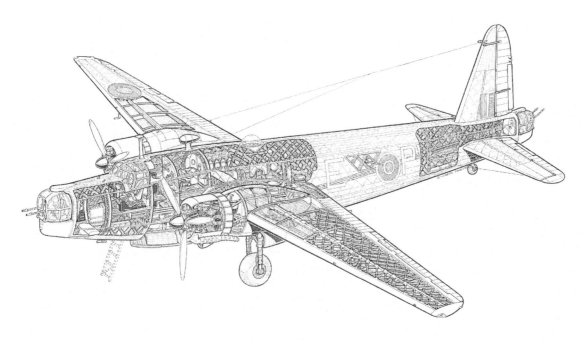

Vickers Armstrong Wellington I C

familiarising themselves with the Vickers Wellington. On the afternoon of the 8th, F/Lt Richmond was again aloft in R1009, and he was joined by F/Lt Shaw and P/O Anstey on a 60 minute familiarisation flight. In the afternoon both would carry out their first flights as captain, F/Lt Shaw taking R1008 while New Zealander Anstey skippered R1009, both trips were faultless. It was the turn of the NCO pilots to get their hands on their new charges on the 9th. The first was Sergeant Geoff Morley who carried out a series of take-off and landings. Representatives of the armament and signals section, plus maintenance flight were temporally detached for four days to gain experience with an operational Wellington squadron. On the 10th, Blenheim R3666 was flown to RAF Raynham, it was the first of the trusty Blenheims to depart. It was also the last flight F/Lt Shaw would fly in the Blenheim.

*On 10 November, I flew P6960 to RAF Watchfield near Swindon to attend a course at No. 1 Blind Approach School. This was my last actual flight in my old aircraft with our good luck emblem painted on the nose. It was a small demon-like figure with stunted wings and a long, doleful looking face. We called it our Mugwump. It was copied from a cartoon in a magazine and bore the caption 'Harbinger of Doom'. Aircrew are a superstitious lot.*

Shaw attended No.1 Standard Blind Approach Course at RAF Watchfield, near Swindon. Watchfield was one of the first airfields to teach Blind/Beam Approach training which meant that when no other aircraft were flying in the country due to the weather, Watchfield's Anson's were airborne teaching pilots how to land in dangerous conditions. It was an intensive course, over the 11 days Shaw would be airborne on each of them. Pilot Officer Dunham arrived on the squadron on the 11th via No.214 Squadron. Peter Dunham had started his RAF career as a LAC air gunner, with sheer determination and a big dollop of skill he had risen through the ranks and was now a qualified observer. On the morning of November 13th, two more Wellington MkIcs arrived from No.44 M.U, Vickers built N2844 and T2801. These were followed in the afternoon by another duel controlled Wellington Mk.Ia, N2937. This somewhat tired old Wellington had previously served with No.37 and 75 Squadrons. Four qualified rear gunners, Sergeants Herbert Riding, Louis Kolitz, Thomas Dunk and Arthur Rose, arrived on the 13th via No.1 RAF Depot, Uxbridge. The delivery of a further two Wellington MkIcs T2885 and R1183 brought the squadron's total to seven MkIc and two duel control Mk.Ias. Concerns about the deterioration of the grassed runways was now a priority. A spell of heavy rain and the weight of the Wellingtons and the even heavier Stirlings had caused some parts of the airfield to become boggy and rutted. These areas were marked off with many red flags.

The Wellington equipped 9 Squadron provided Sergeants Frederick Reed, front gunner and Thomas Bowen, wireless operator on the 14th. The squadron was beginning to increase not only in aircraft but aircrew. Wing Commander Combe was aloft in the duel controlled MkIa on the morning of the 15th, while the commanding officer was airborne the squadron received another Wellington, R1210. This brought the squadron's strength to 8 I.E. aircraft and 2 Dual control. The delivery of a further 8 Wellingtons would begin within the next few weeks. Five of the Blenheims were flown to their new homes on the afternoon of the 15th, two to No.38 M.U Llandow and three to No.33 M.U Lyneham. The continuing deterioration of the airfield and the wet conditions was affecting training, no flights were undertaken on the 17th, and only limited flying was conducted on the 18th. Those fortunate to have been sent on 12 days leave began to arrive back on the 18th. Their arrival back meant that those who had remained were now getting ready to depart for their leave. Once again, the condition of the airfield meant that only a handful of flights were flown on the 19th. It was now becoming a significant problem.

Pilot Officer Byng-Hall arrived from No.29 Squadron on the 19th, an experienced air gunner he had fought during the Battle of Britain. Percy Byng-Hall was born in England in 1907 but went to Canada as a child. Just before the outbreak of the war, he returned to England as a member of the West Nova Scotia Regiment. He transferred to the RAF in May 1940 as a direct-entry Air Gunner joining 29 Squadron on July 7th.

The following day W/Cdr Combe departed on ten days leave, S/Ldr Gillman assumed command. The squadron had a new adjutant, if but temporary. Pilot Officer Mitchell, who not for the first time, assumed the role until relief was found. Seven Blenheims managed to depart despite the boggy conditions on the 21st, collected by pilots from Ferry Command. In the afternoon, a squadron Wellington became bogged down requiring the help of a tractor to tow it to a firmer patch of ground. The following morning three Blenheims fell victim to the treacherous conditions delaying their departure. The complaints about the condition of the runways at Oakington had finally reached group H.Q. On the 22nd, Air Vice Marshal Baldwin arrived to inspect the airfield at 15:00 hours, what he found was an airfield more reminiscent of the Somme than an operational station. Harrison realised that action had to be taken and quickly. At 2300 hour, a message was received from 3 Group H.Q, No.218 Squadron was to move immediately to RAF Marham, and the move was to be completed by the 26th. The following morning a conference was quickly arranged to discuss the impending move, it was a case all hands to the pump. By 14:00 hours the first party ably led by P/O Hugh Magee had left for Marham, it had been a tremendous effort. On the 24th, W/Cdr Combe returned from leave having been recalled. His return was in time to see ten lorry loads of equipment start the journey to Norfolk. On the 25th, the Air Party departed however lousy weather resulted in a swift return to Oakington. The Main Party left at 11:00 hours arriving just after 13:00 hours. The Air Party eventually took off in the afternoon with a break in the weather. They arrived just after 15:15 hours. With most of the squadron in residence at Marham and the chaos of the previous 48 hours over the squadron took stock of their new home.

There was some discontentment amongst the squadron. They had come to enjoy the new facilities and comforts of Oakington even with the arrival of 7 Squadron. Having just settled in they found themselves once again on the move. It was becoming a bit of a habit. More annoying was what they saw on their arrival at Marham. The hangars and barracks were filthy and the whole place needed organising since the departure of No.38 Squadron to Fayid, Egypt only a few weeks prior. Wing Commander Combe immediately ordered a clean-up and requested an interview with the station commander Group Captain Victor Groom DFC and bar MiD. Marham had been operational during the Great War when it was used as a night landing ground for the defence of Norfolk against Zeppelins. Like so many airfields after the end of the war, the airfield languished until the first half of 1935 when work started on a new airfield which became active on April

*The damaged and rather neglected grave of Sergeant Edward Evans DFM. Buried in Southey Green Cemetery, Sheffield this is the last resting place of a brave young airman.*

1st, 1937. The first squadron to arrive was No. 38 Squadron on May 5th, 1937 equipped with Fairey Hendon bombers. In June, No. 115 Squadron re-formed at Marham with the Handley Page Harrow, initially sharing No. 38 Squadron's Hendons until Harrow deliveries were completed in August. Number 38 Squadron received the new Vickers Wellington Mk. I bombers in December 1938, followed in April 1939 by No. 115 Squadron.

November 26th was spent cleaning up and organising equipment and stores. In the afternoon S/Ldr Gillman and the rear party arrived leaving a small party still at Oakington servicing two Wellingtons. The squadron was now officially based RAF Marham. It had been a monumental effort by all the squadron. Squadron Leader Edward Davy joined the squadron via 'B' Flight of 15 OTU on the 26th. Having joined the RAF on a Short Service Commission (SSC) in 1930, he brought a wealth of experience to the squadron.

Conversion resumed almost immediately, however, the initial cheeriness was tragically cut short on the 28th when Sergeant Edward Evans DFM accidentally walked into a Wellington airscrew out at dispersal. Seriously injured he was immediately taken to the Station Sick Quarters (SSQ) where despite the best efforts of the medical staff the 21-year-old died at 21:15 hours. It was a tragic accident to a veteran of the bloody battles of May 1940.

A thick fog covered the region on the 1st, stalling any flying. Twenty-six sergeant aircrew arrived from Oakington to complete the squadron move, joining them was acting Flight Lieutenant Charles Turner. He was posted from No.214 Squadron to take over the duties of squadron Adjutant. There was an emergency on the 5th which needed to be resolved urgently, F/Lt Shaw stepped up to the call, he was aloft in Wellington N2937.

*On 5 December the weather was bad with thick overcast cloud and a call was made for a crew to fly to Oakington to pick up some much-needed medical supplies and our crew volunteered. We were obliged to fly below cloud level, which made for an interesting trip. We reported to flying control at Oakington while the crew loaded the medical supplies. We did not hang around longer than necessary and returned to Marham as visibility was poor. I must admit to feeling a degree of satisfaction on completing the mission as we watched the medical supplies being off-loaded, until an NCO shouted an order to his section, "You'd better get this bloody bog-paper to the latrines!" and the sanitary squad did just that. For some time after that we were known as the 'bumph crew'.*

On December 8th, the squadron learnt the tragic news that Flight Lieutenant Hughes DFC had been killed. It had been a long-held ambition of Johns since leaving Cranwell to fly fighters. Soon after leaving 218 Squadron he had a brief spell with the Radio Servicing Flight at RAF Biggin Hill. On September 26th, 1940 he was posted to No.25 Squadron a night fighter unit based at RAF North Weald where he took command of 'B' Flight. He carried out his first patrols on October 25th and 26th. These turned out to be his only sorties. At the time, the squadron being re-equipped with the then new Bristol Beaufighter. On the evening of December 7th 1940 John Hughes took off from RAF Wittering detailed to check the blackout over Peterborough in Blenheim Mk.IF L1235. During the patrol, the weather deteriorated, and a severe storm developed. Control of the aircraft was lost, and the Blenheim came down near the village of Elton in Huntingdonshire (now Cambridgeshire). Twenty-three-year-old John Hughes and the gunner, Sergeant Jack Friend, were both killed while the radar operator, Sergeant Frank Blenkharn was seriously injured and admitted to Peterborough Hospital. John Hughes is buried in Chilworth Church, he left behind a wife, Patty (nee Walsh) Hughes.

*Left: A beautiful stained-glass window in memory of F/Lt John Hughes DFC. Above, His grave.*

*Flying Officer William Anstey at the controls of a Wellington. This unassuming officer optimised the courage and determination of his country.*

For the next two weeks, the squadron flew almost daily in their attempt to get themselves ready to resume operations. The squadron lost S/Ldr Davy on 16th. He was posted to command No.40 Squadron based at RAF Wyton. To fill the vacant flight commander role, F/Lt Ian Richmond was appointed the unpaid rank of Acting Squadron Leader. It was an agreeable appointment to all the squadron. The uncharacteristic period of beautiful weather continued allowing the crews to refine their newly acquired flying skills on the Wellington. Finally, the squadron was deemed ready to return to operations. On the morning of December 22nd Form B.372 arrived at RAF Marham informing the squadron that the Channel Port of Ostend was to be bombed that night. There was an air of real excitement across the squadron, 218 was back in the front line.

It was no real surprise when the names of two of the squadron's most experienced New Zealanders was chalked up on the Ops board, 'B' Flights S/Ldr Richmond and F/O Anstey. These two friends would be given the honour of carrying out the squadron's first operation on the Wellington from RAF Marham. At 0420 hours, Wellington Mk.Ic R1009 HA-L lifted away from Marham's grass runway followed quickly by Wellington R1210 HA-O skippered by F/O Anstey. Loaded with six 500 pounders and 120 incendiaries both crews found a somewhat subdued target, no flak was encountered, there were however numerous searchlights. It was all a bit of an anti-climax, both crews were back at dispersal by 07:10 hours. Not one to sit on their laurels the squadron was briefed to attack the port of Flushing on the 22nd. Once again S/Ldr Richmond's name was chalked up, he was joined on this occasion by 'A' Flight's S/Ldr Ault in Wellington HA-A R1008 and F/Lt Shaw at the controls of R1025 HA-B, F/Lt Shaw;

215

*On 22 December, the Squadron became operational on Wellingtons and thinking back to our old Blenheim I requested a Mugwump to be painted on the nose of our aircraft. Unfortunately, the airman was no artist, and we ended up with a devil complete with a pitchfork painted on in red 'dope'. I suggested we should change it when we got back, but the crew stated emphatically that this was lucky and in no way should it be changed. We really are a superstitious lot!* Squadron Leader Ault was unable to attack the primary so bombed the docks at Calais, F/Lt Shaw dropped his 6 x 500lb + 1 x 250lb bombs from 13,000 feet starting fires on the primary target, two of which appeared to have sparks shooting from them. This low-key operation would be the last operation before Christmas.

On Christmas Day the Station Commander, Group Captain Groom and all officers available on the station attended the Airmen's Christmas dinner at 1230 hours and waited upon them as was the tradition. Everyone was buoyant. The station band played during the dinner, which seemed to get everyone in the festive spirit. There was an atmosphere of Christmas cheer throughout the squadron. The dining hall reverberated with laughter as the crews, many of whom were survivors of France relaxed and enjoyed a beer and a sherry with their Turkey. Greetings were received from the C-in-C, the Chief of Air Staff and A.O.C No.3 Group. These were read out to the assembled airmen. The dinner ended at 1400 hours, in the evening the officers held their Christmas dinner, which by all accounts was a tremendous success.

On the 28th, the squadron reported that it had seven fully operational crews trained on the Wellington, with three still under training. The following night six of those trained crews would be briefed to attack the docks at Boulogne. As it turned out, the weather would be the only victor on this night. Squadron Leader Ault and F/O Smith attempted to bomb the secondary target of Calais without success. Flying Officer Anstey and Sergeants Ronald Hoos and Geoffrey Morley were unable to locate the target and brought their bombs back. The ever-dependable Flight Lieutenant Shaw was forced to abandon the operation with radio and gyrocompass failure. He was obliged to land at RAF Martlesham Heath on return. Pilot Officer Brian Lymbery arrived from RAF Harwell on the last day of December. He was the last airman to be posted to the squadron in 1940.

### The Following Wellington Mk.Ia and Mk.Ic are known to have been delivered

### November - December 1940

| Serial | Code | Delivered | Maker | Contract | Mark |
|--------|------|-----------|-------|----------|------|
| L4234 | - | 06/11/1940 | Vickers Armstrong Weybridge. | 549268/36 | MkIa |
| L4293 | - | 06/11/1940 | Vickers Armstrong Weybridge. | 549268/36 | MkI |
| R1009 | HA-L | 06/11/1940 | Vickers Armstrong, Chester | B992424/39 | MkIc |
| R1008 | HA-A | 07/11/1940 | Vickers Armstrong, Chester | B992424/39 | MkIc |
| R1025 | HA-B / J | 07/11/1940 | Vickers Armstrong, Chester | B992424/39 | MkIc |

| | | | | | |
|---|---|---|---|---|---|
| N2844 | HA-M | 13/11/1940 | Vickers Armstrong, Chester. | B992424/39 | MkIc |
| T2801 | HA-E | 13/11/1940 | Vickers Armstrong, Weybridge | B38600/39 | MkIc |
| N2937 | HA-? | 13/11/1940 | Vickers Armstrong, Chester. | B549268/36 | **MkIa** |
| T2885 | HA-D | 14/11/1940 | Vickers Armstrong, Weybridge | B38600/39 | MkIc |
| R1183 | HA-N | 14/11/1940 | Vickers Armstrong, Chester | B992424/39 | MkIc |
| R1210 | HA-C / D | 15/11/1940 | Vickers Armstrong, Chester | B992424/39 | MkIc |
| L7798 | HA-S | 15/12/1940 | Vickers Armstrong, Chester. | B992424/39 | MkIc |
| P9299 | HA-R | 05/12/1940 | Vickers Armstrong Weybridge. | B549268/36 | MkIc |
| P9207 | HA-? | | Vickers Armstrong Weybridge. | B549268/36 | MkIa |
| P9291 | HA-? | 15/12/1940 | Vickers Armstrong Weybridge. | B549268/36 | MkIc |
| P9296 | HA-K | 15/12/1941 | Vickers Armstrong Weybridge. | B549268/36 | MkIc |
| R1326 | HA-G | 20/12/1940 | Vickers Armstrong, Chester | B992424/39 | MkIc |
| R1368 | HA-F | 25/12/1940 | Vickers Armstrong, Chester | B992424/39 | MkIc |
| R1135 | HA-S / N | 28/12/1940 | Vickers Armstrong, Chester | B992424/39 | MkIc |
| T2958 | HA-T | 28/12/1940 | Vickers Armstrong, Weybridge | B38600/39 | MkIc |

*The dates recorded in the squadron Operational Record Book and the AM Form 78 Movement Card differ making accurate delivery dates almost impossible.*

The new year started with a low-key attack on the Docks at Antwerp on the 1st, Sgt William Adam undertaking his first operation was joined by the uncontainable S/Ldr Richmond who once again was at the controls of R1007 HA-L. Sergeant Adam was unable to locate the target bringing his bomb load back, his

*The squadron received an influx of Armourers to accommodate the extra work involved in bombing-up the Vickers Wellington, which carried a much bigger bomb load than the trusty Blenheim.*

flight commander experience no trouble dropping his 6 x 500lb plus 120 x 4lb incendiaries on the docks. Large fires and explosions were observed with the whole dock area ablaze when the last of Marham's crews departed. Such was the conflagration that the blaze was visible for over 100 miles.

The docks at Brest were the intended target on the night of the 4th. Six crews were detailed however due to bad weather Group HQ reduced the number to just two by early afternoon. Yet again, S/Ldr Richmond's name was to be found on the crew list, alongside that of F/O Anstey. Inter-com failure resulted in the early return of S/Ldr Richmond. With his navigational lights on and Marham airfield in the distance S/Ldr Richmond and crew were at 1000 feet when tracer fire whistled past their wing, the time was 1926 hours. Shocked into action, Richmond ordered his New Zealand co-pilot P/O Nelson Mansfield to extinguish the navigation lights as he put Wellington R1009 HA-L into a violent turn away from their unseen antagonist. Thankfully, the Germans pilots aim was slightly off, a short burst of cannon fire had missed the lumbering Wellington by a few yards. Having lost the German fighter, reported to have been a Bf110, Richmond wisely deciding to fly a wider than usual circuit. The crew now fully alert hugged the flat Norfolk countryside for the next 30 minutes, eventually landing at 19:00 hours. There were no Bf110s operational on this night, the only German intruders were the Ju88Cs and less agile Do17Z of NJG2 based at Gilze Rijen, not for the first time it was a case of misidentification. Unable to reach the target due to bad weather, F/O Anstey jettisoned his bomb load into the sea, he landed Wellington T2958 at 2020 hours.

The squadron provided six crews on the 9th. The target was an oil refinery (Z.33) at Rotterdam. While No.3 Group dispatched 51 Wellingtons to attack Gelsenkirchen, it also sent 14 crews, including 218's contribution on the 'Freshman' attack against Rotterdam. The weather conditions on route and over the target afforded the crews the best opportunity so far for accurate bombing. All the crews attacked including F/Lt John Mitchell and F/O George Agar, who bombed from 10,000 feet dropping his 6 x 500 pounders and 120 incendiaries on to the largest of the fires. Both skippers were carrying out their first Wellington operation. A number of fires were started, and returning crews were confident that the raid was a success.  Wing Commander Combe's name appeared in Routine Orders on the 9th having been mentioned in despatches by the Air-Officer Commander-in-Chief, it would have been cause for celebration in the mess. The squadron increased it trained pilots to 11 on the morning of the 11th with the arrival of the recently qualified Sergeant Alfred Binnie from No.15 O.T.U Harwell. The Canadian was immediately put in 'A' Flight. Two new pilots arrived on the 13th. From No.9 Squadron, Australian F/O Phillip MacLaren. Born in Perth in 1915 the Aussie had previously served pre-war with both the Australian Navy Reserve and Royal Artillery, in July 1938 he joined the RAF on an SSC. There followed many non-operational postings to No.98 and 52 Squadrons where he was screened and given instructor duties on the Fairey Battle. Classified as an excellent instructor, he inevitably took over the role of deputy flight commander. Keen to get operational, Phillip initially applied to join Coastal Command but was for reasons unknown rejected. Finally, in January 1941 he was posted to No.9 Squadron where mysteriously he remained for only a few days before his posting to 218 Squadron. The squadron also welcomed 23-year-old F/O John Stokes from No.214 Squadron, Stokes like MacLaren was only on his previous squadron for a matter of days before posting.

Tragedy struck on the morning of the 15th when F/O MacLaren crashed on his first Wellington solo at 1130 hours in the dual control Wellington P9207. It is understood that MacLaren may have taken off on completion of maintenance work by the ground crews. With no experienced Wellington pilot to check over the Wellington before take-off and his pre-flight checks, the young Aussie took off. Moments after taking off the port wing dropped, and the aircraft dived into the ground between Wormegay and Pentney. The Wellington immediately burst into flames, killing MacLaren instantly. He had only 1-hour dual experience on the Wellington. He was buried with full military honours at Marham (Holy Trinity) Churchyard.

*RAF  Marham's very own band.*

## Wednesday 15th January 1941

*Vickers Wellington*
*Mk.Ia P9207*
*Contract No :B549268/36*
*Taken On Charge :*
*Pilot: Flying Officer Phillip Frederick MacLaren*
*41191 RAF* **Killed**

On the 15th the squadron briefed six crews for what would be the squadron's first visit to Germany with the Wellington. The target was the heavily defended docks at Wilhelmshaven. As it turned out only two crews eventually took off, Sergeant Donald Hoos at 18:40 hour in Wellington N2844 HA-M followed 5 minutes later by Sgt Geoff Morley at the controls of L7798 HA-P. Only Sgt Hoos found and attacked the target dropping his bomb load just north of the large railway station despite the freezing conditions encountered. Engine trouble prevented Sgt Morley from reaching Wilhelmshaven, they selected the docks at Rotterdam which received the mixed HE and incendiary bomb load.

A period of bad weather followed, operations planned for the 17th, 18th and 19th were all cancelled due to freezing condition and heavy snow. An influx of new officers arrived on the 23rd,

*The grave of F/O MacLaren. He spent less than 48 hours on the squadron before his tragic death.*

P/O Douglas Paterson and his observer P/O Walter Linley came via No.20 O.T.U. The Harwell based No.15 O.T.U provided F/O Denis Clyde-Smith a pre-war regular and air gunner P/O Frederick Chalk. 'Gerry' Chalk had joined the Honourable Artillery Company as a gunner when war broke out. He transferred to the RAF in 1940, widely known in pre-war cricketing circles he had captained the Oxford University team and later went on to captain Kent.

That night six crews were detailed and briefed for operations, but once again the weather cancelled the raid. This trend continued the following night and on the 25th. A number of NCO aircrew arrived on the squadron during the day including Sergeant pilot Regional Richardson from No.20 OTU plus several wireless operators, observers and air gunners. The squadron was told to prepare for operations on the night of the 28th. But once again the weather intervened, it was now becoming an unwanted habit.

Wing Commander Geoffrey Amison MiD arrived on the 2nd from RAF Stradishall to take command of the squadron from the soon to be departing W/Cdr Combe. Twenty-eight-year-old Amison had joined the RAF in 1932 and had learnt to fly at No.3 Training School, Grantham. Gaining his wings, Amison would initially serve with No.9 Squadron before he found himself posted to Ramla, Palestine with No.2 Armoured Car Company in 1937. It was while in Palestine he was award a MiD in recognition of distinguished services rendered during this period. By now a squadron leader a posting to No.38 Squadron followed in August 1939. During November 1940 he joined No.311 (Czechoslovak) Squadron, his role was navigation instructor and O/C "B" Flight. During December 1940 he spent a brief period with No.214 based at R.A.F Stradishall before posting to 218 Squadron. He would be promoted the non-substantive rank of acting wing

*A young-looking Flying Officer Clyde-Smith*

commander on February 6th. A significant milestone was reached on the 3rd. The squadron reached its full aircraft establishment of sixteen MkIc Wellingtons. It still retained two of the MkIas, but these trusty old war horses would be posted away within the next few weeks. There was a slight break in the weather that finally ended the enforced three week lay-off. On the 4th, Flying Officer Crosse and Sergeant Adam were given the Channel port of Ostend to attack. Unfortunately, once airborne the crews encountered dense cloud that blanketed the entire route and the target, both crews failed to bomb. The recently arrived combination of F/O Clyde Smith and his gunner P/O Chalk were posted to No.115 Squadron across the airfield on the 5th where they began their tour against Boulogne on the 7th. On the 6th Wing Commander Combe departed, he was posted to HQ Bomber Command. Perhaps not the most dynamic leader, his forte appeared to be more administrative than operational. In the seven months, he commanded the squadron he flew a single operation. What he did do remarkably well was guide the squadron during its re-equipping and training firstly on the Bristol Blenheim then the Vickers Wellington.

On the 7th nine squadron crews were detailed and briefed for an operation against Boulogne, it was the most substantial squadron effort to date. The raid was by the standards of the day a success. All the crews reported bombing. Some even managed to identify the various docks. Boulogne appeared to be covered in fires, many of which were visible from the North Foreland on the coast of Kent on return. The squadron dropped an impressive 44 x 500 pounders and 1080 incendiaries plus two photo flashes, it was the largest tonnage the squadron had ever dropped. A significant effort was directed against Hanover on the 10th, over 100 Wellingtons would be provided by 3 Group of which nine squadron crews would participate. Cloud over the target area prevented some of the earlier crews from visually identifying the target. Sergeant Adams circled the target at 6000 feet waiting for a break in the cloud. All the while buffeted by flak. Flying Officer Crosse at the controls of Wellington R1326 HA-G circled the target for 30 minutes before a break in the cloud gave the crew a chance to bomb. Both flak and searchlights were considerable, and for the first time, a few fighters were observed. All the crews were again enthusiastic about the results, numerous fires were observed, some of which were classed as large. It was back over England that the squadron encountered serious trouble, from German intruders. Sergeant Morley was attacked by what he reported as a single-engine fighter, while F/O Crosse met a Ju88 over Marham delaying his landing by an hour. While most of the squadron was over Germany, a single crew captained by P/O Mansfield was given the Oil Refineries at Rotterdam to attack. With no flak or searchlights to bother them the raid should have been a 'milk-run'. Nevertheless, the crew were attacked by a Bf110. Thankfully, violent evasive action by P/O Mansfield and some accurate return fire from the rear gunner was enough to shake the fighter off. After crossing the coast, the rear gunner Sgt Louis Kolitz reported a fighter was following them astern, for ten agonising minutes the fighter kept station until it finally disappeared.

It was on this night that a major effort by the German intruders of NJG2 brought panic to the returning bombers over England. Junkers Ju88 C-2s and Do17 Z-10s in four waves departed Gilze-Rijen between 2345hrs and 0442hrs. They had some success, a Marham based Wellington of No.115 Squadron was shot down over West Raynham airfield while a Blenheim of 21 Squadron was brought down while in the circuit at Watton. Further north over Lincolnshire a Hampden was destroyed north of Lincoln.

On the 10th a number recently qualified pilots were posted in. Sergeants Robert Glass, Basil Foster, New Zealanders John Fry, Mason Fraser and Mervnn McNeil and finally Scotsman, John Brown, all arrived from No.15 O.T.U RAF Harwell.

The following night eight crews were detailed and briefed to attack both Bremen and Hanover, it would be a disaster. Six of the crews were detailed to attack the Focke-Wulf works at Bremen, while two crews, F/O Smith and F/Lt Mitchell would re-visit Hanover. The first aircraft aloft was R1008 HA-A skippered by S/Ldr Ault at 1750 hours. Almost immediately the Wellington was enveloped in the cloud which persisted without a break over the entire trip. The flight commander claimed to have dropped his mixed HE and incendiary load over the target area from 12,000 feet causing many fires. Of the remaining crews briefed for Bremen, only the ever-persistent F/Lt Shaw and Sgt Adam were confident they reached what they believed to be the target area. Flight Lieutenant Shaw selected a canister of incendiaries to stir up the flak, which he then bombed. Sergeant Adam had a glimpse of four night fighters over the targets area, one of which got to within 1000 yards before veering off. The cloud which had thwarted the attack on Bremen and Hanover had thickened over England since take-off making conditions even more difficult. With Marham and most of the country blanketed four crews either force landed or abandoned their aircraft. Unable to

*Vickers Armstrong built Wellington Mk.Ic R1008 HA-A. Arriving on the squadron in November 1940 it would be used almost exclusively by the incumbent 'A' flight commander or the squadron's commanding officer.*

land at Marham the crews were diverted north, short of fuel F/O Agar forced landed Wellington R1135 HA-S in a field with the under carriage retracted at Bassingham, a small village in Lincolnshire. None of the crew were injured and damage to the Wellington was classed as slight. The 2nd pilot, Sgt Vandervord recalls.

*Geoffrey Amison MiD, the squadron's third war-time commanding officer. He brought with him some welcomed operational experience. The scar on his cheek was the result of a motoring accident.*

*We came back with our bombs because we could not see anything over Germany or over England and we had to decide what to do. We discussed climbing, putting the Wellington on George and heading it out over the sea. We caught occasional glimpses of the ground through the cloud, so the pilot decided to nip down under the cloud. The next thing I recall was me yelling there was a tree in front of us. Agar calmly lifted the Wellington over the tree, there was a ploughed field in from of us and we made a wheels up landing. We did not have a clue where we were, so we all walked along a nearby road and found a house. We knocked on the door and scared the life out of the occupants. They rang the local police who soon arrived, and we were transported back to Marham.'*

Flying Officer Anstey reached what he thought was Bremen and bombed a group of searchlights. While returning to base, the wireless set failed, an error in navigation brought the Wellington over the defences of London where the Anti-Aircraft defences opened fire. Quickly turning north in the hope of finding an airfield to land the crew were obliged to abandoned Wellington R1210 HA-O over Tebay, Cumbria at 02.15hrs. The aircraft eventually crashed onto the high ground in the Bretherdale Common area, between Kendal and Shap. The crew are believed to have landed nearby and all escaped serious injury. Sergeant Adam crash-landed on the mud banks of the River Severn near Frampton-on-Severn, Gloucestershire at 01:00 hours due to shortage of fuel. The crew were all uninjured apart from Sgt Leonard Millatt, the Wop/Ag who suffered bruising. Their aircraft, Vickers Wellington T2885 HA-D was submerged, it would eventually be struck off charge. Flying Officer Smith reached the general target area, but the cloud prevented visual identification. Unable to identify the target, the crew turned back jettisoning their bomb load over the North Sea. A combination of cloud and mist prevented landing at Marham and the alternative RAF Wyton. Flying north they forced landed 1 mile south of Roos, near Withernsea, South Yorkshire at 0130 hours. All the crew were unharmed, but Wellington T2801 HA-E was severely damaged when Smith landed with the undercarriage fully retracted, like T2885 it never returned to the squadron. None of the crews landed back at Marham, S/Ldr Ault diverted to Wyton, F/Lt Mitchell landed at RAF Lindholme while F/Lt Shaw was forced further north to Driffield, he recalls.

*On 11th February 1941, we were at last briefed on a target in Bremen, Germany and we carried a mixed load of bombs and incendiaries as well as two packets of nickels — i.e. propaganda leaflets. This was the first of many trips to Germany for the Squadron. On occasions, when weather was bad, or not as clear as forecast, we had to bomb on ETA (Estimated Time of Arrival). Although 10/10 cloud prevented the use of searchlights, there was always plenty of heavy flak. This was not an ideal bombing situation, but this was Germany and there was a chance that the bombs would cause some harm to the enemy.On a previous occasion, when we were due to fly in bad weather, I asked the Met. Officer which direction would be best to take if there was a weather clampdown on our return and he said North. When we returned from our raid, the weather was bad and so we continued North. Being unable to land in Lincolnshire, we overflew the Humber and Brough airfield, where I had done my reserve training and we eventually landed at RAF Driffield. It was at times like this that DARKIE was brought into operation. This was a system of searchlight signalling not unlike a lighthouse, designed to aid returning crews to identify airfields.*

**Tuesday 11th February 1941**
*Vickers Wellington*
*Mk.Ic T2885 HA-D 'Don'*
*Contract No : B38600/39*
*Taken On Charge: 14/11/1940*
*To : No.45 Group*
*Pilot : Sergeant William Adam and crew safe.*

**Tuesday 11th February 1941**
*Vickers Wellington*
*Mk.Ic T2801 HA-E 'Edward'*
*Contract No :B38600/39*
*Taken On Charge: 13/11/1940*
*To:No.45 Group*
*Pilot: Flying Officer Donald Smith and crew safe.*

**Tuesday 11th February 1941**
*Vickers Wellington*
*Mk.Ic R1210 HA-O 'Orange'*
*Contract No: B992424/49*
*Taken On Charge: 15/11/1940*
*Fate :S.O.C (Burnt out)*
*Pilot: Flying Officer William Anstey and crew safe.*

**Tuesday 11th February 1941**
*Vickers Wellington*
*Mk.Ic R1135 HA-S 'Sugar'*
*Contract No: 992424/39*
*Taken On Charge: 28/12/1940*
*To: No.43 Group (Repaired returned to squadron)*
*Pilot: Flying Officer George Agar and crew safe.*

The squadron lost two of its recently posted pilots on the 12th, Sgts Glass and Fry were posted to No.214 Squadron based at Stradishall. Six of the diverted crews stranded at various airfields on the 11th finally managed to return on the 13th, all apart from F/Lt Shaw who was still at Driffield, he would return the following day.

The squadron was given three separate targets on the 15th, Sgt McNeil and P/O Mansfield were ordered to attack the docks at Boulogne, Sgt Morley the Ruhrchemie (Ruhr Benzin AG) oil works at Sterkrade. In contrast, the remaining four crews attacked an oil plant north of Duisburg. Ground haze made identification of the oil plants almost impossible but conditions over Boulogne were better. Sergeant McNeil dropped his six 500lb and 120 x 4lb incendiaries stoking up some existing fires. Pilot Officer Mansfield reported two large fires and a number of explosions soon after his bomb load was dropped. Both crews reported intense flak and searchlights, Boulogne's already fierce defences were getting even hotter.

Three crews were detailed to carry out Freshman trips on the 17th. Sergeants Madgwick, McNeil and P/O Patterson were all set to visit the Channel ports when at 16:00 hours the raid was scrubbed due to bad weather. The run of bad luck continued the following night when the crews were again briefed, this time the operation was cancelled at 1500 hours. It was not until the 19th that ten crews were detailed once again for operations. All the Wellingtons were fully fuelled and bombed up despite the widespread sleet and snow which covered Marham throughout the day. It was not until late afternoon that the crews including the unfortunate Sgt Madgwick, McNeil and P/O Patterson were informed that the raid had been cancelled due to the prospect of fog on their return. Heavy snow and ice prevented operations on the 19th and 20th, despite frequent snow squalls ten crews were detailed for operations on the 21st, the target was the docks at Boulogne. Once again, the operation was scrubbed and with it another chance for the three novice crews to notch up an operation. Eventually, on the 22nd the weather had improved sufficiently for ten crews to be briefed for an attack on Brest. Incredibly once again the three Freshman crews were withdrawn at the last minute, the operation was already off to a bad start. A further three crews did not take off due to mechanical trouble, both F/Lt Mitchell and Mansfield suffered engine failure, while F/O Agar lost his intercom. The problems did not end there. Flight Lieutenant Shaw had just retracted his undercarriage of Wellington R1025 HA-B when the cockpit hood unexpectedly blew open. The crew discussed continuing to the target, but it was then discovered the heating system was unserviceable, within twenty minutes the crew were back at dispersal.

The first crew aloft was that of the squadron commander, W/Cdr Amison who joined the crew of his flight commander S/Ldr Ault aboard Wellington R1008 HA-A. It was W/Cdr Amison's first operation with the squadron. The raid turned out was a complete failure. Unable to locate Brest or the alternative target of Lorient the crew returned without bombing. Sergeant Morley was more fortunate, reaching the target at 0446 hours the crew managed to identify the docks dropping six 500lb SAP east to west across the docks. On the 23rd the three Freshman crews finally managed to carry out an operation, P/O Paterson and Sgt McNeil were given the docks at Boulogne while Sgt Madwick was given Calais. Unfortunately, Doug Paterson was unable to bomb when his bomb load failed to release. Sergeant McNeil was more fortunate, he made three bomb runs over the target area and received the full attention of the flak defences for his trouble. Wellington R1328 HA-V had its front turret pierced by a sizeable piece of shrapnel, while two large holes were punctured in the geodetics in the tail plane and starboard wing. With a slight improvement in the weather the group provided 30 Wellingtons for an attack directed against Dusseldorf on the 25th, the squadron provided seven crews, plus two Freshman crews who once again were given Boulogne. Thick cloud hampered the attack over Dusseldorf although fires were seen, opposition over the target was reported as plentiful. Once again the real drama occurred over Marham on the squadron's return. Sergeant Hoos and crew were attacked by a Junkers Ju88C flown by Fw Ernst Ziebarth of 2./NJG2 while orbiting base  on return. Grievously damaged, Sgt Hoos tried vainly to gain what height he could to give his crew the best possible chance to bail out. It was to no avail, battling with the controls, Hoos and his 2nd pilot Sgt Ralph Bramwell managed to crash land Wellington R1009 HA-L close to a K Site near Red Lodge, 2 miles south of Swaffham Norfolk at 2315 hours. The Wellington immediately burst into flames as it slid to a halt in the corner of the frozen field. The crew wasted no time in scrambling clear as the fire quickly spread. Unfortunately, the front gunner, Sgt John Stanley was trapped by both legs in his turret. Courageously the crew re-entered the blazing fuselage to help their trapped crewmate. Despite the flames and heat they managing to recover the now severely burnt gunner. John Stanley was quickly transferred to Kings Lynn Hospital where sadly one of his irreparably damaged legs was amputated and his extensive burns treated. Brumwell and Heywood were sent off to Ely Hospital, Sgt Brumwell had received a broken arm while Sgt Heywood the crew's rear gunner, had dislocated his shoulder. Vickers Wellington R1009 HA-L was burnt out and destroyed, it had completed just eight operations and more worryingly was S/Ldr Ian Richmond's favourite aircraft. Both Hoos and Brumwell did not operate with the squadron again, sadly 25-year-old John Stanley succumbed to his injuries on March 3rd, 1941, he was buried at Hope Cemetery, Flintshire. Ron Hoos was killed with No.35 Path Finder Squadron in May 1943. Ralph Brumwell survived the war after completing two tours, his last with 75(NZ) Squadron in 1944.

## Tuesday 25th February 1941
*Vickers Wellington*
*Mk.Ic R1009 HA-L 'London'*
*Contract No: 992424/39*
*Taken On Charge: 06/11/1940*
*S.O.C*
*Pilot: Sergeant Ralph Hoos and crew.*


It was the coastal harbour town of Wilhelmshaven that was chalked up on the Operations Board on February 28th. This important and modern port was where on June 30th, 1934, the "pocket battleship" Admiral Graf Spee was launched.

The target was the almost completed German Battleship *Tirpitz* which was reported moored in the Bauhafen at Wilhelmshaven. The ship was laid down at the Kriegsmarinewerft Wilhelmshaven in November 1936, and her hull was launched two and a half years later. Work was almost completed on this monster in February 1941 after sea trials. Seven crews were detailed and briefed and would join a further 50 Wellingtons supplied by No.3 Group. The first away was F/Lt Mitchell at 2315 hours in Wellington T2958 HA-T, by 2350 all the crews were airborne and heading towards the North Sea. Conditions on the route and over the target were good. Some crews identified the dock area and adjacent marshalling yards. Searchlight activity was surprisingly ineffective. However, the flak defences were not. The flak above the target was described by returning crews as 'intense'. Command HQ concluded that the raid was highly satisfactory.

By the beginning of 1941, the country was gripped with U-Boat fever, the German success in the North Atlantic had Britain and its Royal Navy almost beaten. The North Atlantic convoys had suffered terrible losses since the fall of France the previous summer. The Royal Navy was not able to oppose the threat as it was woefully under strength, Coastal Command was still flying obsolete aircraft. The few modern aircraft it had did not have the range to make any worthwhile contribution. To add to the U-Boat menace, the German Battle-cruisers *Scharnhorst* and *Gneisenau* were on the prowl in the Atlantic causing mayhem, if this was enough the mighty Battleship *Bismarck* was being prepared and made ready to set sail. It was not just at sea the Germans appeared to have the upper hand, it was also in the air. The Luftwaffe had the long-range Focke-Wulf FW200 Condor. With a range over nearly 2000 miles, this formidable aircraft caused havoc to the convoys, armed with 2000lb of bombs the Condors repeatedly attacked and sank merchant vessels, more importantly, they reported the positions of the convoys to the U-Boat packs. Winston Churchill called these four-engine giants *"The scourge of the Atlantic. "*

By March 1941, Britain faced the alarming prospect of its vital ocean links to Canada and America being severed. The Germans were winning the war in the Atlantic. Prime Minister Winston Churchill was forced into giving a simple instruction, Bomber Command will direct all its effort against the targets that housed or sourced the threat to British shipping. On March 9th, 1941 Air Chief Marshal Sir Wilfred Freeman (Vice Chief of the Air Staff) informed Air Marshal Sir Richard Peirse of a new directive to dedicate his energies to defeating the *"attempt of the enemy to strangle our food supplies and our connection with the United States"*. The directive gave explicit instructions *"We must take the offensive against the U-Boat and the Focke-Wulf wherever and whenever we can"* A list of twelve targets were drawn up, each was divided into individual yards, plants, assembly buildings and factories. The targets chosen were:

| | |
|---|---|
| Kiel | *(Germania Shipyards, Deutsche Werkes and Havaldts werke Dockyards)* |
| Bremen | *(Deschimag Shipyards and Focke-Wulf aircraft Factory)* |
| Vegesack | *(Vulcan Werkes)* |
| Hamburg | *(Blohm un Voss Shipyards and Havaldts )* |
| Augsburg | *(MAN diesel factory)* |
| Mannheim | *(MAN Diesel factory)* |
| Dessau | *(Junkers Aircraft Factory)* |
| Lorient | *(U-Boat Pens)* |
| St.Nazaire | *(U-Boat Pens)* |
| Bordeaux | *(U-Boat Pens* |
| Bordeaux – | Merignac *(Airfields of the FW200 Condors)* |

*A pre-war photograph of Flying Officer William Peter Crosse.*

The above targets would soon be modified as priorities and circumstances changed during the coming months. The C-in-C Bomber Command Air Marshal Sir Richard Peirse was not overly happy about the change in policy. Peirse felt that his command was on the verge of success with his attacks on Germany, especially the attacks on Germany's oil targets. The Air Ministry perhaps believing the accuracy of the reports filtering in from HQ Bomber Command did allow Sir Richard Peirse to devote a proportion of his efforts to continue the attacks directed against oil targets. The Air Ministry and Bomber Command would soon come to realise that the crews were overestimating their bombing accuracy. Lord Cherwell commissioned a report led by David Bensusan-Butt, a civil servant at the Air Ministry to analyse the effectiveness or otherwise of Bomber Command bombing accuracy. The findings which would be published in August would send shock waves throughout Bomber Command and the Air Ministry. However, this was in the future. What a contrast between Peirse and Harris, Peirse fully understood the importance of oil to the Germany economy from the very outset, sadly Harris would never fully accept the importance of oil.

227

The first operation of March was on the 3rd against the Hipper Class cruiser in dry dock at Brest. Eight crews reported bombing the dock area, although the cruiser was not seen photographs taken by S/Ldr Ault who bombed the target from 9000 feet clearly showed the cruiser. Returning crews reported that the flak over Brest as intense as that over Germany. On the 5th a brand-new Wellington arrived from No.23 M.U based at Kirkbride, Cumbria. Vickers Armstrong Limited built R1496 brought the squadron's establishment to 17 Mk.Ic aircraft. Also arriving on the 5th were the crews of Sergeant pilots Harry Rose and Howard Skett from No.19 O.T.U. Harry Rose was one of the brave band of Jewish aircrew who joined RAF Bomber Command. Having witnessed the persecution of Jews under the Nazism pre-war, thousands of young Jews joined the RAF to fight against tyranny and antisemitism fully aware that if captured they risked possible torture and execution. A major operation aimed at Brest Docks and the 'Hipper' cruiser was planned for the 6th, eleven crews were detailed and briefed, including both flight commanders. A message from Group HQ at 1700 hours cancelled the raid due to fear of fog on return. The unwelcome news that the likable and dependable Squadron Leader Ault was to be posted arrived on the 6th, it was a bitter blow to 'A' Flight and the squadron. His replacement would be Squadron Leader Beaman who arrived via No.15 OTU where it is believed he had served since April 1940. William Beaman was born August 1908, in Andover, Hampshire. An ex-Halton Apprentice he arrived at RAF Cranwell as a Flight Cadet in January 1927 and was assigned to B Squadron. A keen sportsman, he represented the college in Boxing and Rugby. He passed out from RAF Cranwell as a P/O in December 1928. In 1933 William married and the following year had a daughter. Pre-war he served with No.15 OTU. Two more pilots arrived on the 6th in the form of Englishman P/O Bernal Pape, and from Tasmania, Francis Bryant both from No.19 OTU, RAF Kinloss.

A maximum effort was required on the 8th. The squadron would provide a respectable 13 crews, once again both flight commanders names were included. However, it was not to be. The raid was cancelled early evening. Squadron Leader Ault would not get a chance to carry out a last operation before posting. What was not cancelled was a booze-fuelled mess party for the departing flight commander. Sadly, he would be killed leading 11 Bristol Blenheims of No.11 Squadron on a near-suicidal attack on the Imperial Japanese Navy off Ceylon on April 9th, 1942. Another briefing and another scrub on the 10th did little for the nerves of the aircrew and the patience of the ground crews. Finally, on the 12th, nine crews took off for operations in near-freezing conditions. A marvellously clear moonlight night and clear conditions were welcome, but it also meant the German nigh fighters would be on the prowl. For the first time the squadron would be visiting Berlin, it had been a long time in coming. Three crews were detailed to attack the telegraph office in Berlin, while seven were given Bremen's Focke-Wulf aircraft factory. Things did not start as planned, ten minutes after take-off P/O Mansfield was compelled to return to base when a trimming tab on the recently arrived Wellington, R1496 HA-O snapped making flying control extremely difficult. Struggling to keep the Wellington airborne the bomb load was jettisoned safe at 400 feet. Showing a remarkable amount of skill Mansfield brought the Wellington safely into land, the Squadron Operational Records Book reported it was *a great effort to keep the aircraft airborne.* The three crews briefed for Berlin had little success, Flight Lieutenant Mitchell suffered starboard engine failure over Holland giving him no option than to turn for home, Berlin was spared his 4 x 500 pounders which were jettisoned over the North Sea. Squadron Leader Richmond was accompanied by S/Ldr Beaman for operational experience, doubts about fuel levels resulted in the crew bombing Hamburg Docks, they landed back at Marham after being aloft for nearly 8 hours. Only F/O Agar located and bombed Berlin where he reported a large amount of flak and numerous searchlights. The crews attacking Bremen announced that the target had been successfully attacked, one Wellington was observed over the target area coned by searchlights and surrounded by flak. Flying with the squadron was a mystery pilot, F/O Robert Sturgess. His name or participation in the raid does not appear in the Squadron ORB, only in the Marham Station Records Book. Reported to have been on attachment from RAF Lossiemouth he was in all probability gaining operational experience, he would survive the war. There was one loss from the Bremen operation, Flying Officer William Crosse and crew were intercepted and shot down at 21:45 hours by Feldwebel Hans Rasper of IV./NJG1. Wellington R1326 HA-G crashed into the river at Gouwe Sloot near Opperdoes, Holland taking with it the gallant pilot and three of his crew. The Canadian 2nd pilot, Sgt Alfred Binnie was quickly captured and taken to the hospital at Alkmaar with wounds to his left thigh. Also wounded was the front gunner, 24-year-old Yorkshireman Sgt Arthur Parfitt.

## Wednesday 12th March 1941

*Vickers Wellington*
*Mk.Ic R1326 HA-G 'George'*
*Contract No : 992424/39*
*Taken On Charge : 25/11/1940*
***Failed to Return***
*Pilot : Flying Officer William Peter Crosse, 41154 RAF **Killed***
*2nd Pilot : Sergeant Alfred Binnie 903772 RAF, PoW*
*Wireless Operator : Sergeant William James Chamberlain, 549631 RAF **Killed***
*Observer :Sergeant John Henry Collopy, 566133 RAF, **Killed***
*Airgunner : Sergeant Ernest Joseph Could, 538866 RAF, **Killed***
*Front Gunner : Sergeant Arthur Parfitt, 9427554 RAFVR, PoW*

*A German guard, wrapped up against the cold, looks at the wreckage of Vickers Wellington Mk.Ic R1326 HA-G in the river at Gouwe Sloot near Opperdoes, Holland.*

*Above, the job of recovering the wreckage begins.*

The mighty port of Hamburg was the target on the night of March 13th, when No.3 Group would provide a healthy 51 crews, while a further 7 Freshman crews would attack the oil storage plants at Rotterdam. The squadron would contribute nine crews led by S/Ldr Richmond against Hamburg, while P/O Lymbery and Sgt Donald were briefed to bomb Rotterdam. Squadron Leader Richmond suffered complete electrical failure onboard Wellington R1400 HA-L soon after take-off, with some difficulty he managed to return to Marham. Pilot Officer Mansfield got as far as Germany before a combination of engine failure, and electrical failure forced him to head for home. Over the Dutch coast, they were involved in a brief exchange with a Bf110 which although in a position to attack mysteriously did not. What followed was an extremely useful raid. On this occasion, S/Ldr Beaman joined the crew of Flight Lieutenant Shaw for operational experience. Over the target area, they were held by 40 searchlights. Shaw desperately flung the Wellington around the sky in an attempt to lose his antagonists. With flak exploding all around his Wellington, F/Lt Shaw used all his experience and muscle to finally find a piece of the sky not illuminated by the much-hated searchlight beams. Eventually, after what seemed a lifetime the flak and searchlights faded, the now exhausted Shaw turned for home. Flight Lieutenant Shaw :

*'On a raid to Hamburg on 13 March, a new Flight Commander came as the second pilot to gain some operational experience. We encountered much heavy flak and received a peppering of shrapnel in the rear and tail assembly, a piece of which severed one of the wires connected to the rear gun turret electric sighting device and put it out of action.*

230

*Sergeant David Vandervord.*

Pilot Officer Paterson was also held by searchlights, for over twenty minutes he was illuminated before he too managed to escape their deadly grip. Pilot Officer Agar and crew were also in the thick of the action, held by 40-50 searchlights they were attacked by two Bf110s which inflicted severe damage to Wellington R1148 HA-S. The crew's rear gunner, Sgt Herbert Riding managed to hit one fighter with a well-aimed burst. The second Bf110 attacked from the starboard beam, Agar turned into the fighter giving the front gunner, Sgt Victor Ashworth an opportunity to engage. Opening fire with an extra-long burst the fighter was seen to dive vertically away. Pilot Officer Agar quickly asked for a report on the damage, and it was not encouraging. Both elevators were severely damaged as was the starboard mainplane, the self-sealing tanks were punctured, and fuel was escaping. The damage did not end there, the hydraulic system was practically useless, and the fuselage was like a colander. They may have escaped the clutches of the fighters, but there was still a real possibility they would not get home. To make matters worse, Sgt David Vandervord, the 2nd pilot who was standing at the Astrodome reporting on the fighter's whereabouts had been hit in the leg by a bullet. The young pilot recalls the encounter *"We got as far as the Zuider Zee when we were caught by two fighters. I don't know how the aircraft survived. We may have shot down one before Agar put the Wellington into a dive towards the ground. I was standing in the Astro-hatch, giving a running commentary on the position of the fighters. I was the only one injured, but the aircraft was shot to pieces. We got down low over the sea and made our way to Marham with one engine on fire and the petrol gauge showing zero. The engine fire would fade then start up again, we eventually crash-landed, and I was then taken to hospital."*

David Vandervord was born in 1921, and he was the middle of three brothers. The family had moved to England from Holland in the 17th century and taken up residence in Essex becoming a prominent family in the county. David joined the RAF in 1939 beginning his training in July at No.34 E&R FTS at Southend. There followed a posting to No.7 EFS at Desford were he joined 'D' Flight. Further postings to No.12 SFTS flying the Avro Anson followed. Having mastered the Anson in October 1940, he was sent to No.15 Operational Training Unit for conversion to the Vickers Wellington. His first flight was on October 8th, by December 12th he was deemed ready for operations arriving at 218 Squadron on December 15th, joining 'B' Flight and the crew of F/O Agar.

Another crew lucky to escape the clutches of the German fighters was Sgt McNeil, they were attacked by Fw Hans Rasper of 4./NJG1 while flying at 15,000 feet. Approaching the Wellington from astern and below Rasper opened fire inflicting considerable damage to Wellington R1328 HA-V. With the port landing gear lowered due to the shattered hydraulic system, the gunners put up a steady stream of well-aimed tracer at the Bf110. Such was the accuracy Fw Rasper was obliged to move out of range, in doing so the Wellington managed to slip away. Intriguingly, the crew claimed the Wellington as destroyed.

The squadron turned for home confident that the raid was a success, their optimism was justified. The Blohm and Voss Shipyards had been badly damaged, nearby timber yards were set on fire, and a reported 119 fires started. While on route home F/Lt Shaw decided to attack an aerodrome, both gunners opened fire on several lights which had not been blacked out. The crews activities were not over, back over England and nearing Swanton Morley a Ju88C intruder of NJG2 was seen and engaged, the rear gunner P/O Byng-Hall opened fire without the use of the gun sight which had been damaged by flak. Firing a long burst of tracer, the fighter broke off the engagement, finally after 6 hours 35 minutes aloft F/Lt Shaw landed Wellington R1025 HA-B on Marham grass runway, it was a real baptism of fire for the new flight commander. Once again F/Lt Shaw recalls the events;

*Fw Hans Rasper at the controls of his Bf110. He would claim two squadron aircraft.*

*'The return flight to the English coast was trouble-free, and we crossed the coast at 1500 ft. On our way back to base, with navigation lights still switched off as was normal, I suddenly saw the faint glow of two engines dead ahead on a rapidly closing collision course and pulled away just in time recognising the other plane as a JU88 equipped as a night fighter. The German then tried to attack from astern and passed close by to starboard, giving our rear gunner, Pilot Officer Byng-Hall a chance to fire the twin Brownings. As the reflector sight was not functional, he 'hose-piped' the JU88 using the tracer bullets for sighting but the intruder was able to carry on and we lost sight of him. At least he knew that we were alert. On landing the rear gunner reported an unidentified aircraft was following us from astern and thought it could be our intruder, so decided to get off the flare-path quickly and took a chance of twisting the undercarriage. The aircraft did not open fire at all and made off. It was most likely an intruder on the 'prowl'. The Flight Commander thanked us for the experience, and next time he flew it was as a Captain with his own crew'.*

The extensively damaged Wellington of Sgt McNeil managed to limp back to Marham were it crashed landed, it would never fly with the squadron again. Miraculously only two of the crew were injured, Kiwi Meryvn McNeil and rear gunner Sgt Harry Hutchinson, they would join David Vandervord in the SSQ.

### Thursday 13th March 1941
*Vickers Wellington*
*Mk.Ic R1328 HA-V 'Victor'*
*Contract No : 992424/38*
*Taken On Charge: 08/02/1941*
*Battle Damage*
*To: No.43 M.U*
*Pilot: Sergeant Meryvn McNeil RNZAF and Crew*

Of the two crews attacking Rotterdam both successfully located and bombed the target, sadly however Wellington R1183 HA-N was severely hit by flak over the target. The crew's wireless operator Sgt Jack Huffinley was mortally wounded while standing next to his pilot. Sergeant Donald managed to nurse the Wellington home despite extensive damage. With his hydraulics severed and the undercarriage damaged Sgt John Donald brought Wellington R1183 HA-N in for a wheels-up landing at Marham, it had been a

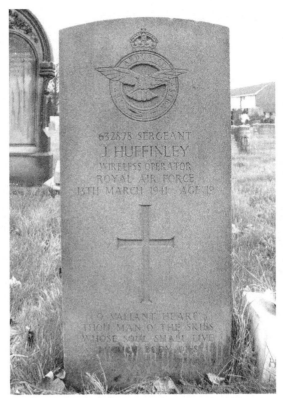

*Sergeant Jack Huffinley was killed on his first operation.*

*Sergeant Morrison Jolly RNZAF from Wallacetown, Southlands New Zealand.*

tremendous effort by the pilot considering it was only his second operation, and first as captain. The body of the 19-year-old Jack Huffinley was taken back to his hometown of Wakefield and buried. He had arrived from No.3 Group Training Flight only a week before. The Rotterdam raid was his first operation on the squadron.

### Thursday 13th March 1941
*Vickers Wellington*
*Mk.Ic R1183 HA-N 'Nuts'*
*Contract No: 992424/39*
*Taken on Charge: 04/11/1940*
*Battle Damage / Wheels up landing*
*To: No.43 M.U*
*Pilot: Sergeant John Donald and crew*

Nine crews were detailed and briefed for an attack on the U-Boats pens at Lorient on the 15th. This number was reduced to just four due to the prospect of bad weather on return. Pilot Officer Paterson and crew were airborne for only ten minutes when they returned to base with a defective starboard engine. Pilot Officer Mansfield experienced an overheating engine over the English Channel resulting in the bomb load being jettisoned. The crew headed for St Eval.

It was left to two of the squadron's most experienced captains to add 218 contributions to the festivities over the U-Boat pens. Flight Lieutenant Shaw dropped his 12 x 250lb bomb in two sticks across the docks, his first stick was unobserved but the second was seen to straddle the dock area. The group diverted him to St Eval on return. Squadron Leader Richmond spent 40 minutes trying to locate the U-Boat pens, and his perseverance paid off. Using the light of numerous flares, he managed to identify and bomb the target. He landed at Boscombe Down on return. All three would return to Marham the following day. Another two crews arrived during the second week of March, from No.11 OTU RAF Bassingbourn, Sgt Kenneth Coates and from No.15 OTU New Zealander Sgt Morrison Jolly.

Berlin was the intended target for the squadrons of No.3 Group on the 18th. But owing to adverse weather, the raid was switched to Kiel. Eight crews were detailed including S/Ldr Beaman who would be undertaking his first operation as captain. Two crews were obliged to make early returns, F/O Agar at the controls of R1025

HA-B with intercom trouble and Sgt Fraser whose escape hatch blew open. Cloud over the target caused some difficulty in identifying the docks. However, despite this and a spirited defence, the raid was another success. Damage to the Deutsche Werke U-Boat Yard was unusually heavy, and much damage was caused to the town itself caused by a large number of incendiaries dropped. Over the previous few months, the squadron had begun to increase the number of incendiaries into the bomb loads. The most numerous type was the 4 lb incendiary bomb. Developed by ICI, it was fast becoming the standard light incendiary bomb used by Bomber Command. First conceived in 1934, the hexagonal bomb was filled with thermite which was easily ignited by a simple internal striker. Ideally suited to any target it was an ideal weapon given Bomber Command's apparent inability to hit small targets. That night alone, the squadron dropped almost a thousand on Kiel.  It was a switch to the U-Boat pens at Le-Havre on the 20th, eight crews were detailed. They were briefed and led once again by both flight commanders, as take-off neared it became increasingly doubtful that the raid would take place as fog swept across the region, finally at 2330 hours the crews were informed that it was a 'scrub'.

Flying Officer Smith misjudged his landing while carrying out a night flying exercise on the 21st. Landing just after 2000 hours he lined up the Wellington on Marham grass runway, misjudging his height the aircraft hit the ground from 30 feet, it immediately bounced upwards catapulting the crew from their seats and landing positions. The Wellington hit the ground again and this time the rear wheel collapsed damaging the rear fuselage. The shaken crew emerged uninjured.

### Friday 21st March 1941

*Vickers Wellington*
*Mk.Ic L7798 HA-S 'Sugar'*
*Contract No: 992424/39*
*Taken On Charge: 15/12/1940*
*Pilot Error*
*Repaired on squadron*
*Pilot: Flying Officer Donald Smith and Crew*


The weather improved the following night slightly to allow P/O Brian Lymbery and crew to carry out a 'Freshman' raid on the E-Boat base and torpedo dump at Ostend. Taking Off at 0340 hours, Wellington N2844 HA-N crossed a completely cloud-covered North Sea. Having reached the target on ETA, it was obvious that any attempt to bomb was out of the question. Turning south the crew skirted along the coast as far as Boulogne in the hope of a break in the cloud. On reaching a cloud covered Boulogne, the crews turned back towards Ostend hoping for some improvement. Once again, their persistence was dashed. Deciding to press on they eventually arrived over Antwerp Docks which was only partially obscured. The crew dropped their 6 x 500lb + 120 x 4lb incendiaries over Docks No.2 and 3 and turned for home landing at 07:45 hours. Sergeant pilot Charles Graham made the short move across the tarmac from 115 Squadron to join the squadron on the 21st where he joined 'B' Flight. The following day he was joined by Sergeants George Plum and William Reid fresh from conversion at No.11 OTU.

There was an air of excitement around Marham on the morning of March 29th. Six crews were briefed and standing by for a daylight operation against the German pocket battlecruisers *Scharnhorst* and *Gneisenau* in Brest. They had arrived in Brest on March 22nd after the successful 'Operation Berlin' in the Atlantic. Both were using the dockyard facilities at Brest for refit and repair. The six crews led by the indomitable F/Lt Shaw waited for the call for action, finally at 16:00 hours they were eventually stood down. While these crews were waiting, a further six Wellingtons were bombed up and fuelled in preparation for an attack that night. Despite the preparation and the crews being briefed this operation was also cancelled.

*Belfast born Sergeant Edmund Shaw completed 8 operations in the 2<sup>nd</sup> pilots' seat. Having completed his tour in the Mediterranean, he returned to England but was tragically killed while flying an Avro Anson of No.21 O.T.U on May 21<sup>st</sup>, 1942.*

Snow and hail greeted the crews the following morning. This continued most of the day. Most would have considered flying out of the question given the terrible flying conditions. As it turned out, they were proved wrong. Twelve crews were detailed to attack Brest with the *Scharnhorst* and *Gneisenau* in dry dock as their objective. It was the start of a ten-month campaign to eliminate two of what the War Cabinet considered the most significant potential danger to the Atlantic convoys. The first crew airborne was Sgt Madgwick. His co-pilot was Sgt Ernest Richardson in Wellington R1511 HA-E at 1855 hours. All but two of the Wellingtons were carrying semi armourer piecing 500 pounders. It was hoped that if these hit the upper armoured decks of the Battlecruisers, they would penetrate deep into the lower decks causing maximum damage, that was the theory. First, you had to find them, then, more importantly, hit them. To the delight of the ground crews there were no early returns, in fact from the 37 Wellingtons supplied by 3 Group only three returned due to technical trouble. As expected, the sky above Brest was a cauldron of flak and searchlights, sea mist and numerous flares also proved troublesome. Sergeant Adam spent 30 minutes trying to find the dry-docks, he reported that *'Flares reflecting back'* hindered his search, he

returned with his entire bomb load. Unlike Sgt Adam, S/Ldr Richmond made his attack with the aid of what he considered *'excellent flares'*. Pilot Officer Paterson made five runs over the docks before he dropped his bombs from the perilously low altitude of 6,500 feet. Sergeant Donald made two runs over the docks. His second run resulted in four of his bombs seen exploding in the main dock area, for their persistence they very nearly fell victim of accurate light flak. While on his second run the crew reported what they believed to be four large and unusual bursts, which they considered were fired by the ships. The use of flares was becoming increasingly common, the problem of illuminating a target at night had long been raised as far back as 1932. It would be No.3 Group that would pioneer the use of flares and 'Raid Leaders' during 1940 long before the advent of the Pathfinders.

It was not all bombs and incendiaries that the squadron dropped. Sometimes it was a bit more personal. Numerous members of the squadron had families living in the cities that had been and were still on the receiving end of the German bombers. Bristol, Cardiff, Portsmouth, Plymouth, Southampton and Swansea were all severely damaged, as were the industrial cities of Birmingham, Belfast, Coventry, Glasgow, Manchester, Sheffield, and of course London. Sometimes it was a case of just wanting to make a small gesture, to get one's own back. One such gesture was remembered by F/Lt Shaw, *'Before take-off, one day, one of the station personnel whose home had suffered enemy bomb damage requested that we throw out a large brick with a rude message for Herr Hitler as a personal act of defiance and we were more than happy to oblige'. The said brick hopefully hit and destroyed a suitable target!*

The squadron lost one of its most experienced captains on the last day of the month when F/Lt John Mitchell was posted to No.7 Squadron based at RAF Oakington. One of the now rare breeds of pre-war pilots he had served continuously on the squadron since arriving as a sergeant in September 1939. Posted with him to 7 Squadron were his 2nd pilot, Sgt Peter Smith, his observer, wireless operator and front gunner. Sadly they were lost on a raid against Berlin on June 3rd 1941when Stirling W7430 was intercepted and shot down on their sixth operation by Fw Ernst Kalinowski who was on detachment to 2./NJG3. The five friends are buried in the Berlin 1939-1945 Cemetery.

*Flying Officer William Anstey and his crew. His co-pilot, Belfast born Sergeant Edmund Shaw would complete six operations with the experienced New Zealander before his departure. Observer Sergeant Norton, Wireless Operator /Airgunner, Sergeant Heyward, Sergeant Black, Front Gunner and Rhodesian rear gunner Sergeant Rose. All the above would serve in the Mediterranean.*

April began with yet another cancelled raid on the 1st, the weather once again the culprit and Brest had a 24-hour reprieve. To offset the departure of F/Lt Mitchell the squadron welcomed from No.57 Squadron New Zealander Sgt Oswald Mathews. The young Kiwi had hardly unpacked, when within a few days he was posted across the tarmac to No.115 Squadron, he would be killed over Munster in July. Another veteran from the French campaign departed on the 2nd when 'B' Flights F/O William Anstey was posted to No.3 Group Training Flight at R.A.F. Stradishall in preparation of his move to the Mediterranean and operations with No.70 Squadron. Ferrying a much-needed Wellington (T2616) he set off for pastures new, firstly to Malta then onto Egypt. From Kabrit and Fuka he would participate in numerous operations. In 1943 he returned to England where he became an instructor firstly with No.1653 HCU based at R.A.F Polebrook, and then R.A.F. Burn. In July 1943 he nearly died when he suffered a burst ulcer, dangerously ill for six months he returned on light duties. In 1946 he sailed for New Zealand. During his time on the squadron, William flown a total of 523 flying hours and survived some of the squadrons most dangerous and costly operations.

Ten crews took off to attack the Cruisers at Brest on the 3rd. This would be P/O Lambert's first operation as captain after completing nine raids in the right-hand seat with F/Lt Shaw. Sergeant Madgwick was in trouble soon after take-off when the wireless set fused due to a static charge aboard Wellington R1511 HA-E. Realising that to continue was impossible the crew jettisoned two SAP 500 pounders in a field near Cranfield aerodrome, where the crew eventually landed. Weather over the target area was too cloudy to allow identification of the docks let alone the Cruisers. The crews had no option than bomb on E.T.A. or the flashes of the subdued flak. Pilot Officer Lambeth spent over an hour above the target area. His persistence was not rewarded, he was obliged to return with his entire bombload. While on the return flight he lost the wireless set forcing him to land at R.A.F. West Raynham.

R.A.F. Marham was attacked at around 01:00 hours on the 4th. A Ju88C circled, then bombed the aerodrome from low altitude while the returning Wellingtons were orbiting to land. Seven 50 kg H.E.s unexploded bombs were discovered next morning, one of which went through a hangar roof. Minor damage to one barrack block was reported. Fortunately, there were no casualties. One Wellington of 115 Squadron was shot down by Lt Heinz Volker of 3./NJG2 at 0120 hours at Terrington St Clement, Norfolk on return from Brest. It is believed that it was Lt Volker who also attacked Marham. Sergeant Ronald Hoos was posted to No.20 O.T.U on the 4th. The Liverpudlian had not flown since his crash landing at Swaffham on return from Dusseldorf on February 25th. Since his arrival on the squadron, he had flown eight daylight operations on the Blenheim and a further six on the Wellington. After a spell instructing at No.20 O.T.U he returned to operations in 1943 with No.35 PFF Squadron. He was killed on May 29th 1943 when his Halifax DT804 TL-C was shot down by a night fighter flown by Lt Heinz-Wolfgang Schnaufer of Stab II./NJG1 while attacking Wuppertal.

*Without doubt the squadron's most flamboyant nose art was found on F/O Anstey's Vickers Wellington R1210 HA-O. The aircraft was destroyed on February 11th, 1941.*

It was a switch to the docks at Calais on the 5th. This operation was however cancelled late afternoon due to marginal weather. The following night the target was once again Calais, the squadron would provide three 'Freshman' crews to attack the Docks. Sergeants John Brown, Charles Graham and New Zealander William Swain took off just after 2000 hours. Interestingly, whereas both Sgt Brown and Graham had previous operational experience, the young Kiwi had none. Brown

237

had flown seven operations as 2nd pilot with Sgt Keith Madgwick, while Graham had flown seven operations with No.115 Squadron's F/Lt King. Strangely and totally against the norm, Swain would operate as captain without undertaking the customary second pilot operations. He had joined 218 only four days prior arriving from No.11 O.T.U. As forecast by the Met Officer the weather over the target prevented visual identification, both Brown and Graham bombed on E.T.A. Swain brought his bombs back to Marham.

The squadron lost Sgt Richardson on the morning of the 7th. He had since his arrival in February from No.20 O.T.U completed seven operations as 2nd pilot with P/O Douglas Paterson. He was now considered ready to captain his own crew and commence operations. Despite his experience over Northern Europe Reginald Richardson was North Africa bound. Posted to No.3 Group Training Flight he and his crew shuttled an urgently needed Wellington to North Africa where he would join No.37 Squadron. On May 4th, 1941 he and his crew were shot down and made PoW while bombing Benghazi. A significant attack on Kiel Harbour was mounted on the night of April 7th, No.3 Group providing a commendable 115 aircraft of the 229 dispatched by Bomber Command. This was the most significant force assembled against one target since the war began. The hope was that this major operation would create a diversion and induce the Germans to withdraw fighter squadrons from the Balkan theatre of operations and simultaneously ease the pressure in Yugoslavia on Greece. That was the plan. However, it first needed to succeed. Given its importance, it was no surprise that both Squadron Leader Beaman and S/Ldr Richmond's names appeared on the Ops board. They would join eight selected crews from 218 Squadron and a further 12 from No.115 Squadron. All twenty Wellingtons were safely airborne by 2300 hours in near-perfect weather conditions. The raid would be carried out in three waves with No.3 Group making up the second and third wave. Crews had no difficulty navigating to the target, F/Lt Shaw reported 'Fires visible 70 miles from target'. On reaching the target the squadron found Kiel enveloped in smoke, large fires raged in the old city and dock area. In amongst the explosions and destruction around them, the Germans manning the flak and searchlights tried valiantly to ensure the skies above Kiel were equally hot. Flying Officer Agar was scheduled to be over the target area between 2048 hours and 2106 hours. He was caught and held by numerous searchlights while on his bomb run. Two Bf110 night fighters wasted no time and quickly attacked the illuminated bomber damaging the rear turret in the process. Putting the Wellington into a steep dive, F/O Agar pointed the nose of the Wellington to the ground in a desperate attempt to lose both the flak and the fighters. Having lost almost 7,000 feet, the Wellington levelled off a few thousand feet above the ground not however before it was hit by light flak. Damage to Wellington R1594 HA-S was relatively light. The starboard fuel tanks were punctured and were leaking. The wireless set was damaged as was the A.S.I., astonishingly none of the crew was injured due to the excellent flying skill of the pilot and steady nerve of the rear gunner Sgt Herbert Riding. Over the Dutch coast P/O Lambeth had a sharp encounter with two Bf110s without either side inflicting damage. Sergeant Fraser was attacked while over the North Sea, the crew's rear gunner, Sgt Harry Hutchinson got in a telling burst on the Ju88, the gunner was positive the fighter was hit and damaged. As predicted by the returning crews widespread damaged had been achieved. Apart from the numerous fires the eastern dock area was particularly hard hit. Useful damage to the U-Boat producing Deutsche Werke and German Werft was also achieved. The armament depot burnt for two days before it was finally brought under control. It had been an extremely effective raid, the squadrons at Marham dropping an impressive 28 tons of bombs for no loss. In an effort to capitalise on the success of the previous night, another major raid was ordered against Kiel. Once again, the squadron provided ten crews led inevitably by both flight commanders. Like the previous raid, the groups were to bomb in waves with 218 Squadron scheduled to bomb between in the first wave between 19:52 hours and 20:30hrs. Number 115 Squadron's ten Wellingtons would attack in the second wave between 21:34 hrs and 22:12 hrs. With the weather once again clear a highly effective raid was carried out. Fires were still burning as the crews made their attack. Having suffered under the weight of bombs the night before it appeared that the defences of Kiel were out for revenge, the flak was described as *'intense and accurate'*. The crew of P/O Lambert were once again in trouble. Held by searchlights the Wellington experienced the unwelcome attention of both the flak defences and prowling fighters. While attempting to escape the flak the starboard engine was hit and damaged and would eventually seize on the flight home. With the Wellington losing height, P/O Lambert ordered that all non-essential equipment be jettisoned. Fearing that they would not make England he instructed his navigator to destroy all the maps and charts just in case a forced landing in Holland was necessary. Over the North Sea, they obtained fixes from Hull. Eventually, Wellington R1497 HA-H was brought in for a wheels-up crash landing at R.A.F. Horsham St Faith. It had been aloft for over 8 hours. Such was the damage it would be over two months before it would return from No.43 Group. Pilot Officer Lambert recalls the life and death struggle on this operation.

*'We crossed the English coast north of Great Yarmouth and set course for the target in NW Germany. It was necessary to avoid friendly shipping convoys that were known to us. They would often open fire on us without warning if they felt threatened. Flying into northern Germany, we always tried when possible to avoid the heavily defended islands, especially Heligoland. We made our way towards the target without much opposition from flak or searchlights. Approaching the target area, it was more exciting, on our bomb run we were caught and held by a cone of searchlights and much flak. The noise from the exploding flak become audible even above the engines of our Wellington. After bombing the aiming point, I dived away to get out of trouble. We had been at 11,000 ft. We set course for our base at Marham some 500 miles away over the North Sea. It soon became apparent that our port engine had been damaged and was out of action. It was becoming difficult and impossible to maintain height. We were flying off the coast of Holland and*

*The NCO crew of Flying Officer Anstey photographed just prior to their posting to the Mediteranean. Sergeant Rose was injured by German shell fire after the crew forced landed in no-mans-land in Iraq. All would return to England on completion of their tours.*

*extremely near to the surface of the sea. We threw everything portable out of the Wellington, guns, ammunition, all the equipment and even the Elsen was hacked off with the fire axe. I judged we were going to make a forced landing and turned on a course for the nearby Dutch coast as home was hundred-odd miles distance. It was then that the rear gunner informed me over the intercom that a night-fighter was closing in on our tail and remarked that he had no guns or ammunition! I signalled an S.O.S. using our navigation lights normally extinguished and waggled the Wellingtons wings by rolling the aircraft to indicate distress. The German fighter drew alongside. He then waggled his wings to indicate that he understood and made off. He must have been a gentleman! We were down to about 200 feet or less, but I found that probably due to using up fuel, I was now able to maintain height and even when needed climb a little. I decided to turn around 180 degrees and make once again for home and the 80-100-mile sea crossing. We limped over the English coast north of Great Yarmouth. I made an emergency landing with little or no fuel left in the badly damaged Wellington. I have been aloft over 8 hours compared with 6hour 35 minutes the previous night'.*

## Monday 7th April 1941

*Vickers Wellington*
*Mk.Ic R1497 HA-H 'Harry'*
*Contract No: 992424/39*
*Taken on Charge: 12/03/1941*
*Battle Damage, Wheels up landing.*
*To: 43 Group*
*Pilot: Flying Officer Anthony Lambert and Crew*


Pilot Officer Agar and S/Ldr Beaman both reported seeing a Wellington shot down and crash while making a run over the target area. It is assumed that this aircraft was a Wellington of No.149 Squadron skippered by Sgt John Cusworth. They are all buried in Kiel. Once again, the raid was a success, large fires could still be seen 50 miles from the target on the return flight. Unlike the first raid, the main weight of bombs fell on the town inflicting severe damage to the commercial and residential areas. The two attacks had killed over 200 German civilians and bombed-out over 8,000. Such was the intensity of the raids that many residents of Kiel decided to flee. It was, up until that time, the most successful attack flown against Germany.

A welcome 24-hour reprieve from operations meant that the squadron aircrew could have an evening to relax and enjoy a drink in the mess or the local pubs. The ground crews were not so lucky, a few Wellingtons had sustained damage over the previous few days as a result of Kiel's flak and Germany's increased fighter activity. These would have to be repaired, test flown and made ready. On the 10th, Bomber Command switched its attention to the *Scharnhorst* and *Gneisenau* at Brest. With the threat of fog in the early hours, the squadron's crews began taking off just after 1930hrs. There were two early returns within 30 minutes, the starboard engine cowling aboard Wellington R1511 HA-E blew off almost immediately on take-off giving Sgt Madgwick no option than to return. He was quickly followed by P/O Lambert in R1368 HA-F who experienced excessive vibration of the tail plane. Conditions over the target were marginal with much ground haze. Nevertheless, the crews carried out some excellent bombing. The Wellingtons of Marham and Stradishall led the attack with the objective of quieting the flak and searchlights defences. Returning crews reported many explosions on and within 50 yards of the *Gneisenau*. The returning crew's observations proved correct. Reports began to filter in a few weeks later that the *Gneisenau* had been struck by four bombs killing and wounding over a hundred personnel.

*Flying Officer Anthony Lambert's Vickers Wellington Ic R1497 HA-H 'Harry' photographed on the morning of April 8th, 1941. The port wing shows a large hole caused by Kiel's flak.*

The success of the operation was marred by the mysterious loss of Scotsman Sergeant John Brown and crew. Obviously in trouble, the wireless operator sent an S.O.S requesting a fix. The aircraft was last plotted ten miles south of Start Point, Devon, sadly it was not seen or heard from again. Sergeant Brown had arrived on the squadron in February and completed the standard seven 2nd pilot operations before he captained his own crew. This was his third operation as captain. His co-pilot was Sgt Arthur Plumb on only his third operation. Theo Boiten in his excellent Nachtjagd Combat Archives volume attributes the loss to German Coastal Flak who reported the Wellington crashing into the sea off Brest. The body of Sgt Anderson eventually washed ashore on the 13th near 'Mezenez' at St Marc, France and was buried in the Brest (Kerfautras) Cemetery on April 17th.

### Thursday 10th April 1941

*Vickers Wellington*
*Mk.Ic R1442 HA-D 'Don'*
*Contract No: 992424/39*
*Taken on Charge: 21/02/1941*
***Failed to Return***
*Pilot: Sergeant John Donald Brown 970094 RAFVR* **Killed**
*2nd Pilot: Sergeant Arthur George Plumb, 904038 RAFVR* **Killed**
*Wireless Operator: Sergeant David Francis Henderson 978536 RAFVR* **Killed**
*Observer: Flight Sergeant Robert Edward Venning Anderson, R/54533 RCAF,* **Killed**
*Rear gunner: Sergeant Tahu William Dabinette, 403106 RNZAF* **Killed**
*Front Gunner: Sergeant George Stewartson Snodden, 977632 RAFVR* **Killed**

It was back to Brittany and Brest Harbour on the 12th in what turned out to be a disappointing night. Complete cloud cover over the region made the task of bombing with any accuracy impossible. Most crews turned for home. The more experience tried the secondary target of Lorient. Flight Lieutenant Shaw bombed Lorient submarine yards dropping his 7 x 500lb + 1 x 250lb GP slightly west of the docks near a bridge. Squadron Leader Richmond also made for Lorient. His bomb load was seen to explode south to north near the southern dry dock area. It was a frustrating raid given the recent run of success. The following day, Flying Officer John Stokes was attached to No.11 OTU Basingbourne. Having completed eight operations with 'A' Flight's experienced F/Lt Shaw, he was considered ready to captain his own crew. At Bassingbourne he would have the difficult task of selecting his own crew.

*Left; Flight Sergeant Robert Edward Venning Anderson RCAF, right, Sergeant Tahu William Dabinette RNZAF*

The group dispatched a total of 40 aircraft on yet another attack on the docks at Brest on the 14th. Conditions had improved slightly affording the six crews the briefest glimpse of the dock area. The ever-persistent F/Lt Shaw circled the target for 45 minutes waiting for an opportunity to bomb. Finally, he was satisfied and dropped his 7 x 500lb SAP on the dock area, which produced a massive explosion. All the squadron crews safely return from what was yet another disappointing raid. Two crews skippered by Sergeant Robert Banks and Sgt Henry Huckle arrived from No.20 O.T.U RAF Lossiemouth on the afternoon of the 16th. It was a switch back to Germany on the 16th with the docks of Hamburg and Berlin the intended targets. These targets were later switched to Bremen. Nine crews were detailed and briefed from 218 Squadron with a further eleven from No.115 Squadron. The objective was the important Duetsche Schiff Maschinenbau A.G factory. The squadron suffered one early return, F/O Agar reported engine trouble which prevented him continuing. Wellington L7798 HA-S was landed safely back at Marham. The first part of the trip was flown in semi daylight. Flight Lieutenant Shaw was attacked by a Ju88, his logbook records the encounter;

*Daylight fight with a JU88. Lots of tail chasing and shooting. JU88 seen by all of us to climb steeply and then plunge vertically through 10/10th clouds. We think we got him!! We had a few holes.*

The Wellington was attacked repeatedly but using all his experience F/Lt Shaw together with P/O Byng-Hall the rear gunner had the measure of the German pilot. The rear gunner firing a total of 400 rounds at his adversary with numerous hits observed.

By the time, the squadron was over Bremen the city was ablaze, several fires were observed some considered large. Typically, of any German target, the flak and searchlights seemed especially vicious. Dozens of searchlights groped the sky above Bremen, flak of every calibre was exploding at various heights and in amongst this were a few fighters. Pilot Officer Mansfield watched two Bf110s patrolling over the burning city waiting to pounce on any unsuspecting victim. Seven of the nine Wellingtons dispatched were carrying incendiaries which were duly dropped on the already burning city. Sergeant Fraser got to within 15 miles of the target before he was forced to jettison his entire bomb-load due to a defective rudder. All the crews returned to Marham delighted with the night's effort. The squadron dropped a commendable 21,000lb of bombs.

Flying Officer Stokes returned from No.11 O.T.U Bassingbourne on the 19th with his new crew, the same day sergeant pilot Raoul Tucker also arrived from Bassingbourne. A solitary Freshman trip was planned for the 20th, Sgt Edward Chidgey was given the oil storage facility at Rotterdam to attack in Wellington N2844 HA-M. Over the North Sea the crew entered a mass of cloud, within seconds the Wellington began to ice-up. Transparent sheets of ice quickly formed on the leading edges, accumulated on the propellers, and started to block the air intakes of the engines and immediately started to choke the carburettors. Ice also built on the windshield, cutting down forward visibility. It was obvious that they could not continue. Wisely, and despite this being his first operation as captain Sgt Chidgey turned for home. It was a frightening baptism. Pilot Officer Pape returned from his detachment to No.4 B.A.T.F on the 20th. On the 21st Sgt Chidgey along with F/O Stokes were briefed for a Freshman trip, despite both Wellingtons being fuelled and loaded with bombs, and both crews briefed the operation was scrubbed an hour before take-off for fear of fog on return. As it turned out, it was a prudent decision.

The following night eight crews were briefed for yet another attack on Brest, while F/O Stokes and Sgt Chidgey were briefed to attack Oostende along with seven other Freshman crews drawn from other squadrons. Number 3 Group would be the only group over Brest and as expected the target was once again the *Scharnhorst* and *Gneisenau*. Only 26 crews were involved with RAF Marham providing the bulk of the crews in what turned out to be a frustrating and costly night. Shortly before take-off, the crews were informed that there was a particularly good chance that they would be diverted on return. Given this news, the unfortunate F/O Stokes and Sgt Chidgey were once again withdrawn from the night's proceedings. Flight Lieutenant Shaw was forced to return when the starboard engine of Wellington R1025

*Sergeant William Henry Swain RNZAF*

*Sergeant Raymond Finch, 2nd pilot.*

HA-B began to give trouble. He was back at dispersal within the hour. On reaching Brest, the small force of bombers encountered a cauldron of flak and searchlights. The intensity of the defences surprised even the most seasoned crew. Sergeant Adam reached the target at 16,000 feet, an unheard-of altitude. Luck was however not on his side, coned by 30 searchlights the Wellington was singled out by the flak. In an effort to escape, Sgt Adams put the Wellington into a dive. After dropping 6,000 feet the crew dropped their 7 x 500lb bombs across the dock area before succeeding in escaping in one piece. Pilot Officer Mansfield was not so lucky. His Wellington was hit by flak on the bomb run, a large chunk of the tail being blown off thankfully without injuring the rear gunner. A Wellington was seen to be held by searchlights over the target area surrounded by bursting flak, within seconds it was observed spinning down obviously out of control. The searchlights followed the stricken Wellington down to 1000 feet seconds before it crashed and exploded. This was the Wellington flown by New Zealander William Swain and crew. Vickers Wellington L7798 HA-S crashed at near Trezeger Farm, Pont ar Glut Milizac (Finistère) 6 miles NW of Brest killing all but the rear gunner Sgt James Clarke RNZAF.

Glaswegian born Sergeant Clarke managed to parachute to safety. On reaching the ground he used his knowledge French to find help. He managed to avoid capture until May 20th with the help of the local Resistance. Hidden in a local farm, arrangements had been made for him to move with the cooperation of the local Maquis when another farmer betrayed him. The mutilated bodies of his crewmates were removed from the wreckage and buried in a single grave on April 25th with full military honours. Occupying the right-hand seat was 23-year-old Sergeant Raymond Finch. Croydon-born Raymond had learnt to fly at the famous Redhill Flying Club in 1939. He had only been on the squadron three weeks, the Brest raid was his 5th operation. The small force of bombers had experienced the full attention of Brest defences, returning crews remarked about the ferocious reception they received. The crews turned for home thankful to escape the flak and searchlights. Unfortunately, their troubles were not over. Marham was fog-bound, resulting in the crews being diverted. Sergeant Madgewick and Pilot Officers Lambert and Mansfield landed at RAF

Abingdon, Oxfordshire. Flying Officer Agar managed find sanctuary at Exeter. Unfortunately, Sergeants Graham and Adam were not so fortunate. Sergeant Adam was refused permission to land at RAF Boscombe. They flew onto Marham in the hope that they might be lucky with the weather there. Unfortunately, Marham was still fog-bound, and they overshot the airfield. The crew then headed for Wyton. With the fuel situation critical aboard Wellington R1368 HA-F the crew had no option than abandoning the aircraft which crashed at 0315 hours just north of Clenchwarton Station, 2 miles west of Kings Lynn. The crew who had been aloft for over seven hours all landed safely apart from Sergeants Dadd and Payne. Both receiving sprained ankles. Sergeant Graham crash-landed near the village of St Minver north Cornwall, due to a combination of fuel shortage, wireless failure and being lost. Wellington R1597 HA-N was severely damaged in the crash. It never returned to the squadron. As for the Freshman operations, these were wisely cancelled.

**Tuesday 22nd April 1941**
*Vickers Wellington*
*Mk.Ic L7798 HA-S - 'Sugar'*
*Contract No : 992424/39*
*Taken On Charge: 14/01/1941*
***Failed to Return***
*Pilot: Sergeant William Henry Swain, 40665 RNZAF **Killed***
*2nd Pilot: Sergeant Raymond Edward Finch, 907613 RAFVR **Killed***
*Wireless Operator: Sergeant Victor Raymond Lloyd 944768 RAFVR **Killed***
*Observer: Sergeant Malcolm Bruce Crooks, 40755 RNZAF, **Killed***
*Rear Gunner: Sergeant James Clarke 402103 RNZAF POW*
*Front Gunner: Sergeant Geoffrey Molyneaux 985594 RAFVR **Killed***

**Tuesday 22nd April 1941**
*Vickers Wellington*
*Mk.Ic R1368 HA-F - 'Freddie'*
*Contract No: 992424/39*
*Taken on Charge: 25/10/1940*
*Abandoned; SoC*
*Pilot: Sergeant William Adam and crew safe.*

**Tuesday 22nd April 1941**
*Vickers Wellington*
*Mk.Ic R1597 HA-N- 'Nuts'*
*Contract No: 992424/39*
*Taken on Charge: 18/03/1941*
*Forced Landed: SoC*
*To: No.43 Group*
*Pilot: Sergeant Charles Graham and Crew safe*

The squadron welcomed Wing Commander Herbert "Jimmy" Kirkpatrick on the 22nd posted from No.9 Squadron based at RAF Honington. Born in Scotland in October 1910 he had learnt to fly with the Oxford University Air Squadron in 1929. On completing his pilot training, his first posting was to No.5 Squadron in India, in 1935 he would become the Personal Assistant to the AOC, RAF India. Returning to England in 1936 he attended an instructor's course at the Central Flying School, on completion he was posted to Oxford

245

University Air Squadron as Adjutant. In 1939 'Jimmy' joined the Air Staff at HQ Fighter Command, which was followed in 1940 with a posting as Chief Flying Instructor with Cambridge University Air Squadron. In April 1941 while serving at 3 Group HQ, he was attached to No.9 Squadron for operational experience. He was by now a wing commander. Having completed just two operations with 9 Squadron, he arrived at Marham. He may have lacked operational experience, but the thickset Scotsman made it up with years of technical and instructional knowledge. The new wing commander did not assume command immediately, as he still had much to learn.

Finally, on the 25th, P/O Stokes and Sgt Chidgey managed to complete their long-awaited Freshman trips. Their target was Oostende an important E-Boat base. The raid would be an anti-climax. Oostende like the rest of Europe, was covered with cloud. Flying Officer Stokes return to base with his bomb load when he was unable to locate his primary and alternative target. Sergeant Chidgey dropped his six 500lb G.Ps on searchlights. On return to Marham Sgt Chidgey overshot on his first attempt at landing. Opening up the throttles he climbed away to compose himself and settled his nerves. After completing another circuit, he approached Marham for the second time. On this occasion he undershot his approach, striking the top of some trees. The Wellington, T2958 HA-T crash landed in a field at Barton Bendish at 0320 hours. All the crew were shaken but otherwise uninjured, Chidgey was held responsible and ordered to have more night flying training.

### Tuesday 25th April 1941
*Vickers Wellington*
*Mk.Ic T2958 HA-T 'Tommy'*
*Contract No: 38600/39/C*
*Taken On Charge: 28/12/1940*
*Crash Landed*
*To: No.43 Group / Vickers SAS*
*Pilot: Sergeant Edward Chidgey and Crew safe*

That night eight crews, including Wing Commander Kirkpatrick, were detailed, and briefed for Kiel, one solitary crew was given Emden. It was another low-key operation by 3 Group. Only twenty-eight Wellingtons drawn from No.115, 214 and 218 Squadrons were involved. For 218 Squadron the night was one of disappointment, frustration, and tragedy.

The first to take-off was Sgt Graham in Wellington R1511 HA-E, he was back at his dispersal within a few hours when he was unable to obtain a wireless bearing over the North Sea. He was not the only early return, P/O Lymbery was forced to abandon the operation 100 miles off Cromer when the starboard engine aboard N2844 HA-M started to show signs of trouble. Flying with him on his first operation was Sergeant Andrew

*Pilot Officer Edward Chidgey with his new wife.*

Kaarsberg RCAF. Pilot Officer Lambert failed to reach the target owing to petrol failure. Deciding to head for the island of Heligoland the crew somehow completely missed the island fortress so continued to the Frisian Islands. Here they found an airfield which they bombed after dropping a flare on their first pass. The bombs were seen to explode near two hangars, annoyingly the 120 x 4lb incendiaries hung up. The crew were diverted to R.A.F. Honnington on return. They had been airborne 7 hours 40 minutes. The remaining crews managed to locate and bomb the docks or general area encountering considerable opposition from flak and searchlights. Squadron Leader Beaman was lucky to return, a navigational error due to loop failure and a change in the briefed winds meant the crew became hopelessly lost. Unable to locate the target or the secondary target they circled over northern Germany from 0100hrs to 0230hrs, desperately trying to establish their position and the correct course for home. By the time they had established their position by back-plotting, it was discovered to their horror that they were over the North Baltic. The crew eventually landed at the airfield at Sutton Bridge, Lincolnshire. The exhausted crew had been aloft for 8 hours 30 minutes, their luck had held, just. Sadly, the squadron's luck did not prevent the tragic loss of F/O George Agar and crew. An S.O.S. was received at 23:56hrs, a bearing taken at the time placed the crew 80 miles from the Dutch coast. The crew are believed to have come down in the North Sea, there were no survivors, and their bodies were never found. Flying Officers Agar's rear gunner was Sgt Wilfred Thornhill, both had started their tours together on the Blenheim and had operated continuously since September 1940, it was their 26th operation together. Also killed was 24-year-old 2nd pilot, P/O Gilbert Redstone RNZAF who had joined the crew fresh from No.15 O.T.U. in March, it was his tenth operation.

**Tuesday 25th April 1941**
*Vickers Wellington*
*Mk.Ic R1507 HA-V - 'Victor"*
*Contract No: 992424/39*
*Taken on Charge: 18/03/1941*
**Failed to Return**
*Pilot: Flying Officer George Brian Shelton Agar, 41240 RAF* **Killed**
*2nd Pilot: Flying Officer Gilbert Peter Lewis Redstone, 40242 RNZAF* **Killed**
*Wireless Operator: Flight Sergeant Clifford William Andrews 563158 RAF* **Killed**
*Observer: Sergeant Victor Edwin Ashworth, 759036 RAFVR,* **Killed**
*Rear Gunner: Flight Sergeant Wilfred Thornhill, 965427 RAFVR,* **Killed**
*Front Gunner: Pilot Officer Charles Edward Blair, 78743 RAFVR,* **Killed**

There was some good news after a horrendous night, one of the pre-war regulars had successfully returned from his last operation. Flight Lieutenant Shaw was at the time the second longest-serving pilot on the squadron behind S/Ldr Ian Richmond. Walter Shaw had joined 218's 'A' Flight in May 1938 from No.6 FTS. The loss of this highly experienced and respected captain was a tremendous blow to the squadron. He, along with Richmond, were the backbone of the squadron. Known for his press-on attitude and steely determination, he freely passed on his knowledge and experienced to the less experienced captains on the squadron. The irreplaceable Flight Lieutenant Walter Shaw was deemed tour expired having completed more than 33 operations on the Battle, Blenheim and Wellington.

*'On 25 April I took part in another blitz on Kiel, dropping six containers of incendiaries and two GP bombs from 15,000 ft. We had our usual rough and noisy ride through the concentrated heavy flak and searchlight defences. As we left the area, many large fires could be seen in Kiel. We landed safely at Marham and after debriefing followed by the operational cooked breakfast, retired to bed. This was my last operational flight with 218 Squadron, which meant a posting away from the Squadron to another unit. I had one last flight in my Wellington taking three non-flying personnel as passengers, one sergeant and two aircraftwomen duly authorised to get experience in the air. It was a nostalgic flight for me, and our red devil crest was still on the nose, which had brought good luck to our crew, but I suspect the next owners would replace it with their own idea of a good luck charm and I sincerely hoped it would work for them as well. After this, I made my farewells to 218 and took up my duties with No. 22 OTU at RAF Station Wellsbourne Mountford, near Stratford on Avon. Shortly after acting as the Flight Commander, I was officially appointed in this capacity with the rank of Squadron Leader with effect from 7 May 1941.'*

He returned to operations with No.83 Pathfinder Squadron in March 1943 when he took command of 'B' Flight. Walter completed a further 23 operations, with targets including Berlin, Hamburg, Essen, Munich and Turin. He was subsequently awarded a well-deserved and long overdue DFC and Bar and three MiDs. Not a well-known bomber captain, he was a true bomber baron in every sense of the word. There is an interesting postscript given by Walter and his reconnection with 218 Squadron.

*'The training programme continued as usual until 30 September 1942 when No. 11 OTU moved to RAF Westcott in Buckinghamshire. This was done to enable units of the American Air Force to move into Bassingbourne. One bright morning, while driving around the perimeter track, I saw a replacement Wellington which had just been flown in by a ferry pilot. Much to my surprise and pleasure, I found it to be my old 218 Squadron battlewagon R1025 and was able to acquire it for my flight. The next thing I noticed about it was that the big red devil mascot we had on the nose had been removed, but it had still survived. At the time, we considered it to be a lucky aircraft, and so it proved to be for us and also for the aircrews who took it over. In 1943 the training commitment at Oakley had increased, and the post for an officer in command had been established with Wing Commander rank, and I had been earmarked for the job. However, before this took place, I received a phone call from Wing Commander Gillman who knew me in pre-war 218 Squadron days at Boscombe Down and who was now commanding 83 Pathfinder Squadron at RAF Wyton. He offered me B Flight with Wing Commander rank if I would like to volunteer to join the Pathfinder force. I had to make my mind up quickly and said yes. So yet again I was on the move and on 2 March 1943 I made my farewells, having collected my chocolate ration and a bottle of Gordon's Gin from the Officers' Mess staff as a good luck present and off I went to 83 Squadron'.*

*Co-Pilot aboard Wellington R1507 HA-V was New Zealander Gilbert Redstone. He arrived on the squadron from No.15 O.T.U in March 1941.*

At 0318 hours Marham was bombed by a Ju88 of NJG.2 which dropped eight bombs damaging the station's main water mains and blowing out 'A' Flights hangar windows. Flying Officer Stokes had a lucky escape on return from his solitary attack on Emden. He was in the process of landing when the Ju88 attacked. His Wellington, R1536 HA-G collected several fragments from the exploding bombs, thankfully none of the crew was injured. As a precaution, the remaining ten Wellingtons of 115 and 218 Squadron were diverted to RAF Honington while the craters were filled, and a search was undertaken for any delayed action bombs. Marham's Q Site was also attacked, twelve HE bombs were dropped, without causing any damage. On the 28th Wing Commander Amison departed to No.12 OTU at RAF Benson. Since he assumed command in February, he had flown a solitary operation, it was certainly not a case of leading by example. Both previous commanding officers had shown a distinct lack of gusto when it came to operations. The following night Sgt Chidgey was detailed for yet another Freshman operation, his target was the docks at Rotterdam. Owing to 10/10th cloud, he was unable to locate the target. The return flight was flown at less than 600 feet, jettisoning his bomb load over the North Sea, he made a safe landing on his return.

The last operation of the month was flown on the 30th, and again Kiel was the intended target. Number 3 Group provided twenty-nine crews drawn from No.115, 149 and 218 Squadrons. Conditions over Kiel prevented any visual confirmation of the Docks, let alone the individual aiming point. Most crews presumed they were in the general proximity by the intense flak emanating from below. Squadron Leader Richmond characteristically decided to seek an alternative target. Finding conditions better over Wilhelmshaven he bombed from 10,000 feet. His mixed incendiary and HE bomb load were seen exploding, these then started some fires. Pilot Officer Lymbery bombed the airfield at Rensburg where he dropped his 2 x 500 pounders, 1 x 250 pounder and 360 incendiaries from 17,000 feet. On leaving the target, the rear gunner noted several small fires and one massive fire which was still visible twenty minutes after departure. Squadron Leader Beaman was once again having difficulty finding the target. For an agonising 50 minutes, the crew tried to get a visual on the docks. Continuously buffeted by accurate flak, the plucky crew finally bombed in the general Kiel area. The raid was a failure. Thankfully, there were no losses suffered by Marham squadrons. The month ended on a positive note. The squadron was justly proud of a notice from the Commander in Chief about the exploits of P/O Lambert.

On the night of 8/9th April 1942, this pilot was captain of a Wellington aircraft detailed to attack Kiel. During the course of this operation his aircraft was caught in a concentration of searchlights and subjected to intense anti-aircraft. Nevertheless P/O Lambert pressed home his attack by diving down onto the target from 11,000 feet to 5000 feet and realised his bombs from the lower height. The port engine was hit hard by anti-aircraft fire and the oiling system affected. There were many holes in different parts of the air frame. With the engine and air frame in such a condition it was found difficult to maintain height. P/O Lambert foreseeing a force landing was probable, set course for the Frisian Islands. All removable items of equipment were jettisoned from the aircraft. Near the Dutch coast an enemy fighter approached to attack but by signalling SOS on an Aldis lamp and putting on the navigation lights, the enemy was prevented from making an attack. At this stage he found that he could maintain height at approximately 1500 feet with an airspeed of approximately 80 m.p.h. He therefore decided to try and reach England and set about getting back. Ten minutes later the port engine started showing signs of problems whilst the starboard engine gave only 3 1/2lb boost. Flying with one engine and with no navigational equipment, the aircraft eventually crossed the coast, but realising the he would have difficulty in maintaining this with the undercarriage down, P/O Lambert decided to land with the undercarriage retracted. This he did successfully at Horsham St Faith without injuries to any of his crew. At all-time Pilot Officer Lambert had displayed great determination and devotion to duty.

Other than two training sorties flown on the morning of the 1st the only excitement was the arrival of two pilots from No.11 O.T.U RAF Bassingbourn. Norfolk born Sergeant Kenneth Shearing and Australian Sergeant Allan Barton RAAF. Both had just completed No.28 Course and were now ready to put their training into practice.

The following day, P/O Denis Clifford observer to F/Lt Shaw was posted to No.18 O.T.U RAF Bramcote on completion of his first tour, he like his pilot, would survive the war. On the 3rd Wing Commander Kirkpatrick led nine crews against Brest. Conditions over the Docks were excellent, which enabled the crews to easily identify the targets, the Cruisers *Scharnhorst* and *Gneisenau*. Undertaking his first operation was the recently posted Sgt Shearing, he accompanied S/Ldr Richmond aboard Wellington R1448 HA-L. This crew bombed from 11,000 feet and obtained four excellent photographs which clearly showed both cruisers and oil storage tanks. So good were the photos that they were sent to Group H.Q. Also flying was the now fully recovered Sgt Vandervord. With his former mentor F/O Agar missing David joined the crew of New Zealander Sgt Mervyn McNeil, it was his first operation in nearly seven weeks.

*Seen here side by side at No.11 OTU. Sergeant Kenneth Shearing and Sergeant Allan Barton RAAF.*

*The crew of New Zealander Sergeant Mervyn McNeil RNZAF. Sergeant Vandervord, 2ⁿᵈ pilot. Observer Sergeant Franks, Wireless Operator, Sergeant Hartley, Front gunner Sergeant Booth and rear gunner Sergeant Dunk.*

Weather conditions hindered the planned operations on the night of May 5th, Hamburg was to be the target, but this was later changed to Mannheim. Nine crews were detailed and briefed with P/O Pape and crew flying a 'Freshman' trip Cherbourg. There was one exciting development on this raid, the appearance on the squadron of the Wellington Mk.II which was equipped with the Rolls Royce Merlin engine. The first Wellington Mk II prototype flew in March 1939. The new engines provided 1,145 hp, an increase of 100 hp over the Pegasus engine. There was however one drawback, they were much heavier – the weight of the Mk II increasing by some 4,000 lbs when compared to the otherwise similar Mk I.C. The Mk II was faster and had a higher service ceiling, but the bomb load and maximum range were both reduced. The reduced maximum bomb load still allowed the Wellington Mk II to be used to test the then-new 4,000 lb which was gradually being introduced replacing the less effect bombs currently in use. This new bomb required a series of changes to be made to the bomb bay, including the removal of a central structure that had divided the bomb bay in two, and the removal of part of the bomb bay doors. Vickers built Wellington Mk.II W5447 arrived on the squadron via 12 M.U. on April 18th.

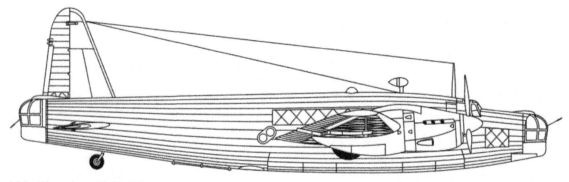

## Wellington Mk.II

Equipped with two Merlin Mk.X engines, it was coded HA-Z, and immediately the senior crews scrambled to be the first to operate the aircraft and drop the new monster bomb, the 4000 pounder! As expected, the most senior and experienced skipper on the squadron was given the honour. Squadron Leader Richmond took off at 2215 hours, by his side was Sgt Shearing. The single bomb was dropped on an autobahn 1 1/2 miles S.E. of Mannheim due to the primary being entirely covered by cloud. The crew remarked that the explosion was 'terrific' producing blue flashes. It was the first of thousands that would cause destruction on an unprecedented scale over Germany. The squadron bade farewell to F/Lt Shaw and his gunner P/O Byng-Hall on the 5th. Percy Byng-Hall was posted to No.20 O.T.U, Lossiemouth. Transferring to the Administrative Branch in July 1942 he returned to Canada. Eventually, he was released from the R.A.F. in early 1946. To offset the loss of F/Lt Shaw, F/O Stokes was promoted to the unpaid rank of Acting F/Lt.

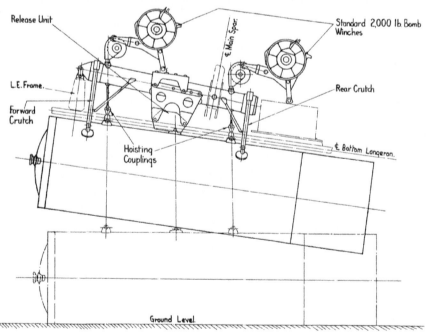

*The Wellington Mk.II was capable of delivering the still relatively new 4000 pounder. To accommodate the monster bomb, the Wellington underwent some modifications to the standard winching and lifting points and strengthening of the bomb bay.*

A further two pilots, Sergeant Reginald Burr and Sgt Kenneth Fisher arrived on the 5th, both from No.21 O.T.U.

Additional movements took place on the 6th, Sergeant William Adam was posted to No.23 O.T.U Pershore, his tour finally over. He had flown nine daylight operations on the Blenheim and a further thirteen on the Wellington with the squadron. In April 1942 he was sent to instruct at No.1653 Heavy Conversion Unit. Reoccurring problems with his health and a few stays in hospital meant that William did not return for a second tour. Born in 1915, he joined the R.A.F in 1931 as an apprentice Metal Rigger at Halton. William eventually retired from the R.A.F. in 1959. He had served for an impressive 28 years. Also posted were two Scottish wireless operators, both old hands from the early days at Oakington. Douglas Methven, the wireless operator to F/Lt Shaw, was sent to instruct at No.22 O.T.U. He would return for a second tour of operations flying with No.101 Squadron. Sadly, while attacking Osnabruck in August 1942 he was killed. Sergeant George Tibbetts went to No.11 O.T.U at Bassingbourn, he lost his life flying with No.202 Squadron when his Catalina flew into high ground near Algeciras, Spain in 1943.

The *Gneisenau* and *Scharnhorst* were again the targets on the 7th, ten crews being chosen. The weather was once again kind to the participating crews, both cruisers and the dock facilities were clearly identified. Five of the Wellingtons were carrying the 2000lb Mk.I High Capacity bomb. This ship buster had made its debut in May 1940. It had been explicitly designed for attacks on shipping in basins, docks, anchorages, aqueducts and canals. The earlier variant was equipped with a cumbersome parachute. These were soon removed due to accuracy issues. Bomber Command had high hopes for this bomb against the 'Toads'. Each of the crews were given individual targets, seven were given the *Scharnhorst* in Dock 8 as their primary target, while the remainder were given Dock 9 which held the *Gneisenau*. The squadron was over the target just after midnight. Wellington R1713 HA-V captained by Sgt Fraser RNZAF had only just reached the target when a Bf110 attacked it. The crew's rear gunner, Sgt Harry Hutchinson was fully alert, giving the crew time to lose the fighter with a dive to port. Squadron Leader Richmond claimed a direct hit on the *Scharnhorst* with one of his 500lb SAP bombs. The claims were not confined to the flight commander, F/Lt Stokes recorded a '*Likely hit*' while P/O Pape reported, '*three bursts observed on jetty and the stern of the ship*'. Immediately after bombing a Bf110 attacked the Pape crew, the encounter was brief and inconclusive. The Marham crews were enthusiastic about the raid on return. The Station records Book records ;

18 aircraft attacked the primary target. Very good visibility enabled the crews to identify the ships easily and good bombing runs were made. Direct hits were claimed on the ship in the torpedo jetty with 2 x 2000lb and 500lb bombs. The aircraft which bombed with the 500lb dived from 11,000ft to 2,000ft the bombs being released at 4,000ft The crew are certain that the ship was definitely hit. 1 x 2000lb bomb aimed at the ship in the dry dock claimed to be very near.

A maximum effort was required from No.3 Group HQ on the morning of the 8th, the target for the night was the Blohm and Voss yards at Hamburg. The first of twenty Wellingtons began taking off from Marham around 2200 hours, each squadron providing ten crews. One of the participating crews was Wing Commander Kirkpatrick. He departed at 2245hrs at the controls of Wellington R1496 HA-O. The squadron also supplied two of the Merlin-powered Wellington Mk.IIs. Squadron Leader Richmond was once again flying W5448 HA-Z while the recently arrived W5447 HA-C was skippered by F/O Smith, both were carrying the new 4000lb bomb. Visibility was perfect over the target, bright moonlight ensuring the crews had an unparalleled view of Hamburg.

Both S/Ldr Richmond and F/O Smith were pleased with the results of the bomb, Smith reporting *'Great flash was seen lighting up the clouds, a Wizard bomb'*. The bomb exploded in the centre of Hamburg. Fighters were active and some crews reported twin-engine Bf110s prowling over the target area. All the crews returned safely from the operation. Once again, the was a buzz around the debriefing room on return, crews were convinced the raid was a success reporting numerous fires on leaving the target area. They were right, a total of 83 fires were reported of which nearly half were classed as large. The 4000 pounders had caused devastation in amongst the densely packed streets and houses causing the German services considerable trouble. A total of 185 people were killed, over 500 wounded and nearly 2000 bombed out. It was the highest fatal casualty figure suffered by the Germans in the war to date.

The success over Hamburg warranted a message from the Secretary of State (Air) Sir Archibald Sinclair to HQ Bomber Command, the message reads.

"My congratulations to you and the Groups and squadrons under your command on last night's heavy and successful raids over Germany. The skill and daring with which they were carried out deserve the highest praise and their scale reveals the growing power of Bomber Command. Archibald Sinclair ends"

The only incident was during landing. Pilot Officer Pape who had failed to reach Hamburg and bombed the secondary target of Kiel instead had just touched down when unbeknown to him and his crew a 500 pounder which had hung-up dropped off its rack striking the tail wheel of Wellington R1536 HA-G. Flying with the crew was Sgt Ron Gill, former wireless operator to F/Lt Shaw. Born in Westcliff-on Sea in September 1916, Ron had joined the Army in 1934, disillusioned with Army life after two years he brought himself out for the princely sum of £25. Joining the RAF in 1937, Ron undertook his initial training at Uxbridge before being sent to Cranwell. Here he excelled in anything to do with the wireless, on completion of his 14 months at Cranwell he passed out as an Aircraftman first class, along with his best mate Wally Ellis, who would also join 218 Squadron. These were the only two cadets to achieve the AC1 rank. The remaining cadets were all classified as Aircraftman 2nd class. In 1938 Ron joined 218 Squadron at Boscombe Down, he had served continuously since then. This would be Ron Gills last raid with the squadron having survived approximately 31 trips over occupied Europe. Screened from operations, Ron was given the task of training new wireless operators arriving at Marham. This he did until the urge to return to Ops had him volunteer for a second tour. Unfortunately, and to Ron's regret he was not posted back to 218 Squadron but No.99 Squadron based at RAF Waterbeach in August 1941. A further six operations were flown, returning from an operation to Frankfurt on September 29th, his Wellington crashed near Bury St Edmunds, his injuries were such that he did not fly again. Over at RAF Mildenhall, the respected Canadian commanding officer of No.149 Squadron, W/Cdr John Powell was due to be posted leaving a vacancy for a new commanding officer. The man chosen to replace him was 218 Squadron's S/Ldr William Beaman, he departed on May 9th. His posting left a flight commanders vacancy, this was ably filled with the arrival of F/Lt Clyde-Smith from No.115 Squadron. It was perhaps the most stress-free posting for the new flight commander, a simple walk from one flight office to another. On the day of his arrival at 218, he was immediately promoted to squadron leader, unpaid! While operational with 115 Squadron's 'A' flight, he had flown an impressive 19 operations attacking targets such as Kiel, Bremen and Berlin.

*Seen here with a group of ground crew is Sergeant Ron Gill (2nd row 2nd right). At the time, he was one of the longest serving members on the squadron.*

It was back to Hamburg on the 10th, Bomber Command HQ was hoping for another success. The squadron provided 12 crews led by the unstoppable S/Ldr Richmond. There was the customary early return, P/O Lambert got as far as Holland before he was forced to return with an overheating starboard engine not before he dropped his bombs on the naval base at Heligoland. Sergeant Madgwick got as far as Westerhaver, Holland before he too encountered trouble. Flying over the flat landscape of northern Holland at 14,000 feet he was caught and held by a number of searchlights. Despite every effort, he was unable to shake them off until finally he pushed the control column forward and dived the Wellington to 8,000 feet. Levelling off the crew too stock, once satisfied they continued onto Hamburg, they were shaken but still in one piece. Over Meldorf, Germany they were yet again held by searchlights, this time accompanied by intense heavy and medium flak which began exploding dangerously close. Sergeant Madgwick pushed the control column forward for a second time, unlike over Holland the searchlights and flak were not so easily fooled. It was not until Sgt Madgwick, and his co-pilot, Sgt Ronald Read levelled the Wellington at a mere 50 feet the flak subsided. All but two of the searchlights had been lost, both front and rear gunners engaged their antagonist spraying down the beams with machine gunfire. Finally, they were clear, apart from numerous holes along the fuselage and a damaged port elevator they were all alive. Given their altitude, the crew turned to Heligoland where they bombed the seaplane base.

Weather over the dock and town was excellent affording the defences the same opportunities as the bomb aimers above, unlimited visibility. Flak and searchlights were plentiful, heavy, and accurate. The Blohm and Voss works were quickly identified and received the attention of the squadron's remaining crews. A ring of fire about a half-mile radius seemed to surround the dock area, with the main conflagration in the city centre. For the crews, at fourteen thousand feet, the raid looked to them successful as they turned for home. While over the North Sea P/O Pape was followed by a Bf110 for seven minutes, no attack developed, but the crew were extra vigilant until the wheels of Wellington R1596 HA-D had touched down at Marham.

There was a change of command at station level on May 11th with the departure of Group Captain Victor Groom OBE DFC and Bar. His replacement was Wing Commander Andrew McKee DFC AFC a forthright and pugnacious New Zealander.

The splendid work of wireless operator Sergeant Hugh Burke on a recent Kiel raid was recognised in a signal which arrived at RAF Marham from the C-in-C.

*On the night of 8/9th April this NCO was a member of a crew of a Wellington aircraft detailed to attack Kiel. In the course of this operation the aircraft was very badly hit and was eventually flown to England across the North Sea on one engine after all removable equipment and maps had been jettisoned from the aircraft. Great dependence, therefore had to be placed upon the assistance which could be obtained by the wireless in order to bring the aircraft back to England. The fixed aerial, however, had been damaged by enemy action, and before any wireless could be obtained. Sergeant Burke with more than half his body outside the astro hatched repaired the damage. The aircraft returned to England on a course guessed by the navigator, who had no means of sextant and by wireless bearings which were obtained by Sgt Burke once he had repaired his wireless. Throughout the whole trip Sgt Burkes coolness and efficiency resulted in the aircraft being brought safely back to an aerodrome in England. He had to change the frequencies and wavebands at the pilot's request with great rapidity and finally homes the aircraft successfully at Horsham St Faith. It is considered that this NCO's coolness and skill resulted in the safe return of the aircraft.*

It was back to Hamburg the following night. Wing Commander Kirkpatrick led the crews away on what turned out to be another successful raid. Sergeant McNeil RNZAF and crew got involved in a vicious encounter with a Bf110 and soon after jettisoned two 500 pounders over the North Sea. The crew's rear gunner claiming a 'Probable'. Hamburg received yet another heavy blow. A reported 88 fires were started, a third of which were classed as large. These operations, although small in comparison to what was to come, had slowly started to ebb away at the population's morale. These latest raids over Northern Germany had sent shock waves throughout German High Command, the scale of the damage was gradually increasing, it was a sign of things to come. Canadian pilot, P/O John Maxwell and his Observer P/O Garnet Jacobson arrived from No.11 OTU on the morning of the 11th. They were quickly followed in the afternoon by fellow Canadian Sgt James Gordon and his all NCO crew. Two pilots, Sgt Burr and Fisher, were sent on a short course at No.4 Blind Approach Training Unit (BATF) based at Wyton before they started operations on the squadron. It was essential that after mastering the basics at OTU they gained experience of Blind flying, their lives and that of their crew depended on it. Marham was on the receiving end of five separate attacks between 0100 hours and 0420 hours by JU88s of NJG2s. One bomb landed outside the mess blowing in all the windows, also damaged was the maintenance hangar and MT section. The equipment stores were set on fire by incendiaries, 15 station personnel were also injured.

It was not all arrivals. The squadron lost the experienced Sgt Madgwick and his crew on the 13th when they were posted to No.115 Squadron. Sergeant Bernard Madgwick was a seasoned and experienced captain having completed 23 operations since his arrival in January. His stay on 115 Squadron was brief, on June 8th he was posted to the Short Stirling equipped No.7 Squadron. Sadly, he was tragically killed on his third operation with the squadron. On return from a raid against Hannover on July 15th, his Stirling, N6022 MG-D ran out of petrol. All the crew successfully bailed out, sadly Madgwick slipped out of his parachute harness and fell to his death. Also posted to No.115 Squadron was Sgt William Reid, he had yet to operate with 218. William would be shot down attacking Bremen on July 13th, 1941 and made a PoW.

Pilot Officer Chalk arrived on the 14th from No.115 Squadron. The rear gunner would again team-up with his old pilot, S/Ldr Clyde-Smith. The exodus from 115 Squadron continued. It would appear that 218's new flight commander had pulled a few strings to get his old crew posted with him, Sergeant Harry Taylor, 2nd pilot, observer Sgt Bruce King RNZAF, and wireless operator/gunners Sgt Brown and Player all arrived on the 14th. Two Canadian pilots joined the ever-growing squadron on the 16th from No.21 OTU RAF Moreton-In-Marsh. Sergeant John 'Jack' Swingler and Sgt Robert Lowe. At 29 years old, Robert was older than most of his companions and unlike Swingler, Lowe arrived with three of his crew. RAF Marham provided twenty-two crews for a raid directed against Cologne on the 16th, with 218 Squadron providing ten crews. Operating on his first raid as flight commander was S/Ldr Clyde-Smith, in veteran Wellington R1008 HA-A.

*Vickers Wellington Mk.Ic R1008 HA-A Apple. This aircraft would be used almost exclusively by Squadron Leader Clyde-Smith for his tour.*

Both the squadron's Wellington Mk.IIs were airborne, as usual, S/Ldr Richmond had bagged W5448 HA-Z, while P/O Lambert was given the opportunity to fly W5447 HA-C. Unusually, both aircraft were carrying conventional bomb loads, and not the 4000 pounder. Unlike the previous attacks on Kiel, the raid was rather disappointing. Arriving over the target, the crews found cloud over the aiming point and scattered fires. Accurate flak caused some inconvenience. Crews bombed the approximate position as judged by the abundance of flak and searchlights. The whole attack did not have the cohesiveness of previous attacks. There was a flurry of postings and promotions at senior level at Marham over the 18th and 19th. Number 115 Squadron's commanding officer, Wing Commander Anthony Evan Evans was replaced by W/Cdr Robert Sharpe. On departure, Evan Evans was immediately promoted to the rank of Group Captain (unpaid) and assumed command of RAF Marham vice Group Captain McKee who was posted to RAF Wyton.

The last two weeks of May 1941 would turn out to be one of frustration, tragedy and farewells. It would also be a period of aircrew movements on a scale not seen since the squadron's hectic weeks of May 1940. On the 18th the squadron was stunned by the tragic news that six airmen had been killed while on what should have been a routine an air-test in one of the Mk.II Wellingtons. The aircraft was being flown by P/O Lymbery and his 2nd pilot, Sgt Coates. All appeared normal until the aircraft was seen approaching Hilgay, 3 miles south of Downham Market at an altitude of 2000 feet. The Wellington suddenly turned sharply to port and fell into a steep dive. Brian Lymbery almost succeeded in regaining control, but the aircraft struck the ground at a flat angle and travelled for several hundred yards disintegrating until the main wreckage came to rest in a wood. All the crew were killed instantly apart from the crew's rear gunner Sergeant Ronald Mew who was found alive but severely burnt to the face and hands. He was taken to Ely Hospital but succumbed to his injuries two days later. He was just twenty years old. The accident was investigated, and the investigating officer concluded that the Wellington's dinghy broke loose and fouled the starboard elevator. It was a tragic waste of an experienced crew. Brian Lymbery had completed 24 operations, 16 flown as captain, and had accumulated 171 flying hours on the Wellington. His 2nd pilot, Kenneth Coates had completed 12 operations all alongside his pilot. Canadian Sgt Wilbur Frederick Webber R/54909 RCAF, the crew's observer, was buried alongside his skipper on May 22nd at Marham Holy Trinity Churchyard. The remaining crew were taken to their hometowns for burial.

**Sunday 18th May 1941**
*Vickers Wellington*
*Mk.II W5448 HA-Z 'Zebra'*
*Contract No : 38600/39*
*Taken On Charge: 16/04/1941*
*Destroyed in crash*
*Pilot: Pilot Officer Brian Edward Lymbery 89063 RAFVR **Killed***
*2nd Pilot: Sergeant Kenneth Wilson Coates, 745552 RAFVR **Killed***
*Observer: Sergeant Wilbur Frederick Webber R/54909 RCAF **Killed***
*2nd Wireless Operator: Sergeant Luther Crawshaw 944323 RAF **Killed***
*1st Wireless Operator: Sergeant George Lee Morris Bayly, 974237 RAFVR **Killed***
*Rear Gunner: Sergeant Ronald George Mew, 649028 RAF **Killed***


There was an air of stunned disbelief throughout the squadron that the crew who had survived the flak and fighters over Kiel, Hamburg and Cologne could be killed in such tragic circumstances on what should have been a simple practice flight. The following day the weather like the mood on the squadron, was miserable, low cloud and rain swept the airfield putting paid to any flying. Or so the crews believed, 12 crews were briefed for an attack on Cologne, but as expected the weather had the final say. What followed over the next few weeks was a sequence of briefings and cancellations. The effect of these cancellations on the aircrews varied, a few, especially the recent arrivals, tended to shrug it off. This was probably due to their enthusiasm to get operational. The others, the more experienced aircrew the effect was one of frustration mixed with relief. The cancellation of an operation played heavily on the nerves of some, irrespective of experience. This was also true of the ground crews. Although not experiencing the same dangers, their work was physical, demanding and at times hazardous. The following gives some idea of what the aircrews and ground crews had to endure, mentally and physically.

| Date | Target | Crew Detailed and Briefed | Cancelled |
|---|---|---|---|
| 19/05/1941 | Cologne | 12 | *Bad Weather* |
| 21/05/1941 | Freshman | 1 | *Bad Weather* |
| 22/05/1941 | Boulogne | 10 | *Unknown* |
| 23/05/1941 | Freshman | 1 | *Unknown* |
| 24/05/1941 | Freshman | 1 | *Bad Weather* |
| 25/05/1941 | Hamburg | 11 | *Bad Weather* |
| 26/05/1941 | Dieppe | 2 | *Bad Weather* |
| 26/05/1941 | Bismark' | Not specified | *Unknown* |
| 27/05/1941 | Bismark | 10 | *HQ Cancelled sunk by RN* |
| 28/05/1941 | Wilhelmshaven | Not Specified | *Bad Weather* |
| 31/05/1941 | Berlin | 13 | *Bad Weather* |

On the 20th the squadron lost two of its highly respected pilots, Canadian F/O Don Smith was deemed tour expired and posted to No.20 OTU. He had flown eleven operations on the Blenheim plus a further twenty-three operations on the trusty Wellington. After a spell of instructing, he would return to operations. In February 1943 he assumed command of the No.428 RCAF Squadron. Sadly, he was shot down and made PoW in September of that year. Also departing was the quiet and unassuming New Zealander P/O Nelson Mansfield. Having completed 31 operations instructor duties beckoned at No.23 OTU. In May 1943 postings to No.97 and No.156 PFF Squadron followed. Once again fate would intervene, Wing Commander Mansfield DFC was killed in January 1944 with 156 Squadron while attacking Braunschweig. On the 24th, a rather dapper English flight Lieutenant arrived from No.15 OTU RAF Harwell where he had served as an instructor, his name was Herbert Price. Born in Bridgewater, Somerset in 1914 Herbert joined the RAF in 1936. Upon his arrival, he was immediately promoted to the unpaid rank of squadron leader. The newly promoted squadron leader had the unenviable task of replacing the soon to be posted S/Ldr Ian Richmond. Keeping up the Kiwi connection Sergeant Charles Dare RNZAF arrived from No.20 OTU on May 25th. Born August 1919 in Auckland and schooled at Auckland Grammar School, he was a keen sportsman and skilled Hockey player. Before departing New Zealand for Canada to train as a pilot, Charles had been accepted into the University of Otago Dental School to do a degree in Dentistry. With the outbreak of war, this was put on hold, and he travelled to Canada to begin his pilot training. Group Captain Evan Evans brief tenure as station commander was concluded on the 24th with the return of G/Cpt McKee AFC DFC. Both Marham's squadrons were put on two hours Stand-By on the early evening of the 26th. With the Royal Navy still in shock from the loss of HMS Hood only a few days prior, the Admiralty were bent on revenge.

With the German Battleship Bismarck at large in the Atlantic and the Royal Navy's reputation in tatters, the Admiralty needed to sink the Bismarck and quickly. Concerned that she may head

*The squadron song, circa 1941. This was Graham Hunter's copy. Graham went on to fly 35 operations with the squadron. He joined 142 Squadron in January 1943 completing a further 30 operation.*

for Brest Harbour and outrun the Royal Navy's ever-growing number of warships, Bomber Command was requested to intervene. The squadrons at Marham waited for the call.

The following day, May 24th the heroic actions of the Fairey Swordfish torpedo bombers of 825 Naval Air Squadron, led by Lt Cdr Eugene Esmonde saved the Admiralty's blushes. A lucky torpedo hit near the port rudder was the turning point and sealed the fate of the mighty Bismarck. Turning in circles and helplessly outnumbered, the Bismarck was finally sunk at 10:35 hours. Despite the sinking, the squadrons were still on stand-by. Two Naval Observers from the Fleet Air Arm arrived to assist in the attack on the German cruiser Prinz Eugen which had accompanied the Bismarck. God forbid that the RAF bombed the wrong ship! Finally, after 48 hours of waiting the squadrons were informed at 1220 hours on the 27th to remove the SAP bombs from the Wellingtons and stand-down. After 11 days inactivity, two 'Freshman' crews managed, despite the weather to carry out an operation. On the 27th, Sergeants Gorden, Jillett and Howard Skett attacked Calais Docks. Wellington L7797 HA-F was hit by flak peppering the rear turret. Despite the intense flak, Sgt Jillett pressed home his attack dropping his bombs across the dock complex causing two large fires. Sergeant Howard Skett managed to escape the attention from the flak, his mixed HE and incendiary load were observed exploding in the target area. Two pre-war survivors, Sgt Ron Gill and James Drummond DFM and veterans of France were promoted to the dizzy heights of flight sergeant on the 27th. Both had seen continuous action since the war was declared in September 1939.

On the 28th the squadron lost Sergeant Ronald Read to the Communication Flight at RAF Halton, he had flown ten operations in the 2nd pilot role with Sgt Bernard Madgwick. The posting of S/Ldr Ian Richmond on the 29th was a bitter blow to the squadron. Although everyone was thrilled, he was going, it was tinged with great sadness. Ian was the last surviving link to the squadron's pre-war days. His press-on attitude was infectious, totally devoted to the squadron and courage by the bucket load he was respected by all. The success of 218 was in no small part because of Richmond. He exuded confidence which reverberated throughout the squadron. Stability in command was a vital element in maintaining morale and the squadrons fighting spirit, both of which New Zealander Richmond, and Englishman Shaw had shown continuously. Apart from his brief detachment Richmond had always been in the thick of the action, never one to shirk his responsibilities he epitomised the squadrons fighting spirit and the contribution of New Zealanders in Bomber Command. Ian had flown 30 operations on 218 Squadron, seven on the Blenheim and the rest on the Wellington. After a farewell party, he departed for No.17 OTU RAF Litchford. In May 1942 he returned to operations with No.15 Squadron flying the Short Stirling, within a month he was shot down while attacking Bremen and made a PoW. He was involved in the mass escape from Stalag Luft III. While a PoW he was in-prisoned with his cousin Group Captain Leonard Trent VC DFC.

*Keeping up the New Zealand connection, the newly qualified pilot, Sergeant Charles Dare RNZAF.*

Despite the drizzle and low overcast eight training sorties were flown on the morning of the 1st. One air-test was flown by S/Ldr Price in preparation for his 'Freshman' trip that night, which was subsequently cancelled late afternoon. Within 24 hours he would have another chance. Squadron Leader Price and crew were the only crew selected for an attack directed against Dusseldorf. He had finally opened his batting with 218. The run of cancellations continued on the 3rd when a major effort on Kiel was planned, 13 crews were detailed and briefed but frustratingly it was cancelled moments before take-off. The following afternoon 13 Wellingtons were prepared for an attack on Bremen. On this occasion the raid was cancelled before briefing, unfortunately not before the Wellingtons were fuelled and bombed up by the overworked ground crews. The patten was set for the next few days. On the 6th, Kiel, cancelled, 8th, Dusseldorf, again cancelled.  Two new pilots arrived on the 5th, Sgt Anthony 'Tony' Moss and Sgt Roland Brewerton, both on completion of No.30 Course at No.11 OTU.

The first 'Black' of the month occurred on the 7th when Wellington R1511 HA-L landed without its undercarriage locked, none of the crew were injured but the aircraft was severely damaged.  The pilot, Canadian Pilot Officer John Maxwell was held responsible, the aircraft never returned to the squadron after its departure to No.43 Group.

### Tuesday 7th June 1941
*Vickers Wellington*
*Mk.Ic R1511 HA-L 'London'*
*Contract No: 992424/39*
*Taken on Charge: 03/03/1941*
*Pilot Error,*
*To: 43 Group*
*Pilot: Pilot Officer John Maxwell and Crew.*


Finally, on the 10th, twelve crews managed to take off in the murk for an attack on the *Prinz Eugen* at Brest. Thirty-eight Wellingtons were supplied by the group who found an effective smokescreen in place on arrival. With little hope of identifying the target visually most crews bombed in the general area, a few isolated bomb bursts were seen. The returning crews knew that the raid was a failure and realised in all probability they would be returning. Sergeant Harry Taylor was obliged to seek refuge at R.A.F. Boscombe Down due to engine trouble on return. It was while landing a 500 pounder which had hung up, dropped off causing slight damaged to the underside of Wellington R1601 HA-H. The crew could count themselves extremely fortunate it did not explode. The following night a single Wellington captained by Sgt Basil Forster carried out his first operation as captain. The target was the docks at Boulogne where they encountered considerable opposition from both flak and searchlights. Over the target, the crew observed several twin-engine fighters looking for trouble. Once the mixed HE and incendiary load were dropped the crew sought the relative safety of lower altitude landing Wellington L7797 HA-F safely back at Marham a few hours later.

In keeping with No.3 Group Instruction No.55 dated June 6th, the squadron would begin a series of operations directed at the German rail network between the Ruhr and the rest of Germany. Each individual bomber group were allocated a specific marshalling yard, No.3 Group was given Hamm. Situated in the North Rhine-Westphalia, it was at the time one of Germany's largest and most modern yards.

The objective was to destroy the marshalling yards, the railway lines and the rolling stock and locomotives that used it. On the 11th the squadron had its first crack at Hamm. Twelve crews were detailed and briefed, plus a solitary Wellington Mk.II captained by S/Ldr Clyde-Smith was given Hanover as his primary. Haze over the target caused some considerable difficulty for the crews. In an attempt to locate the marshalling yards, Squadron Leader Price decided to reduce height contrary to orders. While his colleagues were at 14,000 feet Price was at 9,000 feet desperate for a break in the clouds. Finally, the briefest of glimpses gave the crew the opportunity it needed. The mixed HE and incendiary load were dropped in amongst dozens of existing fires, satisfied the crew turned for home. Despite the crew's optimism, the raid was a failure, the haze and cloud over the target had got the better of the attackers. The squadron dropped nearly 40,000 pounds of bombs, subsequent reports recorded only seven bombs landed in Hamm, none of which fell near the marshalling yards, it was a frustrating night for all involved. The now-familiar arrival of young pilots fresh from O.T.U.s continued on the 12th. Sergeant Arthur Mitchell and Pilot Officer Leslie Parfitt. Both were older than most of their fellow captains, Leslie was 29 while Arthur was 26. Both had arrived from No.20 O.T.U. It was back to Brest and the three cruisers on the 13th. Marham detailed eighteen Wellingtons of which 218 Squadron provided twelve led by S/Ldr Clyde-Smith. Pilot Officer Maxwell failed to take off having experienced engine trouble. All the remaining crews attacked the primary, only one crew reported seeing the cruisers and reported a near miss. An effective smoke screen and low cloud hindering the participating crews. Sergeant Chidgey was caught by several searchlights while on his run-up to the target. To escape their clutches and the crescendo of flak the young pilot frantically slung the Wellington around the sky. His efforts were rewarded, damage to Wellington R1594 HA-S was minimal, a few holes in the wing. Importantly none of the crew was injured.

*Flying Officer Mervyn McNeil RNZAF. The 25-year-old was killed while serving as a staff officer with No.27 O.T.U*

The exodus of talented New Zealanders continued the 14th with the departure of Sergeant Mervyn McNeil who would be joining fellow Kiwi Ian Richmond at No.27 O.T.U. for instructing duties. While screened at Lichfield, the 25-year-old would continue to operate. He completed two operations with a scratch crew. Sadly, he was shot down and killed on August 1st, 1942 while attacking Dusseldorf. His Wellington DV552/N was shot down by Lt Heinz Wolfgang Schaufer of Stab II./NJG1. It was his 21st bombing operation.

The Cologne-Geron Marshalling Yards were the target for twelve crews on the 15th, while once again S/Ldr Clyde-Smith was given Hanover to attack in the Merlin-powered Mk.II. All the squadron Wellingtons were airborne by 2318 hours, within 50 minutes F/Lt Stokes was back at dispersal with a defective front turret aboard R1536 HA-G. He was followed by P/O Bryant who suffered oil pressure failure to his port engine shortly after crossing the Belgian coast. His Wellington, T2806 HA-T landed safely back at Marham retaining all its bombs. Over the target the crews were met with solid cloud, unable to locate the marshalling yards the majority bombed on the concentration of flak and searchlights. Squadron Leader Clyde-Smith also encountered 10/10th cloud over Hanover. He dropped his single 4000 pounder in the estimated position of the town. While on route home north of Amsterdam the Wellington was attacked by a Bf110. In the ensuing combat, Wellington W5447 HA-C was hit by cannon fire in the port wing fuel tank and tail plane.

However, it was not all one-sided, P/O Chalk, the crew's rear gunner, claimed the fighter as shot down. It was for this action both Clyde-Smith and Chalk were recommended for the D.F.C. Fifteen Wellingtons were detailed and briefed to attack Dusseldorf the following night. It was the most significant force yet dispatched by the squadron to date. The number was quickly reduced when S/Ldr Clyde-Smiths Wellington, veteran R1008 HA-A developed starboard engine trouble just before taking off. Although the night was reported as very dark with an industrial haze over Dusseldorf, returning crews were confident that the target had been hit. Squadron Leader Price reported *'The town and streets were clearly seen in the light of a flare. Bombs were falling slightly east of the river bridge. The second stick was dropped across the aiming point'.* Pilot Officer Maxwell and crew recorded the following *'Bombs fell just west of target starting a white fire which was still visible 40 miles away'.* On return the crews were confident of a successful raid, there was however one station commander who had doubts. This unnamed station commander reported *'that the lack of flak was suspicious and that the fires seen may have been dummies'.* Number 3 Group H.Q. dismissed his concerns stating that numerous crews had identified the river and 'should' have located the aiming point. In fact, the raid was again a total failure.

*Pilot Officer Frederick Chalk DFC with his new wife Rosemary Foster on their wedding day, September 15th, 1941. The couple were married by the Bishop of Croydon at Worplesdon Church. Frederick was the former captain of the Kent Cricket XI. On completion of his tour with No.218 Squadron, Frederick undertook pilot training. In September 1942 he was posted to No.124 Squadron flying Spitfires. He was shot down and killed on February 17th, 1943 by Fw190s from JG26. His body remain undiscovered until 1989.*

During the first half of 1941, the R.A.F. had been collecting information on the accuracy and effectiveness of its attacks against targets in Germany. This information arrived from various sources, information via neutral countries, reports from returning crews, and lastly, and the most accurate, target photographs. Photo reconnaissance flights were still in their infancy during the first half of 1941 however they were still able

*Sergeant Gordon Jillett RNZAF.*

to produce detailed and valuable information if on a limited scale. The growing confidence within Bomber Command and its belief in its own ability to hit and destroy selected targets was in direct contrast with the information coming out of Germany. With very few options available, the only credible source of information came from the cameras fitted to the bombers. These target photographs were the only means of determining the accuracy of Bomber Command. In an unparalleled moved, all the bombing photographs were collected during May / June 1941 and sent off for study.

Interestingly, this was not a decision by Bomber Command, or the Air Ministry but Lord Cherwell, scientific advisor to the Prime Minister. Entrusted to carry out this study was a Mr D.M Butt, a civil servant in the War Cabinet. His findings would be released in August. A tragic accident on an air-test resulted in the death of one of 218 Squadron ground crew on the 17th. Aircraftsman 2nd Class Alfred Smith was killed while flying in Wellington R1517 KO-Z of No 115 Squadron. The Wellington was seen to climb slowly to around 500 feet, turned through 180 degrees and then dive towards the ground. At about 15 feet it levelled out and then crashed and burst into flames at Palgrave Farm, Sporle, 2 miles N.E. of Swaffham, Norfolk. Why the 30-year-old was aloft in a 115 Squadron Wellington is unknown. One of the squadron's recent arrivals was posted across the tarmac to No.115 Squadron on the 19th. P/O Sidney Wild had only completed a single operation with F/L John Stokes and crew before new pastures beckoned. Within ten days he was a PoW, shot down while attacking Hamburg. His operational career lasting just over three weeks. Sixteen crews including one 'Freshman' crew were detailed and briefed for Kiel on the night of June 20th. This was a milestone in the history of the squadron, never had it provided this number of crews onto a target. It was a magnificent achievement by all concerned.

Three crews would be forced to return early, Sgt Rose turned back 50 miles from the Norfolk seaside town of Sheringham with turret problem. Sergeant Forster experienced a miss firing engine while Sgt Workman on his 'Freshman' trip to Boulogne reported an overheating engine aboard Wellington R1456 HA-N. All three safely returned to Marham where a rather subdued group of ground crew were waiting. Reliability was paramount to the men who worked on the Wellingtons. When an aircraft returned early due to a mechanical problem, especially an aircraft they worked on they took it hard and personally. The 'Erks' took tremendous pride in their work, the lives of the aircrew depended on it. A former 218 Squadron rigger, *'It was all about trust, the aircrews trusted us to ensure the kite was tip-top on every flight. I did not want my 'kite' to return early due to something I should have done or could have done better and put the crew at risk'.*

The primary target for the 47 bombers provided by No.3 Group was the *Tirpitz* birthed in the Deutsche Werke Kiel A.G shipyard. Low cloud and haze over the docks prevented accurate bombing, crews had to rely on picking out features along the coast to ensure that they were bombing in the general target area. The shipyards escaped the squadron's attention. Most dropped on E.T.A. or the flak and searchlight defences. Three crews reported two massive explosions, one producing an intense white flash while the other a reddish/orange glow. These may have been the explosion of a 4000 pounder. Two crews, Sgt Jillett RNZAF and Sgt Fraser RNZAF, sent out an S.O.S. on the return journey, both reporting engine trouble and both were last heard of in approximately the same position. The crew of Sergeant Gordon Jillett RNZAF sent a message at 03:35 hours reporting engine trouble. A first-class fix from Hull put the crew at 54 degrees N. 030 degrees 17' E just before fading out. The sea was calm so 22 ASRU based at Grimsby dispatched one of its 63ft long HSLs. At first light, two Wellingtons from 218 Squadron and three Short Stirlings were airborne and ordered to search the area. For over an hour the five bombers searched the sea below, at position 54 degrees N. 030 degrees 15' E a patch of oil and a dinghy was located. Sadly, the dinghy was empty, and there was no sign of any survivors from Wellington R1339 HA-J. The crew of Sergeant Mason Fraser were never heard of again. Theo Boiten in his excellent series of Nachtjagd Combat Archives attributes the loss to Oblt Paul Bohn of 4./NJG2 who claimed a Wellington 200km E of Spurn Head.

### Saturday 20th June 1941
*Vickers Wellington*
*Mk.Ic R1339 HA-J - 'Johnnie'*
*Contract No : 992424/39*
*Taken On Charge : 03/02/1941*
**Failed to Return**
*Pilot : Sergeant Gordon Grant Jillett 40233 RNZAF* **Killed**
*2nd Pilot : Sergeant Ronald Henry Burr, 917065 RAFVR* **Killed**
*Observer : Sergeant Nigel Rodney Patrick Goodenough 905643 RAFVR* **Killed**
*Front Gunner : Sergeant William Albert James Davis, 927362 RAFVR* **Killed**
*1st Wireless Operator : Sergeant Bernard Joseph Mees, 925004 RAFVR* **Killed**
*Rear Gunner : Sergeant Alfred Gordon Venn, 1061955 RAFVR* **Killed**


The 23-year-old pilot from Taranaki was on his 18th operation and only his third as captain. Sergeant Ron Burr is believed to have been on his third operation with the crew. All are recorded on the Runnymede Memorial.

### Saturday 20th June 1941
*Vickers Wellington*
*MkIc R1713 HA-V - 'Victor'*
*Contract No: Vickers*
*Taken On Charge: 28/04/1941*
**Failed To Return**
*Pilot : Sergeant Mason John Fraser 40224 RNZAF* **Killed**
*2nd Pilot: Sergeant John Abbott Donald, 1257597 RAFVR Killed*
*Observer: Sergeant Desmond Aubrey Dacre, 391397 RNZAF* **Killed**
*Front Gunner: Sergeant William John Baird, 551811 RAF* **Killed**
*1st Wireless Operator: Sergeant Dennis Higham Harrison, 975057 RAFVR* **Killed**
*Rear Gunner: Sergeant Harry Hutchinson 938149 RAFVR* **Killed**


Twenty-three-year-old Mason Fraser from Hawkes Bay New Zealand was on his 23rd operation, Sgt Donald was on his second trip. The crew are remembered on the panels of the Runnymede Memorial.

The terrible realisation that the squadron had lost not one, but two crews over the North Sea stunned the whole squadron on the morning of the 21st. There was still some possibility they could be found. As the morning turned into the afternoon, it became increasingly apparent that both crews, well into their operational tours were missing. The gloom was lifted was some good news during the day, S/Ldr Clyde-

Smith and his rear gunner P/O Chalk received the news that the C/O's recommendation for the DFC had been approved at group HQ.

*Sergeant Desmond Aubrey Dacre RNZAF poses besides Wellington MkIc R1713 HA-V - 'Victor'. Born in Auckland, New Zealand on March 11th, 1915, Desmond originally served in the New Zealand Army. 'Des' was posted to No.218 Squadron in September 1940. By the time of his death, he had completed 22 operations, all on the Wellington.*

Air Vice-Marshal J.E.A Baldwin CB DSO OBE Air Officer Commanding No.3 Group visited RAF Marham during the day. On the evening, a boxing match was held in No.115 Squadron's 'B' Flight Hangar, it was just the tonic the squadron needed. One of the squadron's longest-serving observers, Pilot Officer Magee was posted to No.57 Squadron on the 21st to assume the role of squadron navigation officer. Hugh Magee had joined the squadron soon after its arrival back from France in the early summer of 1940. He teamed up with P/O Ross Mansfield completing seven Blenheim operations before he joined the crew of S/Ldr Richmond. The thirty-year-old Irishman then completed a further 23 operations. Tragically he was killed while a passenger of a 57 Squadron Wellington on March 16th, 1942. The aircraft was on a cross country flight to Northern Ireland with a planned stop at RAF Aldergrove. While flying in low cloud near Newcastle, Co.Down the Wellington struck the side of a hill near Thomas Mount, killing all but one on board. One of the passengers was 24-year-old WAAF, Section Officer Barbara Blackiston-Houston from Killyleagh. It is understood that both Magee and S/O Blackiston-Houston were returning home on leave.

The group was given two main targets plus two 'Freshman' targets on the 23rd. The Stirlings of No.7 and XV Squadrons plus a number of Mk.II Wellingtons carrying the 4000 pounders would attack the docks at Kiel with the *Admiral Graf Spee* as the intended target. The Marham based 218 Squadron would apply its trade over three German cities, Cologne, Emden and Kiel. Eleven crews were briefed for Cologne led by S/Ldr Clyde-Smith. They encountered a dense layer of haze over the target, which made identification of the aiming point, the Neumarkt impossible. Crews desperately tried to make out landmarks, even the Cathedral which could usually be found defied all attempts to be located. The crews, in the end, bombed the flak and searchlights in the general Cologne area, creating some scattered fires. These fires attracted the attention of the later arrivals who willingly deposited their mixed HE and incendiary loads. These small fires gradually increased in density. It was these that a number of crews reported upon their return. Sergeant Jolly *'A good fire was started by bombs which were still visible when the aircraft entered cloud about 45 miles from the target'*. The raid was yet again a failure. Sergeant Forster experienced a few navigation issues on return. Arriving over England near the heavily defended Thames Estuary the crew, short of petrol, landed at the grass airfield at RAF Detling, Kent.

Wing Commander Kirkpatrick was over Kiel in Wellington Mk.II W5457 HA-Z where he received a less than friendly welcome. Singled out by what appeared to be every flak gun and searchlight in Kiel, the commanding officer slung the Wellington about the sky in a desperate attempt to escape. The 4000lb bomb was discarded over Kiel. It was now a battle for survival. For what seemed an eternity the Wellington was surrounded by flak, Kirkpatrick took violent evasive action, but it was only a matter of time before he was hit. A burst of flak exploded under the tail shredding the horizontal tail plane, fin and rudder. Miraculously the rear turret and the fortunate gunner, Sgt Davidson escaped damage or injury.

Pilot Officer James Drummond DFM, the longest-serving wireless operator/air gunners on the squadron was posted to No.115 Squadron on the 26th. One of the original airmen who flew to France on that bright sunny day in September 1939, he was one of the last of the pre-war NCO aircrew still operating on the squadron. While serving with 115 Squadron, he flew the majority of his operations with flight commander, S/Ldr James Sindal. On October 1st, 1941, James Drummond was posted to No.12 OTU RAF Chipping Warden for instructional duties. He returned to operations in September 1942 with No.460 RAAF Squadron as squadron signals leader. He was posted again in April 1943 to No.100 Squadron, RAF Grimbsy. On August 3rd, 1943, he was shot down and killed by Oblt Hermann Greiner of 11./NJG1 while attacking Hamburg, James was twenty-three years old.

It was back to the Neumarkt at Cologne on the 26th. Bomber command HQ was unimpressed with the previous raid. Pilot Officer Maxwell was cancelled just before take-off owing to unserviceability of his Wellington X3217 HA-E. The operation was again a failure due to violent thunderstorms and icing over the continent. Most crews turned for home, a few selected targets of opportunity. Squadron Leader Price bombed the flare path at Soesterberg while P/O Bryant got as far as Aachen before dropping his bombs on the flak and searchlight defences. Sergeant Banks ventured as far as Antwerp before he and his crew gave up. They bombed the aerodrome at Haamstede producing three good fires which they claimed were amongst a number of dispersed aircraft.

Yorkshire born Sergeant John Thompson arrived from No.20 OTU on the 29th, strangely it would be two months before he flew an operation. The last operation of the month was flown on the 29th. Eleven crews would attack the marshalling yards at Bremen, while P/O Lambert would venture alone to Hamburg in the Mk.II Wellington. The bad weather that had dogged the previous raids had abated giving the participating crews, a chance at last for some accurate bombing. Three crews failed to reach the marshalling yards, Sgt Rose lost the intercom aboard Wellington R1448 HA-L while Sgt Workman got too close to the flak defences over Wilhelmshaven when he ventured off track. Forced to reduce height to escape the flak they were too low to attack the primary target so opted to bomb an oil storage facility at Bremerhaven. Pilot Officer Lambert at the controls of Wellington Mk.II W5447 HA-C also lost the use of the intercom and encountered a problem with navigation. Unwilling to trust to luck the crew attacked the last resort target of

*Light Flak and tracer fire criss-cross the night sky. For the crews of Bomber Command, it was an almost nightly game of hide and seek with the most deadly of foes.*

Rensburg on the Kiel Canal. The exploding 4000 pounder producing a vivid flash which lit up the surrounding area for 20 seconds.

Clear conditions over marshalling yards although welcome by the crews also meant that the flak and searchlight defences were particularly vicious. The sky above Bremen was thick with flak and searchlights which appeared to be working in unison. A bomber was observed held by a single searchlight beam, two more quickly joined in holding the unfortunate crew in their glare until the flak started bursting all around the Wellington. Its fate is unknown.

Such was the visibility crews could identify individual districts and landmarks, Sgt Jolly recognised and bombed the Deutschwerkes producing an intense white fire. With a job seemingly well done the crews turned for home, S/Ldr Clyde Smith reported that fires were still visible 70 miles away. The return journey home, however, was going to be less than easy. Taking full advantage of the weather conditions the German night fighters were airborne and active. Sergeant Jolly and crew were involved in a vicious but thankfully brief encounter with a Ju88, the vigilance of the rear gunner Sgt Challoner saved the crew on this occasion. Pilot Officer Maxwell was attacked just off the English coast by a Bf110 which was successfully beaten off.

Marham lost two crews from the operation. No.115 Squadron lost the experienced F/Lt Bailey DFC in one of their Wellington Mk.IIs while 218 Squadron lost Pilot Officer Francis Bryant and crew. Wellington T2806 HA-T crashed into a moor east of Dedesdorf, Germany close to the right bank of the River Weser, there were no survivors. The crew were initially buried 7 miles from the crash site in the Municipal Cemetery, at Wesermunde-Geestarmunde, Bremerhaven. Pilot Officer Francis Bryant was a 26-year-old Australian. One of three Australian students from the National Aeronautical College chosen to join the Yorkshire Aeroplane Club under the British Civil Guard Plan he was on his way to take up his new appointment in England when war was declared. With his appointment now cancelled he accepted a commission in the RAF in October 1939. He joined the squadron from No.19 OTU in March 1941. Francis had the good fortune of teaming up with S/Ldr Ian Richmond completing 8 operations in the 2nd pilot role. On taking over his own crew he completed a further 12 raids. The Bryant family had the misfortune of losing two sons on the same night. Francis younger brother, Able Seaman Reginald Bryant RANR, was stricken with malignant malaria while his vessel, HMAS Canberra, was at Colombo. He was admitted to the Military Hospital, Colombo but died there on 29th June 1941. The crew's 2nd pilot was fellow Australian Sergeant Allan Barton. He had joined the squadron in late April and had flown all his ten operations with P/O Bryant. A former clerk from Melbourne, Barton enlisted in the RAAF May 27th, 1940. He embarked from Sydney on October 3rd, 1940. The crew's rear gunner was a Battle of Britain veteran.

Flight Sergeant Thomas Marshall joined the RAF in April 1938 as an Aircrafthand. He later remustered as an Airman / Air Gunner and after completing his training joined the Bristol Blenheim Mk.IF equipped No.219 Squadron based at RAF Catterick in August 1940 where he served throughout 1940.

## Monday 29th June 1941

*Vickers Wellington*
*Mk.Ic T2806 HA-T 'Tommy'*
*Contract No: B38600/39.*
*Taken on Charge: 24/04/1941*
**Failed to Return**
*Pilot: Pilot Officer Francis Egerton Bryant, 87049 RAFVR* **Killed**
*2nd Pilot: Sergeant Allan Ernest Ross Barton, 400074 RAAF* **Killed**
*Observer: Pilot Officer Ernest Edward Ellner, 89596 RAFVR RAFVR* **Killed**
*Front Gunner: Sergeant Donald Charles Smallbone ,43284 RAFVR* **Killed**
*1st Wireless Operator: Sergeant John Johnstone Jordan ,949055 RAFVR* **Killed**
*Rear Gunner: Flight Sergeant Thomas Robson Marshall 611372 RAF* **Killed**

The last posting of the month arrived on the 30th, Australian Alan McLean arriving from No.11 OTU. Born October 1918 in Queensland, Alan worked as a Clerk in the Civil Service before he joined the Australian Army. Unhappy with the drudgery of Army life he joined the RAAF embarking from Sydney to Canada in November 1940. On arriving on the squadron, he had the excellent fortune of teaming up with S/Ldr Price as second pilot.The squadron had flown 119 sorties in June for the loss of three experienced crews, plus one Wellington lost in a crash. The Wellingtons could be replaced but the crews could not, especially experienced ones well into their operational tours. The squadron was fortunate that amongst its ranks it had some skilful and courageous Commonwealth pilots. The New Zealanders were the most numerous closely followed by the Australians, while there was a splattering of Canadians to give a North American feel. All three contributed to the success of the squadron operationally. Their arrival brought a certain edge to the squadron, less formal than the rather stuffy pre-war RAF types their blend of flying and mess antics gelled the squadron and went a long way to raise squadron morale.

The new month started with yet another disappointing attack on Bremen on the 2nd. A thick layer of scattered cloud over the city made it virtually impossible for the crews to identify the primary visually. A few, the lucky ones, bombed through the occasional gap in the cloud. Most of the crews dropped their bombs in the general area of the town or on the troublesome searchlights. Flight Lieutenant Stokes at the controls of Wellington Mk.II W5447 HA-R dropped his 4000 pounder on the city. There was a large flash and the resulting explosion which last 5 seconds had the effect of dowsing all the searchlights within a 3-mile radius. Another raid directed against the cruisers in Brest was mounted on the 4th, twelve crews were detailed and led by S/Ldr Clyde Smith in Wellington R1008 HA-A. Weather conditions on the route were excellent however, obviously aware of the approaching threat, the Germans put in place a very effective smokescreen over the docks and town. Ten of the twelve crews were loaded with a single 2000 pounder SAP and 3 x 500 pounders. Sergeant Harry Taylor skippered the MkII while F/O Ralph on his 'Freshman' trip carried 6 x 500lb SAPs. Sergeant Taylor experienced problems with his starboard Merlin halfway across the English Channel. Unable to climb to the briefed bombing height and having problems even maintaining height the plucky crew on their 12th operation decided to continue to target. Their mettle was sadly, not rewarded. Arriving over the target at a mere 5000 feet the crew made their run-up to the target, frustratingly the 4000-pounder hung up. Undeterred the crew decided to make another bomb run, however, north of Brest the bomb suddenly fell off its bomb rack. In total contrast to Sgt Taylor and showing rather less determination P/O Ralph turned for home without bombing when he was unable to climb above 10,000 feet. Some crews used visible landmarks to make a time and distance run over the town. The more fortunate caught a glimpse of the dock area. Sergeant Forster claimed to have observed his bomb load exploding close to No.1 Dock, while fellow sergeant pilot, Robert Banks reported seeing his 2000 pounder explode in the dry docks. The London Gazette published the news of the two DFCs won by S/Ldr Clyde Smith and P/O Chalk on July 4th. Pilot Officer Frederick Chalk's citation follows. Interestingly the squadron had been involved in combats with German night fighters over a dozen times since conversion to the Wellington claiming two destroyed and damaging three others, none of the sergeant air gunners was put up for awards.

*" One night in June 1941, this officer was the rear gunner of an aircraft which took part in an attack on Hanover. On the return journey, whilst over the Amsterdam area, the aircraft was attacked by a Messerschmitt 110 which pressed home two attacks from close range. In the face of accurate cannon and machine gun fire from the enemy. Pilot Officer Chalk fired off two steady bursts which were observed to enter the enemy aircraft causing it to break away with flames coming from the starboard side. By his cool and accurate fire, Pilot Officer Chalk undoubtably saved his aircraft and probably destroyed the attacker. Since February 1941, this officer has participated in 20 operational missions and as shown high courage and devotion to duty throughout.*

The long drawn out and inconclusive campaign against the French ports was now at an end, a new directive from Bomber Command HQ switched the commands attention back to Germany. The squadrons would be used in *'dislocating the German transportation systems and to destroy the morale of the civil population as a whole and of the industrial workers in particular'*. The following were targets to be attacked during the moon period of each month. These targets basically encircled the Ruhr, the intention was clear to prevent and hinder movement of material in and out of Germany's industrial heartland.

*Hamm*
*Osnabruck*
*Soest*
*Schwerte*
*Cologne*
*Duisburg*
*Dusseldorf*

Germany's important inland ports with their links to the Rhine were also targeted, these would be attacked when there was no moon.

*Cologne*
*Dusseldorf*
*Duisburg*

Finally, when the weather was unfavourable Bomber Command would switch its attention to targets further afield.

*Stuttgart*
*Hamburg*
*Bremen*
*Hannover*
*Frankfurt*

It was these targets that would dominate the summer of 1941, for No.218 Squadron it would be a costly and at times frustrating summer. The squadron lost one of its few Canadian pilots on the return from Brest. Sergeant James Gordon RCAF volunteered for service in the Mediterranean. He would eventually join No.37 Squadron. Within a matter of weeks, he failed to return from a raid against the harbour installation at Benghazi, he spent the rest of the war a PoW.

The Marshalling Yards at Munster was the intended target on the 6th. It would be an all No.3 Group effort. The squadron provided twelve Wellingtons which took off just before midnight in excellent conditions. For once, the weather over the target afforded the crews the opportunity for some accurate bombing. Much to the crews surprise the flak and searchlights gave extraordinarily little trouble providing them with the unaccustomed luxury of taking slightly longer over the target area. Sergeant Banks reported ' *50 separate fires in the target area'* while P/O Ralph recorded upon his return that ' *Large fires already burning at the aiming point. There was a tremendous bluish-white explosion which lit up the interior of the aircraft.'* There was some opposition, the crew of Sgt Robert Banks was attacked over the target by a Ju88. The rear gunner, P/O Patrick Cranley opened fire at just 30 yards range with two short bursts. The .303s tore into the Ju88, it faltered and dived away emitting smoke. A minute later, the crew saw what they believed to be an explosion on the ground and claim the aircraft as destroyed. It was not the only fighter encounter that night. Flying Officer Harold Ralph at the controls of Wellington T2887 HA-W was attacked on the return flight by a Bf110. Details are scarce, but the returning crew claimed that Front Gunner, Sgt Bain-Kelle shot it down.

For the first time in some weeks, there was some cause for celebration, a successful operation, and the destruction of two fighters. Flying on this operation in the second pilot role was an old friend of the squadron, S/Ldr James Gillman. He flew with S/Ldr Price aboard R1148 HA-L, it was to be his only operation, and one can only speculate why. He would die over Dortmund in 1943 while commanding No.83 Path Finder Squadron. He was 31 years old.

Eleven crews returned to Munster the following night. All successfully reached the target area between 03:41 hours and 04:28 hours. Navigation to the target was easy, the city was still burning from the previous night's visit. Parts of the city and the marshalling yards could be identified from the glow of the fires and the parachute flares which slowly descended over the target. Munster suffered yet another damaging attack. The fires had started merging on the departure of the squadron and could be seen from the Zuider Zee. A Ju88 attacked Pilot Officer Lambert over the North Sea on the return journey, the crew claimed it as a 'possible'. One pilot was undertaking his first operation on this night, Sgt George Cottier RCAF was sitting alongside P/O Maxwell. While Marham's squadrons were over Germany, the station was attacked by a solitary Ju88 at 01:15 hours dropping eight small HE bombs. His aim was good as damage was inflicted to 218 squadron's 'A' Flight hangar and Watch Office. Fortunately, there were only two minor casualties. One Wellington was however damaged by splinters while being repaired in the hangar.

*Vickers Wellington Mk.Ic R1448 HA-L. Used regularly by Squadron Leader Price the aircraft completed a total of 25 raids during its 12 months on the squadron.*

*Vickers Armstrong built Wellington Mk.Ic T2887 HA-W. The aircraft had previously served with No.115 Squadron before it arrived on No.218 Squadron in April 1941. It flew a total of 16 raids with the squadron.*

The squadron dropped nearly 30,000lb of HE and incendiaries on the Marshalling Yards at Osnabruck on July 9th. It had been a frustrating night for the squadron. Squadron Leader Clyde-Smith was forced to return early when the starboard engine aboard Wellington R1025 HA-J overheated. Unable to land at Marham he diverted to RAF Oakington. Conditions over the continent and target were considered favourable, however, what followed was a disappointing raid. Pilot Officers Pape and Lambert bombed Munster after mistaking the former as the primary target. The remaining crews bombed what they believed to be the primary producing some large fires. Sergeant Banks was attacked by a Bf109 over Holland when it appeared unobserved from the starboard beam. Opening fire at 300 yards with cannon and machine-gun fire the Wellington shuddered under the impact as shells ripped into the port wing and flaps. Sergeant Banks turned the Wellington into the attacker, allowing the front gunner to engage. He then turned away giving the rear gunner, P/O Cranley an opportunity, this he did with an accurate 10-second burst. The Bf109 went into a very steep dive and was seen by the 2nd pilot 700 feet below almost vertical. The crew considered the fighter as a 'probable' as it was in their words about to 'Pile-In'. Marham was fog-bound on the crews return diverting the crews far and wide. Three crews diverted to RAF Abington, two to RAF Benson, RAF Harwell took two while RAF Lyneham accepted one crew. Sergeant Banks made an emergency landing at the fighter base at RAF Manston, Kent. This would be the last operation flown by Squadron Leader Denis Clyde-Smith DFC with the squadron. He would not be posted immediately, his predecessor needed to be appointed. Until his arrival, Denis would continue with his flight commander duties after a spot of well-earned leave. On the 10th, the squadron commanding officer, W/Cdr Kirkpatrick suffered an injury to his scalp and secondary haemorrhage due by bomb fragments caused by the explosion of a bomb from a crashed Wellington. He was quickly dispatched to RAF Hospital Ely. Squadron Leader Price took temporary command.

The squadron was detailed and briefed for an operation against Brest on the 11th. This was subsequently cancelled by 3 Group HQ owing to a forecast of bad weather on return. A well-groomed Australian Squadron Leader arrived on the 12th from No.20 OTU. Augustus Rodney Gibbs was born in the township of Youngs, New South Wales in 1915. He enlisted in the RAAF at Point Cook in 1936, by 1938 he found himself with No.115 Squadron in England. On conclusion of his time with 115 in September 1940 'Rod' was posted to RAF Lossiemouth. On completion of his 'rest period' and promoted to squadron leader he travelled south back at RAF Marham. It would not be until the 13th that the squadron was airborne, the target was the railway station at Bremen. In an overcast and thunderous sky eleven crews took off, it was an ominous start and the crews wondered why the operation had not been scrubbed. Pilot Officer Lambert turned back within the hour with starboard engine trouble. Pilot Officer Jolly and crew followed him when the starboard engine started to vibrate aboard Wellington X9678 HA-R giving the pilot no option than to turn for home. As the crews flew across Holland the weather quickly deteriorated. Sergeant Skett turned for home when he started to encounter icing, Sgt Banks in the Wellington Mk.II W5457 HA-Z got as far as Croningen when the crew called it a day. They dropped the 4000 pounder on the aerodrome at Texel, causing a large red flash and fire. Squadron Leader Price decided to attack an alternative target on account of the thunderstorms and icing. Turning south he flew along the Dutch coast until he located the aerodrome at Haamstede. Here the young squadron leader dive-bombed the target from 1,500 feet dropping his 1x1000lb + 4 x 500lb + 250lb bombs between a number of lights forming a large V before pulling out at 400 feet. All the while, his front and rear gunners were shooting out any searchlights or engaging any worthwhile targets. Sitting beside S/Ldr Herbert Price was Sgt Alan McLean RAAF on his first operation, it was a real baptism for the young Aussie.

*Squadron Leader Rodney Gibbs had originally served with both No.24 Squadron and No.115 Squadron pre-war. He brought a wealth of experience and was immediately considered a worthy replacement to squadron Leader Clyde-Smith DFC.*

Those crews that managed to reach Bremen found it completely covered by a dense layer of cloud. With no possibility of locating the railway station, they bombed the flak and searchlights. The raid was a failure, but thankfully all the squadron crews returned safely despite the unfavourable weather.

Wellington X3217 HA-E was very nearly written off in an incident on the afternoon of the 15th. Sergeant Thomas Cottier RCAF was carrying out a training flight when on return to Marham he misjudged his landing. Stalling the Wellington, the aircraft smashed into the ground from 30 feet buckling the port undercarriage in the process. It was not an auspicious start for him on the squadron. Tom was born in Winnipeg in 1915. He travelled to England pre-war after graduating in science from the University of Manitoba in 1935. Once in England, he taught at a number of schools, when war was declared, he immediately returned to Canada and joined the RCAF. X3217 never flew with the squadron again. Sergeant Cottier had previously only flown a single operation in the 2nd pilot role to P/O Maxwell. The subsequent investigation into the accident pulled no punches and put the blame squarely on the young Canadian.

*'Cottier was posted in from a Stirling Squadron and that he is unlikely to make an efficient pilot. If this were known, he would have been given dual training. Previously trained at an OTU. 218 Squadron commander states that further training as been given and that Cottier will make a capable pilot.'*

### Tuesday 15th July 1941
*Vickers Wellington*
*Mk.Ic X3217 HA-E - 'Edward'*
*Contract No : B.92439/40*
*Taken On Charge : 15/06/1941*
*Heavy Landing to No.48 MU*
*Pilot : Sergeant Thomas Cottier RCAF uninjured*

The intervention and faith shown by the squadron commanding officer, W/Cdr Kirkpatrick resulted in the young Canadian getting the extra flying hours urgently needed, however more near misses were soon to follow.

It was the turn of the railway and goods yards at Duisburg on the 15th. Twelve crews were detailed. Flying with S/Ldr Price was Wing Commander John Fletcher who had recently arrived on the squadron via No.15 OTU. He was to take command of the squadron while W/Cdr Kirkpatrick was still recovering from his injuries. For once there were no early returns and all the crews managed to arrive over the target area. Once over the target, the crews experienced the full fury of the city's flak and searchlight defences. The sky above Duisburg was a cauldron of exploding flak of every calibre. The crews had never experienced such a ferocious reception even over Brest. Squadron Leader Price dropped his bombs over the north of the city where he was hit by anti-aircraft fire which smashed his port engine and ripped chunks out of the geodetics of Wellington R1148 HA-L. The Wellington of Sgt Rose and crew was also severely hit, the tail plane was shredded, and the fuselage was holed in numerous places. The catalogue of damage continued. With his Wellington X9678 HA-R severely damaged by flak, Sergeant George Workman stalled on landing back at Marham. The Wellington never fly with the squadron again. Canadian Sgt John Swingler RCAF and crew were lucky to survive

*Sergeant Thomas Cottier RCAF*

when a burst of flak exploded a few yards from their Wellington. The forward section took the full force of the explosion, fragments of flak ripped into the cockpit smashing the Perspex and leaving two large holes. Flying Officer Ralph's port engine was hit over the target area. The crew struggled to the Dutch coast jettisoning every moveable object aboard Wellington R1025 HA-J on the way. They limped back to Marham at 600 feet. Squadron Leader Price feathered his still smoking engine over the Dutch Coast. He too managed to reach Marham flying below 1000 feet. Miraculously not one crew member was injured despite the battering the squadron received. It was inevitable that the squadron's luck would not last, one crew failed to return.

Deputy flight commander, Flight Lieutenant John Stokes was at the controls of Wellington R1536 HA-G. Having reached and bombed the target, the crew's wireless operator, Sgt Glover sent a NAP message back to base at 0138 hours. This highly experienced crew had the misfortune of being coned by searchlights over Holland. Unable to lose their enemies attention, the Wellington was held in their beams for several minutes. It was inevitable that they would attract the attention of any prowling night fighter. Sadly, they did and an experienced one, Hptm Werner Streib of Stab.I./NJG1 was airborne flying a Bf110 from Venlo airfield. The counter was brief and fatal. The blazing Wellington crashed at 02:00 hours (other reports suggest 00:55hrs) at Leukeshoeve, Roggel 10 km NW of Roermond, there were no survivors.

*Sergeant Henry Dyer RNZAF*

*Sergeant Albert Glover the Wop/Ag aboard Wellington R1536 HA-G. His message was the last contact Marham had with the crew.*

The crew were first laid to rest at Venlo, but since the war, their remains have been taken to Jonkerbos War Cemetery. Twenty-three-year-old Dorset born John Stokes was on his 33rd operation and would have expected to have been screened from operations any day. His brother was Wing Commander Leonard Stokes DFC commanding officer of the Blenheim equipped 107 Squadron. John's co-pilot, P/O Leslie Parfitt had completed eight operations, all flown alongside John. The crew's rear gunner was Sergeant Henry Dyer, RNZAF. He was another Battle of Britain veteran. The son of a policeman, he was born at Paeroa, North Island on May 4th, 1919. In March 1939 he applied for a short service commission but was unsuccessful. He volunteered for aircrew at the outbreak of war. Dyer reported to the Ground Training School Weraroa on March 12th, 1940 and moved to 2 EFTS New Plymouth on 8th April. He did not progress during pilot training and re-mustered as an air gunner. After a gunnery course at the Air Observers School Ohakea, Dyer sailed for the UK aboard the RMS Rangitata on June 7th, 1940. Soon after his arrival he was posted to 5 OTU at RAF Aston Down on July 30th. On completion of his training and being awarded his air gunners badge, he joined No.600 Squadron at RAF Redhill on September 21st, 1940. With the advent of airborne radar and the arrival of Beaufighter, the air gunners were flying less and less. In late 1940 those not wishing to retrain, Dyer amongst them, were transferred to Bomber Command. He was posted to 11 OTU Bassingbourn on February 6th, 1941. Henry now crewed-up, converted to Wellingtons and joined 218 Squadron at Marham, Norfolk on 19th April. He joined John Stokes as his regular gunner and was lost on his 23rd operation. It was yet another savage blow to the squadron. The loss of any crew was keenly felt, but to lose a pilot of John Stokes calibre and experienced was particularly hard to accept, especially when he was to be posted for instructor duties anytime.

## Tuesday 15th July 1941

*Vickers Wellington*
*Mk.Ic R1536 HA-G 'George'*
*Contract No: 992424/39*
*Taken on Charge: 18/03/1941*
***Failed to Return***
*Pilot: Flight Lieutenant John Stokes, 70820 RAF* **Killed**
*2nd Pilot: Pilot Officer Leslie William Parfitt 62293 RAVR* **Killed**
*Observer: Sergeant John Harold Storey, 754355 RAFVR* **Killed**
*Front Gunner: Sergeant Fred Wood, 975313 RAF* **Killed**
*1st Wireless Operator: Sergeant Albert Glover, 948672 RAFVR* **Killed**
*Rear Gunner: Sergeant Henry David Patrick Dyer, 40758 RNZAF* **Killed**

**Tuesday 15th July 1941**
*Vickers Wellington*
*Mk.Ic X9678 HA-R*
*Contract No: B.97887/39*
*Taken on Charge: 20/06/1941*
*Stalled from 20 feet, lost sight of flare path on landing at 0244hrs.*
*Pilot: Sergeant George Workman, 923432 RAFVR uninjured.*
*2nd Pilot: Sergeant Ronald Brewerton, 999259 RAFVR uninjured.*

One of the Wellingtons that returned this night was Wellington R1025 HA-J flown by F/O Harold Ralph. This old-war horse built by Vickers Armstrong had arrived on the squadron in December 1940. Since then, it had survived 38 raids, now showing signs of wear after two forced landings it was decided that J-Jig would be withdrawn from front line operations.

The squadron was informed it would be required for an operation on the 18th, but this was cancelled by No.3 Group HQ early afternoon due to unfavourable weather. On the afternoon of the 20th, 'A' Flight were aloft practising formation flying, it was a novel experience for the crews accustomed to night flying, all agreed there was something in the wind. The following night twelve crews were detailed for an attack on Mannheim, with the centre of the city the intended target.

*Pilot, Sergeant George Workman.*

There was two early returns, the Wellington Mk.II W5447 HA-C developed a problem with the port Merlin, P/O Pape was back at Marham within the hour, he landed with his 4000 pounder. The other early return was Wellington R1719 HA-K with Sgt John Swingler RCAF at the controls. Unable to climb the crew got as far as the Belgium coast before they turned for home. This would be the fifteenth and last operation flown by the young Canadian and his RAF co-pilot, Sgt John Joy. Both would join No.38 Squadron in the Middle East, and both would end up PoWs within the year. Conditions over the Mannheim were clear but hazy giving the crew the opportunity for some accurate bombing, returning crews reported several fires in the target area and seemed confident that the raid was a success. The following morning a number of selected crews were aloft practising formation flying, conditions were not ideal with thundery showers in the region. Nevertheless, a total of 15 flying hours was notched up.

On the 24th, six crews were given the news that most had expected but hoped would never come, the squadron would be flying a daylight operation. It would be the first since November 1940. Six crews were chosen to attack the German Pocket Battleship the Gneisenau at Brest Harbour. Leading the squadron in Wellington R1008 HA-A was S/Ldr Gibbs, sitting beside him was W/Cdr Fletcher. The squadron would be joined by three Wellingtons of No.115 Squadron which would form three Marham formations. Once airborne they would joined a further 25 Wellingtons drawn from No.3 Groups 40, 57, 75(NZ), 99 and 101 Squadrons.

## *OPERATION "SUNRISE"*

| Formation No.1 | Aircraft | Formation No.2 | Aircraft | Formation No.3 | Aircraft |
|---|---|---|---|---|---|
| **218 Sqdn** | Take-off 1126hrs | **218 Sqdn** | Take-off 1128hrs | **115 Sqdn** | Take-off 1130hrs |

| S/Ldr Gibbs | R1008 HA-A | Sgt Banks | R1601 HA-T | S/Ldr Sindall | W5720 KO-J |
| --- | --- | --- | --- | --- | --- |
| F/O Ralph | R1497 HA-H | P/O Jolly | Z8781 HA-S | F/Lt Pooley | R5684 KO-G |
| P/O Pape | R1596 HA-B | Sgt Chidgey | R1726 HA-O | Sgt Prior | X9671 KO-F |

The Wellingtons of No.3 Group would be joined by 24 Wellingtons from No.1 Group, 18 Wellingtons from Yorkshire based No.4 Group and finally 18 Hampden from No.5 Group. Three Flying Fortresses would open proceedings from 30,000 feet. Fighter Command would provide an umbrella of squadrons to protect the opening waves of Hampdens. However, the Wellingtons would have to go in alone.

The three Marham formations headed south flying towards Cornwall then out over the English Channel for the long sea crossing. Conditions were excellent. There was one early return, F/O Ralph broke formation shortly after crossing Lands' End with engine trouble, he landed safely at Portreath with his 7 x 500 SAPs. As the formation neared Brest, they could see smoke drifting over the docks, above the target the sky appeared to be black with bursting flak bursts. More alarming was the presence of Bf109s. Squadron Leader Gibbs dropped his bombs from 14,500 feet in the face of intense flak. His seven SAPs were seen to explode just short of Dock No.1. Leaving the target, his Wellington was immediately set upon by two BF109s just north of the Brest. The crew claimed one possible destroyed. The badly holed Wellington turned for home. Pilot Officer Pape seemed to have been a magnet for the flak gunners. His Wellington was rocked by a barrage of exploding flak, unable to fly straight and level due to the bursting anti-aircraft fire that encircled his Wellington the crew lined up the best they could on the docks below. Finally, the bombs were dropped and after what seemed a lifetime were seen to explode slightly short of the main dock area and on the quayside. The now extensively damaged Wellington tucked in close to its leader and limped for home. The second formation had slightly better luck. Sergeant Banks watched as his bombs straddled the docks, one of the 500 pounders were believed to have clearly hit the camouflaged *Gneisenau*. A burst of flak near the tail rendered the rear turret unserviceable. It was not the time to be without the protection of the rear guns as a Bf109 made an attack north of Brest. Thankfully, there was just enough hydraulic pressure for Sgt Robert Moodie to get in one telling burst at the fighter which he believed he damaged before it dived below the Wellington. Sergeant Chidgey dropped his bombs in one stick from 14,000 feet. The last two of his bombs were seen falling in the water on a line that the crew were confident must have covered the cruiser. Damaged by flak the crew were quickly set upon by two Bf109s. After a short but vicious exchange of fire, the Wellington managed to slip away, numerous holes in the fabric were a small price to pay as they too headed for the comparative safety of the English Channel. Not all the squadron Wellington crews were so lucky, 'B' Flight's Pilot Officer Jolly was set upon by several Bf109s. The Wellington was seen to crash into the sea in the target area. The crew's wireless operator was Sergeant John Knott, who was on his 3rd operation.

*From my training, at OTU, I was posted to 218 Squadron on the 2nd May 1941 as a Wop/Ag on the Vickers Wellington. I flew with various pilots until May 25th, 1941 making the usual cross-country trips, W/T practice, Air Calibration, fighter affiliation, formation flying and of course circuits and landings by night and day. It was a busy time. On June 14th I went to RAF Newmarket for a couple of weeks and with a 'virgin' pilot did a few cross-country trips as well as a little Air-to-Air firing. On June 29th, it was back to RAF Marham to be crewed up, and I found myself with a New Zealand pilot. After a short leave, we did some formation flying and other training flights. Before I knew it, I was on night operations over Germany.*

*On July 24th, 1941, a force of Wellingtons flying in formation in daylight were sent to Brest Harbour to bomb Gneisenau. The Wellington I was in managed to get through the very heavy flak barrage information when we were hit by German fighters. All the rear gunners let loose. Our rear gunner gave a running commentary on the attacks over the intercom. During the attack, the rear of the aircraft caught fire. I was standing next to the pilot. I tapped the 2nd pilot on the shoulder, causing him to turn around. I pointed towards the rear fuselage, which was on fire. I had my parachute on and went down to open the exit door, on kneeling down I caught my parachute release buckle, and the chute opened inside the Wellington. I quickly gathered it up in my arms. By this time, the Canadian observer had his legs dangling out, I gave him the nod and out he went. The front gunner was beside me as I sat on the edge of the exit door, he gave me the nod and out I went headfirst. I must have blacked out for a second. When I came to, I thought that the chute had caught on the aircraft. I quickly looked up, and there was the chute unopened. I must have fallen 4000 feet before the chute finally opened, and I floated down to the sea. A German fighter circled my decent. I later found out this was to guide the launch to pick me up. I sank into the water before I could dispose of the chute. In my shock state, I had forgotten to unbuckle the harness. I pulled my Mae West which just exploded! I finally managed to free myself from the chute underwater. I had come down close to the observer, and we managed to climb aboard a small French fishing boat. A German launch soon turned up, and we were ordered aboard. They took us to the beach where more German soldiers were waiting. We were told to take off our uniforms and handed them to a German soldier. Here we were standing in our pants watched by French women sunbathing. We were taken to a nearby chateau overlooking the beach. Here we were given some dry clothing and a meal which we had with a German Air Force officer, all the while the battle was waging above our heads. The officer handed us a pair of binoculars and indicated to us to look towards the docks, I could see that the battleship looked undamaged. This went on for some time until our uniforms were dried. Eventually, they were returned, and we were driven off to a fighter base and handed over to the Germany Army. We were taken to a nearby town and given a room for the night. A guard stood outside the door the whole night. The following day we were put on a train for Paris'.*

Sadly, there were only two survivors from Wellington R1726 HA-O. The 23-year-old New Zealand pilot, Pilot Officer Morrison Jolly RNZAF and 19-year-old co-pilot, Sergeant 'Tony' Moss went down with the blazing Wellington. It was the Kiwi's 22nd operation and Anthony's 8th, all of which were flown beside P/O Jolly. The crew's rear gunner who courageously defended the Wellington until killed by cannon fire was Polish-born Jew, Pilot Officer Louis Kolitz. He had started his tour with S/Ldr Richmond back in December 1940, this was his 23rd operation with the squadron. It is believed that the Wellington was shot down by a Bf109 of JG2. The bodies of the crew were never found.

### Thursday 24th July 1941
*Vickers Wellington*
*Mk.Ic R1726 HA-O 'Orange'*
*Contract No: B992424/39*
*Taken On Charge: 18/05/1941*
**Failed To Return**
*Pilot : Pilot Officer Morrison Jolly 40648 RNZAF,* **Killed**
*2nd Pilot: Sergeant Anthony Cade Moss, 1170249 RAFVR,* **Killed**
*Observer : Sergeant William Lloyd Jacobson, R/51672 RCAF, PoW*
*Front Gunner: Sergeant Herbert Ronald Barton, 615896 RAFVR* **Killed**
*1st Wireless Operator: Sergeant John Knott, 924849 RAFVR PoW*
*Rear Gunner: Pilot Officer Louis Phillip Kolitz, 80119 RAFVR,* **Killed**

*Wing Commander Fletcher. An accomplished tennis player and all-round sportsman.*

The operation appeared to be a success but was marred by the fighter opposition, which was stronger than expected. A total of ten Wellingtons and two Hampden were lost to a combination of flak and fighters.

With five crews safely back from Brest, the squadron turned its attention to northern Germany and one of the Kriegsmarine's major naval and shipbuilding centres, Kiel Harbour. Six crews started to take off just before midnight. All was well until Sgt Dare neared the German coast when it was discovered the front turret aboard T2887 HA-W was unserviceable. Deciding not to continue the crew bombed the aerodrome at Westerland on the island of Sylt. Sergeant Forster was at the controls of the squadron's Mk.II Wellington, W5447 HA-C, it was his first experience of the Merlin-powered Wellington. The crew found the target, the Deutsche Werks Kiel A.G without difficulty despite the ground haze, dropping their 4000 pounder which produced a vivid burst. Sergeant Taylor was caught and held by searchlights over the target, unable to escape their deadly grip he was forced to jettison his bomb load. Two rookie second pilots were undertaking their operational debut on this raid. Sergeant Roy Boswell joining the crew of Sergeant Ken Shearing while Sergeant James Cottingham sat beside the 26-raid veteran, Sergeant Harry Rose. Over the target Sgt Rose was attacked by a Bf109, the fighter was successfully driven off and claimed as a probably by the rear gunner Sgt Marshall.

A message from the Chief of Air Staff arrived at RAF Marham on the 26th. It was a nice touch, but the participating crews would, given a preference, prefer not to be sent out in daylight again. The squadron knew that they had got off relatively lightly considering the fighter opposition.

*'Please convey to all who took part in yesterday's operation my warm appreciation of the efficiency and determination with which the attack on the enemy warships was conceived and executed. I am sure that all units realise the supreme importance of keeping these German cruisers inactive and the great contribution their attacks have made towards relieving the Royal Navy of some part of its very heavy burden. It was most satisfactory that the number of enemy fighters destroyed by your gunners well exceeded your own losses'*

The Station held its annual Sports Day on the 27th. Fine weather ensured a good turnout of both participants and spectators. In the evening, a station dance was held, this too was well attended. The Brest trip was the 35th and final operation flown by Sergeant Edward 'Ted' Chidgey. He had started his tour back in February completing 12 operations besides New Zealander Nelson Mansfield. He went on to complete a further 23 operations as captain. He was posted to No.27 O.T.U at RAF Lichfield. While instructing, he married a WAAF. He returned for a second tour with No.35 Path Finder Squadron winning a DSO and DFC in the process. He survived the war. it was a fitting and happy ending to a busy month.

The squadron began its August campaign with an attack on the Air Ministry at Berlin on the 2nd. Only two crews were detailed, P/O Pape and the irrepressible S/Ldr Price. Both of the squadron's Wellington Mk.IIs would be used, and both would carry the 4000 pounder. Pilot Officer Pape was the first aloft at 2234hrs in W5447 HA-C, a minute later S/Ldr Price eased W5457 HA-Z into the night sky. Conditions on route were good, however on arrival over Berlin, the crews disappointingly found it blanketed in cloud. Pilot Officer

Pape dropped his bomb from 14,000 feet on what he believed to be the Brandenburg area of Berlin. The crew of S/Ldr Price was not so lucky. They were not even able to find Berlin. They dropped their bomb over the town of Neustrelitz, 60 miles north of Berlin. A massive explosion was observed, followed by an even larger one with a vivid blue flash. Both weary crews landed back at RAF Marham after being aloft almost seven hours.

The following night nine crews were detailed and briefed for an attack on Hanover, it would be a costly night for the squadron. Almost immediately after take-off the crew of P/O Maxwell RCAF experienced problems as they entered dense cloud. The crew's 2nd pilot, Canadian P/O Thomas Cottier recalls the tragic minutes that would see the death of two of his crewmates.

*I was the 2nd pilot on the trip. I was forward with the pilot on take-off. He seemed to have some difficulty setting course due to the plane 'slipping off to port'. We set course 2000 feet above the drome at approx 2330 hours. We ran into thick cloud almost immediately. About 2240 hours, the navigator came forward to see if he could map read and went back to the astrodome. We were near the top of the cloud layer as it was possible to catch a glimpse of the moon when the pilot shouted that the gyro horizon had gone west. He had previously said that the air was extremely bumpy. The plane then seemed to fall off to port and from the astrodome, it appeared to me that we had turned 180 degrees. From then on we were pressed against the roof as if on our backs, then on the floor and then again on the roof. The pilot remained calm, ordered the front gunner out of his turret, then ordered us to bail out, which he did. I bailed out from the rear escape hatch and while doing so noticed the rear gunner coming out of his turret alone the corridor. I shouted to him to bail out, but he apparently did not do so. It was his first operational trip, but he had been instructed and knew what to do in case of an emergency. The trouble started at 5500 feet, and we bailed out at 4000 feet. The time was approx. 2255 hours.*

One can only imagine the desperate battle the young Canadian pilot was having trying to keep the Wellington aloft. Like so many young pilots, his priority was the safety of his crew. Four of the crew managed to escape the Wellington before it crashed at Salhouse, a village that lies south of the River Bure and Salhouse Broad, 6 miles north-east of Norwich. The Canadian navigator P/O Garnet Jacobson recalled; *'I was the crew's navigator on this trip. When the aircraft went out of control, the captain ordered the front gunner out of his turret. While I was helping him out, the order was given to abandon the aircraft. The front gunner jumped followed by me and then the wireless operator'.*

On hitting the ground, the Wellington, X9747 HA-E immediately burst into flame, a 500 pounder then exploded shattering the aircraft and depositing debris over a large area. It is apparent from 2nd pilot's report that the rear gunner, P/O Crabb had vacated his turret and should have had ample time to parachute to safety. A subsequent investigation on the crash suggests that when P/O Crabb went forward, he omitted to take his parachute with him. George James Leonard Crabb was an East Ender, born in West Ham in 1905, older than most on the squadron he was a recent widower. His 29-year-old Irish wife, Mary was killed on April 19th, 1941 when a German parachute mine landed on the Prince of Wales pub at Chigwell, Essex. Mary, along with 30 others were killed. Pilot Officer Crabb was buried in the Chadwell Heath Cemetery. This was his first and only operation with the squadron. The body of the 24-year-old pilot was buried on August 7th in Marham Cemetery. John Maxwell had completed 12 operations. A report into the crash dated September 3rd, 1941 recorded the following.

It appears probable that the pilot while flying up through the cloud attempted to check a suspicion that something had gone wrong with the instruments by an occasional glance at the moon. Later on it seems he stalled the aircraft completely after which he gave the orders for the crew to abandon. It is noteworthy that a letter had very recently been circulating to all Bomber Command stations BC/8776/ENG.30 dated 23.07.1941 drawing attention to the increasing number of failures in artificial horizons and directional giros'.

## Sunday 3rd August 1941

*Vickers Wellington*
*Mk.Ic X9747 HA-E 'Edward'*
*Contract No : B.97887/39*
*Taken On Charge : 22/07/1941*
*Destroyed In Crash*
*Pilot : Pilot Officer John Arthur Maxwell J/3715 RCAF, **Killed***
*2nd Pilot : Pilot Officer Thomas George Cottier, J/4885 RCAF, uninjured*
*Observer : Pilot Officer Garnet Franklin Jacobson, J/3500 RCAF uninjured*
*Front Gunner : Sergeant Gordon Sidwell, 993621 RAFVR, uninjured.*
*1st Wireless Operator : Sergeant George Hoult, 98423 RAFVR, uninjured.*
*Rear Gunner : Pilot Officer George James Leonard Crabb, 82975 RAFVR **Killed***

*Pilot Officer John Maxwell RCAF stayed at the controls of his Wellington to allow his crew the best chance of survival. His selfless act cost him his life.*

Unaware of the tragedy that had overtaken one of their colleagues, the rest of the squadron crossed the North Sea without further incident. The raid was scheduled to take place between 0045hrs and 0210hrs, one crew that never reached the target was that of Wing Commander Fletcher. Engaged by flak south of Bremen, Wellington Z8781 HA-S was hit and set on fire, what happened next is described by the crew's Scottish navigator, Sgt Alexander.

*On the order being given to bail out, I went forward and found W/Cdr Fletcher at the controls keeping the aircraft as far as I could judge straight as possible in a steep dive. The hatch and the turret door were open. Sgt Bridwell was standing with a parachute attached at the hatchway, there was no sign of Sgt Spong, Sgt Dodd or the front gunner F/Sgt Crail. Communication with each other was impossible, and as the aircraft was diving steeply and in flames, I bailed out at once. The aircraft crashed below me, and by the time I reached the ground it was completely enveloped in flames and I judged anyone still on board must have been killed. I was obliged to make off as some German civilians were approaching. I was informed later by the Germans that all the crew apart from myself and Sgt Spong were dead. I could not find out where they were buried.*

The Wellington, the victim of flak from 8.Flak Division crashed near Moordeich/Stuhr at 0104 hours. Three of the crew were found in the burnt out wreckage including W/Cdr Fletcher. One member, believed to be Sgt Bridwell was discovered some distance from the crash, his parachute unopened. The two 250lb bombs were found close to the wreckage confirming that the crew never reached Bremen. The severely burnt bodies were taken to the Municipal Mortuary Bremen before being buried on the 8th in the Bremen Walle Cemetery.

**Sunday 3rd August 1941**

*Vickers Wellington*
*Mk.Ic Z8781 HA-S 'Sugar'*
*Contract No : B71441/40*
*Taken On Charge : 27/06/1941*
**Failed To Return**
*Pilot : Wing Commander John Lionel Howe Fletcher 05218 RAF* **Killed**
*2nd Pilot : Sergeant Frank Craighton Dodd, 1104391 RAFVR,* **Killed**
*Navigator: Sergeant Robert James Alexander, 979955 RAFVR, PoW*
*Front Gunner : Flight Sergeant Frank Grail 965679 RAFVR* **Killed**
*1st Wireless Operator : Sergeant Terence Alfred Evelyn Bridewell, 945177 RAFVR,* **Killed**
*Rear Gunner : Sergeant Eric Stanley Spong, 544575 RAFVR, PoW*

This was the Commanding Officers first operation as captain having flown his previous two trips with his flight commanders. He chose to take the experienced crew of the recently departed Sgt Edward Chidgey, he would also use the formers new Wellington. The crew's 2nd pilot, 19-year-old Sgt Frank Dodd was on his 5th operation, while the replacement front gunner Sgt Frank Grail was on his first.

John Lionel Howe Fletcher was born on June 13th, 1910, the youngest son of Horatio and Lilian Fletcher, of Uppercroft Wadhurst, Sussex. He was born into a wealthy family, his father Horatio was the director of a successful coal exporting company, *H Fletcher Coal Exports and Agency* based in London's Fenchurch Street. Educated at Cambridge University John flew with the University Air Squadron between 1929 and 1932, being commissioned in the Reserve of Air Force Officers in March 1930. In 1932 he was commissioned into the RAF with a rank of Pilot Officer. On completion of his pilot training John was posted in August 1933 to No.32 (F) Squadron flying the Bristol Bulldog based at RAF Biggin Hill. After two years he was posted briefly to the Central Flying School then to the Station Flight, RAF Duxford. In 1937 he joined No. 600 (City of London) Squadron flying the Hawker Demon as flight commander. Based at RAF Hendon he took part in many of the major air displays during the period. His time on the squadron was concluded with a posting to No.6 (Aux) Group HQ in December 1938. During this time, it was not just flying John had a passion for, he was also an accomplished lawn tennis player. He had represented both Cambridge and the RAF on a number of occasions and was the RAF's Lawn Tennis Champion three years in succession.

*A German sentry stands guard over the wreckage of Wing Commander Fletchers Wellington Z8781 HA-S. The crumpled rear turret is on the left, the escape doors wide open.*

*Wing Commander John Lionel Howe Fletcher RAF.*

A posting to the Air Ministry followed working for the Directorate of Operational Requirements. Perhaps feeling that his time on fighters was over, he was at the time twenty-eight. John was posted to No.15 O.T.U based at RAF Harwell then almost immediately to No.1 School of Army Co-Operation whose function was to liaise between the tactical needs on the ground for the Army and the RAF. This was John's last posting before his arrival on the squadron. With W/Cdr Kirkpatrick still recovering from his injuries, it was the inexperienced W/Cdr Fletcher that stepped in to take command. Sadly, the squadron diaries do not record if this was a temporary measure or permanent posting. Immediately upon his arrival John Fletcher demonstrated that despite his lack of operational experience he would lead by example and from the front, tragically this courageous approach so typical of many pre-war regular officers would cost him his life. The Scottish navigator, Sergeant Alexander adventures had only just begun on landing in Germany. Fluent in German the following records the young Glaswegians escape attempt.

*Eighteen year old Wireless Operator / front gunner aboard Wellington Mk.Ic Z8781 HA-S 'Sugar', Sergeant Terence Alfred Evelyn Bridewell.*

We took off from Marham in a Wellington aircraft at 2300 hours on August 3rd 1941. Before we reached the target, the aircraft was hit by flak. The aircraft caught fire and the pilot gave the order to abandon aircraft. I bailed at 0200 hours on August 4th and landed in a field near Bremen close to the aircraft which was burning. I landed near a house and several people were gathering near the aircraft, so I threw away my parachute and crawled away from the vicinity. Sometime later I buried my harness and mae west.

I hid in a ditch until 2100 hrs on August 4th when I discovered from a signpost that I was 9km south of Bremen. I decided to get to Stettin, and I made a detour of the outskirts of Bremen and hid in a barn. I remained there until 0600 hours on August 6th when I left the barn, after having appropriated a civilian jacket, which I discovered. In one of the fields near the farm I obtained a peached cap from a scarecrow. I found a hayrack and I carried this on my shoulder. I walked to the river Weser and then turned south along the western riverbank. I crossed over the river by a bridge with a stream of workers going to a factory on the other side. I passed the factory and walked along a main road until I came to the outskirts of Bremen, when I began walking east across country. I noticed a lot of German soldiers in the vicinity, so I hid in a filed until 22.00 hours.

I then made my way to a main road and began walking along it. I saw a bicycle outside a public house and I stole it. I then cycled along a autobahn towards Hamburg until 0500 hours on the 6th when I hide in a barn until 1000 hours. I then resumed cycling along the autobahn.

Soon afterwards I was stopped by two German officials who asked me what I was doing on the autobahn. I speak fluent German and was able to answer their questions without difficulty. They asked where I came from, where I was going to, where I was born etc. They then asked me for my identity papers, and I stated that I left them at home. At this stage I lost my temper and said I was sorry I had been cycling along the autobahn, but I did not know this was forbidden and that I wanted to get to Hamburg quickly. In answer to my questions, they directed me to an ordinary road to Hamburg which crossed the autobahn at this point. I thanked them and rode off along an ordinary road. I cycled throughout the remainder of that day and the next two days and nights resting from time to time.

I arrived in Hamburg about 0600 hours on August 9th and joined a stream of workers entering the town from the outskirts. I rode to the western outskirts and hid in a clump of bushes until the evening. About 2200 hours I began to ride along the autobahn towards Lubeck. I rode at night and hid in barns and haystacks during the day until I arrived in Lubeck about 0700 hours on August 11th. I cycled through Lubeck and located the docks. I discovered the docks were unfenced, but that guards were located at intervals of approximately 200 yards around the perimeter. I cycled to the outskirts of Lubeck and hid in a graveyard until 2350 hours. I then returned to the dock area and after removing boots I went on board a ship. It was not flying a flag. I hid behind a boat on deck, but I was not satisfied with my hiding place. I went to the ships galley and stole some bread and jam, which I ate. I also took a slab of cake which I put in my pocket. I then left the ship and hid in a shed in the garden of a house on the outskirts of Lubeck. I was discovered by a gardener during the following afternoon. I told him I was Swedish sailor and I had lost my ship. He seemed to accept my story and advised me to go to the police. I said I would do and left the garden. I then returned to the cemetery where I had previously hidden. I remained there until evening when I went to the docks and discovered a small ship flying a Swedish flag. I removed my boots and went aboard. I hid under the bowsprit and at 0600hrs on the 13th the ship sailed. I remained hidden and at 1100 hours I was amazed when a boy member of the ship's crew placed a tureen of soup near me. The boy did not speak. I ate the soup. At 1500 hours the same boy came to my hiding place in order to get a pot of paint. He saw me and appeared to be very startled. I did not speak. He went away and returned a few minutes later with another boy who appeared to be very surprised when he saw me. The two boys then informed another member of the ship's crew who also had a look at a me. No one spoke to me and I did not speak to them. The three of them then turned and walked away.

I left my hiding place and approached the ship's captain who was in his cabin with one of the members of the crew who had seen me. I attempted to speak to them in English and German, but they did not understand. The captain then smiled and said "MALMO" I left the cabin and saw several ships of various nationalities were sailing close to the ship I was on. A few minutes later, a motor launch came along side and a German in a brown uniform came aboard. He spoke to the ship's captain and then came to where I was standing and asked me if I was British. I stated that I was. He then said, 'come with me'. I protested, in German against being taken off a neutral ship, but he forced me to go onto his launch. I was taken to a German ship where I was stripped and searched. I was provided with meal and sailors clothes. At 1200 hours, on August 14th a passing ship stopped, and I was transferred to it. I was taken to Warnemünde where I arrived at 1500 hours and taken to an aerodrome and put into cells. On August 15th I was taken under escort, by train to Dulag Luft, Frankfurt. From the time I bailed out at 0200 hours on August 4th until my capture at 1500 hours on August 13th my only food was a few apples and pears, which I stole and some corn. This was in addition to the bread and cake I stole from the ship on August 11th.

The brave young Scot was not done yet, while a POW at Stalag Luft III E Kirchain he was involved in another escape attempt. In early 1942 he and a few other prisoners managed to dig a tunnel under the wire of the compound. On May 11th, 1942 he escaped, travelling by night he managed to get as far as Berlin where he was captured on May 21st, 1942. This was not the end of his escapades. With the Russian advance into Germany in 1945, the inmates of Stalag 357 were ordered to move west. The vast column of weary PoWs were not guarded as closely as they should have been allowing the young Scot to slip away from the column unobserved. Hiding in nearby woods, he waited for the column to pass and set off in the hope of reaching Allied lines. On April 16th, 1945 three days after his escape, his luck runs out when two SS troops captured him. Fearing for his life, he was amazed when the *SS* commander handed him over to Germans civilians near Munster. He was eventually taken to a French PoW Camp, where he was liberated by British troops a few days later. The brave and resilient young navigator was awarded a well-deserved OBE in December 1945 in recognition to his *'distinguished service'*.

There was stunned disbelief on the morning of the 5th. Two crews had gone, one of them the commanding officer. The squadron had never lost a commanding officer on operations. John Fletcher was the first, but sadly not the last. The announcement in the London Gazette of the award of the DFC to S/Ldr Herbert Price did little to raise the squadron spirit. The citation read;

*On a night in July 1941, this officer was detailed to attack Duisburg. In spite of searchlights concentration and heavy anti-aircraft fire, he spent 40 minutes locating the target, which was eventually successfully bombed. His aircraft was repeatedly hit, and his rear turret put out of action. Over Holland, on the return journey, his aircraft was intercepted by an enemy aircraft which was shaken off by skilful avoiding action. The port engine failed, and his aircraft began to lose height rapidly. All available articles were jettisoned but Squadron Leader Price was nevertheless compelled to fly at 600 feet. By skilful piloting, however, he landed at his base. He has always shown the utmost coolness, courage and determination.*

The only crew to encounter mechanical problems on route was that of Sgt Robert Banks who was obliged to bomb the docks at Calais which he did with some success. The mixed HE and incendiary load were seen

288

to burst across Dock 4 and 5, causing a vivid blue and green flash and started a fire that was visible from Clacton on return. The remaining Mannheim force delivered an extremely accurate raid inflicting some worthwhile damage. Both flight commanders delivered their single 4000 pounder without mishap. Squadron Leader Price dropped his bomb on the centre on Karlsruhe producing a *'Huge red burst, like molten lava'.* Squadron Leader Gibbs witnessed this explosion as he arrived over the target dropping his bomb and two flash bombs from 9,000 feet causing a fire that was visible 80 miles away. Two 'Freshman' operations were flown on the 7th, P/O Mitchell and Sgt Tucker were given the docks at Boulogne to attack, only the crew of Arthur Mitchell managed to locate and bomb the target. This was Mitchell's first operation as captain having flown 11 operations as second pilot. Sergeant Raoul Tucker was unable to find the target due to the cloud. He returned to Marham minus two 500 pounders which were jettisoned over the North Sea. This was also Tucker's first operation as captain having previously completed 16 operations in the left-hand seat. Joining him in the cockpit and opening his batting on the squadron was second pilot Sgt Victor Haley.

Hamburg was the intended target on the 8th. The raid was a failure. Only 44 aircraft were briefed to attack the Blohm and Voss works, 218 Squadron provided six crews. Sergeant Forster returned early due to port engine failure aboard Wellington L7797 HA-F, he was followed by the crew of F/O Ralph who experienced icing. What was left of the squadron found Hamburg covered in dense cloud, identifying the Blohm and Voss works was impossible. The crews either dropped on ETA or the flak. One crew, however, decided to find an alternative target. Squadron Leader Price unwilling to drop his bombs over a cloud-covered Hamburg turned his attention to the fires visible at Kiel. A small force of Hampdens and Whitleys were attacking the submarine yards, seeing the glow in the distance S/Ldr Price added his 5 x 500 pounders on the fires below. Diverted to RAF Linton-On-Ouse the crew spent an enjoyable evening as the guests of No.4 Group. The following morning the weather over Marham had cleared sufficiently for the crew to return. Unfortunately, during take-off the undercarriage was retracted too soon, the Wellington gradually sank back onto the runway damaging R1448 to the extent that it was almost three months before it returned to squadron service. It was an uncharacteristic and fundamental error on the part of S/Ldr Price DFC who had at the time 617 flying hours on the Wellington.

### Saturday 9th August 1941
*Vickers Wellington*
*Mk.Ic R1448 HA-L 'London'*
*Contract No : B992424/39*
*Taken On Charge : 22/02/1941*
*Undercarriage raised too soon on take-off.*
*Pilot : Squadron Leader Herbert Price DFC*
*2nd Pilot : Sergeant Alan McLean RAAF*


The squadrons of RAF Marham provided 21 of the 29 aircraft dispatched to the railway station at Rheydt, a few miles south of Munchen Gladbach on the 11th. The first of 218 Squadron's eleven Wellingtons aloft was skippered by Sgt Ken Shearing in N2844 HA-M at 0044hrs. It was not until the force was over the Belgium coast that Sgt Shearing encountered problems. Failure of the W/T and intercom forced the crew to seek a secondary target to attack, this they did in the form Bruge Aerodrome. The crews all HE load was dropped from 12000 feet on a number of faint lights, the resulting explosions starting a number of fires. Another crew experiencing technical trouble was that of Sgt Huckle. They bombed the docks at Calais from 10000 feet when only one of the rear guns functioned. Over the target the crews encountered considerable flak, Sgt Fisher was badly hit seconds after bombing. His hydraulic system was damaged, resulting in the bomb doors failing to rise. In addition to this, one of the petrol tanks were holed, the starboard aileron buckled, and the fuselage was punctured in numerous places. By sheer luck, none of the crew was injured. Not so fortunate was Pilot Officer Mitchell. A burst of flak shattered this cockpit canopy, splinters of which hit the pilots face. The results were difficult to assess due to cloud, however returning crews were confident of success. Arriving back over England Sgt Kenneth Fisher was obliged to crash land his Wellington at RAF Martlesham Heath, Suffolk. It was on this raid that two Wellingtons of No.115 Squadron flew the first trial of the still secret and experimental Gee navigational system.

## Monday 11th August 1941

*Vickers Wellington*
*Mk.Ic R1596 HA-O 'Orange'*
*Contract No : 992424/39*
*Taken On Charge: 15/04/1941*
*Crashed on Return. To No.43 Group for repair.*
*Pilot: Sergeant Kenneth Fisher and Crew*


Pilot Officer Graham Hunter, an observer with Sgt Tucker, recalls this operation:

*This was my first operational trip and first over Germany. Also, it was my first trip using Oxygen. Climbing to about 8,000 feet, I asked Sgt Tucker how to switch on the oxygen, as I had not been shown this while in training. He told me to turn the switch until the needle flicked. I did precisely this, not knowing that I should have turned the switch well beyond that point. We climbed to 18,000 feet, which the skipper always used as his operational height. I flew the whole trip without oxygen, but at 19 years of age and with big lungs, I seemed to cope. It was only when the Wop received a direct course for Marham when we were nearing the English coast that I suddenly felt exhausted. I remember putting my parachute on the floor and going to sleep! The next thing I remember was a sudden sharp pain in my stomach and popping noises. The stomach pains were caused by the G-Force due to the violent turns to avoid a Ju88 Intruder that had latched onto us. The popping sound was from the rear gunner losing off a few rounds. Luckily, Marham's ground defences were on the ball and opened up on the Intruder. I vaguely remember someone yelling at me "Are you alive". Once I was fully awake, the crew told me what had happened, they were a bit shook up, but naturally, it had no effect on me!'*

Bomber Command was out in force on the 12th visiting a number of targets. Number 3 Group was particularly busy visiting Hanover, Essen, Berlin and Le Havre providing an impressive 132 bombers. Eight crews were supplied by 218 Squadron, two crews flying the Wellington Mk.IIs would attack Berlin while the remainder would attack the Krupps Werks at Essen. Neither S/Ldr Price nor Sgt Huckle reached the 'Big City' due to weather conditions on the route. Squadron Leader Price DFC bombed Stettin Docks while Kiel received the 4000 pounder of Sgt Huckle and crew. The attack on Hanover was equally unsuccessful, thick cloud and haze made the target impossible to identify, resulting in scattered bombing. On return Sergeant, Tucker was attacked and damaged by a Ju88 while in Marham's circuit at 02:50 hours. Accurate return fire from the crew's rear gunner Sgt Grewcock was sufficient to deter any further attacks. Not so lucky was the crew of P/O Woods of No.115 Squadron. They were attacked four times by Ofw Peter Laufs of I./NJG2 killing the New Zealand rear gunner. Wellington T2568 KO-D crashed at 02:20 hours at Smiths Farm, Scottow, four miles south of Walsham, Norfolk.

There was no let-up in raids, Bomber Command continued its attacks on Germany with Hannover, Brunswick and Magdeburg being visited on the 14th. The squadron detailed and briefed eleven crews for the night's activities, nine would attack Hannover while once the squadron's two Merlin-powered Wellington Mk.IIs were given Madgeburg on the river Elbe. The crew of Sgt Fisher were withdrawn before take-off with a defective engine. The Wellington Mk.IIs were first away, S/L Gibbs was airborne at 2110 hours in W5447 HA-C followed almost immediately by W5457 HA-Z with Sgt Dare at the controls. Both crews managed to locate the target area in deteriorating weather, thick cloud once again preventing identification of the target visually.

Unable to pinpoint the aiming point both 4000 pounders were dropped on ETA or flak positions. The raid on Hannover proved costly for the squadrons at Marham. The attack, although producing some fires, was hampered by patchy cloud and haze. The squadron arrived over the city towards the end of the attack bombing either small isolated fires or the flak or searchlights. Opposition from the city's flak defences was stiff, but not unduly troublesome as the force of over one hundred bombers turned for home. At 0057 hour the crew of P/O Mitchell sent a messaged back to base reporting that the target had been successfully bombed, it was the last time they were heard from. Having attacked the target, P/O Mitchell slowly banked veteran Wellington R1008 HA-A to port and headed for home. South of Bremen the crew were engaged and held by several searchlights, immediately accurate flak began to burst all around the aircraft, tragically unlike the defences over Hannover, these were deadly accurate. The Wellington was quickly hit and set on fire apparently giving the crew no time to escape. The blazing Wellington crashed at 02:36 hours between Blocken and Obernheide a few miles south of Bremen. There were no survivors. The following morning the site was visited by German troops, smoke rising from the crumpled and still burning aircraft made locating it easy. Once the fires had finally burnt out the grizzly job of finding and identifying the crew began. Due to the impact and subsequent fire, the bodies of the severely burnt crew were incorrectly identified and recorded. This mistake was not rectified until 1948. Once removed from the wreckage the crew were buried on August 18th in the Wallerfriedhof Cemetery. Arthur Mitchell had flown fifteen operations since his arrival in June, eleven of those as second pilot. Flying beside him was 20-year-old Sgt Kenneth Smith, a young lad from Croydon. Kenneth had completed seven trips since his arrival.

### Thursday 14th August 1941

*Vickers Wellington*
*Mk.Ic R1008 HA-A 'Apple'*
*Contract No : 992424/39*
*Taken On Charge: 06/1/1940*
**Failed To Return**
*Pilot : Pilot Officer Arthur Page Mitchell 43977 RAF* **Killed**
*2nd Pilot : Sergeant Keith Ernest Smith, 1174439 RAFVR ,* **Killed**
*Navigator: Pilot Officer Ernest Wakefield, 67083 RAFVR,* **Killed**
*Front Gunner : Sergeant Alfred Ronald Bell, 931537 RAFVR* **Killed**
*1st Wireless Operator : Sergeant Charles James Mathews, 751430 RAFVR* **Killed**
*Rear Gunner : Flight Sergeant Keith Francis Lewis, 625523 RAF,* **Killed**

Sadly, for the squadron, they would lose another crew this night in mysterious circumstances. Pilot Officer Wilson and crew had bombed the target and were making their way back to Marham. Either due to damage or navigational error they requested a number of fixes on the return route. One of the first was timed at 04:02 hours, a second-class fix from Hull positioned them well off-track west of Saint-Omer. Sixteen minutes later another fix had them slightly north-east of Arras. While P/O Wilson was groping his way around France desperate to establish his position back at Marham the first crews had already landed from Hanover and making their way to de-briefing. Soon after the last fix at 04:18 hours, the Wellington crashed near Ferques, six miles south of the Pas-de-Calais. There was only one survivor, the rear gunner Sgt Roy

Barnard. The cause of the loss is unclear. Unconfirmed reports suggest that the aircraft run out of fuel and the 26-year-old pilot attempted a crash landing. The bodies of the crew were initially buried with full military honours in the Soldiers Cemetery near Chateau de Ledquent, near Marquise France. Tragically this was P/O Winston Wilson's first operation as captain. He had previously completed ten trips learning the ropes besides the experienced S/Ldr Denis Clyde Smith. The second pilot, Sgt James Cottingham, was undertaking his first operation with P/O Wilson, he would have soon been captaining his own crew having completed six trips.

### Thursday 14th August 1941
*Vickers Wellington*
*Mk.Ic  X9753 HA-G 'George'*
*Contract No : B124362/40*
*Taken On Charge : 27/07/1941*
***Failed To Return***
*Pilot : Pilot Officer Winston Claude Wilson, 87444 RAFVR **Killed***
*2nd Pilot : Sergeant James Charles Cottingham, 930649 RAFVR **Killed***
*Navigator: Sergeant Gordon Alexander Munro, 998367 RAFVR **Killed***
*Front Gunner : Sergeant Peter Prosser, 994378 RAFVR **Killed***
*1st Wireless Operator : Sergeant Alexander Ian Pryce Anderson, 909949 RAFVR, **Killed***
*Rear Gunner : Sergeant Roy Barnard, 1375489 RAFVR PoW*


Across the airfield, No.115 Squadron recorded the loss of a crew who ditched in the North Sea. Three Wellingtons were sent to search one of which found a dinghy and all the crew who appeared quite cheerful. The captain of the Wellington dropped rations and then gained height to radio back to base the crew's location. Sadly, it was the last time the crew were seen. The squadron was ordered to prepare for a raid on the 17th, this was subsequently cancelled due to thundery conditions over the bases. The following night with an improvement in the weather the railway yards at Duisburg would be attacked by seven crews. A further two Wellington Mk.IIs would visit Cologne. Sadly, the run of bad luck would continue.

Cloud over the target caused problems identifying the railway yards, a few separate fires were observed none of which appeared near the aiming point. Sergeants Tucker and Dare both reported their bombs falling across the general target area. They were the only positive comments from an otherwise frustrating night. Sergeant Kenneth Fisher dropped his all HE load from 14,000 feet at 0203 hours. Satisfied that their second operation as a crew was complete, they landed back at RAF Marham. It was as the tired crew were clambering out of the aircraft a shocked armourer informed them that their single one-thousand pounder and five 500 pounders were still on board! One can only imagine their horror! Somehow the bombs had failed to drop, and more alarming the observer and pilots had failed to notice!

*The mangled wreckage of Vickers Wellington Mk.Ic  X9753 HA-G 'George.*

There was one crew missing from Duisburg, skippered by the experienced Sergeant Kenneth 'Ken' Shearing. At 0206 hours Wellington N2844 HA-M was intercepted and shot down over the Zuider Zee by Fw Siegfried Ney of 4./NJG1. The blazing bomber crashed a few miles north of Den Oever at a location referred to as Afsluitdijk. There were no survivors. The body of the young pilot and two of his crew were never found and are presumed still with the aircraft. The sea would provide three bodies over the coming months. All would wash ashore. The first on September 1st was that of the rear gunner, P/O Pockney. The thirty-five-year-old was found near Lemmer. He was buried in the Lemmer General Cemetery on September 3rd. On October 8th, the body of Sergeant Roy Boswell the 2nd pilot washed ashore at 'Afsluit Dijk' dam. The last crew member to be found was the RAAF observer, Sgt Alexander Wilson, who washed ashore at Oude Zeug on October 12th. The 31-year-old was initially buried in the Military Cemetery at Huis Duinen near Den Helder on the 14th.

A highly popular individual in his hometown back in Australia, the news of his death, resulted in the town's flags being run at half-mast and a two-minute silence observed. Older than most this New Zealand born airman's dream was to become a pilot. However, this was dashed. Nevertheless, he reapplied for observer training in the hope that this

*Sergeant Ken Shearing enjoying his pipe. The young pilot's body was never found. He along with two of his crew mates are remembered on the walls of the Runnymede Memorial*

would speed up his involvement in the war and active service. Sergeant Kenneth Charles Shearing was lost on his 23rd operation, seventh as captain. He was one of those captains that appeared not to have a steady crew. Over the six previous operations, he had flown with four different wireless operators, five different front gunners, and five rear gunners. The only regular crewmember was his fellow pilot, Sergeant Roy Boswell. Roy had been on the squadron less than a month and had completed six operations all alongside Kenneth.

*Vickers Armstrong built Mk.IC N2844 HA-M. The aircraft arrived on the squadron November 11th, 1940 via No.44 MU. It was not until December 29th, 1940 that Sgt Donald Hoos took N2844 to the docks of Boulogne on what would be the first of 27 raids it would fly with the squadron. The Wellington failed to return from Duisburg on August 18th, 1941. Note the reapplication of the squadron codes and reduced RAF roundel.*

*Fw Siegfried Ney 4./NJG1. He claimed the destruction of Wellington N2844 HA-M on August 18th and Wellington X9674 HA-A on the night of October 31st, 1941. The photograph was taken around March 1941.*

**Monday 18th August 1941**

*Vickers Wellington*
*Mk.Ic N2844 HA-M 'Monkey'*
*Contract No : 992424/39*
*Taken On Charge : 11/11/1940*
**Failed To Return**
*Pilot : Pilot Officer Kenneth Charles Shearing, 758034 RAFVR **Missing***
*2nd Pilot : Sergeant Roy Gerald Boswell, 622252 RAF **Killed***
*Navigator: Sergeant Alexander MacGregor Wilson, 400314 RAAF **Killed***
*Front Gunner : Sydney Arthur Maguire, 1378011 RAFVR **Missing***
*1st Wireless Operator : Sergeant Lothian Julyan George, R/69557 RCAF, **Missing***
*Rear Gunner : Pilot Officer Ewart Duncan Pockney 76925 RAFVR, **Killed***

The Group provided just three Wellingtons on the attack on Cologne. Two were supplied by 218 Squadron, while 115 Squadron provided the third. The small Marham force would join a predominately Hampden contingent and a few Whitleys provided by No.4 Group. Sergeant McBride delivered his 4000 pounder from 15,000 feet which was dropped on the west bank producing a huge explosion which the crew described as a '*large mushroom*'. Unfortunately the crew of Sgt Huckle flying Wellington Mk.II W5457 HA-Z were intercepted on route to Cologne by Ofw Gerhard Herzog of 3./NJG1 after being held by searchlights. The encounter was short and vicious. Fortunately, on this occasion, most of the crew managed to take to their parachutes when at 70000 feet. The Wellington smashed into the ground at Azfeld at 02:30 hours sadly taking with it the crews front gunner Sgt Robert 'Bert' McKinnell. The pilot, Sgt Huckle records the final desperate moments aboard the bomber.

*'My crew, all except Sgt McKinnell, managed to bail out, he did not due I believe to fear. The Germans who captured me informed me that he was found under the aircraft with his chute on, sadly dead. When I bailed out, I was under the impression that all the others had left the aircraft. But as I went out the hatch, I saw McKinnell crouched over the bombsight with his chute clipped on, and he was staring out through the hatch. I called to him as I left the aircraft as I was unable to stop myself'.*

The body of the young Scotsman was initially buried with Full Military Honours in the Azfeld Eiffel Churchyard but was re-interred in the Rheinberg War Cemetery in August 1948. Born 1920 in Troqueer, Kirkcudbrightshire he was the Son of Robert and Elizabeth (Jolly) McKinnell from Dumfries. Pre-war he was a keen member of the Laurieknowe Church choir and the church football team. Thirty-year-old George Huckle had arrived on the squadron in April of completion of his training at No.20 OTU. He had flown the customary 2nd pilot's operations with Sgt Edward Chidgey completing ten operations by his side. On collecting his own crew, he undertook a further eight operations as captain. Sergeant Roy Pridham had completed seven operations since joining the squadron in July, all were flown with Sgt Huckle.

## Monday 18th August 1941
*Vickers Wellington*
*Mk.II  W5457 HA-Z 'Zebra'*
*Contract No : 38600/39*
*Taken On Charge : 28/05/1941*
### Failed To Return
*Pilot : Sergeant Henry George Huckle, 904171 RAFVR PoW*
*2nd Pilot : Sergeant Roy Kenneth Pridham, 1165303 RAFVR, PoW*
*Observer :  Sergeant Adrian John Condon, 407017 RAAF, PoW*
*Front Gunner : Sergeant Robert Smith McKinnell 998292 RAFVR,* **Killed**
*1st Wireless Operator : Sergeant Andrew Learmonth 1051248 RAFVR, PoW*
*Rear Gunner ; Sergeant Leslie Stephens, 1377640 RAFVR, PoW*

It would have been a subdued mess the following morning, two more crews 'Gone for Burton'. Both well into their tours, August was fast becoming a costly month.

On August 18th, the long-awaited Butt Report was finally released, its findings come as an unpleasant shock to many. The report initiated by Lord Cherwell produced a storm of disbelief both in the Cabinet and Air Ministry who typically looked to someone to point the blame. David Bensusan-Butt had methodically scrutinised over 600 target photos taken between June and July and compared them with crew's post raid debriefing notes. From examining the report to the actual photographs, he concluded.

*a) Of those aircraft recorded as attacking their target, only one in three got within 5 miles.*

*b) Over the French ports, the proportion was two in three; over Germany as a whole, the proportion was one in four; over the Ruhr, it was only one in ten.*

*c) In the full moon, the proportion was two in five; in the new moon, it was only one in fifteen.*

*d) All these figures relate only to aircraft recorded as attacking the target; the proportion of the total sorties which reached within 5 miles is less than one-third. ...*

The startling conclusion seemed to follow that only about one-third of aircraft claiming to reach their target actually reached it. Naturally, senior

*2nd Pilot Sergeant Roy Kenneth Pridham completed 7 operations in the right-hand seat before becoming a Prisoner of War.*

*His Excellency Sir Alan Burns Governor Designate of the Gold Coast inspects the crews outside A Flight Hangar, note the smashed windows. Behind Sir Alan is the unmistakable figure of Group Captain McKee DFC AFC.*

Air Staff were outwardly sceptical of the findings. However, behind closed doors, they were furious that the Commands hard work and accomplishments over the previous years had been put in doubt. Slighted, Senior RAF commanders argued that the Butt report's statistics were faulty and immediately commissioned another report. Despite the repercussions at the senior level, the aircrew and squadron commanders were aware of the problems facing them. With limited navigational equipment and bombing aids almost non-existent the accuracy of any raid depended on two factors, the weather, and the tenacity of the crews. On August 20th, His Excellency Sir Alan Burns Governor Designate of the Gold Coast, accompanied by Mr Sabine of the Colonial Office arrived at RAF Marham just after midday to inspect the squadron. They were met by the Air Officer Commanding No.3 Group, Air Vice Marshal Baldwin and Marham's Station Commander, Group Captain McKee DFC AFC. The visit was to officially recognise the adoption of the squadron by the people of the Gold Coast. Always escorted by the Station Commander, the honoured guests visited the Operations Room and other sections in the Station Headquarters. On completion of this part of the visit, the AoC bade farewell leaving by air. The Governor and Mr Sabine were driven to the Mess where squadron personnel were introduced in the Ante Room. An 'After lunch drinks' was arranged in the 'Ladies Room'. Attended by Group Captain McKee DFC AFC, Squadron Leader Price DFC who was acting on behalf of Wing Commander Kirkpatrick, Lieutenant Colonel Clarke, Squadron Leader Parkin, Squadron Leader Spence, Squadron Leader Bruce, Flight Lieutenants Hoare, Taylor, Isbell DFC and finally F/Lt Dunham. After lunch, a parade of the entire squadron personnel who could be spared from essential duties was inspected by his Excellency outside 'A' Flight hangar. His Excellency took the salute standing on a dais as the Squadron and Squadron band marched past. A tour of the airfield was then undertaken, here Sir Allan was able to see a number of hastily painted Wellingtons christened with towns in the Gold Coast. Finally, the NCO aircrews were presented in "A" Flights crew room. After the inspection, the Governor had tea with senior officers, and later dinner. During the evening he attended a station boxing match. Before departing, Sir Alan asked if the Squadron would appreciate some small gift from the peoples of the Gold Coast. The squadron's medical officer, F/Lt Phillips, suggested a 'sun-ray-lamp', Sir Allan promised to see what he could do.

With its adoption by the peoples of the Gold Coast, the squadron would officially be known as No.218 (Gold Coast) Squadron. The choice of name was intended partly as a compliment and, partly as a means of associating outlying parts of the Empire as closely as possible with the overall war effort. In an attempt to bond the squadron and the peoples of the Gold Coast even closer, a number of the squadron's Wellingtons had the names of local towns and cities applied to them.

The squadron welcomed a tall, tough-looking New Zealander on the 21st who would over the coming months carve out a reputation on the squadron. His name was Phillip Lamason, he and his crew arrived from No.23 OTU to begin their tour. On the 26th 'B' Flight carried out a low-level bombing exercise on the light tanks of the 5th Royal Inniskilling Dragoon Guards at the artillery and bombing range at Grimston Warren, Norfolk. It was reminiscent of the activities flown by the squadron pre-war and more recently in France with the BEF.

No operations were flown until the 26th when Sergeant John Thompson and crew were detailed and briefed for a 'Freshman' trip to Boulogne Docks. The mixed HE and incendiary load were seen to explode between docks 4 and 6, producing a small fire. They were back at their dispersal with 3½ hours of take-off. Eight crews were part of a small force of No.3 Group Wellingtons provide to attack Mannheim on the 27th. The night's operation would not start well and would quickly get worse. The experienced Sergeant Rose managed to taxi into a barbed wire fence as he manoeuvred to take off. Despite both the crews and ground crews' best intentions Wellington R1601 HA-T and its crew were not going to participate in the night's activities. The remaining crews departed just before 21:00 hours. There was one early return. The usually dependable Merlin Mk.IIs notched up their first abort when Sergeant Banks was obliged to bomb the aerodrome at Haamstede. Having reached as far as Trier the crew wisely decided to seek an alternative target when the port engine aboard W5449 HA-Y began showing signs of trouble. Over the target, the

*His Excellency Sir Alan Burns takes the salute standing on a dais as the station band and personnel march past.*

bombers found Mannheim free of cloud although there was some ground haze. For once no incendiaries were carried, the Wellingtons were loaded entirely with  High  Explosive which were dropped

*Above: A member of the ground crew paints the name 'Akyem Abuakwa' on the nose of Wellington R1448 HA-L. This was a powerful kingdom of the Akyem people of the Eastern Gold Coast.   Below: Squadron Leader Price DFC and His Excellency Sir Alan Burns pose in front a squadron Wellington. The Wellington has been named 'Mamprusi' a native tribe of northern region of the Gold Coast.*

from between 13000 feet to 16000 feet. Crews were confident that the raid was a success, numerous fires were reported close to the aiming point as the participating crews turned for home from what was an uncannily quiet operation. Returning from Mannheim were two pilots back from their first operation, Sgt James Hinwood had accompanied Sgt Lowe and crew while Irishman Sgt William Gregg joined the crew of Sgt Banks.

While the squadron was returning from Germany, a Ju88 Intruder of I./NJG2 carried out a low-level attack on Marham. At around 01:55 hours, it dropped ten bombs from 200 feet, the damage was slight, but the Drem light system and flare path were temporally put out of action, more worryingly was one bomb failed to explode. The decision was quickly taken to divert both squadrons if the station could not be repaired and cleared in time for the return of the squadron. Two of the squadron crews safely diverted, while two crashed, one at base the other at RAF West Raynham. Sergeant Fisher crash-landed Wellington R1596 HA-O on Marham's flare path when his windscreen oiled resulting in a blind landing, the undercarriage collapsed but no one was injured. The Wellington required the attention of No.43 MU. It would be two months before it returned to operations. Sergeant James McBride severely damaged Wellington X9663 HA-D when he undershot his approach while landing at RAF West Raynham resulting in extensive damage to the port engine, port undercarriage and bomb-beam. The pilot was slightly injured, but the remaining crew all escaped unharmed, the Wellington never returned to the squadron.

### Wednesday  27th August 1941
*Vickers Wellington*
*Mk.Ic R1596 HA-O 'Orange'*
*Contract No : B992424/39*
*Taken On Charge : 12/04/1941*
*Crashed on Return*
*To : No.43 M.U*
*Sergeant Kenneth Fisher and Crew*


### Wednesday  27th August 1941
*Vickers Wellington*
*Mk.Ic X9663 HA-D 'Don'*
*Contract No : B97887/39*
*Taken On Charge :*
*Crashed on Return*
*To : No.43 MU*
*Sergeant James McBride and Crew*


Number 115 Squadron lost three Wellingtons on return, the crew S/Ldr Sindall bailed out of their Wellington when fuel become critical, the aircraft crashing near Alburgh, Norfolk. Flight Lieutenant Pooley's Wellington crashed short of fuel near North Walsham the crew again taking to their parachutes. Finally, F/Lt Foster crashed at RAF West Raynham in poor visibility, the aircraft catching fire, but not before all the crew escaped uninjured.

Nine crews were involved in the raid directed against Mannheim on the 29th. Participating was W/Cdr Kirkpatrick back from his enforced spell of sick leave. The crews were airborne just after 2100 hours. There was only one early return. Sergeant Dare encountered a severe electrical storm and icing south of Bruges, forcing him to jettison his entire bomb load and returned to Marham. Conditions over the target were not ideal, 10/10th cloud preventing visual identification of the aiming point. Sergeant Rose flying the Merlin-

301

powered Mk.II W5449 HA-Y reported that his single bomb was dropped on the approximate area of the aiming point. The squadron's other Wellington Mk.II, W5447 HA-C, was being flown by Squadron Leader Gibbs. He was forced to drop his 4000 pounder on ETA. The only crew to see anything of the target was that Sgt John Thompson. This was Thompson's second operation as captain. He reported, *'Bombs fell 100 yards south of existing fires in two large buildings 1/4 mile north of aiming point D. Target identified by double canal north of aiming point D.*

While the squadron was over Germany, Sgt Robert Banks with Sgt Edward 'Ted' Crosswell flying as second pilot attacked Le Havre dropping their mixed load from 12,000 feet on the docks. It was a disappointing end to a torrid month for the squadron and Bomber Command. The publication of the Butt Report had dampened the crew's spirits but had not affected the squadron's commitment to press home their attacks despite the negative views expressed from certain quarters. The loss of six crews, including its commanding officer however did have an effect. Not since the frantic action over France and Belgium in May 1940 had the squadron suffered such crippling losses. The only positive was the return of the respected Wing Commander Kirkpatrick now recovered from the incident in July.

The cathedral city of Cologne was the target for the first raid on September 1st. Eight crews were briefed, S/Ldr Gibbs would be the senior captain, the remaining seven crews were all captained by sergeant pilots. Sergeant McBride was able to take off when the hydraulics to the front turret aboard the Wellington Mk.II W5447 HA-C ruptured forcing him to abandon the operation. Once again, the squadron recorded the early return of a crew. Sergeant Forster suffered port engine malfunction over Holland resulting in the bombs being jettisoned safe. The good weather over England was not replicated over Cologne, low cloud and haze making accurate bombing difficult. Despite the conditions, the crews used what landmarks were available and with some difficulty pressed home their attack.

Sergeant Dare dropped his 4000 pounder on a built-up area on the west side of the river but was disappointed when the expected explosion failed to happen. Carrying out his first operation since his arrival from No.7 Squadron was Squadron Leader Gerald Spence MiD who joined the crew of 'A' Flight commander, S/Ldr Gibbs. Sergeant Basil Forster was declared tour expired on return from Cologne having flown an impressive 33 operation since his arrival from No.15 O.T.U in February. After the usual end of tour drinks in the mess, he was sent on a Flying Instructors Course before posting to No.21 O.T.U based at RAF Moreton-in-the-Marsh. He returned to operations in 1944 flying the Avro Lancaster with No.195 Squadron based at RAF Wratting Common. He would command 'B' Flight and completed a further 15 operations. Promoted to squadron leader, he ended the war with a well-earned DFC and retired from the RAF in 1960 as Wing Commander Forster MBE, DFC AFC.

It was a welcome switch to the E-Boat Base and torpedo dump at the Port of Ostend on the 2nd, only four crews were detailed from Marham, all from 218 Squadron. Squadron Leader Gibbs DFC took off just after 2022 hours at the helm of a brand-new Wellington, X9810 HA-K. Sitting alongside Gibbs on his first trip was twenty-one-year-old Sgt Terrence Helfer. The crew had just bombed and were leaving the target area when hit by flak. What followed was a remarkable fight for survival, the following is taken from a newspaper published at the time.

*Vickers Wellington Mk.Ic X9787 HA-S. Note the odd shaped code letter S*

A remarkable story of how a RAF squadron leader, trapped underneath the water in a bomber which had come down in the sea fought his way out, and then, half drowning, was supported in the sea by his front gunner until he could reach the dinghy. Near Ostend a shell from a heavy anti-aircraft gun burst directly under the bomber with what the pilot described as a "sickening bump". Down went the aircraft almost out of control with its engines racing alarmingly. At about 4000 feet above the sea, the pilot managed to steady the engines and to flatten out. The bomb doors and landing gear had dropped down and the petrol and oil pipes appeared to be damaged. There was nothing to do but turn for home.

The crew were ordered to throw overboard everything that was moveable, but even after this had been done the bomber still was not light enough to maintain height. Both engines were missing badly, and after a time the aircraft began to drop at a rate of about 500ft a minute. Nose heavy, it touched the water at about 90mph, bounced and then came down on the port wing and crashed into the sea. The fuselage was almost broken in two. Four of the crew managed to get out through the break, but the pilot, who had got stuck to his controls, and the front gunner, who had come out of his turret and gone back beside the observers seat were trapped inside the aircraft. The pilot's cockpit, with the pilot still in it was about 10 ft under the sea, but the front gunner, now further back in the aircraft was above the level of the water. The bomber had caught fire after it had come down, and now with its tail and part of the fuselage out of the water was sinking fast. "the first thing I realised was that I was down beside the bombsight in the nose of the aircraft" said the pilot. "I could feel the bombsight under the water. I struggled back to my seat and then tried to get out through the pilots escape hatch, but I could not because half of it was jammed and with my full kit on, I could not get through. For a moment I gave up.

It did not seem possible I could get away with it. The whole of the front of the aircraft was completely underwater. I held my breath for as long as I could, and then began taking in water. At times it was a great relief not to hold my breath. I was albeit drowned when I saw a bright light above me.. I then saw more lights further up. I don't know how long I was under water, but when I was near to the second light, I found there was break in the fuselage. The sergeant front gunner was just getting through it. I was in a pretty bad way, but I was still conscious. As I got my head above the water I saw a dinghy, and with the help of the sergeant, who was in a better shape than I, I started swimming towards it. The rest of the crew were already in the dinghy and they began paddling towards us. While we were in the water the sergeant tried to blow up my flotation jacket with his mouth, but he could not manage it. I can remember telling him to go and leave me but be wouldn't leave me. I cannot remember getting into the dinghy. I can only remember an eternity with my head under the water. I can remember the crew telling me to sit up, and then helping me to do so. I could not even talk, it was just too painful. I spent the whole night trying to get the salt water out of my lungs". For three days the crew drifted in the sea, on the first morning visibility was only about 200 yards. A bell was heard by the men and using the tins as paddles, they made towards the sound. The mist began to clear, and they saw a boat in the distance. The tide was running strongly towards it, but it was too strong, and they were swept past it when it was only 200 yards away. In the late afternoon they saw the masts of a sunken ship. Each of the crew took it in turns to keep watch. On the second morning the pilot, according to the rest of the crew, was stronger than any of them. " I was sore around the ribs that's all" he said. Some hours after dawn, another buoy was sighted, this time the current defeated them when they got to within 20 yards of it. For the rest of the day, they continued to drift about in the dinghy. They rationed carefully their supplies of water, biscuits, malted milk tablets and chewing gum. All the time they were getting nearer to the English coast, and on the third day they could see buildings on the shore and could hear trains running in the distance. But they were still being washed in the out by the tides. They had come down in the sea at 10 o'clock on the night of Tuesday September 2nd. On Friday night, September 5th at 1145 the tide carried them near enough to the coast to enable them to paddle ashore.

The weary crew finally came ashore near Margate, Kent. They could not have landed at a more heavily defended and mined area on the South coast. Having presumed that the crew were lost, the operations room at Marham received the welcome news from RAF Manston that the crew were in fact safe, if but exhausted. It was Squadron Leaders Gibbs 36th operation, and last with 218 Squadron.

### Tuesday 2nd September 1941
*Vickers Wellington*
*Mk.Ic  X9810 HA-K 'King'*
*Contract No : B97887/39*
*Taken On Charge : 23/08/1941*
### Failed To Return
*Pilot:  Squadron Leader Augustus Rodney Gibbs DFC 267505*
*2nd Pilot: Sergeant Terence Helfer, 1186112 RAFVR Injured slight burns.*
*Observer: Sergeant Reginald Lawrence Ross, 92779 RAFVR*
*Front Gunner: Sergeant Jack Purcell, 1169029 RAFVR Injured, sprained ankle.*
*1st Wireless Operator: Sergeant James Adamson, 1050913 RAFVR*
*Rear Gunner : Sergeant Kenneth William George England, 1375251 RAFVR*

After a period of sick leave, S/Ldr Gibbs DFC was eventually posted to RAF Waterbeach. He would return to operations in 1943 with the Wellington equipped No.142 Squadron. On August 16th, 1943 he took off from the Tunisian airfield at Hani West to bomb the marshalling yards at Viterbo, Italy, he never returned.

There was no let-up the following night when ten crews joined over 100 bombers on an attack directed against the 'Toads' at Brest. All the crews managed to become airborne despite the fear of fog on return. Yet again the squadron chalked up an early arrival, on this occasion, it was Sgt Banks. Both engines aboard Wellington R1511 HA-L began to show signs of overheating giving him no option than turn for home. The squadron arrived over Brest to find it strangely quiet, visibility was excellent, but the usual smokescreen hampered identifying the aiming point. Unbeknown to the squadrons of 3 Group, the bombers of No.1, 4 and 5 Group had been recalled due to the likelihood of widespread fog on return. Somehow the recall message had not been received by 3 Group who continued alone. The usual vicious flak met the crews as they bombed between 10,000 feet and 14,500 feet. With just the 3 Group squadrons over the target, the crews ran the gauntlet of both flak and searchlights. Sergeant Lowe and P/O Ralph were both coned on their bomb run. Both managed to escape by taking violent evasive action, but in doing so, were unable to observe the accuracy of their bombing. The only positives from an otherwise disappointing raid was a number of returning crews claimed that explosions had been seen across No.1 Dock. On return to England, the weather had clamped down, forcing the squadrons to divert. Five of the squadron's crews landed at RAF Alconbury, while the remainder managed to find sanctuary at Mildenhall and Wyton. The squadron was informed that it would be required for an operation to Kiel on the 5th, but this was cancelled late afternoon. The following day the squadron was detailed for an attack on Huls this too was cancelled due to weather. Bomber Command turned its attention to Berlin (Whitebait) on the 7th, a respectable ten crews were detailed and would join over 180 bombers on this most distant and difficult of targets. Number 3 Group made up the bulk of the bombers involved providing 75 aircraft. Every 3 Group squadron was operating on this night.

Two of the squadrons most senior captain's names were chalked up on the operations board, W/Cdr Kirkpatrick and 'A' Flight Commander, S/Ldr Price DFC. Both took along for the experience new arrivals. Welshmen Sgt Maldwyn Griffiths accompanied the commanding officer while Sergeant John Webber joined his flight commander in Wellington Mk.II W5449 HA-Y.

### No.3 Group Form B.603 - 7/8th September 1941

| Base | Squadron | Berlin (Whitebait) | Kiel (Ant) | Boulogne CC.29(a) |
|---|---|---|---|---|
| Mildenhall | 149 Squadron | 6 Wellingtons | 2 Wellingtons | 4 Wellingtons |
| Honington | 9 Squadron | 7 Wellingtons | 3 Wellingtons | 1 Wellington |
| Honington | 311 (Czech) Squadron | 6 Wellingtons | 3 Wellingtons | |
| Marham | 115 Squadron | 7 Wellingtons | 3 Wellingtons | 2 Wellingtons |
| Marham | 218 Squadron | 10 Wellingtons | | 2 Wellingtons |

| Wyton | 15 Squadron | 7 Stirlings | 1 Stirling | |
|---|---|---|---|---|
| Wyton | 40 Squadron | 3 Wellingtons | 3 Wellingtons | 3 Wellingtons |
| Oakington | 101 Squadron | 7 Wellingtons | 2 Wellingtons | |
| Oakington | 7 Squadron | 5 Stirlings | 2 Stirlings | |
| Feltwell | 75(NZ) Squadron | | | 1 Wellington |
| Feltwell | 57 Squadron | | | 2 Wellingtons |
| Stradishall | 214 Squadron | 10 Wellingtons | 1 Wellington | |
| Stradishall | 138 (SD) Squadron | | | |
| Waterbeach | 99 Squadron | 7 Wellingtons | 2 Wellingtons | 4 Wellingtons |
| **TOTALS** | | **75 aircraft** | **22 aircraft** | **19 aircraft** |

*The above table shows the contribution of No.3 Group, which was from the very start of the war, one of the most potent bomber groups.*

There was one incident just before take-off when the crew of F/O Ralph were all electrocuted while running up the engines aboard Wellington R1025 HA-J. Such was the force of the electrical current that the rear gunner, P/O Dalton was completely knocked out. It was a peculiar accident that resulted in the crew being withdrawn from the raid.

With an improvement in the weather the squadron as well as the rest of No.3 Group departed their East Anglian bases and crossed the North Sea without trouble from either cloud or fog. A total of 13 early returns marred the group's contribution, one of this number was the crew of Sgt Dare within an hour of take-off. His starboard engine started cutting out just as he crossed the Norfolk coast 10 miles off Cromer, the mixed bomb load was jettisoned into the sea. Berlin was spared another bomb load when the crew of Sgt Banks was forced to bomb Magdeburg at 23:15 hours when the front gunner became ill and was unable to operate his turret. Sergeant Robert Banks was on his 24th operation having arrived on the squadron via No.20 OTU in April. A dark, stocky individual he had recently taken over the crew of P/O Langley when they arrived via No.15 OTU on August 29th. The union was not a happy one. Many fires were visible the closer to Berlin the crews become. Visibility was excellent, allowing the observers huddled over their bombsights time to affix their position and more importantly identify the aiming point. All the crews dropped their bombs over Berlin. Sergeant McBride reporting, *'One stick SE-NW. Bursts were seen on the aiming point. Target easily identified by moonlight on water, large red fires seen on arrival'*. Squadron Leader Price DFC reported his 4000 pounder; *' Bomb fell just west of aiming point exploding satisfactorily'*.

Useful damage was reported in Berlin's eastern district of Lichtenberg and the more northern district of Pankow, including four war-producing factories and ten transport centres. Given the excellent conditions it was no surprise that the German defences were active, and inflicted Bomber Commands highest loss rate thus far, 15 bombers shot down. This figure would have been higher if it had not been for the flying skill of Squadron Leader Price. The crew had just crossed the Dutch coast when the port engine caught fire. The following is transcribed from a BBC radio recording given by S/Ldr Price DFC in 1941.

*This was my 50th raid, and somehow it seemed very fitting to celebrate a half-century with a trip to Berlin. I had been there three times before, but none of the previous raids came anywhere near this one. Which as you know was the biggest yet made against Berlin. Our squadron, which is incidentally the 'Gold Coast' Squadron formed part of a very powerful force that Bomber Command put out. We could see the western defences of Berlin, the Flak and the searchlights in action when we were still forty miles away. They seemed very busy, and we knew the earlier aircraft were doing their stuff. It was obvious from all the activities that there was a continuous procession of bombers over the city.*

*Just south of Berlin we saw one of our bombers very low down caught in a cone of searchlights. He was so low that the searchlights were running almost parallel to the ground. I think it was held for at least 3 or 4 minutes then an enemy fighter attacked him. My crew saw more of it than I did because I was rather busy keeping an eye on the flak and searchlights. The crew said they saw tracers shooting between the two aircraft and the next thing they reported was the fighter was going down in flames and exploded on the ground. There were five big fires already going when we got to Berlin. These were orange and red fires with masses of smoke and flames, two of them were nearly in the centre of the city. We flew over and had a look at one of them. You could see buildings ablaze with flames coming out of the window. Conditions were absolutely ideal for bombing. The moon was so bright that if we were flying at the same height in daylight, we could have hardly seen more. Streets, buildings and railway lines, everything stood out absolutely clearly. Perhaps it will give you some idea how bright it was when I say I could even pick out the Brandenburger Tor. Everything was in our favour. You don't often get it as good as that. There was not even a bit of haze to cover the city. We had our set target, which was one of the big railway stations, but in fact, we could have bombed anywhere we liked, in other words, we had the city at our mercy as it were. We got to Berlin about a quarter of an hour after midnight, and we left about quarter to one. During that time we saw a number of other people bombing, then we dropped our bomb. We were carrying on of the new bombs. Some humourist had written on it " This might have been a leaflet". When it went off, there was a mighty explosion which lit up the sky. Our wing commander, who was at this time on his way home, told me afterwards that he saw this terrific flash over his shoulder and called out to ask what on earth had happened. The rear gunner told him it was one of the big bombs going off.*

*Then out we came the same way we had gone in, again here we did not have much trouble. We had a grand journey back almost flak and searchlight free. But just after crossing the Dutch coast, the port engine started backfiring and caught alight. But the second pilot who was flying the aircraft at the time-pressed the extinguisher and put out the flames. The engine went on backfiring and eventually failed altogether. We threw out a bit of stuff to make the plane lighter and came along very nicely on one engine. When we got back over the aerodrome that engine packed-up too and we kind of half stalled, I saw a nice-looking field and decided to put down in that. But just as we were going in a haystack loomed up in front, but I don't know how I managed it, but I got the aircraft rising again and up we went over the haystack and some trees, plus some telegraph wires and we landed in the next field. Fortunately, no one had been hurt. No sooner than we landed than up come three Home Guard with rifles at the ready, but when they saw the Wellington*

*A happy bunch of 'B' Flight NCO airmen pose for a photograph 1941*

*Back row: Sgt Barton, R/G (Killed) - Sgt Knott Wop/Ag (PoW) - Sgt Clarke, Wop/Ag – Sgt Hartley, Wop/Ag (Killed) Sgt Huckle, Pilot, (PoW) Sgt Harrison, F/G (Killed) - Sgt Salisbury – Sgt Alexander, Obs, (PoW) Sgt Hutchinson R/G (Killed) - Sgt Wilkes, F/G - Sgt Workman, Pilot – Sgt Banks, Pilot and Sgt Baird, Wop/Ag (Killed)*

### Front Row

*Front row: Sgt Fraser, Pilot (Killed) – Sgt Kolitz, R/G (Killed) - Sgt Riding, R/G – Sgt Chidgey, Pilot - Sgt Graham, Pilot and Sgt Vandervoord, Pilot.*

everything was "alright". When we got back to the aerodrome and talked things over with the rest of the crews who had been out, we were all convinced that this raid on Berlin was one of the most successful we had ever been on anywhere.'

The Wellington landed in a wheat field at Hall Farm, Barton Bendish a few miles south of Marham at 0430 hours. Thankfully, none of the crew was injured due to airmanship of S/Ldr Price. The Wellington which had only arrived from 115 Squadron on August 2nd had notched up five raids before it was SoC

### Sunday 7th September 1941

*Vickers Wellington*
*Mk.II  W5449 HA-Y 'Yorker'*
*Contract No : 38600/39*
*Taken On Charge : 02/08/1941*
*Crashed landed.*
*SoC*
*Pilot :  Squadron Leader Herbert Price DFC*
*2nd Pilot : Sergeant John Webber*

Two more pilots making their operational debut on the squadron this night were New Zealanders Sgts Phil Lamason and Ivan McPhail. Sergeant Lamason joined the crew of Australian Sgt Alan McLean who along with Sgt Roland Brewerton and McPhail were briefed to bomb the docks at Boulogne. In what was described as brilliant moonlight, the crews carried out an effective attack. Both managed to watch as their mixed bomb loads exploded across docks 4 and 7 producing several fires. These fires were still visible 40-50 miles on the return trip. The squadron's ranks were bolstered by the appearance of an experienced New Zealander on the 9th, fresh from a stint at No.3 Training Flight. His name was Flying Officer Arthur George Lee Humphreys.

There was a great deal of excitement around the squadron on the 10th. The squadron would be making its first visit across the Alps to Italy. The target for the squadrons of Marham was the Royal Arsenal at Turin while other squadrons would be attacking Turin's main railway station. Due to the range the Wellingtons were fitted with long-range tanks and the usual standard bomb load was dramatically reduced to around 1,500lb. One of the first names chalked up for the operations board was S/Ldr Price DFC. The recent Berlin incident had been quickly forgotten and this trip across the Alps was very much something that appealed to him and his crew. The crews began to lift off at around 1940 hours. They joined 44 other aircraft drawn from No.3 Group as they made their way towards the south coast. This number was quickly whittled down when 11 aircraft returned early. Nine of the early returns were based at RAF Wyton who provided 8 Wellingtons and 7 Stirling's. Wellington X9674 HA-H flown by Sergeant John Thompson was obliged to jettison part of his load when the hastily fitted long-range tanks became faulty. There was a great deal resting on the navigational skills of the observers as the bombers flew south crossing the French coast and deep into the south of France. This was unknown territory for most of the observers accustomed to attacks on the French coast and Germany. Thankfully, the weather conditions were ideal, almost unlimited visibility allowed the crews to pick out landmarks to establish the aircraft's position. Soon the imposing snow-capped Alps loomed ahead and once cleared Turin was only another few minute's flying time. Surrounded on the western and northern side by the Alps and the eastern side by the high hills of the Monferrato. With four major rivers passing through the city, the Po and three of its tributaries it was not a hard target to locate. Quickly identified by the crews they began their attack. Haze over the Royal Arsenal and smoke from the previous attackers caused some anxiety as the first bombs were dropped from between 12,000 - 15,000 feet. Most crews bombed on existing fires reporting a number of large explosions in the process. One crew not content to attack from the briefed height was that of S/Ldr Price DFC. They bombed from the perilously low altitude of 2,000 feet dropping their mixed load 1/2 mile south of the aiming point. On their return, the crew reported that a *'Big square building blazed-up very quickly.'* Thankfully, there was little in the way of serious opposition from the defenders of Turin. The biggest danger, especially for the crew of S/Ldr Price, was being bombed from above. As the squadron crews started their climb back over the Alps numerous fires were still burning and visible 20 miles distant. Surprisingly, the force encountered no opposition on the return route, the first crew to land back at Marham was P/O Livingstone. He had been airborne for 8 hours 30 minutes. As expected, the last crew to land was that of S/Ldr Price, he and his crew touched down after being aloft for a staggering nine hours thirty-six minutes. The squadron had dropped a total of 12,000lb on bombs on this most distant of targets. Nine crews were detailed for an attack on Frankfurt on the 12th, the crew of S/Ldr Price was cancelled just before take-off. Squadron Leader Spence would have joined him, but serviceability issues aboard X9787 HA-S prevented take-off. Sergeant Brewerton was airborne only a matter of minutes when he was forced to return to base with port engine trouble. He landed R1601 HA-T with its full load. Sergeant Fisher was very nearly the victim of flak near Oostende. A burst of flak exploded close enough to damage the Wellington preventing the crew from gaining altitude, so they wisely turned for home. The night was fast becoming a disaster. Things would get worse when the squadron lost one of its more experienced New Zealand skippers on the raid. Sergeant Charles Dare RNZAF lifted off from Marham at 21:04 hours aboard Wellington X960 HA-N. They experienced no opposition until they arrived over the target. Over the city, they were quickly coned by searchlights and engaged by accurate flak. Hit and set on fire Sgt Dare immediately realised that the aircraft was doomed. Wasting no time, he gave the order to bail-out. Holding the now blazing Wellington stable all the crew managed to jump to safety. Finally, when satisfied his crew had left the plucky New Zealander took to his parachute. The blazing Wellington crashed at Pfingstweidstrabe, a few hundred yards from the city zoo, the oldest zoo in Germany. All the crew managed to take to their parachutes before X9670 HA-N crashed into a few houses at 23:29 hours. Within an hour of the Wellington crashing, they had all been located and captured. The only injury suffered was to the wireless operator, Sgt Robert Moody, who broke his right leg on landing. The crew would keep together while PoWs up until a few weeks before liberation. This was the young Kiwis 12th operation as captain. He had previously completed 12 operations in the right-hand seat with Sgt Banks and P/O Mitchell. The crews recently posted 2nd pilot, Sgt Leslie Booth, had managed to survive three operations since his arrival, all flown with the Dare crew. What was left of the squadron carried out an effective and damaging raid on Frankfurt. Large fires were seen, and crews were confident that the attack was a success despite the cloud cover. One returning crew reported that the flames were visible 30 miles after leaving the target.

**Friday 12<sup>th</sup> September 1941**

*Vickers Wellington*
*Mk.Ic X9670 HA-N. 'Nuts'*
*Contract No: B97887/39*
*Taken On Charge: 23/07/1941*
**Failed To Return**
*Pilot: Sergeant Charles Dare, 401373 RNZAF PoW*
*2nd Pilot: Sergeant Leslie Booth, 1107264 RAFVR PoW*
*Observer: Sergeant Ian Leitch, 924403 RAFVR, PoW*
*Wireless Operator / Gunner: Sergeant Robert Purdy, 922942 RAFVR, PoW*
*1st Wireless Operator: Sergeant Kenneth Birchenough, 950131 RAFVR, PoW*
*Rear Gunner: Sergeant Robert Moodie, 187103 RAFVR, PoW*

'A' Flight's Squadron Leader Spence and crew undertook their first operation on the 16th. The target was the docks at Le Havre. Meeting no opposition other than a few isolated flak bursts the crew attacked from 12,500 feet. The mixed HE and incendiary bomb load were seen to explode across Dock 6 and 7 resulting in a reddish fire. Neither of Marham's squadrons was required for the raid against Hamburg on that night. Sadly, however, tragedy was never far away even when not operating. At 03:15 hours a Wellington on No.57 Squadron attempted to land at Marham without brakes due to damaged inflicted over Germany. The Wellington had safely landed on the flare path when it suddenly swung off and hurtled across the field towards a number of dispersed Wellingtons. The 57 Squadron machine struck a parked Wellington of 218 Squadron and both aircraft immediately burst into flames. Four of the crew managed to scramble clear but tragically, the pilot Sgt Arthur Witherington, and his wireless operator Sgt Kenneth Clark were burnt to death.

*Wreckage of Sergeant Dare's Vickers Wellington Mk.Ic X9670 HA-N - 'Nuts' being inspected by Luftwaffe personnel.*

**Tuesday 16th September 1941**

*Vickers Wellington*
*Mk.Ic  R3153 HA-*
*Contract No : B3913/39*
*Taken On Charge : 25/03/1941*
*Burnt-Out.*
*SoC*

It was a sobering and frightful accident. The crew were so close to safety only for it to be snatched away at the last critical second. Strangely, Wellington R3153 does not appear to have undertaken any operations with the squadron. There was some reason to celebrate on return from the operation. Sergeant Robert Banks had completed his first tour of operations. He arrived on the squadron in April 1941 via No.20 O.T.U and commenced operations on April 22nd besides Sgt Charles Graham. His relationship with his crew was not a happy one, Sgt Howard Hewer, wireless operator, '*a few days after our return from Karlsruhe we were called to the crew room in the hangar. One of the flight commanders, a flight lieutenant, was there to greet us. Sergeant Banks was not there, but another sergeant pilot was standing beside the officer. The flight lieutenant explained that Sgt Banks had reached the end of his tour and he introduced our new captain to us, Bill Dixon. We did not see Banks again. He left as quietly as he arrived. We never socialised with him, he had a wife off base, but I thought it strange that he never said goodbye. After all, we were a good reliable crew. He had, however, seen us through some very harrowing operations. He deserved a rest.*

Sadly, after a well-deserved period of rest Robert Banks, since promoted to flight lieutenant would be killed attacking Frankfurt in September 1944 with 625 Squadron.

*Squadron line up, 1941.*

The squadron was not required on the 17th or 18th. It was a brief pause in what had been a busy but productive few week of operations. On the 19th eight crews were detailed for a raid against the distant target of Stettin, on the Baltic coast. A major centre of the weapons industry it also an important deep-water port. The bad luck that beset the operation of the 12th returned on this night. One crew were cancelled owing to a burst tail wheel while taxing. Then another crew was withdrawn with a defective front turret. Then to add insult to injury, an unknown crew taxied into a hedge on the south side of the aerodrome. It was not the start the squadron was hoping for. To add to the chaos, the customary early return was experienced. The crew of Sgt McGlashan abandoned the operation over the North Sea due to intercom failure. On only their second operation together they jettisoned their incendiaries and returned to base. What was left of the depleted squadron attacked Stettin's main station and the Schuppenspeicher Warehouse. With the bomb loads considerably reduced due to the distance, each Wellington carried a 1500lb mixed load the attack was never going to produce a conflagration. However, a few good fires were started in both the north and south of the town. Despite the amount of time over enemy airspace opposition was surprisingly light, no fighters were encountered, and flak was described as light.

The squadron was stood down on return from Stettin. Given Wing Commander Kirkpatrick's high standards and more importantly, the standard demanded by Marham's station commander, Group Captain Andrew McKee there would have been some strong words and much annoyance by both officers at the squadron's recent poor performance.

*Squadron Leader Ian Ricmond, Pilot Officer Bryant 2nd Pilot, Pilot Officer Bryant, Observer, Sergeant Alsbury, Front Gunner/Wop, Sergeant Green Wop/Ag, Sergeant Kolitz, Rear Gunner.*

The mood would not have been helped by the arrival on a 24-hour visit of Marshal of the RAF, Lord Trenchard on the 25th. Members of the Officers Mess were ordered to 'dine-in' and were given an informal after dinner talk by the ageing Air Marshal. The planned operation to Mannheim that night had been cancelled owing to bad weather. The following morning, he addressed the aircrews and ground personnel of the squadron in front of 'A' Flight's Hangar. This impromptu 'Pep' talk was received with genuine appreciation by all concerned. The Air Marshal modestly referred to and compared his experience in the Great War to the assembled crews and their bombing war. That night two recent arrivals were given Emden to attack, one of the crews was a highly experienced and seasoned bomber pilot. Flying Officer Arthur Humphreys was born in Rangiora, New Zealand in 1919. His operational career began in April 1940 when he was posted on completion of his training to No.214 Squadron. His association with 214 lasted only a matter days before he was sent to No.75(NZ) Squadron, where he would complete his first tour of 23 operations.

*Flying Officer Arthur Humphrey in the centre with some of his crew. Sadly, the only other identified member of the crew is Pilot Officer Graham Hunter 1st right.*

His first operation with 218 Squadron was not a success. He was obliged to jettison his mixed bomb load over the North Sea and return to Marham as instructed. Sergeant Victory Haley for some reason did not hear the instruction to abort the raid due to rapidly deteriorating weather, he and his crew continued onto Emden where they delivered two 500 pounders and 120 x 4lb incendiaries on a cloud-covered target.

The last operation of the month would see the squadron visiting Le Havre, Hamburg and Stettin. One of the first crews away was that of Wing Commander Kirkpatrick who departed at 1942 hours in Wellington Mk.II

W5447 HA-C. He was quickly followed by S/Ldr Price in the squadron's other Vickers-built Mk.II, Z8375 HA-Z. Both were detailed to bomb Hamburg. Joining the crew of S/Ldr Price was Wing Commander Peter Heath, a pre-war regular who was on the squadron for operational experience. The next to take off were the seven crews ordered to attack Stettin. Sergeant Fisher got as far as Heligoland before he decided to abort the operation with intercom trouble. They dropped their entire load on the island causing a small fire before they turned for home. On reaching the target the crews were met with a few well-established fires, these were duly bombed producing two very distinct larger fires which were visible from over 70 miles on the return trip. Sergeant Thompson's Wellington, X9697 HA-was hit by flak over the target area. The Canadian second pilot, Sgt Richard Forsyth, had a lucky escape when flak splinters entered the cockpit via the starboard window. A piece of flak struck the Canadian a glancing blow across the forehead inflicted a slight facial wound. An unprecedented number of recently posted pilots would operate on this night in the second pilot role. Sergeants William Bowhill, Cyrdi Jetten and Australian, Sergeant William Fraser RAAF, would all visit Stettin, all would safely return from their first operation on the squadron. Wing Commandeer Kirkpatrick dropped his single bomb from 14,000 feet slightly east of the aiming point. He remarked on his return, 'Good explosion showing up rows of houses and streets, two members of the crew saw debris going in various directions'. A photograph was attempted, but evasive action was required when the flak started to get a little too close for comfort. Squadron Leader Price was equally busy trying to evade Hamburg's defences. His 4000 pounder gave a 'satisfactory explosion'. Finally, the last two crews departed some six hours after their companions, the target for Sergeants Tompkin and Vezina RCAF was the Docks at Le Havre. Both were carrying out their debut operation as captain having completed the customary spell occupying the right-hand seat. Sergeant Tompkins found the docks hidden by a blanket of cloud, bombing on ETA the crew dropped their mixed HE and incendiary load from 10,000 feet. Sergeant Vezina was unable to locate the target, he jettisoned safe his entire bomb load on the return flight, landing at 0612 hours. Joining the crew of Sgt Vezina was another recent arrival, Sgt Frank Griggs RAAF who arrived on the squadron on September 2nd via No.20 O.T.U. September ended with the squadron having flown 84 sorties, for the loss of three Wellingtons and one crew. Disappointingly the numbers of early returns had slowly begun to rise. The majority were caused by mechanical malfunctions of some of the older Wellingtons. However, W/Cdr Kirkpatrick made it clear that these 'boomerangs' would need to decrease and not increase over the coming winter months.The squadron's first operation of October was directed again the port of Rotterdam-Schiedam by 13 crews led by 'A' Flight's S/Ldr Spence. Wing Commander Heath would be travelling south to Dunkirk aboard one of the squadron's veteran Wellingtons, R1025 HA-J. For once there was not a single early return, a triumph for the ground crews. A number of fires were visible as the crews neared the Dutch coast. In excellent visibility, all bombed the primary target. Many fires were started notably between docks 21 and 24. A large warehouse was seen blazing furiously on Dock 15. Many explosions were observed in St Jans Haven and the petroleum storage area at Kortenoordse. Also ablaze was the area between Dock 30 and 31, these fires resulted in a number of large colourful explosions. Wing Commander Heath arrived over Dunkirk at 21:07 hours meeting accurate flak. Weather was not as clear as Rotterdam, but an accurate raid developed with numerous fires started across the dock area. All the Wellingtons apart from W/Cdr Heaths were loaded with mixed 500 and 1000lb HEs, the squadron dropped a respectable total of 55,480lbs of bombs.

There was an uncharacteristic lull in operations immediately on return from Rotterdam. The squadron was finally detailed for an operation on the 7th. The target was the port city of Bordeaux on the Garonne River in southwestern France. This operation and those planned for the 8th and 9th were all cancelled due to bad weather. Finally, on the 10th, 22 Marham Wellingtons took off to attack this distant target. The squadron's provided 11 crew apiece, leading 218 Squadron's contribution was W/Cdr Heath in Wellington X9833 HA-A, he was joined by Sergeant Simmons on his first operational trip. All the crews arrived over Bordeaux to find it covered by cloud apart from Sgt Webber. While at 10,000 feet on the outward journey, the two .303 machine guns in the rear turret suddenly 'ran away'. Pilot Officer Dalton, the rear gunner, quickly broke the ammunition link and attempted clear the malfunctions guns. With no rear defence the crew decided to seek a target of opportunity, this they believed they found in an airfield under construction at Merdrignac, Brittany.

The remaining crews, unable to pin-point the primary target, had no option than bomb on ETA or the flashes of the flak below. On this raid the crews were given a specific time to attack, it was a new tactic and one that the crews were unaccustomed to. At around 0330hrs the crews started their bomb runs meeting a spirited flak defence. In the distance the snow-capped Pyrenees were visible, there was some comfort in that if in trouble the crews could make for neutral Spain or unoccupied Vichy France. It was believed at the time that the raid was to cover an operation by British Commandos to attack the FW200 Condor bases along the French coast.

This rather disappointing raid, unfortunately, cost the squadron two crews, Sergeant Victor Haley and Sgt Alan McLean. Soon after leaving the target area, the crew of Sgt Victor Haley were in trouble, possibly the result of flak damage the wireless operator sent a message back to RAF Marham stating that they were 'Bailing out, engine trouble'. Wellington R1511 HA-L crashed at St Antoine de L'Isle. All the crew managed to escape via parachute apart from the crew's observer, Sergeant Judge who was killed. The 29-year-old from Lincolnshire was buried in the Villenave D'Ornon Communal Cemetery.

### Friday 10th October 1941
*Vickers Wellington*
*Mk.Ic  R1511 HA-L 'London'*
*Contract No : 992424/39*
*Taken On Charge : 03/03/1941*
**Failed To Return**
*Pilot : Sergeant Victor George Haley 1251661 RAFVR PoW*
*2nd Pilot : Sergeant William Johnson Bowhill, 921741 RAFVR PoW*
*Observer: Sergeant Horace Hill Judge, 998283 RAFVR, **Killed***
*Front Gunner : Sergeant Peter Llewellyn Jones, 911913 RAFVR PoW*
*1st Wireless Operator : Sergeant Alexander Richard Langley, 1183833 RAFVR PoW*
*Rear Gunner : Sergeant Duncan MacDiamid,1023034 RAFVR, PoW*


Sergeant Haley, a former pre-war Clerk recalls the events of his 12th and last operation immediately before the order to bail out.

*'We took off from RAF Marham at 2000hrs on October 10th to bomb the oil tanks slightly north of Bordeaux. We reached our objective but shortly after we turned for home the starboard propellor flew off. I turned the Wellington towards the unoccupied zone and gave the order to bail out at approximately 0400hrs.*

His crew were quickly captured by the Germans who were tipped off by a local French farmer with whom they were hiding. Sergeant Haley was more fortunate, the following is from his Escape and Evasion Report.

# Squadron Ground Crew

*The success of any squadron depended on the dedication, skill and hard work of the ground crew. Their work was dangerous and unglamorous but vital. Behind the scenes there were hundreds of personnel on the squadron who ensured that the squadron ticked. Often working out at a distant dispersal in all weathers they applied their trade with diligence and cheerfulness. Left: Five unidentified ground crew photographed with Vickers Wellington MkIc R1210. Right : One of those who kept the squadron performing was Alfred Fox who joined the squadron in September 1940 as a flight mechanic. He served until 1942 when he was posted to No.1657 CU.*

I came down outside a farm at Le Pizou and having made a low drop, was rather winded. The farmer came out and took me to his house, where I stayed for about half an hour. He gave me food and an old pair of dungarees and a jacket and hid my flying clothes and parachute. He also gave me a diagram on a piece of paper showing how to cross the line of demarcation, avoiding Mon Pont Sur L' Tesla where there was a force of about 300 German soldiers. At about 0430 hours I set out alone and walked to about 1030hrs. I was trying to get to a small village called Very. I crossed the line of demarcation between Mont Pont and St Remy.  I was challenged as being English by a farmer at St Remy. When I told him who I was, he took me to his farm where I remained from the 12th October to December 11th while the farmer tried without success to  get in touch with an organisation to help me escape. Living on the farm was an Englishman who had made his home at Lille since the end of the last war and was a refugee from the occupied zone.  This Englishman eventually organised my journey for me, helped to provide me with civilian clothes, and gave me 1000 francs. I left St Remy alone on December 11th by taxi to Ste Foy-La-Grande. There I was met by an Alsatian who provided me with food, clothes, maps, compass and 1000 francs, and put me on a bus for La Reole where I caught the Bordeaux - Marseilles night express to Narbonne. I then went by train to Perpignan. From there on December 12th I went on foot along the main Le Perthus Road from which I turned off via Bages, Brouilla, St Genis to the Ville Longue, near the frontier. From here I crossed the Pyrenees on foot without a guide.

After crossing the mountains, I called at a chateau to ask for food. There a Spaniard, who spoke French and a little English advised me to give myself up immediately to the police, assuring me that the British Consul would be able to reclaim me. I took his advice and gave myself up to the Guardia Civil at the village of Cantallops on December 13th. I was imprisoned at Figueras on the 14th, 15th and 16th December and at Barcelona between the 16th and 20th of December. At Zaragoza, between the 21st and 23rd December.  I was then moved to Miranda concentration camp, where I remained to February 19th 1942.  When I surrendered to the Civil Guard on December 13th, I declared myself a British pilot. I had with me 2000 French francs and 13/6d sterling, but no action was taken against me on a charge of smuggling.  From Miranda I went to Madrid, arriving on February 19th 1942 and leaving to Gibraltar on February 23rd 1942.

On May 26th, 1942 the London Gazette announced the award of the Military Medal to Sergeant Haley, the citation reads;

*This airman was a member of a crew of an aircraft that crashed on return from an attack on Bordeaux. Evading capture on bailing out he showed great resource in journeying across France, and overcoming many obstacles he finally made his way without a guide over the Pyrenees into Spain from where, after a period of detention, he was repatriated*

Londoner Sergeant William Bowhill was shot down on his 3rd operation, like his captain he was a pre-war clerk. Captured on the 11th at Saint Metard, he and the remaining crew would remain, guests of the Third Reich, until liberated in April 1945.

The mostly Australian crew of Sgt Alan McLean reached the cloud covered target and circled for half an hour dropping their bombs one at a time. Having deposited their entire bomb load, the NGZ signal was sent at 03:17 hours. At the mouth of the Garonne river, they were engaged by flak, five flak bursts exploded slightly ahead of Wellington X9677 HA-V, none of the crew was injured, and the only damaged reported was to the intercom which was put out of action. All appeared calm until at 04:30 hours when the port engine began to show signs of trouble. At 05:16 hours a third-class bearing was obtained which showed the Wellington was well off track.

With the engine coughing and engine temperature rising the crew called base for a D/F at 06:26hrs, but the signal strength was too weak for a bearing to be received. At around 06:45 hours the port engine finally failed, the Wellington began to lose height. Not sure of their exact location due to cloud and heavy rain the captain asked the crew whether they should bail out or stay with the aircraft while he slowly descended into the darkness to try and establish his location. The crew all agreed to remain with their pilot. Gingerly both pilots sank into the cloud, finally, at 1000 feet they emerged only to be greeted by the inhospitable sea below. The decision to remain aboard was a wise one. Almost immediately the starboard engine which had shown no sign of trouble coughed and then inexplicably failed. The pilot immediately instructed the crews to go to their dinghy stations and inflate the floatation gear. Showing remarkable calm, both pilots turned the Wellington into the wind and brought the aircraft down onto the sea as gently as the situation allowed. The Wellington hit the sea and immediately broke up in the rough swell, within 30 seconds it began to sink. McLean scrambled out of the quickly sinking Wellington via the emergency cockpit cover, Sgt Honeyman the co-pilot went out through the astrodome. The front gunner managed to escape when a hole appeared as the Wellington broke in two just aft of the main spar. These three managed to right the dinghy which had been hand released by the second pilot and scramble aboard. The wireless operator, Sgt Stephenson, was seen on the wing of the aircraft, he attempted to jump for the dinghy. Sadly, he was washed away by a large wave and not seen again.

The three occupants of the dinghy momentarily glimpsed Sgt Pugh near the rear turret. He, too, was not seen again. The rear gunner, Sgt Ireland was seen floating face down in the sea. The Wellington had ditched at approximately 07:00 hours five miles S.E of St Albans Head. Within three hours trawlers were sighted by the now freezing survivors, McLean fired a distress flare, thankfully this was seen by the crew of H.M.T 'Grimsby Town' who quickly steamed towards the dinghy and its survivors. All three were hauled aboard, stripped of their wet clothing, and provided with dry, warm clothes and a large tot of rum. On arrival at Portsmouth, they were quickly transferred to the R.N Hospital at Haslar. An extensive search was carried out for the missing crew by the St Ives Lifeboat, apart from a section of the wing and a wheel nothing was found.

**Friday 10th October 1941**
*Vickers Wellington*
*Mk.Ic X9677 HA-V 'Victor'*
*Contract No : B.7887/39*
*Taken On Charge : 00/06/1941*
Ditched
*Pilot : Sergeant Alan Maxwell McLean, 402387 RAAF Survived*
*2nd Pilot : Sergeant Archibald Cowen Honeyman, 404549 RAAF Survived*
*Observer: Sergeant James Douglas Pugh, 926529 RAFVR **Killed***
*Front Gunner : Sergeant Lionel Maurice Benstead 404428 Survived*
*1st Wireless Operator : Sergeant Robert Worrall Stephenson, 404418 RAAF **Killed***

*Rear Gunner : Sergeant Eric William Ireland, 902411 RAFVR **Killed***

Sergeant Alan McLean's actions and considerable flying skill had been instrumental in saving some of his crew. It was unfortunate that the weather on that night was particularly bad and the sea was described as very rough. Alan McLean was on his 16th operation, 8 of which were as captain, Honeyman was on his 3rd. After a period of rest, the three survivors eventually join No.215 Squadron. In June 1942 their luck sadly ran out, all three were killed when Wellington Ic BB514 blew up over Ghafaugaon, India. The Bordeaux raid was the last flown by Wing Commander Peter Heath on the squadron. He would eventually take command of No.40 Squadron in November. Another long-range operation was planned for the 12th when eleven crews were detailed to attack Nuremberg, the site of pre-war massed Nazis rallies. Two crews failed to reach the target, Sgt McKay was aloft less than an hour before he returned, a faulty pilot escape hatch being the culprit. Sergeant John Webber experienced compass trouble. He got as far as Sankt Ingbert, 2 miles N.E of Saarbrucken. Seeing the faint lights of a flare path below, they decided to bomb. Conditions over Nuremberg were excellent. An enormous fire was already established as the crews made their bomb runs. The primary target, the main railway and rail junction, was easily identified and singled out for some accurate bombing. Wing Commander Kirkpatrick at the controls of Wellington Mk.II Z8375 HA-Z bombed prematurely, his 4000 pounder exploding in the city a mile from the primary, the result of a faulty intercom. The whole of the centre of Nuremberg appeared to be ablaze, W/Cdr Kirkpatrick reported '*Huge red and green and yellowish fires seen 50 miles after leaving'*. Sadly, the crew's enthusiasm was misplaced, bombs had been dropped all over southern Germany, towns such as Lauingen, sixty-six miles from Nuremberg reported heavy bombing. Even smaller towns were not immune, Lauffen on the river Neckar a decoy site for Stuttgart received a number of bomb loads, Lauffen is located 90 miles from Nuremberg! The crews began landing just before 0500 hours, Sgt McGlashan had just landed and was taxing Wellington Z8910 HA-F along the flare path when it was struck by Wellington Z9877 KO-Q flown by Sgt Ronald Runagall of No.115 Squadron. Thankfully, none of the crew was seriously injured, but Z8910 was a '*write-off'*. A brand-new aircraft it had been on the squadron only five weeks.

**Sunday 12th October 1941**
*Vickers Wellington*
*Mk.Ic  Z8910 HA-F 'Freddie'*
*Contract No : B71441/40*
*Taken On Charge: 04/09/1941*
*Damaged Beyond Repair*
*Pilot : Sergeant John McGlashan RAFVR*
*2nd Pilot : Sergeant Terence Helfer  RAFVR*

A Vickers Wellington, X9786 of No.57 Squadron made a belly landing at Marham on return from Dusseldorf on the 13th. Having suffered port engine failure over Germany F/Lt Donaldson brought the Wellington into land without flaps, it was an excellent effort on the part of the crew. Possibly realising that the attack on Nuremberg on the 12th was not a success Bomber Command HQ ordered 80 bombers back to the city on the 14th, fifty-nine of which were provided by No.3 Group. 218 Squadron provided ten crews led by both flight commanders, Squadron Leader Spence and S/Ldr Price, who had just returned from some well-earned leave. If the previous visit was disappointing this raid would be equally frustrating and costly. Six Wellingtons failed to take off, and a further six returned early from the force of fifty-nine provided by Group, one of the early returns was from 218 Squadron. Sergeant Fisher suffered excessive engine vibration to the port Hercules of Wellington Z8865 HA-O. The crew jettisoned 'Safe' a single a 1000 pounder to reduce weight as they made their approach to Marham. Unbeknown to the crew, the bomb had not dropped and was still in the bomb-bay. Having received permission to land, Sgt Fisher guided the Wellington onto the flare-path, following a normal approach, full flaps were applied. Without warning the Wellington suddenly sank owing to the excessive load. The Wellington struck the ground 100 yards from the eastern boundary, crashed through three trees, a boundary hedge and finally hit a fuel bowser before coming to a halt. Mercifully, the Wellington did not catch fire, but it was in a sorry state. Broken in two, the crew scrambled clear of the wreckage aware that it still had bombs on board. Sergeant Joseph Borrowdale, the crew's observer, suffered a fractured leg, while Sgts Jetten and Mews were both bruised.

## Tuesday 14th October 1941

*Vickers Wellington*
*Mk.Ic*
*Z8865 HA-O 'Orange'*
*Contract No : B71441/40*
*Taken On Charge : 31/08/1941*
*Struck off Charge*
*Pilot : Sergeant Kenneth Fisher RAFVR*
*2nd Pilot : Sergeant Cyrdi Jetten RAFVR Injured*
*Observer: Sergeant Joseph Borrowdale RAFVR Injured*
*Front Gunner : Sergeant A.J Smith RAFVR*
*1st Wireless Operator : Flight Sergeant J.G Clarke RAFVR*
*Rear Gunner : Sergeant A Mews RAFVR Injured.*


Conditions on the route and over the target were described as terrible, Nuremberg was covered in 10/10th cloud. Squadron Leader Spence was unable to locate the target so bombed a flak position near Mannheim. Sergeant Webber jettisoned his entire bomb load over Waldurn, a small town 25 miles S.E of Wurzburg. Flying Officer Humphreys bombed a number of fires 30 miles east of target. Those crews that reached the general area of Nuremberg bombed on ETA or the flashes of the flak guns below. All apart from S/Ldr Price who ventured down to the recklessly low altitude of 5000 feet in an attempt to pinpoint the target. Despite his best efforts, all he could find was yet more cloud. Eventually, the 4000 pounder was dropped, the ensuring explosion damaging the Wellingtons fuselage when it was struck by bomb splinters, fortunately none of the crew was injured. Sergeant Vezina and crew had bombed the general area of Nuremberg. Trouble started on the route home when a shortage of petrol resulted in a wheels-up crash-landing at Hampden Park, near Eastbourne at 0615 hours. The crew, all safe were taken to RAF Friston from where they were returned to Marham. Wellington Mk.Ic R1025 HA-J had arrived on the squadron in November 1940 and had flown an impressive 39 raids. Such was the damaged that the Wellington never returned to the squadron.

## Tuesday 14th October 1941

*Vickers Wellington*
*Mk.Ic*
*R1025 HA-J 'Johnnie'*
*Contract No :992424/39*
*Taken On Charge : 06/11/1940*
*Wheels Up Landing*
*Repaired in Works*
*Pilot : Sergeant Joseph Vezina RCAF*

*Flight Lieutenant Peter Dunham DFC*

One pilot had reason to celebrate on return from Nuremberg. Sergeant Kenneth Fisher had just flown his 24th and last operation on the squadron. He survived the war and remained in the RAF until 1963!

The run of bad luck continued the 16th when eight crews were detailed to attack the main power station at Duisburg, while two crews were given Dunkirk. One of the crews was skippered by Sergeant James Hinwood. 218 Squadron had continued with a policy that resulted in the senior officer in the crew being classified as captain, in this case, Flight Lieutenant Peter Dunham, a trained observer and second tour veteran. The crew had been given the dubious honour of operating the first of the modified Wellington Mk.Ic with the upgraded Pegasus 18 engines to carry the 4000 pounder. Wellington Z8957 HA-L had only arrived on the squadron on October 10th from No.12 Maintenance Unit. This *423 variant* had an extra 2 1/2 pound of boost and had the bomb doors removed, the normal bomb beams and the intermediate bomb doors were removed, and special vertical members were inserted in the centre-section spar bracing, with fittings on the forward frame to suit suspension of the 4000lb bomb. Jim Hinwood recalls the pre-flight Air-Test;

*On the 16th of October 1941, I was detailed to air test a new aircraft, which only had flown 2 hours. I remember the controls were very stiff and it all smelt very new. The air test lasted 15 minutes, and then the bomb was loaded. The bottom of the bomb stuck out into the slipstream and was painted matt black. The Mk.IIs were better performers but did not have the range, hence the new modified Mk.Ics.*

The first crews to take off were the two 'Freshman' who departed just after 1900 hours. Sergeant McGregor RNZAF failed to locate the target on this his first raid as captain. New Zealander, Sergeant McPhail bombed the docks at Dunkirk from the perilously low altitude to 2,100 feet and was damaged by flak for his trouble. Both crews were safely home as the remainder of the squadron began lifting off for Germany. Z8957 HA-L took off from Marham at 0125hrs carrying a 'cookie', the first occasion on which a 218 Squadron Mk Ic had carried a blockbuster. Sergeant Jim Hinwood recorded the events of that night.

*Take off was 01.25hrs on the 17th. Take off was up the hill past Lady Woods and at the fence, I lifted off and then touched down again briefly in the field outside the boundary. It really was touch and go. We climbed rather slowly, and after about 15 minutes as we reached 3,000 feet, the port motor started to misfire badly with lots of flames from the exhaust. I throttled back, but the prop would not feather on the Pegasus engines. As height could not be maintained on one, we continued to the coast to drop the bomb into the sea. Inside the fuselage, alongside the navigator's position, the aircraft floor had been raised and a bomb beam fitted. The beam, the bomb release hook and a manual release lever were above floor level. Two Vickers hoists were also in place, one in the front beam, the other behind. The hoists were initially used to lift the bomb into the bomb bay by means of two steel cables to the hoist, the hoists and cables being left in place*

322

*to stabilise the bomb during the take-off and climb. Once clear of the coast the co-pilot had slackened of the cables, releasing them from the anchorage point. The co-pilot was also responsible for the manual release in an emergency.*

*We crossed the coast north of Great Yarmouth and the co-pilot, Sgt McKay, went back to jettison the bomb. The fuselage of the Wimpy is not over large and with the raised floor, bomb beam and hoists there is not a great deal of room for someone wearing an Irvin flying jacket and Mae West. Anyway, when the release was pulled one cable was not clear so that the bomb fell off the hook and the front end dropped into the slipstream whilst the back end pushed the floor up even higher. There was only one thing to do, using the fire axe. The co-pilot Sgt McKay chopped through the ply-wood floor and then through the cable which was resting against the bomb casing. By this time, we were down to 1,600 feet, and the good engine running at maximum continuous power was getting very hot. The last strands of the cable parted, and we turned for the coast. With the port engine still spitting flames, we could not dump the full fuel load. The coast was crossed inbound at Lowestoft, but as we were still losing height, the first crew member was told to jump at 1,300 feet using the rear escape hatch. The co-pilot and rear gunner were followed by the front gunner at 1,100 feet and the wireless operator at 900 feet. The observer, F/Lt Peter Dunham, was the captain, unusually, but he was on his second tour. So, after checking that the rest of the crew were clear, and handing me my chest type parachute, he left from the front hatch. I closed the throttles at 700 feet, trimmed the aircraft and dropped from the seat only to find my harness had caught up in the seat-lowering handle. Struggling free, I went out of the hatch headfirst, well below 500 feet by now, and pulled my ripcord. I landed in a ploughed field impacting on my shoulders with my parachute canopy streaming behind me. The flight had lasted 45 minutes. The aircraft landed in a field in which a potato crop was being harvested. None of the crew was injured, but Sid Turner hurt his knee when climbing over a gate, and Ken Wheeler fell into a dyke. Peter Dunham and I finished the night at the house of a local Policeman in Cantley between Yarmouth and Norwich, while the rest of the crew found a pub. Next day we were collected by personnel from Horsham St Faith and returned to Marham by road.*

It had a been a close call for the crew and especially for the 20-year-old pilot, James Hinwood who was on his first operation as captain. Over the target the squadron found Duisburg covered in a thick blanket of cloud. Unable to pinpoint the primary target crews resorted to bombing the flashes of the flak guns below. It was not all one way. Wellington X9787 HA-S was fortunate to survive a flak burst that punctured a large hole in the starboard fuel tank. Sergeant John Webber and his Australian co-pilot Sgt Cook RAAF did well in bringing the crippled Wellington home with rapidly dwindling fuel. Duisburg would see the first operation of F/Lt Wilfred 'Bill' Williams DFC since his arrival on the squadron on October 10th. There was a change of command on the 18th, Group Captain Andrew McKee AFC DFC was replaced by Group Captain Archibald Hugh Herbert McDonald former pre-war commanding officer of No. 40 Squadron. Not everyone was upset to see the abrasive New Zealander replaced.

Pilot Officer Harper was the only crew aloft from the squadron on the 20th, and he was in good company. 115 Squadron's commander, W/Cdr Freeman, would join him on a raid directed against the port of Antwerp. The attack was a failure due to cloud with both bringing their bombs back to Marham. A major raid on Bremen was flown on the 21st, Marham provided 18 Wellingtons, nine from both squadrons. The weather was the only victor on this night, haze, plus searchlights prevented all but two crews from identifying the target, the Vulcan Shipyards. Flying Officer Humphreys bombed Stuhr airfield in Wellington Mk. II Z8375 HA-Z when he was unable to locate Bremen positively. The 4000 pounder which hung up for 10 seconds produced a vivid explosion that illuminated the airfield for five seconds.

*Squadron Leader Wilfred Maurice Williams DFC RNZAF.*

It was the turn of the dockyards at Kiel on the night of October 23rd, only seven crews were detailed led by S/Ldr Price who departed at 1755 hours. He was followed almost immediately by 'B' Flight commander S/Ldr Spence. The rear turret aboard Wellington R1346 HA-B was discovered to be faulty soon after crossing the enemy coast south of Den Helder. Despite the best efforts of the rear gunner, the stoppage could not be fixed. The pilot, Sgt Bernard Tompkins had no option but turn for home. Another crew that returned early was that of Sgt John McGlashan. They had crossed the North Sea without the heating system working aboard Wellington R1596 HS-K. On entering enemy airspace, the crew started climbing to 15,000 feet where the temperature plummeted inside the aircraft, with no heating the conditions become unbearable. Searching for an alternative target the crew tried without success to locate the airfield at Westerland which they had passed only a few minutes prior. Unable to do so, they dropped their all HE load on the town of Westerland producing three large explosions. What remained of the squadron were disappointed to find the docks covered by thick cloud.

Crews either bombed on ETA or the flak guns, S/Ldr Spence dropped his single 1000 pounder and two 500 pounders of the flak defenders, reporting on his return, *'Bombs fell in target area amongst flak, some of which apparently were put out of action'*. Other than the customary training flights no operations were flown until the 29th when Form B.648 arrived from No.3 Group HQ informing the squadron that it would be required for operations that night, the target was Hamburg. It was not until late afternoon that further news was received cancelling the operation owing to weather conditions. Sergeant Tompkins was aloft in Wellington X9888 HA-A on a training flight on the 29th. At 800 feet all appeared to be going well until problems with the starboard engine where encountered. Unable to maintain height Sergeant Tompkins looked for the nearest airfield to land. Eventually RAF Rougham was sighted but, in his haste to land with a badly misfiring engine, their luck ran out. The Wellington, X9833, stalled and spun in from 50 feet crashing at Washpit Farm, Rougham at 12:50 hours. Two of the crew were injured, including Sgt Tompkins. The aircraft caught fire on impact and was burnt-out.

### Wednesday 29th October 1941

*Vickers Wellington*
*Mk.Ic*
*X9833 HA-A 'Apple'*
*Contract No :B.97887/39*
*Taken On Charge: 21/08/1941*
*Burnt-Out Struck off Charge*
*Pilot : Sergeant Bernard Tompkins, injured.*
*2nd Pilot : Sergeant Frank Griggs RAAF.*
*Observer : Sergeant Carroll, Injured*

The squadron was informed by the Police of the death of one of the squadron's air gunners on the 29th. Sergeant Reginald England was motorcycling home on leave to see his Fiancée in Carlisle when he was in a collision with an Army truck. The collision proved fatal, and Reginald died of his injuries. The driver of the truck, which belonged to the Royal Tank Regiment did not stop leaving the young gunner in the road. The driver was subsequently found and charged with dangerous driving. The body of Reginald England was taken back to Merseyside and cremated in Birkenhead Crematorium.

The preparations for Hamburg were not wasted, within 24 hours the squadron was preparing 10 crews for a raid on the shipyards at Bremen. The first crew away was that of Sgt Hinwood at 18:10 hours in Wellington W5727 HA-V. This was a brand-new machine which had only arrived on the squadron days prior. Also airborne was the squadron commander, W/Cdr Kirkpatrick in Wellington Mk.II Z8375 HA-Z. He was accompanied in the cockpit by Sgt Stanley Coggin, a 22-year-old making his operational debut on the squadron. Weather conditions were far from ideal, solid overcast over the North Sea continued over northern Holland and further into northern Germany. With no let-up in the weather and Bremen protected by dense cloud a number of crews bombed the secondary target and other targets of opportunity. Sergeant Brewerton disposed of his load on the docks at Den Helder. Emden received three bomb loads. Sergeant McGregor bombed the main railway junction, while Sgts Webber and P/O Harper dropped in the Emden 'area'. Flight Lieutenant Williams dropped his 4000 pounder on Hamburg while Sgt Hinwood dropped his entire bomb load on the airfield at Oldebrook, Holland. Another airfield attacked was Eelde by the

*A fresh-faced Stanley Coggin.*

crew of Sergeant Thompson. Joining the crew on his first operation was Canadian Sgt Harold Millichamp at 32-year-old from Toronto. Unable to reach Bremen the crew had turned back, south of Den Helder they were attacked by a Do215 of 4./NJG1 flown by Ofw Siefried Ney at 2328 hours. The following is a report submitted by Ney soon after.

*'Once I was in the box, I was directed by Lt Tank of 7./Ln.Rgt 203 ground control on to a bogey flying east to west at 3900m. After some correction my Bordmechaniker Fw Warbelow saw the hostile at 200m range, above and to the starboard. I positioned myself under the machine and recognised it as a Wellington. Then I pulled my DO215 up and fired from behind and below causing the Wellington starboard engine to emit a dazzling flash and several large burning pieces flew off. The rear gunners defensive fire fell silent right away. As I now found myself higher than that of the Wellington. I flew the second attack from below and behind, the fire expanding further and fire spreading on to the fuselage. I positioned myself off to the port and attacked again from the side, below and the left. Since the Wellington was taking wild evasive action and was apparently out of control, she pulled up burning. I only had limited airspeed, sideslipped to port and spun down from 3900 to 1000m before regaining control of my machine. During the spin I had set the airscrew pitch to 9 o'clock and forgotten to restore it in all the excitement, so the engine wasn't pulling. I could not communicate with my crew as my helmet connection had come out and no one knew what was up. My thought was to reach the coast but shortly before I noticed my mistake and both engines ran normally once again. Meanwhile, I learned from ground control that the Wellington had crashed in flames'.*

The above report gives a fascinating insight into the encounter between Ofw Ney and the crew of Sgt John Thompson. The frantic attempts to evade the cannons of Neys Do215 and Thompson's skill in keeping aloft the crippled Wellington is testament to his and his crew determination to survive. Somehow, the two pilots managed to coax the crippled Wellington over the North Sea and land back at Marham. Damage was extensive, the tail plane, fuselage and port wing and fuel tank were shredded. The port engine was misfiring, and port nacelle almost hanging off. With the intercom u/s due to the encounter the crew were unable to contact the rear gunner once the attacks by the fighter had stopped. The crew's wireless operator was sent back to see what was wrong, he found the gunner slumped over his guns and the rear turret badly holed. Unable to remove the gunner it was not until the crew landed back at Marham it was discovered that Sgt John Northcote, a 19-year-old from Manchester was dead, a single bullet wound to his forehead had killed him instantly. Tragically this young gunner was killed on his 30th operation, and he could have expected to be taken off operations within days. His body was taken home to Manchester and buried in the Manchester Southern Cemetery on Wednesday November 5th, 1941. Vickers built Wellington X9674 HA-H was repaired by No.54 MU, it would not return to squadron service until December 31st. The only crews who claimed to have bombed Bremen were Wing Commander Kirkpatrick and Sgt McGlashan who had been joined by a young Scottish born 2nd pilot, Sgt George Niblo RCAF taking part in his first operation. While the squadron crews were battling the weather over northern Germany Sergeant Lamason was over the docks at Boulogne. In excellent conditions the crew watched as their mixed HE and incendiary load exploded across the entrance of No.4 dock producing two huge flashes. Joining Lamason on his first operation as captain was Sgt Richard 'Dick' Medus who was opening his batting with the squadron.

This ended a difficult month for the squadron and more importantly the whole of Bomber Command. Things would however not improve in November. The squadron was not involved in the disappointing raid against Kiel on the 1st. It would have to wait until the 3rd before it was called into action. The first target of the month were the 'Toads' at Brest. Only two crews were involved, S/Ldr Price at the controls of Wellington Mk.II Z8375 HA-Z and Sgt Webber in a modified Wellington Mk.Ic, Z8965 HA-L. Both were aloft just

*The crew of New Zealander Sergeant Phil Lamason RNZAF*

326

before 17:30 hours loaded with a single 4000 pounder. The usual tenacious Herbert Price circled the docks for 8 minutes for a break in the cloud. All the while the defences were pumping up a large amount of flak. Finally, after much deliberation, the crew located the ship's position in relation to the searchlights near Dock 8. Bombing from 12000 feet the bomb was dropped in the face of stiff opposition from both medium and heavy flak. A massive explosion was observed through the low cloud in the area they believed the 'Toads' were birthed. On leaving the target, the crew checked their run and position by identifying Pointe Saint-Mathieu. They were delighted to confirm what they believed to have been the right track and heading. Sergeant Webber was fortunate to see a break in the cloud two miles from the Docks, immediately identifying their position they attacked from 13,800 feet. Both Wellingtons were damaged, S/Ldr Price's front turret was badly holed while circling the target. During the late morning of the 4th, the squadrons of Marham received a rather strange message from group HQ at Exning requested that RAF Feltwell and RAF Marham detail thirty of their best crews to raid the Ruhr and make the 'maximum nuisance of themselves'.

What this meant is unclear, this request was later cancelled. That night seven crews were detailed to attack the Krupps works at Essen, while three 'Freshman' crews were given Oostende to visit. Once again, the weather over Northern Germany proved to be the only winner. A blanket of thick impenetrable cloud covered Essen. Frustrated, crews once again sought out targets of opportunity or bombed on ETA. Squadron Leader Spence bombed Duisburg. His fellow flight commander, S/Ldr Price DFC at the controls Wellington Mk.II Z8375 HA-Z dropped his 4000 pounder in the general area of Essen. Sergeant Hinwood stooged around Essen, hoping for a break in the cloud. His patience was not rewarded, in the end he bombed Munster. The three crews detailed to attack Oostende were equally hindered by the weather. Sergeant McKay spent 40 minutes trying to locate the docks, frustrated, he turned for home the cloud having got the better of him. Sergeant Cook RAAF was on his first operation as captain. He had beside him Sgt Kenneth Deadman, a 25-year-old from Liverpool on his first operation. Both operations were despite the commendable efforts by the crew's failures and no damage was caused to either targets. Group Captain McKee AFC DFC returned to Marham on the 17th, Group Captain MacDonald was off to pastures new, he was required at RAF Tempsford.

A major operation directed against the German capital was planned for the 7th. The C-in-C Bomber Command, Air Chief Marshal Sir Richard Peirse, decided to mount a major effort against Berlin despite the forecast of storms and freezing weather on the route and the concerns of some of his group commanders. It would be a maximum effort for No.3 Group who would provide 88 Wellingtons and Stirlings against Berlin, and provide a further 9 aircraft to attack Mannheim, twenty-six to Oostende and 8 to 'nuisance themselves in the Ruhr'

Squadron Leader Spence was the first away at 17:30 hours. For once there were no early returns, it was the only positive on an otherwise disappointing night. After battling the weather condition on route, the crews found a blanket of cloud covered Berlin. Bombs were dropped on ETA or crews joined those carrying out 'Roving' attacks on targets of opportunity in the Ruhr. Sergeant Lamason RNZAF was fortunate to return. While on his bomb run over Berlin his Wellington, X9785 HA-O came in for some close attention of the flak defences. The damage to his aircraft was widespread, both wings were severely holed, and the port oil tank punctured. Both turrets were put out of action, the Astro hatch was blown out, and the pilot's perspex smashed. The young New Zealander and his co-pilot Sgt 'Dick' Medus somehow managed to keep the Wellington aloft and with considerable skill coax it back to Marham. Sadly, Marham reported the loss of one crew, Sergeant John McGlashan. The crew are known to have bombed 'Berlin' as a message was received back at Marham at 2034hrs, there was no other contact. Damaged by flak, the Wellington crashed at Fellerhöfer 9 miles south of Krefeld. All the crew managed to parachute to safety.

**Tuesday 7th November 1941**

*Vickers Wellington*
*Mk.Ic*
*Z1069 HA-J 'Johnnie'*
*Contract No : B97887/39*
*Taken On Charge : 03/11/1941*
**Failed To Return**
*Pilot : Sergeant John Reid Curtis McGlashan 1264539 RAFVR PoW*
*2nd Pilot : Sergeant William Fraser Aus/404342 RAAF, PoW*
*Observer : Sergeant Alfred Herbert Bowater, 937787 RAFVR, PoW*
*Front Gunner : Sergeant John Dobson, 1051598 RAFVR, PoW*
*1st Wireless Operator : Sergeant Ronald Sydney Charles Stewart, 1151561 RAFVR, PoW*
*Rear Gunner : Sergeant Frederick Charles Adams, 1377902 RAFVR, PoW*

*Sergeant John Reid Curtis McGlashan RAFVR*

John Reid Curtis McGlashan was born in Hampstead, London, on December 12th, 1921, the son of a chartered accountant. Educated at Fettes, he was 18 when he joined the RAF in 1940, training as a pilot before joining No.218 Squadron. He completed the customary second pilot operations besides Sgt Forster completing eight trips before captaining his own crew. He was shot down on his 19th operation. According to his family, the German officer who greeted McGlashan on the ground at gunpoint really did observe, *"For you, the war is over"* McGlashan was to spend the rest of the war as a prisoner-of-war in a series of five prison camps, including Stalag Luft IV, where he helped to set up and run the RAF School for Prisoners of War. This offered PoWs lectures on 34 subjects from Latin to hotel management. Although many of them went on to pass exams, McGlashan believed the real value of the courses lay in preserving morale in the camp. He also taught bridge. At Stalag Luft VI McGlashan was awarded the YMCA sports medal for all-around sportsmanship. After the war he went up to Christ Church, Oxford, on a Classics scholarship, winning a rugby blue on his 24th birthday in 1945. His co-pilot had arrived via No.20 O.T.U and completed nine operations with F/O Arthur Humphreys. This was his first and only operation with McGlashan.

The activities on the night of November 7th/8th set two new records at the time. The number of aircraft dispatched, 392 and, more alarmingly, recorded 37 bombers that failed to return, double the previous highest for night operations. This one night had far-reaching consequences not only for Bomber Command but Air Chief Marshal Sir Richard Peirse.

The squadron lost two of its flight commanders after the Berlin raid. Squadron Leader Gerald Spence was posted within days to help rebuild No.40 Squadron based at RAF Alconbury after the majority of its flying and ground crews were posted to Malta. He would command the squadron only a matter of weeks until replaced by Acting Wing Commander Peter Heath on November 26th. Peter Heath would continue to command the squadron until February 14th, 1942 when the home echelon of 40 Squadron was renumbered 156 Squadron. Heath would continue to lead until he was killed attacking Gennervilliers on May 29th, 1942.

Gerald Spence was then sent to fill the vacant post of the commanding officer of No.149 Squadron on the departure of another ex 218 Squadron flight commander, William Beaman who had been posted on the 11th to command No.99 Squadron. The Berlin raid was the last operation flown by the irrepressible Squadron Leader Herbert Price DFC. All the squadron was pleased to see this courageous flight commander survive his tour, his press on attitude and sheer determination was an inspiration to all. He would be posted to No.3 Group HQ as Squadron Leader Operations for a well-earned rest within the month. On May 31st, 1942 he assumed command of No.156 Squadron based at RAF Alconbury due to the loss of Peter Heath two days prior. Tragically, Herbert's spell of command was cut short when he failed to return from Hamburg on July 28th. He had at the time completed an estimated 61 operations.

The squadron was detailed for an operation against Essen on 8th. However, No.3 Group HQ cancelled the operation at the 11th hour due to adverse weather conditions. It was the start of five days of inaction other than training flights and Air-tests. Marham was visited by members of the Bomber Defence Committee on the 12th. The Committee under the chairmanship of Mr W.S Farren, Chief Superintendent of R.A.E Farnborough, discussed and talked at length with the squadron's air gunners to understand the issues and problems that they were encountering on operations. It was an ideal opportunity for the crews and 'boffins' to work together. Bomber Command was painfully aware of the limitations of the existing bomber defences. It was hoped that these meetings would help eliminate any mistakes regarding R.A.E Farnborough ideas and theories regarding the protection of bombers. This 'hands-on' approach was typical of the forward-thinking Mr W.S Farren who up until weeks before was the Director of Technical Development in the Ministry of Aircraft Production.

Both Marham's squadrons were finally called to action on November 15th. 218 Squadron was given two targets. Ten crews would attack Kiel, while two would visit Emden. Of the twelve Wellingtons dispatched five crews would be carrying the 4000 pounder.

### No.218 Squadron Vickers Wellington Mk.Ic and Mk.II 4000lb Bomb Carriers

| Date | Serial | Codes | From | Mark | Engine | Maker | Contract | Fate |
|---|---|---|---|---|---|---|---|---|
| 16/04/1941 | W5448 | HA-Z | No.12 M.U | Mk.II | Merlin X | Vickers Armstrong | B/71441/40 | Crashed. |
| 18/04/1941 | W5447 | HA-C | No.12 M.U | Mk.II | Merlin X | Vickers Armstrong | B/71441/40 | To No.305 Sqdn |
| 28/05/1941 | W5457 | HA-Z | No.28 M.U | Mk.II | Merlin X | Vickers Armstrong | B/71441/40 | FTR |

| | | | | | | | | |
|---|---|---|---|---|---|---|---|---|
| 11/07/1941 | **W5536** | *Not Coded* | No.115 Sqdn | Mk.II | Merlin X | Vickers Armstrong | B/71441/41 | To No.305 Sqdn<br><br>*No Ops flown with 218* |
| 02/08/1941 | **W5449** | **HA-Y** | No.115 Sqdn | Mk.II | Merlin X | Vickers Armstrong | B/71441/40 | **Crashed.** |
| No Date | **Z8375** | **HA-Z** | No.115 Sqdn | Mk.II | Merlin X | Vickers Armstrong | B/71441/40 | To No.405 Sqdn |
| 28/09/1941 | **Z8399** | *Not Coded* | No.115 Sqdn | Mk.II | Merlin X | Vickers Armstrong | B/71441/40 | To No.115 Sqdn<br><br>*No Ops flown with 218* |
| 04/11/1941 | **Z8437** | **HA-X** | No.12 M.U | Mk.II | Merlin X | Vickers Armstrong | B/71441/40 | To No.405 Sqdn |
| 08/11/1941 | **Z8431** | **HA-J** | No.12 M.U | Mk.II | Merlin X | Vickers Armstrong | B/71441/40 | To No.405 Sqdn |
| 13/10/1941 | **Z8957** | **HA-L** | No.12 M.U | Mk.Ic | Pegasus XVIII | Vickers Armstrong | B/71441/40 | **Crashed.** |
| No Date | **Z8965** | **HA-L** | No.57 Sqdn | Mk.Ic | Pegasus XVIII | Vickers Armstrong | B/71441/40 | To No.214 Sqdn |
| 14/10/1941 | **Z8982** | **HA-E** | No.51 M.U | Mk.Ic | Pegasus XVIII | Vickers Armstrong | B/71441/40 | To No.214 Sqdn |
| 15/11/1941 | **Z8970** | **HA-W** | No.51 M.U | Mk.Ic | Pegasus XVIII | Vickers Armstrong | B/71441/40 | To No.214 Sqdn |

*The above lists all known squadron Wellington MK.Ic and Mk.II that dropped or were capable of carrying the 4000lb Blast Bomb between April and November 1941.*

*A wonderful painting by the war artist David T Smith painted in 1941. This is one of two completed by the artist on his visit to RAF Marham. This painting shows Wellington Mk.II W5457 HA-Z undergoing maintenance in 'A' Flight hangar.*

The two raids on this night typify the problems facing the group and more importantly the difficulties the C-in-C Bomber Command had to face almost nightly during this period. Number 3 Group provided forty-nine bombers for the Kiel raid, plus a further 19 would attack Emden. Of the sixty-eight aircraft detailed, eleven failed to take off. Two further bogged down. At RAF Honington three of the five Wellingtons of No.9 Squadron detailed were unable to take off. These were covered in hoar frost and could not be cleared before take-off time. With the Group's numbers whittled down to 52, a further seven returned early due to ice. These problems were not unique to No.3 Group, they were replicated throughout the command. Once airborne the crews quickly encountered freezing conditions, and to add to their problems they encountered much stronger winds than the Met men forecast. The aircraft of No.4 Group detailed to attack Kiel were recalled due to the fear of the weather closing down their Yorkshire airfields. There was no such recall for No.3 Group. Over the long flight over the North Sea the squadron recorded four early returns, three due to severe icing.

The first return was Sgt McPhail in Wellington X9785 HA-O who experienced icing at 9000ft. Both wings were covered by a quickly worsening film of ice. With the Wellington vibrating and refusing to climb the crew turned for home retaining their bomb load. He was promptly followed by Sgt Brewerton in Wellington Z8437 HA-X who experienced identical problems. Sergeant McKay had ice form on both wings leading edge, engine nacelles, tail, and rudder of Wellington W5727 HA-V. It had also started to cover the cockpit canopy and windscreen making forward vision impossible. To make matters worse, the Wellington began to vibrate and shudder under the weight of ice. Unable to climb and with the controls quickly stiffing up, and no forward view Sgt McKay wisely jettisoned his entire bomb load and turned for home and warmer air. The final early return was Sergeant Webber and crew. They lost the port engine aboard Wellington Z8965 HA-L due to a split oil tank. They reached half away across the inhospitable North Sea before they jettisoned the bomb load from 12000ft. It was an ominous start to what would be a terrible night.

None of crews managed to reach Kiel, all were blown helplessly north of track and found themselves over Denmark. Wing Commander Kirkpatrick ended up off the Danish coastal town of Gjerrid on the eastern coast of Denmark, some 200 miles north of Kiel. Sergeant Vezina attacked Aarhus on Jutland peninsula's east coast. Sergeant Forsyth found himself blown so far north he ended up over Skagen, a port town at the most northern end of Denmark's Jutland peninsula. Flight Lieutenant Livingstone faired a little better, he bombed Horsens, a city on the east coast of Jutland around 90 miles north of Kiel. Sergeant Tomkins deposited his entire bomb load on a flak battery at Spiekeroog, one of the East Frisian Islands. Now the crews had the unenviable task of navigating back to Marham. An SOS was received at 02:02hrs from the crew of Australian Sgt Alan Cook at the controls of veteran Wellington, R1135 HA-N. A second-class fix from the MF D/F station at Hull based on this transmission gave their position at 56:53 N - 03:30 E. This put the crew in the middle of the North Sea and halfway between Scotland and Denmark. Sadly, they were not heard from again, it was the crews second operation. Tragically, despite the fix no Air/Sea Rescue was possible due to the extreme range involved. Only the body of Sgt Drury was recovered. He washed ashore at Sklinna on the island of Leka, Norway at the end of December 1941. The body was brought to Bronnoysund on the mainland where he was buried on January 1st, 1942 in the Bronnoysund Old Cemetery as an 'unknown'. The badly decomposed body was given a full military funeral. The young lad from Liverpool was taken to Trondheim (Stavne) Cemetery for reburial post war.

*Sergeant Alan Cook RAAF and crew are believed to have ditched in the North Sea. The chances of survival even in more favourable weather conditions were slim. In November, with a freezing sea and sub-zero winds their fate was sealed.*

### Saturday 15th November 1941
*Vickers Wellington*
*Mk.Ic*
*R1135 HA-N 'Nuts'*
*Contract No : B992424/39*
*Taken On Charge: 28/12/1940*
**Failed To Return**
*Pilot : Sergeant Alan Cook, Aus/400696 RAAF,* **Killed**
*2nd Pilot : Sergeant Kenneth David Deadman, 1014105 RAFVR,* **Killed**
*Observer : Sergeant Jack Burton Drury, 968019 RAFVR,* **Killed**
*Front Gunner :Sergeant Robert Ville Hannam, 1006118 RAFVR,* **Killed**
*1st Wireless Operator : Sergeant Fred Charles Reeve, 1168648 RAFVR,* **Killed**
*Rear Gunner : Sergeant Robert Edmund 'Ted' Glenny, 1021175 RAFVR,* **Killed**

Alan Cook had successfully completed seven operations before his disappearance, six flown as 2nd pilot besides Sgt John Webber. Sergeant Deadman had completed just two operations prior to his death. Tragically, the crew's rear gunner, 19-year-old Robert 'Ted' Glenny from Warrenpoint, County-Down was on his first operation.

The crew of Sergeant Richard Forsyth experienced trouble on the return flight. Blown northwards the

Wellington began showing signs of trouble when both engines started to misfire. A quick check of the fuel gauges showed both main fuel tanks had almost run dry of petrol. Switching over to the nacelle tanks both engines immediately picked up, however the problem was short lived. Within 10 minutes both engines cut again and despite the pilots attempts to coax a few more minutes flying time which would see them safely clear the Yorkshire coast and its defences and find a suitable place to land. With both engines now dead, the Wellington quickly began to lose altitude. Both pilots frantically searched for a place to force land. Fighting the controls, Sgts Forsyth and Niblo managed to bring the Wellington down on a frozen field near New Marske south of Redcar. The Wellington unfortunately over-ran the selected field and ploughed into woodland. The fuselage broke in two while the Fraser-Nash nose turret was almost crushed flat. The underside of the aircraft was severely crumpled on hitting the frozen ground. The time was 06:00 hours, the crew had been aloft for 8 hours 19 minutes. During the forced landing, the crew's front gunner, Sgt Collins was killed, Sgt Nibo sustained a fractured left leg while the crew's observer was badly bruised. Wellington Z8853 HA-H was written off but both engines were salvaged and reused.

*Only the body of the young observer, Sergeant Jack Burton Drury was recovered. He is buried in the Trondheim (Stavne) Cemetery.*

Sergeant Niblo and Gordon were taken to the local E.M.S. Hospital at Winterton for treatment. The body of the young gunner was brought home to Harrow, Middlesex. He was buried on November 21st, at the Harrow (Pinner) New Cemetery. This was Charles' first operation. The loss rate on this trip was sobering especially for 3 Group who bore the brunt of the nights activities. Five crews were missing, two ditched and five crashed in the U.K., for negligible results. It was yet another black mark against the C-in-C Bomber Command and there were more rumblings of discontent. No operations were flown on the 16th, sleet and snow being forecast. However, this did not prevent 115 Squadron sending out a crew to search for one of their Wellingtons that ditched off Whitby. For once, there was a happy ending. A Destroyer picked up the crew who were then transferred by launch and brought safely to shore. On the 17th the A.O.C. called a conference of all his station commanders to discuss the recent losses on operations. It must have been a rather tense meeting.

**Saturday 15th November 1941**

*Vickers Wellington*
*Mk.Ic*
*Z8853 HA-H 'Harry'*
*Contract No : B71441/40*
*Taken On Charge : 28/10/1941*

*Forced Landed UK*
*Pilot : Sergeant Richard A Forsyth R/65238 RCAF*
*2nd Pilot : Sergeant George Niven Niblo R/58479 RCAF. Injured.*
*Observer : Sergeant Derrick Birks 1154263 RAFVR*
*Front Gunner : Sergeant  Charles Lloyd Allan Collins 1254914 RAFVR* **Killed**
*1st Wireless Operator : Sergeant Alexander Bruce Gordon 921998 RAFVR. Injured.*
*Rear Gunner: Sergeant  Frederick Herbert Slatford 1183344 RAFVR*


The squadron was not required to operate again until 23rd. However, the squadron did not sit idle, 75 training flights were flown amounting to some 80 hours flying. On the 23rd a single crew was detailed and briefed; the target was the docks at Dunkirk. Canadian, Pilot Officer Cottier along with his Australian co-pilot Sgt Savage were unable to identify the target due to cloud, resulting in the bomb load being jettisoned. It was another solitary crew detailed for operations on the 26th. Sergeant Joseph Vezina RCAF and crew departed Marham at 1715 hours aboard Wellington Z1103 HA-A. This was a brand-new machine that had only arrived via No.44 M.U a few weeks before.

The crew had successfully located and bombed Emden and were on their return flight when they encountered flak from the Frisian Islands. The crew's observer Sgt Boss carried out a routine fuel check and recorded 130 gallons of fuel. Fifteen minutes later, and to his shock another examination showed that 50 gallons of fuel had been lost, presumably the result of flak damage. Unable to confirm their position and

*Another unidentified squadron Vickers Wellington. This aircraft has notched up 10 operations and a fighter 'kill'.*
*A caricature of the Swedish born American actress Greta Garbo and her famous 'I want to be alone' line, or in*
*this case 'One Alone'!.*

relying on D/R due to cloud the crew believed they were just 100 miles from the English coast. Helfer brought the Wellington down to 3500 feet to establish his position once the coast was crossed. He flew at this height for some time and when the coastline did not appear, he asked for a priority fix at 22:21 hours. To his horror, this established that they were still over 100 miles from the English coastline. The nacelle tanks had already been pulled at 22:00 hours, he had no additional fuel, the main fuel gauges were showing a gradual but constant reduction. For some inexplicable reason, the W/T receiver decided to stop working making an already perilous situation even more difficult. Without a bearing the crew would be unable to fix their exact location. Thankfully, the transmitter was still functioning, and an S.O.S. was sent at 22:30 hours. Squeezing every drop of petrol out of the tanks the Wellington finally reached the English coast off the north Norfolk coast at 22:55 hours. A few searchlights were observed pointing west along the coast, a green verey flare was also seen. Deciding to turn in the direction of the searchlights the Wellington flew along the now almost horizontal beams.

*Sergeant Kenneth England the rear gunner aboard Wellington Z1103 HA-A. Sadly this 19-year-old lad from Watford would be killed on operations in May 1942.*

Hugging the coastline desperately searching for somewhere to land the crews luck finally failed when both engines started to splutter and misfire. Sergeant Helfer realised that he needed to quickly land while he still had the use of the fast-fading engines. Believing that the beaches would be mined, he decided to ditch the Wellington. The floatation bags were inflated at 1,500 feet in preparation. Showing remarkable skill Helfer brought the Wellington down onto the sea 1 mile off Wells. The Wellington hit the waves, bounced twice, and settled on the surface. Once stationary the dinghy released automatically from the starboard nacelle as the aircraft began quickly filling with water. The dazed crew scrambled into the dinghy, once aboard the tie line was cut and the dinghy slowly drifted off. The Wellington remained afloat for almost five minutes thanks to the floatation bags before it sank below the waves. Sergeant Helfer ordered a distress flare fired. For the next two hours the crew drifted until a light was seen flashing in the distance. This was answered by torch giving the S.O.S. signal. An R.A.F. Launch piloted by the Cox'n of the Well Lifeboat dispatched from Wells Harbour approached the dinghy from the seaside. All the crew were taken aboard, cold, bruised but very much alive.

## Wednesday 26th November 1941
*Vickers Wellington*
*Mk.Ic*
*Z1103 HA-A 'Apple'*
*Contract No : B.97887/39*
*Taken On Charge : 28/10/1941*
*Ditched of Norfolk Coast*
*Pilot : Sergeant Terence Helfer, 1186112 RAFVR.*
*2nd Pilot : Sergeant Taylor NFD*
*Observer: Sergeant Reginald Lawrence Ross, 92779 RAFVR*
*Front Gunner : Sergeant Jack Purcell, 1169029 RAFVR*

*1st Wireless Operator : Sergeant James Adamson, 1050913 RAFVR*
*Rear Gunner : Sergeant Kenneth William George England, 1375251 RAFVR*

It had been the crews second ditching. They had survived a few days afloat in September off the coast of Kent. Sergeant Helfer's decision not to land on the beach for fear of mines proved correct, it had been heavily mined the previous summer. Once again luck was on their side.

The following night, nine crews, five of which were carrying a 4000 pounder were heading for the marshalling yards at Dusseldorf. Two returned early, one was skippered by the recently promoted Squadron Leader Bill Williams DFC, flying his first operation in nearly three weeks. Problems with the starboard Merlin aboard Z8431 HA-J meant that he could not climb above 9000 feet. Having crossed the North Sea and not wishing to waste the bomb the crew selected the airfield at Haamstede as a suitable target and watched with satisfaction as it produced a vivid crimson flash as it exploded. The crew of Sgt Hinwood experience a loss of oil pressure in the port engine of Wellington W5727 HA-V soon after crossing the English coast. They dropped their single 500lb bomb but retained all the incendiaries. Stronger than forecast winds once again caused problems especially for the inexperienced observers. Isolated fires were seen a considerable distance west of target, these were quickly ignored as dummies or more likely the inexperienced crews caught out by the strong wind.

Those who located Dusseldorf found it covered with industrial haze. All the squadron crews reported bombing the general target area, no ground details were visible, but this did not stop some concentrated bombing. There was practically no flak or searchlight activity encountered. Those carrying the 4000 pounders had the most satisfaction, the explosions of these 'block-busters' were easily identified. Wing Commander Kirkpatrick was at the helm of Wellington Mk.II Z8375 HA-Z. He reported on his return, *'Bomb seen to burst with a terrific force and the whole built up area appeared to boil. This appearance was probably caused by a large reddish fire, which flared up on departure and was visible from thirty to forty miles away'.* Sergeant Brewerton was equally impressed, *'Bomb dropped E to W of marshalling yards. Burst seen, large column of light-coloured smoke rising to 1-2000 feet high'.*

The operation was the last flown by the squadron in November, the last few days were spent on the ground, a spell of bad weather preventing any flying.

# Chapter 11: December 1941 to April 1942 – The Arrival of the Stirling

Widespread fog over the region meant that apart from one solitary training flight on December 5th the squadron remained grounded. Things improved slightly on the 6th when thirteen training flights and air-tests were completed in wintery conditions. A rumour had started to circulate around the various messes that the squadron was to convert from the trusty Wellingtons to the massive four-engine Short Stirling. The old hands were mortified at the prospect. They had come to trust the rugged qualities of the old 'Wimpy'. Like all rumours, everyone was guessing what was happening, for the time being, at least the crews would continue operating with the Wellington.

Finally, on the 7th conditions improved sufficiently to allow twelve crews to participate on a raid against the 'Toads' at Brest, while a 'Freshman' crew captained by Sgt William Gregg was given Dunkirk. The squadron would field no less than six Wellingtons capable of lifting the 4000 pounder, it was the largest number dispatched to date by the squadron. There was one early return, Sgt McKay's starboard engine aboard Wellington R1601 HA-T began showing signs of trouble soon after take-off. At an altitude of 9,000 feet, the engine started producing dense black smoke and eventually cut giving the pilot little option other than to abort. Having jettisoned all six 500lb bombs 'safe' Sgt McKay headed for RAF Boscombe Down. Somehow in the confusion instead of landing at Boscombe Down the crew landed at RAF Middle Wallop. Overshooting the shorter than expected runway the Wellington careered out of control at the end of the runway before coming to an undignified stop in a large hedge. The shaken but uninjured crew quickly vacated the Wellington which had suffered a badly crumpled nose and turret. The Wellington was repaired on-site and would eventually return to the squadron in February 1942. It had clocked up an impressive 28 raids.

**Sunday December 7th 1941**

*Vickers Wellington*
*Mk.Ic*
*R1601 HA-T 'Tommy'*
*Contract No : B992424/39*
*Taken On Charge : 15/04/1941*
*Overshot Landing*
*Pilot : Sergeant Sergeant John Robert McKay, 1058793 RAFVR*
*2nd Pilot : Sergeant Archibald Cowen Honeyman, Aus/404549 RAAF*
*Observer: Pilot Officer Grant*
*Front Gunner : Sergeant Smith*
*1st Wireless Operator : Flight Sergeant Clarke*
*Rear Gunner : Sergeant Fuller*

Those crews who arrived over Brest early found it relatively clear of cloud. To the delight of the attackers, the usual dense smoke screen had yet to take effect. This gave the observers an opportunity for some unhindered bombing. The usual flak barrage greeted the crews as they made their bomb runs. Sergeant Vezina was unfortunate, he was caught by both flak and searchlights which spoilt his run into the target. It took all the young Canadian's strength and flying skill to escape. New Zealander, Sergeant McGregor dropped his 4000 pounder near Dock No.8 while Sgt Hinwood dropped his single bomb on Dock No.6. By now the smokescreen had started to cover the dock area making identification difficult. Sergeant Brewerton at the controls of Wellington Z8437 HA-X attacked from 13000 feet dropping his 4000lb bomb in the general dock area. This produced a substantial explosion which was followed almost immediately by an equally large explosion the result of another 4000 pounder detonating. New Zealander, Sgt Phil Lamason on only his 4th operation as captain, was entrusted with one of the squadron's few MkIc type 432 Wellingtons designed to carry the 4000lb bomb. Having bombed the target, the temperature on the port engine started to drop and show signs of trouble. Turning for the quickest route home, the crew settled down for the long sea crossing. Sitting in the 2nd pilot's seat was a 21-year-old Englishman from South Shields, named Sergeant Sidney Falconer. This was his first operation on the squadron. He would over the following months make a name for himself on the squadron. All seemed well until the offending engine suddenly cut over Wiltshire forcing the crew to land at RAF Colerne at 2200 hours. This proved to be Wellington Z8965 HA-L sixth and the last operation on the squadron, after repair it was transferred to No.214 Squadron on December 28th. The crew of F/Lt Humphreys somehow completely missed Brest and mistakenly bombed the docks at Lorient where they dropped their single bomb. The Freshman crew found Dunkirk eerily quiet, no searchlights or flak was encountered. Just after bombing an aircraft was seen on fire, this fell into the sea and burnt for 7 minutes. It is possible the crew had witnessed the loss of a 104 Squadron, Wellington Z8426 EP-E skippered by Sgt Reginald Anson, there were no survivors.

On December 10th Bomber Command was instructed to turn its attention towards attacks on the Biscay Ports. The following night eleven crews were on their way back to Brest. The crew of Sergeant Roland Brewerton were obliged to take to their parachutes en route when the port engine aboard Wellington W5727 HA-V caught fire. The pilot ordered the bomb load jettisoned and instructed the crew to bail-out, which they did from 2000 feet. Sergeant Brewerton made a successful belly landing at 1620 hours in a field near the small village of Charlton, 1 mile north of

Upavon, Wiltshire. The damage was restricted to both props and fuselage of the Wellington. The more pressing problem was that unbeknown to Roland, the bomb load, 6 x 500lb SAPs had still been on board when he crash-landed. For some reason, his order to jettison had either been unheard or a mechanical problem caused them to hang-up.

### Thursday December 11th 1941

*Vickers Wellington*
*Mk.Ic*
*W5727 HA-V 'Victor'*
*Contract No : B.71441/40/39*
*Taken On Charge : 24/10//1941*
*Forced Landing*
*Pilot : Sergeant Roland Brewerton, 999259 RAFVR*
*2nd Pilot : Sergeant William Longmore, 117857 RAFVR*
*Observer: Sergeant Cox*
*Front Gunner : Pilot Officer Taylor*
*1st Wireless Operator : Sergeant Williamson RCAF*
*Rear Gunner : Sergeant McDonald*

The rear gunner Sergeant 'Bill' McDonald recalls the events of that night;

*In mid-December 1941 we flew from Marham to Brest via Portland Bill. We had been there a few times during that week. The aircraft was a Wellington 1c. Hit in the port engine whilst over the target we staggered back over the Channel looking for Portland. At an estimated distance of 35 miles from Portland, and with the prop of the dead engine windmilling away, it seemed unlikely that we would make our landfall. The smouldering fire that developed from a grinding prop seemed likely to spread and did as we lost height alarmingly. It was snowing at the time, and the prospect of ditching was not a pleasant thought. However, a short time later, it became a much more acceptable alternative as the fire suddenly spread down the port side of the aircraft. Jump, ditch, press-on? There is nothing so conducive to quick decision-making in an aircraft as fire. We decided, very quickly, to jump. Removing my helmet and tucking my coffee flask inside my Irvin I dropped clear of the Wellington. I cannot recall consciously pulling the 'D' ring on the chute, but I vividly recall the near emasculation caused by a badly adjusted harness, as the chute opened. After the initial, brief euphoric sensation of a successful opening of the canopy I was preoccupied with the business of a landing. If over the sea as I imagined, I was, when should I hit the quick release? Too soon and I would fall like a sack of potatoes from too great a height. Too late and I would become entangled in the falling canopy and lines. As I descended, I became aware of white patches below which I took to be the white wave tops. I could also hear the crump of gunfire or bombing. While vainly trying to guess my height, I took an enormous thump on the right side of my head and body which prevented any further speculation about height, water, snow and gunfire. I remember coming round, still in a very dazed condition, aware of a very sore head and an even more painful mouth. I had bitten my tongue. One other thing puzzled me too. I seemed to be in a hollow of sorts and above, over the rim of the hollow, two or three searchlights were visible. Lying in this hollow with a confused feeling of relief at surviving but worried about my whereabouts I formed an uneasy feeling that we had been flying on a reciprocal course; that we had bailed out over Brest; that I was lying in a bomb crater near the docks and that the crumps that I heard were bomb bursts.*

*After waiting a further 10 minutes or so for my head to clear I started scrambling around searching for my coffee flask, which I never found but discovered that I was still gripping the 'D' ring in my hand. Climbing out of the crater, I started walking. The snow had now turned to sleet, and it was impossible to guess which direction was north or south as I wandered around aimlessly in what seemed to be scrubland. After perhaps 30 minutes the land was more cultivated, and here and there I disturbed cattle. No searchlights were visible, and a vast silence surrounded me.*

*I cannot remember how much further I walked before coming to a road. By this time, and as my head cleared, I felt my suspicions about landing in Brest were unfounded. I still wished for a drink but continued on this road with more optimism hoping to find some form of habitation when coming towards me was a very dim light which turned out to be that of a cyclist. I called to the cyclist who by this time was no more than 10 paces from me, and I was astounded to see him turnabout and flee in the direction from which he had come at top speed. By this time, I was too weary to consider the reasons for the strange antics of cyclists and I continued walking until I came to a row of houses. There was, I think, a row of four and they were on the right-hand side of the road as I walked; there were none on the left-hand side and there did not appear to be any others in the immediate vicinity. The time would be about 1.45 a.m.*

*It must have been a shock for the lady who opened the door to my knock, but she kept it well hidden or was accustomed to having muddy and bloodstained airmen at her door. After explaining why, I was there and apologising for the inconvenience it must cause her, I was shaken by her casually phrased question, 'Been to Brest, have you?' I was given a chair and was eagerly awaiting that drink of water. But it did not come. First, she went upstairs to wake her two small children who stood in front of me, staring as though I was something from another planet, which is probably what I did resemble. Still no water. The lady said that she would only be a moment and I thought, at last, a drink, but no, she had gone next door and next door again to rouse the children who, over a 10 minute period arrived in ones and twos to join the other two in front of me, the braver ones timidly touching my sleeve. Then, finally, the water; it tasted delicious.*

*Lest it be thought that this good lady merely used me as a diversion to amuse her children, I should also record that she treated my injured face and mouth, provided a good hot, strong cup of tea from her meagre rations and also contacted the police who came to collect me. My flying ration of a bar of chocolate and a handful of raisins was a very poor way of showing my gratitude, but the children seemed to enjoy the chocolate and the break in their routine.*

*I was driven to Devizes Police Station, where they suggested a generous tot of Scotch would be beneficial. It might also help to heal my tongue! They explained that we had landed in the southern part of Salisbury Plain and close by there had been a night shoot. When we had left the aircraft, as standard procedure, the Wireless Operator had sent the bale out code and clamped his key down. The RAF had picked up the signal and informed the police in the appropriate areas which, in turn, had contacted the army authorities and called off the firing. The searchlights were to mark the estimated area in which they thought that we would be. Hearing all this explained my hallucinations and other fantasies. From police authority, I was handed over to RAF authority; namely RAF Upavon, where I met two other members of the crew. We were debriefed and later flown back to base in a DH Rapide. Our minor ordeal was over.*

This was Sgt Roland Leslie Brewerton's 25th and last operation with the squadron. Shortly after he was posted to No.22 OTU, he survived the war. Vickers Wellington W5727 would be repaired and eventually return to squadron strength in March 1942.

Unlike the previous visit, the weather over the Brest was lousy. Complete cloud cover on the route and over the target resulted in the crews bombing on ETA or a number of flares dropped by two Short Stirlings of No.XV Squadron. Participating on his first operation since his arrival a few days prior was Squadron Leader Beverley Ridley Ker from 23 OTU. Born in 1906, the young Ker was no stranger to adventure. Having obtained his pilot's licence in 1932, he flew from Newcastle's then the new municipal airport, Woolsington to Oslo alone, a distance of some 12000 miles. A rather serious individual, his reputation as a rather tough, straight-talking arrogant man preceded him. A former farmer, he was granted a commission into the RAF as P/O on probation on 27th March 1934 and eventually rose to F/Lt on 16th March 1941. He would take command of 'A' Flight.

On the 16th Marham reverberated to the sound of four Hercules Mk.XI engines, the sound of a Hercules was nothing new, however these were the engines of Short Stirling Mk.I N6127. The mess rumours that the squadron was going to convert had become a reality. Built by Short and Harland Ltd Belfast this massive aircraft with a wingspan 99ft and a length of 87ft and perched on two massive if troublesome undercarriage towered over the low-slung Wellingtons. Even the crews of No.115 Squadron, who would generally keep themselves to them themselves were intrigued. But for the time being, it was back to normality

*Taken in 1932, a young and rather serious looking Beverley Ker. He was not a man who made friends easy. His bullish demeaner would upset many on the squadron especially the Commonwealth and Dominion crews.*

The cancelled Brest operation was back on, 48 hours later six crews including Wing Commander Kirkpatrick were heading south for another crack at the Cruisers in Brest Harbour. Sergeant Vezina started experiencing problems with his starboard engine soon after take-off. These problems increased when he started gaining altitude, at 11,000 feet, the engine caught fire. Sergeant Vezina had this to say about the incident that followed;

*Starboard engine caught fire at 11000 feet. Immediately I turned off the switches and glided to about 7000 feet. I turned on the switches again and the fire came on again. I tried to keep my height on the port engine but it was unsuccessful, so I ordered the crew to bail-out at about 8,000 feet.*

All the crew managed to safely bail-out, only the crew's rear gunner, Sgt Jim Crump was injured, fracturing his ankle on landing. The young Canadian pilot with some skill managed to crash-land the Wellington 500 yards west of Holm Farm, Paverstock, Dorset at 1945 hours. Most of the crew landed near Chilfrome Mill, near Maiden Newton. Pilot Officer Reginald Brown, the crew's observer, appears to have delayed his escape as he landed close to where the Wellington had crashed. The Wellington hit the ground producing a muffled explosion. Living close by to the now wrecked Wimpy was a Mrs Egerton and her husband, the local Home Guard Leader. Woken by the noise they quickly dressed and started walking towards the glow of the fire. Here they found P/O Brown wondering in a field close to the crash site. He appeared to be dazed and confused. Concussed, and suffering from shock he was quickly taken to the home of Mrs Egerton. It was a lucky encounter. Pilot Officer Reg Brown was immediately given some hot soup and a pair of her son pyjamas before ordered to bed to rest. Soon afterwards, the telephone rang. Both Mr and Mrs Egerton decided to initially ignore it, however it continued ringing throughout the evening. Finally, they answered, a frustrated Home Guard, the local Civic Defence and RAF all demanded information. At midnight one caller asked that Mr Egerton wake up the young airman and drive him to Dorchester. This was refused, Mr Egerton stating that the young man needed the rest! The calls continued up until 0200 hours. The following morning refreshed and after a good breakfast, Reg Brown thanked Mr and Mrs Egerton for their hospitality and kindness and returned to RAF Marham. Interestingly, he told his hosts that, *they should never have bailed out, for they could have got back OK*. That same morning Mrs Egerton walked the short distance to the crash site. Wreckage from the Wellington was strewn over an area of 400 yards. The field was now guarded by the RAF who refused her entry into the field. It was while back on the squadron that Reginald Brown posted a thank you card on which he wrote, *To the nicest people I have ever dropped in on.*

## Tuesday December 16th 1941
*Vickers Wellington*
*Mk.Ic*
*X9785 HA-O*
*Contract No : B.97887/39*
*Taken On Charge : 24/10/1941*
*SoC : 30/12/1941*
*Forced Landing*
*Pilot : Sergeant Joseph Fernand Paul Vezina R/162799 RCAF*
*2nd Pilot : Sergeant Harding*
*Observer: Pilot Officer Reginald Wiseman Brown 104694 RAFVR*
*Front Gunner : Sergeant George Toynbee-Clarke RNZAF*
*1st Wireless Operator : Sergeant Willett*
*Rear Gunner : Sergeant Jim Crump, 1377496 RAFVR, Injured*

Sergeant Crump was admitted to the Bridport, Dorset Hospital with a fractured ankle. The subsequent investigation into the crash revealed that No.6 cylinder stub and blown out, this had given the pilot the impression that the engine was on fire. The issue of not maintaining height on one engine was not explained. The station commander Group Captain McKee in his summoning up of the whole incident pulled no punches.

This pilot seems to have found great difficulty in maintaining height on one engine after jettisoning his bomb load. He will be given thorough re-training in this aspect of flying. A further factor which made it difficult for him to find an aerodrome was unsatisfactory W/T communication. The pilot of this aircraft is a French Canadian and in an emergency is rather inclined to be excitable. It is considered that a cool and collected pilot could have got this aircraft safety down on an aerodrome. From investigations the mechanical failure was the broken exhaust stub.

*Group Captain*
*RAF Station Marham*
*17.12.1941*

This was the last operation flown by the young Canadian. He had completed 19 operations, 12 of them as captain. During that time, he had made two forced landings, on each occasion all his crew survived unscathed. Within a few days, he was posted to the newly formed No.419 RCAF Squadron based at RAF Mildenhall. Sadly, he would be killed on February 12th, 1942 during Operation 'Fuller'. He was just twenty years old.

Sergeant Helfer was only airborne a few hours in Wellington X9755 HA-K when he returned to RAF Marham. Unable to climb above 9000 feet and with the aircraft decidedly nose-heavy he aborted the operation. Conditions over the target initially were clear, once again, flares dropped by the Stirlings provided some much-needed illumination. Wing Commander Kirkpatrick watched between flak bursts as two of his 500 pounders exploded close to the 'Toads'. Pilot Officer Cottier RCAF dropped his bombs in one stick across the Port De Commerce area of Brest, four distinctive explosions were seen. Despite the flak which was described as heavy all the crews returned unscathed. Sergeant Hinwood landed at RAF Boscombe Down due to fuel shortage. This would be the 17th and last operation flown by Sergeant Thomas Cottier RCAF and crew who would be posted along with fellow Canadian Sgt Vezina to No.419 Squadron. Thomas would have the distinction of being the squadron's first loss. On January 15th, the crew ditched off Spurn Head on return from Hamburg, Thomas Cottier, his wireless operator and air gunner was sadly drowned, Thomas's body would not be found until April 1942.

On the 17th another Short and Harland built Short Stirling, N6126 landed at Marham fresh from the parent factory. This was followed on the 23rd by N6128 bringing the squadron strength to three. The squadron would be the fourth to be equipped in the group. However, it would not become operational until February.

There followed another long period of operational inactivity after the Brest operation not that the squadron was complaining. With Christmas fast approaching there was an air of festive spirit sweeping RAF Marham. To add to the joviality and not needing an excuse for a party, the squadron was delighted to read in the London Gazette the

*Sergeat Joseph Vezina RCAF's time on the squadron was nothing if not eventful.*

announcement on December 23rd of the award of the DFC to both Wing Commander Herbert Kirkpatrick and Flight Lieutenant Peter Dunham. Wing Commanders Kirkpatrick's citation reads;

> *This officer has commanded the squadron for some time except for a few weeks due to an injury received while trying to save members of his squadron when an aircraft crashed, and a bomb exploded. He had displayed great coolness, leadership and courage.*

Peter Dunham's citation is slightly more interesting:

> *This officer has participated in attacks on a wide variety of important targets in Germany and the occupied territory. Throughout he had displayed great courage and leadership, of descending to low altitude to ensure accuracy of bombing. On two occasions, when acting as captain, fighters have attacked his aircraft, but in both instances the enemy was destroyed, and the mission completed. Flight Lieutenant Dunham has displayed great ability and devotion to duty. Although normally employed as an instructor, he has also acted as captain of aircraft.*

*Thomas Cottier RCAF. Sadly, this brave young pilot was found floating in the River Humber in April 1942, almost four months after he was reported missing.*

The squadron received a flurry of Seasonal messages from the senior ranks of the RAF. The AOC-In-C sent the following, " *To all Ranks of Bomber Command I send my Warmest Christmas Greetings and praise for work well done'* PEIRSE.  Lord Trenchard wrote, *"All good wishes to you and your Command for Christmas and the New Year. Congratulations on the work you have done in this war"*.

It is fitting that the last word should be from the A.O.C No.3 Group.

> 'This is the third Christmas of the war. For the third time I, as your Air Officer Commanding would wish you a happy Christmas. A wish for all ranks of the RAF, Dominion and Allied Air Forces, WAAF and the Army units stationed on aerodromes in the group. In the year that has past we have done well. In the year that is about to begin let us see that we do even better. To this end I commend all the courage and the energy that is in each one of you.'

After the booze fuelled Festive Break it was back to war. On December 28th six crews were detailed and briefed for a raid against Wilhelmshaven. The weather was for once ideal over the target. However, the crews had to endure freezing conditions. Unlimited visibility provided the observers with an opportunity to exact some end of year misery to the townsfolk of this important

German port. Such was the visibility the crews could pin-point where their bombs dropped. Sergeant Griggs flying at 16,000 feet watched as his 5 x 500lb bombs exploded across the city's central railway station. Sergeant Helfer's all HE load burst close to a large lock gate producing vivid explosions while Sgt McPhail watched as his bombs exploded on the dock front. A few fires were started in the centre of the city, Sergeant McGregor added to these by dropping his two 1000 pounders and 160 x 4lb incendiaries into the flames below. Other than the bitterly cold conditions the returning crews were confident that the raid was a long-overdue success. Reports via Switzerland later established that the raid inflicted some substantial damage to the city, especially around the vital train station.

Widespread fog covered the region, preventing any further operations. On the December 31st, the squadron learnt that Wing Commander Kirkpatrick DFC's time in command was at an end, he was off to No.3 Group HQ. He had commanded the squadron since April and in that time had flown 13 operations. All but two against targets in Germany, including Berlin. With a reputation as a

*Scottish born Herbert Kirkpatrick DFC seen here while a Group Captain. Unlike his predecessors he would lead by example often flying on the most dangerous of raids. The award of the DFC was in recognition of his leadership and courage at a time when the squadron was suffering heavy losses.*

first-rate commanding officer and bomber pilot, his successor had a significant role to fill. In June 1942 he was posted to RAF Wyton as Station Commander. In May 1943 he would become No.3 Group's SASO and alongside AVM Harrison guide the group for the rest of the war.

Fog covered Marham on the morning of January 1st, 1942. No flying was undertaken. The new squadron commander arrived by road mid-morning, his name, Wing Commander Paul Holder DFC. Born in Port Elizabeth, South Africa in September 1911 his father was Chief Electrical Engineer and managing director of the tramway company. In 1913, Paul and his family moved back to England settling in Somerset. Paul Holder had quite an academic record before joining the RAF having gained a first in his MSc in Engineering from Bristol University in 1933 (he also attended the University of Illinois), becoming a Robert Blair Fellow in 1934 and gaining his PhD in 1935. He joined the RAF as a University entrant in 1935 and following his training at No 3 FTS, Grantham, he was posted to No.57 Squadron flying Hawker Hinds at RAF Upper Heyford in December 1936.

Number 108 Squadron reformed at Upper Heyford on January 4th, 1937 from 'B' Flight of No 57 Squadron. One of the squadron's first officers was F/O Holder. In February, the squadron moved to Farnborough, and in July it moved again to Cranfield. Late 1937 he was posted to the Middle East where, in January 1938 he joined No 84 Squadron. Equipped with Vickers Vincent the squadron was based at Shaibah in Iraq. By 1940 he was the station Administration Officer at RAF Habbaniya. When the station was attacked and besieged by the Iraqi Army in 1941, he took command of the makeshift bomber squadron assembled from the stations training aircraft. It was during the siege that he had two narrow escapes. Twice he was forced down, on one occasion he managed to escape his aircraft before it exploded. On the second occasion, he landed on a golf course, the plane turned over, and he found himself upside down in a bunker. He was awarded the DFC for these operations. Following the 'Battle of Habbaniya', he returned to the UK and joined the air staff at HQ Bomber Command.

*The wedding of Wing Commander Holder DFC and Miss Mary Kidd at the Parish Church of Portishead, December 1941.*

Short Brothers built Stirlings N3707, N3709 and N3710 arrived on the squadron during the first week of January, their stay was brief as they were quickly sent to No.7 Squadron. One Stirling that stayed was Short and Harland Belfast built, N6089. This aircraft arrived on the 5th and was immediately coded HA-L. To help speed up the conversion of crews, a new unit was created on January 1st. Formed from No.26 Conversion Flight, No.1651 Conversion Unit was formed at RAF Waterbeach. This new unit would be commanded by Wing Commander Stewart Menaul DFC, he would be ably assisted by S/Ldr Richard Speare DFC fresh from No.26 CF and S/Ldr Reginald Cox DFC of No.7 Squadron. The instructors were tour expired former members of 7 or XV Squadron. Group also instructed each of its stations equipped with the Short Stirling to form a Conversion Flight. The flights would be established on the basis of 4 Stirlings with no reserves. They would be independent of but affiliated to the Stirling Squadron numbered accordingly and added in accordance with WAR/BC177.

**Short Stirling Mk I**

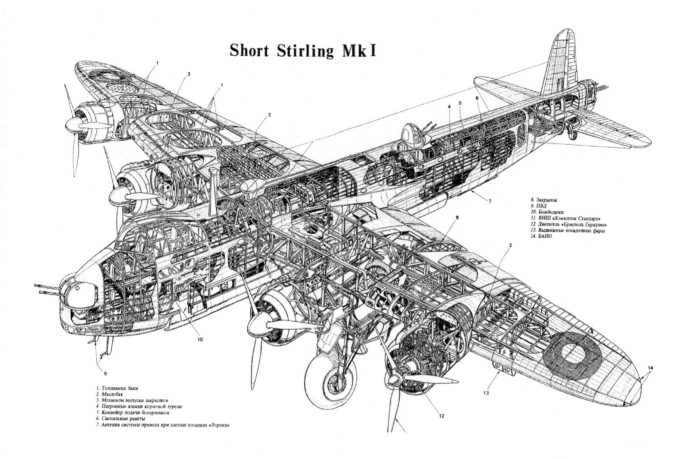

1. Топливные баки
2. Маслобак
3. Механизмы выпуска закрылков
4. Патронные ящики кормовой турели
5. Конвейер подачи боеприпасов
6. Сигнальные ракеты
7. Антенна системы привода при слепых посадках «Лоренц»

8. Закрылок
9. ПВД
10. Бомболюки
11. ВИШ «Хэмилтон Стандард»
12. Двигатель «Бристоль Геркулес»
13. Выдвижные посадочные фары
14. БАНО

During the late morning of the 3rd, the squadron was informed it would be required that night. The target was once again Brest. This order was later cancelled due to the threat of bad weather. This would be the start of a series of attacks on this target over the coming weeks and months. On the 5th six crews were part of a force of nearly fifty aircraft from No.3 Group tasked with bombing the Arsenal Power Station at Brest. The Arsenal, located on the river Penfeld, consisted of a number of important quays and basins, plus numerous military installations essential to the German Kriegsmarine operations into the Atlantic. The first Wellington aloft was Z1101 HA-F flown by S/Ldr Williams DFC, beside him was W/Cdr Holder DFC. Also joining the crew was Pilot Officer Reginald Brown now fully recovered from the accident on December 16th. Broken cloud over the target plus the welcome addition of flares helped the crews identify some key features over the dock area. A concentration of incendiaries attracted the majority of the bomb loads, Sgt Webber bombed from 19,000ft on flak flashes. The only problems encountered was the failure of the heating system aboard three Wellingtons, crews reported temperatures as low as -30. Group seems happy with the night's results stating the *'Raid appeared successful'*.

On the 6th the squadron learnt about the announcement of the British Empire Medal awarded to Sgt Jack Purcell for his courageous actions in saving S/Ldr Gibbs in September 1941. It was just the fillip the NCOs on the squadron needed.

*Sergeant Purcell was the front gunner of an aircraft which, whilst carrying out an attack on Ostend, received a direct hit from heavy anti-aircraft fire. Although an attempt was made to bring the aircraft back to England, it eventually crashed in the sea some ten miles from the coast. On impact, the captain was thrown down into the bomb compartment but, after being submerged in fifteen feet of water, he eventually escaped, in a semi-drowned condition, through the broken off tail of the aircraft. Sergeant Purcell, who was suffering from burns about the face and hands, had helped the captain to climb out from the wreckage and then supported and encouraged him for about half an hour until it was possible to reach the dinghy. In spite of the captain's continual suggestions that Sergeant Purcell should leave him and get to the dinghy himself, the sergeant refused to do so. There is little doubt that the captain's life was saved as a result of the determination and bravery shown by Sergeant Purcell. He subsequently displayed courage, cheerfulness and powers of endurance during the three days which the crew spent floating in the dinghy.*

It was back to Brest on the 7th. Five crews were provided by the squadron on what turned out to be a rather low-key and disappointing raid. Sergeant Helfer was forced to abort the operation just 15 minutes from the target when the port engine failed. His all-HE bomb load was jettisoned into the sea. The crew landed at RAF Middle Wallop on return. Squadron Leader Williams reported his mixed load exploding through the cloud producing some small fires.

During the early hours of the 10th three crews led by W/Cdr Holder DFC were part of a force of 18 aircraft provided by 3 Group on yet another raid on Brest. The squadron was over the target around 0630 hours. Flak was plentiful and accurate as the crews began their bomb runs. Sergeant McGregor's Wellington, R1346 HA-B was coned by searchlights over the outskirts of Brest. Flak quickly latched onto the Wellington, almost immediately the aircraft was rocked as bursts exploded just a few yards below the aircraft damaging the hydraulics and puncturing large holes in the fuselage and port wing. Managing to escape both the flak and searchlights the crew discovered that the bomb bay doors would not close. To add to the problems, they watched helplessly as the undercarriage started too slowly lower. The hydraulic pump that operated the undercarriage and the bomb doors were located in the damaged port wing which looked more like a sieve than a wing. Sergeant Griggs pinpoint Brest Arsenal through a small gap in the clouds, W/Cdr Holder was not so lucky, he dropped his 6 x 500 pounders on flak flashes.

Sergeant McGregor RNZAF managed to coax his severely damaged Wellington back to the South Coast of England where it crashed landed at 08:40 hours at the RAF fighter station at Exeter. All the crew managed to vacate the Wellington, unfortunately the damaged Wellington had come to a rest on the main runway causing an obstruction, much to everyone's annoyance. Unfazed the crew returned to Marham after breakfast.

### Saturday January 10th 1942
*Vickers Wellington*
*Mk.Ic*
*R1346 HA-B 'Beer'*
*Contract No : B.992424/39*
*Taken On Charge : 15/05/1941*

348

*RoS (Vickers)*
*Forced Landing*
*Pilot : Sergeant John McGregor, NZ403465 RNZAF*
*2nd Pilot : Sergeant Walker*
*Observer: Sergent Hobden*
*Front Gunner : Sergeant Finney*
*1st Wireless Operator : Sergeant Davidson*
*Rear Gunner : Sergeant Cox*

Wellington R1346 was one of the squadron's veterans having flown on 38 raids since its arrival in May. Repaired, it would eventually return to the squadron on March 21st. A solitary 'Freshman' crew was dispatched to Boulogne on the 10th. Sergeant Shirley Davidge had completed his time in the right-hand seat having completed ten operations as 2nd pilot. Now deemed ready to captain his own crew he departed Marham at 1745 hours. Besides him was a young Dutch pilot, Sergeant William Rieter on his first operation. The raid was an anti-climax. A thick layer of cloud obscured Boulogne, and despite the crew's attempts to find an alternative target, they eventually had to jettison the bomb load. They landed at RAF Bodney on return.

*AVM John Baldwin was the group commander chosen to command RAF Bomber Command on the removal of Peirse.*

Major changes at No.3 Group and Bomber Command HQ on the 10th would influence the future direction of the command. Number 3 Groups AoC, AVM John Baldwin was given temporary command of Bomber Command on the departure of the long-suffering Richard Peirse. Criticism of Peirse's command began to gain momentum immediately after the disastrous raid on November 7/8th 1941. This disaster added to the Butt Report, and continual heavy losses gave Peirse's critics sufficient clout to put ever-increasing pressure on both the Air Staff and the Prime Minister to replace him. In the end, he had to go. With Baldwin's departure, No.3 Groups SASO, Acting Group Captain John Astley Gray DFC GM took command. Up until November 1941, Gray had been station commander at RAF Honington. He was awarded the George Medal when he and the Honington Station medical officer entered a blazing Wellington of No.9 Squadron to rescue the trapped crew.

The squadron dispatched another trio of aircraft against Brest on the 11th. Taking off at 1530 hours the crews would join 22 other aircraft provided by the group in attacking the Scharnhorst and Gneisenau. It was not long after take-off that the wireless set aboard Wellington R1496 HA-R caught fire forcing the crew to abort. Sergeant Hinwood landed the Wellington at RAF Boscombe Down due to bad weather at Base. The usually effective smoke screen had not covered the docks when the crews arrived. Instead, the crews encountered intense flak above the docks and the whole area of Brest, crews remarking that it was *'particularly fierce'*.

Searchlights held Sergeant Griggs RAAF and despite throwing the Wellington around the sky the tell-tell sound of holes being blasted through the geodetics reverberated around the aircraft. A large chunk of the nacelle was blown from the starboard wheel housing and numerous holes appeared in the floor of the bomb bay. The crew's wireless operator Sgt Allen reported over the intercom that he had been hit by shrapnel, this was followed by Sgt Morrison sitting in the front turret. He had also been hit, a piece of flak striking him in the jaw. Having dropped their 6 x 500lb SAP's they headed for home. Sergeant Helfer carried out a glide attack from 13000 feet in the hope he could fool the flak defences. It must have worked as he did not report any damage upon return. Sergeant Griggs managed to land his Wellington at RAF Exeter at 2110 hours.

### Saturday January 10th 1942
*Vickers Wellington*
*Mk.Ic*
*X9755 HA-K 'King'*
*Contract No : B.124362/40*
*Taken On Charge : 22//11/1941*
*CAT AC/FB*
*RoS (Vickers)*
*Forced Landing*
*Pilot : Sergeant Frank Moreton Griggs 035376 RAAF*
*2nd Pilot : Sergeant Geoffrey Jeary 126109 RAFVR*
*Observer: Pilot Officer Green*
*Front Gunner :Sergeant Morrison, Injured*
*1st Wireless Operator : Sergeant Allen, Injured*
*Rear Gunner : Sergeant Hendry*


The damage to X9755 required the attention of the Vickers repair team. It would not be until March 7th the aircraft was returned to the squadron. Two crews were operational on the 14th, Sgt Millichamp and crew were given the docks at Rotterdam while Sgt Davidge was given Emden, both operations were unsuccessful.

Wing Commander Holder decided that the Hamburg operation of January 15th would be his next trip. He was joined by four crews from 218 Squadron and a further 22 from No.3 Group. Two crews were forced to abort. Over the North Sea, the port engine aboard Wellington R1596 HA-A suddenly started showing signs of overheating. Unable to climb above 6000 feet Sgt Edward Crosswell, on his first operation as captain wisely turned for home. Sergeant John McKay on his first operation since his accident on December 12th got halfway across the North Sea before he abandoned the sortie due to W/T failure. The problems continued, W/Cdr Holder found himself way off track. The crew obviously lost, found themselves over Fyn Island, Denmark over 160 miles north of Hamburg. Unable to locate Hamburg, the all incendiary load fell in open countryside near an isolated railway line. The raid on Hamburg achieved extraordinarily little damage, but thankfully for the squadron at least there were no losses or incidents. Number 3 Group dispatched 12 Wellingtons to Emden on the 20th, two crews were provided by the squadron, once again the raid was a failure. The following night Sergeant Maurice Smithson and crew carried out a *'Freshman'* trip to Boulogne. The target was identified from 14000 feet. The crew met practically no opposition and dropped their 12 x 250lb + 180 x 4lb incendiaries on a somewhat subdued Boulogne.

The following night another 'Freshman' trip was undertaken, Canadian Sgt Millichamp attacked the docks at Dunkirk. In excellent visibility, the crew were able to identify the docks where 16 x 250 pounders were accurately delivered. Two large fires were started which produced two distinct columns of smoke. The crew were back at Marham having only being airborne 2 hours 30 minutes. It was a 'piece of cake'!

The final operation of a noticeably quiet month was flown on the 28th when the squadron dispatched three crews against the rail yards at Munster. The weather conditions en route and over the target area were appalling. Sergeant Crosswell and crew got halfway across the North Sea before they jettisoned safe after entering a magnetic storm. Sergeant John Mackay bombed the flare path of Haamstede aerodrome owing to icing. The only crew to reach Munster was Sgt Smithson. It very nearly ended in tragedy. Soon after bombing the Wellington encountered severe icing. Such were the conditions that the Wellington became uncontrollable and entered into a spine. The captain realising the predicament quickly gave the order to bail-out, however, the front gunner could not vacate his turret. The delay in removing the gunner meant that Smithson had time to pull out of the spin but in doing so he had dropped from 19,500 feet to 2,500 feet. With practically no instruments, this exceptional young pilot managed to save his crew and bring them and Wellington Z1070 HA-B safely back to Marham.

The squadron had flown just 31 sorties in January for the loss of two damaged Wellingtons. Two factories fresh Short Stirlings were delivered to the squadron on the 26th and 31st January. Stirling

*The crew of Sergeant Ted Crosswell seen here just before their departure to the Mediterranean. Left; Sergeant Len Mayer, Sergeant Jim Munro, Sergeant George Fuller, Sergeant Howard Hewer and Sergeant Ted Crosswell.*

N3712 arrived on the 26th and was given the code HA-Y, followed on the 31st by N3714. Most of the crews were busy working up on the Stirlings, which would soon make its operational debut. An intense training programme was organised, pilots and crews would need to acquire a minimum 25 flying hours on the Stirling before being considered experienced enough to commence operations. However, the foul January weather in Norfolk and Suffolk combined with the serviceability issues with the new bomber soon demonstrated just how ambitious that figure was. Thick ice and snow during January would continue into February making the necessary practice flights more and more infrequent. Some pilots and their crews flew their last operations with the squadron in February. Demands for bomber crews in the Middle East meant that Sergeants Mackay, Longmore, Jetten, Crosswell and Smithson would depart for pastures new, some would end up in the Middle East while others would apply their trade in the Far East. The squadron did not undertake any operations for the first 11 days of February. It did however accept another batch of Short Stirlings. On the 6th N3713 and N3717 arrived, followed on the 11th by N3718. One of the earliest pilots chosen to convert to the Stirling was New Zealander Sgt Phil Lamason. On successfully completing his conversion course Phil Lamason was sent back to the squadron. Now considered an 'expert' he was tasked with giving S/Ldr Ker dual control flying lessons. Squadron Leader Ker was known as a hard taskmaster, but it seemed the two hit it off. After a number of familiarising flights with the new aircraft S/Ldr Ker was deemed sufficiently trained to master the mighty Stirling. With the arrival of the Stirling and its reliance on Electrical power, it was no surprise that there was soon an increase in the number of electricians on the squadron. Due to the number of technical personal needed to keep the Stirling operational, there was steady influx of new postings. This proved to be a problem, and accommodation was now an issue. To ease the situation, all newly arrived 218 personnel were to be billeted in huts in the grounds of Narborough Hall situated 3 miles from the airfield. This meant that transport into and out of the station had to be provided every morning and evening. On the night of the February 11th the German Battleship *Scharnhorst, Gneisenau* and heavy cruiser *Prinz Eugen* and escorts slipped out of Brest and were making their way north skirting the French Coastline. Panic at The Admiralty was matched by that of the RAF. Operation FULLER, the planned response to this very scenario was put into operation. Conceived in April 1941 by both the Royal Navy and the RAF it should have been a well-executed and organised response. It was anything but. It was not until late afternoon of the 12th that the squadron was called to action, six crews were detailed, including three of the squadron's new and unproven Stirlings. At 14:30 hours Squadron Leader Ker lifted off in N3700 HA-O loaded aimed with 15 x 500 pounders. He was quickly followed by Sgt Bernard Tomkins in Stirling N6089 HA-L and F/O Allen at the controls of N6128 HA-T. A few minutes before departure the Wellingtons of Sgt Webber, R1596 HA-A and Sgt McGregor's RNZAF Wellington R1496 HA-R were both surprisingly cancelled. The only Wellington to take off was R1448 HA-N captained by Sgt Griggs at 14:50 hours. Within minutes of departure, a hydraulic issue with the Wellingtons front turret resulted in the crew's early return to Marham. An hour later, repairs made and with the turret now fully operational the plucky crew took off again, the time was 16:46 hours. Squadron Leader Ker located one large ship and their destroyers 40 miles off the Hague at 16:00 hours. Weather conditions at all heights were poor. In amongst the clouds, swarms of German single and twin-engine fighters hunted tirelessly for any possible danger for their charges. An endless barrage of light and medium flak plus murderous MG fire poured from the cruisers and the escorting destroyers. Into this cauldron the four aircraft of 218 found themselves. The following account is from the Combat Reports submitted by the crew upon their return:

Stirling Mk.I 'O' 218 Sqdn. Flying at an indicated air speed of 165 on a course of 216 was about to turn into attack the German Battleships when a Do217 appeared about 200ft below the starboard bean flying on a converging course. The E/A was 600-800 yards distant when first seen and flying at a greater speed than our aircraft. The E/A opened fire at 500 yards with a beam gun and minor damage was caused to the bomb doors. The Stirlings front gunner (Sgt Christy) opened fire at 400 yards with two bursts of 200 rounds each and claims to have hit the E/A. Both aircraft now turned away from each other, the E/A into cloud and our to make an attack on the Battleship which was however not located owing to the cloud and the bad visibility. Apart from side slipping no special evasive action was taken by our aircraft which was manoeuvring to attack the Battleship when the E/A was first seen, and the captain continued on his main objective. The E/A was not seen again, and no claim is made by our front as to damage caused.

Some heavy flak, either from the battleship or escorting destroyers was encountered throughout the combat and our rear gunner states that as the aircraft turned away from each other he saw the E/A flashing what he took to be a message to the Battleship but was unable to read it. Our aircraft had IFF on throughout the engagement.

Unable to locate the Battleships S/Ldr Ker returned to Marham with his bomb load. Flying Officer Allen sighted two destroyers 10 miles NE of S/Ldr Ker. With the cloud base as low as 800 feet the crew circled for 36 minutes hoping to sight the larger ships. Their patience eventually paid off when the two larger ships were sighted. Attacking from 1500 feet the 11 x 500 pounders were dropped in the face of considerable light flak and machine gun fire and repeated fighter attacks. The crew's rear gunner, Sgt McBride reported two distinct red flashes about 100-150 yards from the starboard side of the lead ship. Somehow, despite the flak and fighters Stirling N6128 HA-T landed back at RAF Marham with just a damaged bomb door. The following details are from the Combat Report.

At 1515 hours on the 12th of February 1942 Aircraft 'T' made a sortie against the Scharnhorst and Gneisenau. Visibility was about 2000 yards at 3500 feet. When approx 6 minutes from the target area, time 1555hrs three Me110s were sighted at a range of 1000 yards flying on the red quarter in a non-formation order. One Me110 shortened range and commenced an attack from dead astern. The rear gunner (Sgt McBride) opened fire with a sighter burst at 500 yards. The fighter returned fire with 4-6 machine guns. The enemy fighter pressed home its attack until at 120 yards he broke away to starboard. During the whole time the rear gunner continued firing. During the break away the mid-upper gunner (Sgt Gregory) made a 3 second burst at the E/A. The E/A then made a second attack from the starboard beam. The rear gunner fired several long bursts at the aircraft and on the break away to port the E/A presented an exceptional target by exposing the underpart of the fuselage to a five second burst by the mid upper gunner which raked the aircraft from nose to stern. The E/A was last seen in an almost vertical dive and it was lost to sight through cloud. The remaining two Me110s did not develop an attack. Several other single fighters were sighted but no interceptions were made. Over the target intense and very accurate light flak and machine gun fire was encountered. The E/A was not seen to hit the sea.

Number of rounds fired : Rear turret 620
Mid Upper : 250

Sergeant Tompkins was unable to locate the German ships despite flying as low as 1000 feet. It was on one sweep they were engaged by a Bf110, a short but vicious encounter developed, thankfully the crew managed to enter some cloud and safety. No damage was sustained to the Stirling. The crew returned with their bombload. Sergeant Griggs found the *Scharnhorst* and *Gneisenau* after breaking cloud 40 miles off the Dutch coast. With the Destroyer escort on either flank, the crew decided to attack from ahead against the ships that were in line astern. From 300 feet a seriously low altitude, the crew commenced their attack, flak and Mg fire erupted around the Wellington, Sgt Rogers in the front turret opened fire with his twin .303 machine guns. It was a pitiful response but helped the crew's nerves. Surrounded by flak the crew dropped 7 x 500 pounders, the rear gunner in between spraying the decks with MG fire reported that the bombs had undershot by 100 yards. The crew were fortunate, the only damage sustained was to the rear turret and aerial, both of which were rendered unserviceable. This brave crew turned for home landing at Marham at 18:25hrs. Considering the German opposition, it was a clean sweep for the squadrons at Marham.

The Germans bold dash up the English Channel had exposed many failings in both RAF planning and performance. The inability of Coastal Command to effectively stop the German cruisers, and the ineffectiveness of Bomber Command against moving ships. Despite the courageous actions on the day, the response was negligible and disjointed. There were lots to learn.

On the 13th the squadron recorded its first Stirling accident. Sergeant Lamason RNZAF had just completed a successful cross-country flight in Stirling N3713. Bringing the Stirling into land on RAF Lakenheath's runway the undercarriage suddenly collapsed. The giant bomber skidded to an unceremonious halt, the crew, all of whom were uninjured quickly vacated the aircraft.

### Friday February 13th 1942
*Short Stirling*
*Mk.I*
*N3713  HA-?*
*Contract No : 763825/38*
*Taken On Charge : 06/02/1942*
*CAT B/FB*
*RIW (Sebro)*
*Undercarriage Failure*
*Pilot : Sergeant Phil Lamason RNZAF*
*2nd Pilot : Sergeant Sidney Falconer*
*Observer:*
*Front Gunner :*
*1st Wireless Operator :*
*Mid Upper Gunner*
*Rear Gunner :*

The following night two crews, Sgt Lamason at the controls of N6089 HA-L and Sgt Gregg in Stirling N3700 HA-O carried out the squadron's first bombing operation over mainland Europe. The target were the docks at Le Havre and a 'Nickle' trip to Paris. Both crews successfully delivered their all HE bomb load. A number of blue bursts were observed by Sgt Lamason while Gregg noted two large flashes in the dock area. Low on fuel due to the time the crew had spent trying to locate the docks Sgt Gregg was unable to deliver his 'Nickels' to Paris. On landing a 500 pounder that had jammed between the bomb doors suddenly dropped on the runway at Oakington. On inspection, the tail fin was found jammed in the bomb door. It was a lucky escape for the crew. On the 16th another undercarriage incident at Marham resulted in the loss of Stirling N3714 for a few months when the troublesome undercarriage could not be lowered.

**Monday February 16th 1942**
*Short Stirling*
*Mk.I*
*N3714 HA-?*
*Contract No : 763825/38*
*Taken On Charge : 31///01/1942*
*CAT Ac/FA*
*ROS (Sebro)*
*Undercarriage Failure*
*Pilot : Flying Officer Donald Westbrook Allen 88245 RAF*

The following day the Stirling's undercarriage curse struck again. Sergeant Bernard Tompkins was landing N3718 on Marham grass runway when once again the undercarriage unexpectedly collapsed. Like N3714 it would be months before it returned to squadron strength.

**Tuesday February 17th 1942**
*Short Stirling*
*Mk.I*
*N3718 HA-C 'Charlie'*
*Contract No : 763825/38*
*Taken On Charge : 11///02/1942*
*CAT Ac/FA*
*ROS*
*Undercarriage Failure*
*Pilot : Sergeant Bernard Tompkins.*

The problem with the undercarriage was due to its size. The massive wheels were carried between a pair of oleo pneumatic shock structs of either Shorts or Turner design. Each main undercarriage unit was electrically operated by a separate motor. The landing gear was so long that it could not retract into the nacelle, it was therefore divided into parts. A complicated two stage system was designed and introduced. First the gear was taken vertically upwards, then backwards. Even the undercarriage doors comprised of four separate sections, the complexity of the whole undercarriage design was to prove troublesome. When compared to the Avro and Handley Page designs it certainly was.

On February 22nd, Baldwin's brief time at the helm of Bomber Command was terminated. His replacement was Arthur Travers Harris.

On the 24th F/Sgt Harold Millichamp RCAF and Sgt Shirley Davidge arrived back on the squadron having completed their conversion course at No.1651 Conversion Flight. The month of February end with yet another undercarriage failure. Sergeant Tompkins was once again the unfortunate captain involved. Coming into land at Marham, he had just touched down when the pylon struct on the port side broke preventing the wheel from locking down. The Stirling sank onto its wing causing considerable damage. The aircraft was recategorized 'E' for reduction to produce parts and spares

**Friday February 27th 1942**
*Short Stirling*
*Mk.I*
*N3715 HA-*
*Contract No : 763825/38*
*Taken On Charge : 31//01/1942*
*CAT 'E'*
*Reduced to spares*
*Undercarriage Failure*
*Pilot : Sergeant Bernard Tompkins.*

*Sergeant Harold Millichamp RCAF seen here at No.11 O.T.U*

On February 28th yet another new unit was created, this one would be intricately linked to the squadron. No.218 Conversion Unit was established to complete the training undertaken and completed with No.1651 Conversion Unit. The numerous intricacies of the Stirling not covered by the general conversion program at 1651 CU would be taught and learnt.

Formed at RAF Marham the flight was to be independent of but affiliated to No.218 Squadron. But the flight would, however, come directly under the station commander. Chosen to command was S/Ldr Ker, he would be aided by Sgt Phil Lamason. The flight was initially equipped with four Stirlings, W7454 -W, N6128 - T, N6129 - X and N6078 - P.

Training and conversion were the priority now, No.218 CF moved to RAF Lakenheath on the 3rd, it made sense as Marham's grass runways were looking decidedly rutted. On the 3rd, Form B.744 was received from No.3 Group HQ. Four crews, all recently converted were chosen to attack the Billancourt Renault Factory. Built on Île Seguin, an island in the river Seine southwest area of Paris, it was a modern factory built on the lines of Fords in America.

One of the first names down on the crew list was that of W/Cdr Holder DFC, he would be joining the crew of F/Lt Livingston aboard Stirling W7473 HA-F. Accompanying the crew of F/Lt

Humphreys was the recently posted Squadron Leader Arthur Waite Oldroyd AFC. The first crew to departed was S/Ldr Ker at 1825 hours in Stirling W7469 HA-M, once airborne the crews would join over 60 Wellingtons and Stirlings provided by No.3 Group who would in turn merge with over 150 other bombers drawn from 1, 4 and 5 Groups. Each of the four Stirlings carried 4 x 1000 pounders plus 6 x 500 pounders. Slowly they gained cruising altitude while heading south, then out over the English coast. Conditions on route were ideal, apart from a full moon. Over the target area the factory was easily identified by the fires already started by the preceding bombers. Flight Lieutenant Livingston was able to make out the 'Body Press Shop' and 'Vehicle Assembly Shops' from the glare of the fires and flares dropped by a number of experienced crews. From just over 2000 feet F/Lt William Livington dropped the entire bomb load in one stick, violent white explosions were seen close to the vehicle assembly shops. Debris shot into the air to almost the same height as the Stirling. A massive flash lit up the sky as bombs from another aircraft hit the power station. Flight Lieutenant Humphrey managed to identify and bomb the Vehicle Assembly Shop from the perilously low altitude of 1100 feet. The Stirling was rocked by the explosions of its own bombs and others which was not surprising given the extraordinarily low height. The target was left a mass of flames, numerous fires were observed throughout the factory complex with columns of thick black smoke rising into the sky.

One such column was from a gasometer which was seen burning furiously. The raid appeared to be an outstanding success, this was subsequently confirmed by PRU reconnaissance. Numerous hits on the power station, engine workshops and assembly shops were confirmed. In all over 300 high explosive bombs fell in the factory complex destroying over 40% of the buildings. Squadron Leader Ker landed at Thorney Island due to a combination of fuel shortage and undercarriage trouble on return.

USINE DE BILLANCOURT

*The vast Renault factory straddled both sides of the Seine and occupied the island of Seguin.*

The only negative on an otherwise excellent nights work was back at Marham. Having successfully bombed Billancourt the crew of F/O Allen had just touched down when there was a loud explosion followed immediately by a large flash which was immediately followed by flames. Unbeknown to the crew two 1000 pounders had 'hung-up' one of which had become dislodge on landing. The shattered Stirling, which was practically in two slithered to a halt, flames almost entirely engulfing the rear section. Pilot Officer Frank Gales the crew's navigator was the first out of the wreckage. On discovering that his crew mates were still trapped inside he courageously re-entered the blazing bomber despite having sustained a broken ankle and badly bruised elbow. With the assistance of the 2nd pilot Sgt Laidlaw, they managed to extract three of the crew from the forward section. Despite the flames the flight engineer, Sgt Herring and the seriously injured wireless operator, Sgt Harvey were the first to be pulled out. The last to be found and rescued was the wireless operator / air gunner Sgt Gregory. Sadly, both Sergeants Gregory and Harvey succumbed to their injuries. Flying Officer Allen, P/O Gales and Sgts Laidlaw and Herring were taken to Ely Hospital. Herring was classed as critical with life threatening wounds to his back. Sergeant McBride was admitted to Marham SSQ. Both Sergeant Laidlaw and P/O Gales had shown remarkable bravery in re-entering the blazing bomber without consideration of their own safety. Sadly, this selfless act went unrewarded.

**Tuesday March 3rd 1942**
Short Stirling
*Mk.I*
*N3712 HA-Y*
*Contract No : 763825/38*
*Taken On Charge : 26/01/1942*
*CAT E/FB*
*SoC*
*Hang-Up - Explosion on landing.*
*Pilot : Flying Officer Donald Westbrook Allen, 88245 RAFVR, injured*
*2nd Pilot : Sergeant Willian John Laidlaw, 1022530 RAFVR, injured*
*Navigator : Pilot Officer Phillip Frank Gales, 106042 RAFVR, Injured*
*Wireless Operator : Sergeant William Rodney Gregory,1005402 RAFVR*
**Killed**

*Flying Officer Donald Westbrook Allen seen here standing in front of a squadron Short Stirling. The name on the nose is 'Fante'*

*The squadron's first fatalities on the Short Stirling were 20-year-old Sergeant Harvey and 18-year-old Sergeant Gregory.*

*Wireless Op/Gunner : Sergeant Kenneth Bertram Harvey,954434 RAFVR* **Killed**
*Rear Gunner : Sergeant A.M McBride, 973468 RAFVR, Injured.*
*Flight Engineer : Sergeant C.W Herring, 576229 RAFVR, Injured.*

The second 1000 pounder was discovered next morning 30 yards from the Stirling. The failure to release the two bombs over the target was due to the fouling of the mechanical release gear. No blame was attached to the navigator, as the bomb release panel had shown all the bombs had been dropped. The bodies of the two killed were taken to their hometowns for burial. Twenty-year-old Sergeant Kenneth Harvey was buried on March 7th at Great Dunmow Churchyard, Essex. Eighteen-year-old William Gregory was buried in Liverpool (West Derby) Cemetery on March 9th.

Since the squadron's conversion, its crews had been busy getting to grips with the navigational aid known as TR1335 or Gee. The squadron had yet to use this still relatively new and secret device operationally. It would make its operational appearance with the squadron against the Krupps works at Essen on March 8th. Only four squadron Stirling's had been equipped, all would participate. Joining the crew of F/Lt Livingston was an old friend of the squadron, the respected War Artist David Thornton Smith. Somehow, he had wrangled all the necessary approval from the Air Ministry and Ministry of Information to participate on an operation over Germany. The decision to attack Essen was not made until 16:00 hours due to doubts over the weather condition over the target. Every available bomber equipped with TR1335 was to be used on this its first outing. The Krupps works were the intended target, but the centre of the old town was given as the aiming point. Flares dropped by TR1335 equipped aircraft would illuminate the target which in turn would then be backed up by an incendiary force. The fires from the incendiaries would attract the main striking force. All four Stirlings took off just after midnight. Immediately after becoming airborne, the crew of Sgt William Gregg had difficulty retracting the undercarriage of Stirling N3717 HA-S. Decided to stay near the aerodrome they set about trying to resolve the problem. Almost an hour after taking off the crew of Sgt Gregg finally managed to retract the stubborn undercarriage and set off for Essen. Weather conditions on the route were ideal with an almost full moon, over the target visibility was excellent apart from some ground haze.

By the time the four Stirlings reached the target fires were visible across vast swathes of Essen, one large fire was visible on the eastern end of the Krupps works. Flight Lieutenant Humphreys dropped his all-incendiary load from 13,000 feet reporting '*Large red fire seen burning in target area with a number of smaller ones'.* Each of the crews attacked the target, the persistence shown by Sgt Gregg was not rewarded as his TR1335 failed over the North Sea. Arriving late over the target area, the crew decided altitude was the safest option. From 18,200 feet they deposited 22 x 250lb + 4 x 500lb bombs slightly N W of the aiming point. Other than flak damage to the port outer engine of Flight Lieutenant Humphreys Stirling the returning crews reported no damage, which was surprising given the intensity of the flak over the target area. The raid was not the success Bomber Command had hoped for. Of the 211 aircraft dispatched, 168 claimed to have bombed the target area. Unfortunately, photographic evidence revealed that the main target area and the centre of the old town showed little damage while the important Krupps works were completely missed. Most of the bomb fell on the outskirts of Essen and as far as Duisburg and Oberhausen. On return to Marham F/Sgt Bernard Tompkins was once again in trouble. On landing the starboard outer engine aboard Stirling W7474 HA-D jammed in the 'open' position. This resulted in the aircraft overshooting the grass runway, the Stirling swung to port striking a searchlight position. Thankfully, the crew were uninjured, and the searchlight post was unoccupied. Damage to the aircraft was minimal and repaired on the station.

**Saturday March 8th 1942**
Short Stirling
*Mk.I*
*W7474 HA-D*
*Contract No : B982939/39*
*Taken On Charge : 14/02/1942*
*CAT Ac/FB*
*RoS*
*Starboard Outer engine issue*
*Pilot : Sergeant Bernard Tompkins and crew*

The following night two pilots from 218 CF were back over Essen. Squadron Leader Ker departed at 1930hours in a brand-new Stirling Mk.I W7506 HA-K, fifteen minutes later he was followed by F/Sgt Lamason in another recently arrived aircraft, W7502 HA-N. Once again, a number of fires had already been started when both crews arrived. Flight Sergeant Lamason RNZAF dropped his all-incendiary load from 15,500ft meeting stiff opposition from the city's flak defences. Squadron Leader Ker deposited his 21 x 250 pounders on a number of fires. Just after bombing his Stirling was hit by heavy flak in the port outer engine nacelle. Other than several gagged holes in the nacelle the Hercules appeared undamaged. Both crews returned safely to Marham. The campaign against Essen continued on the 10th when four crews were detailed and briefed. Flight Lieutenant Humphreys was the first aloft at 1915 hours, within nine minutes all four were climbing for altitude over the flat fens. Haze over the target hindered visual identification of the aiming point although numerous flares and fires were observed. Over Essen, intense flak greeted the crews, Flight Sergeant Lamason was unfortunate to be caught and held by a number of searchlights. Lamason instinctively put the Stirling into a steep dive knowing that to be held in the beams would be fatal. This tried and tested manoeuvre worked as the Stirling slipped safely into the darkness.

All four crews reported issues with the temperamental T1335 sets. Flight Lieutenant Humphreys failed to locate Essen so bombed Oberhausen. In all, the squadron dropped nearly seven thousand 4lb incendiaries. This the third consecutive raid on Essen was another disappointment. On the 13th 218 CF returned to Marham after its brief stay at Lakenheath. That night Bomber Command turned its attention to the Cathedral city of Cologne. Five crews were detailed, operating again was the Squadron Commander W/Cdr Holder DFC. The flare dropping force opened proceedings with a number of well-placed flares, lessons learnt over Essen appeared to be working, for the first time both the TR1335 sets, and their operators appeared to click. These initial flares were accurately backed up with incendiaries.

*The size of the Short Stirling is captured in this photograph of Short Stirling Mk.I N3725 HA-D seen in the summer sun awaiting a load of incendiaries.*

361

Numerous fires across the centre of Cologne were visible miles from the target. Once over Cologne conditions were ideal, the Hindenburg Bridge and Cologne's main railway station were easily picked out in the light of the flares. At 2205 hours Flight Lieutenant Humphreys watched as his twenty-one 250 pounders exploded between the Hohenzollern and Hindenburg Bridges producing numerous fires. Flight Lieutenant Livingston bombed the old town with his all HE bomb load from 17,500 feet. Making his operation debut on the Stirling was Canadian F/Sgt Harold 'Hal' Millichamp RCAF. Aided by the large quantities of flares the crew dropped their all-incendiary load across the centre of Cologne noting *'Fires already burning across the town to south West and North West. Many scattered red and yellow fires all over the town'*.

Returning crews were enthusiastic about the raid. They were right to be. Cologne had suffered its most destructive attack so far. Post raid reconnaissance showed a number of industrial factories in the northern suburb Nippe were damaged, some severely. The Franz Clouth Chemical works and rubber factory showed considerable damage as did the important Nippe Marshalling Yards. The raid was arguably the first TR1335 success. On the 14th the squadron took delivery of a new Stirling, Austin Motors-built W7507. Unfortunately, while landing it crashed. Damage must have been minor as it was ready for operations within 10 days.

On return from Cologne, the squadron was effectively stood down, although it was informed that it would be required to attack the Krupps works on the 16th. This was subsequently cancelled by group at 1300 hours due to weather. The squadron missed the raids on Essen on March 18th and 21st. It was not however idle, 34 training flights were carried out, mostly mastering the TR1335 sets. It was during this period of inactivity that the group began a brief dalliance with daylight operations to Essen. On the 18th, No.115 Squadron was chosen to provide six Wellingtons to attack Essen using cloud cover. Thankfully lack of cloud meant the Wellingtons aborted and returned safely to Marham. Despite this setback Bomber Command HQ intended to continue with these suicidal operations. The following day 101 Squadron provide just two Wellington, once again lack of cloud forced the two crews to abort. On the 20th it was the turn of 75(NZ) and 57 Squadron and again on the 21st Marham's 115 Squadron was to dispatch six crews, mercifully for all concerned, there was insufficient cloud on both occasions.

It was not until the morning of the 25th that the squadron was informed it would be required that night, and all available Stirlings were to be made ready. The usual pre-operational air-tests took place throughout the afternoon, by early evening ten Stirlings and crews were detailed and briefed. The target was once again Essen. Short Stirling N6071 HA-G developed engine trouble just before take-off and was withdrawn. The first Stirling to lumbered down Marham's grass runway was N6070 HA-A flown by F/Sgt Hinwood. This was 20-year-old James Hinwood's first operation on the Stirling. He was an experienced pilot having flown 25 operations on the Wellington since his arrival August 1941. Other pilots making their Stirling debut was Sergeants Shirley Davidge, John Webber, John McGregor RNZAF and Squadron Leader Arthur Waite Oldroyd AFC who now held the 'B' Flight command role.

Over 100 Wellingtons and Stirlings slowly started climbing for altitude from No.3 Group's East Anglian bases. Marham provided a quarter of the group's contribution, No.115 Squadron supplying an impressive 17 Wellingtons. This mighty force would join Wellingtons, Manchesters and Hampdens drawn from No.1 and 5 Groups. A total force of over 250 bombers were all converging on Essen. Number 3 Groups contribution was divided into flare, incendiary and striking forces, 218 was part of the incendiary force. German night fighters were extremely active between the Dutch Coast and the Ruhr, numerous sightings of both twin and single-engine fighters were reported. Essen was cloudless with good visibility, but as expected industrial haze and an effective smoke screen proved troublesome. The crews attacked Essen from between 12,000 - 16,000 feet, some on TR1335 while others bombed visually. All reported a large red glow and numerous fires, F/Lt Humphreys reported *Bombs fell across a large factory with two smoke stacks already on fire. Eight smaller fires burning on arrival'*. Sitting beside the New Zealander was Squadron Leader Harold Ashworth on his first operation with the squadron. An experienced pre-war pilot, he had just celebrated his 40th birthday on March 13th, which was well over the average age of an operational pilot. Returning crews were confident that the raid was a success, many claiming that the Krupps works had been hit. Once again, this optimism proved misplaced, photographs showed that a large number of crews had inadvertently bombed the German decoy site at Rheinberg, 18 miles from Essen. It was yet another disappointing raid. Undeterred Bomber Command HQ ordered a return visit the following night.

Once again, the squadron provided nine crews. On this occasion, the crew of F/Sgt Lamason RNZAF was chosen to be part of the initial flare dropping force. His Stirling, N3725 HA-D would be loaded with 4 x 250lb bombs and 12 bundles of flares. The industrial haze that had hindered the previous visits was unusually missing, however, the flak and searchlights appeared to have doubled in number and intensity. Flight Lieutenant Humphreys was hit by flak over the target cutting the rudder cables. The sky above Essen was a mass of flares, flak bursts and burning bombers. More alarming was the presence of fighters in amongst the bombers. Flight Sergeant

*New Zealander Phil Lamason and some of his crew pose under the port inner engine of Stirling W7574 HA-H.*

Bernard Tompkins was attacked by two Ju88s over the target area. The crew's rear gunner, Sgt Howes, opened fire on a Ju88 which had closed to within seventy-five yards, his aim appeared to be good as the Ju88 went down in flames. Soon afterwards the mid-upper gunner, Sgt Brooks engaged a Bf110, hits were registered, but no definite results were seen. Bomber Command claimed a successful raid, but it came at a cost. Returning crews spoke excitably of large fires visible 50 miles from Essen during interrogation, surely this time it had received a telling blow. Ten Wellingtons and a Stirling failed to return. A further 13 were damaged by flak and a further two were damage by enemy fighters. Frustratingly the raid was yet another failure, little if any damaged was inflicted on the Krupps works. Despite Bomber Command HQ's determination to destroy Krupps it knew to attack a target on three consecutive nights was exposing its crews to unacceptable risks, for the time at least, Essen was forgotten.

The squadron was given a well-deserved day off on the 27th. However, it was not without its excitement. 218 Conversion Flight commander, Squadron Leader Ker was giving dual instruction to Sgt Boyd. The flight went well until landing at 23:05hrs when the starboard undercarriage of W7454 'G' collapsed. The Stirling immediately sunk onto its wing, damaging both starboard engines, undercarriage, and outer wing. None of the crew was injured, but damage to the Stirling was extensive. It would not return to 218 CF until the end of July.

*Sir Arthur Travers Harris. The first six months of his command were anything but smooth. Despite continues set backs his dogged atitude and belief in those under his command paved the way to future truimpths.*

**Friday March 27th 1942**
Short Stirling
*Mk.I*
*W7454 'G'*
*Contract No : B982939/39*
*Taken On Charge 218 CF : 28/02/1942*
*RoS/Sebro*
*Starboard Undercarriage Failure*
*Pilot: Squadron Leader B.R Ker*
*Pupil Pilot: Sgt George Kilpatrick Boyd*
*1060543 RAFVR*

On the morning of the 28th of March 1942, Form B.763 arrived at RAF Marham informing the squadrons that they would be required that night. After the recent frustrations over Essen, Harris turned his attention north. Bomber Command needed to demonstrate to its critics it could deliver a crippling blow against Germany. The target chosen to do this was Lubeck, on the Baltic coast. Easy to locate and with comparatively light defences this ancient city was deemed suitable for testing the effects of a large raid with incendiary bombs. During the morning, the Secretary of State for Air Archibald Sinclair arrived at RAF Marham with Group Captain Sir Louis Greig. They were introduced to all captains by W/Cdr Holder DFC. Both were keen to learn about the Stirling. After the brief visit, which lasted just over an hour, they departed but concluded by congratulating the squadron on its fine performance, and to' *keep it up'!*

One of the major ports of Germany, Lubeck straddled the river Trave. With several shipyards including the U-Boat building Lübecker Flender-Werke within the port area, it was a prime target. Connected to the rest of Germany by the important Elbe–Lübeck Canal, Lubeck like Hamburg was vital to Germany's war production. Vast quantities of imported material were unloaded in Lubeck and then transported by canal into the industrial heart of the Ruhr.

Nine aircraft were prepared for the night's operation, the usual pilots were briefed, seven of whom were NCOs. The first Stirling lifted off just before 20:00 hours. The pilot was F/Sgt Jim Hinwood in N6070 HA-A. There were two novel features to this operation. Firstly, the raid was divided into two distinct waves, the first and second waves separated by 40 minutes. The first wave was made up of experienced crews loaded entirely with flares and incendiaries, they would open proceedings at 2245 hours, zero hour. The second wave was all TR1335 equipped aircraft although Lubeck was beyond TR1335 range. This wave which included 218 Squadron, would bomb from 23:25 hours.

The unique feature of the raid was that the second wave would be loaded almost exclusively with incendiaries. Given the narrow streets and tightly packed timber building of the old city, Bomber Command was relying on it to burn. Group provided over 100 aircraft, 80% of which were carrying all incendiary loads. The oldest part of the city was on an island in the centre of the river. This would be one of two aiming points, the other was a machine tool factory. Beyond the range of TR1335 the apparatus was used preliminary for navigation up until a point where old fashion map reading took over. Thankfully, northern German was bathed in the light of the full moon. The most experienced crews of 3 Group would open proceeding. These arrived over the target at around 2245 hours. Crews could not believe the conditions, having been frustrated by the industrial haze over Essen over the past few weeks Lubeck was laid out like a map below. Given the lack of opposition, they started their bomb run from between 5,000 - 6,000 feet. Bathed in what appeared to hundreds of flares the old town was illuminated like daylight. Numerous fires had already taken hold as F/Sgt Gregg deposited his 21 x 250lb Incendiaries across the aiming point. Such was the visibility he could clearly make out Ratzeburger See and numerous bridges along the River Trave. Flight Sergeant Lamason RNZAF watched as his stick of incendiaries straddled the old town, while F/Lt Humphreys dropped his bomb load into a sea of flames which silhouetted the twin spires of Lubeck's Gothic Cathedral on the southern tip of the island. The main railway station, streets and individual buildings could all be identified as the crews roared across Lubeck. One crew remarked *'It was just one big party'.* As the they turned away for the long flight home, the old city was starting to burn. Flight Lieutenant Humphrey was at the controls of Stirling W7507 HA-P, having crossed the Kiel canal he was in sight of the North Sea when they were attacked by a Bf110 flown by Lt Leopold Fellerer of 5./NJG2. The following account records the encounter;

Aircraft 'P' captained by F/Lt Humphreys was attacked by an enemy aircraft after successfully bombing the target. They were on their return and while crossing the Kiel canal, the mid-upper gunner reported a twin-engine enemy aircraft on the starboard beam. The enemy machine attacked almost at once. His first burst of cannon fire hit the starboard wing and fuselage and one shell pierced the cabin Perspex and exploded against the armour plate behind F/Lt Humphrey's head. Soon afterward the mid-upper and rear turrets were put out of action, the rear gunner being wounded. The pilots communication with the rear turret being rendered useless. During further attacks our aircraft was forced down to 200 feet but mainly due to the excellent collaboration between himself and the wireless operator, who had taken up position in the astro position, F/Lt Humphreys was eventually able to evade the enemy fighter and set course for home. Throughout the combat F/Lt Humphreys showed great skill and courage and the ability to remain completely unruffled. He made a perfect landing at base despite severe damage to his aircraft. Which included landing flaps that had been rendered practically useless. His petrol tanks were badly holed and neither of the starboard wing tanks contained more than 15 gallons on landing.

For their actions on this night F/Lt Arthur Humphreys was awarded the DFC, while the crew's wireless operator, Sergeant Kenneth Wheeler was awarded the DFM. Their joint citation published on April 17th, 1942 reads;

*As captain of aircraft and wireless operator respectively. Flight Lieutenant Humphreys and Sergeant Wheeler participated in an attack on Lubeck on the night of 28th March, 1942 On the return journey, whilst over the Kiel Canal, the aircraft was subjected to a series of attacks by an enemy fighter. The rear gunner was wounded, the mid-upper and rear turrets were put out of action, and other damage was sustained by the aircraft. During the action, Flight Lieutenant Humphreys' aircraft was forced down to some 200 feet but, largely due to the excellent collaboration between himself and Sergeant Wheeler, he finally succeeded in evading his attacker and flew his damaged aircraft back to base where he made a safe landing. Throughout the combat, this officer displayed high skill and courage and was greatly assisted by Sergeant Wheeler who steadfastly remained at his post, giving clear directions of the enemy's tactics. Both Flight Lieutenant Humphreys and Sergeant Wheeler have carried out many sorties over enemy territory.*

On return Austin built W7507 recorded a catalogue of damage, repairs were even beyond the capabilities of the squadron's ground crews. It had flown only three operations since it crashed on delivery on March 14th, each raid was captained by F/Lt Humphreys. The crew's rear gunner, Sgt Norman John Stronell was admitted to RAF Marham SSQ where his wound to his knee and hand were cleaned and dressed.

**Saturday March 28th 1942**
Short Stirling
*Mk.I*
*W7507 HA-P 'Pip'*
*Contract No : B982939/39*
*Taken On Charge 14/03/1942*
*Cat /B salvage*
*No.54 MU*
*Battle damage*
*Pilot : Flight Lieutenant Arthur Humphreys*
*Pupil Pilot : Sergeant Robert Yates*
*Rear Gunner : Sergeant Norman Stronell, Injured*

Bomber Command had, in this one raid effectively destroyed over 200 acres or 40% of the inner city of Lübeck. Bomber Command estimated that over 2000 houses had either been totally destroyed or damaged beyond repair. It was not just residential damage, the central electric power station and four large factories had been destroyed and between 5 - 10 others seriously damaged. The important railway station and workshops had also been badly hit. It was later learnt that 1,468 (or 7.1%) of the buildings in Lübeck were destroyed, 2,180 (10.6%) were seriously damaged and 9,103 (44.3%) were lightly damaged, these represented 62% of all buildings in Lübeck. The direction of the attack was evident by a corridor of about 300 yards wide from Lübeck Cathedral to St. Peter's Church, the town hall and St. Mary's Church. Another area of damage was north of the Aegidienkirche. St. Lorenz, a residential suburb in the west of the Holstentor, was also severely damaged. The German police reported 301 people dead, three people missing, and 783 injured. More than 15,000 people lost their homes. The objectives set out prior to this raid had been totally met, it was Bomber Commands first major success against a German target.

March had been the squadron's first full operational month with the Short Stirling. It had flown 46 sorties dropping over 250,000 pounds of bombs in the process. It was a solid start. By the end of March, the squadron had received at least on paper the following Short Stirling Mk.Is.

| **Arrived** | **Serial** | **Contract** | **Built By** | **Code** | **From** | **To** |
|---|---|---|---|---|---|---|
| 12/12/1941 | N3706 | 763825/38 | Short Bros (R&B) Ltd Swindon | - | - | No.7 Squadron. 16/01/1942 |
| 16/12/1941 | N6127 | 774677/38 | Short and Harland Ltd. Belfast | - | - | No.149 Squadron. 15/02/1942 |
| 17/12/1941 | N6126 | 774677/38 | Short and Harland Ltd. Aldergrove | - | - | No.149 Squadron. 14/02/1942 |
| 23/12/1941 | N6128 | 774677/38 | Short and Harland Ltd. Aldergrove | - | - | No.7 Squadron. 24/12/1941 |
| 02/01/1942 | N3709 | 763825/38 | Short Bros (R&B) Ltd Swindon | - | - | No.7 Squadron. 16/01/1942 |
| 02/01/1942 | W7466 | B982939/39 | Austin Motors Ltd | - | - | No.7 Squadron. 05/01/1942 |
| 03/01/1942 | N3710 | 763825/38 | Short Bros (R&B) Ltd Swindon | - | - | No.7 Squadron 05/01/1942 |
| 05/01/1942 | W7467 | B982939/39 | Austin Motors Ltd | - | - | No.7 Squadron. 17/01/1942 |

| 05/01/1942 | N6089 | 774677/38 | Short and Harland Ltd. Belfast | HA-L | 7 Sqdn | - |
|---|---|---|---|---|---|---|
| 06/01/1942 | W7468 | B982939/39 | Austin Motors Ltd | - | - | No.7 Squadron. 10/01/1942 |
| 08/01/1942 | N6129 | 774677/38 | Short and Harland Ltd. Aldergrove | - | 7 Sqdn | No.218 CF. 28/02/1942 |
| 16/01/1942 | N3700 | 763825/38 | Short Bros (R&B) Ltd St Marston | HA-A | 7 Sqdn | - |
| 11/02/1942 | W7473 | B982939/39 | Austin Motors Ltd | HA-F | - | - |
| 12/02/1942 | W7475 | B982939/39 | Austin Motors Ltd | HA-H | - | - |
| 14/02/1942 | W7474 | B982939/39 | Austin Motors Ltd | HA-D | - | - |
| 16/01/1942 | W7454 | B982939/39 | Austin Motors Led | - | 149 Sqdn | No.218 CF. 28/02/1942 |
| 25/01/1942 | W7469 | B982939/39 | Austin Motors Led | HA-M | - | - |
| 26/01/1942 | N3712 | 763825/38 | Short Bros (R&B) Ltd Swindon | HA-Y | - | Cat E/FB SoC |
| 28/01/1942 | R9297 | 774677/38 | Short and Harland Ltd. Aldergrove | - | 7 Sqdn | No.7 Squadron. 31/01/1942 |
| 28/01/1942 | R9298 | 774677/38 | Short and Harland Ltd. Aldergrove | - | 7 Sqdn | No.7 Squadron. 27/02/1942 |
| 31/01/1942 | N3714 | 763825/38 | Short Bros (R&B) Ltd Swindon | HA-Q | - | Cat E/FB SoC |
| 31/01/1942 | N3715 | 763825/38 | Short Bros (R&B) Ltd Swindon | - | - | Cat B/FA SoC |
| 06/02/1942 | N3717 | 763825/38 | Short Bros (R&B) Ltd Swindon | HA-S | - | - |

| | | | | | | | |
|---|---|---|---|---|---|---|---|
| 14/02/1942 | W7474 | B982939/39 | Austin Motors Ltd | **HA-D** | - | | - |
| 17/02/1942 | N6070 | 774677/38 | Short and Harland Ltd. Aldergrove | **HA-A** | - | | - |
| 11/02/1942 | N3718 | 763825/38 | Short Bros (R&B) Ltd Swindon | **HA-C** | - | | - |
| 16/02/1941 | N3713 | 763825/38 | Short Bros (R&B) Ltd Swindon | - | - | | Cat B/FA-RIW/Sebro |
| 21/02/1942 | N3720 | 763825/38 | Short Bros (R&B) Ltd Swindon | **HA-B** | - | | - |
| 23/02/1942 | N3721 | 763825/38 | Short Bros (R&B) Ltd Swindon | **HA-C** | - | | - |
| 24/02/1942 | N6071 | 774677/38 | Short and Harland Ltd. Aldergrove | **HA-G** | - | | - |
| 24/02/1942 | N6072 | 774677/38 | Short and Harland Ltd. Aldergrove | **HA-J** | - | | - |
| 27/02/1942 | W7506 | B982939/39 | Austin Motors Ltd | **HA-K** | - | | - |
| 03/03/1942 | W7502 | B982939/39 | Austin Motors Ltd | **HA-N** | - | | - |
| 08/03/1942 | N3722 | 763825/38 | Short Bros (R&B) Ltd Swindon | **HA-E** | - | | - |
| 08/03/1942 | N6077 | 774677/38 | Short and Harland Ltd. Aldergrove | **HA-V** | - | | - |
| 10/03/1942 | N6076 | 774677/38 | Short and Harland Ltd. Aldergrove | - | - | | No.XV Squadron. 12/03/1942 |
| 10/03/1942 | W7503 | B982939/39 | Austin Motors Ltd | **HA-R** | - | | - |

| 14/03/1942 | W7507 | B982939/39 | Austin Motors Ltd | **HA-P** | - | - |
|---|---|---|---|---|---|---|
| 15/03/1942 | N3725 | 763825/38 | Short Bros (R&B) Ltd Swindon | **HA-D** | - | - |
| 21/03/1942 | N6078 | 774677/38 | Short and Harland Ltd. Aldergrove | **HA-P** | - | - |

*New Zealander Derek Bullock. One of a number of outstanding 'Kiwi' captains that served with the squadron.*

The month of April started with the squadron in excellent spirits, the recent success over Lubeck and a practically clean sheet with losses went a long way to bolster morale. Other than a few teething issues with the Stirlings undercarriage the crews appeared to be confident in its performance. The Conversion flight under the competent command of S/Ldr Ker was now operating daily. A good-looking New Zealander arrived on the 1st fresh from conversion at No.1651 CU based at RAF Waterbeach. Derek Bullock was born in Hamilton, New Zealand on February 22nd, 1919. Before his enlistment, in the RNZAF he had worked for the NZ Co-op Pig Marketing Association as an office clerk. He embarked for the United Kingdom in September 1941, and after completing spells at various flying schools, he eventually arrived at No.19 O.T.U on November 13th, 1941. Here he trained on the ungainly Whitley before posting to No.1651, and conversion to the Stirling.

A welcome switch to a French target on the 2nd meant a shorter time over enemy territory and less flak. The target chosen was the Matford Factory at Poissy. It was at the time believed to be the most modern and efficient factory in France. The factory was located only 14 miles from the centre of Paris. Five crews were detailed, including the squadron commander W/Cdr Holder DFC. In brilliant moonlight and near-perfect visibility the target was identified. Flight Sergeant Lamason claimed that 10 out of his 11 bombs were direct hits on the factory complex, equally confident was F/Sgt Hinwood. He too reported 10 of his HEs exploding in amongst the fires throughout the factory. Wing Commander Holder lost an engine aboard W7503 HA-R on route, deciding to press on they then overshot the turning point. Now hopelessly late, they wisely decided to abort. While crossing the French coast, they were hit in the starboard mainplane and fuselage by flak. Thankfully, nothing vital was hit, and all the crew escaped unharmed. Twenty miles off the coast of France, the crew jettisoned the entire bomb load into the sea. The returning crews claimed yet another success, the flat elongated roofs of the factory were seen on fire, six individual fires were reported within the factory complex including one large fire at the factory's power station.

A significant raid directed against Cologne was scheduled for the 5th. A total of 263 aircraft would participate, 118 of them were provided by No.3 Group. No.218 Squadron would supply ten, once again led by Wing Commander Holder DFC. The raid was planned for two waves, 127 aircraft would attack first, 30 minutes later the remaining bombers would attack.

The squadron lost one crew to engine failure. Sergeant Webber lost his starboard inner engine soon after crossing the Norfolk Coast and he was obliged to jettisoned 'safe' 21 x 250 pounders. Despite the promise given at briefing that the weather conditions over Cologne would be clear, it was anything but. Dense broken cloud and industrial haze made visual identification of the aiming point extremely difficult. Wing Commander Holder somehow managed to identify the target by the river and its numerous bridges, TR1135 confirmed that he was over Cologne, but nothing else. By the time the squadron arrived over the target, there were countless flares and incendiaries, but no concentration. Flight Lieutenant William Livingston reported, *'No fires observed in town at this hour, Some flares and fires at Bonn'*. Sergeant Shirley Davidge remarked, *'Heavy concentration of searchlights and a dummy fire in target area'*. One crew put up a commendable show. Flight Sergeant Bernard Tompkins was unable to fully retract the port undercarriage aboard N6071 HA-G after take-off. Not wishing to miss the raid they continued onto the target dropping their 21 x 250 pounders visually on some scattered flares. While on route home they suffered port inner engine failure forcing the crew to return to Marham on just three engines. Flying on his first operation alongside Tompkins was Sgt Reginald Elsom a former Grocery Manager from Loughborough, Leicestershire. Little did he know that he would be one of just a handful to survive his tour with No.218 Squadron from this period. Reg would be awarded a DFM for completing his tour of thirty operations in September but would be killed while instructing with 22 OTU on October 13th, 1942, before he could collect his award.

The raid appeared to be a success, especially to the crews from Stradishall, Honington, Wyton and Mildenhall. However, there were some concerns raised from 75(NZ), 218, 57 and 115 Squadrons who did not consider the raid successful and told Group HQ and reported the fact. As it turned out, the attack was a failure. Scattered flares drew the majority of incendiaries which in turn attracted the HE carried by the second wave. No.1 Group was given its own target, the Maschinenbauanstalt Humboldt mechanical engineering firm. This was missed entirely. It was back to the Ruhr and Essen on 6th. Bomber Command was still hoping for a decisive blow that would destroy the Krupps works. The raid was marred by severe storms and icing on route and almost complete cloud cover over the target. Flight Lieutenant Humphreys was obliged to bomb Gladbach when he lost the starboard outer engine aboard W7506 HA-K. Joining him once again in the 2nd pilot seat was

S/Ldr Ashworth. 'B' Flights Squadron Leader Oldroyd managed to locate Essen using TR1335 dropping his 15 x 250lb bombs from 17,000 feet 1/2 mile north of the aiming point. The raid was yet another failure. A record-breaking 272 crews were made available for an attack on the city and docks of Hamburg on the 8th. Hamburg had been spared a visit since early January. It was time it was revisited. Given the successful raid on Lubeck, it was hoped that another attack on a coastal target with numerous identifiable features could be replicated. The squadron would provide six crews, one of which was captained by Scotsman, Sgt George Boyd who was making his debut as captain. The squadron notched one early return. The issue of the non-retracting undercarriage aboard N6071 HA-G reappeared forcing the crew of F/Sgt Tompkins to jettison the high explosive bomb load once again and return to Marham. It was a lousy night for No.3 Group, of the 112 crews detailed, nine failed to take off, and an alarming 31 returned early due to either mechanical failure or icing.

The weather that had affected the previous Essen raids was still very much evident as the crews encountered both electrical storms and icing over the North Sea and Northern Germany. A solid layer of cloud meant that the crews equipped with TR1335 had the advantage over those not yet equipped. Those crews that battled the elements and managed to reach the target found it blanketed by cloud. Once again, the Senior Met Officer at Group had got it very wrong. Each of the squadron crews was forced either to bomb on a few isolated flares or TR1335 fix. The squadron dropped a total of 84 x 250lb bombs plus 6 x 1000lb and 3 x 500lb. The raid was yet another failure. The Bomber Command HQ's fixation with Essen continued on the 10th. The crews were promised clear conditions over the Ruhr. At the briefing at Marham it raised a few disparaging remarks, confidence in the Met men was at an all-time low.

It was a thankless job, the Met Office was responsible for meeting the RAF's requirements at the beginning of WW2 - although, like the military, it was understaffed and ill-equipped for the conflict. Forecasts for flying operations were prepared by HQ Group Met Offices (GMO), based on advice issued by HQ Met Office, and sent by teleprinter to the operational airfields where civilian forecasters briefed the aircrew. One of the biggest problems was operations involving squadrons from two or more Groups. Unsettled weather could result in uncertain forecasts, perhaps leading to one Group cancelling an operation whilst another Group allowed its aircraft to operate as planned. An airfield in Cambridge or Suffolk might be clear for the returning bombers, while an airfield in North Yorkshire may find itself completely fog bound. Forecasting conditions over England was one thing, over Germany was certainly different. To aid the Met Office, Met Reconnaissance flights began over the North Sea from about April 1941. It was not until November 7th, 1941 that these Met Flights ventured over Germany. The first was flown by P/O Frank Wilson in Spitfire P9550 of 1401 Met Flt, but it ended tragically when he crashed in the sea off Eastbourne during the return flight. It was not until the following spring flights were resumed.

Command had requested that all available aircraft be used and loaded with a high proportion of incendiaries. The No.3 Group provided 102 Wellingtons and Stirlings, of which No.218 Squadron provided nine. Flying on his first raid as captain was 'A' Flight's Squadron Leader Harold Ashworth. A pre-war Timber Importer he had gained his pilot's licence in 1928. An experienced civil pilot, he was commissioned in the RAF as a P/O in December 1939 for the duration of hostiles. The squadron's other flight commander, 24-year-old S/Ldr Oldroyd was also aloft, he was joined by P/O John Abberton in the co-pilot's seat. Contrary to the briefing the crews found the target covered by cloud, of the nine crews dispatched, only three claimed to have bombed the target. The majority attacked Cologne on TR1335, while S/Ldr Ashworth bombed Dusseldorf due to a defective DR compass, collecting a few flak holes for his trouble. The three crews that claimed to have reached Essen were Sgt Webber, and F/Sgts Millichamp RCAF and Tompkins. All three reported that their all-incendiary loads were dropped on flares starting a number of fires in a built-up area. The raid despite the commendable effort by those that endured the storms and icing was a failure.

*Short Stirling N6129 HA-X of No.218 Conversion Flight. A brand new Short and Harland built aircraft it arrived at Marham on January 8th, 1942. It was almost immediately transferred to the conversion flight where it completed 4 operations before being shot down into the sea off the Island of Sylt in July 1942. It had accumulated over 228 flying hours when lost.*

On the 12th, HQ's sights were once again directed towards Essen. The Met Officer yet again promised clear weather over the Ruhr, a large cheer reverberated around the briefing room. In preparation for the raid the hard-working ground crews had made available 11 aircraft, it was a marvellous achievement. Both Flight Commanders joined the rest of the squadron as they departed RAF Marham just after 2200 hours. The bombers each carrying an all-incendiary load slowly climbed for altitude as they first crossed the Norfolk coast and then headed out across the North Sea. As usual No.3 Group provided the bulk of the bombers, 124 Wellingtons and Stirlings would

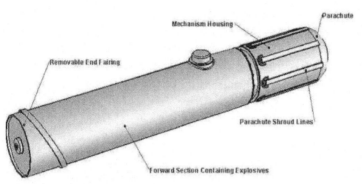

**Mk.I Air Deployable Anti-Ship Mine**

join a further 126 aircraft drawn from No.1, 4 and 5 Groups. There was just one early return. Pilot Officer Finch, a pilot making his only appearance on the squadron was taken ill over the North Sea. The crews arrived over the target just after 0100 hours and to their delight found the target almost free of cloud. Some sizeable fires had already developed around a concentration of flares. Ground details could be seen despite the industrial haze. Squadron Leader Oldroyd reported a dummy fire 7 miles south of Essen and another south-west of the target. Given the clear conditions, it was no surprise that the Ruhr's flak defences were more active than normal. Two squadron Stirlings sustaining minor damage, while a further forty from the 179 bombers that claimed to have attacked also reported flak damage. One of the squadrons Stirling's hit was flown by Sgt John Webber. They were forced to land Stirling N3717 HA-S at RAF Manston, Kent on return due to fuel shortage a result of a holed wing tank. For once there was some good news. The initial TR1335 dropped markers were both accurate and concentrated, these attracted the incendiary force who carried out some accurate bombing. The Krupps works were finally hit and sustained some damage, however, S/Ldr Oldroyd's observation of dummy fires proved correct. Much of the bombing was scattered all over the Ruhr some bombs even dropping on the town of Schweln, 20 miles south east of Essen. This was the last of the raids on Essen and concluded a disappointing and frustrating campaign against Hitler's armaments heartland. For the squadron at least it could celebrate the fact that they had not lost a crew, not so fortunate was No.115 Squadron across the airfield. Since the beginning of March, they had lost five Wellingtons crews.

On the 13th the squadron found itself undertaking a new type of operation, mining, or *'gardening'*. This was the RAF term given to the dropping of aerial mines from bomber aircraft into the sea. The mines were *'sown'* near ports and harbours, inland waterways, estuaries and in busy shipping lanes. Throughout Europe, the coastline was split into various targets and also given distinct code names. The responsibility of delivering and *'planting'* of airborne sea mines was taken over by Bomber Command on March 25th, 1942. The squadron prepared five aircraft each loaded with four x 1500lb sea mines, the first name on the Ops board was that of W/Cdr Holder DFC. The first crew aloft was that of New Zealander F/Sgt Lamason at 2110 hours at the controls of N3725 HA-D. The target chosen was the Garden area coded *'Nectarines'*. This was an area of sea from the Island of Terschelling to the Island of Wangerooge commonly known as the Frisian Islands. This mass of water was divided into three due to its size, area I, II and III. These would feature heavily in the months to come. Using their TR1335 sets all the crews apart from Sgt Davis who experienced TR1335 set failure, planted the mines or *'Vegetables'* in *'Nectarines III'*. Wing Commander Holder DFC planted his four mines with a 4$_{1/2}$ second interval from 500 feet damaging the undercarriage housing to W7469 HA-M in the process. His position was confirmed and pinpointed from the island of Baltrum. It was an excellent start to what would become a regular feature. Much of the group's early success was in no small part due to the tremendous help provided by No.5 Group. They had started minelaying back in April 1940 and had gained considerable experience in the art of 'Gardening'. Eight crews were detailed for a significant raid directed against the industrial and communication centres in Dortmund on the 14th. It was the start of a frantic period of operations for the squadron. Wing Commander Holder was joined by both flight commanders on what would be the most substantial force yet sent to the city. The route to target was cloudless with visibility extending some 5-10 miles. The fires from the first wave could be seen miles from the Dortmund, long before the squadron started their bomb runs. Once over the city, the crews encountered accurate and intense flak. What appeared to be hundreds of searchlights swept the skies looking for an unfortunate crew to latch onto. Also evident were fighters, a number of twin-engine Ju88 and Bf110s were reported making an appearance. Squadron Leader Ashworth found himself coned over the city while making his bomb run. With some considerable effort, he finally managed to shake them off, which enabled the crew to watch as their all incendiary load burst across the centre of Dortmund. Both Flight Sergeants Millichamp RCAF and McGregor were hit by flak as was W/Cdr Holder's Stirling which had two large, jagged holes in the port wing courtesy of Dortmund's flak gunners. While on route home Squadron Leader Ashworth was passing north of Essen when once again, he was caught by searchlights which seemed to be working in conjunction with night-fighters. Almost immediately they sighted a twin-engine fighter 600 yards to port, the rear gunner, Sgt William Watt opened fire with two short bursts which appeared to put off both the searchlights and the fighter. The crew of F/Sgt McGregor found itself in trouble 22,000 feet over the target. Dazzled by searchlights, both McGregor and his 2nd pilot, P/O Ball put the Stirling into a near-vertical dive. Such was the angle of decent the Elsan become dislodged and found itself, and its contents near Sgt Don Finney's wireless position. The observer's maps, charts, pencils, plus all his equipment seemed to just float in mid-air much to Sgt Hobden's dismay. The heavy wooden sextant container box ended up wrapping itself around the pilot's armour plating. Reaching almost 420 mph and in a body numbing dive the mid-upper gunner, Sgt Davidson politely asked over the intercom, *'are you ever going to pull this fucking thing out'*. It took both pilots to pull the aircraft out of its dive, once level they were down to below 7,000 feet. The crew managed to get home without further mishap. All the Stirlings started to land just before dawn on the 15th, other than a few holes, it was another clean sheet. Returning crews put the defences over Dortmund on par with Essen, but still managed to drop a total of 52,320lb of incendiaries on the city. Sadly, the raid was an utter failure. Bombing photographs showed bombs falling across a 40 mile stretch of the Ruhr; damage to Dortmund was negligible.

The following night the squadron detailed seven NCO crews on a follow-up attack against Dortmund. This number was reduced when Sgt Davidge was withdrawn just before take-off due to engine trouble to Stirling N3722 HA-F. The total was further depleted with the early return of Sgt Stanley Coggin and crew who suffered intercom failure. They were followed by F/Sgt John Webber with a defective rear turret. Those crews that found Dortmund encountered thick cloud and icing, and the bombing was once again scattered. Bombing photographs were plotted between 5 and 51 miles from Dortmund! The raid was yet another embarrassing fiasco. It was becoming increasingly difficult to hide the frustration both at group level and command level at the apparent failure of the crews to locate and mark the targets even when in range of the TR1335 sets. Despite changes in tactics, the introduction of flare droppers and TR1335 accuracy was still very much a hit or miss affair. Rumblings at the Air Ministry and in Parliament added to the pressure on Harris and his group commanders. The squadron welcomed Sergeant Robert Yates a recently qualified pilot fresh from conversion on the 16th. He would soon be in the thick of the action. Squadron Leader Ashworth and crew were flown down to RAF Manston by F/Sgt Millichamp RCAF in W7506 HA-K on the morning of the 16th. Stirling N3717 HA-S which had landed short of fuel on

*Inspection of Short Stirling W7503 HA-R a day after its near vertical dive over Dortmund. This Austin Motors built Stirling arrived on the squadron on March 10th, 1942. Flight Sergeant McGregor and crew would complete seven operations with this aircraft.*

return from Hamburg on the 12th was finally ready for collection. Taking off at 12:40 hours S/Ldr Ashworth was back at Marham within the hour. There was cause for celebrations on the 17th with the announcement of the DFC to F/Lt Arthur Humphreys and the DFM to Sergeant Kenneth Wheeler. A brief break in operations gave the squadron the opportunity to make ready 12 aircraft for an attack on the port of Hamburg. The ever-efficient ground crews had pulled out every stop to provide this number, the largest provided since conversion. The squadron started taking off a few minutes before midnight, once airborne they joined a force of over 150 bombers heading towards northern Germany.

In good weather and clear sky, the crews headed north. North of Hamburg two crews encountered prowling night fighters. Two miles north of Reher Sgt Wilf Davis was attacked by a Bf110 at 02:38hours. Thankfully both gunners were alert to the danger and engaged the fighter, which wisely dived away and was lost. Seven minutes later at 02:45hrs, Sgt Boyd was attacked while at 17000 feet. On this occasion, the Stirling, N3700 HA-B received minor damage. Once again, accurate return fire from both gunners seemed to deter the German pilot from further attacks. Over the target the searchlights were in abundance, and flak was intense. Flight Lieutenant Humphreys DFC and F/Sgt Gregg were both hit, the latter losing the rear turret when flak punctured the hydraulic system. Seven crews reported a large conflagration in the Altona area, a district in western Hamburg.

One crew who very nearly *'Got the chop'* was Sgt Wilf Davies and crew. They had already survived an encounter with a Bf110 and now found themselves coned by a number of searchlights. Unable to shake them off and despite all his attempts to manoeuvre out of the beams the young pilot had no option but to put the nose of the Stirling down and dived directly towards the city below. The Stirling quickly began to vibrate as the speed and angle of dive increased. As the Stirling got closer and closer to the ground, the searchlights started to disengage until the crew were wrapped in the welcome blanket of darkness. With an airspeed reaching 400 mph both pilots began desperately to pull back on the control columns, it took every ounce of the strength of both Davies and Sgt Guntrip to pull the vibrating Stirling out of the dive. Once level, Wilf Davies checked the altimeter having glanced out of the cockpit and saw to his horror chimneys and factories almost at their level. It was a close-run thing, the Stirling had lost almost 15,000 feet in the dive and now found itself below 1000 feet over the outskirts of Hamburg. A few seconds more, the crew and the Stirling would have ploughed into the ground smashing them all to pieces. Once the shocked crew had recovered from the near-vertical dive they headed for home. Stirling W7502 HA-N had lost a propellor either due to flak or the dive which contributed to the vibration, eventually, the still shaken crew reached Marham for a safe landing. At de-briefing returning crews reported that fires were visible 40-50 miles from the target. Post raid reconnaissance provided no evidence of fresh damage. A planned operation against Le Havre was cancelled on the 20th due to weather. On the 22nd seven crews were detailed for a gardening operation, they would be making the squadron's first visit the Baltic Sea, a long and dangerous trip. Each of the Stirlings was loaded with 4 x sea mines plus 2 x 250lb MC bombs. The first crew aloft was F/Sgt Hinwood in Stirling N6070 HA-A at 2100 hours. Soon after the departure of the seven Baltic crews, two *'Freshman'* crews were on their way to Le Havre. Sergeants George McAuley and Richard Medus were carrying out their

*The crew of W7473 HA-F skippered Sergeant Shirley Davidge. All would be killed in a tragic accident soon after take-off.*

first operations as captain. Both found the docks and deposited their 18 x 500 pounders across docks 9 and 13. They were back at Marham in under four hours. Over the Baltic Sea, F/Lt Livingstone and crew chanced upon a number of ships sailing 8 miles east of Schonhagen. Showing remarkable courage, the crew attacked from 1000 feet machine-gunning the decks of one ship and bombing another with the two 250 pounders. Wing Commander Holder having planted his mines bombed a flare path on an aerodrome at position 5528N/1140E from 8000 feet. Three hours after the return of the Le Havre pair the mining crews started to land, the last to land after being airborne for 7 hours 22 minutes was S/Ldr Oldroyd in Stirling N3722 HA-F. The following night six NCO crews were detailed and briefed for the first of a series of raids directed against the important Baltic port of Rostock and specifically the Heinkel Works. One of the crews detailed was skippered by Sergeant Shirley Davidge who departed at 22:57 hours in Stirling W7473 HA-F. Soon after take-off the crew were in trouble, the port inner engine began to misfire and lose power. Realising that they could not continue with the operation, the crew jettisoned the 24 x 250lb cans of incendiaries over the Wash and turned back to Marham. The Stirling got as far as Clenchwarton a small village located about 1 1/2 miles west of the River Great Ouse, about 2 miles from King's Lynn. It was in this sleepy village that Sgt Davidge and his crew lost their lives. Reports suggest that Davidge may been attempting to crash land as he was seen to make a steep turn to port immediately prior to the Stirling crashing to the ground at Ingrams Farm at 23:30 hours. Sadly, there were no survivors from the crew. There is however an account of the incident as recalled by Mr J Mann.

*As far as I can recall, I was 10 years-old at the time the bomber was going out on a raid to Germany. Soon after take-off it developed engine trouble. The pilot radioed back to base for permission to return, but there was an air raid alert, and the base could not put the landing lights on. They were told to head out to sea and the crew bail-out. The bombs were jettisoned safely over the Wash. Some of the bomb load landed near Clenchwarton Marshes. No doubt they are still there today. The pilot spotted a field near Clenchwarton known locally as Ingram Field, about 100 yards from the local school. It was a long narrow field near a number of greenhouses, belonging to Mr Ingram. The Pilot though he could make a belly landing in this field, so he tried to bring the aircraft in. Unfortunately, the pilot had not noticed a large Oak Tree on the edge of the field. The aircraft wing hit the tree which spun the aircraft around almost 360 degrees. The aircraft struck the ground completely smashing the rear fuselage. The aircraft then burst into flames. The local A.F.S arrived but only had hand powered fire pumps and no foam, there was not much they could do but watch the aircraft and its crew burn to death. I remember going to school next morning and seeing the large single rudder sticking skywards. Ironically, this part of the aircraft had escaped most of the fire as it had broken off on impact and was laying seven yards from the rest of the smouldering aircraft. I was told that the gunner was alive when the aircraft crashed but he could not operate the rear turret doors which were buckled and was overcome with the heat. Sadly, he perished with the rest of his crew. After school that day I went back to Ingrams field to look at the remains of the bomber, there was not much left, just a big burnt patch and large hole. I went into Ingrams potting sheds, where I had a terrible shock. On the potting shed benches was a large tarpaulin, I looked underneath and to my horror I found the crew all lying beside each other all terribly burnt. It was a sight I have never forgot!*

A subsequent investigation discovered that the port inner engine cut due to the seizure of No.12 cylinder. The situation was further complicated by the accusation by the investigation team that the pilot turned into the defective engine, however this has never been fully established. The bodies of the young crew were taken to their hometowns for burial which ranged from Armagh in Northern Ireland to Cornwall and Yorkshire.

### Thursday 23rd April 1942

Short Stirling
Mk.I
W7473 HA-F 'Freddie'
Contract No : B/982939/40
Taken On Charge : 11/02/1942
CAT E 'Burnt'
SoC
Engine Failure
Pilot : Sergeant Shirley Vincent Davidge, 1186826 RAFVR, **Killed**
2nd Pilot : Sergeant Willem Joseph Gerard Rieter, 1271309 RAFVR, **Killed**
Observer : Sergeant John Hartley, 989820 RAFVR, **Killed**
Wireless Operator : Sergeant Archibald John Thorburn, 960871 RAFVR, **Killed**
Wireless Op/Gunner : Sergeant Jamie Kitchener Windle Paul, 1380822 RAFVR, **Killled**
Rear Gunner : Sergeant William James Cook, 540952 RAF, **Killed**
Flight Engineer : Sergeant Abson Squires, 545944 RAF, **Killed**

*Sergeant Willem (Wim) Rieter RAFVR seen here while undergoing pilot training.*

The young Dutchman, Sgt Willem Rieter was taken for burial at Brookwood Cemetery, the local newspaper, the Surrey Advertiser reported on his burial.

*The funeral of Sergeant Willem Joseph Gerard Rieter.*

**Surrey Advertiser - Saturday 02 May 1942**

**AIRMAN'S FUNERAL**

The funeral took place at Brookwood on Wednesday of Sergeant Pilot W. Rieter, who lost his life when an aeroplane he was piloting crashed. He was 24 years of age and Dutch, and had been living with Mr. and Mrs. Dodman, of Charlton, Oyster Lane, Byfleet. When war broke out, he went to Holland to serve in the Forces. A short time later he returned to this country to continue his studies. He volunteered for the R.A.F. and gained his wings in September last, becoming a bomber pilot. He had taken part in several raids over Germany. A service was held first at the Roman Catholic Church, West Byfleet, Father Sullivan officiating. The coffin, which was covered with the Dutch flag, was carried by members of the R.A.F.

Sergeant Davidge was, by the time of his death, an experienced bomber pilot. Since his arrival on the squadron in August 1941, he had completed ten operations on Wellingtons in the 2nd pilot role, plus a further three as captain. On completion of his conversion to the Stirling, he had completed a further six operations. Sergeant Willem (Wim) Rieter had completed six operations all sitting beside Sgt Davidge. The Dutchman was probably only a few weeks away from captaining his own crew.

The area around the important Heinkel works was already ablaze when the squadron crews arrived over the port. A number of fires were blazing away in the old town. Sergeant Medus and crew dropped their bomb load on the New town, south of the old city producing five excellent fires. Sergeant Davis started five small fires, remarking ' *Several large fires seen in target area'*. Sergeant Webber dropped his all incendiary load from 10,000 feet across the old town, on departing he caught a glimpse in the light of the fires of the magnificent Schwerin Castle. The five NCO crews arrived back at Marham just before daybreak on the 24th, Sgt Webber had been flying for over seven hours. The raid was partially successful, but the main weight of bombs had fallen on the old town and suburbs. The Heinkel works the designated target for No.5 Group was untouched. Given a window of good weather, Bomber Command kept up the pressure on Rostock the following night when 125 aircraft were detailed. The squadron provided four Stirlings, once again all captained by NCO skippers. Like the previous night visibility and the weather to the target was excellent, still 50 miles away from Rostock, the fires could already be seen in the distance. Unlike the previous night, the fires appeared to be much more concentrated. Arriving over the

*The now fully qualified bomber pilot, Sergeant Willem Joseph Gerard Rieter.*

town between 13,000 - 15,000 feet the squadron meet slightly more opposition than the previous night but reported it as ' *Not at all serious'*. Flight Sergeant Tompkins reported 'Terrific fires covering ten blocks burning on arrival in New Town, SW of aiming Point'. Sergeant Davis on his second visit to Rostock added his all-incendiary load onto a mass of fires in the old town. On turning for home Rostock appeared to be ablaze, F/Sgt Hinwood reported that the fires could be seen from Romo Island, over 100 miles distant. There was an air of satisfaction at the debriefing, it appeared to be a job well done. Returning from his 35th and last operation was observer, P/O Graham Hunter. Born in Bromley, Kent in 1921, Graham had started his career on the squadron back in July 1941 on his arrival from 20 O.T.U based at RAF Lossiemouth. Unusually Grahams early operations were flown as a spare. It was not until he eventually teamed up with Sgt John Webber in October 1941 he settled into a crew. In May he was posted to 21 O.T.U at RAF Moreton-in-Marsh for instructional duties. He returned to operations in 1943 with No.142 Squadron in the Mediterranean theatre where he completed a further 30 operations. On completion of his second tour, he was awarded a well-deserved DFC in November 1943.

There was stunned disbelief the following day when the squadron was informed that it was Rostock again that night. The squadron had never attacked the same target on three consecutive nights.

Three NCO crews were detailed and briefed while a further six crews including both Flight Commanders and the recently promoted P/O Phil Lamason RNZAF were given a unique operation. The Skoda Works in Pilsen, Czechoslovakia was the distant target given to just No.218 Squadron. The city of Pilsen was a major weapons producer, with a population of 130,000 in 1942, a staggering 35,000 worked for Skoda.

Skoda became an arsenal for the German military, producing the Panzer tanks, Jagdpanzer tank destroyers, and almost exclusively produced thousands of rounds of 10" howitzer shells and tens of thousands 88mm and 37mm anti-aircraft shells a month. After the German invasion, the Nazis divided Czechoslovakia into the Protectorate of Bohemia and Moravia and governed the region with its usual brutality. Skoda's importance was not lost on German propaganda. Much was made about its apparent immunity to RAF raids and its contribution to the German war effort. Sometime in late 1941, the Czechoslovakian underground got in contact with SOE in London requesting that the works be bombed to *'Maintain morale in the face of constant propaganda to the effect that the RAF was unable to bomb a target within the Protectorate'.* Detailed plans of the Skoda Armament works were smuggled out and found their way to London. After much deliberation between organisations in London, the exiled Czechoslovakian Government, and the Czech Underground a small-scale raid comprising of between 6-8 aircraft was agreed. The operation would be code named 'CANONBURY'. The details of the operation would only be sent on the day of the operation when the preparations on the ground could be carried out, secrecy was paramount. On the late afternoon of the 25th a pre-arranged broadcast was received to the sounds of Dvoraks Slavonic Dance No.8. At 18:40 hours the code *' Be patient, the day of reckoning will come'* was broadcast. This message was then passed through to the Air Ministry then No.3 Group HQ and finally to 218 Squadron at Marham. Operation CANONBURY was on that night.

*Sergeant Harold Reuben Millichamp RCAF*

The six selected crews were drawn equally from both flights, three from 'A' Flight led by S/Ldr Ashworth and three from S/Ldr Oldroyd's 'B' Flight. The crews were briefed separately from the 15 other crews drawn from No.115 and No.218 Squadrons due to the nature of the operation. This was unlike any Bomber Command operation previously undertaken and was shrouded with mystery. Pilsen was almost at the limit of the Stirlings range and would require the crews to be over enemy-held territory for a considerable period. Navigation was critical, beyond the range of TR1335 (Gee) the success of the operation was placed squarely on the accuracy of the navigators. One of the navigators was P/O John Banting, a 27-year-old south Londoner. John had the distinction of being part of the very first draft of RAF aircrew to be trained in navigation in the United States under the 'Arnold Scheme'.

*Sergeant Philip Harold Bullock RAF*

He along with nine others was hand-picked from observer students at No.1 Navigation School, Eastbourne in March 1941 to be the first to commence training in the Pan American Airways Navigation Section based at the University of Miami. It was a gruelling course, with much emphasis on astronavigation and countless hours of classroom studies. Given the distance involved and the unknown terrain the participating crews would be assisted by members of the Czech Underground. As they neared the target a number of fires would be started on the ground at predetermined locations to aid navigation. Barns were to be set alight at Skvrany a few miles west of Pilsen. Another barn was to be set on fire a few miles south of Pilsen. Just after 21:00 hours, the first of the six bombers started to depart from RAF Marham, each loaded with 6 x 1000 pounders. The crews would gain altitude to 10,000 feet and fly at this height for the majority of the outward flight. With a predetermined route the crews would have been flying within minutes of each other in the darkness. Weather on route was initially good on the outward leg of the flight. It was approximately 20 miles south-west of Wiesbaden that the crew of Pilot Officer Harold 'Hal' Millichamp RCAF were attacked and shot down by Ofw Karl Haisch flying a Bf110 C-4 D5+HM of 4./NJG1. In what must have been a vicious encounter, Stirling W7606 HA-K plummeted to the ground crashing at Lohrer Muhle, 200 meters from the road between Huffelsheim - Rudesheim - Bad Kreuznach, Germany. The subsequent crash left a crater 100ft wide and 30 ft deep, there were no survivors. The time was 00.06 hours. The combat was not all one-sided. The crew's gunners managed to inflict some damage to one of the Bf110s engines forcing Ofw Haisch to make a belly landing. This encounter was seen by two crews who reported that at 00:10 hours, an aircraft flying behind them at approximately 10,000 feet was seen shot down.

**Saturday 25th April 1942**
Short Stirling
*Mk.I*
*W7506 HA-K*
*Contract No : B/982939/38*
*Taken On Charge : 27/02/1942*
*CAT E/FB (Missing)*
*SoC*
**Failed To Return**
*Pilot :  Pilot Officer Harold Reuben Millichamp, J/15307 RCAF* **Killed**
*2nd Pilot : Sergeant Thomas Cunningham Bird, 1006950 RAFVR,* **Killed**
*Observer : Pilot Officer John Albert Stokes Banting, 107988 RAFVR,* **Killed**
*Wireless Operator : Sergeant  Thomas MacFarlane, 1062947 RAFVR,* **Killed**
*Wireless Operator/Gunner : Sergeant David Holly Bird, 1181384 RAFVR (Canadian)* **Killed**
*Mid Upper Gunner : Sergeant Stuart Alan Bain Kellie, 1378331 RAFVR* **Killed**
*Rear Gunner : Sergeant Percy George Detmold, 12811232 RAFVR* **Killed**
*Flight Engineer : Sergeant Philip Harold Bullock, 570264 RAF* **Killed**

*Sergeant Thomas Cunningham Bird RAFVR killed on his first operation with the squadron.*

Hal Millichamp at 32 was older than most on the squadron. Born in Toronto, Canada he had joined the squadron mid-October 1941 on completion of No.39 Course at No.11 Operational Training Unit. On the same course was fellow Canadian, Sgt George Niblo, both would be sent to 218 Squadron then still equipped with the Wellington. Hal's first six operations were flown in the right-hand seat for operational experience. He had the good fortune of flying five of the raids with the experienced 'B' Flight Commander, S/Ldr Williams DFC. It was not until January 1942 he captained his own crew flying two operations before converting to the Stirling. During March and April, Hal completed a further eight raids bringing his total to 16 operations. In total contrast, 21-year-old Yorkshireman Sergeant Bird had only just arrived on the squadron having completed No.43 Course at No.11 O.T.U. This was his first operation. Also, on his first operation with the crew was the experienced Sergeant Stuart Kellie. The remains of the crew were recovered and initially buried in the Communal Cemetery at Bad Kreuznach. They were exhumed on April 2nd, 1948 and taken for reburial at Rheinberg War Cemetery.

The remaining five crews pressed on, about 100 miles from the target the weather started to deteriorate, an ominous layer of solid cloud stretched across southern Germany and more importantly over the final run into the target. This placed yet more strain on the overworked navigators. With no ground detail available astronavigation was now the only means of navigating. With the promise of clear weather gone, the crews had two options, continue onto the target and rely on the skill of the navigator, or descend below the clouds. Two crews, Squadron Leader Oldroyd and P/O Lamason opted for the low-level approach. At this lower altitude, it was hoped that the blazing barns would be visible. Just after 01:00 hours, the Air Raid sirens started to sound at Pilsen. At considerable risk, the first barn was set alight by the underground at 01:32 hours. This was located on the Bory Fields situated on the Goldscheidrovka Farm. Twenty minutes later, the second barn at Skvrnany Street Nade was set alight by the Czech Underground. These brave young men had fulfilled their part. It was now up to the five squadron crews.

Just after 02.03 hours, the first of the 1000 pounders started to explode across Pilsen. The city's flak and searchlight defences were already fully alerted and desperately trying to locate the bombers. Showing remarkable courage, the crew of S/Ldr Oldroyd roared into the target at the perilously low altitude of 1,500 feet. At this height, there was no margin for error. Despite being severely damaged by light flak, the crew dropped their six 1000 pounders just north of the target starting a number of fires. Pilot Officer Lamason attacked from 2,500 feet, but even at this low altitude, he was unable to see the results of his bombing due to cloud. Two crews opted for a high-level attack, which given the weather conditions meant they would bomb blindly on ETA.

Flight Lieutenant Humphries deposited his 6 x 1000lb bombs from 8,000 feet reporting *'Flashes or bursts seen through clouds'*. Squadron Leader Ashworth bombed from even higher at 10,000 feet. He reported *'No results seen. Reflection of a large fire seen on cloud'*. Neither crew could confirm that that had bombed the Skoda works. The final crew was that of F/Lt Livingstone, he attacked on ETA from 4,000 feet, reporting upon his return, *'No results seen owing to clouds'*. Despite the spirited defence over Pilsen, only two aircraft received flak damage, one unsurprisingly was S/Ldr Oldroyd's Stirling N3722 HA-E the other was Phil Lamason's Stirling, N3721 HA-C. Given all the activity, it was no surprise given the commotion enemy night fighters were active. Pilot Officer Lamason had a vicious encounter with a Bf110 night fighter. Excellent crew discipline and a skilled pilot prevented what could have been, yet another crew chalked up as *'Missing'*. The first crew to land back at Marham was P/O Lamason at 05:50 hours. He had been airborne for 8 hours 30 minutes. Five minutes later F/Lt Livingston landed Stirling W7469 HA-M, he was followed at 06:00 hours by 'A' Flight's S/Ldr Ashworth and crew. There followed an agonising 30-minute wait for the next crew to land, at 06:30 hours Short Stirling W7521 HA-U touched down on Marham's grass runway, at the controls was New Zealander F/Lt Humphreys, they had been airborne 9 hours.

Finally, at 06:45 hours and in the light of the early morning sun, S/Ldr Oldroyd touched down. The tired crew clambered out of the Stirling, undoubtedly stiff and with the roar of the four Hercules engines still ringing in their ears they set off for debriefing. The crew had been flying for 9 hours 30 minutes, the majority of which was over enemy territory. There was still some hope that the last crew, that of P/O Millichamp could have landed at another aerodrome or even ditched. This hope would have been dashed soon after interrogation with the reporting of a blazing bomber south of Mainz. Due to his actions on this night, P/O Phil Lamason was awarded an immediate award of the DFC, it was gazetted in May 1942, the citation reads:

Despite the courage and tenacity of the crews, the Skoda Works were not hit. The majority of the bombs fell south-east of Pilsen. A number of bombs fell around the Rudolf Company complex and the Koterov railway and marshalling yards. Further afield, and to the east of Pilsen, the village of Bozkov reported broken windows to a factory and 26 damaged houses. The Skoda works may have escaped the bombers, but the effect it had on the local populous outweighed any material damage. It was a tremendous boost to morale, not only to the local population but the Czech underground movement. The raid had shown that Bomber Command could reach any target despite the boasts by the puppet Czech Government to the contrary. On the squadron, there was a tremendous sense of pride by all the ranks that they, the 'Gold Coast' Squadron had been chosen to carry out this operation over the more established and experienced Stirling squadrons within the group. Operation 'CANONBURY' was the only bombing operation of the war which involved the cooperation and involvement of a resistance organisation. The question remains why was No.218 (Gold Coast) Squadron chosen to undertake such an important operation. One possible reason could have been the recent visit by the Secretary of State for Air, Sir Archibald Sinclair just two weeks earlier. It is not beyond the realms of possibility that Sir Archibald was so impressed by the crews and their recent success over Lubeck that when Operation CANONBURY was agreed and put before him, he proposed 218 Squadron. His parting comments to the assembled crews when leaving on his visit was congratulating the squadron on the 'very fine performance it had kept up'. Sadly, however, the answer to this may never be known.

Over four hundred miles north, the three crews detailed to bomb Rostock found the target a mass of flames on arrival. Fires appeared concentrated, and as the attack developed four of the larger fires seemed to merge into one vast conflagration. Sergeant Medus dropped all 24 of his 250 pounders in one salvo on the old town. Sergeant Coggin and F/Sgt Webber bombed the north-eastern corner of the town where the largest fires seemed to be burning. Sergeant Coggin reported on his return that the flames were visible from the island of Sylt. All three crews landed safely just after 05:00 hours. The squadron was stood down on the 26th and missed the fourth and final raid on Rostock. The lessons learnt on the previous raids had not been wasted, on this last operation Bomber Command produced a devastating raid on the port and town. It was an ominous sign of things to come for Germany. This was the last operation flown by Flight Sergeant James Hinwood. Born in Broughton, Hampshire in 1922, 'Jim' joined the RAF in July 1940. After completing his initial training, he was posted to No.20 O.T.U at Lossiemouth in June 1941. For the next two months, he refined his flying skills until posted to the squadron on August 18th, 1941. He was now a seasoned and highly skilled bomber pilot having completed 36 operations. After the usual end of tour 'piss-up', Jim was posted to No.101 Conversion Flight for instruction duties. Bomber

Command switched its attention to Cologne on the 27th with a small-scale raid by 97 bombers. Number 3 Group provided the bulk of the aircraft with 67 Wellington and Stirlings, five of which were supplied by 218 Squadron. One of the first away was S/Ldr Ashworth in R9313 HA-Q his now personal Stirling. Over the English Channel three of the Hercules engines aboard R9313 started showing signs of trouble. Realising that reaching Cologne was impossible S/Ldr Ashworth ordered the all-incendiary load to be jettisoned into sea 15 miles north of Dunkirk. It was later discovered that the airscrew exactors which worked the throttle, mixture, and pitch controls had failed. The squadron was scheduled early over the target backing up the flare force with incendiaries. There was little indication that the raid would develop into the success it did. Flight Sergeant George McAuley dropped his all-incendiary load from 15,500 feet starting three large fires, he reported on his return, *'Numerous fires chiefly on east bank of river. A number of very large fires seen in this one area'.* The squadron dropped over 7,500 four-pound incendiaries on Cologne while the Wellington equipped No.115 squadron dropped twenty 2000 pounders. Considering the low numbers of bombers involved nine industrial buildings and over 1500 houses were damaged or destroyed.

*Armourers loading 250lb GP bombs onto Short Stirling N3721 HA-P 'Peter'.*

The weather on the 28th was marginal grounding any flights planned by 218 CF. It would be a welcome break. The flight had flown continuously every day of the month thus far. This was a tremendous effort by everyone concerned, from the lowest 'Erk' to the man at the helm, S/Ldr Ker.

The weather, however, did not prevent five aircraft from 218 Squadron carrying out a four-hour low-level cross country and bombing exercise. Flying at just 150 feet and in loose formation, the five Stirlings headed north to Spalding in Lincolnshire, from here they continued further north until they arrived at Dishforth in North Yorkshire. On reaching Dishforth, they turned to port and headed towards the Cumbrian coast and St Bees, turning south they flew over the rugged features of Wales until they arrived at Aberdovey on the River Dyfi in Gwynedd. Finally, the crews turned on the final leg for home, on what was an epic cross-country flight.

Form B.795 was received from Group HQ on the morning of the 29th. The squadron would provide five crews for an attack on the Gnome and Rhome aero-engine factory at Gennevilliers in the northern suburb of Paris. With the fall of France in 1940, Gnome et Rhome was ordered to produce the BMW 801 engine. They were a major supplier of engines to the Luftwaffe, producing both their own designs as well as German ones under licence. Once again Bomber Command HQ only committed a small number of bombers, 88 would be detailed of which No.3 Group would provide the bulk with 45 Wellingtons and just six Stirlings, the squadrons of Marham supplying a respectable 21 aircraft. The first of five crews aloft from No.218 Squadron was that of S/Ldr Oldroyd AFC at 21:15 hrs at the controls of N3720 HA-B. Undertaking his first operation as captain was P/O Bullock RNZAF. After completing six operations sitting beside his late friend, P/O 'Hal' Millichamp RCAF the young Kiwi was deemed ready to take over his own crew. As forecast by the Met officer, the crews experienced excellent weather conditions on route with no cloud and full visibility. Flying between 6,000 and 8,000 feet the squadron experienced considerable light flak and searchlights activity over the target. Despite the defences, some accurate bombing followed. The crews of Sergeants McAuley and Medus both claimed to have bombed the Gnome Rhone works. Flying Officer Bullock reported *'Bombs seen to fall NE corner of electrical works. Two bursts seen. Gnome Rhone works on fire, also black smoke from the Goodrich Rubber Factory'*. Squadron Leader Oldroyd AFC reported that on dropping his bombs, *'A bright green explosion was seen'*. As the crews turned for home, Gennevilliers was a sea of flames although some crews believed that the bombing was on the wrong side of the Seine River. Surprisingly given the amount of light flak only one Stirling received minor damage, all five returned safely to Marham. Unfortunately, over at 115 Squadron, they reported the loss of Sgt Walter Reynolds and crew. A Daylight reconnaissance operation was flown the following day and revealed that the Gnome-Rhone works had escaped damage, but significant damage was achieved to other important buildings. The Power Station roof was severely damaged, the Thomson Houston Factory which produced electrical motors showed signs of substantial damage as did the Goodrich Rubber Tyre Works. Also, hard hit was the Levy factory which appeared to be gutted. It was not the result that was planned, but Bomber Command HQ would, given the frustrations and disappointment over the month settle for that amount of damage to an important target. April had been a hectic month for the squadron. It had flown 113 sorties for the loss of just one crew. Only one other squadron had flown more sorties, No.115 which had undertaken an impressive 176. There was however some news to cheer about, 218 Squadron topped the group with bombs dropped, reporting a new record of over 600,000 pounds. Apart from operational sorties an impressive 81 training flights were also completed. It was not just 218 Squadron that was busy, 218 CF found itself flying on all but one day of the month. Squadron Leader Ker was instrumental in this, his style of command was forthright, no-nonsense, and disciplined. He was ably assisted by his deputy flying instructor, F/O Arthur Jones. The flight had amassed some 177 flying hours flown during the day and a further 55 at night. Seven crews had been trained.

The existence of the conversion flight was still very much in the balance. Hitherto the normal method of conversion of new crews onto the Stirling was via the Conversion Unit at Waterbeach, then onto a conversion flight and finally a squadron to carrying out 'Freshman Trips'. To speed up the conversion process crews were now being posted directly to the Conversion Flights from the O.T.Us. Number 218 CU was the first of its kind, if successful No.7 and No.149 Squadron would quickly follow.

*Gnome and Rhome aero-engine factory at Gennevilliers in the northern suburb of Paris.*

# Chapter 12: May 1942 to August 1942 – The 1000 Plan

The squadron took breath on the 1st. It could look back at its achievements in April with some pride. Little did they realise what May 1942 would bring.

Five crews were given two separate 'Garden' areas to mine on the 2nd, S/Ldr Ashworth and F/Sgt McGregor were detailed to plant their 'Vegetables' in the 'Quince' area, while P/O Bullock, F/Sgt Gregg and Sgt McAuley were given the 'Forget-Me-Not' garden. Just prior to take off Stirling N6078 HA-P experienced engine trouble, Sgt McAuley wisely aborted the operation. The crews would not be alone. Bomber Command dispatched 96 aircraft on this night, 55 from No.3 Group. Each of the four crews successfully planted their four mines from less than 500 feet. Fog in the 'Forget-Me-Not' area prevented the crews from pin-pointing their positions. The weather was not a problem in the Baltic Sea, both S/Ldr Ashworth and F/Sgt McGregor successfully planted their 4 sea mines after identifying landfall on the Island of Langeland. Squadron Leader Ashworth found a tanker steaming in the Fehmarn Belt, this was duly attacked with 2 x 500lb bombs, the crew claiming a near miss. Flight Sergeant McGregor's Stirling W7503 HA-R was hit by flak in the port wing and port outer engine on the return flight. The damaged engine was feathered resulting in a long flight back to Marham.

Pilot Officer William McCarthy and crew were the squadrons sole representative on the night of

May 3rd. Their target was the docks at St Nazaire. This was the 22-year-old first operation as captain having completed six trips beside Sgt James Hinwood. Joining the crew on his first operation on the squadron was P/O Owen Sanderson RAAF. On arrival, the crew had difficulty pinpointing the docks from 10,000 feet due to sea mist. Help was at hand when a number of explosions were seen in the target area. The crew quickly dropped their 14x500lb bombs directly into fires which presumably had found the docks. The opposition was surprisingly stiff, flak, both light and heavy made bombing difficult. While on his bomb run Pilot Officer McCarthy was forced to take evasive which prevented the crew from observing their results. It was an ideal 'Freshman' operation for gaining experience! It was only on the return trip that it was realised that a 500 pounder had hung up.

The following day the squadron would be given another challenging nights work. Once again, Bomber Command HQ had put its trust in the squadron. Six crews were given the task of revisiting the Skoda Works at Pilsen, for Operation CANONBURY II. Four crews were detailed to

*Pilot Officer William McCarthy RAFVR.*

attack Stuttgart while a solitary crew was given the long flight to the south of France. Lyon, the capital city in France's Auvergne-Rhône-Alpes region, would be 'Nickelled'

Pilot Officer Lamason was the first of the Pilsen force to take-off. He departed at 2135hrs in Stirling N3725 HA-D. He was followed by S/Ldr Oldroyd AFC and F/Sgts Webber and Gregg and finally P/O Bullock at 21:55 hours. The sixth crew was withdrawn before take-off. The crew of F/Sgt Webber bombed Mainz due to reasons unknown, however, there is some suggestion that the crew had become lost. The remaining bombers arrived over Pilsen around 01:45 hours. Squadron Leader Oldbury AFC was loaded with a number of flares, possibly with the intention of identifying the target for the rest of the squadron. Flak had been bolstered since the squadrons last visit. Three armoured trains mounting anti-aircraft guns had arrived from Essen only a few days prior and a new flak commander had also arrived. Both light and heavy flak exploded around S/Ldr Oldroyd's aircraft inflicting considerable damage but thankfully missing the crew and engines. All six 1000 pounders were dropped from 7,500 feet. Pilot Officer Lamason RNZAF reported that his bombs landed north-west of the target, or very near to it, as did P/O Bullocks. He reported; *'Bombs believed fell NW of target or on target which started a fire near a red flare'*. The flare would have been one of the six dropped by S/Ldr Oldroyd. It is believed that F/Sgt Gregg also bombed the target from the recollections of Sergeant Robert MacAfee RCAF, the crew's mid-upper gunner. *' Had trouble crossing coast on way out near Ostend, very heavy flak, but no damage. Reached target a few minutes late, flak very heavy and one large fire on the ground. Had difficulty bombing due to flak and left target with two 1000 pounders'*.

Once again, the main Skoda Works had escaped damage. Four bombs landed in the area between the railway lines and Koterow, while five bombs exploded over 2 miles west near Blovice. The real damage was achieved at Zieglaruv Dul which was a subsidiary of the Skoda specialising in filling artillery shells. Further heavy damage was inflicted at an ammunition factory at Hoysov which worked directly for Skoda. The crews now had the difficult task of getting home. Sergeant Gregg and crew are believed to have strayed over the flak defences of Frankfurt and paid the price. Short Stirling N6070 HA-A crashed into the Goldstein Strasse, Frankfurt Am Main, there was only one survivor, the crew's Canadian mid-upper gunner. Sergeant Robert MacAfee describes the events, *'Off course sometime later and pinpointed Frankfurt, dropped the remaining two bombs from 7-8,000ft. Then the flak barrage came up. Shell burst in the cabin and seemed to set fire to all the aircraft in the front of the main spar. No intercom or lights, aircraft went into a very steep dive. I got out immediately and seemed to hit the ground at the same time. The aircraft exploded very close to where I landed'*.

### *Monday 4th May 1942*
*Short Stirling*
*Mk.I*
*W6070 HA-A 'Apple'*
*Contract No : 774677/38*
*Taken On Charge : 17/02/1942*
*CAT E/FB (Missing)*
*SoC*

*Failed To Return*

*Pilot : Flight Sergeant William Humphrey Gregg, 994457 RAFVR* **Killed**

*2nd Pilot : Pilot Officer Joseph Ogden Heap, 46921 RAF* **Killed**

*Observer : Sergeant Leonard Aspinall Mayer, 1051991 RAFVR* **Killed**

*Wireless Operator : Sergeant Kenneth Wheeler 923992 RAFVR DFM* **Killed**

*Wireless Operator/Gunner : Sergeant Thomas Wythe, 1108923 RAFVR ,* **Killed**

*Mid Upper Gunner : Sergeant Robert Lewis MacAfee, R/64752 RCAF PoW*

*Rear Gunner : Sergeant Rowland Lennock, 1378346 RAFVR* **Killed**

*Flight Engineer : Sergeant Thomas Randall Sherwood, 569100 RAF* **Killed**

*Pilot Officer Joseph Ogden Heap.*

The crew are buried side by side in the Durnach War Cemetery. Twenty-five-year-old William Gregg hailed from County Down, Northern Ireland. If William had returned from Pilsen, he would have expected to be taken off operations at any time. He had completed 33 operations since his arrival on the squadron in August 1941. Fellow pilot, Pilot Officer Heap had flown just seven operations, all with F/Sgt Gregg. New to the crew was Sergeant Wheeler DFM who had replaced Sgt Gordon on May 2nd.

The crews having bombed, now had the long and dangerous task of getting home. With the Germans now fully alerted it would be a battle for survival. Squadron Leader Oldroyd was held by searchlights and on the receiving end of some accurate flak while crossing the Rhine area. Near Brussels they were intercepted by a Ju88. After a mammoth 20-minute life and death struggle S/Ldr Oldroyd and his gunners finally managed to break-off the combat. They landed at RAF Manston short of fuel after being airborne over 71/2 hours.

For his skill in attacking the Skoda Works and escaping both the night fighter and flak, S/Ldr Oldroyd AFC was awarded an immediate DFC. Also recognised was his navigator, F/O Reginald Brown. The citation reads;

> *Squadron Leader Oldroyd and Flying Officer Brown were the captain and navigator respectively of an aircraft, detailed to attack the Skoda Works at Pilsen. Dense cloud was experienced in the last 200 miles to the target but, owing to the navigational skill of Flying Officer Brown, the objective was reached and located 5 minutes before the estimated time. Very heavy anti-aircraft fire was encountered, and the aircraft was repeatedly hit. Despite this, Squadron Leader Oldroyd remained over the target for a considerable time. On the return journey the aircraft was held by searchlights and subjected to further anti- aircraft fire, which was evaded successfully. Later, the aircraft was engaged by a Junkers 88, fire from which caused damage to the oil system, the port landing wheel and the petrol tanks. Throughout this combat Squadron Leader Oldroyd displayed skill and courage of a high standard which contributed largely to the safe return of his aircraft and crew. Flying Officer Brown has continually displayed great skill and courage and has always identified his targets under extremely difficult and hazardous conditions.*

The four crews briefed for Stuttgart found the target covered in 7/10th cloud and to make matters worse considerable ground haze. Both Sergeant McAuley and F/Sgt Tompkins reported that they bombed the target area depositing the all-incendiary load from 14,000ft. Sergeant Medus and McGregor were slightly more cautious, Sgt 'Dick' Medus reported *' bombs were believed to be dropped in a built-up area, small explosions'.* Flight Sergeant McGregor did not even attempt a photograph owing to the poor visibility while F/Sgt Johnson jettisoned due to the haze. On leaving the target area Sgt George McAuley lost his port outer engine due to flak. This was duly feathered and after checking with his crew for any injuries the young Irishman headed for home. Flying lower than usual the crew were subjected to a barrage of accurate flak as they crossed the French coast. Thankfully, none of the crew were injured, Stirling W7521 HA-U was not so lucky. Large, gagged holes appeared in both wings and almost immediately the flight engineer Sgt George Neale reported that they were losing fuel. Quickly transferring the remaining fuel to the undamaged fuel tanks, the crew headed slowly across the North Sea. Shortly after crossing the Norfolk coast the three remaining engines started to show signs of trouble, quickly realising that he would not make Marham Sgt McAuley looked for a suitable place to force land. With the engines now almost useless with a suspected airlock in the fuel system George showed remarkable flying skill in crash landing the Stirling at 04:55 hours near Mulbarton, a small village 5 miles south of Norwich. None of the crew were injured but the aircraft, an Austin Motors built Stirling was declared a write-off.

### Monday 4th May 1942
Short Stirling
*Mk.I*
*W7521 HA-U 'Uncle'*
*Contract No : B982939/38*
*Taken On Charge : 12/04/1942*
*CAT E/FB*
*SoC 07/05/1942*
*Forced Landed*
*Pilot : Sergeant George McAuley 122267 RAFVR*
*2nd Pilot : Pilot Officer Richards*
*Observer : Sergeant S.E Stevens, 1270512 RAFVR*
*Wireless Operator :  Sergeant B.W Roberts 1375123 RAFVR*

*Wireless Operator/Gunner : Sergeant Stronnel*
*Mid Upper Gunner : Sergeant E.Nettleton 994389 RAFVR*
*Rear Gunner : Sergeant  A.E Burkitt, 900855 RAFVR*
*Flight Engineer : Sergeant  G.L.A. Neale 528927 RAF*

Squadron Leader Ashworth and crew had the lonely but rather more pleasant trip to the south of France. Six crews were drawn from Bomber Command, but only one from No.3 Group was selected for the raid. Squadron Leader Ashworth's target was to 'Nickle' the area around Lyons and St Etienne. The crew successfully completed their assignment dropping 600 bundles of various propaganda leaflets (type F.43 and F.37) to the inhabitants of the south of France. Having managed to escape the attentions of any prowling night fighters over France they eventually crossed the English coast dodging the trigger happy British Anti-Aircraft Batteries along the south coast. Over Sussex, the crew had the misfortune of encountering a modified American twin-engine Douglas Turbinlite of No.1455 Flight and a Hawker Hurricane of No.1 Squadron up on patrol. The Havoc equipped with a 2,700 million candela searchlight in the nose was an early attempt to thwart the German bomber raids over England. Guided on to the enemy aircraft by ground radar and its own basic radar, it would turn on its searchlight to illuminate the attacking enemy bombers. The accompanying fighter, usually Hurricanes would then shoot it down. That was the theory. The pilot of the Hurricane (BD770) was P/O Frederick Murray. Prior to the fateful encounter Murray had flown on three sorties over the previous 24 hours. A fruitless intruder operation during the early hours of the 4th was flown, that same day he was airborne again at 22:25 hours in Hawker Hurricane BD770 on this occasion accompanied by a Havoc Turbinlite of No.1455 Flight on what turned out to be another frustrating and unproductive operation patrolling the south coast. Obviously, a keen type and not one for sitting ideally about he was airborne once again at 03:20 hours on the morning of the 5th. Pilot Officer Murray departed RAF Tangmere in company with Squadron Leader George Oliver Budd at the controls of the Havoc Turbinlite. Over the Sussex Downs, the crew of the Stirling would have been looking forward to their bacon and eggs and getting some sleep after the long flight to the south of France. It was not to be, unbeknown to the crew the Havoc/Hurricane combination had been vectored onto them. It was a few minutes before 04:30 hours when the Stirling was located.

*Type F.43 leaflet dropped by S/Ldr Harold Ashworth and crew.*

The Havoc switched on the nose searchlight and illuminated the bomber. Incredibly P/O Murray attacked, how he did not recognise a four-engine Stirling in the early morning light is a mystery. Opening fire, the Hurricanes 4 x 20mm cannons made short work of the Stirling's wings. Fire quickly engulfed the bomber as the damaged fuel tanks spewed out what remaining fuel was left, this immediately caught fire like a blowtorch. Wasting no time, S/Ldr Ashworth gave the order to bail out. Miraculously none of the crew was hit in the initial attack. All manage to take to their parachute as the blazing Stirling smashed into a meadow at Gatehouse Farm, Lurgashall, Horsham, Sussex. Returning to RAF Tangmere the triumphant duo was eager to claim an enemy bomber destroyed. The jubilation soon turned to horror as news started to filter through. The 8-man Stirling crew were collected and incredibly taken to RAF Tangmere, where it is reported *'a riot almost started'*. It is not known how soon after the interception the pilots realised that they had made a calamitous error. The only positive thing was that the shaken crew of R9313 all survived, bruised but very much alive. As if to hide the apparent embarrassment of shooting down an RAF Stirling, the Adjutant of No.1 Squadron when filling out the Operational Records Book for this date decided not to record any of the events by simply recording against P/O Murray's sortie *'Nothing to Report'.!!*

**Monday 4th May 1942**
Short Stirling
*Mk.I*
*R9313 HA-Q*
*Contract No : 774677/38*
*Taken On Charge : 07/04/1942*
*CAT E Burnt-Out*
*SoC 13/05/1942*
*Friendly Fire Incident*
Pilot : Squadron Leader Harold Ashworth 76467 RAFVR
2nd Pilot : Pilot Officer Colin MacQueen Farquharson, 108074 RAFVR
Navigator : Pilot Officer Alan Green, 104402 RAFVR
Wireless Operator : Flight Sergeant St.John
Bombaimer : Sergeant Medhurst
Mid Upper Gunner : Sergeant William Watt, 1108788 RAFVR
Rear Gunner : Sergeant T Mulroy, 5355969 RAFVR
Flight Engineer : Sergeant William John Hayden, 620195 RAFVR

Four of the crew sustained minor injuries, Pilot Officer Farquharson suffered a fractured right elbow while S/Ldr Ashworth had a deep cut above his eyebrow. Sergeant Mulroy sustained heavy bruising to the head, while Sergeant Medhurst suffered from delayed shock. It was a bad night for the squadron, one crew lost, one shot down by our own fighters and three Short Stirlings written off. It was not the start the squadron was hoping for. On the 6th, four crews were briefed for a raid directed against Stuttgart, while W/Cdr Holder DFC would revisit Lyon. Australian Sergeant John Savage was given Nantes to bomb for his 'Freshman' trip. The second of the series of attacks on Stuttgart was not a success. A German decoy site at Lauffen, 15 miles north of Stuttgart attracted a large number of crews despite the lack of cloud over the city. Regardless of the returning crews' optimism on the success of the raid, it was a failure. Wing Commander Holder DFC had no problem finding his target. Indifferent to any type of 'black-outs' the streetlights in Lyon were ablaze as the Stirling swept over the city at 3000 feet dropping half of it 810 bundles of leaflets. Like the previous raid, the crew then visited St Etienne situated 34 miles southwest of Lyon in the beautiful Auvergne-Rhône-Alpes. Here the remaining packages of leaflets were dropped. Unfortunately, 240 bundles hung up in the bomb containers. The crew landed without mishap back at RAF Marham 0450 hours.

A major operation was flown against Warnemunde and to its Heinkel works on the 8th. There were some novel features to this raid. Twelve bombers were detailed to bomb and suppress the flak defences with both 500lb HE and 40lb fragmentation bombs. Also, a force on 19 bombers was to attack the Heinkel works from low level. Nine crews were detailed and briefed from No.218 Squadron. Sergeant Boyd was the first away at 2140 hours in N3720 HA-B, within 20 minutes all nine were aloft. Unlike the previous operations, the German night fighters were out in force on this night. Fighters from NJG1, NJG2 and NJG3 were up and patrolling from Holland to southern Denmark. The first encounters were recorded as the bombers crossed the North Sea coast near Schleswig. Fortunately for the squadron, they were not troubled as they arrived over their primary target, the Ernst Heinkel Flugzeugwerke. Number 3 Group's contribution of 66 bombers would attack the target over four waves, No.218 Squadron was scheduled for the second wave timed between 0051hrs - 0141hrs. Given the factory's importance, it was no surprise that the opposition over the target was fierce. The flak was ferocious, and the searchlights were blinding. The searchlight suppression was not particularly effective as crews struggled to identify the Heinkel works. Sergeant Boyd reported *'Intense searchlight activity made it impossible to pinpoint accurately'.* Thankfully not all the crews found the conditions as challenging. Flight Lieutenant Humphreys dropped his all HE bomb load from 9,000ft and watched as they appeared to land near a large shed causing a massive green explosion. Flying on his first operation with the squadron was a young New Zealander, Pilot Officer Roy Spear RNZAF a 23-year-old from Christchurch. He joined the crew of F/Sgt McGregor aboard N6077 HA-V. Contrary to the returning crews reports the raid was yet another failure, little if any damage was inflicted on the Heinkel works. Unfortunately for Bomber Command, the operation resulted in the loss of twenty bombers and their crews to a combination of flak and night fighters. The Lancaster equipped No.44 (Rhodesia) Squadron lost four of the six aircraft it provided, including its squadron commander, Wing Commander Patrick Lynch-Blosse DFC. The squadron was one of those chosen to attack the Heinkel works at low-level. Wing Commander Lynch-Blosse had only arrived on the squadron via No.25 OTU on the 6th to replace the departing W/Cdr Roderick Learoyd VC. He was awarded the DFC with 115 Squadron in 1940. Also, hard hit was the RAF Driffield based 158 Squadron, they reported the loss of four Wellingtons. Other than a single flak hole in one Stirling all the squadron returned to RAF Marham.

Bomber Command effectively stood down on return from Warnemunde, other than a few cloud covered raids and minor minelaying trips no significant operations were mounted until the 17th. That is not to say the squadron relaxed, over 80 flights were carried out including low-level bombing, cross country, formation flying and the usual air-tests. The squadron welcomed F/O Arthur Jones on the 10th. He had been heavily involved with 218 CF since its formation back in February. Now, he was ready to start his second tour. On the 16th the station MO and a doctor from Group HQ carried out medical examinations on the air gunners of the squadron. Their opinion was that since the gunners were last examined there had been a marked deterioration in the physical efficiency of the gunners. The only way to cure this was for them to be given more P.T training. What the gunners thought of this is not on record, but I am sure it was not appreciated! More

*The crew of Flight Sergeant John McGregor seen here at the rear exit door of Stirling N6077 HA-V. Left; Sgt Finney, Wireless Operator, Sgt Hobden, Observer, F/Sgt McGregor, Pilot ,Sgt Moyes,Wireless Operator, Sgt Medhurst, Rear Gunner and Sgt Davidson, Mid Upper Gunner.*

worryingly was a case of Paratyphoid 'B' admitted to the SSQ. Due to the seriousness of this condition and fear it could possibly spread an inoculation scheme was immediately started. However, to inoculate over 2700 personnel serving on the station was going to take time. The Station Commander implemented a scheme where any personnel that travelled to and from the station had to be checked out by the M.O. Any individual going on leave had to be inoculated prior, only then would the Station Medical Officer, S/Ldr Michael Maley sign their leave pass. In fact, there had already been a few fatal cases in the villages local to Marham.

Finally, on the 17th Form B.813 arrived at Marham, both squadrons would be required that night on the groups most ambitious mining effort to date. Thirty-two Stirlings would be accompanied by 28 Wellingtons. The squadron provided 11 Stirling's including both Flight Commanders. The operation would be an all 3 Group affair. The target for all the squadron crews was the Daffodils mining area, a stretch of sea south of Copenhagen. Squadron Leader Oldroyd DFC AFC was the first away in the pouring rain at 2220 hours in Stirling N3722 HA-E. The weather was for once as the Met Officer predicted, foul. There was one early return. Soon after take-off S/Ldr Ashworth was forced abort when the port outer aboard W7530 HA-Q failed, the four mines and two 500 pounders were jettisoned. Austin Motors built W7530 was a brand-new Stirling having arrived on the squadron on May 8th. It was immediately coded 'Q' Queenie replacing R9313 shot down by the overzealous RAF Fighters on return from Lyon. Using his squadron leader rank, the flight commander claimed W7530 for his own. Unlike on the squadron's previous outing, they would encounter stiff opposition on route to the 'Garden' area. Taking off a few minutes after midnight from his base on the Island of Sylt was Oblt Rudolf Schoenert and his Funker, Feldwebel Hans

Richter. The crew flying Bf110 F-4 R4-BM were part of 2./NJG2 who were aloft and on the hunt. Flight Lieutenant Humphrey and crew had made the long North Sea crossing and were nearing the Danish Coast. It was here that the two met in a vicious encounter that would see the experienced New Zealander and his crew take to their parachutes, and the blazing Stirling smash

*Pilot Officer Eliot Ralph Barnfather RAAF on the left looks towards the camera while his skipper, Flight Lieutenant Arthur Humphrey has a conversation with 'Mick' The Terrier.*

into the ground near Lyne, 9 miles south of Tarn, Denmark. The first to be captured was Sgt Roland Layfield, he was found by the Danish Police at 0228hrs on the main road to the north of Starbaek Mill. Aware of the plight of his crewmate, he guided the Police to a field were the crew's 2nd pilot was hiding. Sergeant Richard Hill had suffered a badly broken ankle on landing but more worrying he had received a sizeable wound to his thigh. He was carried to a car and immediately driven to the Varde County Hospital while Layfield was taken to the Police Station at Varde. The next crewman to be found was Sergeant William Lawrence at 0500hrs. He too had broken his ankle on landing and had suffered numerous wounds to his legs and torso. Like Sgt Hill, he was taken to Varde County Hospital for treatment. The Australian navigator, Pilot Officer Eliot Barnfather, was found dead under his parachute at 0600 hours. It is reported that he died from wounds to his stomach area, other reports suggest his parachute did not open fully. The body of the 27-year-old from Geelong, Victoria was taken to the chapel at Varde County Hospital. At around 1030hrs Sergeant George Toynbee-Clarke was located north of the crash site near Vostrup. Dazed, and with a severe head wound he was taken to Tarn where the towns Doctor, Reinhold Nielson treated his wounds. Once treated he was transported to the Police Station at Varde. Almost 24 hours after their encounter with Oblt Rudolf Schoenert the two remaining crew members were finally located. At 2235hrs, Flight Lieutenant Arthur Humphreys DFC and the crew's rear gunner, Sergeant Joh Taylor were discovered at a farm at Egknud, 3 miles south-east of the crash site. They were handed over to the Police and taken to join the rest of the crew. All were eventually handed over to the local German Wehrmacht to spend the rest of the war in a prisoner of war camps. Flight Lieutenant Arthur Humphreys DFC was repatriated on February 6th, 1945 onboard the ship 'Arundel Castle' due to 'sores'. The body of P/O Barnfather was taken for burial at the Fourfelt Cemetery at Esberg on May 23rd, 1942.

**Sunday 17th May 1942**

Short Stirling
*Mk.I*
*N6071 HA-G 'George'*
*Contract No : 774677/38*
*Taken On Charge : 24/02/1942*
*CAT E Missing*
*SoC 19/05/1942*
***Failed To Return***
Pilot : Flight Lieutenant Arthur George Lee Humphrey, 36241 RAF DFC PoW
2nd Pilot : Sergeant Richard Innes Hill, 402059 RNZAF PoW
Observer  : Pilot Officer Eliot Ralph Barnfather, 400393 RAAF, **Killed**
Wireless Operator : Flight Sergeant Roland Layfield, 550786 RAFVR, PoW
Mid Upper Gunner : Sergeant George Toynbee-Clarke, 971164 RAFVR, PoW
Rear Gunner : Sergeant Sergeant William Arthur Lawrence, 611762 RAFVR, PoW
Flight Engineer : Sergeant John Nichols Thomas Taylor, 568172 RAFVR,

Pilot Officer Eliot Ralph Barnfather RAAF was a barrister and solicitor from Geelong, Victoria before enlistment. He initially trained at 8 EFTS before being shipped to Canada to continue his training under the Empire Air Training Scheme (EATS) at No 2 Air Observers' School (2AOS), Edmonton, Alberta. He received his 'brevet' as an air observer on June 22nd, 1941. Sergeant Richard Hill was on his 4th operation all flown besides Arthur. Incredibly F/Lt Humphreys had flown 31 operation on this his 2nd tour. In total, the young Kiwi had flown 57 operations since he began his bombing career in April 1940. Losing a crew was never good, but to lose a pilot of F/Lt Humphreys' experience was a bitter blow, especially when so close to finishing his 2nd tour of operations.

The crew of Sergeant Medus were involved in a brief encounter with a Bf110 while flying at 5000 feet. The Stirling was attacked from the port side low. Taken completely unawares the cannon fire thankfully did not hit anything vital. The crew's rear gunner, Sgt Davey, returned fire with two long bursts which seemed to deter the German pilot. It had been a close shave for the crew. Squadron Leader Oldroyd planted his four mines in the last resort target due to low cloud in the primary. Also hindered by the cloud was Sergeant Coggin and crew, they dropped their four mines 40 miles north of Zingst in the Baltic Sea. Soon after the starboard inner engine aboard R9311 HA-L failed forcing the crew to make the long sea crossing on three engines. Flying Officer Jones on his first operation since his arrival successfully dropped his parachute mines from 400 feet. On the return flight, the crew were engaged by two light machine gun positions at Gedser Head a town at the southern tip of the Danish island of Falste. Both gunners, P/O Brown and Sgt Murray returned fire, from just 700 feet the position was hosed with machine-gun fire, both gun positions fell silent. It was a sobering night for the group, eight crews failing to return, 7.5% of the force dispatched. There was some good news. Flight Sergeant Bernard Tompkins was declared tour expired on the 19th and posted to 218 CF for instructional duties. He had completed 20 operations on the Vickers Wellington and a further 16 on the Stirling, incredibly despite flying 36 operations he was not recommended for a DFM, a shocking oversight. Bernard survived the war and retired from the RAF in 1969 a squadron leader.

*The shattered remains of Short Stirling N6071 HA-G 'George' after the encounter with Oblt Rudolf Schoenert over Lyne, Denmark.*

Mannheim was the main target for 197 bombers of the evening of May 19th. Seventy Wellingtons and Stirlings were provided by the squadrons of No.3 Group. A further 30 Group aircraft would attack the docks at St Nazaire. Wing Commander Holder DFC briefed seven crews for the Mannheim operation and just one 'Freshman' crew for St Nazaire. The raid on Mannheim would be a total failure. Of the 61 photographs taken over the 'target', an embarrassing four could only be plotted within 5 miles of the aiming point. Most of the bombing was 15-20 miles west of Mannheim, and these bombing photographs showed many fires in open countryside. The apparent inability of the crews to locate and bomb targets even in good weather was becoming a problem that no amount of bravado on the part of the C-in-C Bomber Command could hide. There was no hiding the truth, despite the crews of Bomber Command best endeavours they were missing targets more than hitting them. These failures were not wasted on those in the Air Ministry or Admiralty who were keen to see a change in policy and direction of Bomber Command. To compound a miserable night, 11 bombers failed to return including one from No.218 Squadron. Sergeant Stanley Coggin and his all NCO crew failed to return.

The circumstances surrounding their loss is unclear, they are one of the numerous crews that met their fate over the North Sea. Taking off in Short Stirling DJ977 HA-F at 2316 hours nothing was heard from them after take-off. Slightly older than most on the squadron at 32, Stanley arrived at Marham in October 1941 joining 'B' Flight. He completed nine operations on the Wellington, four of which were flown with W/Cdr Kirkpatrick. After Stirling conversion, he teamed up with F/Lt Humphreys completing a further three trips as the second pilot. He was finally given his own crew in the beginning of April successfully completing seven operations. Recent research by the respected author and historian Theo Boiten may have established that the crew were shot down by Ofw Heinz Struning of 7./NJG2 who claimed a Stirling at 0335hrs.

*Some of the crew of Sergeant Stanley Alfred Coggin standing beside Short Stirling Mk.1 R9311 HA-L. It is understood the photograph was taken on May 18th, 1942 the morning after the mining trip to the Baltic. Short and Harland built R9311 lasted less than a month on the squadron. It was Struck Off Charge after Sergeant Falconer ripped off the port wheel on take-off for the 1000 bomber raid on Cologne on May 30th. Below, Sergeant Coggin 2nd right while Sergeant Parker the crew's 2nd pilot is 2nd left.*

**Tuesday 19th May 1942**
Short Stirling
*Mk.I*
*DJ977 HA-F 'Freddie'*
*Contract No : 763825/38*
*Taken On Charge : 22/04/1942*
*CAT E/FB Missing*
*SoC 20/05/1942*
***Failed To Return***
*Pilot : Sergeant Stanley Alfred Coggin, 1182229 RAFVR **Killed.***
*2nd Pilot : Sergeant Robert Peter Melton Parker, 655328 RAFVR **Killed***
*Observer : Sergeant Peter Hallam Ward, 755983 RAFVR **Killed***
*Wireless Operator : Sergeant Thomas McDonagh, 964668 RAFVR **Killed***
*Front Gunner Sergeant William Heriot Goodrum, 905933 RAFVR **Killed***
*Mid Upper Gunner : Sergeant Frederick Nelson Hanish, 1375359 RAFVR **Killed***
*Rear Gunner : Flight Sergeant Hugh Arthur Worthington, 535943 RAF **Killed***
*Flight Engineer : Sergeant John Henry 'Harry' Stephenson, 653773 RAF **Killed***

Tragically on the morning of the 19th, Peter Ward wrote a letter home to his brother Thomas, it would be his last. The letter is reproduced below sadly given its age parts are illegible.

---

*****75593 Sgt P Ward***
***Sgt Mess***
***RAF Marham***
***Norfolk***
***19-5-1942******

*My Dear Tommo,*

*I am glad to hear that you have survived the ........... come and are back on the old job for a rest.*

*What a life they do lead you in your ...... Not a minute of peace. Anyone would think there was a war on!!!!*

*I suspect the old-boy has told you that I've done a few ops. He told everyone when I was last on leave, so I suspect he has !!! You know what he is. We had a bit of a shaker the other night when an engine cut out over the baltic, but old Stan, the skipper, brought us back 600 miles on three quite comfortably. I think we could have done it on two if the need arose. Anyhow, it was an experience, and I will know what to expect if it happens again.*

*I had a very good leave although as always it went far too quickly. We all went out on the town on Friday and saw ........... at the Hippodrome and it was a dammed good show too. Then we had a couple of drinks and caught the 10pm train from Liverpool Street. Jack come up on his bike, and a fine job it is too. It really is in spanking condition and a real*

---

Peter was the youngest of four children born to Captain John Hallum Ward and Annie Jane Ward (nee Lumsden). His oldest brother, Jack, was a skilled engineer and was in a reserved occupation for the duration of the war. Thomas, (Tommo) served with the BEF and was evacuated from Dunkirk on June 6th, 1940 aboard 'HMS Havent' (which was sunk). He would continue in the Army until VE Day. Lastly, there was a sister, Joan. The Old Man was Peter's grandfather.

An incident on take-off had brought into question the suitability of Marham for the squadron and its Stirlings. A recent operation had seen seven fully laden Stirlings successfully take off but in doing so had churned up the soft ground so severely that the flare path had to be realigned to enable the Wellingtons of No.115 Squadron to take off. It was now only a matter of time before the squadron would need to be moved.

For the next nine days the squadron was withdrawn from operations. Other than a few small-scale mining operations Bomber Command prepared for one of the biggest bombing operations of the war to date. Training was the order of the day on the squadron with emphasis on low-level bombing and formation flying. Rumours began to circulate of another attempt at the Skoda Works at Pilsen. Maybe it would be third time lucky. On the 29th the squadron was given three separate targets to attack. Four specially selected crews were briefed for another raid against the Gnome and Rhone works at Gennevilliers as weather conditions over Germany were unfavourable. Three crews were given the 'Nectarines' Garden to mine while three 'Freshman' crews would attack the docks and town of Cherbourg. The first away were the 'Freshman' crews. Sergeant Geoffrey Jeary, Sgt Robert Yates and Sgt Sidney Falconer departed at 22:20 hours. Next to depart were the minelayers, Sergeants John Savage, F/Sgt John Johnson and finally F/O Allen. At midnight S/Ldr Ashworth lifted off W7530 HA-Q from Marham's increasingly battered grass runway, in quick succession he was followed by P/O Derek Bullock RNZAF, F/O Arthur Jones and finally S/Ldr Oldroyd DFC AFC.

*Looking every bit the experienced bomber crew they were. 'A' Flight's Pilot Officer William 'Bill' McCarthy is flanked by Pilot Officer Thomas Scanlan, Observer, and rear gunner Pilot Officer Alexander Rowe.*

All three of the minelayers found their Garden area and dropped their 4 x 1000lb magnetic parachute mines from 400 feet. Flight Sergeant Johnston watched in morbid fascination as an aircraft crashed in flames in the target area, just a few miles from where he was making his bomb run. This was a No.15 Squadron Stirling flown by F/O Francis Doyle, the victim of an encounter with Fw Hans Berschwinger of 4./NJG2. Sadly, there were no survivors. The only other incident in an otherwise quiet operation was experienced by Sgt Savage who dropped all four mines simultaneously due to a problem with the release gear. Over Cherbourg, the three crews encountered 8/10th -10/10th cloud at 8,000ft. To add to the difficulties a spirited flak and searchlight barrage was in operation. Only Sgt Jeary and crew managed to identify the target area dropping their 20 x 500lb general purpose bombs on the docks. Both Sergeants Falconer and Yates jettisoned half of the bomb load and returned home.

The four chosen to re-visit the Gnome and Rhone works at Gennevilliers found broken cloud over Paris. Flak was the major problem, heavy flak was not unduly troublesome, but the light and medium flak made up for it in sheer volume. By the time the four crews arrived over the target area smoke was already rising and many fires were observed around the aiming point. On the run-up to target bundles of 'Nickles' were released, both Squadron Leaders Ashworth and Oldroyd DFC AFC bombed from 8,000 feet dropping their 8 x 500lb + 6 x 1000lb high explosives between the power station and the docks. Squadron Leader Oldroyd remarking ' *Visible identification by the 'Y' shape and island one-mile south-west of the target. Smoke from power station chimneys. Five of our bursts seen.'*

Pilot Officer Bullock RNZAF bombed from 2000 feet despite the danger of falling bombs. His bravery was rewarded, he reported *'All bombs seen to burst in the target area. Fires seen at sewage works just beyond target'.* The young New Zealander was lucky. His Stirling W7475 HA-H was severely hit by flak. He reported on his return *' Aircraft aerials were shot away by flak'.* Not so fortunate was F/Lt Jones and crew who were shot down just before bombing, crashing at Colombes, a suburb a few miles south-west of the target. Sadly, there were no survivors. The 8-man crew were initially buried at Dugny Cemetery in the north-eastern suburbs of Paris, located 9 miles from the centre of Paris. Twenty-four-year-old Arthur Jones was the son of John and Margaret Jones in Pwhlheli, Caernarvonshire, Wales. He was posted to XV Squadron in December 1940 and flew a total of thirty-five operational sorties whilst serving with the squadron.

*Against a grey overcast sky, what remains of the burnt-out wreckage of Short Stirling W7535 HA-C and the crew of Flight Lieutenant Arthur Jones. The Stirling crashed at Colombes, a suburb a few miles south-west of the target. Note the 500 pounder and crumpled rear turret.*

On 8th August, the granting of a commission in the rank of pilot officer was gazetted. Four months later Jones was declared 'tour expired' and posted to No.26 Conversion Flight for instructional duties. Since his arrival from 218 CF he had completed two operations.

**Friday 29th May 1942**
Short Stirling
*Mk.I*
*W7535 HA-C 'Charlie'*
*Contract No : B982939/39*
*Taken On Charge : 13/05/1942*
*CAT E/FB Missing*
*SoC 20/05/1942*
***Failed To Return***
*Pilot : Flight Lieutenant Arthur Wyn Idwal Jones, 102593 RAFVR* **Killed.**
*2nd Pilot : Sergeant John Kneeshaw, 1378284 RAFVR* **Killed**
*Observer : Sergeant Ronald John Craig Young, 1257537 RAFVR* **Killed**
*Air Observer : Sergeant Frederick Herbert Slatford, 1183344 RAFVR* **Killed**
*Wireless Operator : Sergeant Thomas Edward Murray, 979137 RAFVR* **Killed**
*Air Gunner : Sergeant John William Davis, 642788 RAF* **Killed**
*Rear Gunner : Pilot Officer Stanley Brown, 104401 RAFVR* **Killed**
*Flight Engineer : Sergeant Frederick Armstrong, 571552 RAF* **Killed**

Sergeant 'Fred' Slatford was nearing the end of his operational tour, he had survived a near fatal crash back in November 1941 on return from Kiel and was only a few operations short of being deemed 'tour-expired'. Sadly, the Jones family were to lose a second son with Bomber Command. Arthurs younger brother, Sgt David Vincent Jones was killed on August 13th, 1943 while serving with 619 Squadron. The Lancaster he was flying, JA844 collided with another bomber over Sussex on return from an operation to Milan. His aircraft crashed just off the Littlehampton coast. He is buried in Treflys Churchyard, Caernarvonshire

The squadron was aware that something big was going to happen, but what was still unknown. The Station Commander, 'Square' McKee had been making himself busy over the previous few days frequently visiting both No.115 and No.218 Squadrons commanding officers. He had also made rare appearance around the maintenance hangars asking questions and requesting details of the state and availability of the aircraft. No doubt spurred on by the forthright Base Commander and realising something was afoot the squadrons hard-working, and conscientious ground crews worked tirelessly to get the maximum number of bombers ready. Thankfully, other than the tragic loss of F/Lt Jones, only one Stirling received minor damage on the Gennevilliers raid. It was now a battle against time to get the Stirlings inspected, air-tested, refuelled, and re-armed. On the morning of May 30th, the tension increased even more, the weather looked favourable for that night.

As the day progressed it became clear to everyone that something hugely different was going to take place, this was confirmed when the Station Commander, Group Captain McKee telephoned 218 Squadrons Commanding Officer in the afternoon and gave the South African some probably unwelcome news. The squadron would at the AoC personal request take him to Cologne that night. It was an honour to be chosen, but it came with challenges. Who amongst his most capable pilots would he choose to take Baldwin? The operation turning out to be something special. Now it had the added responsibility of ensuring the AoC survived the night. Like any good commanding officer, he backed himself. He would take AVM Baldwin. Why of all the squadrons in No.3 Group Baldwin chose No.218 Squadron is unknown, regardless of the reason he did, the squadron had to get on with it and make sure he returned!

The recent disappointing raids undertaken by Bomber Command had put tremendous pressure on the C-in-C. His predecessor had been removed from the post for not achieving the results demanded and expected by his superiors, Harris was going the same way. Unlike Pierse, Arthur Harris had a number of advantages, the most notable being Gee. He also had growing numbers of the four-engine Halifax and Stirling bombers at his disposal, plus the mighty Avro Lancaster was increasingly arriving within the command. Another advantage was the escalating numbers of well-trained crews arriving from the training units. Harris knew he had to do something big. He had a radical and risky idea. On May 18th he went to see Sir Charles Portal and outlined his plan; he

*The operations board at RAF Marham for the 1000 bomber raid against Cologne on May 30th, 1942. A total of 31 bombers would participate from Marham, including one, Stirling W7530 HA-Q which would take the AoC to Cologne. Note AVM Baldwin's name chalked on the Ops board.*

wanted to put 1000 bombers over a single target. It would mean committing the whole strength of his command, plus the vast majority of the Operational Training Units. The magical figure of 1000 would however only be reached with the cooperation of Coastal Command. Initially, Coastal Command agreed to help, but as expected at the last minute, they withdrew their offer, a petty decision on the part of the Admiralty. In the event, by sheer hard work, Bomber Command and Training Command reached the required numbers. The target chosen was the industrial city of Cologne. The tactic was simple, overwhelm the city defences by attacking in the space of 90 minutes.

The briefing room at RAF Marham was standing room only, 152 aircrews from 218 Squadron were joined by a further 96 from No.115 Squadron, 248 young aircrew were assembled and listened intently as the details of the raid were explained by the Station Commander and both Squadron Commanders. The Gee equipped squadrons of No.1 and No.3 Group would open the attack in the first 15 minutes, zero hour was planned for 0055 hours. The onus, however, would very much be on No.3 Group. There was not a man on the squadron that did not want to fly on this operation. One of them was Squadron Leader Ker over on the Conversion Flight, he would be flying, and the flight would contribute four aircraft, 'O' - 'X' -'Y' and 'Z'.

## The Crews : 1000 Bomber raid Cologne *'Operation Millennium'*

| Code | Pilot | Serial | Take Off | Landed | Flying Time | Bomb Load | Notes |
|------|-------|--------|----------|--------|-------------|-----------|-------|
| A | F/Sgt Johnston | DJ976 | 2315hrs | 0305hrs | 3.45min | 1890 x 4lb Inc | DCO |
| B | Sgt Boyd | N3720 | 2310hrs | 0325hrs | 4.15mins | 1890 x 4lb Inc | DCO |
| D | P/O Lamason | N3725 | 2310hrs | 0315hrs | 4.10mins | 192 x 30lb Inc | DCO |
| E | **S/Ldr Oldroyd** | N3722 | 2315hrs | 0255hrs | 3.40mins | 1890 x 4lb Inc | DCO |
| H | P/O Bullock | W7475 | 2315hrs | 0305hrs | 3.45mins | 1890 x 4lb Inc | DCO |
| K | F/Sgt Webber | W7474 | 2305hrs | 0400hrs | 4.55mins | 192 x 30lb Inc | DCO |
| L | Sgt Falconer | R9311 | 2350hrs | 0555hrs | 6.05mins | 6 x 1000lb + 7 x 500lb GP | DCO |
| M | Sgt Jeary | W7469 | 2350hrs | 0425hrs | 4.35mins | 6 x 1000lb + 7 x 500lb GP | DCO |
| N | Sgt Davis | W7502 | 2315hrs | **FTR** | ---- | 192 x 30lb Inc | DCO |
| O | **S/Ldr Ker** | N3700 | 0005hrs | 0440hrs | 4.35mins | 6 x 1000lb + 7 x 500lb GP | DCO |
| P | Sgt Medus | N6078 | 2305hrs | 0400hrs | 4.55mins | 192 x 30lb Inc | DCO |
| Q | **W/Cdr Holder** | W7530 | 2330hrs | 0335hrs | 4.05mins | 1890 x 4lb Inc | DCO |
| R | P/O Ball | W7503 | 2305hrs | 0405hrs | 5hrs | 1890 x 4lb Inc | DCO |
| T | Sgt Savage | DJ974 | 2315hrs | 0335hrs | 5.20mins | 1890 x 4lb Inc | DCO |

| | | | | | | |
|---|---|---|---|---|---|---|---|
| U | Sgt McAuley | N3753 | 2310hrs | 0320hrs | 4.10mins | 1890 x 4lb Inc | DCO |
| V | F/O Allen | N6077 | 2255hrs | 0335hrs | 4.40mins | 192 x 30lb Inc | DCO |
| X | Sgt Yates | N6129 | 2350hrs | 0410hrs | 4.20mins | 6 x 1000lb + 7 x 500lb GP | DCO |
| Y | P/O McCarthy | N6084 | 2355hrs | 0415hrs | 4.20mins | 6 x 1000lb + 7 x 500lb GP | DCO |
| Z | F/Sgt McGregor | W7464 | 2345hrs | 0355hrs | 4.10mins | 6 x 1000lb + 7 x 500lb GP | DCO |

*Two close friends on the squadron were Australian Pilot Officer Geoff Corser RAAF and New Zealander Pilot Officer Roy Spear RNZAF. Seen here soon after their award of the DFC on completion of their first operational tour. Geoff started his tour against Cologne on May 30th, 1942.*

Wing Commander Holder DFC commandeered the crew of 'A' Flights S/Ldr Ashworth. It is not known what the Flight Commanders feelings were, missing out on the raid and having his crew pinched! Most of the squadron would be carrying incendiaries. These would be the Gee equipped aircraft which would be tasked with setting the Cathedral city on fire for the following bombers drawn from No.91 and No.92 Groups and Flying Training Command. The final waves would be from No.4 and No.5 Group who would bring the raid to completion. There was only one hiccup on take-off, Sgt Falconer ripped off the port wheel while taking off when it hit raised ground just beyond the runway. After a quick check that nothing vital had been damaged and the engine was undamaged the crew to a man agreed to press on to Cologne. It was a brave decision by a young crew.

It is a testament to the ground crew's ability that not a single Stirling turned back due to a malfunction. The hours spent working in the rain and wind had paid off. The route to Cologne was almost straight, crossing the North Sea the whole armada would make landfall slightly

410

north of the Island of Overflakkee and head directly to the target. It was no surprise that the German defences were active, night fighters of NJG1 and NJG2 were already airborne long before the bombers entered German airspace. The squadrons of No.1 and No.3 Group would have their own target, the centre of the old town would be their aiming point. Number 91 and No.92 Group would bomb 1 mile north of the Old City while No.4 and No.5 Group would bomb 1 mile south. Fires had already taken hold as the first of the squadron Stirlings approached the German border. When still over 50 miles from the target the searchlights and flak could easily be seen in the excellent visibility. Soon the first glimpses of the fires came into view, burning intensely but slightly scattered. Over the City, the sky was a cauldron of flak and a few brave German night fighter pilots. The bombing heights varied dramatically on the squadron. Squadron Leader Ker bombed from 11,000 feet while Squadron Leader Oldroyd added his all-incendiary load from 18,000 feet, one of the highest recorded on the raid by a No.3 Group crew. A recently posted pilot was undertaking his first operation on this night. Australian, Pilot Officer Edward 'Geoff' Corser RAAF a 22-year-old from Brisbane had

*Sergeant Ronald Joseph Guntrip, RAFVR 2nd pilot aboard Short Stirling W7502 HA-N 'Nuts.*

joined the squadron from No.10 OTU on May 15th. He would open his batting flying on this, the most remarkable raid flown by Bomber Command to date. Sergeant Savage reported '*There was a sea of flames all over the target, for this reason, our bomb bursts were not observed, but they fell in the centre of the town'.* Wing Commander Holder DFC bombed from 16000 feet, sitting beside him was the 49-year-old commanding officer of No.3 Group, Air Vice-Marshal John Baldwin. He had no difficulty identifying the target; both the AOC and W/Cdr Holder could clearly see from the light of the fires the twin 516ft spires of Cologne Cathedral. Over the target, Sgt Mulroy the rear gunner reported over the intercom the presence of a fighter on the starboard quarter. Wing Commander Holder kept the Stirling steady and prepared for the inevitable cannon fire and the order to corkscrew. Thankfully, the fighter had its sights on another victim. A relieved Holder sought the relative safety of the blackness away from a now burning city.

The crews were confident that the operation was a complete success, P/O Ball took one final look at the city below as he turned for home, ' *It was a sea of flames, smoke was at this time rising to 12,000 feet'* he remarked at the debriefing. Having bombed the target, the crews headed south towards Euskichen a town in North Rhine-Westphalia, here they then turned for home skirting north of St Trond and passing over the Dutch Coast at Zeeland. It was on this homeward leg that the crew of Sergeant Davis were engaged by flak from 1./Res.Flak.Abt.212 based near to Aachen.

Coned by 20-30 searchlights the pilots did everything they could to escape the blinding glare, soon the inescapable flak began to burst around the Stirling. It was only a matter of seconds before the Stirling began to shudder under their impact.

In the mid-upper turret, Sgt Albert Smith was hit by a shell fragment which penetrated his chest. Lowering himself down into the fuselage, he tried desperately to communicate with his crew up front. The Stirling was in a bad way, both port engines were either on fire or smouldering wrecks, the port outer had lost its propeller the result of a direct flak burst. Somehow, the battered Stirling was still flying. Sergeant Smiths calls were thankfully answered with the appearance of the flight engineer who somehow managed to drag the injured gunner to the rest position. Having applied what First Aid he could he prudently clipped on Sgt Smiths parachute as a precaution. This simple act would ultimately save the gunners life. Once satisfied, the flight engineer went forward and re-joined the pilots desperately struggling to keep the Stirling airborne. Unknown to Sgt Smith there was a tragedy unravelling in the Stirling's nose. Flak had torn to pieces the parachute of F/Sgt 'Joe' Borrowdale the crew's observer. The shredded chute was spilling out of its canvas pack in the confines of the bomb aimers position. Without a moment's hesitation the American front gunner, Sgt Tate told his crewmate that they would jump together on one chute. It would be dangerous for both men, but it was Borrowdale's only chance. With both Sgt Davis and Guntrip losing the fight to keep the Stirling aloft, the injured Sgt Smith, Tate and Borrowdale bailed-out. Sergeant Smith smashed into the ground and passed out. Sergeant 'Tex' Tate and 'Joe' Borrowdale survived the initial jump, but when the parachute deployed the force was so great the 26-year-old from Cumberland slipped to his death. Turning to watch the fate of his Stirling, Tate watched helplessly as bomber turned onto its back and smashed into the ground near Huppenbroich, taking with it five of the crew. Both survivors were quickly found, Smith receiving some excellent medical care from his captures. Both would spend the rest of the war as Prisoners of War.

### Saturday 30th May 1942
Short Stirling
*Mk.I*
*W7502 HA-N 'Nuts'*
*Contract No : 982939/39*
*Taken On Charge : 03/03/1942*
*CAT E/FB Missing*
*SoC 31/05/1942*
***Failed To Return***
*Pilot : Sergeant Arthur Wilfred Davis, 125321 RAFVR* **Killed.**
*2nd Pilot : Sergeant Ronald Joseph Guntrip, 1378901 RAFVR* **Killed**
*Observer : Flight Sergeant Joseph Lewthwaite Borrowdale, 1151361 RAFVR* **Killed**
*Wireless Operator : Sergeant Harold ' Harry' Allen, 1355784 RAFVR* **Killed**
*Front Gunner, Sergeant Howard 'Tex' Tate, R/98078 RCAF, PoW*
*Mid Upper Gunner : Sergeant Albert Smith, 1016992 RAFV, PoW*
*Rear Gunner : Sergeant Kenneth William George England, 1375251 RAFVR* **Killed**
*Flight Engineer : Sergeant Edward James White, 647117 RAFVR* **Killed**

Joseph Lewthwaite Borrowdale was the son of Mr and Mrs Joseph H Borrowdale of Hensingham, his father was a successful Tailor. Joseph was a sickly child, on the first day of the Spring Term in 1932 his poor health was immediately obvious to the teaching staff. On being examined by a specialist, he was advised to leave school at once. From that day on he was educated privately. He went to South Africa on a government appointment to Witwatersrand on reaching school leaving age. When war broke out, he joined the crew of a floating whale factory and worked his passage to England to join the RAF in 1940. The crew lie side by side in the Rheinburg War Cemetery, Germany.

The crew of Sgt Sidney Falconer having successfully bombed Cologne now had the tricky problem of landing back at Marham. In the grey damp light of Sunday morning Sgt Falconer circled Marham trying to use up the remaining fuel. Finally, satisfied Sidney Falconer on only his second operation as captain began his approach for a wheels-up landing.

At 05:55 hours Sidney brought Stirling R9311 HA-L into land. The flat slab like fuselage of the Stirling made belly landings that little bit easier, with a sickening crump the Stirling slid to a halt on Marham damp grass runway. Given the circumstances it had been a first-class effort by the crew, all of which clambered out of the buckled R9311 without injury. Standing around in the rain the crew waited to be collected and transported to debriefing, they were the last crew to land. It was the start of a remarkable but tragically short career for the young pilot from South Shields.

**Saturday 30th  May 1942**
Short Stirling
*Mk.I*
*R9311 HA-L*
*Contract No : 774677/38*
*Taken On Charge : 06/04/1942*
*CAT B/FB*
*SoC 23/06/1942*
*Crash Landing*
*Pilot : Sergeant Sidney Falconer, Uninjured.*
*2nd Pilot : Sergeant Humphreys, Uninjured.*
*Observer  : Sergeant  Birks, Uninjured*
*Wireless Operator : Sergeant Wolstencroft, Uninjured.*
*Front Gunner, Sergeant E.J Harding, Uninjured.*
*Mid Upper Gunner : Flight Sergeant  J.L Lawler, Uninjured.*
*Rear Gunner : Sergeant E.A Green, Uninjured.*
*Flight Engineer : Sergeant Wilkes, Uninjured.*

At debriefing all the discussions revolved around the fires at Cologne, not since the attack on Lubeck had the crews been so enthusiastic. A real feeling of achievement and no small measure of satisfaction was felt by all the squadron, it was after all a job well done. Even Air Vice-Marshal John Baldwin got caught up in the excitement. Invigorated by the air crews, he joined them for their customary breakfast of eggs and beacon.

Subsequent daylight reconnaissance showed that the raid was a complete success, when photographed the next morning fires were still raging in the centre of Cologne and numerous residential and industrial areas. Over 600 acres of the city was destroyed, over half of which was Cologne's city centre. It was estimated that a staggering 3,000 houses and 250 factory buildings were destroyed or severely damage. The cost in lives was unknown, not that the majority of the crews really cared. It was only a year before that London, Manchester, Liverpool, Coventry and Bath and countless other British cities all experienced nightly attacks from the Luftwaffe bombers. For many aircrews, it was payback time.

On the morning of the 31st, Form B.827 arrived from Group HQ, Bomber Command was undertaking another 1000 bomber operation that night against Hamburg. Harris, keen to capitalise on the success over Cologne was eager to produce yet another knock-out blow, this time against the important docks and yard facilities, it would also fulfil his obligations to the battle raging in the Atlantic. This put a tremendous strain on the air crews but especially the ground crews who would have to work feverishly throughout the day to get the required number of aircraft ready. As it was, the raid was cancelled early afternoon, much to everyone one's relief.

*The boyish good looks of Sidney Godfrey Falconer. Seen here while a flight lieutenant with a DFC and DFM. He was killed aged just 23 in May 1943 in a tragic flying accident.*

414

*Short Stirling N3725 HA-D arrived on the squadron March 15th, 1942 carrying out its first operation on March 25th with Flight Sergeant Lamason RNZAF to Essen. It eventually notched up an impressive 31 raids totalling some 223 flying hours before it crashed on September 14th, 1942 near Stoke Ferry, Norfolk. Above the impressive bomb tally is the name 'Mamprusi'. These were a people from the northern area of the Gold Coast. Below the bomb symbols is a flying Jumbo emblem. Note the 2000 pounder, a bomb N3725 never carried.*

It was no surprise to anyone when the news arrived that a second 1000 bomber raid was planned for the night of June 1st, the target was Essen. It would be the last opportunity for a while to use the aircraft from No.91 and No.92 Groups and Training Command. They were needed elsewhere. Unlike Hamburg, Essen was well inside the range of TR1335. The attacking force would be divided into three waves, the first, a flare force of 20 specially selected TR1135 aircraft. These were followed by an incendiary force of 125 'heavies' specially chosen for their experience with TR1335. Finally, the third and final was made up of the main force. This type of technique using Gee-equipped aircraft to initially mark the target was code-named 'Shaker'. Marham would provide 18 Wellingtons and 15 Stirlings from its two squadrons. Six crews of No.218 Squadron were chosen for the incendiary force. Once again, the station's Commanding Officer outlined the night's proceedings, special emphasis was placed on accuracy, especially by the opening waves. The attack was planned to start at 0050 hours. The crews began departing just after 2300 hours. There were two early returns. Sergeant McAuley experienced shuddering aboard N3753 HA-U soon after take-off, not willing to miss another '1000 bomber' raid the crew initially decided to press on. Their pluck was not rewarded, soon issues with a misfiring engine meant that the crew would have to return to Marham on three engines. More worryingly was an unresponsive rudder and vibration that could not be identified. The young Irish pilot ordered the bomb load to be jettisoned and turned for home. On reaching Marham Sgt McAuley undershot his first approach, hitting trees he damaged the Stirling's undercarriage and tailplane. The damage was such that any prospect of a

*The damaged Stirling N3753 HA-U 'Uncle' photographed the morning after the crash landing.*

normal landing was now out of the question. Circling the airfield, Sgt McAuley came in for a belly landing on the soft grass slightly off the main runway. Slithering to a halt the Stirling on just its second operation was a write-off.

## Monday 1st June 1942
Short Stirling
*Mk.I*
*N3753 HA-U 'Uncle'*
*Contract No : 763825/38*
*Taken On Charge : 14/05/1942*
*CAT B/FB*
*SoC 22/06/1942*
*Crash Landing*
*Pilot : Sergeant G McAuley, Uninjured.*
*2nd Pilot : Pilot Officer J Frankcomb Uninjured.*
*Observer : Pilot Officer G Tudor, Uninjured*
*Wireless Operator : Sergeant B Roberts, Uninjured.*
*Front Gunner, Sergeant H Davies, Uninjured.*
*Mid Upper Gunner : Sergeant E Nettleton, Uninjured.*
*Rear Gunner : Sergeant A Burkitt, Uninjured.*
*Flight Engineer : Sergeant G Neale, Uninjured*

George McAuley was born at Play Hill, Cairncastle, Larne in 1921. He was educated at Larne Grammar School and was joint head boy during the 1939-1940 season, his last at the school. A cheerful young lad with a big smile he excelled at rugby, running and boxing. It was not all sport, an excellent student he had originally hoped to study medicine. George's father was a WW1 veteran who had served in the Merchant Navy. At the outbreak of WW2, he re-enlisted and served as a Chief Engineer, interestingly, he had the distinction of being torpedoed in both campaigns and surviving. Sadly, at just 19, George was one of the young pilots on the squadron and would not inherit his father's Irish Luck. Sergeant McAuley was followed by the crew of P/O McCarthy. They had the misfortune to lose all three turrets, a very unusual occurrence.

Layers of cloud hid the bombers from an almost full moon as they crossed the North Sea. On nearing the Dutch coast, the tell-tale signs of trouble were quickly evident. Blazing bombers were observed, the unmistakable sign of prowling night fighters. Flying Officer Allen reported seeing ten unidentified aircraft with green lights in their nose at 16,000 feet while flying over the Hague at 00:32hrs. It is not beyond the realms of possibility that these were inexperienced crews from Training Command who simply forgot to turn off their navigational lights. Sergeant Yates watched as a Ju88 with a white light in its nose close in on an unsuspecting Wellington, the outcome was inevitable. Almost exactly on time, the first of the flares were blindly released over Essen by the TR1335 equipped Flare Force. Essen was partially covered in cloud and combined with industrial these initial flares were difficult for the following wave to identify. Not only were they difficult to see, but they were also woefully inaccurate. One flare dropper released its flares nine miles WNW of Essen over Hamborn. Sadly, the hoped for concentration of flares did not materialise. With limited options available to them the incendiary force either bombed the scattered flares, or the more experienced used their TR1135 sets and bombed independently. Sergeant George Boyd dropped his all-incendiary load from 16,000 feet. With the raid only just starting the more experienced crews had their doubts about the accuracy of the marking, Sergeant Boyd reported ' *All bombs dropped in a built-up area, thought to be Essen'.* Flight Sergeant Webber was equally puzzled, *'No searchlights or flak were seen, but an aircraft was seen to burst into flames and fell to the ground'.* Sergeant Medus reported the demise of a bomber over the target area, which was seen shot down all the while dropping its incendiaries and flares as it plummeted to earth. The majority of the squadron crews were rather vague about the accuracy of their bombing, all apart from F/Sgt Webber. He was the only crew to identify a landmark positively. Sadly, the area he bombed was miles from Essen. Many large fires were taking hold as the squadron's crews departed the target area, the biggest conflation was near Oberhausen NW of Essen. It was this fire that P/O Lamason RNZAF reported seeing from Eindhoven on the return leg. Thirty miles off the coast of Norfolk S/Ldr Ker and his 218 CF Stirling crew were shot at by a convoy. The recognition flares were fired and eventually, the flak, which was inaccurate abruptly stopped. Just after 03:00 hours Squadron Leader Ashworth and crew were preparing to land back at Marham. With the runway in sight, the Stirling was reportedly attacked by two single-engine fighters which appeared to fire a short burst at W7530 HA-Q from less than 50 yards. So unexpected and quick was the encounter the gunners had no time to respond before the fighters were lost to view. The shaken crew eventually landed at 04:30hrs. The only German activity on this night was over Ipswich by Luftwaffe bombers. No Intruders were active, and certainly, no German single-engine fighter could reach Marham. Who or what attacked the crew is a mystery?

Unlike the raid on Cologne the returning crews were somewhat subdued, there was little excitement, except that of getting safely home to their bacon and eggs. The operation was a failure, it failed in its primary objective to bomb Essen and more importantly destroy or at the very least damage the Krupps works. The only positives were that severe damage had been inflicted on Oberhausen, and that was sheer luck. The main railway station was severely damaged as were numerous buildings in the proximity. An additional 70 residential and commercial building and factories were also severely affected. Further afield at Mulheim, over ten miles SW of Essen many factory buildings were burnt out, at Duisburg a railway yard was damaged. The bombing was scattered all over the Ruhr. Harris and his staff blamed the weather. The much-vaunted TR1335 was not proving to be the saviour it was hoped. Thankfully, the casualties were relatively light, 31 bombers and crews were lost, including one from 115 Squadron.

*Australian John Savage seen here after leaving the squadron on completion of his first operational tour.*

No operations were flown on the 2nd, 218 Squadron's ground crews fussed over their charges while only two aircraft were aloft, one was P/O McCarthy's R9332 HA-G which suffered complete turret failure on route to Essen. A switch north, away from the Ruhr was planned for the 3rd The important docks and submarine yards at Bremen were the intended targets. Only seven crews were detailed and briefed, the senior captain being S/Ldr Ashworth who was the first away at 22:55 hour in W7530 HA-Q. A force of over 170 bombers lifted off from their bases dotted along the east coast of England. Once airborne they headed out over the North Sea, of the total dispatched, 51 aircraft were provided by No.3 Group. Once again, the now-standard procedure of a flare dropping force opening proceedings was planned. 3 Group would provide fifteen TR1335 equipped aircraft of which Marham's 115 Squadron would provide seven. It was to turn out to be a frustrating and costly night for the squadron. Pilot Officer Ball abandoned the operation over the North Sea with rear turret failure. Flight Lieutenant Allen lost the starboard inner engine aboard N6077 HA-V. This would not normally be a problem. Pilots were trained to fly on three and possibly two engines in an emergency. However, of this occasion, what followed was a life-or-death struggle with a Stirling that became increasingly uncontrollable. All lateral control was lost resulting in the Stirling swinging drunkenly around the sky. Using every bit of his experience, F/Lt Don Allen somehow managed to keep the Stirling flying and head back at Marham. Showing commendable skill, he brought the Stirling in for a rather bumpy landing. Shaken but otherwise unscathed the crew headed for debriefing while N6077 HA-V was moved to the maintenance hangar. Over Holland, the crew of Flight Sergeant John Webber had the misfortune of being intercepted by Oblt Ludwig Becker of 6./NJG2 10,000 feet above Den Helder. In the ensuing encounter only the crew's rear gunner, Sgt Keith Cox survived. Short Stirling W7474 HA-K crashing at 0027 hours near 'Het Kuitje' 1 mile south of Den Helder.

**<u>Wednesday 3rd June 1942</u>**
Short Stirling
*Mk.I*
*W7474 HA-K 'King'*
*Contract No : B982939/39*
*Taken On Charge : 14/02/1942*
*CAT B/FB*
*SoC 14/02/1942*
***Failed to Return***
*Pilot : Flight Sergeant John Webber, 1262680 RAFVR, **Killed***
*2nd Pilot : Pilot Officer James Garscadden, 106113 RAFVR, **Killed***
*Observer : Pilot Officer John Douglas Insch, 100055 RAF, **Killed***
*Wireless Operator : Flight Sergeant Harold Cyril Broadbent, 971256 RAFVR DFM, **Killed***
*Front Gunner : Flight Sergeant Leo Louis Joseph FARLEY, R/60963 RCAF, **Killed***
*Mid Upper Gunner : Sergeant Norman Cyril Frederick Sibley, 1334367 RAFVR, **Killed***
*Rear Gunner : Sergeant Keith Cox 1019151 RAFVR, PoW*
*Flight Engineer : Sergeant Leonard James Smith, 616593 RAFVR, **Killed***

*The wreckage of Short Stirling W7474 HA-K being inspected by Luftwaffe personnel.*

The loss of the Webber crew was a bitter blow to all the squadron. All the crew were experienced. It was particularly hard knowing that 19-year-old John Webber was tantalisingly close to completing his operational tour. His war began in September 1941 with a raid against Berlin with S/Ldr Price DFC when they crash-landed on return. He completed 17 operations on the Wimpy before converting to the Stirling. Once converted he undertook a further 14 operations bringing his total count to 31. Regrettably, he did not live to wear the pilot officer tunic so richly deserved, his promotion being published in July 1942. Flight Sergeant Broadbent was awarded his DFM for service with No.99 Squadron, awards to wireless operators, even good ones were a rarity. Five of the crew were buried as 'unidentified' airman on June 9th, 1942. Only the bodies of Leo Farley and

*Two of the crew killed aboard Short Stirling W7474 HA-K 'King'. Left Twenty-two-year old Flight Sergeant Leo Farley RCAF the crews front gunner. Right, Pilot Officer James Garscadden 2ⁿᵈ pilot. Aged twenty-nine and married, he was older than most on the squadron at the time.*

Norman Sibley were identified, they were initially buried at Huisduinen Military Cemetery on June 30th. They now rest in the Bergen-Op-Zoom Cemetery.

Away from the squadron, Pilot Officer John 'Jack' Abberton was in the process of polishing off his training in the Conversion Flight before joining the squadron. In a letter home dated June 6th he writes about a few experiences, *'The squadron boys have been swimming today and twice yesterday, we on the Con Flight have not been at all. You can guess we love the Con.Flight!! Last night we broke two tailwheels on our kite, BAGS OF PANIC!! We had the C/O out looking at the kite. He was quite decent, and it was quite amusing! I must close, as there is a terrific argument going on in the mess and I cannot think to write!'* It would be one of his last letters home.

On the evening of the 6th the squadron visited Bremen, eleven crews were involved. Squadron Leader Ashworth somehow managed to arrive over the target area 21 minutes early, with no flares and Bremen's defences deadly quiet they circled the city below. Sitting beside him was Marham's Station Commander, Group Captain McKee. The flight was probably undertaken without the knowledge or agreement of either the C-in-C AVM Harris or McKees immediate boss Baldwin. It was a risky decision by the group captain, if shot down and captured alive the German propaganda machine would have had a field day. As it was, his courageous, if but foolhardy decision to operate ended well, it also went a long way to instil confidence in both of Marham's squadrons. Just after 0110 hours, the first of the flares began to appear, at once Bremen searchlights flicked on and the murderous flak, both light and medium calibre hosed the sky above the docks and town. One crew more than most had a good reason to be annoyed over Bremen. Pilot Officer Lamason having dodged the flak and searchlights discovered he was unable to bomb when the bomb doors failed to open. Despite the flight engineers' best efforts, they remained firmly shut, it was a very irritated crew that returned to Marham.

*A wonderful photograph of a group of squadron 'erk's at RAF Marham. Unfortunately, their names are unknown. The success of the squadron could never have been achieved without the dedication, skill, and sheer hard work of the ground crews.*

Flares, of which there were plenty were well placed over the old Town and eastern sector of the Docks. These attracted the majority of the bombs producing what was classed as 'satisfactory' fires. Some useful damage was achieved, the docks and nearby warehouses were hit and the German Destroyer Z-25 sustained blast damage. The biggest success was in the residential areas were considerable damage was inflicted. The Stirlings began to arrive back at Marham in the early morning sunshine. It had been a frustrating night, one crew 'missing', two aborts and a full bomb load returned due to a mechanical issue.

It was back to northern Germany and Emden on the 6th, eleven crews were once again selected and briefed. In excellent conditions 103 Wellingtons and Stirlings of No.3 Group gradually climbed to altitude, there was just one early return from the squadron. Bad luck once again seemed to favour the crew of F/Lt Donald Allen when all four engines aboard R9354 HA-N overheated. The Stirling, a Short and Harland built aircraft had only arrived on the squadron a few days prior. This was its first raid. The bomb load, consisting of 192 x 30lb incendiaries were jettisoned into the sea. Once again, the unfortunate F/Lt Allen and crew were the first back for their bacon and egg breakfast. The Wellingtons of RAF Feltwell and Marham would open the attack at 0115 hours with a number of Flares dropped at 3-minute intervals using their TR1135 sets. There was no cloud over the target and apart from slight haze, Emden lay below like a map. Bombing from between 12-15000 feet the crews easily identified the dock area and old town. A few fires were already starting to merge as the squadron, part of the 2nd wave began the long flight home. Sergeant Geoffrey Jeary reported, ' *One very large building in the SE of the town a mass of flames. Fires still visible 90 miles away'*. Post raid reconnaissance later showed that the raid had inflicted considerable damage, some 300 houses had been destroyed with a further 200 damaged. Some useful damage was also reported in the dock area, 10 acres of dock yards had been flattened, the building owned by Schulte and Bruns had been burnt out as well as the Herings Fischerei A.G. Also affected was the towns gas works and large railway station and sidings. There would have been an air of satisfaction and relief at both Group and Command HQ on seeing the reconnaissance photographs.

Both Bremen and Emden had suffered serious damage, the flare force of No.3 Group was finding its feet and the main force bombers were beginning to bomb the flares and not the fringes of the target. It was all change the following night when seven crews were selected for a mining operation. Their target was the Nectarine 1 Garden area. The first crew aloft departed at 23:20 hours, sitting in the 2nd pilots seat of N3720 HA-B flown by F/Sgt Boyd was a 28-year-old New Zealander carrying out his first trip. Sergeant Keith Ryan RNZAF was fresh from No.20 OTU. Each of the bombers was loaded with 4 x 1,500lb parachute mines. After the long haul to northern Germany over the previous two raids the seven crews experienced a trouble-free and relatively brief operation dropping 27 mines in their allotted garden from between 400 and 700 feet.

On the 8th, Pilot Officer John Abberton was given a 'Nickle' operation to France. Flying Stirling N6077 HA-V the crew visited Caen, Evreux and Le Treport, strangely this operation is not recorded in either the squadron or station ORB. This raid was followed by yet another mining operation on the 9th. Once again seven crews were detailed and briefed for a return trip to the Nectarines Garden area. Sergeant Geoff Jeary lost his rear turret due to a burst hydraulic pipe on route. The all NCO crew decided to press on. It was a bold decision. Other than P/O McCarthy being unable to pinpoint his allotted position all the crews successfully dropped their mines. Much to all the squadrons surprise they were again briefed for a mining operation on the 11th. Six crews were aloft including S/Ldr Oldroyd DFC AFC who had just returned from some well-earned leave.

The target was again the busy shipping lanes off the Dutch coast. Twenty No.3 Group Stirlings, including 218 Squadrons contribution were given Nectarines II to mine. Unlike the previous outings, there was a concerted effort by the German defences to oppose this operation. German night fighters were active over Northern Holland, a Lancaster of No.5 Group falling victim to a Bf110 of 5./NJG2. Flak ships were now an ever-present danger. Aware of the areas that Bomber Command mined the German Kriegsmarine quickly started positioning 'Vorpostenboot' or flak boats and even barges. Bristling with both light, medium, and heavy flak these proved to be a genuine danger to the low flying bombers. All six crews successfully identified the island of Schiermonnikoog before dropping their mines, P/O MacAuley ventured a little too close to the island. German flak positions quickly found their mark and put seven holes in the wings and bomb bay doors of Stirling N3721 HA-S. Although not as dangerous as long flights over the Fatherland gardening was becoming a little bit dicier. On this night four bombers failed to return, luckily none from Marham.

*German flak ships like the one above proved deadly in the Garden areas. Heavily armed with light, medium and heavy flak guns they posed a serious threat to the low flying aircraft. Constantly moving from one position to another bomber crews were unaware of the location until it was often too late.*

Tragedy struck in the most unfortunate way on the 12th. At 2130 hours alone Do 217 flying in low cloud, dropped 4 x 500 kg HE bombs over Kings Lynn. Three of the bombs caused little damage apart from wrecking a cattle market. The 4th scored a direct hit on the 'Eagle' Hotel in Norfolk Street, demolishing the building. In the hotel celebrating a 21st birthday was a number of 218 Squadron personnel. In the explosion that followed 42 people were killed, 24 servicemen and 18 civilians. Three of the servicemen were from 218 Squadron, Sergeant William Cooper, Sergeant James Laurie and air gunner Sergeant George Jones. It was the worst single air raid incident in Norfolk throughout the war. Thirty-year-old Sgt Laurie was taken home to be buried in Dumfriesshire. Sergeant Jones was buried in Marham Cemetery, while Sergeant Cooper was taken home to be buried in the Gatcombe (St.Olave) Churchyard on the Isle of Wright. There followed a period of relative inactivity. Other than a real push by the flight commanders for a series of exercises over the bombing ranges. Despite the slightly drizzly weather ten aircraft completed a low-level bombing expertise on the 14th. This was repeated on the 16th. Aerial gunnery was the order of the day on the 17th, when ten crews were airborne in cloudy conditions. Finally, on the 18th, the squadron was informed that it was required that night. Three crews were detailed for another Gardening operation. The target was once again the Nectarines. The first away was P/O McCarthy at 2340hrs in W7475 HA-H, he was quickly followed by P/O Ball and Sgt McAuley. Loaded with four 1000lb mines, the trio headed towards Cromer and out over the North Sea. Visibility was exceptional, keeping low the Stirlings carried out an unmolested operation, all 12 parachute mines were seen to release and splash into the sea. It had not taken Group HQ long to realise that these operations were ideal for 'Freshman' crews to learn their trade. During the coming moon period, the maximum number of 'Freshman' were to be included for operational experience. News started to filter through that the squadron might be on the move. It had long been known that the landing ground at Marham was taking a terrible pounding from the massive Stirlings. Despite good drainage, the area was becoming increasingly rutted. Any prolonged rain would make take-off and landing a tricky undertaking in the sludge and mud. A new airfield a few miles S.W at

*Armourers manhandling two 500lb GP bombs beneath the nose of a squadron Short Stirling. The height above the ground of the cockpit is evident in this lovely photograph of two dispersed Stirlings at RAF Marham.*

Downham Market was nearing completion. With three concrete runways, it would be an ideal aerodrome for the heavy brigade of No.3 Group.

A lone Spitfire Mk.Vb of No.610 Squadron made an appearance on the afternoon of the 20th, obviously, in trouble, the Coltishall based fighter made an impromptu forced landing. With its undercarriage retracted, the sleek fighter skidded to halt at 218 CF dispersal area. The pilot, F/Sgt W.M 'Jacko' Jackson RCAF prowess obviously impressed S/Ldr Ker who witnessed the whole event. Never one to dispense praise lightly, he remarked that it took *'Skill and initiative'* on the part of the pilot to land safely. In an unusual move, S/Ldr Ker even wrote to F/Sgt Jacksons Commanding Officer commending his actions. Another crack at Emden was scheduled for the night of June 20th, over 200 bombers would be involved of which No.3 Group would provide 71. Marham fielded 13 Wellingtons and nine Stirlings. Two recent arrivals to the squadron would join the flight commanders on this their first operation.

Accompanying Squadron Leader Oldroyd DFC AFC was a F/Lt Arthur Samson. Born 1915 in Newfoundland, he had enlisted in RAF Reserve in 1936 being commissioned 1940. Joining S/Ldr Ashworth was Flight Lieutenant Desmond Plunkett. A Former Wimbledon schoolboy, Desmond had only arrived on the squadron on the 12th. Both Arthur and Desmond had flown on the 1000 bomber operation against Cologne on May 30th and Essen on June 1st with No.22 OTU. Another pilot carrying out his first operation was Sgt Geoffrey Milligan RCAF a 20-year-old from Edmonton, Alberta. He had served briefly on 57 Squadron before posting to 218 CF for conversion

*Sampling 218 Squadron's donated Tea Wagon, Marham 1942. This is the McGregor crew. Left, Sgt Medhurst, rear gunner (Partially obscured by the WAAF) Wireless Operator Sgt Finney, Sgt Davidson, Mid Upper gunner, Pilot, Sgt McGregor, Sgt Moyes, Wireless operator/ gunner, unknown, unknown. Sitting on the table is New Zealand Roy Spear.*

to the Stirling. Geoffrey would accompany the crew of F/Sgt Johnston aboard W7475 HA-H. Just after 23:30 hour, the first of the Stirlings departed and headed for the departure point of Cromer. The most experienced TR1335 set operators from the Wellington equipped squadrons of Marham, Oakington, Honington and Feltwell would open proceedings at 01:15 hours dropping flares, these would be backed up every 3 minutes for the duration of the raid. There was just one early return, P/O Medus and his co-pilot, P/O Corser RAAF were forced to return due to a malfunction of the rear turret over the North Sea. Unfortunately, the forecast of clear skies above Emden proved incorrect, the crews flying between 12-15,000 feet encountered dense broken cloud over the target and ground haze below. Above the docks and city, the crews were not unduly bothered by searchlights however the flak was reported to be particularly heavy. German twin-engine fighters of NJG2 were also airborne and active although not bothersome over the target area. Only one crew managed to get fleeting glimpses of the ground, P/O Ball watched as his all-incendiary load landed on the northern docks. The squadron crews were not overly complimentary with the marking preferring to rely on their own TR1335 sets. Pilot Officer McCarthy reported conditions over the target as *'bad'*, F/Sgt Boyd was more fortunate. He identified the target by the flares over the dock area where he reported *'saw our own incendiaries burn, one red fire in town area seen'*. It was on the return route that the crew of Squadron Leader Ashworth had the misfortune to encounter a Ju88 C-6 flown by Lt Johannes Werth of 7./NJG2 based at Gilze-Rijen airfield. Over the Wognun, north Holland the two crews engage in a bitter and deadly encounter. Unfortunately, the odds were just too great for the experienced crew. At 0200 hours Short Stirling W7530 HA-Q crashed into farmland taking with it the 40-year-old Squadron Leader Ashworth and two of his

425

gunners. Five of the crews managed to parachute to safety including F/Lt Plunkett on his first and last operation with the squadron.

## Sunday 20/21st June 1942

Short Stirling
*Mk.I*
*W7530 HA-Q 'Queenie'*
*Contract No : B982939/39*
*Taken On Charge : 08/05/1942*
*CAT E/FB Missing*
*SoC 20/06/1942*
***Failed to Return***
*Pilot : Squadron Leader Harold Ashworth 76467 RAFVR **Killed***
*2nd Pilot : Flight Lieutenant Desmond Plunkett 78847 RAFVR PoW*
*Navigator/Observer : Pilot Officer Alan Green, 104402 RAFVR PoW*
*Wireless Operator : Pilot Officer Reginald Horace Attwood 80197 RAF PoW*
*Mid Upper Gunner : Sergeant William Watt, 1108788 RAFVR **Killed***
*Wireless operator/Front Gunner Sergeant William Edwin Whitehead, 994746 RAFVR **Killed***
*Rear Gunner : Sergeant Thomas Mulroy, 537282 RAFVR PoW*
*Flight Engineer : Sergeant William John Hayden, 620195 RAFVR PoW*

In June 1943 the London Gazette announced the award of the DFC to Squadron Leader Harold Ashworth awarded with effect from 2nd June,1942. There is no citation, but it is not beyond the realms of possibility he was put forward for the DFC due to his involvement in the Pilsen operations of which he took an active part. Desmond Plunkett landed in the midst of a herd of cattle. He was later arrested in a nearby village. A fiery man with a thick bristly moustache he went on to play a key role in the Great Escape in March 1944. Desmond Launcelot Plunkett was born on February 21st, 1915 at Guntur in the Madras Presidency of India, where his father was a civil engineer. After the family had returned to England, Desmond was educated at King's College, Wimbledon. His first job was with the Hawker aircraft company at Kingston upon Thames, Surrey. In 1936 he found work with a company that designed and built gliders, and in the same year, he had his first experience of flying, at the famous Redhill Flying Club. He then joined the RAF Volunteer Reserve, graduating as a flying instructor in 1939. Despite many requests for active service, he was retained as an instructor for the first two years of the war. Finally, in 1941, Plunkett was posted for training as a bomber pilot with the rank of flight lieutenant, the notification coming only a few days before his wedding to Patricia Wildblood in November 1941. Before the escape from Stalag Luft III, Plunkett had been involved in earlier attempts of a 'Home-run'. His first plan had been to conceal himself in a cart which was removing ash from the camp.

*The crew of Squadron Leader Harold Ashworth RAFVR standing in front of Short Stirling W7530 HA-Q 'Queenie'. This was a new machine, arriving from No.149 Squadron on May 8th, 1942. It was immediately commandeered by the flight commander. The crew completed five operations in 'Queenie'. Below; The impressive memorial to the crew at the crash site.*

*Two photographs of the crumpled wreckage of S/Ldr Ashworth's Stirling, W7530 H-Q.*

He and another airman duly climbed into the cart and buried themselves in the ash; but because the coals lying underneath were still red hot, their trousers caught fire! A second attempt, to escape via a tunnel, had been foiled by the German guard dogs. A third, to scale the perimeter fence by ladder, was also unsuccessful. And a further effort to dig a tunnel was abandoned after the excavators found themselves delving into the local sewage works. It was after this that Roger Bushell instructed Plunkett to concentrate on mapmaking. Roger Bushell put Desmond in charge of a team of 14 men who were employed in mapmaking. Putting his previous learnt skills to good effect his team produced local maps indicating the quietest routes leading away from the camp, as well as more extensive maps showing escape routes through Czechoslovakia to Switzerland and France, and through the Baltic to Sweden. By bribing a guard, Plunkett obtained a large and detailed map of Europe which formed the basis of an eventual supply of some 2,500 maps in five colours. He abandoned tracing as being too time-consuming; instead, he conjured up an ingenious mimeograph using gelatine created from the crystal jelly sent in Red Cross parcels. Plunkett and his team were able to produce not only maps but also forged passes, permits and other "official" documents. Desmond was No.13 on the night of the escape, a place and number he specifically asked for. Having crawled the length of 'Harry' he successfully managed to get to the relative safety of the nearby woods. With his companion, a Czech airman named Bedrich Dvorak, he went to the local railway station and boarded a train for Breslau. Luck played a noticeably big part in Desmond's survival. The two men succeeded in getting into Czechoslovakia where, after several days in the relative luxury of a hotel, they hid in a barn. They eventually got as far as the Austrian border before being arrested. He spent a number of weeks a guest of the Gestapo where he was frequently tortured and beaten. He was eventually released by the Gestapo into the custody of Hradin prison at Prague. Later, in January 1945, he was sent to Stalag Luft I on the Baltic Sea, from where he was repatriated after VE Day

*Flight Lieutenant Desmond Plunkett had plenty of flying experience, but little operational experience prior to his arrival.*

*The Observer aboard Stirling W7530 HA-Q was Pilot Officer Alan Green. He spent the rest of the war a PoW.*

*Flight Lieutenant Samson would assume command of 'B' Flight on the death of S/Ldr Ashworth. This experienced and courageous pilot brought a wealth of experience to the squadron. He needed to; S/Ldr Ashworth was a hard act to follow.*

Bomber Command HQ classified the raid as only moderately successful blaming the haze as the contributing factor. What damage there was mostly centred in the town causing some useful if limited damage to a number of industrial buildings and sheds. There was little to show for eight bomber crews shot down. Obviously disappointed in the previous attempts to inflict a telling blow on Emden a force of over 200 bombers were briefed for one last attack on the 22nd. Almost half the force would be supplied by No.3 Group with 218 Squadron providing eleven crews led on this occasion by Wing Commander Holder DFC who was the last airborne at 2359hrs in Stirling N3725 HA-D. Joining him in the cockpit was F/Lt Samson, who was destined to take over the vacant 'B' Flight commander role. The weather and visibility were good, and crews had little difficulty in identifying the target, which was already well ablaze as the crews arrived. Unlike the previous attack, the flares dropped by TR1335 equipped Wellingtons of No.3 Group were concentrated and regularly backed up. Wing Commander Holder dropped his all-incendiary load from 16,000 feet reported on his return, '*Bombs fell in town NE of docks. Many small fires burning. One good fire in centre of town caused green explosion up to 2000 feet*'. As the crews turned for home the fires were gradually increasing in size and intensity. It was on the homeward leg of the operation where one of the squadrons most experienced crews met their end. At 0301hrs Short Stirling N6078 HA-P captained by Pilot Officer Richard Medus plummeted into the sea 25 miles NW of Zandvoort, a Dutch coastal town west of Amsterdam. There were no survivors from the crew who was claimed by the night fighter crew of Oberfeldwebel Beier, Unteroffizier Kleinenbrands and Unteroffizier Riemer of Ergänzungsstaffel NJG 2. They had taken off from Gilze-Rijen airfield in Ju 88 C-6 R4+WR.

## **Monday 21st/22nd June 1942**
Short Stirling
*Mk.I*
*N6078 HA-P ' P - Peter'*
*Contract No : 774677/38*
*Taken On Charge : 21/03/1942*
*CAT E/FB Missing*
*SoC 23/06/1942*
**Failed to Return**
*Pilot: Pilot Officer Richard William Medus,122992 RAFVR,* ***Killed***
*Observer: Flight Sergeant Joseph Simeon David Gosselin R/55226 RCAF,* ***Killed***

*Wireless Operator: Flight Sergeant Alexander Colin Stelman R/75683 RCAF, **Killed***
*Wireless Operator: Sergeant John Frederick 1108776 RAFVR, **Killed***
*Air Gunner: Sergeant Edward Victor Davey 1383321 RAFVR, **Killed***
*Air Gunner: Flight Sergeant Allan Harry Gudgeon R/55316 RCAF, **Killed***
*Flight Engineer: Sergeant Robert Wigham, 946411 RAFVR, **Killed***

Regrettably, none of the crew were recovered, all seven are remembered on the walls of the Runnymede Memorial.

Unteroffizier Riemer recorded the following, ' *Attack took place from below and behind to port. Enemy aircraft sank burning into the sea'*. Twenty-Year-Old Pilot Officer Richard 'Dick' Medus had flown on 31 operations since his arrival on the squadron in October 1941. He would be posthumously awarded a well-deserved DFC in July 1943 with effect from January 20th, 1942. It was small consolation to his parents William James Medus and Elizabeth Maude Rosa Medus, of Thames Ditton, Surrey. Unusually there were three Canadians in the crew. Flight Sergeant Gudgeon had previously seen service with Fighter Command with No.151 Squadron in 1941. This was a night fighter unit equipped with the Boulton Paul Defiant. He then served briefly with No.410 RCAF Squadron before posting to No.218 Squadron in May 1942. Alexander Stelman's parents were both Romanians having immigrated to Canada in the 1920s. This, the final raid directed against Emden was the most effective. Over 86% of the aircraft taking part claimed to have bombed the target. Post raid reconnaissance showed considerable damage had been inflicted to the town and dock area. The Cassens shipyard was severely damaged as was

*Flight Sergeant Alexander Colin Stelman RCAF standing under the port wheel of Stirling N6078 HA-P*

the Nordseewerke, a shipbuilding company, located in Emden harbour plus the government yard and stores building. Damage was also meted out to the residential areas of the town, between 40 - 50 houses were totally destroyed, and a number of commercial and public building gutted by fire. Emden had endured 4 raids in two weeks, over 800 sorties had been flown for the loss of 31 crews. Despite Bomber Commands best endeavours Emden survived the bombardment reasonably intact. The docks and infrastructure had been damaged but with typical Germanic efficiency this was quickly repaired. The crippling blow that was so desperately wanted at High Wycombe had eluded them. On the 23rd a single crew from 218 Squadron captained by P/O John Abberton and a Wellington from 115 Squadron were detailed for a 'Freshman' trip, the target was St Nazaire. Unable to identify the target owing to 10/10th cloud P/O Abberton returned to Marham jettisoning

*The crew of Pilot Officer Richard William Medus waiting for the order to take-off for an operation in June 1942.*

6 x 500 pounders on the way, the remaining 5 bombs were brought back. Also airborne was Sgt Leonard Hartley of 218 Conversion Flight, who was given a 'Bullseye' exercise.

After a brief pause in operations Harris reassembled his '1000 Bomber Force' for a raid on Bremen, if the weather conditions were unfavourable Duisburg would be attacked. The operation was coded 'Millenium Two'. Harris included in this force the previously unused Bostons and Mosquitoes of the daylight specialists, No.2 Group. As usual the Admiralty did everything they could to excuse themselves, however Winston Churchill's timely intervention resulted in the addition of over 100 Hudsons and Wellingtons. The squadrons and units of No.3 Group detailed an impressive 196 aircraft with No.1483 Flight based at RAF Stradishall providing an impressive 20 Wellington, Marham provided 18 Wellingtons and 14 Stirlings. The attack would be carried out in three waves. An advance force of TR1335 equipped bombers would open the attack at 0120 hours. They would be followed by the first wave consisted of 50 Stirlings and 50 Halifaxes who were to attack the centre of the town at zero hour + 10 minutes, these would be followed by more TR1335 equipped aircraft. The main force would bomb between zero hour + 20 and zero hour + 55 who would attack the town centre and southern dock area. One of the first squadron crews aloft was F/Sgt Boyd at 2310 hours in Stirling N3720 HA-B, he was loaded with 7,500lbs of four-pound incendiaries. Once airborne the crews headed for the departure point over Southwold, a small coastal town on the coast of Suffolk. There were no early returns from the squadron although No.3 Group did report a total of 24. The forecast weather unfortunately did not materialise, ominous banks of cloud began to gather the nearer the force got to the northern Dutch coast. More worryingly was the early presence of German fighters. One of the first bombers to be shot down was the Stirling of Pilot Officer Brian Ball and crew. They were intercepted at 0039 hours by

Oberleutnant Ludwig Becker of 6./NJG 2 based at Leeuwarden airfield. The bomber and its crew crashed into the Ijsselmeer off Wieringen, North Holland, there were no survivors.

**Friday 25th/26th June 1942**
Short Stirling
*Mk.I*
*W7503 HA-R 'Robert'*
*Contract No : 982939/39*
*Taken On Charge : 10/03/1942*
*CAT E/FB Missing*
*SoC 26/06/1942*
***Failed to Return***
*Pilot: Pilot Officer Brian Francis Ball, 108148 RAFVR,* **Killed**
*Observer: Flight Sergeant Richard Francis Carroll, 994961 RAFVR,* **Killed**
*Wireless Operator: Sergeant Kenneth George Rogers, 1166334 RAFVR* **Killed**
*Wireless Operator: Sergeant Arthur Leslie Brooks, 1177569 RAFVR* **Killed**
*Air Gunner: Sergeant Denniss Vincent Howes, 1282831 RAFVR ,* **Killed**
*Air Gunner: Sergeant John Frederick Howes, 540188 RAFVR* **Killed**
*Flight Engineer: Sergeant Edward Reed Douglass, 570275 RAF,* **Killed**

Only the body of Sgt Rogers was found, he washed ashore near Makkum a village on the banks of the IJsselmeer on July 7th, he is buried in the Wonseradeel (Makkum) Protestant Cemetery. Flight Sergeant Carrol was one of the handful of airmen from the Republic of Ireland that served on the squadron. Born in 1916 he was the son of Patrick and Clara Carroll, of Ennis, Co. Clare. Thirty-year old Brian Ball arrived on the squadron in March undertaking his first operation with F/Sgt McGregor on April 6th to Essen. He completed seven operations besides McGregor before he was given his own crew. On May 19th, he took his crew to St Nazaire, followed by the *1000 Bomber Raids* on Cologne and Essen. This his third 1000 raid was his 8th and last as captain. Pre-war he had been awarded a B.A (Hons) in Electrical Engineering. Sergeant Waters and crew were hit by flak soon after crossing the Dutch coast. Both starboard engines were hit and faltered which resulted in the Stirling going into a sickening spin. It took every ounce of Sgt Ralph Waters strength and flying skill to keep some sort of control. After what seemed an eternity the exhausted pilot finally managed to get the Stirling level, the 6 x 1000 pounders + 4 x 500 pounders were immediately jettisoned. The flak which had knocked out the engines also punctured No.5 fuel tank which quickly emptied. The weary Sgt Waters now had the long flight home to contend with.

A thin layer of cloud which the Met had hoped would clear before the raid was frustratingly still covering much of Bremen obscuring the town and important docks. The success of the operation was now totally dependent on the TR1335 set operators. The first waves relying totally on the Gee fixes surprisingly started a number of fires which quickly grew to a substantial size. The majority of the squadron were confident that they bombed the target either using TR1335 or aided by the flares and fires. Pilot Officer Abberton reported ' *Target identified by many fires'* while Sgt McAuley recorded, ' *No bomb bursts seen, but a very large fire seen which could not possibly have been a dummy'.* The crews bombing from heights varying from 11,000 feet to 17,000 feet meeting stiff opposition from Bremen's flak batteries. Sergeant Falconer summed up the defences, *'Exceptionally accurate heavy and light flak was experienced'.* Despite the flak, fighters and the cloud the fires grew in intensity as the raid progressed. This concentration of bombing was almost totally due to Gee being used primarily as a blind bombing device. By 0225 hours the raid had run its course, large fires were seen below the clouds which reflected the reds, orange and sometimes blues flames below. The damaged Stirling of Sergeant Waters managed to land safely at Marham at 0330 hours. Stirling DJ974 HA-T was immediately towed into the repair hangar where the aircraft required extensive repair. Given the number of bombers over Bremen, the damage was not large considering the scale of the attack. Some useful damage to industrial properties had been inflicted, most notably to the important Focke-Wulf aircraft factory which had sustained considerable damage. The loss in men and aircraft was considerable, 48 bombers failed to return. Bomber Command was not able to emulate the success of Cologne. The weather had beaten it once again. There was however some improvement on the recent 1000 Bomber raid on Essen which was basically a failure. On the morning of June 26th, Bomber Command had a lot to ponder, even with over 1000 at its disposal that knock-out blow still eluded them.

On the 27th and much to the crews surprise they were detailed and briefed for another crack at Bremen. Ten crews would join a further 46 Stirlings and Wellingtons of No.3 Group. This attack was planned as a blind bombing raid unless the target was free of cloud. The planners had specifically planned the route to give the TR1135 trained set operators the best possible approach to the target. The squadron crews began taking off just before midnight once again laden with all incendiary loads. Pilot Officer 'Jack' Abberton was forced to abandon the operation when his rear gunner reported his turret faulty. Unable to continue, the load was jettisoned from 3,000 feet midway across the North Sea. For once the Met briefing was correct, the weather was 10/10th cloud on route and over northern Germany. Over Holland the crew of Sgt Falconer were engaged by three Ju88s. The Stirling was extensively damaged. The cockpit instruments were smashed, both turrets put out of action and the fuselage peppered along the entire length of the aircraft. The following appeared in the London Gazette on July 17th and described the dramatic events on this night.

*'This airman was captain of an aircraft detailed to attack Bremen. In the light of' 'the full moon, shortly after crossing the Dutch coast, the aircraft was intercepted by 3 enemy fighters whose pilots made simultaneous attacks from the port quarter, starboard and dead astern positions. Sergeant Falconer took violent evasive action but, in spite of this, his aircraft sustained severe damage. Just when it seemed that he had eluded his attackers, another enemy fighter appeared, firing a burst which raked the bomber from front to rear. The complete combat, lasting for 20 minutes, was fought from 15,000 feet, down to sea level. With 2 of his crew wounded, the aircraft's turrets useless, the astrodome, blind-flying panel and oxygen system shot away, as well as other damage sustained, Sergeant Falconer set course for this country. Although subjected to strong concentrations of light anti- aircraft fire near the enemy coast, he flew the aircraft safely back to base. Throughout, this airman displayed great courage, skilful captaincy and devotion to duty.'*

Sergeant Sidney Falconer jettisoned his incendiaries load 3 miles S.E of Makkum at 01:30 hours. The disabled Stirling eventually crash-landed back at Marham at 0247 hours. Both gunners had suffered gunshot wounds and were quickly taken to the SSQ. Sidney's Stirling, R9333 HA-F needed extensive repair. Classified Cat B/FB it would need the attention of Sebro (Short Brothers Repair Organisation) and would not return to the squadron until February 1943.

*The crew of Sergeant Jeary pose in front of Short Stirling R9333 HA-Y. Left; 2nd pilot Sergeant George Crombie, Pilot, Sergeant Geoff Jeary, Flight Sergeant Reg Norton, Wireless Operator, Sergeant Richard Anderson Observer and Sergeant Fred Ebbern, Flight Engineer.*

Two recently posted pilots would be experiencing their first bombing raid on this night. Flying with Sgt Geoff Jeary for operational experience was P/O John Gruber. Sergeant Colin Jerromes accompanied P/O Colin Farquharson aboard Stirling N6070 HA-V. Jerromes was a protege of F/Lt Desmond Plunkett, having learnt to fly at No.5 EFTS at RAF Meir under Plunkett's guidance in 1941. The first bombs started to burst across Bremen around 01:20 hours, as forecast the target was completely cloud covered. All the squadron crews bombed on TR1335 or the glow of the fires started by the proceeding bombers. Pilot Officer McCarthy and Sgt McAuley both reported upon their return a large fire NW of the target. Both agreed that this was oil-based decoy. Flak over the target was intense, and sightings of fighters were numerous. Pilot Officer McCarthy was hit by flak on his bomb run, which confirmed to him that he was at least over the target.

On the route home the crew of Sgt Ralph Waters fell foul of the German Marine flak, the blazing Stirling crashed into the mudflats at the mouth of the Jade at Hohenstiefersiel, near Horumersiel at 0228 hours. The wreckage burnt for several hours until the area was submerged by the incoming tide. The following morning the wreckage again started to burn probably due to a hung-up incendiary. The wreckage which was lying in a busy watercourse was blown up by the German Navy as it posed a danger to shipping. Two bodies were recovered near to the wreckage, plus three unopened parachutes. The bodies were collected by German Navy personnel and taken to Wilhelmshaven. These were the identified as the pilot, and Sgt Dick, both were buried on July 2nd.

**Sunday 27th/28th June 1942**

Short Stirling
*Mk.I*
*DJ974 HA-T 'Tommy'*
*Contract No : 763825/38*
*Taken On Charge : 01/05/1942*
*CAT E/FB Missing*
*SoC 28/06/1942*
***Failed to Return***
*Pilot: Sergeant Ralph Waters, 1193368 RAFVR,* ***Killed***
*Observer:  Pilot Officer Horace Martin Simon, 116027 RAFVR,* ***Killed***
*Wireless Operator: Sergeant George Anderson Gow, 974840 RAFVR* ***Killed***
*Wireless Operator: Sergeant John Armstrong, 998998 RAFVR Killed*
*Wireless Operator: Flight Sergeant Thomas Campbell Parry, R/58177 RCAF,* ***Killed***
*Air Gunner:  Sergeant Frederick Dick, 1067547 RAFVR* ***Killed***
*Flight Engineer: Sergeant John Kingston Lew Heath, 925390 RAFVR* ***Killed***

It was not until 1950 that the remaining crew members were recovered from the wreckage and buried at Hanover War Cemetery. Sergeant Ralph Waters had begun his operational tour in January joining the crew of Sgt John Webber. It was with this crew that he flew an unprecedented 14 operations before he captained his own crew. Having collected a crew from No.10 OTU he proceeded to No.218 CF where he is recorded as flying a minelaying operation on June 10th. A further two operations were flown before his death over North-Holland. The last crew to land back at Marham was Sgt Yates at 05:40 hours, the remaining few patches of mist were burning off in the early morning sun as the crew clambered out of Stirling N3721 HA-S. None of the aiming point photographs showed any ground details, however some useful damage had been inflicted to the Atlas Werks and the Korff Refinery, both having been damaged on the previous raid. The loss of yet another crew, the fifth for the month hit the squadron hard. These were friends that would have been seen around the various messes, local pubs, cafes and cinemas every day. Thirty-seven, sons, husbands, brothers or sweethearts gone, the air war was taking a steady toll on the crews of Bomber Command.

On the morning of the 29th, the news that the squadron was to return to Bremen again that night was sweeping around the station. To visit a heavily defended target in Germany three times in a matter of a few short days was almost unknown at the time. Crews were not accustomed to this type of concentrated attack on a single selected target. Twelve crews were detailed and briefed. This number was reduced to ten when two Stirlings, HA-V N6077 captained by P/O McGregor and R9357 HA-E skippered by Sgt Jeary were reported unserviceable just prior to take-off. Once again, the operation was planned to be a TR1335 operation with the most experienced set operators in the first wave. With a duration of just 60 minutes, the second wave was to carry where possible entirely 30lb incendiary bombs. Bomber Command despatched 284 aircraft of which No.3 Group would supply almost half. There were the usual early returns, P/O Farquharson was obliged to turn for home when the rear turret was reported as faulty, the 30lb incendiaries were jettisoned in The Wash. A layer of low cloud was experienced almost to the target where it increased to 8/10th but there were thankfully some gaps. Visibility above the cloud was ideal for night fighters, especially the Bf110s of NJG2. The main attack started at around 0030 hours, the squadron was evenly divided between both waves and interestingly bombed from altitudes ranging from 15,000 feet to an unheard of 18,000 feet. One of the first over the target was S/Ldr Oldroyd DFC AFC, he dropped his entire load in or near the dock area reporting *'several large fires already in the town'*. Pilot Officer Abberton who was scheduled for the second wave was one of the few to get a momentary glimpse of the target in a gap in the cloud. He reported, *'target identified visually, while bursts were not actually seen. It is felt that they were accurately placed. Many fires were burning when we left the target area'*. The raid was surprisingly successful, the concentration of bombing achieved was better than could have been hoped for, TR1335 was finally delivering. During a period of 24 minutes over 180 bombers dropped their bomb loads on Bremen. The following day a photo-

*Irishman Pilot Officer George McAuley. He would be awarded a DFC in July but would sadly fail to return from a minelaying sortie on August 20th the victim of flak.*

reconnaissance flight revealed considerable fresh damage, a few sheds and workshops at the Hansa Lloyd Dynamo works and Hansa Lloyd Automobile Works had been totally destroyed. A dozen factories received fresh damage. Severe damage was also inflicted to the Neustadt Guter Bahnhof freight yard. Thankfully all the squadron aircraft returned safely to RAF Marham having dropped an impressive 53,640lbs of incendiaries. Losses were acceptable given the success, 12 bombers failed to return, sadly 8 of which were from 3 Group.

The month of June had seen the squadron suffer its fair share of drama and casualties. Five crews had failed to return, it was a bitter blow. The loss was especially hard when one of the losses was a respected flight commander and a crew so desperately close to completing a tour. The loss of men of this calibre and experience had a marked if brief effect on morale, especially for the less experienced. If a 'Gen' crew could get the chop, what hope was there! Thankfully, these young men put aside these feeling very quickly and got on with the job in hand. Fortunately, the squadron had strong leadership in Wing Commander Holder DFC and 'A' Flights S/Ldr Ashworth DFC AFC.

The final 1000 Bomber Raid had been flown, although the success in terms of damage inflicted was less than anticipated and claimed by Bomber Command HQ and the British media the three raids had achieved one thing. The numerous doubters who took every opportunity to discredit Bomber Commands achievements were now silent, for the time being at least. In Germany, the knowledge that a force of over 1000 bombers could be assembled and attack any town in range sent shock waves through their command. This knowledge affected German civilian morale, making this yet another success for Bomber Command. German civilians now lived in constant fear of bombing, bombing on a scale that was unimaginable only a year before.

The rumours that the squadron was on the move proved correct, the luxury of a peace-time station with all its many attributes was soon to be exchanged for a partially completed building site. The move began on June 30th, the Bremen raid brought June 1942 to a conclusion. The squadron had flown 113 sorties dropping in the process 532,330 lbs of HE and incendiaries bombs. June had also witnessed the squadron plant a creditable 87 parachute mines, the largest amount sown by any squadron in the group.

*The crew of Flight Sergeant Robert Yates. Seen here at RAF Downham Market. Left; unknown. Sergeant Arthur Richardson, Flight Sergeant Robert Yates, Pilot, Sergeant George Boxall, Flight Sergeant Robert Dixon and Flight Sergeant John McGann. They would Fail to Return from a raid against Frankfurt on August 24th 1942 the victim of an encounter with Major Kurt Holler of Stab III./NJG4.*

# Chapter 13: July 1942 – All Change

July 1st dawned with a layer of mist blanketing Marham. This forestalled any flying during the morning, giving everyone apart from the ground crews a breather. The aircrew had the luxury of either relaxing in the mess or if permitted take a trip into town. It was not until late afternoon the mist finally cleared, allowing nine crews to carry out the customary air tests and exercises. The following day the squadron received Form B.857 from No.3 Group HQ, informing both squadrons that they would be required that night, the target, Bremen. The squadron lost the services of John McGregor's Observer, P/O Reginald Hobden on the 1st. He was posted to the Conversion Flight as Navigational Instructor on completion of his operational tour.

Nine crews would be required for the raid, and they would join over 300 bombers on yet another attempt to deliver that elusive crippling blow to the docks at Bremen. The weather conditions towards take-off were not favourable, a prospect of thunderstorms over England put the operation in doubt. Finally, with the weather improving the decision to attack was given. One of the first crews away was Sgt Geoffrey Jeary in Stirling N3718 HA-C at 23:15hrs. This aircraft had arrived on the squadron in February, but the undercarriage had collapsed on landing. After months of repair, it was now finally ready to operate for the first time. For once there were no early returns from the squadron although an alarming 46 crews did abort, 13.26% of the force dispatched. The tried and tested method of attack which proved so successful a few days before was once again implemented. The bombers were to carry where possible a maximum incendiary load comprising of 50% 30lb and 50% 4lb incendiaries. Once airborne, the crews headed towards the departure point of Cromer on the north Norfolk coast.

While on route to target an SOS was received at 00:28hrs sent by the wireless operator of Sergeant Geoffrey Jeary. This placed them north of the Dutch Frisian Islands approaching the German coastline. Nothing was heard from this crew again. Unlike the previous attack, the crews found Bremen clear of cloud, which presented the flak and searchlight defenders an opportunity to engage the bombers with a barrage of accurate vicious flak. Pilot Officer Owen Sanderson was coned and received several holes in Stirling N3763 HA-Q while on his bomb run, he was fortunate to elude their attention. Conditions were so good crews could pick out individual areas of Bremen, P/O Bullock watched as his entire load of 30-pound incendiaries exploded across the old town.
In contrast, F/O Farquharson's load fell across the river into town centre producing two fires in amongst some large building. A crew reported a seeing a burning train between Delmenhorst and Bremen. Once again many crews bombed from the near maximum altitude of their Stirling Mk.Is. Sergeant Savage in R9354 HA-N and F/Sgt Johnston at the controls of DJ976 HA-A both bombed from 18,000 feet. Fighters were active, Flying Officer Farquharson and crew claimed a Bf110 destroyed while Sergeant Savage had a brief but vicious encounter with three Bf110s which he successfully managed to evade. Despite the crews, enthusiasm, and reports of *the town a mass of flames'* post raid reconnaissance established that there was no fresh damage in Bremen. There was however some good news, in Delmenhorst, a district 2 miles west of Bremen severe damage was

*Sergeant Richard John Anderson RCAF. He was the navigator aboard N3718 HA-C that disappeared without trace on the raid against Bremen.*

inflicted on the vital wool-producing Nordd Wollkammerei un Kammgarn Spinnerei factory. Almost 5000 square-yards of the factory was destroyed plus many more buildings. This residential area also suffered the loss of nearly 3 acres burnt-out. By 0225 hours the last of the bombs had fallen, the raid which was planned to be of a duration of just 30 minutes, in fact, lasted 69 minutes. There were skirmishes with the fighters of NJG2 and NJG3 along the entire route home up until the North Sea. Oblt Heinrich Prinz zur Sayn-Wittgenstein of 9./NJG2 made one claim at 03:05 hours, a Short Stirling over the sea 30 miles West of Hook van Holland. Theo Boiten in his excellent Nachtjagd series of books attributes the loss of Sgt Jeary and crew to Oblt Heinrich Prinz zur Sayn-Wittgenstein. However, there remains the mysterious SOS message received by the crew at 00:28 hours.

### Friday 2nd/3rd July 1942
Short Stirling
*Mk.I*
*N3718 HA-C 'Charlie'*
Contract No : 763825/38
Taken On Charge: 11/02/1942
CAT E/FB Missing
SoC 02/07/1942
***Failed to Return***

Pilot: Sergeant Geoffrey George Jeary 126109 RAFVR, **Killed**
Observer: Sergeant Richard John Anderson, R/77386 RCAF **Killed**
Wireless Operator: Flight Sergeant Ronald Ernest Pithers, 905958 RAFVR **Killed**
Wireless Operator/Air Gunner: Flight Sergeant Walter Watson, 1112566 RAFVR Killed
Wireless Operator/Air Gunner: Flight Sergeant Reginald Noton, R/59356 RCAF **Killed**
Air Gunner:  Flight Sergeant Harold Ernest Magladry, R/74322 RCAF Killed
Flight Engineer: Sergeant Jack Mainwaring, 572972 RAF Killed

Alas the crew were never found. Sergeant Geoff Jeary, a pre-war schoolteacher, had begun his operational career back in December 1941. Under the able tuition of Sgt William Gregg, he had completed seven operations flying the trustworthy Wellington before Greggs untimely death. In March and on completion of his Stirling conversion he joined the crew of F/Lt William Livingston and completed a further six operations in the right-hand seat. Having gained the required skill, he collected his own crew and started operations as captain by the end of May. Geoffrey and his crew participated in all three 1000 Bomber Raids. It was the crew's 11th operation and Sgt Jeary's 24th.

Flight Sergeant Harold Ernest Magladry was another ex-Defiant air gunner having previously served on No.151 and No.410 RCAF Squadron. He arrived on the squadron on May 20th.

The crews began landing back at Marham just after 04:30 hours in the early morning sun, little did they realise that the squadron was returning from its last raid flown from this peace-time built station. Late morning two crews, Sgt Savage and P/O McCarthy were aloft on an Air Sea Rescue search. Presumably, this was for their missing comrades. After a fruitless search of nearly four hours, the crews returned to Marham. The squadron did not operate on the 4th but carried out a number of training flights. These training flights continued on the 5th. Behind the scenes, the squadron was preparing itself for the move to Downham Market. Group had in their wisdom instructed the squadron that the impending move must be completed on the 7th. It was no easy task moving over 650 men, 20 Stirlings, equipment, tools, stores and a thousand other bits and pieces that makes a squadron tick. Number 218 Conversion Flight which had been doing commendable work converting crews under S/Ldr Ker would continue to operate from Marham. On the 6th the squadron began the backbreaking move, everything needed to be boxed up, labelled and loaded onto the waiting transport. Thankfully, the weather was kind, especially for the ground crews who perhaps had the most challenging job of all. The main move started at dawn on the 7th, and predictably it was raining making the move even more demanding. Thirteen Short Stirlings flew directly to Downham Market. It was a short trip, less than 10 minutes in the murk. With the aircraft on their way the main road convoy set off on the short journey, thankfully the roads connecting both stations were almost straight, no narrow bends and tight corners that seemed to be the norm in this part of Norfolk. A herculean effort by all the personnel would see the squadron complete the move by 23:59 hours!

# Chapter 14: Downham Market Isn't Much of a Place!

The squadron's new home, and a home it would occupy for the next 21 months was more like a building site than an operational airfield. Hundreds of contractors were still finishing off various dispersals and taxiways. Heaps of building materials, and piles of concrete, gravel and cement littered the airfield making taxing, take off and landings tricky. The living quarters were far from finished plus there was still work to complete on a number of prefabricated buildings and offices. The crews accustomed to the luxury of Marham were far from impressed, John Abberton in a letter home to his younger brother dated July 28th wrote, *'Downham Market isn't much of a place!'*. Sadly, John, a married man from Staffordshire, would be killed within two weeks. The squadron would be the sole resident, the annoyance of the often enthusiastic and at times damn rowdy crews of No.115 Squadron was now in the past. Friendships that had been forged in the night skies over Germany and the pubs and messes were broken. The bond, a happy one full of rivalry and banter between 115 and 218, was now just a memory.

For 218 Squadron what remained of 1942 would see the squadron vitally wiped out. By Christmas 1942 the squadron would report 28 crews missing including its commanding officer, two flight commanders and a deputy flight commander. These five months are remembered as the squadrons 'Blackest' period. But that's another story.

*Perched twenty plus feet off the ground, an engine fitter tweaks the port outer Hercules engine of a Short Stirling soon after the squadrons arrival at RAF Downham Market. Below starboard inner gest some attention from the a 'Erk' while another secures the astro hatch.*

*The still incompleted RAF Downham Market photographed on August 27th 1942. Above, runway 'C' is directly ahead with Oak Woods on the right. Within a year the whole area at the bottom of the photograph would be deleveloped. Below: The techinical site and early accomidation site. Just visible is the unique control tower lower right hand corner.*

# About the Author

Steve 'Smudger' Smith is a 56-year-old Londoner with a passion for RAF Bomber Command, particularly the exploits of No.3 Group. For the past 20 years, he has been privileged to be the official No.218 (Gold Coast) Squadron Association historian and archivist. Steve is also the historian for No.623 Squadron and author of a book on their exploits titled *'A Short War'*. Steve's other books include *'St Vith to Victory'* a history of the squadron, *'A Stirling Effort'* the Stirling operations flown from RAF Downham Market. 'In Time' details No.218 Squadron's pivotal role in the introduction of the blind bombing aid GH in 1944. A joint venture with the historian Chris Ward resulted in the publication of *'No.3 Group RAF Bomber Command, An Operational History'*. Steve lives in Bexleyheath with his wife, Jill and two Border Terriers, Fred & Dolly.

Steve can be contacted via the publisher, mtwpublications@gmail.com

Printed in Great Britain
by Amazon

40900404R00249